MEN AT SEA

MEN AT SEA

The Best Sea Stories of All Time from Homer to William F. Buckley, Jr.

Edited and with an Introduction
by Brandt Aymar

BARNES
&NOBLE
BOOKS
NEW YORK

This edition published by Barnes & Noble, Inc., by
arrangement with the Promotional Reprint Company Limited, U.K.

1994 Barnes & Noble Books

ISBN 0 88029 907 X

Printed and bound in Finland

To
John Marshall,
a shipmate on many voyages

Acknowledgments

"The Burning of the *Morro Castle*" from *Fire at Sea* by Thomas Gallagher, copyright 1959 by Thomas Gallagher, reprinted by permission of Henry Holt and Company.

"The Loss of the *Endurance*" from *South* by Sir Ernest Shackleton, courtesy William Heinemann, Ltd.

"Life in the Forecastle" from *Casuals of the Sea* by William McFee, courtesy of The Modern Library, Random House, Inc.

"Southward Ho to the Pole" from *Discovery* by Richard Evelyn Byrd, copyright 1935 by Richard Evelyn Byrd, published by permission of Richard Byrd III.

"Teddy Tucker, Bermuda Diver" from *Sea Fever* by Robert F. Marx, copyright 1972 by Robert F. Marx, published by permission of Robert F. Marx.

"The Battle of *Bonhomme Richard* and *Serapis*" from *Knight of the Seas, The Adventurous Life of John Paul Jones*, by Valentine Thomson, reprinted by permission of Liveright Publishing Corporation. Copyright 1939 by Liveright Publishing Corporation. Copyright renewed 1966 by Valentine Thomson.

"U.S.S. *Skate* Surfaces at North Pole" from *Surface at the Pole* by James Calvert, copyright 1960 by James Calvert, published by permission of McGraw-Hill Book Company.

"Slaver: The *Amistad*" from *Tall Ships and Great Captains* by A.B.C. Whipple, copyright © 1951, 1956, 1960 by A.B.C. Whipple. Reprinted by permission of Harper & Row, Publishers, Inc. Reprinted by permission of A.B.C. Whipple.

"The Ambush and Death of Magellan" from *Ferdinand Magellan, Circumnavigator* by Charles McKew Parr, copyright 1953, 1964 by Charles McKew Parr. Reprinted by permission of Harper & Row, Publishers, Inc.

"The Torpedoing of the *Lusitania*" from *Lusitania* by David Butler, copyright © 1982 by David Butler. Reprinted by permission of Ballantine Books, a division of of Random House, Inc., and MacDonald & Co. (Publishers) Ltd.

"The Capture of the *Manila Galleon*" from *The Privateers: A Raiding Voyage to the Great South Sea* by Fleming MacLiesh and Martin L. Krieger, copyright © 1962 by Random House, Inc. Reprinted by permission of Random House, Inc.

"The Sinking of the *Squalus*" from *Blow All Ballast!* by Nat A. Barrows, copyright 1940 by Dodd, Mead & Company, Inc., copyright renewed 1968 by Dorothea W. Barrows. Reprinted by permission of Dodd, Mead & Company, Inc.

"Halfway" from *Kon Tiki* by Thor Heyerdahl, copyright © 1950, 1978, 1984 by Thor Heyerdahl. Published in the United States by Rand, McNally & Company. Reprinted by permission of Hyman Unwin Ltd.

"*Gipsy Moth* Capsizes in the Tasman Sea" from Gipsy Moth *Circles the World* by Sir Francis Chichester, copyright 1967 by Sir Francis Chichester. Published by permission of John Farquharson, Ltd.

"The Fog" from *Saved: The Story of the* Andrea Doria by William Hoffer, copyright 1979 by William Hoffer. Published by permission of Summit Books, a division of Simon & Schuster, Inc.

"The Cannons of the *Atocha*" from *Treasure* by Robert Daley, copyright © 1977 by Robert Daley. Reprinted by permission of Sterling Lord Literistic, Inc.

"Hospital Ship Rams U-Boat" from *San Andreas* by Alistair MacLean, copyright © 1984 by Alistair MacLean. Reprinted by permission of Doubleday & Company. Reprinted by permission of Collins Publishers.

"The Mutiny" from *The* Caine *Mutiny* by Herman Wouk, copyright 1951 by Herman Wouk. Reprinted by permission of Doubleday Publishing Group.

"Reaching Marbella" from *Atlantic High* by William F. Buckley, Jr., © 1982 by William F. Buckley, Jr. Reprinted by permission of Doubleday, a division of Bantam, Doubleday, Dell Publishing Group, Inc.

"The Fight with the Sharks" from *The Old Man and the Sea* by Ernest Hemingway in *The Hemingway Reader*, copyright 1953 by Charles Scribner's Sons, copyright renewed © 1981 by Charles Scribner's Sons. Reprinted with the permission of Charles Scribner's Sons, a Division of Macmillan Inc.

"The Battle of Jutland" from *25 Centuries of Sea Warfare* by Jacques Mordal, translated by Len Ortzen, translation copyright 1965 by Len Ortzen and Souvenir Press Ltd. of London.

"First Crossing of the Atlantic" from *Christopher Columbus, Mariner* by Samuel Eliot Morison, copyright 1942, 1955 by Samuel Eliot Morison, copyright © renewed 1983 by Emily Morison Beck. Published by permission of Little, Brown and Company, in association with The Atlantic Monthly Press.

"The Sinking of the *Bismarck*" from *The Last Nine Days of the* Bismarck by C. S. Forester, copyright © 1959 by Little, Brown and Company. Published by permission of Little, Brown and Company.

"The Defeat of the *Yorktown*" from *Incredible Victory* by Walter Lord, copyright © 1967 by Walter Lord. Reprinted by permission of Harper & Row, Publishers, Inc. Reprinted by permission of Hamish Hamilton Ltd.

Contents

Sea Disasters

Sea Divers

Sea Explorers

Sea Life

Sea Mutinies

Sea Phantoms

Sea Pirates and Privateers

Sea Storms

Sea Survivors

Sea Whalers and Sealers

Sea Wrecks

MEN AT SEA

Introduction

There are estimated to be some one hundred forty billion square miles of oceans covering the Earth's surface. Once all this was deserted and desolate. *Then men put to sea.* Their explorations, adventures, battles, wrecks, disasters, incredible survivals, mutinies, piracy, plunders, and devasting storms have been recorded since ancient times in their never-ending tales. This book attempts to include some of the most notable.

Faced with a task somewhat analogous to emptying an ocean with a thimble, the anthologist must select what he personally prefers, organize it in an orderly fashion, and trust that the reader will relish the result as much as the compiler.

The selections in this anthology all concern men of action at sea. Men who challenged the sea and the unknown. Men who viciously fought each other on the sea. Men who daringly pitted themselves against the denizens of the deep. Men who, amazingly, lived to tell of their most harrowing experiences at sea. Omitted are the many wonderful works about the nature of the sea itself, about sea archaeology, and about scientific studies of the oceans. They do not belong in a work portraying men of action at sea.

I have arranged my selections alphabetically under thirteen headings, each a category of the literature of the sea. We begin with "Sea Adventurers." One of the greatest, and certainly one of the earliest of sea adventure stories, is the *Odyssey* by Homer. In a translation by Theodore Buckley he tells of the perilous and terrifying passage of Odysseus's ship between Scylla, the monster of the rocks, and the mysterious Charybdis. How Odysseus and his crew barely escape a horrible fate makes for chilling reading.

Richard Henry Dana, Jr., son of a well-to-do Massachusetts family, interrupted his undergraduate life at Harvard and, on August 14, 1834, shipped out from Boston Harbor in the small 180-ton brig *Pilgrim* to begin a two-year voyage that would take him around Cape Horn, to California, and back. One purpose of his book, *Two Years Before the Mast,* was to publicize the hardships and injustices suffered by American sailors of that period. Thus the selection here includes a flogging scene aboard ship. While "the flogging was seldom, if ever, alluded to by us in the forecastle," the men vowed to help expose the captain's violence as soon as the ship returned to Boston.

Though he is perhaps best known for his voyage around the world in 1896, Joshua Slocum's voyage in the *Liberdade*, a thirty-five-foot sailing canoe built

1

in Brazil, is included here. In 1888 the captain, his wife, Hettie, and sons Victor and Garfield sailed from Rio de Janeiro to Washington, D. C. The trip was filled with adventures galore, as well as unexpected hazards, all colorfully described by this famous master mariner.

Nothing daunts the true sea adventurer. Certainly not Thor Heyerdahl, who with five companions built *Kon-Tiki*, a 40-foot raft of balsa logs, then sailed it on a 4,300-mile, 101-day voyage across the Pacific. Their purpose was a scientific experiment to duplicate how the ancient Peruvians made just such a voyage on a similar craft from South America to Tahiti. In "Halfway" they tell of their daily life aboard the raft, of the huge number of fish that accompanied them, of meeting many whales and dolphins, of their subsistence problems.

Sir Francis Chichester's magnificent venture, told in his own salty words in Gipsy Moth *Circles the World*, captured the imagination of the world. One of the most harrowing moments on this fabulous voyage was when, in the Tasman Sea in Australia on "a night as foul and black as you could see," his sturdy ship capsized and rolled over. The resultant chaos was incredible. How the skipper finally coped with the situation, restored order, and still decided to carry on is only part of the reason he is acclaimed as one of the greatest adventurers of his time.

Throughout history, nations have not ceased to wage war on each other, and so the largest category in this anthology covers sea battles. It opens with the battle of Salamis as described by Herodotus. Here, in 480 B.C., the Greek fleet under Themistocles fought against the superior Persian fleet of Xerxes to save their very civilization. By a clever strategy on the part of the Athenians and their allies the Aeginetans, the Persian vessels were caught between the two and destroyed.

In the novel *Ben-Hur* by Lewis Wallace, the Jewish hero is one of 120 slaves chained to the benches of a Roman warship. For three years he has been their captive. Then as his ship engages a pirate enemy, there appears to be a hope of escape.

Another story of escape, this time of a ship itself, is told by Richard Hakluyt. In 1585 the *Primrose* of London with twenty-eight Englishmen outwitted ninety-seven Spaniards who sought to detain them at Bilbao. Taking with them several important Spaniards as prisoners, they finally reached England safely.

The defeat of the Spanish Armada by Queen Elizabeth's English ships under the command of Sir Francis Drake is told by Charles Kingsley in his remarkable novel *Westward Ho!,* wherein the ship of its hero, Sir Amyas Leigh, fights valiantly to contribute to that victory.

In another classic novel, *The Pilot,* James Fenimore Cooper uses the American War of Independence as the background for the battle, off the coast of England, between the American warship *Ariel* and the British *Alacrity.* As the two ships came together and the crews joined in hand-to-hand combat, the novel's hero, Tom, dealt a fatal blow to the unfortunate commander of the *Alacrity.* It was one of the bloodiest sea battles of the American Revolution.

The hero of the most famous sea battle of the American Revolution was, of course, John Paul Jones. In his captivating biography, *Knight of the Seas*, Valentine Thomson recounts the historical engagement between the *Bonhomme Richard* and the *Serapis*. With his ship almost destroyed and staggering under the devasting onslaught of his British adversary, when asked by their captain, "Do I understand that you have struck?" the undaunted Jones gave his ringing answer, "No, I have just begun to fight."

Robert Southey's account of the Battle of Trafalgar, written in 1813 just eight years after the historic conflict, is the highlight of his book *The Life of Nelson*. No better firsthand description of the fighting and the consequent tragic death of this British admiral has ever been told. How ironic that Nelson's twice-given, humanitarian orders to the *Victory* to cease firing at the *Redoubtable* should be the cause of his own demise.

In his book *The Naval War of 1812*, Theodore Roosevelt credits the excellent gunnery of the *Constitution* over the very poor firepower of the *Guerrière* for a stunning American sea victory. Completely outmaneuvering his opponent, Captain Hull gained victory in a little less than thirty minutes.

For a Civil War selection I have chosen the firsthand account by a Southern officer, John McIntosh Kell, aboard the defeated *Alabama*. The action took place off Cherbourg, France, in an arranged battle with the Union's man-of-war *Kearsarge*. It was an unequal engagement that never would have been fought, except for a fatal error on the part of the officers of the *Alabama*.

The Spanish-American war on the seas climaxed with Admiral George Dewey's superior naval strategy in the Battle of Manila Bay. In his *Autobiography* he hair-raisingly describes the complete destruction of the Spanish vessels, as well as the silencing of the Manila shore batteries. As he modestly put it, "The order to capture or destroy the Spanish squadron had been executed to the letter. Not one of its fighting vessels remained afloat."

The British and German fleets of World War I met, if not head-on, at least in one gigantic running encounter on May 31, 1916, off Jutland. Admiral Sir John Jellicoe's Grand Fleet was pitted against Admiral Reinhard Scheer's High Sea Fleet in "the greatest naval battle the world has ever known." In his mammoth work, *25 Centuries of Sea Warfare*, Jacques Mordal, maneuver by maneuver, has detailed the Battle of Jutland for all posterity. After Jutland the German High Sea Fleet hardly ever put to sea again.

World War II saw sea action on both the Atlantic and Pacific Oceans, involving battleships, destroyers, submarines, airplanes, convoy escorts, and all other types of vessels attached to the warring fleets. The stories here reflect the incredible daring, bravery, desperate gambles, heroic action, decisive battles, and tragic loss of men at sea during this most costly of wars.

In May 1941 the 42,000-ton *Bismarck*, the world's largest and most dangerous ship of war yet launched, left the harbor of Gdynia. She was Hitler's proudest and deadliest battleship. Winston Churchill thundered, "Sink the *Bismarck*. The eyes of the whole world are upon us." In one of his most dramatic and suspenseful writings of the sea, C. S. Forester reconstructs her tracking by the British ships in *The Last Nine Days of the* Bismarck, until the fatal moments when the approaching *Dorsetshire* fired her torpedos into the already stricken ship. The *Bismarck* rolled over and sank.

Alistair MacLean has been thrilling readers with great maritime tales for over a quarter of a century. In *San Andreas* a very unlikely ship, a hospital vessel, carrying the wounded on a perilous voyage from Halifax to Aberdeen, is attacked by a U-boat. To save her wounded passengers from certain death she is forced into offensive action, ramming and sinking the enemy submarine.

Known best for his book on the sinking of the *Titanic*, Walter Lord, in *Incredible Victory*, covers the Battle of Midway, the turning point of the war against Japan in June 1942. But victory also takes its toll and here, hour by hour, is the tragic sinking of the crippled *Yorktown*.

There can be nothing more horrendous than when disaster strikes at sea. The pages of such terrifying tales have filled volumes of maritime history. In one of Victor Hugo's masterpieces of fiction, *Ninety-Three*, there is an episode of perhaps the most dreadful thing that could happen at sea. A cannon breaks loose from its fastenings and is suddenly transformed into a supernatural beast. From that moment on, the man-of-war *Claymore* is doomed. Two men escape together, one dedicated to saving the king of France, the other to establishing the republic.

Crushed by the huge blocks of the packed ice of the Antarctic, Sir Ernest Shackleton's ship, *Endurance*, became a total loss, stranding him and his men hundreds of miles from the nearest civilization. In *South* he tells of his ship's death struggle.

"Captain Will Turner's ship was the ill-fated *Lusitania*. On May 7, 1915, she was hit by a single German torpedo. Within eighteen minutes she sank, taking with her 1,200 of the 1,900 people aboard. In his magestic novel, *Lusitania*, David Butler alternates the action from the conning tower of the German submarine U20 to the bridge where Captain Turner is going through the horrifying ordeal of losing his beloved vessel.

The burning of the *Morro Castle* in 1938 brings back vivid memories for me. I had planned to take a vacation trip to Cuba that summer and would be returning to New York on the *Morro Castle*. Instead, I went to Bermuda, coming back on the *Monarch of Bermuda*. Early in the morning before our arrival in New York, the room steward knocked on my door and cried out, "Look out of your porthole, the *Morro Castle* is in flames!" We picked up many survivors that day and witnessed a number of gruesome death scenes. Thomas Gallagher, in *Fire at Sea*, takes us aboard this raging inferno and unmasks the confused, cowardly behavior of chief engineer Abbott.

Disaster struck the men of the U.S. submarine *Squalus* on her routine test dive that May day in 1939. Leaving her New London, Connecticut, base, she began her submersion. All seemed in perfect order until suddenly the telephone taker in the control room poured out an incredible message. The engine rooms were flooding. *Blow All Ballast*, by Nat A. Barrows, follows the suspenseful moments as the sub continued descending out of control until she hit hard and fast on the bottom.

A dense fog enveloped two passenger ships on a collision course the afternoon of July 25, 1956, off the island of Nantucket. Captain Piero Calamai stood on the bridge of the great Italian luxury liner, the *Andrea Doria,* directing her approach to New York harbor. In *Saved* William Hoffer recounts the events that followed. An approaching ship unaccountably rushed directly toward the *Andrea Doria.* Despite desperate maneuvers on the part of the *Andrea Doria,* there was no way to stop the Swedish liner *Stockholm* from plowing with full force into her starboard side.

What Jules Verne imagined in 1869 in his classic adventure story of a strange underwater craft, today's sea divers have turned into reality. In *Twenty Thousand Leagues Under the Sea,* in the *Nautilus* the inscrutable Commander Captain Nemo roams the oceans of the world inflicting horrible vengeance on his fellowmen. "Captain Nemo's Revenge" is an example of how he accomplishes his dire purpose.

Teddy Tucker is Bermuda's most famous treasure diver. In a fascinating, brief biography from his book, *Sea Fever,* Robert F. Marx, himself an expert diver, follows Teddy Tucker on his many quests for undersea wealth and fame.

In *Treasure,* the story of the most successful and most tragic treasure hunt of modern times, Robert Daley brings to a climax the many years of search for the Spanish galleon *Atocha,* lost somewhere in the Florida Keys in 1622. "The Cannons of the *Atocha*" tells how the treasure king, Mel Fisher, after an eleven-year search, finally locates some valuable remains of this ship, but with tragic results.

For the category of stories about sea explorers, I have, not surprisingly, opened with Christopher Columbus. Of the millions of pages written about this outstanding mariner and navigator, Samuel Eliot Morison's rewriting of his life and voyages is the most straightforward narrative of them all. So here, from his *Christopher Columbus, Mariner,* is his "First Crossing of the Atlantic," packed with all the terror, excitement, and near pandemonium of one of the great adventure stories of all time.

Ferdinand Magellan, Portuguese navigator, circled the globe under the Spanish flag in 1519. In his acclaimed biography, *Ferdinand Magellan, Circumnavigator,* Charles McKew Parr, distinguished present-day historian, writes of Magellan's last fateful battle at Mactan in the Philippines. Hopelessly outnumbered, the Spaniards tried to retreat. Only the wounded Magellan valiantly held off the enemy so his comrades could escape. But to no avail! "They rushed upon him with iron and bamboo spears, and with their cutlasses, until they killed our mirror, our light and comfort, our true guide." A great career was over.

Governor William Bradford's famous history of the Pilgrims naturally included their voyage to the New World aboard the *Mayflower.* In this modern English version of his *The History of Plymouth Settlement,* Governor Bradford chronicles the entire voyage, from her departure on September 6, 1620, to the landing on Plymouth Rock on December 16 of the same year. Nine days later the grateful Pilgrims began to erect the first house for common use, to receive them and their goods.

More than two hundred years after the death of Magellan, the famous explorer, Captain James Cook, met his death on a Hawaiian island under remarkably similar circumstances, also at the hands of the native people. His ships, the *Discovery* and the *Resolution*, had returned to Keragegooah Bay to ride out a gale when trouble with the natives began. The fracas culminated with an Indian giving Captain Cook a lethal blow with a club. He was seen alive no more.

In *Discovery: The Story of the Second Byrd Antarctic Expedition*, Rear Admiral Richard Evelyn Byrd relives the sea journey of his ship, *Ruppert*, from Wellington, New Zealand, to a location where the ship was blocked by the ice and could proceed no farther. The trip had been packed with excitement, bad weather, some very horrendous episodes, iceberg sightings, and stowaways. It was now up to aviation to renew the assault on the Antarctic.

Commander James Calvert gives us an eyewitness account in *Surface at the Pole* of how his nuclear-powered submarine U.S.S. *Skate* made history by surfacing at the North Pole. It was her second trip, but the first to finally break through the ice: "the first ship in history to sit at the very top of the world."

What life at sea is like has been portrayed in many different ways by various writers. Of them, the illustrious author of nineteenth-century sea stories, Frederick Marryat, is noted for his humor. So instead of using a selection from one of his better-known novels, such as *Mr. Midshipman Easy*, here is a tidbit from his book *Stories of the Sea*, entitled "The Midshipman." On the H.M. frigate *Unicorn*, Midshipman Edward Templemore is constantly laughing, for which the first lieutenant, at his wits' end, requests the captain to put him on report. However, Captain Plumbton, being fond of his very junior officer, issues him an invitation instead: "So come and dine with me; at my table. You know, I allow laughing in moderation."

William McFee knows "Life in the Forecastle" from personal experience. He portrays the readjustment of Hannibal from a young man of London into a stoker on a ship traversing the seven seas. He soon learns to respect the tough men in the forecastle as he discovers a new world far removed from his former urban life.

What is life like aboard history's most famous clippership, the *Flying Cloud*? Morley Roberts, in "Aloft on the *Flying Cloud*," takes us along on a neophyte's first climb up the towering mast, as he fearfully follows the old salt Bram to the top. Rung by rung they climb, past the crosstrees, up to the royalyard, ever higher to the yard of the skysail. Here the boy swings his leg across the yard and sits shaking and triumphant, a true salt at last.

Who has not read Ernest Hemingway's *The Old Man and the Sea*? Here is an excerpt in which, after the old man's skiff has been towed way out to sea off Cuba by the giant marlin he has hooked, he lashes the fish to the boat and sails back for home. Along the way his catch is attacked by sharks and the old man must kill many of them. In the end he does not want to look at the fish; "he knew that half of him had been destroyed."

In 1980 William F. Buckley, Jr., again gathered together his friends and set sail across the Atlantic on a thirty-day journey from St. Thomas in the Virgin Islands to Marbella, Spain, aboard *Sealestial*. After a trip packed with winds and calms, nasty watches and ceaseless ruminations, close companionship liberally doused with drinks and wine, they gratefully tied up at Marbella's immigration dock.

The mutineers on the slave schooner *Amistad* became a nationwide cause célèbre, pitting abolitionists against proslavery forces. But to the blacks chained in its hold it was a matter of life and death. Under the leadership of Cinque, son of an African chief, they freed themselves after many hours of picking at locks with a recovered nail. The captain and most of the crew were murdered or drowned. Don José Ruíz, Don Pedro Montez, and Antonio, the cabin boy, were spared, the former two to navigate and the boy to interpret the mutineers' language. By devious means of navigation Montez brought the ship into Montauk Point at the end of Long Island, a far distance from the Africa Cinque imagined they were heading for. There they were taken captive by the U.S. surveying brig *Washington*.

In his famous novel of World War II, *The* Caine *Mutiny*, Herman Wouk brings to mind the true experiences of Admiral William Halsey's fleet battling a killer typhoon in the Pacific in 1944. But there the resemblance ends. This is the fictional story of the psychotic Captain Queeg of the U.S.S. *Caine*, who loses control of himself and his ship in the face of a raging tornado. Faced with inevitable disaster, Executive Officer Lieutenant Stephen Maryk has no choice but to do the unthinkable—relieve the captain of the command of his ship.

There are many legends of phantom ships in the annals of the sea. Here is one, as told by William Bassett in *Wander-Ships*. Fishing off the Grand Banks of Newfoundland, the *Étoile de Saint Malo* is heading home after seven months. Suddenly she strikes a giant mass of submerged ice and immediately sinks. Only the aged master and his boy, jumping into the trawl boat, survive. As the days pass with no sight of a ship, the grandfather weakens. In his feverish state he begins to hallucinate about the glories, the pleasures, and the eternal happiness aboard a giant ship called *La Grande Chasse Foudre*, where all sailors finally go to rest. When a rescue ship appears and picks them up, the grandfather is dead. He has joined the crew of the giant ship.

In "The Craft of Death" R. T. Ross writes of a dying man adrift on a raft. He is revived by a last glimmer of hope as he sees a large boat with masts and sails set approaching. The man, in a final desperate effort, pulls himself over the edge of the ship, falling prostrate on the deck. When he can collect himself he looks around. To his horror he notices dead men all about. It is then that he picks up and reads a note in the hand of one of the bodies. "All dead of the black plague but myself."

On April 24, 1840, the narrator of this mysterious tale takes passage on a barque named *Lord of the Isles*. It is sailing from Rio de Janeiro to Bristol,

England, and he is the lone passenger. In *The Phantom Death* by W. Clark Russell, first the captain, then the chief mate, then the second mate all mysteriously die during successive nights, apparently from poison. Unjustly accused, the passenger is locked in his cabin, until the culprit who caused these phantom deaths is uncovered.

In *Hard Cash* novelist Charles Reade tells of how a Portuguese pirate overtakes Captain Dodd's ship the *Agra* on its return voyage from the China Seas. The attack is fierce as both sides engage in battering each other's vessels. Coming together at one point, the *Agra* is boarded by members of the pirate crew, who are summarily thrashed to death. Another pirate ship joins the first, but Captain Dodd masterfully navigates the *Agra* to elude her, too. In the end the *Agra* successfully escapes as the pirate ships finally give up the chase.

During the eighteenth century, when piracy was particularly rampant, it was often difficult to distinguish between a pirate and a privateer. The notorious Captain Kidd was hanged in 1701 for piracy, but not before, with letters of intent from the queen, he had seized many ships and lands belonging to Spain and had enjoyed a number of years as governor of Jamaica. But Captain Teach, known as Black-Beard, was a different story. This seagoing villain pillaged ships up and down the coast of Virginia until the governor of that colony issued a proclamation offering a reward of one hundred pounds for Teach's capture and/or demise, with lesser sums for any other vessel and crew engaged in piracy. To which end he placed Robert Maynard, first lieutenant of the man-of-war *Pearl* and her sistership *Luire* in charge of the expedition. Howard Pyle recounts the bloody "End of Black-Beard, The Pirate" as Lieutenant Maynard caught up with and boarded the pirate's sloop. After particularly fierce fighting, during which the sea was tinctured with blood, Black-Beard received twenty-five wounds. As he was cocking another pistol, he fell down dead.

Captain William Fly was another notorious pirate, his hunting ground stretching north from Nantucket to the fishing banks. Charles Johnson chronicled the dire deeds of many pirates. Fly, sailing as boatswain under Captain Green of Bristol, left from Jamaica in the *Elizabeth* snow for the coast of Guinea in April 1726. Some days later, after proposing his design to his brothers in iniquity, Fly took over the ship and murdered the captain and his mate. Then the pirate's snow ravaged ships up and down the coast, until Fry himself was overpowered and brought with the other prisoners to Great Brewster. There they stood trial and were hung.

Two English ships, the *Duke* and *Duchess*, sailed from Bristol in 1708 carrying letters of marque from the crown authorizing them to prey on enemy shipping. They crossed the Atlantic, raided in the Caribbean, and beat their way around the Horn. They then raided Spanish cities along the west coast of South America, captured many ships, and took vast amounts of wealth. However, their main purpose was to meet up with the famed Spanish ship, the *Manila Galleon*, laden with the riches of the Indies that sailed each year from Manila. Luckily they intercepted her off the coast of Baja California, captured her, and seized her vast wealth. In *The Privateers* authors Fleming MacLiesh and Martin Krieger, basing their account on the ships' logs, retell one of the notable voyages in the history of piracy.

Joseph Conrad's stirring narrative of sea life is contained in his novel *The Nigger of the Narcissus*. There is no more harrowing account of a violent storm and its devastating effects on the ship's crew than that portion of the novel devoted to "The Gale." How the *Narcissus* manages to weather the unspeakable fury of the "wind that rushed in one long unbroken moan above their head" and "the towering waves that swept the decks from end to end," it is difficult to imagine. With superhuman effort Captain Allistoun and his crew bring her through.

Twelve men survived "The Loss of the *Centaur* Man-of-War," which foundered in the Atlantic Ocean in September 1782, during the greatest naval catastrophe to result from the violence of the elements, which caught the British fleet shortly after leaving shore. Three thousand lives were lost. In this firsthand account, the narrator along with others who took to the pinnace escaped from the doomed ship. Suffering from exposure, hunger, and thirst, they finally reached land.

The master storyteller of horror tales, Edgar Allan Poe, turns to the sea for this excerpt from *The Narrative of Arthur Gordon Pym*. During the voyage of the American brig *Grampus* to the South Seas in 1827 a mutiny took place. However, the ship was fortuitously recaptured by the captain's son, Augustus Barnard, and three loyal companions, including the narrator. During the scuffle the brig encountered such a vicious gale that she was all but sunk, her superstructure demolished. The brig now became a mere log, rolling at the mercy of every wave. Sometime later a hermaphrodite brig bore down on the survivors, offering a hope of rescue. When only fifty feet away a hellish stench nearly overwhelmed the survivors, for thirty human bodies lay scattered about the ship in the most loathsome state of putrefaction. Then the death ship sailed on. Days of indescribable horrors passed, in which the four were reduced to cannibalism, drawing straws to determine the victim. The days that followed saw the death of Augustus. Six days later the schooner *Jane Guy* came upon the two remaining survivors and picked them up.

The Open Boat by Stephen Crane is such an accepted masterpiece of sea literature that it is included here in its entirety. Based on the true experiences in 1893 of four men from the sunken steamer *Commodore,* the author writes of how each of the four—the captain, the cook, the oiler, and the correspondent—fared in the tortuous days in the tiny lifeboat.

In Frank Stockton's sea story "The Landsman's Tale" a stranger comes to a little town on the New England coast, where he attends a local public meeting. Judging him a landsman, the villagers are taken quite by surprise when, as his turn comes to recount a story, he begs their permission to tell one, not of the land, but of the sea. His tale is of a good-sized American schooner, probably bound for the Sandwich Islands. Every one of the crew was fond of books, to which end they carried on board, as their prize possession, a library. The ship was suddenly hit by a hurricane that carried away all the masts and nearly turned over. A furious blast blew off the heel. Then she righted. At this point they had to abandon her, but all they had was a collapsed hunting boat, only large enough for the men and a small space for one box. But they needed to take two, one containing condensed foods of various kinds sufficient to last some days, the other containing their precious portable library. Which would the crew vote to take?

"I was fast asleep when the *Titanic* struck." So begins the survival story of Henry Sleeper Harper, one of the passengers aboard the ill-fated pride of the Cunard line as she struck an iceberg. His narrative describes the inability of the passengers to imagine that the ship could sink, the mess the crew members made in their clumsy attempts to lower the lifeboats, the confusion of the lifeboat rowers in trying to get clear of the stricken ship, and their immense feeling of relief as they paddled toward the rescue ship *Carpathia*. This story appeared shortly after the sinking in the April 27, 1912, issue of *Harper's Weekly*.

The greatest whaling story ever told is Herman Melville's *Moby Dick*. Even though it is so familiar to readers all over the world, to leave out the three-day chase to capture Moby Dick by the purpose-crazed Captain Ahab would be a whale of an omission.

A somewhat unusual whale hunt was experienced by the ship *Arethusa* near the Falkland Islands on her way to round the Horn. A dreadful casualty occurred when one of the boats approaching a group of whales speared one of them. At once the air was darkened by the ponderous tail of the infuriated monster burying the starboard boat in a cloud of foam. It was smashed to pieces, the men swimming for their lives. Mr. Johnson, the third mate, never made it and drowned. How the *Arethusa* avenged his death makes suspenseful reading.

The most unlikely place to enjoy a Christmas dinner is on top of a whale. But that's exactly where the stranded whalers have their holiday repast in Frank Bullen's *The Cruise of the* Cachalot. They bomb-gun the whale and during the violent explosion lose their boat. They find themselves stranded on top of their now-dead antagonist. Cutting off some good-sized chunks of meat, they have their "feast"—thinking all the while how queer a Christmas dinner they were eating.

In *The Sea Wolf*, one of Jack London's best known novels, the sealing schooner *Ghost*, skippered by the brutal Wolf Larsen, reaches the great seal herd of the Bering Sea. Casting off, the six hunter boats are soon lost sight of over the horizon. Late in the day the winds increase to such a velocity that the whipped-up waves overtop the ship. For hours the badly damaged sealer searches for her boats. Three are found and the men rescued. Three are lost.

One of the earliest recorded shipwrecks is found in the Bible's Acts of the Apostles XXVII. St. Paul was being escorted as a prisoner on a sea journey on the way to face Caesar in Rome. The ship reached the city of Lasea, where Paul advised them, because the season of bad weather was upon them, to stay.

But the captain insisted on proceeding. Caught in a tempest the ship seemed doomed and all aboard lost. The ship was wrecked and it was only by following Paul's advice that they all escaped safely to land.

During the eighteenth and nineteenth centuries the number of shipwrecks reached a peak. The two narratives included here are typical of such accounts. In 1786 the passenger ship *Halsewell*, an East Indiaman, set out from England. It got no farther than the coast of Dorsetshire, where she was beset by several violent gales, sprung a leak, and crashed onto the rocks. Many lives were lost in the pitiful attempts of the passengers and crew to reach the doubtful safety of a group of rocks. They then were forced to scale an almost perpendicular cliff to attain the summit above. Of the more than 240 who sailed on the *Halsewell*, only 54 survived this terrible ordeal.

A careless accident started a fatal fire aboard the *Kent*, East Indiaman, shortly after she left the English downs for Bengal and China on February 19, 1825. One of the officers went down into the hold to check the cargo and discovered a spirit cask to be adrift. Unfortunately, at a sudden heavy lurch, he dropped the lantern he was carrying. At the same time the loose cask was stove in, spilling out the spirits. The whole place was instantly ablaze. The fire was well out of control and the ship demolished to the point of sinking when the brig *Cambria* appeared and rescue efforts were begun. But the two ships were caught in a full-scale gale, dangerously hampering such efforts. This then is the story of how the heroic Captain Cobb and his men succeeded in transferring 600 passengers and crew to the tiny 200-ton brig, which then fought its way through the gale to the safety of Falmouth Harbour.

The last story in this anthology is that part of Daniel Defoe's *Robinson Crusoe* in which our hero visits the wreck a number of times in his attempts to take off all the stores and equipment possible for the long years that lay ahead for him as a castaway on a deserted island.

This collection of stories, narratives, and selections from famous sea novels attempts to give a representative sampling of what men experienced when they went to sea. With the wealth of sea lore available, it necessarily touches but the tip of the iceberg. So the criterion for choice is a personal one, but always keeping a weather eye to covering as many major categories of sea literature as possible. I hope reading them will afford you a rare insight into the many-faceted aspects of a sailor's life and, in the end, will leave you happily all at sea.

Brandt Aymar

SEA ADVENTURERS

Escape from Scylla-Charybdis, then Shipwreck

by HOMER,

translated by THEODORE ALOIS BUCKLEY

"But when the ship left the stream of the river Ocean, and came back to the wave of the wide-wayed sea, to the island of Aeaea, where are the abodes and dancing-places of Aurora, the mother of dawn, and the risings of the sun: having come here, we drew up our ship on the sands, and we ourselves disembarked upon the shore of the sea. Here lying down to sleep we awaited divine morning: but when the mother of dawn, rosy-fingered morning, appeared, then I sent forward my companions to the house of Circe, to bring the corpse, the dead Elpenor. And immediately cutting trunks, where the shore projected the farthest, we buried [him] in sorrow, shedding the warm tear. But when the corpse was burnt, and the arms of the dead, having built a tomb, and having erected a column over it, we fixed the well-fitted oar at the top of the tomb.

"We indeed went through every thing; nor yet returning from Hades did we escape Circe, but she came very quickly, hastening: and her female attendants with her brought bread, and much flesh, and dark-red wine. And she, the divine one of goddesses, standing in the middle of us, addressed us:

"Wretched ones! who alive have come under the house of Pluto, twice dead, when other men die but once. But come, eat food and drink wine here through the whole day; and ye shall sail together with morn appearing; but I will show you the way; and will instruct you in every thing; that ye may not grieve at all, suffering harm either on the sea or on land by some grievous bad counsel.'

"Thus she spoke; but our noble mind was forthwith persuaded. Thus, then, during the whole day until sun-set, we sat feasting on abundant flesh and sweet wine; but when the sun had sunk, and darkness came on, they indeed slept near the cables of the ship; but she, taking me by the hand, at a distance from my dear companions, made me sit down, and reclined opposite, and inquired every thing of me; and I related all things rightly to her. And then indeed venerable Circe addressed me with words:

" All these things indeed have thus been performed; but do thou listen, how I will tell thee, and a deity himself will make thee remember it. First indeed thou wilt come to the Sirens, who charm all men, whoever comes to them. Whosoever through ignorance has approached and heard the voice of the Sirens, by no means do his wife and infant children stand near him when he returns home, nor do they rejoice. But the Sirens, sitting in a meadow, soothe him with a shrill song, and around there is a large heap of bones of men

15

rotting, and skins waste away round about. But sail beyond; and anoint the ears of thy companions, moulding sweet wax, lest any one of the others should hear; but do thou thyself hear, if thou wilt. Let them bind thee hands and feet in the swift ship, upright in the mast hole; and let cables be bound from it; that, delighted, thou mayest hear the voice of the Sirens: but if thou entreatest thy companions, and biddest them loose thee, let them then bind thee in still more bonds. But when thy companions shall have sailed beyond these, then I cannot tell thee accurately which will afterwards be thy way; but do thou thyself consider in thy mind; but I will tell thee of both ways. There indeed are lofty rocks; and near them the vast wave of dark Amphitrite resounds; the blessed gods call them the Wanderers; here nor birds pass by, nor timid doves, which carry ambrosia to father Jove; but the smooth rock always takes away some one of them, but the father sends another to make up the number. From this not yet has any ship of men escaped, whichever has come to it; but the wave of the sea and the storms of destructive fire take away planks of ships and bodies of men together. That sea-traversing ship alone has sailed by it, Argo, a care unto all, which sailed from Aetes: and now perhaps it would have quickly dashed it there against mighty rocks, but Juno sent it on, since Jason was dear [to her]. But as to the two rocks, the one reaches the wide heaven with its sharp top, and a dark-grey cloud surrounds it: this indeed never withdraws, nor does a clear sky ever possess its top, either in the summer or in the autumn; nor could a mortal man ascend it, or descend, not if he had twenty hands and feet; for the rock is smooth, like unto one polished around. But in the middle of the rock there is a shadowy cave towards the west, turned to Erebus; where do thou, O illustrious Ulysses, direct thy hollow ship. Nor could a young man darting an arrow from a bow from a hollow ship reach the deep cave. Here Scylla dwells, shrieking out terribly; her voice indeed is as of a new-born whelp, but she herself is a vast monster; nor would any rejoice seeing [her], not even if a god should meet her. She has twelve slender feet in all; and she has six very long necks; and on each there is a terrific head, and in it three rows of teeth, thick and frequent, full of black death. She is sunk in the middle through her hollow cave: and she holds forth her heads out of the terrible abyss, and fishes there, watching about the rock, for dolphins, and dogs, and if she can any where take a larger whale, which deep-groaning Amphitrite feeds in countless numbers. By whom unharmed never at any time do sailors boast that they have fled by in their ship; but snatching a man with each of her heads from a dark-prowed ship, she bears him away. But thou wilt see the other rock lower, O Ulysses, each near to the other; and thou couldst reach it with an arrow. In this there is a large wild fig-tree flourishing with leaves; under this divine Charybdis sucks in black water. For thrice in a day she sends it out, and thrice she sucks it in terribly: mayest thou not come thither when she is gulping it; for not even Neptune could free thee from ill. But by all means sailing to the rock of Scylla, drive thy ship quickly beyond; since it is much better to regret six companions in a ship, than all together.'

"Thus she spoke; but I answering addressed her; Come then, tell me this truly, O goddess; if I can by any means escape out from destructive Charybdis, should I be revenged upon her, when she has harmed my companions?'

"Thus I spoke; but she, the divine one of goddesses, immediately answered: 'O wretched one, are warlike deeds and labour still a care to thee? nor wilt thou yield to the immortal gods? She is not indeed mortal, but is an immortal evil, terrible, and difficult, and fierce, nor to be fought with. Nor is there any defence; it is best to flee from her: for if thou shouldst delay, arming thyself, by the rock, I fear lest again attacking thee she would reach thee with so many heads, and would take away so many men. But sail on very quickly and call for help to Crataeis, the mother of Scylla, who brought her forth a destruction to mortals, who will immediately hinder her from attacking thee afterwards.

"'And thou wilt come to the island Trinacria; where are fed many oxen and fat sheep of the Sun, seven herds of oxen, and as many beautiful flocks of sheep, and fifty in each; but there is no increase of them, nor do they ever perish; but goddesses are their shepherdesses, the fair-haired nymphs, Phaethusa, and Lampetie, whom divine Neaera bore to the sun who journeys above. Whom having nourished and brought them forth, their venerable mother sent them away to the Trinacrian island, to dwell afar off, to guard their father's sheep and crumpled-horned oxen. If thou leavest these unharmed, and carest for thy return, thou mayest yet come to Ithaca, although suffering evils; but if thou harmest them, then I foretell to thee destruction to thy ship and thy companions; and although thou shouldst thyself escape, thou wilt return late, in misfortune, having lost all thy companions.'

"Thus she spoke; but golden-throned morning immediately came. The divine one of goddesses then went away through the island; but I, going to my ship, excited my companions to embark themselves, and to loose the halsers. But they immediately went on board, and sat down on the benches, and sitting in order they smote the hoary sea with their oars. Then the fair-haired Circe, an awful goddess, possessing human speech, sent a prosperous gale behind our dark-prowed ship, that filled the sails, an excellent companion. Immediately having got ready all our tackle in the ship, we sat down; and the wind and the helmsman directed it. Then sorrowing in my heart, I addressed my companions:

"'O my friends, it is not fit that one or two only should know the oracles, which Circe, divine one of goddesses, has spoken unto me; but I will tell you, that being aware we may either die, or avoiding it may escape death and Fate. First she commands us to shun the voice of the divine Sirens, and their flowery mead; she ordered me alone to hear their voice; but do ye bind me in a difficult bond, that I may remain there firmly, upright in the mast-hole: and let cables be fastened from it. But if I entreat you, and command you to loose me, do ye then press me with still more bonds.'

"I indeed telling every thing, related it to my companions: but in the mean time the well-made ship came quickly to the island of the Sirens; for a harmless prosperous gale urged it on. Immediately then the wind ceased, and there was a windless calm, and a deity hushed the winds to sleep. And my companions rising up, furled the sails of the ship, and placed them in the hollow ship; and they sitting on their oars, whitened the water with their polished blades of fir. But I having cut in small pieces a large circle of wax with the sharp brass, pressed it with my strong hands: and the wax immediately became warm, for the great force compelled it, and the shining of the sun, the king, the son of Him that journeys on high: and I anointed it in turn upon the ears of all my companions. But they bound me both hands and feet together in the ship, upright in the mast-hole, and they fastened cables from it; and they themselves sitting down smote the hoary sea with their oars. But when we were so far distant as one makes himself heard shouting out, going on swiftly, the ship passing the sea quickly, driving near, did not escape them, but they prepared a tuneful song.

" 'Come hither, O much-praised Ulysses, great glory of the Grecians, stop thy ship, that thou mayest hear our voice; for no one has yet passed by here in a black ship, before he has heard the sweet voice from our mouths; but he goes away delighted, and acquainted with more things. For we ken all things, whatever the Grecians and Trojans suffered by the will of the gods in spacious Troy; and we know whatever things are done in the food-abounding earth.'

"Thus they spoke, uttering a sweet sound; but my heart wished to hear them, and I ordered my companions to loose me, nodding with my eye-brows; but they falling forward rowed; and Perimedes and Eurylochus immediately rising, bound me with more bonds, and pressed me still more. But when it passed by them, and we no longer heard the voice of the Sirens, nor their song, my beloved companions immediately took away the wax, which I anointed on their ears, and loosed me from the bonds. But when we had now left the island, immediately I saw smoke and a vast wave, and heard a noise. The oars flew from the hands of them terrified; and all making a noise [went] down the stream; but the ship was stopped there, since they no longer urged the extended oars with their hands. But I went through the ship, and incited my companions with mild words, standing near each man:

" 'O my friends, we are not by any means ignorant of misfortunes. This evil indeed does not come greater upon us than when the Cyclops shut us in his hollow cave by powerful force; but we escaped even from thence by my valour, and counsel and prudence; and I think that you will some time remember these things. But now come, let us all obey, as I direct; do ye smite the deep billow of the sea with your oars, sitting on the benches, if Jove will by chance grant us to escape from and avoid this death. But to thee I order thus, O helmsman, and lay it up in thy mind, since thou art managing the rudder of the hollow ship; keep the ship off from this smoke and wave; and do thou observe the rock, lest rushing out thence she escape thy notice, and thou cast us into evil.'

"Thus I spoke; and they quickly obeyed my words. But I did not speak of Scylla, an unavoidable evil, lest my companions, terrified, should cease from rowing, and huddle themselves within. And then I forgot the terrible command of Circe, for she ordered me not to arm myself; but I, having put on my noble arms, and taking two long spears in my hands, went to the deck of the ship's prow; for I expected that rocky Scylla, who brought harm to my companions, would appear from thence first. Nor could I perceive her any where; but my eyes toiled, looking every where to the dark rock. And we sailed through the strait, mourning, for on one side was Scylla, and on the other divine Charybdis terribly sucked in the briny water of the sea. When she vomited it out, it all murmured, bubbling up as a cauldron on a large fire, and the foam fell on high upon both the lofty rocks. But when she drank up the briny water of the sea, it all appeared bubbling up within; and thundered terribly about the rock, and the earth appeared below with azure sand; and pale fear seized them. We indeed looked to this, fearing destruction. And Scylla in the mean time took six of my companions from the hollow ship, who were best in their hands and their strength. And looking to the swift ship and to my companions at the same time, I now perceived the feet and hands above of them raised on high; and calling out, they addressed me by my name, there for the last time, sorrowing at heart. As when on a jutting rock a fisherman with a very long rod throwing food as a snare for little fishes, sends the horn of a rustic ox into the sea, and then snatching it [a fish] up, throws it out panting; so they panting were raised up to the rocks: and there at the door she fed upon them crying out, stretching out their hands to me in dreadful calamity. That of a truth was the most miserable of all the things that I witnessed with mine eyes, whatever I suffered, searching out the ways of the sea.

"But when we escaped the rocks, both terrible Charybdis and Scylla, we came immediately afterwards to the blameless island of the god; there were beautiful oxen with wide foreheads, and many fat sheep of the Sun that journeys above. Then I, still going on the sea in a black ship, heard the lowing of oxen in stalls, and the bleating of sheep: and there came into my mind the word of the blind prophet, Theban Tiresias, and of Aeaean Circe, who charged me very often to avoid the island of the mortal-rejoicing Sun. Then I addressed my companions, sorrowing in my heart:

"'Hear my words, O companions, although suffering evils, that I may tell you the oracles of Tiresias, and of Aeaean Circe, who charged me very often to avoid the island of the Sun that journeys above; for she said that from hence would be a most terrible evil unto us. But drive the black ship beyond the island.'

"Thus I spoke; but their dear heart was broken down. And Eurylochus immediately answered me with a harsh speech; 'Thou art severe, O Ulysses; thou hast exceeding might, nor art thou fatigued as to your limbs; surely all of them are of iron, [since] thou dost not suffer thy companions, wearied out with toil, and [oppressed with] sleep, to go upon the land, where we may again prepare an agreeable supper in the sea-girt island; but thou commandest us to wander in vain through the swift night, straying from the island in the misty sea. During the nights troublesome winds arise, the destruction of ships: how could any one escape from utter destruction, if a storm of wind should by chance come on a sudden, either from the South or hard-blowing West, which especially destroy ships, against the will of the gods, who are kings? But let us indeed now obey black night, and let us get ready supper, remaining near the swift ship; and, embarking in the morning, let us enter on the wide sea.'

"Thus spoke Eurylochus; and my other companions approved: and then I knew that the deity meditated evils: and addressing him I spoke winged words:

"'O Eurylochus, surely now ye compel me much, being alone; but come, all of you, now swear a strong oath to me, if we find any herd of oxen, or great flock of sheep, no one will kill either ox, or even sheep, through his infatuation: but quiet do ye eat the food which immortal Circe gave us.'

"Thus I spoke; and they immediately swore as I commanded: but when they had sworn and finished the oath, we stationed the well-made ship in the hollow port, near the sweet water: and my companions went out of the ship, and then skilfully prepared supper. But when they had taken away the desire of drinking and eating, then calling to mind their dear companions whom Scylla eat, having taken them out from the black ship, they wept; and sweet sleep came upon them weeping. But when it was the third part of the night, and the stars went down, cloud-collecting Jove raised against us a strong wind, with a mighty whirlwind, and covered earth and heaven at the same time with clouds; and night arose from heaven. But when the mother of dawn, rosy-fingered morning, appeared, we moored our ship, drawing it into a hollow cave; there were the beautiful dancing-places and the seats of Nymphs; and then I, having formed an assembly, spoke unto them all:

"'O my friends, there is food and drink in the swift ship; but let us abstain from the oxen, lest we suffer any thing. For these are the oxen and fat sheep of a dread god, the Sun, who overlooks all things, and hears all things.'

"Thus I spoke; and their noble mind was persuaded. But the South wind blew without ceasing for a whole month, nor was there any other wind afterwards except the East and South. But they, whilst they had food and red wine, so long abstained from the oxen, being desirous of life; but when all the provisions were now consumed out of the ship, then wandering of necessity they followed after booty, fish and birds, acceptable, whatever came to their hands, with crooked hooks: but hunger wore down their belly. Then I went away through the island, that I might pray to the gods, if any one would show me the way to return. But when now I avoided·my companions, going through the island, having washed my hands where there was a shelter from the wind, I made vows to all the gods who inhabit Olympus: and they poured sweet sleep over my eyebrows. But Eurylochus was the beginner of evil counsel unto my companions.

"'Hear my words, O companions, although suffering evils: all deaths are hateful to wretched mortals; but, through hunger, it is most miserable to die and draw on one's fate. But come, having driven away the best of the oxen of the Sun, we will sacrifice to the immortals who possess the wide heaven. But if we come to Ithaca, our father-land, we will immediately build a rich temple to the Sun, who journeys on high, where we may place many and excellent images. But if by any means wrathful on account of the straight-horned oxen, he should wish to destroy our ship, and the other gods follow, I had rather at once lose my life gaping in the wave, than waste away any longer, remaining on a desert island.'

"Thus spoke Eurylochus; and my other companions approved. But immediately having driven the best of the oxen of the Sun from near at hand, (for the beautiful black oxen, with their broad foreheads, pastured not far away from the dark-prowed ship,) they stood around them, and prayed to the gods, having cropped the tender leaves of a lofty-tressed oak; for they had not white barley on the well-benched ship.

"But when they had prayed, and slain and skinned them, they cut off the thighs, and covered them with fat, doubling them, and they set the raw parts upon them: nor had they wine to make libations over the burnt sacrifices, but making libations with water, they roasted all the entrails. But when they had burnt the thighs, and tasted the bowels, they cut up the other parts, and fixed them on spits: and then sweet sleep rushed away from my eyebrows: and I hastened to the swift ship and the shore of the sea. But as I was now going near the ship rowed on both sides, then the sweet vapour of the fat came upon me: and mourning, I cried out to the immortal gods:

"'O father Jove, and ye other blessed gods, who exist for ever, certainly ye laid me to sleep in a pitiless sleep, to my harm, but my companions remaining here have devised a heinous deed.'

"But quickly to the Sun, who journeys above, came Lampetia, wearing a large garment, as a messenger, that we (my companions) had slain his oxen. And he immediately addressed the immortals, enraged at heart:

"'O father Jove, and ye other blessed gods, who exist for ever, punish the companions of Ulysses, the son of Laertes, who have insolently slain mine oxen, in which I rejoiced both coming to the starry heaven, and turning back again to earth from heaven. But if they do not repay me a proper return for my oxen, I will go down to Pluto's, and will shine amongst the dead.'

"But him cloud-collecting Jove answering addressed: 'O Sun, do thou by all means shine amongst the immortals and mortal men, over the fruitful plain. And then I, striking a little their swift ship with a white thunderbolt, will quickly cleave it in the middle of the dark sea.'

"But these things I heard from fair-haired Calypso; and she said that she had heard them from the messenger Mercury. But when I came to the ship and the sea, I chided them one after another, standing near them, nor could we find any remedy; for the oxen were now dead. Then the gods immediately showed prodigies to them; the skins crawled, and the flesh lowed on the spits, both roast and raw; and there was a voice as of oxen. For six days then my beloved companions feasted, driving away the best of the oxen of the Sun: but when Jove, the son of Saturn, brought on the seventh day, then the wind ceased raging with a tempest: and we, straightway embarking, committed ourselves to the wide sea: having erected the mast and drawn up the white sails.

"But when we had now left the island, nor did any other land appear, but the heaven and the sea, then the son of Saturn reared an azure cloud above the hollow ship; and the sea became dark beneath it. But it ran for no very long time; for immediately came the clamouring West wind, rushing with a mighty tempest: and the storm of the wind broke both the cables of the mast; and the mast fell backwards, and all the tackle was thrown in confusion into the hold; and he struck the head of the helmsman backward in the ship, and broke all the bones of his head together; and he fell like unto a diver from the deck, and his noble mind left his bones; and Jove thundered together, and hurled a thunderbolt upon the ship: and it was entirely whirled round, stricken with the thunderbolt of Jove, and it was filled with sulphur; and my companions fell from the ship. And they, like unto gulls, were borne on the waves around the black ship; for the deity took away their return. But I kept going about through the ship, until the storm loosed the sides from the keel; and the wave bore it along naked. And it broke out the mast at the keel: but a thong was thrown upon it, made from the skin of an ox. With this I bound both together, the keel and the mast: and sitting upon them I was borne by the destructive winds.

"Then indeed the West wind ceased raging with a storm, and quickly the South wind came on, bringing grief to my mind, that I should again measure my way to destructive Charybdis. I was borne along during the whole night; and together with the rising sun I came to the rock of Scylla, and terrible Charybdis. She gulped up the briny water of the sea; but I, raised on high to the lofty fig-tree, held clinging to it, as a bat, nor could I any where either fix myself firmly with my feet, or ascend: for the roots were far off, and the branches were wide apart, and both long and vast, and they overshadowed Charybdis. But I held without ceasing, until she vomited out again the mast and keel; and it came late to me wishing for it: as late as a man has risen from the forum to go to supper, adjudging many contests of disputing youths, so late these planks appeared from Charybdis. And I put down my feet, and my hands over them, to be carried along, and I fell with a noise in the middle on the long planks, and sitting upon them, I rowed with my hands. Nor did the father of men and of gods permit Scylla to behold me any more; for I could not have escaped bitter destruction. From thence I was borne along nine days; but in the tenth night the gods drove me to the island Ogygia; where fair-haired Calypso dwelt, an awful goddess, possessing human speech, who received me kindly, and took care of me. Why should I recount these things to thee? for I have already related them yesterday in thine house, to thee and thy illustrious wife; but it is hateful to me to recount again things that have been told full plainly."

The Flogging and Arrival
in San Diego

by RICHARD HENRY DANA, JR.

For several days the captain seemed very much out of humour. Nothing went right or fast enough for him. He quarrelled with the cook, and threatened to flog him for throwing wood on deck, and had a dispute with the mate about reeving a Spanish burton; the mate saying that he was right, and had been taught how to do it by a man *who was a sailor!* This the captain took in dudgeon and they were at sword's points at once. But his displeasure was chiefly turned against a large, heavy-moulded fellow from the Middle States, who was called Sam. This man hesitated in his speech, was rather slow in his motions, and was only a tolerably good sailor, but usually seemed to do his best; yet the captain took a dislike to him, thought he was surly and lazy, and "if you once give a dog a bad name"—as the sailor-phrase is—"he may as well jump overboard." The captain found fault with everything this man did, and hazed him for dropping a marline-spike from the main yard, where he was at work. This, of course, was an accident, but it was set down against him. The captain was on board all day Friday, and everything went on hard and disagreeably. "The more you drive a man, the less he will do," was as true with us as with any other people. We worked late Friday night, and were turned-to early Saturday morning. About ten o'clock the captain ordered our new officer, Russell, who by this time had become thoroughly disliked by all the crew, to get the gig ready to take him ashore. John, the Swede, was sitting in the boat alongside, and Mr. Russell and I were standing by the main hatchway, waiting for the captain, who was down in the hold, where the crew were at work, when we heard his voice raised in violent dispute with somebody, whether it was with the mate or one of the crew I could not tell, and then came blows and scuffling. I ran to the side and beckoned to John, who came aboard, and we leaned down the hatchway, and though we could see no one, yet we knew that the captain had the advantage, for his voice was loud and clear—

"You see your condition! You see your condition! Will you ever give me any more of your *jaw?*" No answer; and then came wrestling and heaving, as though the man was trying to turn him. "You may as well keep still, for I have got you," said the captain. Then came the question, "Will you ever give me any more of your jaw?"

"I never gave you any, sir," said Sam; for it was his voice that we heard, though low and half choked.

"That's not what I asked you. Will you ever be impudent to me again?"

"I never have been, sir," said Sam.

"Answer my question, or I'll make a spread eagle of you! I'll flog you, by G—d."

"I'm no Negro slave," said Sam.

"Then I'll make you one," said the captain; and he came to the hatchway, and sprang on deck, threw off his coat, and, rolling up his sleeves, called out to the mate: "Seize that man up, Mr. Amerzene! Seize him up! Make a spread eagle of him! I'll teach you all who is master aboard!"

The crew and officers followed the captain up the hatchway; but it was not until after repeated orders that the mate laid hold of Sam, who made no resistance, and carried him to the gangway.

"What are you going to flog that man for, sir?" said John, the Swede, to the captain.

Upon hearing this, the captain turned upon John; but, knowing him to be quick and resolute, he ordered the steward to bring the irons, and, calling upon Russell to help him, went up to John.

"Let me alone," said John. "I'm willing to be put in irons. You need not use any force"; and, putting out his hands, the captain slipped the irons on, and set him aft to the quarter-deck. Sam, by this time, was *seized up,* as it is called; that is, placed against the shrouds, with his wrists made fast to them, his jacket off, and his back exposed. The captain stood on the break of the deck, a few feet from him, and a little raised, so as to have a good swing at him, and held in his hand the end of a thick, strong rope. The officers stood round, and the crew grouped together in the waist. All these preparations made me feel sick and almost faint, angry and excited as I was. A man—a human being, made in God's likeness—fastened up and flogged like a beast! A man, too, whom I had lived with, eaten with, and stood watch with for months, and knew so well! If a thought of resistance crossed the minds of any of the men, what was to be done? Their time for it had gone by. Two men were fast, and there were left only two men besides Stimson and myself, and a small boy of ten or twelve years of age; and Stimson and I would not have joined the men in a mutiny, as they knew. And then, on the other side, there were (besides the captain) three officers, steward, agent, and clerk, and the cabin supplied with weapons. But besides the numbers, what is there for sailors to do? If they resist, it is mutiny; and if they succeed, and take the vessel, it is piracy. If they ever yield again, their punishment must come; and if they do not yield, what are they to be for the rest of their lives? If a sailor resist his commander, he resists the law, and piracy or submission is his only alternative. Bad as it was, they saw it must be borne. It is what a sailor ships for. Swinging the rope over his head, and bending his body so as to give it full force, the captain brought it down upon the poor fellow's back. Once, twice,—six times. "Will you ever give me any more of your jaw?" The man writhed with pain, but said not a word. Three times more. This was too much, and he muttered something which I could not hear; this brought as many more as the man could stand, when the captain ordered him to be cut down.

"Now for you," said the captain, making up to John, and taking his irons off. As soon as John was loose, he ran forward to the forecastle. "Bring that man aft!" shouted the captain. The second mate, who had been in the forecastle with these men the early part of the voyage, stood still in the waist, and the mate walked slowly forward; but our third officer, anxious to show his zeal, sprang forward over the wind-lass, and laid hold of John; but John soon threw him from him. The captain stood on the quarter-deck, bareheaded, his eyes flashing with rage, and his face as red as blood, swinging the rope, and calling out to his officers, "Drag him aft! Lay hold of him! I'll *sweeten him!*" etc., etc. The mate now went forward, and told John quietly to go aft; and he, seeing resistance vain, threw the blackguard third mate from him, said he would go aft of himself, that they should not drag him, and went up to the gangway and held out his hands; but as soon as the captain began to make him fast, the indignity was too much, and he struggled; but, the mate and Russell holding him, he was soon seized up. When he was made fast, he turned to the captain, who stood rolling up his sleeves, getting ready for the blow, and asked him what he was to be flogged for. "Have I ever refused my duty, sir? Have you ever known me to hang back or to be insolent, or not to know my work?"

"No," said the captain, "it is not that that I flog you for; I flog you for your interference, for asking questions."

"Can't a man ask a question here without being flogged?"

"No," shouted the captain; "nobody shall open his mouth aboard this vessel but myself"; and he began laying the blows upon his back, swinging half round between each blow, to give it full effect. As he went on his passion increased, and he danced about the deck, calling out, as he swung the rope, "If you want to know what I flog you for, I'll tell you. It's because I like to do it! because I like to do it! It suits me! That's what I do it for!"

The man writhed under the pain until he could endure it no longer, when he called out, with an exclamation more common among foreigners than with us: "O Jesus Christ! O Jesus Christ!"

"Don't call on Jesus Christ," shouted the captain; *"He can't help you. Call on Frank Thompson!* He's the man! He can help you! Jesus Christ can't help you now!"

At these words, which I never shall forget, my blood ran cold. I could look on no longer. Disgusted, sick, I turned away, and leaned over the rail, and looked down into the water. A few rapid thoughts, I don't know what—our situation, a resolution to see the captain punished when we got home— crossed my mind; but the falling of the blows and the cries of the man called me back once more. At length they ceased, and, turning round, I found that the mate, at a signal from the captain, had cast him loose. Almost doubled up with pain, the man walked slowly forward, and went down into the forecastle. Every one else stood still at his post, while the captain, swelling with rage and with the importance of his achievement, walked the quarter-deck, and at each turn, as he came forward, calling out to us: "You see your condition! You see where I've got you all, and you know what to expect! You've been mistaken in me! You didn't know what I was! Now you know what I am! I'll make you toe the mark, every soul of you, or I'll flog you all, fore and aft, from the boy up! You've got a driver over you! Yes, *a slave-driver—a nigger-driver!* I'll see who'll tell me he isn't a NIGGER slave!" With this and the like matter, equally calculated to quiet us, and to allay any apprehensions of future trouble, he entertained us for about ten minutes, when he went below. Soon after, John came aft, with his bare back covered with stripes and wales in ever direction, and dreadfully swollen, and asked the steward to ask the captain to let him have some salve, or balsam, to put upon it. "No," said the captain, who heard him from below; "tell him to put his shirt on; that's the best thing for him, and pull me ashore in the boat. Nobody is going to lay-up on board this vessel." He then called to Mr. Russell to take those two men and two others in the boat, and pull him ashore. I went for one. The two men could hardly bend their backs, and the captain called to them to "give way!" but finding they did their best, he let them alone. The agent was in the stern sheets, but during the whole pull—a league or more—not a word was spoken. We landed; the captain, agent, and officer went up to the house, and left us with the boat. I and the man with me stayed near the boat, while John and Sam walked slowly away, and sat down on the rocks. They talked some time together, but at length separated, each sitting alone. I had some fears of John. He was a foreigner, and violently tempered, and under suffering; and he had his knife with him, and the captain was to come down alone to the boat. But nothing happened; and we went quietly on board. The captain was probably armed, and if either of them had lifted a hand against him, they would have had nothing before them but flight, and starvation in the woods of California, or capture by the soldiers and Indians, whom the offer of twenty dollars would have set upon them.

After the day's work was done we went down into the forecastle and ate our plain supper; but not a word was spoken. It was Saturday night; but, there was no song—no "sweethearts and wives." A gloom was over everything. The two men lay in their berths, groaning with pain, and we all turned in, but, for myself, not to sleep. A sound coming now and then from the berths of the two men showed that they were awake, as awake they must have been, for they could hardly lie in one posture long; the dim swinging lamp shed its light over the dark hole in which we lived, and many and various reflections and purposes coursed through my mind. I had no real apprehension that the captain would lay a hand on me; but I thought of our situation, living under a tyranny, with an ungoverned, swaggering fellow administering it; of the character of the country we were in; the length of the voyage; the uncertainty attending our return to America; and then, if we should return, the prospect of obtaining justice and satisfaction for these poor men; and I vowed that, if God should ever give me the means, I would do something to redress the grievances and relieve the sufferings of that class of beings with whom my lot had so long been cast.

The next day was Sunday. We worked as usual, washing decks, etc., until breakfast-time. After breakfast we pulled the captain ashore, and, finding some hides there which had been brought down the night before, he ordered me to stay ashore and watch them, saying that the boat would come again before night. They left me, and I spent a quiet day on the hill, eating dinner with three men at the little house. Unfortunately they had no books; and, after talking with them, and walking about, I began to grow tired of doing nothing. The little brig, the home of so much hardship and suffering, lay in the offing, almost as far as one could see, and the only other thing which broke the surface of the great bay was a small, dreary-looking island, steep and conical, of a clayey soil, and without the sign of vegetable life upon it, yet which had a peculiar and melancholy interest, for on the top of it were buried the remains of an Englishman, the commander of a small merchant brig, who died while lying in this port. It was always a solemn and affecting spot to me. There it stood desolate, and in the midst of desolation; and there were the remains of one who died and was buried alone and friendless. Had it been a common burying-place, it would have been nothing. The single body corresponded well with the solitary character of everything around. It was the only spot in California that impressed me with anything like poetic interest. Then, too, the man died far from home, without a friend near him—by poison, it was suspected, and no one to inquire into it—and without funeral rites; the mate (as I was told), glad to have him out of the way, hurrying him up the hill and into the ground, without a word or a prayer.

I looked anxiously for a boat during the latter part of the afternoon, but none came until towards sundown, when I saw a speck on the water, and as it drew near I found it was the gig, with the captain. The hides, then, were not to go off. The captain came up the hill, with a man, bringing my monkey-jacket and a blanket. He looked pretty black, but inquired whether I had enough to eat; told me to make a house out of the hides, and keep myself warm, as I should have to sleep there among them, and to keep good watch over them. I got a moment to speak to the man who brought my jacket.

"How do things go aboard?" said I.

"Bad enough," said he; "hard work and not a kind word spoken."

"What!" said I, "have you been at work all day?"

"Yes! no more Sunday for us. Everything has been moved in the hold, from stem to stern, and from the water-ways to the keelson."

I went up to the house to supper. We had frijoles (the perpetual food of the Californians, but which, when well cooked, are the best bean in the world), coffee made of burnt wheat, and hard bread. After our meal, the three men sat down by the light of a tallow candle, with a pack of greasy Spanish cards, to the favourite game of "treinta y uno," a sort of Spanish "everlasting." I left them and went out to take up my bivouac among the hides. It was now dark; the vessel was hidden from sight, and except the three men in the house there was not a living soul within a league. The coyotes (a wild animal of a nature and appearance between that of the fox and the wolf) set up their sharp, quick bark, and two owls, at the end of two distant points running out into the bay, on different sides of the hill where I lay, kept up their alternate dismal notes. I had heard the sound before at night, but did not know what it was, until one of the men, who came down to look at my quarters, told me it was the owl. Mellowed by the distance, and heard alone, at night, it was a most melancholy and boding sound. Through nearly all the night they kept it up, answering one another slowly at regular intervals. This was relieved by the noisy coyotes, some of which came quite near to my quarters, and were not very pleasant neighbours. The next morning, before sunrise, the longboat came ashore, and the hides were taken off.

We lay at San Pedro about a week, engaged in taking off hides and in other labours, which had now become our regular duties. I spent one more day on the hill, watching a quantity of hides and goods, and this time succeeded in finding a part of a volume of Scott's *Pirate* in a corner of the house; but it failed me at a most interesting moment, and I betook myself to my acquaintances on shore, and from them learned a good deal about the customs of the country, the harbours, etc. This, they told me, was a worse harbour than Santa Barbara for southeasters, the bearing of the headland being a point and a half more to windward, and it being so shallow that the sea broke often as far out as where we lay at anchor. The gale for which we slipped at Santa Barbara had been so bad a one here, that the whole bay, for a league out, was filled with the foam of the breakers, and seas actually broke over the Dead Man's Island. The *Lagoda* was lying there, and slipped at the first alarm, and in such haste that she was obliged to leave her launch behind her at anchor. The little boat rode it out for several hours, pitching at her anchor, and standing with her stern up almost perpendicularly. The men told me that they watched her till towards night, when she snapped her cable and drove up over the breakers high and dry upon the beach.

On board the *Pilgrim* everything went on regularly, each one trying to get along as smoothly as possible; but the comfort of the voyage was evidently at an end. "That is a long lane which has no turning," "Every dog must have his day, and mine will come by and by," and the like proverbs, were occasionally quoted; but no one spoke of any probable end to the voyage, or of Boston, or anything of the kind; or, if he did, it was only to draw out the perpetual surly reply from his shipmate: "Boston, is it? You may thank your stars if you ever see that place. You had better have your back sheathed, and your head coppered, and your feet shod, and make out your log for California for life!" or else something of this kind: "Before you get to Boston the hides will wear all the hair off your head, and you'll take up all your wages in clothes, and won't have enough left to buy a wig with!"

The flogging was seldom, if ever, alluded to by us in the forecastle. If any one was inclined to talk about it, the others, with a delicacy which I hardly expected to find among them, always stopped him, or turned the subject. But the behaviour of the two men who were flogged towards one another showed a consideration which would have been worthy of admiration in the highest walks of life. Sam knew John had suffered solely on his account; and in all his complaints he said that, if he alone had been flogged, it would have been nothing; but he never could see him without thinking that he had been the means of bringing this disgrace upon him; and John never, by word or deed, let anything escape him to remind the other that it was by interfering to save his shipmate that he had suffered. Neither made it a secret that they thought the Dutchman Bill and Foster might have helped them; but they did not expect it of Stimson or me. While we showed our sympathy for their suffering, and our indignation at the captain's violence, we did not feel sure that there was only one side to the beginning of the difficulty, and we kept clear of any engagement with them, except our promise to help them when they got home.*

Having got all our spare room filled with hides, we hove up our anchor, and made sail for San Diego. In no operation can the disposition of a crew be better discovered than in getting under way. Where things are done "with a will," every one is like a cat aloft; sails are loosed in an instant; each one lays out his strength on his handspike, and the windlass goes briskly round with the loud cry of "Yo heave ho! Heave and pawl! Heave hearty, ho!" and the chorus of "Cheerily, men!" cats the anchor. But with us, at this time, it was all dragging work. No one went aloft beyond his ordinary gait, and the chain came slowly in over the windlass. The mate, between the knight-heads, exhausted all his official rhetoric in calls of "Heave with a will!" "Heave hearty, men! heave hearty!" "Heave, and raise the dead!" "Heave, and away!" etc., etc., but it would not do. Nobody broke his back or his handspike by his efforts. And when the cat-tackle-fall was strung along, and all hands, cook, steward, and all, laid hold, to cat the anchor, instead of the lively song of "Cheerily, men!" in which all hands join in the chorus, we pulled a long, heavy, silent pull, and, as sailors say a song is as good as ten men, the anchor came to the cat-head pretty slowly. "Give us 'Cheerily!'" said the mate; but

---

* Owing to the change of vessels that afterwards took place, Captain Thompson arrived in Boston nearly a year before the *Pilgrim,* and was off on another voyage, and beyond the reach of these men. Soon after the publication of the first edition of this book, in 1841, I received a letter from Stimson, dated at Detroit, Michigan, where he had re-entered mercantile life, from which I make this extract:—"As to your account of the flogging scene, I think you have given a fair history of it, and, if anything, been too lenient towards Captain Thompson for his brutal, cowardly treatment of those men. As I was in the hold at the time the affray commenced, I will give you a short history of it as near as I can recollect. We were breaking out goods in the fore-hold, and, in order to get at them, we had to shift our hides from forward to aft. After having removed part of them, we came to the boxes, and attempted to get them out without moving any more of the hides. While doing so, Sam accidentally hurt his hand, and, as usual, began swearing about it, and was not sparing of his oaths, although I think he was not aware that Captain Thompson was so near him at the time. Captain Thompson asked him, in no moderate way, what was the matter with him. Sam, on account of the impediment in his speech, could not answer immediately, although he endeavoured to, but as soon as possible answered in a manner that almost any one would, under the like circumstances, yet, I believe, not with the intention of giving a short answer; but being provoked, and suffering pain from the injured hand, he perhaps answered rather short, or sullenly. Thus commenced the scene you have so vividly described, and which seems to me exactly the history of the whole affair without any exaggeration."

there was no "cheerily" for us and we did without it. The captain walked the quarter-deck, and said not a word. He must have seen the change, but there was nothing which he could notice officially.

We sailed leisurely down the coast before a light fair wind, keeping the land well aboard, and saw two other missions, looking like blocks of white plaster, shining in the distance; one of which, situated on the top of a high hill, was San Juan Capistrano, under which vessels sometimes come to anchor, in the summer season, and take off hides. At sunset on the second day we had a large and well-wooded headland directly before us, behind which lay the little harbour of San Diego. We were becalmed off this point all night; but the next morning, which was Saturday, the 14th of March, having a good breeze, we stood round the point, and, hauling our wind, brought the little harbour, which is rather the outlet of a small river, right before us. Every one was desirous to get a view of the new place. A chain of high hills, beginning at the point (which was on our larboard hand coming in), protected the harbour on the north and west, and ran off into the interior, as far as the eye could reach. On the other sides the land was low and green, but without trees. The entrance is so narrow as to admit but one vessel at a time, the current swift, and the channel runs so near to a low stony point that the ship's sides appeared almost to touch it. There was no town in sight, but on the smooth sand beach, abreast, and within a cable's length of which three vessels lay moored, were four large houses, built of rough boards and looking like the great barns in which ice is stored on the borders of the large ponds near Boston, with piles of hides standing round them, and men in red shirts and large straw hats walking in and out of the doors. These were the hide-houses. Of the vessels: one, a short, clumsy little hermaphrodite brig, we recognised as our old acquaintance, the *Loriotte;* another, with sharp bows and raking masts, newly painted and tarred, and glittering in the morning sun, with the blood-red banner and cross of St. George at her peak, was the handsome *Ayacucho.* The third was a large ship, with topgallant-masts housed and sails unbent, and looking as rusty and worn as two years' "hide droghing" could make her. This was the *Lagoda.* As we drew near, carried rapidly along by the current, we overhauled our chain, and clewed up the topsails. "Let go the anchor!" said the captain; but either there was not chain enough forward of the windlass, or the anchor went down foul, or we had too much headway on, for it did not bring us up. "Pay out chain!" shouted the captain; and we gave it to her; but it would not do. Before the other anchor could be let go we drifted down, broadside on, and went smash into the *Lagoda.* Her crew were at breakfast in the forecastle, and her cook, seeing us coming, rushed out of his galley, and called up the officers and men.

Fortunately, no great harm was done. Her jib-boom passed between our fore and main masts, carrying away some of our rigging, and breaking down the rail. She lost her martingale. This brought us up, and as they paid out chain, we swung clear of them and let go the other anchor; but this had as bad luck as the first, for, before any one perceived it, we were drifting down upon the

Loriotte. The captain now gave out his orders rapidly and fiercely, sheeting home the topsails, and backing and filling the sails, in hope of starting or clearing the anchors; but it was all in vain, and he sat down on the rail, taking it very leisurely, and calling out to Captain Nye that he was coming to pay him a visit. We drifted fairly into the *Loriotte,* her larboard bow into our starboard quarter, carrying away a part of our starboard quarter railing, and breaking off her larboard bumpkin and one or two stanchions above the deck. We saw our handsome sailor, Jackson, on the forecastle, with the Sandwich-Islanders, working away to get us clear. After paying out chain, we swung clear, but our anchors were, no doubt, afoul of hers. We manned the windlass, and hove, and hove away, but to no purpose. Sometimes we got a little upon the cable, but a good surge would take it all back again. We now began to drift down toward the *Ayacucho;* when her boat put off, and brought her commander, Captain Wilson, on board. He was a short, active, well-built man, about fifty years of age; and being some twenty years older than our captain, and a thorough seaman, he did not hesitate to give his advice, and from giving advice he gradually came to taking the command; ordering us when to heave and when to pawl, and backing and filling the topsails, setting and taking in jib and trysail, whenever he thought best. Our captain gave a few orders, but as Wilson generally countermanded them, saying, in an easy, fatherly kind of way, "Oh, no! Captain Thompson, you don't want the jib on her," or "It isn't time yet to heave!" he soon gave it up. We had no objections to this state of things, for Wilson was a kind man, and had an encouraging and pleasant way of speaking to us, which made everything go easily. After two or three hours of constant labour at the windlass, heaving and yo-ho-ing with all our might, we brought up an anchor, with the *Loriotte*'s small bower fast to it. Having cleared this, and let it go, and cleared our hawse, we got our other anchor, which had dragged half over the harbour. "Now," said Wilson, "I'll find you a good berth"; and, setting both the topsails, he carried us down, and brought us to anchor, in handsome style, directly abreast of the hide-house which we were to use. Having done this, he took his leave, while we furled the sails and got our breakfast, which was welcome to us, for we had worked hard and eaten nothing since yesterday afternoon, and it was nearly twelve o'clock. After breakfast, and until night, we were employed in getting out the boats and mooring ship.

After supper two of us took the captain on board the *Lagoda.* As he came alongside he gave his name, and the mate, in the gangway, called out to Captain Bradshaw, down the companion-way, "Captain Thompson has come aboard, sir!" "Has he brought his brig with him?" asked the rough old fellow, in a tone which made itself heard fore and aft. This mortified our captain not a little, and it became a standing joke among us, and, indeed, over the coast, for the rest of the voyage. The captain went down into the cabin, and we walked forward and put our heads down the forecastle, where we found the men at supper. "Come down, shipmates! come down!" said they, as soon they saw us; and we went down, and found a large, high forecastle, well lighted, and a crew of twelve or fourteen men eating out of their kids and pans, and drinking their tea, and talking and laughing, all as independent and easy as so many "wood-sawyer's clerks." This looked like comfort and enjoyment, compared with the dark little forecastle, and scanty, discontented crew of the brig. It was Saturday night; they had got through their work for the week, and being snugly moored, had nothing to do until Monday again. After two years' hard service they had seen the worst, and all, of California; had got their cargo nearly stowed, and expected to sail in a week or two for Boston.

We spent an hour or more with them, talking over California matters, until the word was passed—"Pilgrims, away!" and we went back to our brig. The Lagodas were a hardy, intelligent set, a little roughened, and their clothes patched and old, from California wear; all able seamen, and between the ages of twenty and thirty-five or forty. They inquired about our vessel, the usage on board, etc., and were not a little surprised at the story of the flogging. They said there were often difficulties in vessels on the coast, and sometimes knock-downs and fightings, but they had never heard before of a regular seizing-up and flogging. "Spread eagles" were a new kind of bird in California.

The Voyage of the *Liberdade*

by JOSHUA SLOCUM

> Away, away, no cloud is lowering o'er us,
> Freely now we stem the wave;
> Hoist, hoist all sail, before us
> Hope's beacon shines to cheer the brave.
>
> Massaneillo

When all had been saved from the wreck that was worth saving, or that could be saved, we found ourselves still in the possession of some goods soon to become of great value to us, especially my compass and charts which, though much damaged, were yet serviceable and suggested practical usefulness; and the chronometer being found intact, my course was no longer undecided, my wife and sons agreeing with what I thought best.

The plan, in a word, was this: We could not beg our way, neither would we sit idle among the natives. We found that it would require more courage to remain in the far-off country than to return home in a boat, which then we concluded to build and for that purpose.*

My son Victor, with much pride and sympathy, entered heartily into the plan, which promised a speedy return home. He bent his energies in a practical direction, working on the boat like an old builder.

Before entering on the project, however, all responsibilities were considered. Swift ocean currents around capes and coral reefs were taken into account; and above all else to be called dangerous we knew would be the fierce tropical storms which surely we would encounter.

But a boat should be built stout and strong, we all said, one in which we should not be afraid to trust our lives even in the storm.

And with the advantage of experience in ships and boats of various sizes and in many seas, I turned to the work of constructing, according to my judgment and means, a craft which would be best adapted to all weathers and all circumstances. My family with sympathetic strength pulling hard in the same direction.

Seaworthiness was to be the first and most prominent feature in our microscopic ship; next to this good quality she should sail well; at least before free winds, for we counted on favourable winds; and so they were experienced the greater part of the voyage that followed.

Long exposures and many and severe disappointments by this time, I found, had told on health and nerve, through long quarantines, expensive fumigations, and ruinous doctors' visits, which had swept my dollars into hands

---

*This alternative I was obliged to accept, or bring my family home as paupers, for my wealth was gone—need I explain more? This explanation has been forced from me.

other than mine. However, with still a "shot in the locker," and with some feelings of our own in the matter of how we should get home, I say, we set to work with tools saved from the wreck—a meagre kit—and soon found ourselves in command of another ship, which I will describe the building of, also the dimensions and the model and rig, first naming the tools with which it was made.

To begin with, we had an axe, an adze and two saws, one 1-2 inch auger, one 6-8 and one 3-8 auger-bit; two large sail-needles, which we converted into nailing bits; one roper, that answered for a punch; and, most precious of all, a file that we found in an old sail-bag washed up on the beach. A square we readily made. Two splints of bamboo wood served as compasses. Charcoal, pounded as fine as flour and mixed in water, took the place of chalk for the line; the latter we had on hand. In cases where holes larger than the 6-8 bit were required, a piece of small jack-stay iron was heated, and with this we could burn a hole to any size required. So we had, after all, quite a kit to go on with. Clamps, such as are used by boat builders, we had not, but made substitutes from the crooked guava tree and from *massaranduba* wood.

Trees from the neighboring forest were felled when the timber from the wrecked cargo would not answer. Some of these woods that we sought for special purposes had queer sounding names, such as *arregebah, guanandee, batetenandinglastampai,* etc. This latter we did not use the saw upon at all, it being very hard, but hewed it with the axe, bearing in mind that we had but one file, whereas for the edged tools we had but to go down to a brook hard by to find stones in abundance suitable to sharpen them on.

The many hindrances encountered in the building of the boat will not be recounted here. Among the least was a jungle fever, from which we suffered considerably. But all that, and all other obstacles vanished at last, or became less, before a new energy which grew apace with the boat, and the building of the craft went rapidly forward. There was no short day system, but we rested on the Sabbath, or surveyed what we had done through the week, and made calculations of what and how to strike on the coming week.

The unskilled part of the labor, such as sawing the cedar planks, of which she was mostly made, was done by the natives, who saw in a rough fashion, always leaving much planing and straightening to be done, in order to adjust the timber to a suitable shape. The planks for the bottom were of ironwood, $1\frac{1}{4} \times 10$ inches. For the sides and top red cedar was used, each plank, with the exception of two, reaching the whole length of the boat. This arrangement of exceedingly heavy wood in the bottom, and the light on top, contributed much to the stability of the craft.

The ironwood was heavy as stone, while the cedar, being light and elastic, lent buoyancy and suppleness, all that we could wish for.

The fastenings we gathered up in various places, some from the bulwarks of the wreck, some from the hinges of doors and skylights, and some were made from the ship's metal sheathing, which the natives melted and cast into nails. Pure copper nails, also, were procured from the natives, some ten kilos, for which I paid in copper coins, at the rate of two *kilos* of coin for one *kilo* of nails. The same kind of coins, called *dumps,* cut into diamond-shaped pieces, with holes punched through them, entered into the fastenings as burrs for the nails. A number of small eyebolts from the spanker-boom of the wreck were turned to account for lashing bolts in the deck of the new vessel. The nails, when too long, were cut to the required length, taking care that the ends which were cut off should not be wasted, but remelted, along with the metal sheathing, into other nails.

Some carriage bolts, with nuts, which I found in the country, came in very handy; these I adjusted to the required length, when too long, by slipping on blocks of wood of the required thickness to take up the surplus length, putting the block, of course, on the inside, and counter-sinking the nut flush with the planks on the outside; then screwing from the inside outward, they were drawn together, and there held as in a vise, the planks being put together "lap-streak" fashion, which without doubt is the strongest way to build a boat.

These screw-bolts, seventy in number, as well as the copper nails, cost us dearly, but wooden pegs, with which also she was fastened, cost only the labor of being made. The lashings, too, that we used here and there about the frame of the cabin, cost next to nothing, being made from the fibrous bark of trees, which could be had in abundance by the stripping of it off. So, taking it by and large, our materials were not expensive, the principal item being the timber, which cost about three cents per superficial foot, sawed or hewed. Rosewood, ironwood, cedar or mahogany, were all about the same price and very little in advance of common wood; so of course we selected always, the best, the labor of shaping being least, sometimes, where the best materials were used.

These various timbers and fastenings, put together as best we could shape and join them, made a craft sufficiently strong and seaworthy to withstand all the buffetings on the main upon which, in due course she was launched.

The hull being completed, by various other contrivances and makeshifts in which, sometimes, the "wooden blacksmith" was called in to assist, and the mother of invention also lending a hand, fixtures were made which served as well on the voyage as though made in a dockyard and at great cost.

My builders balked at nothing, and on the 13th day of May, the day on which the slaves of Brazil were set free, our craft was launched, and was named *Liberdade* (Liberty).

Her dimensions being—35 feet in length over all, 7 1-2 feet breadth of beam, and 3 feet depth of hold, who shall say that she was not large enough?

Her model I got from my recollections of Cape Ann dories and from a photo of a very elegant Japanese *sampan* which I had before me on the spot, so, as it might be expected, when finished, she resembled both types of vessel in some degree.

Her rig was the Chinese *sampan* style, which is, I consider, the most convenient boat rig in the whole world.

This was the boat, or canoe I prefer to call it, in which we purposed to sail for North America and home. Each one had been busy during the construction and past misfortunes had all been forgotten. Madam had made the sails—and very good sails they were, too!

Victor, the carpenter, ropemaker and general roustabout had performed his part. Our little man, Garfield, too, had found employment in holding the hammer to clinch the nails and giving much advice on the coming voyage. All were busy, I say, and no one had given a thought of what we were about to encounter from the port officials further up the coast; it was pretended by them that a passport could not be granted to so small a craft to go on so long a voyage as the contemplated one to North America.

Then fever returned to the writer, and the constructor of the little craft, and I was forced to go to bed, remaining there three days. Finally, it came to my mind that in part of a medicine chest, which had been saved from the wreck, was stored some *arsenicum,* I think it is called. Of this I took several doses (small ones at first, you may be sure), and the good effect of the deadly poison on the malaria in my system was soon felt trickling through my veins. Increasing the doses somewhat, I could perceive the beneficial effect hour by hour, and in a few days I had quite recovered from the malady. Absurd as it was to have the judgment of sailors set on by pollywog navigators, we had still to submit, the pollywogs being numerous.

About this time—as the astrologers say—a messenger came down from the *Alfandega* (Custom House), asking me to repair thither at midday on the morrow. This filled me with alarm. True, the messenger had delivered his message in the politest possible manner, but that signified nothing, since Brazilians are always polite. This thing, small as it seems now, came near sending me back to the fever.

What had I done?

I went up next day, after having nightmare badly all night, prepared to say that I wouldn't do it again! The kind of administrator I found, upon presenting myself at his office, had no fault to charge me with; but had a good word, instead. "The little *Liberdade,*" he observed, had attracted the notice of his people and his own curiosity, as being "a handsome and well-built craft." This and many other flattering expressions were vented, at which I affected surprise, but secretly said, "I think you are right, sir, and you have good taste, too, if you are a customs officer."

The drift of this flattery, to make a long story short, was to have me build a boat for the *Alfandega,* or, his government not allowing money to build new— pointing to one which certainly would require new keel, planks, ribs, stem and stern-post—"could I not repair one?"

To this proposition I begged time to consider. Flattering as the officer's words were, and backed by the offer of liberal pay, so long as the boat could be "repaired," I still had no mind to remain in the hot country, and risk getting the fever again. But there was the old hitch to be gotten over; namely, the passport, on which, we thought, depended our sailing.

However, to expedite matters, a fishing license was hit upon, and I wondered why I had not thought of that before, having been, once upon a time, a fisherman myself. Heading thence on a new diplomatic course, I commenced to fit ostensibly for a fishing voyage. To this end, a fishing net was made, which would be a good thing to have, any way. Then hooks and lines were rigged and a cable made. This cable, or rope, was formed from vines that grow very long on the sandbanks just above tide water, several of which twisted together make a very serviceable rope, then being light and elastic, it is especially adapted for a boat anchor rope, or for the storm drag. Ninety fathoms of this rope was made for us by the natives, for the sum of ten milreis ($5.00).

The anchor came of itself almost. I had made a wooden one from heavy sinking timber, but a stalwart ranchman coming along, one day, brought a boat anchor with him which, he said, had been used by his slaves as a pot-hook. "But now that they are free and away," said he, "I have no further use for the crooked thing." A sewing-machine, which had served to stitch the sails together, was coveted by him, and was of no further use to us; in exchange for this the prized anchor was readily secured, the owner of it leaving us some boot into the bargain. Things working thus in our favor, the wooden anchor was stowed away to be kept as a spare bower.

These arrangements completed, our craft took on the appearance of a fishing smack, and I began to feel somewhat in my old element, with no fear of the lack of ways and means when we should arrive on our own coast, where I knew of fishing banks. And a document which translated read: "A license to catch fish inside and outside of the bar," was readily granted by the port authorities.

"How far outside the bar may this carry us?" I asked.

"Quien sabe!" said the officer. (Literally translated, "Who knows?" but in Spanish or Portuguese used for, "Nobody knows, or I don't care.")

"Adios, señor," said the polite official; "we will meet in heaven!"

This meant you can go since you insist upon it, but I must not officially know of it; and you will probably go to the bottom. In this he and many others were mistaken.

Having the necessary document now in our possession, we commenced to take in stores for the voyage, as follows: Sea-biscuits, 120 lbs.; flour, 25 lbs.; sugar, 30 lbs.; coffee, 9 lbs., which roasted black and pounded fine as wheaten flour, was equal to double the amount as prepared in North America, and afforded us a much more delicious cup.

Of tea we had 3 lbs.; pork, 20 lbs.; dried beef, 100 lbs.; *baccalao secca*, (dried codfish) 20 lbs.; 2 bottles of honey, 200 oranges, 6 bunches of bananas, 120 gallons of water; also a small basket of yams, and a dozen sticks of sugar-cane, by way of vegetables.

Our medicine chest contained Brazil nuts, pepper and cinnamon; no other medicines or condiments were required on the voyage, except table salt, which we also had.

One musket and a carbine—which had already stood us in good stead—together with ammunition and three cutlasses, were stowed away for last use, to be used, nevertheless, in case of necessity.

The light goods I stowed in the ends of the canoe, the heavier in the middle and along the bottom, thus economizing space and lending to the stability of the canoe. Over the top of the midship stores a floor was made, which, housed over by a tarpaulin roof reaching three feet above the deck of the canoe, gave us sitting space of four feet from the floor to roof, and twelve feet long amidships, supported by a frame of bamboo, made store-room and cabin. This arrangement of cabin in the centre gave my passengers a berth where the least motion would be felt: even this is saying but little, for best we could do to avoid it we had still to accept much tossing from the waves.

Precautionary measures were taken in everything, so far as our resources and skill could reach. The springy and buoyant bamboo was used wherever stick of any kind was required, such as the frame and braces for the cabin, yards for the sails, and, finally, for guard on her top sides, making the canoe altogether a self-righting one, in case of a capsize. Each joint in the bamboo was an air-chamber of several pounds buoyant capacity, and we had a thousand joints.

The most important of our stores, particularly the flour, bread and coffee, were hermetically sealed, so that if actually turned over at sea, our craft would not only right herself, but would bring her stores right side up, in good order, and it then would be only a question of baling her out, and of setting her again on her course, when we would come on as right as ever. As it turned out, however, no such trial or mishap awaited us.

While the possibility of many and strange occurrences was felt by all of us, the danger which loomed most in little Garfield's mind was that of the sharks.

A fine specimen was captured on the voyage, showing five rows of pearly teeth, as sharp as lances.

Some of these monsters, it is said, have nine rows of teeth; that they are always hungry is admitted by sailors of great experience.

How it is that sailors can go in bathing, as they often do, in the face of a danger so terrible, is past my comprehension. Their business is to face danger, to be sure, but this is a needless exposure, for which the penalty is sometimes a life. The second mate of a bark on the coast of Cuba, not long ago, was bitten in twain, and the portions swallowed whole by a monster shark that he had tempted in this way. The shark was captured soon after, and the poor fellow's remains taken out of the revolting maw.

Leaving the sharks where they are, I gladly return to the voyage of the *Liberdade*.

The efficiency of our canoe was soon discovered, for on the 24th of June, after having sailed about the bay some few days to temper our feelings to the new craft, and shake things into place, we crossed the bar and stood out to sea, while six vessels lay inside "bar-bound," that is to say by their pilots it was thought too rough to venture out, and they, the pilots, stood on the point as we put out to sea, crossing themselves in our behalf, and shouting that the bar was *crudo*. But the *Liberdade* stood on her course, the crew never regretting it.

The wind from the sou'west at the time was the moderating side of a *pampeiro* which had brought in a heavy swell from the ocean, that broke and thundered on the bar with deafening roar and grand display of majestic effort.

But our little ship bounded through the breakers like a fish—as natural to the elements, and as free!

Of all the seas that broke furiously about her that day, often standing her on end, not one swept over or even boarded her, and she finally came through the storm of breakers in triumph. Then squaring away before the wind she spread her willing sails, and flew onward like a bird.

It required confidence and some courage to face the first storm in so small a bark, after having been years in large ships; but it would have required more courage than was possessed by any of us to turn back, since thoughts of home had taken hold on our minds.

Then, too, the old boating trick came back fresh to me, the love of the thing itself gaining on me as the little ship stood out; and my crew with one voice said: "Go on." The heavy south Atlantic swell rolling in upon the coast, as we sped along, toppled over when it reached the ten fathom line, and broke into roaring combers, which forbade our nearer approach to the land.

Evidently, our safest course was away from the shore, and out where the swelling seas, though grand, were regular, and raced under our little craft that danced like a mite on the ocean as she drove forward. In twenty-four hours from the time Paranagua bar was crossed we were up with Santos Heads, a run of 150 miles.

A squall of wind burst on us through a gulch, as we swept round the Heads, tearing our sails into shreds, and sending us into Santos under bare poles.

Chancing then upon an old friend, the mail steamship *Finance*, Capt. Baker, about to sail for Rio, the end of a friendly line was extended to us, and we were towed by the stout steamer toward Rio, the next day, as fast as we could wish to go. My wife and youngest sailor took passage on the steamer, while Victor remained in the canoe with me, and stood by, with axe in hand, to cut the tow-line, if the case should require it—and I steered.

"Look out," said Baker, as the steamer began to move ahead, "look out that I don't snake that canoe out from under you."

"Go on with your mails, Baker," was all I could say, "don't blow up your ship with my wife and son on board, and I will look out for the packet on the other end of the rope."

Baker opened her up to thirteen knots, but the *Liberdade* held on!

The line that we towed with was 1⅓ inches in diameter, by ninety fathoms long. This, at times when the steamer surged over seas, leaving the canoe on the opposite side of a wave astern, would become as taut as a harp-string. At other times it would slacken and sink limp in a bight, under the forefoot, but only for a moment, however, when the steamer's next great plunge ahead would snap it taut again, pulling us along with a heavy, trembling jerk. Under the circumstances, straight steering was imperative, for a sheer to port or starboard would have finished the career of the *Liberdade*, by sending her under the sea. Therefore, the trick of twenty hours fell to me—the oldest and most experienced helmsman. But I was all right and not over-fatigued until Baker cast oil upon the "troubled waters." I soon got tired of that.

Victor was under the canvas covering, with the axe still in hand, ready to cut the line which was so arranged that he could reach it from within, and cut instantly, if by mischance the canoe should take a sheer.

I was afraid that the lad would become sleepy, and putting his head "under his wing" for a nap, would forget his post, but my frequent cry, "Stand by there, Victor," found him always on hand, though complaining some of the dizzy motion.

Heavy sprays dashed over me at the helm, which, however, seeming to wash away the sulphur and brimstone smoke of many a quarantine, brought enjoyment to my mind.

Confused waves rose about us, high and dangerous—often high above the gunwale of the canoe—but her shapely curves balanced her well, and she rode over them all in safety.

This canoe ride was thrilling and satisfactory to us all. It proved beyond a doubt that we had in this little craft a most extraordinary sea-boat, for the tow was a thorough test of her seaworthiness.

The captain of the steamer ordered oil cast over from time to time, relieving us of much spray and sloppy motion, but adding to discomforts of taste to me at the helm, for much of the oil blew over me and in my face. Said the captain to one of his mates (an old whaler by the way, and whalers for some unaccountable reason have never too much regard for a poor merchantman) "Mr. Smith."

"Aye, aye, sir," answered old Smith.

"Mr. Smith, hoist out that oil."

"Aye, aye, sir," said the old "blubberhunter," in high glee, as he went about it with alacrity, and in less than five minutes from the time the order was given, I was smothering in grease and our boat was oiled from keel to truck.

"She's all right now," said Smith.

"That's all right," said Baker, but I thought it all wrong. The wind, meanwhile, was in our teeth and before we crossed Rio Bar I had swallowed enough oil to cure any amount of consumption.

Baker, I have heard, said he wouldn't care much if he should "drown Slocum." But I was all right so long as the canoe didn't sheer, and we arrived at Rio safe and sound after the most exciting boat-ride of my life. I was bound not to cut the line that towed us so well; and I knew that Baker wouldn't let it go, for it was his rope.

I found at Rio that my fishing license could be exchanged for a pass of greater import. This document had to be procured through the office of the Minister of Marine.

Many a smart linguist was ready to use his influence in my behalf with the above-named high official; but I found at the end of a month that I was making headway about as fast as a Dutch galliot in a head sea after the wind had subsided. Our worthy Consul, General H. Clay Armstrong, gave me a hint of what the difficulty was and how to obviate it. I then went about the business myself as I should have done at first, and I found those at the various departments who were willing to help me without the intervention of outside "influence."

Commander Marquis of the Brazilian navy, recommended me to His Excellency, the Minister of Marine, "out of regard," he said, "for American seamen," and when the new document came it was *"Passe Especial,"* and had on it *a seal as big as a soup plate.* A port naval officer then presented me to the good *Administradore,* who also gave me a *passe especial,* with the seal of the *Alfandega.*

I had now only to procure a bill of health, when I should have papers enough for a man o' war. Rio being considered a healthy place, this was readily granted, making our equipment complete.

I met here our minister whose office, with other duties, is to keep a weather eye lifting in the interest of that orphan, the American ship—alas, my poor relation! Said he, "Captain, if your *Liberdade* be as good as your papers" (documents given me by the Brazilian officials), "you may get there all right;" adding, "well, if the boat ever reaches home she will be a great curiosity," the meaning of which, I could readily infer, was, "and your chances for a snap in a dime museum will be good." This, after many years of experience as an American shipmaster, and also ship owner, in a moderate way, was interesting encouragement. By our Brazilian friends, however, the voyage was looked upon as a success already achieved.

"The utmost confidence," said the *Journal Opiz,* of Rio, "is placed in the cool-headed, audacious American mariner, and we expect in a short time to hear proclaimed in all of the journals of the Old and New World the safe arrival of this wonderful litttle craft at her destination, ourselves taking part in the glory." *"Temos confiança na pericia e sangue frio do audaciauso marinhero Americano por isso esperamos que dentro em pouco tempo veremos o seu nome proclamado por todos os jornaes do velho e novo mundo.*

A nos tambem cabera parte da gloria."

With these and like kind expressions from all of our *friends,* we took leave of Rio, sailing on the morning of July 23rd, 1888.

July 23rd, 1888, was the day, as I have said, on which we sailed from Rio de Janeiro.

Meeting with head winds and light withal, through the day we made but little progress; and finally, when night came on we anchored twenty miles east of Rio Heads, near the shore. Long, rolling seas rocked us as they raced by, then, dashing their great bodies against defying rocks, made music by which we slept that night. But a trouble unthought of before came up in Garfield's mind before going to his bunk: "Mamma," cried he as our little bark rose and fell on the heavy waves, tumbling the young sailor about from side to side in the small quarters while he knelt seriously at his evening devotion, "mamma, this boat isn't big enough to pray in!" But this difficulty was gotten over in time, and Garfield learned to watch as well as to pray on the voyage, and full of faith that all would be well, laid him down nights and slept as restfully as any Christian on sea or land.

By daylight of the second day we were again underway, beating to the eastward against the old head wind and head sea. On the following night we kept her at it, and the next day made Cape Frio where we anchored near the entrance to a good harbor.

Time from Rio, two days; distance, 70 miles.

The wind and tide being adverse, compelled us to wait outside for a favorable change. While comfortably anchored at this place, a huge whale, nosing about, came up under the canoe, giving us a toss and a great scare. We were at dinner when it happened. The meal, it is needless to say, was finished without dessert. The great sea animal—fifty to sixty feet long—circling around our small craft, looked terribly big. He was so close to me twice, as he swam round and round the canoe, that I could have touched him either time with a paddle. His flukes stirring the water like a steamer propeller appeared alarmingly close and powerful!—and what an ugly mouth the monster had! Well, we expected instant annihilation. The fate of the stout whale-ship *Essex* came vividly before me. The voyage of the *Liberdade,* I thought, was about ended, and I looked about for pieces of bamboo on which to land my wife and family. Just then, however, to the infinite relief of all of us, the leviathan moved off, without doing us much harm, having felt satisfied, perhaps, that we had no Jonah on board.

We lost an anchor through the incident, and received some small damage to the keel, but no other injury was done—even this, I believe, upon second thought, was unintentional—done in playfulness only! "A shark can take a joke," it is said, and crack one too, but for broad, rippling humor the whale has no equal.

"If this be a sample of our adventures in the beginning," thought I, "we shall have enough and to spare by the end of the voyage." A visit from this quarter had not been counted on; but Sancho Panza says, "when least aware starts the hare," which in our case, by the by, was a great whale!

When our breath came back and the hair on our heads settled to a normal level, we set sail, and dodged about under the lee of the cape till a cove, with a very enticing sand beach at the head of it, opened before us, some three miles northwest of where we lost the anchor in the remarkable adventure with the whale. The "spare bower" was soon bent to the cable. Then we stood in and anchored near a cliff, over which was a goat-path leading in the direction of a small fishing village, about a mile away. Sheering the boat in to the rocky side of the cove which was steep to, we leaped out, warp in hand, and made fast to a boulder above the tidal flow, then, scrambling over the cliff, we repaired to the village, first improvising a spare anchor from three sticks and a stone which answered the purpose quite well.

Judging at once that we were strangers the villagers came out to meet us, and made a stir at home to entertain us in the most hospitable manner, after the custom of the country, and with the villagers was a gentleman from Canada, a Mr. Newkirk, who, as we learned, was engaged, when the sea was smooth, in recovering treasure that was lost near the cape in the British war ship *Thetis*, which was wrecked there, in 1830. The treasure, some millions in silver coins and gold in bars, from Peru for England, was dumped in the cove, which has since taken the name of the ship that bore it there, and as I have said, came to grief in that place which is on the west shore near the end of the cape.

Some of the coins were given to us to be treasured as souvenirs of the pleasant visit. We found in Mr. Newkirk a versatile, roving genius; he had been a schoolmaster at home, captain of a lake schooner once, had practiced medicine, and preached some, I think; and what else I do not know. He had tried many things for a living, but, like the proverbial moving stone had failed to accumulate. "Matters," said the Canadian, "were getting worse and worse even, till finally to keep my head above water I was forced to go under the sea," and he had struck it rich, it would seem, if gold being brought in by the boat-load was any sign. This man of many adventures still spoke like a youngster; no one had told him that he was growing old. He talked of going home, as soon as the balance of the treasure was secured, "just to see his dear old mother," who, by the way, was seventy-four years old when he left home, some twenty years before. Since his last news from home, nearly two decades had gone by. He was "the youngest of a family of eighteen children, all living," he said, "though," added he, "our family came near being made one less yesterday, by a whale which I thought would eat my boat, diving-bell, crew, money and all, as he came toward us, with open mouth. By a back stroke of the oars, however, we managed to cheat him out of his dinner, if that was what he was after, and I think it was, but here I am!" he cried, "all right!" and might have added, "wealthy after all."

After hearing the diver's story, I related in Fortuguese our own adventure of the same day, and probably with the same whale, the monster having gone in the direction of the diver's boat. The astonishment of the listeners was great; but when they learned of our intended voyage to *America do Norte*, they crossed themselves and asked God to lend us grace!

"Is North America near New York?" asked the village merchant, who owned all the boats and nets of the place.

"Why, America is *in* New York," answered the ex-schoolmaster.

"I thought so," said the self-satisfied merchant. And no doubt he thought some of us very stupid, or rude, or both, but in spite of manners I had to smile at the assuring air of the Canadian.

"Why did you not answer him correctly?" I asked of the ex-schoolmaster.

"I answered him," said Newkirk, "according to his folly. Had I corrected his rusty geography before these simple, impoverished fishermen, he would not soon forgive me; and as for the rest of the poor souls here, the knowledge would do them but little good."

I may mention that in this out-of-the-way place there were no schools, and except the little knowledge gained in their church, from the catechism, and from the fumbling of beads, they were the most innocent of this world's scheme, of any people I ever met. But they seemed to know all about heaven, and were, no doubt, happy.

After the brief, friendly chat that we had, coffee was passed around, the probabilities of the *Liberdade*'s voyage discussed, and the crew cautioned against the dangers of the *balacna* (whale), which were numerous along the coast, and vicious at that season of the year, having their young to protect.

I realized very often the startling sensation alone of a night at the helm, of having a painful stillness broken by these leviathans bursting the surface of the water with a noise like the roar of a great sea, uncomfortably near, reminding me of the Cape Frio adventure; and my crew, I am sure, were not less sensitive to the same feeling of an awful danger, however imaginary. One night in particular, dark and foggy I remember, Victor called me excitedly, saying that something dreadful ahead and drawing rapidly near had frightened him.

It proved to be a whale, for some reason that I could only guess at, threshing the sea with its huge body, and surging about in all directions, so that it puzzled me to know which way to steer to go clear. I thought at first, from the rumpus made that a fight was going on, such as we had once witnessed from the deck of the *Aquidneck,* not far from this place. Our course was changed as soon as we could decide which way to avoid, if possible, all marine disturbers of the peace. We wished especially to keep away from infuriated swordfish, which I feared might be darting about, and be apt to give us a blind thrust. Knowing that they sometimes pierce stout ships through with their formidable weapons, I began to feel ticklish about the ribs myself, I confess, and the little watch below, too, got uneasy and sleepless; for one of these swords, they knew well, would reach through and through our little boat, from keel to deck. Large ships have occasionally been sent into port leaky from the stab of a sword, but what I most dreaded was the possibility of one of us being ourselves pinned in the boat.

A swordfish once pierced a whale-ship through the planking, and through the solid frame timber and the thick ceiling, with his sword, leaving it there, a valuable plug indeed, with the point, it was found upon unshipping her cargo at New Bedford, even piercing through a cask in the hold.

July 30th, early in the day, and after a pleasant visit at the cape, we sailed for the north, securing first a few sea shells to be cherished, with the *Thetis* relics, in remembrance of a most enjoyable visit to the hospitable shores of Cape Frio.

Having now doubled Cape Frio, a prominent point in our voyage, and having had the seaworthiness of our little ship thoroughly tested, as already told; and seeing, moreover, that we had nothing to fear from common small fry of the sea, (one of its greatest monsters having failed to capsize us,) we stood on with greater confidence than ever, but watchful, nevertheless, for any strange event that might happen.

A fresh polar wind hurried us on, under shortened sail, toward the softer "trades" of the tropics, but, veering to the eastward by midnight, it brought us well in with the land. Then, "Larboard watch, ahoy! all hands on deck and turn out reefs," was the cry. To weather Cape St. Thome we must lug on all sail. And we go over the shoals with a boiling sea and current in our favor. In twenty-four hours from Cape Frio, we had lowered the Southern Cross three degrees—180 miles.

Sweeping by the cape, the canoe sometimes standing on end, and sometimes buried in the deep hollow of the sea, we sunk the light on St. Thome soon out of sight, and stood on with flowing sheet. The wind on the following day settled into regular south-east "trades," and our cedar canoe skipped briskly along, over friendly seas that were leaping toward home, doffing their crests onward and forward, but never back, and the splashing waves against her sides, then rippling along the thin cedar planks between the crew and eternity, vibrated enchanting music to the ear, while confidence grew in the bark that was HOMEWARD BOUND.

But coming upon coral reefs, of a dark night, while we listened to the dismal tune of the seas breaking over them with an eternal roar, how intensely lonesome they were! no sign of any living thing in sight, except, perhaps, the phosphorescent streaks of a hungry shark, which told of bad company in our wake, and made the gloom of the place more dismal still.

One night we made shelter under the lee of the extensive reefs called the Paredes (walls), without seeing the breakers at all in the dark, although they were not far in the distance. At another time, dragging on sail to clear a lee shore, of a dark and stormy night, we came suddenly into smooth water, where we cast anchor and furled our sails, lying in a magic harbor till daylight the next morning, when we found ourselves among a maze of high reefs, with high seas breaking over them, as far as the eye could reach, on all sides, except at the small entrance to the place that we had stumbled into in the night. The position of this future harbor is South Lat. 16° 48', and West Long. from Greenwich 39° 30'. We named the place "PORT LIBERDADE."

The next places sighted were the treacherous Abrohles, and the village of Caravellas back of the reef where upon refitting, I found that a chicken cost a thousand reis; a bunch of bananas, four hundred reis; but where a dozen limes cost only twenty reis—one cent. Much whaling gear lay strewn about the place, and on the beach was the carcass of a whale about nine days slain. Also leaning against a smart-looking boat was a gray-haired fisherman, boat and man relics of New Bedford, employed at this station in their familiar industry. The old man was bare-footed and thinly clad, after the custom in this climate.

Still, I recognized the fisherman and sailor in the set and rig of the few duds he had on, and the ample straw hat (donkey's breakfast) that he wore, and doffed in a seaman-like manner, upon our first salute. *"Filio do Mar do Nord Americano,"* said an affable native close by, pointing at the same time to that "son of the sea of North America," by way of introduction, as soon as it was learned that we, too, were of that country. I tried to learn from this ancient mariner the cause of his being stranded in this strange land. He may have been cast up there by the whale for aught I could learn to the contrary.

Choosing a berth well to windward of the dead whale—the one that landed "the old man of the sea" there, maybe!—we anchored for the night, put a light in the rigging and turned in. Next morning, the village was astir betimes; canoes were being put afloat, and the rattle of poles, paddles, bait boxes, and many more things for the daily trip that were being hastily put into each canoe, echoed back from the tall palm groves notes of busy life, telling us that it was time to weigh anchor and be sailing. To this cheerful tune we lent ear and hastening to be underway, were soon clear of the port. Then, skimming along near the beach in the early morning, our sails spread to a land breeze, laden with fragrance from the tropic forest and the music of many songsters, we sailed in great felicity, dreading no dangers from the sea, for there were none now to dread or fear.

Proceeding forward through this belt of moderate winds, fanned by alternating land and sea-breezes, we drew on toward a region of high trade winds that reach sometimes the dignity of a gale. It was no surprise, therefore, after days of fine-weather sailing, to be met by a storm, which so happened as to drive us into the indifferent anchorage of St. Paulo, thirty miles from Bahia, where we remained two days for shelter.

Time, three days from Caravellas; distance sailed, 270 miles.

A few fishermen lounged about the place, living, apparently, in wretched poverty, spending their time between waiting for the tide to go out, when it was in, and waiting for it to come in when it was out, to float a canoe or bring fish to their shiftless nets. This, indeed, seemed their only concern in life; while their ill-thatched houses, forsaken of the adobe that once clung to the wicker walls, stood grinning in rows, like emblems of our mortality.

We found at this St. Paulo anything but saints. The wretched place should be avoided by strangers, unless driven there for shelter, as we ourselves were, by stress of weather. We left the place on the first lull of the wind, having been threatened by an attack from a gang of rough, half-drunken fellows, who rudely came on board, jostling about, and jabbering in a dialect which, however, I happened to understand. I got rid of them by the use of my broken Portuguese, and once away I was resolved that they should stay away. I was not mistaken in my suspicions that they would return and try to come aboard, which shortly afterward they did, but my resolution to keep them off was not shaken. I let them know, in their own jargon this time, that I was well armed. They finally paddled back to the shore, and all visiting was then ended. We stood a good watch that night, and by daylight next morning, Aug. 12th, put to sea, standing out in a heavy swell, the character of which I knew better, and could trust to more confidently than a harbor among treacherous natives.

Early in the same day, we arrived at *Bahia do todos Santos* (All Saints' Bay), a charming port, with a rich surrounding country. It was from this port, by the way, that Robinson Crusoe sailed for Africa to procure slaves for his plantation, and that of his friend, so fiction relates.

At Bahia we met many friends and gentle folk. Not the least interesting at this port are the negro lasses of fine physique seen at the markets and in the streets, with burdens on their heads of baskets of fruit, or jars of water, which they balance with ease and grace, as they go sweeping by with that stately mien which the dusky maiden can call her own.

At Bahia we refitted, with many necessary provisions, and repaired the keel, which was found upon hauling out, had been damaged by the encounter with the whale at Frio. An iron shoe was now added for the benefit of all marine monsters wishing to scratch their backs on our canoe.

Among the many friends whom we met at Bahia was Capt. Boyd and his family of the Barque *H. W. Palmer.* We shall meet the *Palmer* and the Boyds again on the voyage. They were old traders to South America and had many friends at this port who combined to make our visit a pleasant one. And their little son Rupert was greatly taken with the "*Riberdade*," as he called her, coming often to see us. And the officials of the port taking great interest in our voyage, came often on board. No one could have treated us more kindly than they.

The venerable *Administradore* himself gave us special welcome to the port and a kind word upon our departure, accompanied by a present for my wife in the shape of a rare white flower, which we cherished greatly as coming from a true gentleman.

Some strong abolitionists at the port would have us dine in an epicurean way in commemoration of the name given our canoe, which was adopted because of her having been put afloat on the thirteenth day of May, the day on which every human being in Brazil could say, "I have no master but one." I declined the banquet tendered us, having work on hand, fortifying the canoe against the ravaging worms of the seas we were yet to sail through, bearing in mind the straits of my great predecessor from this as well as other causes on his voyage over the Caribbean Seas. I was bound to be strengthened against the enemy.

The gout, it will be remembered, seized upon the good Columbus while his ship had worms, then both ship and admiral lay stranded among menacing savages; surrounded, too, by a lawless, threatening band of his own countrymen not less treacherous than the worst of cannibals. His state was critical, indeed! One calamity was from over high living—this I was bound to guard against—the other was from neglect on the part of his people to care for the ship in a seaman-like manner. Of the latter difficulty I had no risk to run.

Lazy and lawless, but through the pretext of religion the infected crew wrought on the pious feelings of the good Admiral, inducing him at every landing to hold mass instead of cleaning the foul ship. Thus through petty intrigue and grave neglects, they brought disaster and sorrow on their leader and confusion on their own heads. Their religion, never deep, could not be expected to keep *Terredo* from the ship's bottom, so her timbers were ravished, and ruin came to them all! Poor Columbus! had he but sailed with his son Diego and his noble brother Bartholomew, for his only crew and companions, not forgetting the help of a good woman, America would have been discovered without those harrowing tales of woe and indeed heart-rending calamities which followed in the wake of his designing people. Nor would his ship have been less well manned than was the *Liberdade,* sailing, centuries after, over the same sea and among many of the islands visited by the great discoverer—sailing too, without serious accident of any kind, and without sickness or discontent. Our advantage over Columbus, I say, was very great, not more from the possession of data of the centuries which had passed than from having a willing crew sailing without dissent or murmur—sailing in the same boat, as it were.

A pensive mood comes over one voyaging among the scenes of the New World's early play-ground. To us while on this canoe voyage of pleasant recollection the fancied experience of navigators gone before was intensely thrilling.

Sailing among islands clothed in eternal green, the same that Columbus beheld with marvelous anticipations, and the venerable Las Casas had looked upon with pious wonder, brought us, in the mind's eye, near the old discoverers; and a feeling that we should come suddenly upon their ships around some near headland took deep hold upon our thoughts as we drew in with the shores. All was there to please the imagination and dream over in the same balmy, sleepy atmosphere, where Juan Ponce de Leon would fain have tarried young, but found death rapid, working side by side with ever springing life. To live long in this clime one must obey great Nature's laws. So stout Juan and millions since have found, and so always it will be.

All was there to testify as of yore, all except the first owners of the land; they alas! the poor Caribbees, together with their camp fires, had been extinguished long years before. And no one of human sympathy can read of the cruel tortures and final extermination of these islanders, savages though they were, without a pang of regret at the unpleasant page in a history of glory and civilization.

From Bahia to Pernambuco our course lay along that part of the Brazilian coast fanned by constant trade winds. Nothing unusual occurred to disturb our peace of daily course, and we pressed forward night and day, as was our wont from the first.

Victor and I stood watch and watch at sea, usually four hours each.

The most difficult of our experiences in fine weather was the intense drowsiness brought on by constantly watching the oscillating compass at night; even in the daytime this motion would make one sleepy.

We soon found it necessary to arrange a code of signals which would communicate between the "wheel" and the "man forward." This was done by means of a line or messenger extending from one to the other, which was understood by the number of pulls given by it: three pulls, for instance, meant "Turn out," one in response, "Aye, aye, I am awake, and what is it that is wanted?" one pull in return signified that it was "Eight bells," and so on. But three quick jerks meant "Tumble out and shorten sail."

Victor, it was understood, would tie the line to his arm or leg when he turned in, so that by pulling I would be sure to arouse him, or bring him somewhat unceremoniously out of his bunk. Once, however, the messenger failed to acoomplish its purpose. A boot came out on the line in answer to my call, so easily, too, that I suspected a trick. It was evidently a preconceived plan by which to gain a moment more of sleep. It was a clear imposition on the man at the wheel!

We had also a sign in this system of telegraphing that told of flying-fish on board—manna of the sea—to be gathered up for the *cuisine* whenever they happened to alight or fall on deck, which was often, and as often they found a warm welcome.

The watch was never called to make sail. As for myself, I had never to be called, having thoughts of the voyage and its safe completion on my mind to keep me always on the alert. I can truly say that I never, on the voyage, slept so sound as to forget where I was, but whenever I fell into a dose at all it would be to dream of the boat and the voyage.

Press on! press on! was the watchword while at sea, but in port we enjoyed ourselves and gave up care for rest and pleasure, carrying a supply, as it were, to sea with us, where sail was again carried on.

Though a mast should break, it would be no matter of serious concern, for we would be at no loss to mend and rig up spars for this craft at short notice, most anywhere.

The third day out from Bahia was set fine weather. A few flying-fish made fruitless attempts to rise from the surface of the sea, attracting but little attention from the sea gulls which sat looking wistfully across the unbroken deep with folded wings.

And the *Liberdade* doing her utmost to get along through the common quiet, made but little progress on her way. A dainty fish played in her light wake, till tempted by an evil appetite for flies, it landed in the cockpit upon a hook, thence into the pan, where many a one had brought up before. Breakfast

was cleared away at an early hour; then day of good things happened—"the
meeting of the ships."

"When o'er the silent sea alone
   For days and nights we've cheerless gone,
Oh they who've felt it know how sweet,
   Some sunny morn a sail to meet.

"Sparkling at once is every eye,
   'Ship ahoy! ship ahoy!' our joyful cry
While answering back the sound we hear,
   'Ship ahoy! ship ahoy! what cheer, what cheer.'

"Then sails are backed, we nearer come,
   Kind words are said of friends and home,
And soon, too soon, we part with pain,
   To sail o'er silent seas again."

On the clear horizon could be seen a ship, which proved to be our staunch
old friend, the *Finance*, on her way out to Brazil, heading nearly for us. Our
course was at once changed, so as to cross her bows. She rose rapidly, hull up,
showing her lines of unmistakable beauty, the stars and stripes waving over all.
They on board the great ship, soon descried our little boat, and gave sign by a
deep whistle that came rumbling over the sea, telling us that we were recognized. A few moments later and the engines stopped. Then came the hearty
hail, "Do you want assistance?" Our answer "No" brought cheer on cheer
from the steamer's deck, while the *Liberdade* bowed and courtesied to her old
acquaintance, the superior ship. Captain Baker, meanwhile, not forgetting a
sailor's most highly prized luxury, had ordered in the slings a barrel of potatoes—new from home! Then dump they came, in a jiffy, into the canoe,
giving her a settle in the water of some inches. This was a valuable addition to
our stores. Some other fresh provisions were handed us, also some books and
late papers.

In return for all these goods we gave sincere thanks, about the only thing we
could spare—above the shadow of the canoe—which was secured through a
camera by the Rev. Doctor Hodge, the worthy missionary, then on his way to a
field of labor in Brazil.

One gentleman passed us a bottle of wine, on the label of which was written
the name of an old acquaintance, a merchant of Rio. We pledged Mr.
Gudgeon and all his fellow passengers in that wine, and had some left long
after, to the health of the captain of the ship, and his crew. There was but little
time for words, so the compliments passed were brief. The ample plates in the
sides of the *Finance*, inspiring confidence in American thoroughness and
build, we had hardly time to scan, when her shrill whistle said "good-bye,"
and moving proudly on, the great ship was soon out of sight, while the little
boat filling away on the starboard tack, sailed on toward home, perfumed with

the interchange of a friendly greeting, tinged though, with a palpable lonesomeness. Two days after this pleasant meeting, the Port of Pernambuco was reached.

Tumbling in before a fresh "trade" wind that in the evening had sprung up, accompanied with long, rolling seas, our canoe came nicely round the point between lighted reef and painted buoy.

Spray from the breakers on the reef opportunely wetting her sails gave them a flat surface to the wind as we came close haul.

The channel leading up the harbor was not strange to us, so we sailed confidently along the lee of the wonderful wall made by worms, to which alone Pernambuco is indebted for its excellent harbor; which extending also along a great stretch of the coast, protects Brazil from the encroachment of the sea.

At 8 P.M., we came to in a snug berth near the *Alfandega*, and early next morning received the official visit from the polite port officers.

Time from Bahia, seven days; distance sailed, 390 miles.

Pernambuco, the principal town of a large and wealthy province of the same name, is a thriving place, sending out valuable cargoes, principally of sugar and cotton. I had loaded costly cargoes here, times gone by. I met my old merchant again this time, but could not carry his goods on the *Liberdade*. However, fruits from his orchards and a run among the trees refreshed my crew, and prepared them for the coming voyage to Barbadoes, which was made with expedition.

From Pernambuco we experienced a strong current in our favor, with, sometimes, a confused cross sea that washed over us considerably. But the swift current sweeping along through it all made compensation for discomforts of motion, though our "ups and downs" were many. Along this part of the coast (from Pernambuco to the Amazon,) if one day should be fine, three stormy ones would follow, but the gale was always fair, carrying us forward at a goodly rate.

Along about half way from Cape St. Roque to the Amazon, the wind which had been blowing hard for two days, from E.S.E., and raising lively waves all about, increased to a gale that knocked up seas, washing over the little craft more than ever. The thing was becoming monotonous and tiresome; for a change, therefore, I ran in toward the land, so as to avoid the ugly cross sea farther out in the current. This course was a mistaken one; we had not sailed far on it when a sudden rise of the canoe, followed by an unusually long run down on the slope of a roller, told us of a danger that we hardly dared to think of, then a mighty comber broke, but, as Providence willed, broke short of the canoe, which under shortened sail was then scudding very fast.

We were on a shoal, and the sea was breaking from the bottom! The second great roller came on, towering up, up, up, until nothing longer could support the mountain of water, and it seemed only to pause before its fall to take aim and surely gather us up in its sweeping fury.

I put the helm a-lee; there was nothing else to do but this, and say prayers.

The helm hard down, brought the canoe round, bows to the danger, while in breathless anxiety we prepared to meet the result as best we could. Before we could say "Save us, or we perish," the sea broke over with terrific force and passed on, leaving us trembling in His hand, more palpably helpless than ever before. Other great waves came madly on, leaping toward destruction; how they bellowed over the shoal! I could smell the slimy bottom of the sea, when they broke! I could taste the salty sand!

In this perilous situation, buried sometimes in the foam of breakers, and at times tossed like a reed on the crest of the waves, we struggled with might and main at the helm and the sheets, easing her up or forcing her ahead with care, gaining little by little toward deep water, till at last she came out of the danger, shook her feathers like a sea bird, and rode on waves less perilous. Then we had time and courage to look back, but not till then.

And what a sight we beheld! The horizon was illumined with phosphorescent light from the breakers just passed through. The rainstorm which had obscured the coast was so cleared away now that we could see the whole field of danger behind us. One spot in particular, the place where the breakers dashed over a rock which appeared awash, in the glare flashed up a shaft of light that reached to the heavens.

This was the greatest danger we had yet encountered. The elasticity of our canoe, not its bulk, saved it from destruction. Her light, springy timbers and buoyant bamboo guards brought her upright again and again through the fierce breakers. We were astonished at the feats of wonder of our brave little craft.

Fatigued and worn with anxiety, when clear of the shoal we hauled to under close reefs, heading off shore, and all hands lay down to rest till daylight. Then, squaring away again, we set what sail the canoe could carry, scudding before it, for the wind was still in our favor, though blowing very hard. Nevertheless the weather seemed fine and pleasant at this stage of our own pleased feelings. Any weather that one's craft can live in, after escaping a lee shore, is pleasant weather—though some may be pleasanter than other.

What we most wished for, after this thrilling experience, was sea room, fair wind, and plenty of it. That these without stint would suit us best, was agreed on all hands. Accordingly then I shaped the course seaward, clearing well all the dangers of the land.

The fierce tropical storm of the last few days turned gradually into mild trade winds, and our cedar canoe skipped nimbly once more over tranquil seas. Our own agitation, too, had gone down and we sailed on unruffled by care. Gentle winds carried us on over kindly waves, and we were fain to count fair days ahead, leaving all thoughts of stormy ones behind. In this hopeful mood we sailed for many days, our spirits never lowering, but often rising higher out of the miserable condition which we had fallen into through misfortunes on the foreign shore. When a star came out, it came as a friend, and one that had been seen by friends of old. When all the stars shone out, the hour at sea was cheerful, bright, and joyous. Welby saw, or had in the mind's-eye, a day like many that we experienced in the soft, clear "trades" on this voyage, when writing the pretty lines:—

> The twilight hours like birds flew by,
>   As lightly and as free,
> Ten thousand stars were in the sky,
>   Ten thousand on the sea.

> For every rippling, dancing wave,
>   That leaped upon the air,
> Had caught a star in its embrace,
>   And held it trembling there.

"The days pass, and our ship flies fast upon her way."

For several days while sailing near the line we saw the constellations of both hemispheres, but heading north, we left those of the south at last, with the Southern Cross—most beautiful in all the heavens—to watch over a friend.

Leaving these familiar southern stars and sailing towards constellations in the north, we hoist all sail to the cheery breeze that carried us on.

In this pleasant state of sailing with our friends all about us, we stood on and on, never doubting once our pilot or our ship.

A phantom of the stately *Aquidneck* appeared one night, sweeping by with crowning skysails set, that fairly brushed the stars. No apparition could have affected us more than the sight of this floating beauty, so like the *Aquidneck*, gliding swiftly and quietly by, from her mission to some foreign land—she, too, was homeward bound!

This incident of the *Aquidneck's* ghost, as it appeared to us, passing at midnight on the sea, left a pang of lonesomeness for a while.

But a carrier dove came next day, and perched upon the mast, as if to tell that we had yet a friend! Welcome harbinger of good! you bring us thoughts of angels.

The lovely visitor remained with us two days, off and on, but left for good on the third, when we reached away from Avis Island, to which, maybe, it was bound. Coming as it did from the east, and flying west toward the island when it left, bore out the idea of the lay of sweet singer Kingsley's "Last Buccaneer."

> If I might but be a sea dove, I'd fly across the main
> To the pleasant Isle of Avis, to look at it once again.

The old Buccaneer, it may have been, but we regarded it as the little bird, which most likely it was, that sits up aloft to look out for poor "Jack." *

---

* There's a sweet litttle cherub that sits up aloft,
   To look out for a berth for poor Jack.--*Dibdin's Poems.*

A moth blown to our boat on the ocean, found shelter and a welcome there. The dove! we secretly worshipped.

With utmost confidence in our little craft, inspired by many thrilling events, we now carried sail, blow high, blow low, till at times she reeled along with a bone in her mouth quite to the mind of her mariners. Thinking one day that she might carry more sail on the mast already bending hopefully forward, and acting upon the liberal thought of sail we made a wide mistake, for the main-mast went by the board, under the extra press and the foremast tripped over the bows. Then spars, booms and sail swung alongside like the broken wings of a bird but were grappled, however, and brought aboard without much loss of time. The broken mast was then secured and strengthened by "fishes" or splints after the manner in which doctors fish a broken limb.

Both of the masts were very soon refitted and again made to carry sail, all they could stand; and we were again bowling along as before. We made that day a hundred and seventy-five miles, one of our best days' work.

I protest here that my wife should not have cried "More sail! more sail!" when, as it has been seen the canoe had on all the sail that she could carry. Nothing further happened to change the usual daily events until we reached Barbadoes. Flying-fish on the wing striking our sails, at night, often fell on deck, affording us many a toothsome fry. This happened daily, while sailing throughout the trade-wind regions. To be hit by one of these fish on the wing, which sometimes occurs, is no light matter, especially if the blow be on the face, as it may cause a bad bruise or even a black eye. The head of the flying-fish being rather hard makes it in fact a night slugger to be dreaded. They never come aboard in the daylight. The swift darting bill-fish, too, is a danger to be avoided in the tropics at night. They are met with mostly in the Pacific Ocean. And the South Sea Islanders are loath to voyage during the "bill-fish season."

As to the flight of these fishes, I would estimate that of the flying-fish as not exceeding fifteen feet in height, or five hundred yards of distance, often not half so much.

Bill-fish darting like an arrow from a bow, has, fortunately for sailors, not the power or do not rise much above the level of the waves, and can not dart further, say, than two hundred and fifty feet, according to the day for jumping. Of the many swift fish in the sea, the dolphin perhaps, is the most marvelous. Its oft told beauty, too, is indeed remarkable. A few of these fleet racers were captured, on the voyage, but were found tough and rank; notwithstanding some eulogy on them by other epicures, we threw the mess away. Those hooked by my crew were perhaps the tyrrhena pirates "turned into dolphins" in the days of yore.

On the 19th day from Pernambuco, early in the morning, we made Bar-badoes away in the West. First, the blue, fertile hills, then green fields came into view, studded with many white buildings between sentries of giant wind-mills as old nearly, as the hills. Barbadoes is the most pleasant island in the

Antilles; to sail round its green fringe of coral sea is simply charming. We stood in to the coast, well to windward, sailing close in with the breakers so as to take in a view of the whole delightful panorama as we sailed along. By noon we rounded the south point of the island and shot into Carlysle Bay, completing the run from Pernambuco exactly in nineteen days. This was considerably more than an hundred miles a day. The true distance being augmented by the circuitous route we adopted made it 2,150 miles.

Many old friends and acquaintances came down to see us upon our arrival at Barbadoes, all curious to inspect the strange craft. While there our old friend, the *Palmer*, that we left at Bahia, came in to refit, having broken a mast "trying to beat us," so Garfield would have it. For all that we had beaten her time four days. Who then shall say that we anchored nights or spent much time hugging the shore? The *Condor* was also at Barbadoes in charge of an old friend, accompanied by a pleasant helpmeet and companion who had shared the perils of shipwreck with her husband the year before in a hurricane among the islands.

Meeting so many of this class of old friends of vast and varied experiences, gave contentment to our visit and we concluded to remain over at this port till the hurricane season should pass. Our old friend, the *Finance* too, came in, remaining but a few hours, however, she hurried away with her mails, homeward bound.

The pleasant days at Barbadoes with its enchantment flew lightly by; and on the 7th of October we sailed, giving the hurricane the benefit of eight days. The season is considered over on the 15th of that month.

Passing thence through the Antilles into the Caribbean Sea, a new period of our voyage was begun. Fair breezes filled the sails of the *Liberdade* as we glided along over tranquil seas, scanning eagerly the islands as they came into view, dwelling on each, in our thoughts, as hallowed ground of the illustrious discoverers—the same now as seen by them! The birds, too, of "rare plumage," were there, flying from island to island, the same as seen by the discoverers; and the sea with fishes teemed, of very gorgeous hue, lending enchantment to the picture, not less beautiful than the splendor on the land and in the air to thrill the voyager now, the same as then; we ourselves had only to look to see them.

Whether it was birds with fins or fishes with wings, or neither of these that the old voyagers saw, they discovered yet enough to make them wonder and rejoice.

"Mountains of sugar, and rivers of rum and flying-fish, is what I have seen, mother," said the son on his return home from a voyage to these islands. "John," said the enraptured mother, "you must be mistaken about the fish;

now don't lie to me, John. Mountains of sugar, no doubt you saw, and even rivers of rum, my boy, but *flying-fish* could never be."

And yet the *fish* were there.

Among the islands of great interest which came in view, stretching along the Caribbean Sea, was that of Santa Cruz, the island famous for its brave, resolute women of days gone by, who, while their husbands were away, successfully defended home and happiness against Christian invaders, and for that reason were called fierce savages. I would fain have brought away some of the earth of the island in memory of those brave women. Small as our ship was, we could have afforded room in it for a memento thus consecrated; but the trades hauling somewhat to the northward so headed us off that we had to forgo the pleasure of landing on its shores.

Pushing forward thence, we reached Porto Rico, the nearest land in our course from the island of Brave Women, standing well in with the southeast capes. Sailing thence along the whole extent of the south coast, in waters as smooth as any mill pond, and past island scenery worth the perils of ten voyages to see, we landed, on the 12th of October, at Mayaguez in the west of the island, and there shook the kinks out of our bones by pleasant walks in tropic shades.

Time, five days from Barbadoes; distance 570 miles.

This was to be our last run among the trees in the West Indies, and we made the most of it. "Such a port for mariners I'll never see again!" The port officials, kind and polite, extended all becoming courtesies to the quaint *"barco piquina."*

The American Consul, Mr. Christie, Danish Consul, Mr. Falby, and the good French Consul, vied in making our visit a pleasant one.

Photographers at Mayaguez desiring a picture of the canoe with the crew on deck at a time when we felt inclined to rest in the shade on shore, put a negro on board to take the place of captain. The photographs taken then found their way to Paris and Madrid journals were, along with some flattering accounts, they were published, upon which it was remarked that the captain was a fine-looking fellow, but "awfully tanned!" The moke was rigged all ataunto for the occasion, and made a picture indicative of great physical strength, one not to be ashamed of, but he would have looked more like me, I must say, if they had turned him back to.

We enjoyed long carriage drives over rich estates at Mayaguez. We saw with pain, however, that the atmosphere of the soldier hung over all, pervading the whole air like a pestilence.

Musketed and sabred, and uniformed in their bed-ticking suits; hated by the residents and despised by themselves, they doggedly marched, counter-marched and wheeled, knowing that they are loathsome in the island, and that their days in the New World are numbered. The sons of the colonies are too civil and Christianlike to be ruled always by sword and gun.

On the 15th of October, after three days' rest, we took in, as usual before sailing from ports, sufficient fresh supplies to carry us to the port steered for next, then set sail from pleasant Mayaguez, and bore away for the old Bahama Channel, passing east of Hayti, thence along the north coast to the west extremity of the island, from which we took departure for the headlands of Cuba, and followed that coast as far as Cardinas, where we took a final departure from the islands, regretting that we could not sail around them all.

The region on the north side of Cuba is often visited by gales of great violence, making this the lee shore; a weather eye was therefore kept lifting, especially in the direction of their source, which is from north to nor'west. However storms prevailed from other quarters, mostly from the east, bringing heavy squalls of wind, rain and thunder every afternoon, such as once heard will never be forgotten. Peal on peal of nature's artillery for a few hours, accompanied by vivid lightning, was on the cards for each day, then all would be serene again.

The nights following these severe storms were always bright and pleasant, and the heavens would be studded with constellations of familiar, guiding stars.

My crew had now no wish to bear up for port short of one on our own coast, but, impatient to see the North Star appear higher in the heavens, strung every nerve and trimmed every sail to hasten on.

Nassau, the place to which letters had been directed to us we forbore to visit. This departure from a programme which was made at the beginning was the only change that we made in the "charter party" throughout the voyage. There was no hap-hazard sailing on this voyage. Daily observations for determining latitude and longitude were invariably made unless the sun was obscured. The result of these astronomical observations were more reliable than one might suppose, from their being taken on a tittlish canoe. After a few days' practising, a very fair off-hand contact could be made, when the canoe rose on the crest of a wave, where manifestly would be found the best result. The observer's station was simply on the top of the cabin, where astride, like riding horseback, Victor and I took the "sights," and indeed became expert "snap observers" before the voyage ended.

One night in the Bahama Channel, while booming along toward the Banks to the nor'west of us before stiff trades, I was called in the first watch by Victor, to come up quickly, for signs of the dread "norther" were in the sky. Our trusty barometer had been low, but was now on the cheerful side of change. This phenomenon disturbed me somewhat, till the discovery was made, as we came nearer, that it was but the reflection of the white banks on the sky that we saw, and no cause at all for alarm.

Soon after this phenomenon the faint glimmer of Labos Light was descried flickering on the horizon, two points on the weather bow. I changed the course three points to windward, having determined to touch at the small Cay where the lighthouse stands; one point being allowed for leeway, which I found was not too much.

Three hours later we fetched in under the lee of the reef, or Cay, as it is commonly called, and came to in one and a half fathoms of water in good shelter.

We beheld then overhead in wonderful beauty what had awed us from the distance in the early night—a chart of the illuminating banks marked visibly on the heavens.

We furled sails and, setting a light in the rigging, turned in; for it lacked three hours yet of daylight. And what an interesting experience ours had been in the one short night! By the break of day my crew were again astir, preparing to land and fill water at a good landing which we now perceived farther around the point to leeward, where the surf was moderate.

On the Cay is stored some hundred thousand gallons of rain water in cisterns at the base of the iron tower which carries the light; one that we saw from the canoe at a distance of fourteen miles.

The keeper of the light, a hardy native of Nassau, when he discovered the new arrival at his "island," hoisted the British Board of Trade flag on a pole in the centre of this, his little world, then he came forward to speak to us, thinking at first, he said, that we were shipwrecked sailors, which indeed we were, but not in distress, as he had supposed when hoisting the flag, which signified assistance for distressed seamen. On learning our story, however, he regarded us with grave suspicions, and refused water to Victor, who had already landed with buckets, telling him that the captain would have to bring his papers ashore and report. The mate's report would not be taken. Thus in a moment was transformed the friend in need to *governor of an island*. This amused me greatly, and I sent back word to my veritable Sancho Panza that in my many voyages to islands my mate had attended to the customs reports; at which his Excellency chafed considerably, giving the gunnels of his trousers a fitful tug up now and then as he paced the beach, waiting my compliance with the rules of the island. The governor, I perceived, was suspicious of smugglers and wreckers, apparently understanding their ways, if, indeed, even he were not a reformed pirate himself.

However, to humor the punctiliousness of his Excellency, now that he was governor of an island, I placed my papers in my hat, and, leaping into the surf, waded ashore, where I was received as by a monarch.

The document I presented was the original *Passe Especial*, the one with the big seal on it, written in Portuguese; had it been in Choctaw the governor would have read it with the same facility that he did this, which he stared at knowingly and said, "all right, take all the water you want; it is free."

I lodged a careful report of the voyage with the governor and explained to his Excellency the whereabouts of the "Island of Rio," as his grace persistently called Rio de Janeiro, whence dated my papers.

Conversing on the subject of islands, which was all the world to him, the governor viewed with suspicion the absence of a word in my documents, referring even to an islet; this, in his mind, was a reprehensible omission; for surely

New York to which the papers referred was built on an island. Upon this I offered to swear to the truth of my clearance, "as far as known to me," after the manner of cheap custom-house swearing with which shipmasters, in some parts of the world, are made familiar. "Not on the island!" quickly exclaimed the governor, "'for thou shalt not disglorify God's name,' is written in the Bible."

I assured the governor of my appreciation of his pious sentiment of not over-swearing, which the Chinese adopt as a policy—laudable however, and one that I would speak of on my return home, to the end that we all emulate the laws of the island; whereupon the governor, greatly pleased, urged me to take some more water, minding me again that it was free.

In a very few minutes I got all the water I wished for; also some aurora shells from the governor's lady, who had arisen with the sun to grace the day and of all things most appropriate held in her generous lap beautiful aurora shells for which—to spoil the poem—I bartered cocoanuts and rusty gnarly yams.

The lady was on a visit only to her lord and master, the monarch of all he surveyed. Beside this was their three children also on a visit, from Nassau, and two assistant keepers of the light which made up the total of this little world in the ocean.

It was the smallest kingdom I had ever visited, peopled by happy human beings and the most isolated by far.

The few blades of grass which had struggled into existence, not enough to support a goat, was all there was to look at on the island except the lighthouse, and the sand and themselves.

Some small buildings and a flagstaff had once adorned the place, but to-gether with a coop of chickens, the only stock of the islanders—except a dog—had been swept away by a hurricane which had passed over the island a short time before. The water for which we had called being now in the canoe, and my people on board waiting for me, I bade the worthy governor good-bye, and, saluting his charming island queen in a seamanlike manner, hastened back to my own little world; and bore away once more for the north. Sailing thence over the Great Bahama Banks, in a crystal sea, we observed on the white marl bottom many curious living things, among them the conch in its house of exquisite tints and polished surface, the star-fish with radiated dome of curious construction, and many more denizens of the place, the names of which I could not tell, resting on the soft white bed under the sea.

"They who go down to the sea in ships, they see the wonders of the Lord," I am reminded by a friend who writes me, on receipt of some of these curious things which I secured on the voyage, adding: "For all these curious and beautiful things are His handiwork. Who can look at such things without the heart being lifted up in adoration?"

For words like these what sailor is there who would not search the caves of the ocean? Words too, from a lady.

Two days of brisk sailing over the white Bahama Banks brought us to Bimini. Thence a mere push would send us to the coast of our own native America. The wind in the meantime hauling from regular nor'east trade to the sou'west, as we came up to Bimini, promising a smooth passage across, we launched out at once on the great Gulf Stream, and were swept along by its restless motion, making on the first day, before the wind and current, two hundred and twenty miles. This was great getting along for a small canoe. Going at the same high rate of speed on the second night in the stream, the canoe struck a spar and went over it with a bound. Her keel was shattered by the shock, but finally shaking the crippled timber clear of herself she came on quite well without it. No other damage was done to our craft, although at times her very ribs were threatened before clearing this lively ocean river. In the middle of the current, where the seas were yet mountainous but regular, we went along with a wide, swinging motion and fared well enough; but on nearing the edge of the stream a confused sea was met with, standing all on end, in every which way, beyond a sailor's comprehension. The motion of the *Liberdade* was then far from poetical or pleasant. The wind, in the meantime, had chopped round to the nor'east, dead ahead; being thus against the current, a higher and more confused sea than ever was heaped up, giving us some uneasiness. We had, indeed, several unwelcome visitors come tumbling aboard of our craft, one of which furiously crashing down on her made all of her timbers bend and creak. However, I could partially remedy this danger by changing the course.

"Seas like that can't break this boat," said our young boatswain; "she's built strong." It was well to find among the crew this feeling of assurance in the gallant little vessel. I, too, was confident in her seaworthiness. Nevertheless, I shortened sail and brought her to the wind, watching the lulls and easing her over the combers, as well as I could. But wrathful Neptune was not to let us so easily off, for the next moment a sea swept clean over the helmsman, wetting him through to the skin and, most unkind cut of all, it put out our fire, and capsized the hash and stove into the bottom of the canoe. This left us with but a *damper* for breakfast! Matters mended, however, as the day advanced, and for supper we had a grand and glorious feast. Early in the afternoon we made the land and got into smooth water. This of itself was a feast, to our minds.

The land we now saw lying before us was hills of America, which we had sailed many thousands of miles to see. Drawing in with the coast, we made out, first the broad, rich forests, then open fields and villages, with many signs of comfort on every hand. We found it was the land about Bull's Bay on the coast of South Carolina, and night coming on, we could plainly see Cape Roman Light to the north of us. The wind falling light as we drew in with the coast, and finding a current against us, we anchored, about two miles from the shore, in four fathoms of water. It was now 8 P.M., October 28, 1888, thirteen days from Mayaguez, twenty-one days from Barbadoes, etc.

The following was the actual time at sea and distances in nautical miles from point to point on the courses steered, approximately:

	Days	Distance
From Paranagua to Santos	1	150
" Santos to Rio de Janerio (towed by *Finance*)	¾	200
" Rio to Cape Frio	2	70
" Cape Frio to Carvellas	4	370
" Carvellas to Saint Paulo	3	270
" Saint Paulo to Bahia	½	40
" Bahia to Pernambuco	7	390
" Pernambuco to Barbadoes	19	2,150
" Barbadoes to Mayaguez	5	570
" Mayaguez to Cape Roman	13	1,300
	55½	5,510

Computing all the distances of the ins and outs that we made would considerably augment the sum. To say, therefore, that the *Liberdade* averaged roundly a hundred miles a day for fifty-five days would be considerably inside the truth.

This was the voyage made in the boat which cost less than a hundred dollars outside of our own labor of building. Journals the world over have spoken not unkindly of the feat; encomiums in seven languages reached us through the newspapers while we lay moored in Washington. Should the same good fortune that followed the *Liberdade* attend this little literary craft, when finished, it would go safe into many lands. Without looking, however, to this mark of good fortune, the journal of the voyage has been as carefully constructed as was the *Liberdade,* and I trust, as conscientiously, by a hand, alas! that has grasped the sextant more often than the plane or pen, and for the love of doing. This apology might have been more appropriately made in the beginning of the journal, maybe, but it comes to me now, and like many other things done, right or wrong, but done on the impulse of the moment, I put it down.

No one will be more surprised at the complete success of the voyage and the speedy progress made than were we ourselves who made it, with incidents and events among which is the most prominent of a life at sea.

A factor of the voyage, one that helped us forward greatly, and which is worthy of special mention, was the ocean current spoken of as we came along in its friendly sway.

Many are the theories among fresh water philosophists respecting these currents, but in practical sailing, where the subject is met with in its tangible form, one cause only is recognized; namely, the action of the wind on the surface of the water, pushing the waves along. Out on the broad ocean the effect at first is hardly perceptible, but the constant trades sending countless millions of waves in one direction, cause at last a mighty moving power, which the mariner meets sometimes as an enemy to retard and delay, sometimes as a friend, as in our case, to help him on his way. These are views from a practical experience with no theory to prove.

By daylight on the twenty-ninth, we weighed anchor and set sail again for the north. The wind and current was still adverse but we kept near the land making short boards off and on through the day where the current had least effect. And when night came on again came to once more close in with Cape Roman light. Next day we worked up under the lee of the Roman shoals and made harbor in South Santee, a small river to the north of Cape Roman, within range of the light, there to rest until the wind should change, it being still ahead.

Next morning, since the wind had not changed, we weighed anchor and stood farther into the river looking for inhabitants, that we might listen to voices other than our own. Our search was soon rewarded, for, coming around a point of woodland, a farmhouse stood before us on the river side. We came alongside the bank and jumped ashore, but had hardly landed when, as out of the earth a thousand dogs so it seemed, sprung up threatening to devour us all. However, a comely woman came out of the house and it was explained to the satisfaction of all, especially to a persistent cur, by a vigorous whack on the head with a cudgel, that our visit was a friendly one; then all was again peaceful and quiet. The good man was in the field close by, but soon came home accompanied by his two stalwart sons each "toting" a sack of corn. We found the Andersons—this was the family name—isolated in every sense of the word, and as primitive as heart could wish. The charming simplicity of these good people captivated my crew. We met others along the coast innocent of greed, but of all unselfish men, Anderson the elder was surely the prince.

In purchasing some truck from this good man, we found that change could not be made for the dollar which I tendered in payment. But I protested that I was more than content to let the few odd cents go, having received more garden stuff than I had ever seen offered for a dollar in any part of the world. And indeed I was satisfied. The farmer, however, nothing content, offered me a coon skin or two, but these I didn't want, and there being no other small change about the farm, the matter was dropped, I thought, for good, and I had quite forgotten it, when later in the evening I was electrified by his offering to carry a letter for us which we wished posted, some seven miles away, and call it "square," against the twenty cents of the morning's transaction. The letter went, and in due course of time we got an answer.

I do not say that we stuck strictly to the twenty-cent transaction, but I fear that not enough was paid to fair-dealing Anderson. However all were at last satisfied and warming into conversation, a log fire was improvised and social chat went round.

These good people could hardly understand how it was, as I explained, that the Brazilians had freed the slaves and had no war, Mr. Anderson often exclaiming, "Well, well, I d'clar. Freed the niggers, and had no wah. Mister," said he, turning to me after a long pause, "mister, d'ye know the South were foolish? They had a wah, and they had to free the niggers, too."

"Oh, yes, mister, I was thar! Over thar beyond them oaks was my house."

"Yes, mister, I fought, too, and fought hard, but it warn't no use."

Like many a hard fighter, Anderson, too, was a pious man, living in a state of resignation to be envied. His years of experience on the new island farm had been hard and trying in the extreme. My own misfortunes passed into shade as the harder luck of the Andersons came before my mind, and the resolution which I had made to buy a farm was now shaken and finally dissolved into doubts of the wisdom of such a course. On this farm they had first "started in to raise pork," but found that it "didn't pay, for the pigs got wild and had to be gathered with the dogs," and by the time they were "gathered and then toted, salt would hardly cure them, and they most generally tainted." The enterprise was therefore abandoned, for that of tilling the soil, and a crop was put in, but "the few pigs which the dogs had not gathered came in at night and rooted out all the taters." It then appeared that a fence should be built. "Accordingly," said he, "I and the boys made one which kept out the stock, but, sir, the rats could get in! They took every tater out of the ground! From all that I put in, and my principal work was thar, I didn't see a sprout." How it happened that the rats had left the crop the year before for their relations—the pigs—was what seemed most to bother the farmer's mind. Nevertheless, "there was corn in Egypt yet;" and at the family circle about the board that night a smile of hope played on the good farmer's face, as in deep sincerity he asked that for what they had they might be made truly thankful. We learned a lesson of patience from this family, and were glad that the wind had carried us thither.

Said the farmer, "And you came all the way from Brazil in that boat! Wife, she won't go to Georgetown in the batto that I built because it rares too much. And they freed the niggers and had no wah! Well, well, I d'clar!"

Better folks we may never see than the farmers of South Santee. Bidding them good-bye next morning at early dawn we sailed before a light land wind which, however, soon petered out.

The *S.S. Planter* then coming along took us in tow for Georgetown, where she was bound. We had not the pleasure, however, of visiting the beloved old city; for having some half dozen cocoanuts on board, the remainder of small stores of the voyage, a vigilant officer stopped us at the quarantine ground. Fruit not being admitted into South Carolina until after the first of November, and although it was now late in the afternoon of the first, we had to ride quarantine that night, with a promise, however, of *pratique* next morning. But there was no steamer going up the river the next day. The *Planter* coming down though supplied us with some small provisions, such as not procurable at the Santee farm. Then putting to sea we beat along slowly against wind and current.

We began now to experience, as might be expected, autumn gales of considerable violence, the heaviest of which overtaking us at Frying-pan Shoal, drove us back to leeward of Cape Fear for shelter. South Port and Wilmington being then so near we determined to visit both places. Two weeks at these ports refreshed the crew and made all hands willing for sea again.

Sailing thence through Corn-cake Inlet we cut off Cape Fear and the Frying-pan Shoals, being of mind to make for the inlets along the Carolina coast and to get into the inland waters as soon as practicable.

It was our good fortune to fall in with an old and able pilot at Corn-cake Inlet, one Capt. Bloodgood, who led the way through the channel in his schooner, the *Packet,* a Carolina pitch and cotton droger of forty tons register, which was manned solely by the captain and his two sons, one twelve and the other ten years old. It was in the crew that I became most interested, and not the schooner. Bloodgood gave the order when the tide served for us to put to sea. "Come, children," said he, "let's try it." Then we all tried it together, the *Packet* leading the way. The shaky wet wind that filled our sails as we skimmed along the beach with the breakers close aboard, carried us but a few leagues when it flew suddenly round to nor'east and began to pipe.

The gale increasing rapidly inclined me to bear up for New River Inlet, then close under our lee; with a treacherous bar lying in front, which to cross safely, would require great care.

But the gale was threatening, and the harbor inside, we could see, was smooth, then, too, cried my people: "Any port in a storm." I decided prompt: put the helm up and squared away. Flying thence, before it, the tempest-tossed canoe came sweeping in from sea over the rollers in a delightfully thrilling way. One breaker only coming over us, and even that did no harm more than to give us all the climax soaking of the voyage. This was the last sea that broke over the canoe on the memorable voyage.

The harbor inside the bar of New River was good. Adding much to our comfort too, was fish and game in abundance.

The *Packet,* which had parted from us, made her destined port some three leagues farther on. The last we saw of the children, they were at the main sheets hauling aft, and their father was at the helm, and all were flying through the mist like fearless sailors.

After meeting Carolina seamen, to say nothing of the few still in existence further north, I challenge the story of Greek supremacy.

The little town of South Port was made up almost entirely of pilots possessing, I am sure, every quality of the sailor and the gentleman.

Moored snug in the inlet, it was pleasant to listen to the roar of the breakers on the bar, but not so cheerful was the thought of facing the high waves seaward, therefore the plan suggested itself of sufficiently deepening a ditch that led through the marshes from New River to Bogue Sound; to let us through, thence we could sail inland the rest of the voyage without obstruction or hindrance of any kind. To this end we set about contrivances to heave the canoe over the shoals, and borrowed a shovel from a friendly schooner captain to deepen the ditch which we thought would be necessary to do in order to ford her along that way. However, the prevailing nor'east gales had so raised the water in the west end of the sound as to fill all the creeks and ditches to overflowing. I hesitated then no longer but heading for the ditch through the marshes on a high tide, before a brave west wind took the chances of getting through by hook or by crook or by shovel and spade if required.

The "Coast Pilot," in speaking of this place, says there is never more than a foot of water there, and even that much is rarely found. The *Liberdade* essayed the ditch, drawing two feet and four inches, thus showing the further good fortune or luck which followed perseverance, as it usually does, though sometimes, maybe, it is bad luck! Perhaps I am not lucid on this, which at best must remain a disputed point.

I was getting lost in the maze of sloughs and creeks, which as soon as I entered seemed to lead in every direction but the right one. Hailing a hunter near by, however, I was soon put straight and reassured of success. The most astonished man, though, in North Carolina, was this game hunter when asked if he knew the ditch that led through where I wished to go.

"Why, stranger," said he, "my gran'ther digged that ditch."

I jumped, I leaped! at thought of what a pilot this man would be.

"Well, stranger," said he, in reply to my query, "stranger, if any man kin take y' thro' that ditch, why, I kin;" adding doubtfully, however, "I have not hearn tell befo' of a vessel from Brazil sailing through these parts; but then you mout get through, and again ye moutent. Well, it's jist here; you mout and you moutent."

A bargain was quickly made, and my pilot came aboard, armed with a long gun, which as we sailed along proved a terror to ducks. The entrance to the ditch, then close by, was made with a flowing sheet, and I soon found that my pilot knew his business. Rush-swamps and corn-fields we left to port and to starboard, and were at times out of sight among brakes that brushed crackling along the sides of the canoe, as she swept briskly through the narrows, passing them all, with many a close hug, though, on all sides. At a point well on in the crooked channel my pilot threw up his hat, and shouted, with all his might:

"Yer trouble is over! Swan to gosh if it ain't! And ye come all the way from Brazil, and come through gran'ther's ditch! Well, I d'clar!"

From this I concluded that we had cleared all the doubtful places, and so it turned out. Before sundown my pilot was looking for the change of a five-dollar-piece; and we of the *Liberdade* sat before a pot-pie, at twilight, the like of which on the whole voyage had not been tasted, from sea fowl laid about by our pilot while sailing through the meadows and marshes. And the pilot himself, returning while the pot-pie was yet steaming hot, declared it "ahead of coon."

A pleasant sail was this through the ditch that gran'ther dug. At the camp fire that night, where we hauled up by a fishing station, thirty stalwart men talked over the adventures of their lives. My pilot, the best speaker, kept the camp in roars. As for myself, always fond of mirth, I got up from the fire sore from laughing. Their curious adventures with coons and 'gators recounted had been considerable.

Many startling stories were told. But frequently reverting to this voyage of the *Liberdade*, they declared with one voice that "it was the greatest thing since the wah." I took this as a kind of complimentary hospitality. "When she struck on a sand reef," said the pilot, "why, the captain he jumped right overboard and the son he jumped right over, too, to tote her over, and the captain's wife she holp."

By daylight next morning we sailed from this camp pleasant, and on the following day, November 28, at noon, arrived at Beaufort.

Mayor Bell of that city and many of his town folk met us at the wharf, and gave me as well as my sea-tossed crew a welcome to their shores, such as to make us feel that the country was partly ours.

"Welcome, welcome home," said the good mayor; "we have read of your adventures, and watched your progress as reported from time to time, with deep interest and sympathy."

So we began to learn now that prayers on shore had gone up for the little canoe at sea. This was indeed America and home, for which we had longed while thousands of miles across the ocean.

From Beaufort to Norfolk and thence to Washington was pleasant inland sailing, with prevailing fair winds and smooth sea. Christmas was spent on the Chesapeake—a fine, enjoyable day it was! with not a white-cap ripple on the bay. Ducks swimming ahead of the canoe as she moved quietly along were loath to take wing in so light a breeze, but flapping away, half paddling, half swimming, as we came toward them, they managed to keep a long gun-shot off; but having laid in at the last port a turkey of no mean proportions, which we made shift to roast in the "caboose" aboard, we could look at a duck without wishing its destruction. With this turkey and a bountiful plum duff, we made out a dinner even on the *Liberdade*.

Of the many Christmas days that come crowding in my recollections now; days spent on the sea and in foreign lands, as falls to the lot of sailors—which was the merriest it would be hard to say. Of this, however, I am certain, that the one on board the *Liberdade* on the Chesapeake was not the least happy among them all.

The day following Christmas found us on the Potomac, enjoying the same fine weather and abundant good cheer of the day before. Fair winds carried us through all the reaches of the river, and the same prosperity which attended our little bark in the beginning of the voyage through tempestuous weather followed her to the end of the journey, which terminated in mild days and pleasant sunshine.

On the 27th of December, 1888, a south wind bore us into harbor at Washington, D. C., where we moored for the winter, furled our sails and coiled up the ropes, after a voyage of joys and sorrows; crowned with pleasures, however, which lessened the pain of past regrets.

Having moored the *Liberdade* and weather-bitted her cables, it remains only to be said that after bringing us safely through the dangers of a tropical voyage, clearing reefs, shoals, breakers, and all storms without a serious accident of any kind, we learned to love the little canoe as well as anything could be loved that is made by hands.

To say that we had not a moment of ill-health on the voyage would not tell the whole story.

My wife, brave enough to face the worst storms, as women are sometimes known to do on sea and on land, enjoyed not only the best of health, but had gained a richer complexion.

Victor, at the end of the voyage, found that he had grown an inch and had not been frightened out of his boots.

Little Garfield—well he had grown some, too, and continued to be a pretty good boy and had managed to hold his grip through many ups and downs. He it was who stood by the bow line to make fast as quick as the *Liberdade* came to the pier at the end of the voyage.

And I, last, as it should be, lost a few pounds' weight, but like the rest landed in perfect health; taking it altogether, therefore, only pleasant recollections of the voyage remain with us who made it.

With all its vicissitudes I still love a life on the broad, free ocean, never regretting the choice of my profession.

However, the time has come to debark from the *Liberdade,* now breasted to the pier where I leave her for a time; for my people are landed safe in port.

Halfway

by THOR HEYERDAHL

The weeks passed. We saw no sign either of a ship or of drifting remains to show that there were other people in the world. The whole sea was ours, and, with all the gates of the horizon open, real peace and freedom were wafted down from the firmament itself.

It was as though the fresh salt tang in the air, and all the blue purity that surrounded us, had washed and cleansed both body and soul. To us on the raft the great problems of civilized man appeared false and illusory—like perverted products of the human mind. Only the elements mattered. And the elements seemed to ignore the little raft. Or perhaps they accepted it as a natural object, which did not break the harmony of the sea but adapted itself to current and sea like bird and fish. Instead of being a fearsome enemy, flinging itself at us, the elements had become a reliable friend which steadily and surely helped us onward. While wind and waves pushed and propelled, the ocean current lay under us and pulled, straight toward our goal.

If a boat had cruised our way on any average day out at sea, it would have found us bobbing quietly up and down over a long rolling swell covered with little white-crested waves, while the trade wind held the orange sail bent steadily toward Polynesia.

Those on board would have seen, at the stern of the raft, a brown bearded man with no clothes on, either struggling desperately with a long steering oar while he hauled on a tangled rope, or, in calm weather, just sitting on a box dozing in the hot sun and keeping a leisurely hold on the steering oar with his toes.

If this man happened not to be Bengt, the latter would have been found lying on his stomach in the cabin door with one of his seventy-three sociological books. Bengt had further been appointed steward and was responsible for fixing the daily rations. Herman might have been found anywhere at any time of the day—at the masthead with meteorological instruments, underneath the raft with diving goggles on checking a centerboard, or in tow in the rubber dinghy, busy with balloons and curious measuring apparatus. He was our technical chief and responsible for meteorological and hydrographical observations.

Knut and Torstein were always doing something with their wet dry batteries, soldering irons, and circuits. All their wartime training was required to keep the little radio station going in spray and dew a foot above the surface of the water.

Every night they took turns sending our reports and weather observations out into the ether, where they were picked up by chance radio amateurs who passed the reports on to the Meteorological Institute in Washington and other destinations. Erik was usually sitting patching sails and splicing ropes, or carving in wood and drawing sketches of bearded men and odd fish. And at noon every day he took the sextant and mounted a box to look at the sun and find out how far we had moved since the day before. I myself had enough to do with the logbook and reports and the collecting of plankton, fishing, and filming. Every man had his sphere of responsibility, and no one interfered with the others' work. All difficult jobs, like steering watch and cooking, were divided equally. Every man had two hours each day and two hours each night at the steering oar. And duty as cook was in accordance with a daily roster. There were few laws and regulations on board, except that the night watch must have a rope round his waist, that the lifesaving rope had its regular place, that all meals were consumed outside the cabin wall, and that the "right place" was only at the farthest end of the logs astern. If an important decision was to be taken on board, we called a powwow in Indian style and discussed the matter together before anything was settled.

An ordinary day on board the *Kon-Tiki* began with the last night watch shaking some life into the cook, who crawled out sleepily on to the dewy deck in the morning sun and began to gather flying fish. Instead of eating the fish raw, according to both Polynesian and Peruvian recipes, we fried them over a small primus stove at the bottom of a box which stood lashed fast to the deck outside the cabin door. This box was our kitchen. Here there was usually shelter from the southeast trade wind which regularly blew on to our other quarter. Only when the wind and sea juggled too much with the primus flame did it set fire to the wooden box, and once, when the cook had fallen asleep, the whole box became a mass of flames which spread to the very wall of the bamboo cabin. But the fire on the wall was quickly put out when the smoke poured into the hut, for, after all, we had never far to go for water on board the *Kon-Tiki*.

The smell of fried fish seldom managed to wake the snorers inside the bamboo cabin, so the cook usually had to stick a fork into them or sing "Breakfast's ready!" so out of tune that no one could bear to listen to him any longer. If there were no sharks' fins alongside the raft, the day began with a quick plunge in the Pacific, followed by breakfast in the open air on the edge of the raft.

The food on board was above reproach. The cuisine was divided into two experimental menus, one dedicated to the quartermaster and the twentieth century, one to Kon-Tiki and the fifth century. Torstein and Bengt were the subjects of the first experiment and restricted their diet to the slim little packages of special provisions which we had squeezed down into the hole between the logs and the bamboo deck. Fish and marine food, however, had never been their strong suit. Every few weeks we untied the lashings which held down the bamboo deck and took out fresh supplies, which we lashed fast forward of the bamboo cabin. The tough layer of asphalt outside the cardboard proved resistant, while the hermetically sealed tins lying loose beside it were penetrated and ruined by the sea water which continually washed round our provisions.

Kon-Tiki, on his original voyage across the sea, had no asphalt or hermetically sealed tins; nevertheless he had no serious food problems. In those days, too, supplies consisted of what the men took with them from land and what they obtained for themselves on the voyage. We may assume that, when Kon-Tiki sailed from the coast of Peru after his defeat by Lake Titicaca, he had one of two objectives in mind. As the spiritual representative of the sun among a solely sun-worshipping people, it is very probable that he ventured straight out to sea to follow the sun itself on its journey in the hope of finding a new and more peaceful country. An alternative possibility for him was to sail his rafts up the coast of South America in order to found a new kingdom out of reach of his persecutors. Clear of the dangerous rocky coast and hostile tribes along the shore, he would, like ourselves, fall an easy prey to the southeast trade wind and the Humboldt Current and, in the power of the elements, he would drift in exactly the same large semicircle right toward the sunset.

Whatever these sun-worshipers' plans were when they fled from their homeland, they certainly provided themselves with supplies for the voyage. Dried meat and fish and sweet potatoes were the most important part of their primitive diet. When the raftsmen of that time put to sea along the desert coast of Peru, they had ample supplies of water on board. Instead of clay vessels they generally used the skin of giant bottle gourds, which was resistant to bumps and blows, while even more adapted to raft use were the thick canes of giant bamboos. They perforated through all the knots in the center and poured water in through a little hole at the end, which they stopped with a plug or with pitch or resin. Thirty or forty of these thick bamboo canes could be lashed fast along the raft under the bamboo deck, where they lay shaded and cool with fresh sea water—about 79° Fahrenheit in the Equatorial Current—washing about them. A store of this kind would contain twice as much water as we ourselves used on our whole voyage, and still more could be taken by simply lashing on more bamboo canes in the water underneath the raft, where they weighed nothing and occupied no space.

We found that after two months fresh water began to grow stale and have a bad taste. But by then one is well through the first ocean area, in which there is little rain, and has arrived in regions where heavy rain showers can maintain the water supply. We served out a good quart of water per man daily, and it was by no means always that the ration was consumed.

Even if our predecessors had started from land with inadequate supplies, they would have managed well enough as long as they drifted across the sea with the current, in which fish abounded. There was not a day on our whole voyage on which fish were not swimming round the raft and could not easily be caught. Scarcely a day passed without flying fish, at any rate, coming on board of their own accord. It even happened that large bonitos, delicious eating, swam on board with the masses of water that came from astern and lay kicking on the raft when the water had vanished down between the logs as a sieve. To starve to death was impossible.

The old natives knew well the device which many shipwrecked men hit upon during the war—chewing thirst-quenching moisture out of raw fish. One can also press the juices out by twisting pieces of fish in a cloth, or, if the fish is large, it is a fairly simple matter to cut holes in its side, which soon become filled with ooze from the fish's lymphatic glands. It does not taste good if one has anything better to drink, but the percentage of salt is so low that one's thirst is quenched.

The necessity for drinking water was greatly reduced if we bathed regularly and lay down wet in the shady cabin. If a shark was patrolling majestically round about us and preventing a real plunge from the side of the raft, one had only to lie down on the logs aft and get a good grip of the ropes with one's fingers and toes. Then we got several bathfuls of crystal-clear Pacific pouring over us every few seconds.

When tormented by thirst in a hot climate, one generally assumes that the body needs water, and this may often lead to immoderate inroads on the water ration without any benefit whatever. On really hot days in the tropics you can pour tepid water down your throat till you taste it at the back of your mouth, and you are just as thirsty. It is not liquid the body needs then, but, curiously enough, salt. We experienced days like this when the wind had died away and the sun blazed down on the raft without mercy. Our water ration could be ladled into us till it squelched in our stomachs, but our throats malignantly demanded much more. On such days we added from 20 to 40 per cent of bitter, salt sea water to our fresh-water ration and found, to our surprise, that this brackish water quenched our thirst. We had the taste of sea water in our mouths for a long time afterward but never felt unwell, and moreover we had our water ration considerably increased.

One morning, as we sat at breakfast, an unexpected sea splashed into our gruel and taught us quite gratuitously that the taste of oats removed the greater part of the sickening taste of sea water!

The old Polynesians had preserved some curious traditions, according to which their earliest forefathers, when they came sailing across the sea, had with them leaves of a certain plant which they chewed, with the result that their thirst disappeared. Another effect of the plant was that in an emergency they could drink sea water without being sick. No such plants grew in the South Sea islands; they must, therefore, have originated in their ancestors' homeland. The Polynesian historians repeated these statements so often that modern scientists investigated the matter and came to the conclusion that the only known plant with such an effect was the coca plant, which grew only in Peru. And in prehistoric Peru this very coca plant, which contains cocaine, was regularly used both by the Incas and by their vanished forerunners, as is shown by discoveries in pre-Inca graves. On exhausting mountain journeys and sea voyages they took with them piles of these leaves and chewed them for days on end to remove the feelings of thirst and weariness. And over a fairly short period the chewing of coca leaves will even allow one to drink sea water with a certain immunity.

We did not test coca leaves on board the *Kon-Tiki*, but we had on the foredeck large wicker baskets full of other plants, some of which had left a deeper imprint on the South Sea islands. The baskets stood lashed fast in the lee of the cabin wall, and as time passed yellow shoots and green leaves of potatoes and coconuts shot up higher and higher from the wickerwork. It was like a little tropical garden on board the wooden raft.

When the first Europeans came to the Pacific islands, they found large plantings of sweet potatoes on Easter Island and in Hawaii and New Zealand, and the same plant was also cultivated on the other islands, but only within the Polynesian area. It was quite unknown in the part of the world which lay farther west. The sweet potato was one of the most important cultivated plants in these remote islands where the people otherwise lived mainly on fish, and many of the Polynesians' legends centered round this plant. According to tradition it had been brought by no less a personage than Tiki himself, when he came with his wife Pani from their ancestors' original homeland, where the sweet potato had been an important article of food. New Zealand legends affirm that the sweet potato was brought over the sea in vessels which were not canoes but consisted of "wood bound together with ropes."

Now, as is known, America is the only place in the rest of the world where the potato grew before the time of the Europeans. And the sweet potato Tiki brought with him to the islands, *Ipomoea batatas,* is exactly the same as that which the Indians have cultivated in Peru from the oldest times. Dried sweet potatoes were the most important travel provisions both for the seafarers of Polynesia and for the natives in old Peru. In the South Sea islands the sweet potato will grow only if carefully tended by man, and, as it cannot withstand sea water, it is idle to explain its wide distribution over these scattered islands by declaring that it could have drifted over 4,000 sea miles with ocean currents from Peru. This attempt to explain away so important a clue to the Polynesians' origin is particularly futile seeing that philologists have pointed out that on all the widely scattered South Sea islands the name of the sweet potato is *kumara,* and *kumara* is just what the sweet potato was called among the old Indians in Peru. The name followed the plant across the sea.

Another very important Polynesian cultivated plant we had with us on board the *Kon-Tiki* was the bottle gourd, *Lagenaria vulgaris.* As important as the fruit itself was the skin, which the Polynesians dried over a fire and used to hold water. This typical garden plant also, which again cannot propagate itself in a wild state by drifting across the sea alone, the old Polynesians had in common with the original population of Peru. Bottle gourds, converted into water containers, are found in prehistoric desert caves on the coast of Peru and were used by the fishing population there centuries before the first men came to the islands in the Pacific. The Polynesian name for the bottle gourd, *kimi,* is found again among the Indians in Central America, where Peruvian civilization has its deepest roots.

In addition to a few chance tropical fruits, most of which we ate up in a few weeks' time before they spoiled, we had on board a third plant which, along with the sweet potato, has played the greatest part in the history of the Pacific.

We had two hundred coconuts, and they gave us exercise for our teeth and refreshing drinks. Several of the nuts soon began to sprout, and, when we had been just ten weeks at sea, we had half a dozen baby palms a foot high, which had already opened their shoots and formed thick green leaves. The coconut grew before Columbus' time both on the Isthmus of Panama and in South America. The chronicler Oviedo writes that the coconut palm was found in great numbers along the coast of Peru when the Spaniards arrived. At that time it had long existed on all the islands in the Pacific.

Botanists have still no certain proof in which direction it spread over the Pacific. But one thing has now been discovered. Not even the coconut, with its famous shell, can spread over the ocean without men's help. The nuts we had in baskets on deck remained eatable and capable of germinating the whole way to Polynesia. But we had laid about half among the special provisions below deck, with the waves washing around them. Every single one of these was ruined by the sea water. And no coconut can float over the sea faster than a balsa raft moves with the wind behind it. It was the eyes of the coconut which sucked in the sea water so that the nut spoiled. Refuse collectors, too, all over the ocean took care that no edible thing that floated should get across from one world to the other.

Solitary petrels and other sea birds which can sleep on the sea we met thousands of sea miles from the nearest land. Sometimes, on quiet days far out on the blue sea, we sailed close to a white, floating bird's feather. If, on approaching the little feather, we looked at it closely, we saw that there were two or three passengers on board it, sailing along at their ease before the wind. When the *Kon-Tiki* was about to pass, the passengers noticed that a vessel was coming which was faster and had more space, and so all came scuttling sideways at top speed over the surface and up on to the raft, leaving the feather to sail on alone. And so the *Kon-Tiki* soon began to swarm with stowaways. They were small pelagic crabs. As big as a fingernail, and now and then a good deal larger, they were tidbits for the Goliaths on board the raft, if we managed to catch them.

The small crabs were the policemen of the sea's surface, and they were not slow to look after themselves when they saw anything eatable. If one day the cook failed to notice a flying fish in between the logs, next day it was covered with from eight to ten small crabs, sitting on the fish and helping themselves with their claws. Most often they were frightened and scurried away to hide when we came in view, but aft, in a little hole by the steering block, lived a crab which was quite tame and which we named Johannes.

Like the parrot, who was everyone's amusing pet, the crab Johannes became one of our community on deck. If the man at the helm, sitting steering on a sunshiny day with his back to the cabin, had not Johannes for company, he felt utterly lonely out on the wide blue sea. While the other small crabs scurried furtively about and pilfered like cockroaches on an ordinary boat, Johannes sat broad and round in his doorway with his eyes wide open, waiting for the change of watch. Every man who came on watch had a scrap of biscuit or a bit of fish for him, and we needed only to stoop down over the hole for him to come right out on his doorstep and stretch out his hands. He took the scraps out of our fingers with his claws and ran back into the hole, where he sat down in the doorway and munched like a schoolboy, cramming his food into his mouth.

The crabs clung like flies to the soaked coconuts, which burst when they fermented, or caught plankton washed on board by the waves. And these, the tiniest organisms in the sea, were good eating too even for us Goliaths on the raft, when we learned how to catch a number of them at once so that we got a decent mouthful.

It is certain that there must be very nourishing food in these almost invisible plankton which drift about with the current on the oceans in infinite numbers. Fish and sea birds which do not eat plankton themselves live on other fish or sea animals which do, no matter how large they themselves may be. Plankton is a general name for thousands of species of visible and invisible small organisms which drift about near the surface of the sea. Some are plants (*phyto*-plankton), while others are loose fish ova and tiny living creatures (*zoo*-plankton). Animal plankton live on vegetable plankton, and vegetable plankton live on ammoniac, nitrates, and nitrites which are formed from dead animal plankton. And while they reciprocally live on one another, they all form food for everything which moves in and over the sea. What they cannot offer in size they can offer in numbers.

In good plankton waters there are thousands in a glassful. More than once persons have starved to death at sea because they did not find fish large enough to be spitted, netted, or hooked. In such cases it has often happened that they have literally been sailing about in strongly diluted, raw fish soup. If, in addition to hooks and nets, they had had a utensil for straining the soup they were sitting in, they would have found a nourishing meal—plankton. Some day in the future, perhaps, men will think of harvesting plankton from the sea at the same extent as now they harvest grain on land. A single grain is of no use, either, but in large quantities it becomes food.

The marine biologist Dr. A. D. Bajkov told us of plankton and sent us a fishing net which was suited to the creatures we were to catch. The "net" was a silk net with almost three thousand meshes per square inch. It was sewn in the shape of a funnel with a circular mouth behind an iron ring, eighteen inches across, and was towed behind the raft. Just as in other kinds of fishing, the catch varied with time and place. Catches diminished as the sea grew warmer farther west, and we got the best results at night, because many species seemed to go deeper down into the water when the sun was shining.

If we had no other way of whiling away time on board the raft, there would have been entertainment enough in lying with our noses in the plankton net. Not for the sake of the smell, for that was bad. Nor because the sight was appetizing, for it looked a horrible mess. But because, if we spread the plankton out on a board and examined each of the little creatures separately with the naked eye, we had before us fantastic shapes and colors in unending variety.

Most of them were tiny shrimplike crustaceans *(copepods)* or fish ova float-ing loose, but there were also larvae of fish and shellfish, curious miniature crabs in all colors, jellyfish, and an endless variety of small creatures which might have been taken from Walt Disney's *Fantasia*. Some looked like fringed, fluttering spooks cut out of cellophane paper, while others resembled tiny red-beaked birds with hard shells instead of feathers. There was no end to Nature's extravagant inventions in the plankton world; a surrealistic artist might well own himself bested here.

Where the cold Humboldt Current turned west south of the Equator, we could pour several pounds of plankton porridge out of the bag every few hours. The plankton lay packed together like cake in colored layers—brown, red, gray, and green according to the different fields of plankton through which we had passed. At night, when there was phosphorescence about, it was like hauling in a bag of sparkling jewels. But, when we got hold of it, the pirates' treasure turned into millions of tiny glittering shrimps and phosphorescent fish larvae that glowed in the dark like a heap of live coals. When we poured them into a bucket, the squashy mess ran out like a magic gruel composed of glow-worms. Our night's catch looked as nasty at close quarters as it had been pretty at long range. And, bad as it smelled, it tasted correspondingly good if one just plucked up courage and put a spoonful of it into one's mouth. If this consisted of many dwarf shrimps, it tasted like shrimp paste, lobster, or crab. If it was mostly deep-sea fish ova, it tasted like caviar and now and then like oysters.

The inedible vegetable plankton were either so small that they washed away with the water through the meshes of the net, or they were so large that we could pick them up with our fingers. "Snags" in the dish were single jellylike coelenterates like glass balloons and jellyfish about half an inch long. These were bitter and had to be thrown away. Otherwise everything could be eaten, either as it was or cooked in fresh water as gruel or soup. Tastes differ. Two men on board thought plankton tasted delicious, two thought they were quite good, and for two the sight of them was more than enough. From a nutrition standpoint they stand on a level with the larger shellfish, and, spiced and properly prepared, they can certainly be a first-class dish for all who like marine food.

That these small organisms contain calories enough has been proved by the blue whale, which is the largest animal in the world and yet lives on plankton. Our own method of capture, with the little net which was often chewed up by hungry fish, seemed to us sadly primitive when we sat on the raft and saw a passing whale send up cascades of water as it simply filtered plankton through its celluloid beard. And one day we lost the whole net in the sea.

"Why don't you plankton-eaters do like him?" Torstein and Bengt said contemptuously to the rest of us, pointing to a blowing whale. "Just fill your mouths and blow the water out through your mustaches!"

I have seen whales in the distance from boats, and I have seen them stuffed in museums, but I have never felt toward the gigantic carcass as one usually feels toward proper warm-blooded animals, for example a horse or an elephant. Biologically, indeed, I had accepted the whale as a genuine mammal, but in its essence it was to all intents and purposes a large cold fish. We had a different impression when the great whales came rushing toward us, close to the side of the raft.

One day, when we were sitting as usual on the edge of the raft having a meal, so close to the water that we had only to lean back to wash out our mugs, we started when suddenly something behind us blew hard like a swimming horse and a big whale came up and stared at us, so close that we saw a shine like a polished shoe down through its blowhole. It was so unusual to hear real breathing out at sea, where all living creatures wriggle silently about without lungs and quiver their gills, that we really had a warm family feeling for our old distant cousin the whale, who like us had strayed so far out to sea. Instead of the cold, toadlike whale shark, which had not even the sense to stick up its nose for a breath of fresh air, here we had a visit from something which recalled a well-fed jovial hippopotamus in a zoological gardens and which actually breathed—that made a most pleasant impression on me—before it sank into the sea again and disappeared.

We were visited by whales many times. Most often they were small porpoises and toothed whales which gamboled about us in large schools on the surface of the water, but now and then there were big cachalots, too, and other giant whales which appeared singly or in small schools. Sometimes they passed like ships on the horizon, now and again sending a cascade of water into the air, but sometimes they steered straight for us. We were prepared for a dangerous collision the first time a big whale altered course and came straight toward the raft in a purposeful manner. As it gradually grew nearer, we could hear its blowing and puffing, heavy and long drawn, each time it rolled its head out of the water. It was an enormous, thick-skinned, ungainly land animal that came toiling through the water, as unlike a fish as a bat is unlike a bird. It came straight toward our port side, where we stood gathered on the edge of the raft, while one man sat at the masthead and shouted that he could see seven or eight more making their way toward us.

The big, shining, black forehead of the first whale was not more than two yards from us when it sank beneath the surface of the water, and then we saw the enormous blue-black bulk glide quietly under the raft right beneath our feet. It lay there for a time, dark and motionless, and we held our breath as we looked down on the gigantic curved back of a mammal a good deal longer than the whole raft. Then it sank slowly through the bluish water and disappeared from sight. Meanwhile the whole school were close upon us, but they paid no attention to us. Whales which have abused their giant strength and sunk whaling boats with their tails have presumably been attacked first. The whole morning we had them puffing and blowing round us in the most unexpected places without their even pushing against the raft or the steering oar. They quite enjoyed themselves gamboling freely among the waves in the sunshine. But about noon the whole school dived as if on a given signal and disappeared for good.

It was not only whales we could see under the raft. If we lifted up the reed matting we slept on, through the chinks between the logs we saw right down into the crystal-blue water. If we lay thus for a while, we saw a breast fin or tail fin waggle past and now and again we saw a whole fish. If the chinks had been a few inches wider, we could have lain comfortably in bed with a line and fished under our mattresses.

The fish which most of all attached themselves to the raft were dolphins and pilot fish. From the moment the first dolphins joined us in the current off Callao, there was not a day on the whole voyage on which we had not large dolphins wriggling round us. What drew them to the raft we do not know, but, either there was a magical attraction in being able to swim in the shade with a moving roof above them, or there was food to be found in our kitchen garden of seaweed and barnacles that hung like garlands from all the logs and from the steering oar. It began with a thin coating of smooth green, but then the clusters of seaweed grew with astonishing speed, so that the *Kon-Tiki* looked like a bearded sea-god as she tumbled along among the waves. Inside the green seaweed was a favorite resort of tiny small fry and our stowaways, the crabs.

There was a time when ants began to get the upper hand on board. There had been small black ants in some of the logs, and, when we had got to sea and the damp began to penetrate into the wood, the ants swarmed out and into the sleeping bags. They were all over the place, and bit and tormented us till we thought they would drive us off the raft. But gradually, as it became wetter out at sea, they realized that this was not their right element, and only a few isolated specimens held out till we reached the other side. What did best on the raft, along with the crabs, were barnacles from an inch to an inch and a half long. They grew in hundreds, especially on the lee side of the raft, and as fast as we put the old ones into the soup kettle new larvae took root and grew up. The barnacles tasted fresh and delicate; we picked the seaweed as salad and it was eatable, though not so good. We never actually saw the dolphins feeding in the vegetable garden, but they were constantly turning their gleaming bellies upward and swimming under the logs.

The dolphin (dorado), which is a brilliantly colored tropical fish, must not be confused with the creature, also called dolphin, which is a small, toothed whale. The dolphin was ordinarily from three feet three inches to four feet six inches long and had much flattened sides with an enormously high head and neck. We jerked on board one which was four feet eight inches long with a head thirteen and one-half inches high. The dolphin had a magnificent color. In the water it shone blue and green like a bluebottle with a glitter of golden-yellow fins. But if we hauled one on board, we sometimes saw a strange sight. As the fish died, it gradually changed color and became silver gray with black spots and, finally, a quite uniform silvery white. This lasted for four or five minutes, and then the old colors slowly reappeared. Even in the water the dolphin could occasionally change color like a chameleon, and often we saw a "new kind" of shining copper-colored fish, which on a closer acquaintance proved to be our old companion the dolphin.

The high forehead gave the dolphin the appearance of a bulldog flattened from the side, and it always cut through the surface of the water when the predatory fish shot off like a torpedo after a fleeing shoal of flying fish. When the dolphin was in a good humor, it turned over on its flat side, went ahead at a great speed, and then sprang high into the air and tumbled down like a flat pancake. It came down on the surface with a regular smack and a column of water rose up. It was no sooner down in the water than it came up in another leap, and yet another, away over the swell. But, when it was in a bad temper—for example, when we hauled it up on to the raft—then it bit. Torstein limped about for some time with a rag round his big toe because he had let it stray into the mouth of a dolphin, which had used the opportunity to close its jaws and chew a little harder than usual. After our return home we heard that dolphins attack and eat people when bathing. This was not very complimentary to us, seeing that we had bathed among them every day without their showing any particular interest. But they were formidable beasts of prey, for we found both squids and whole flying fish in their stomachs.

Flying fish were the dolphins' favorite food. If anything splashed on the surface of the water, they rushed at it blindly in the hope of its being a flying fish. In many a drowsy morning hour, when we crept blinking out of the cabin and, half asleep, dipped a toothbrush into the sea, we became wide-awake with a jump when a thirty-pound fish shot out like lightning from under the raft and nosed at the toothbrush in disappointment. And, when we were sitting quietly at breakfast on the edge of the raft, a dolphin might jump up and make one of its most vigorous sideway splashes, so that the sea water ran down our backs and into our food.

One day, when we were sitting at dinner, Torstein made a reality of the tallest of fish stories. He suddenly laid down his fork and put his hand into the sea, and, before we knew what was happening, the water was boiling and a big dolphin came tumbling in among us. Torstein had caught hold of the tail end of a fishing line which came quietly gliding past, and on the other end hung a completely astonished dolphin which had broken Erik's line when he was fishing a few days before.

There was not a day on which we had not six or seven dolphins following us in circles round and under the raft. On bad days there might be only two or three, but, on the other hand, as many as thirty or forty might turn up the day after. As a rule it was enough to warn the cook twenty minutes in advance if we wanted fresh fish for dinner. Then he tied a line to a short bamboo stick and put half a flying fish on the hook. A dolphin was there in a flash, plowing the surface with its head as it chased the hook, with two or three more in its wake. It was a splendid fish to play and, when freshly caught, its flesh was firm and delicious to eat, like a mixture of cod and salmon. It kept for two days, and that was all we needed, for there were fish enough in the sea.

Gipsy Moth Capsizes
in the Tasman Sea

by SIR FRANCIS CHICHESTER

I passed Sydney Heads at 12.15, and at 14.30 the last of the accompanying boats left me. I had trouble with the propeller shaft, which I couldn't stop rotating. The brake would not work, so I had to dive down under the cockpit, head first and feet up, to fix the thing. I didn't enjoy these upside-down antics, and I felt horribly seasick. By 18.00 I was becalmed, but the calm didn't last long. There was a dense roll of clouds above the horizon, and wind began coming in from the south, at first lightly, but soon blowing up. By 19.00 it was coming at me in a series of savage bursts. At first I ran off northwards at 8 knots, then I took down all sail and lay ahull—that is, battened down, without sail, to give completely to the sea like a cork—in a great deluge of rain, reducing visibility to about 50 yards. Soon it got dark, and it was *very* dark— absolutely pitch dark. I was seasick and turned in but didn't get much rest. After about three quarters of an hour I heard the self-steering oar banging about, and went on deck to deal with it. The wind then was about 35 knots, and I thought that *Gipsy Moth* could stand a jib and get moving again. I set a working jib, but it was too much for her. So I replaced it with a storm jib. With this I left her to fight her way slowly east at about 2 knots and turned in again, determined to sleep all night.

I stayed in my bunk until just after 04.00, when the wind began coming still more strongly and I went up to drop the storm jib and lie ahull again. We stayed like this for most of the day; it was too rough for even a storm jib with the wind blowing at 50 knots or more. In the afternoon I did set a storm jib, reefed to only 60 square feet,* a mere rag of sail, chiefly to try to cut down thumping in the heavy seas. I hoped that the thumping was due to the self-steering gear, and not to the new false keel.

In spite of the storm, radio conditions were good, and at 8 A.M. I had a good radio talk with Sheila which cheered me up. I was still sick from time to time, but slowly began to feel better, and gave myself some brandy, sugar and lemon, which I managed to keep down. The weather forecasts were bad with renewed cyclone warnings. This was Tropical Cyclone Diana, which was reported to be moving SE at about 20 mph. I tried to work out where it was in relation to me, and I reckoned that the worst of it would pass some 270 miles

---

*I had had reefing points fitted to this sail in Sydney.

to the east of my noon position. That was something, but the whole area of the Tasman Sea was violently disturbed with winds from 40 to 60 knots, gusting up to 80 knots in squalls. There was nothing I could do about it. I did not worry over much, but just tried to exist until the storm passed.

That Monday night was as foul and black a night as you could meet at sea. Although it was pitch dark, the white breakers showed in the blackness like monstrous beasts charging down on the yacht. They towered high in the sky. I wouldn't blame anyone for being terrified at the sight. My cross-tree light showed up the breaking water, white in the black darkness, and now and then a wave caught the hull and, breaking against it, sluiced over the decks. As I worked my way along the deck I thought: "Christ! What must it be like in a 120-knot wind!" I dropped the remaining storm sail, furled and tied it down. *Gipsy Moth* had been doing 8 knots with the little sail set, and I thought she would be less liable to damage lying ahull with no forward speed. As I worked my way aft again after finishing the job on the foredeck, I looked at the retaining net amidships, holding the two big genoas bagged up, and the 1,000 feet of warp in several coils. I knew that I ought to pass a couple of ropes over the net between the eye bolts at each side for storm lashings—I had always done this before on the passage out. But these ropes had not been re-rigged in Sydney and I was feeling ghastly, I thought due to sea sickness. (From something which happened later I can only deduce that the chief cause of my trouble was the Australian champagne I had drunk. For some reason this acted like poison on me.) Whatever the cause of my trouble, I weakened, and decided to leave the extra lashing until the morning. When I got below and had stripped off my oilskins I rolled into my bunk and put all the lights out. This was about two hours after dark. The bunk was the only place where one could wait below, for it was difficult to stand up, and I should have been continually thrown off if I had sat on the settee. However, lying on my back in the bunk, I dropped into a fitful sleep after a while.

I think I was awake when the boat began to roll over. If not, I woke immediately she started to do so. Perhaps when the wave hit her I woke. It was pitch dark. As she started rolling I said to myself, "Over she goes!" I was not frightened, but intensely alert and curious. Then a lot of crashing and banging started, and my head and shoulders were being bombarded with crockery and cutlery and bottles. I had an oppressive feeling of the boat being on top of me. I wondered if she would roll over completely, and what the damage would be; but she came up quietly the same side that she had gone down. I reached up and put my bunk light on. It worked, giving me a curious feeling of something normal in a world of utter chaos. I have only a confused idea of what I did for the next hour or so. I had an absolutely hopeless feeling when I looked at the pile of jumbled-up food and gear all along the cabin. Anything that was in my way when I wanted to move I think I put back in its right place, though feeling as I did so that it was a waste of time as she would probably go over again. The cabin was 2 foot deep all along with a jumbled-up pile of hundreds of tins, bottles, tools, shackles, blocks, two sextants and oddments. Every settee locker, the whole starboard bunk, and the three starboard drop lockers had all emptied out when she was upside down. Water was swishing about on the cabin sole beside the chart table, but not much. I looked into the bilge which is 5 feet deep, but it was not quite full, for which I thought, "Thank God."

This made me get cracking with the radio, at forty-five minutes after midnight, and two and a quarter hours after the capsize. I was afraid that the radio telephone would go out of action through water percolating it, and that even if it didn't, if the boat went over again the mass of water in the bilge must inevitably flood the telephone and finish it. I had to try to get a message through to say that I was all right, so that if the telephone went dead people would not think that I had foundered because of that. I called up on the distress frequency 2182 and got Sydney Radio straight away. As usual they were most efficient and co-operative. I asked them to give my wife a message in the morning to say that I had capsized, but that I was all right and that if they got no more messages from me it would only be because the telephone had been swamped and packed up, and not because I had foundered. I asked particularly that they should not wake up Sheila in the middle of the night, but call her at seven o'clock in the morning. I said that I did not need any help.

I am not sure when I discovered that the water was pouring in through the forehatch. What had happened was that when the boat was nearly upside down, the heavy forehatch had swung open, and when the boat righted itself the hatch, instead of falling back in place, fell forwards onto the deck, leaving the hatchway wide open to the seas. It may seem strange that my memory is so confused, but it was a really wild night, the movement was horrible and every step was difficult.

I must have got out on deck to pump the water below the level of the batteries. I found the holding net torn from its lashings. One of my 600-foot genoas had gone, a drogue, and 700 feet of inch-and-a-half plaited warp. The other big genoa was still there in its bag pressed against the leeward lifeline wires. I don't remember how I secured it. I found the forehatch open and closed that. A section of the cockpit coaming and a piece of the side of the cockpit had been torn away. I was extremely puzzled at the time to know how this could have happened. The important thing was that the masts were standing, and the rigging appeared undamaged. I think it was then that I said to myself, "To hell with everything," and decided to have a sleep. I emptied my bunk of plates, cutlery and bottles, etc. One serrated-edged cutting knife was embedded close to where my head had been, and I thought how lucky I was. I had only a slightly cut lip; I do not know what caused that.

My bunk was soaking wet, which was no wonder, considering that in the morning I could see daylight through where the side of the cockpit had been torn away just above the bunk. But I did not give a damn how wet it was, turned in, and was soon fast asleep. I slept soundly till daylight.

When I awoke the boat was still being thrown about. All that day it was blowing a gale between 40 and 55 knots. I was still queasy and unable to face eating anything. I had not had a proper meal since leaving Sydney. Now and then I had some honey and water, but even that was an ordeal, for I had not filled up my vacuum flasks with hot water before starting as I always intend to do before a voyage, so that I can have honey and water hot as soon as I feel queasy. And I was faced with this awful mess; it looked like a good week's work to clear up, sort and re-pack everything. I have rarely had less spirit in me. I longed to be back in Sydney Harbour, tied up to the jetty. I hated and dreaded the voyage ahead. Let's face it; I was frightened and had a sick feeling of fear gnawing inside me. If this was what could happen in an ordinary storm, how could a small boat possibly survive in a 100-knot greybearder?

After this I made another tour of inspection, surveying the damage. Some extraordinary things had happened. The long mahogany boat hook which had been lashed down at the side of the deck was jammed between the shrouds about 6 feet up in the air. By a great stroke of luck the locker under one of the cockpit seats, which had a flap lid with no fastening at all, was still full of gear, including the reefing handles for the main boom and the mizzen boom. I suppose the jumble of ropes and stuff which filled this locker (so that it was practically impossible to find anything in it) had jammed so tightly when upside down that nothing had spilled out. On the other hand, sundry winch handles, which had been in open-topped boxes specially made for them in the cockpit, had all disappeared.

Down below some queer things had happened. To start with, there was that foul smell. I sniffed the bilges, but it did not come from there. I tried the batteries, but they fortunately had been clamped down securely in the bilge and were perfectly all right. At last I tracked it down to the vitamin pills, pink vitamin C. The bottle had shot across the boat from the cupboard above the galley sink, and had smashed to pieces on the doghouse above my head. The pills had spread all over the windows in the doghouse, where they partly dissolved in sea water. I tried to mop them up but the melting vitamin mixture smeared into the joint between the Perspex and wood of the windows and into every possible crack and cranny. For the time being I had to put up with the stink. The irony of it was that I never used a vitamin pill on the whole passage!

I worked at the pump intermittently, stopping for a rest after every 200 strokes (the water had to be "lifted" 10-11 feet) and doing some other job as a change from pumping. When at last I got to the bottom of the bilge I found an assortment of plates and crockery, and also I found plates beside the motor, and one right aft of the motor. I was much puzzled at the time to know how these plates had got into such extraordinary positions, but realized later what had happened. The motor had a wooden casing covering it in at its forward end in the cabin, and the top of this is a step which hinges upwards. This lid had flown open, so that the plates had shot through the gap and when the boat righted herself, the lid had closed down again. One of the strangest things happened at the forward end of the cabin, where I kept on finding minute particles of razor-sharp, coloured glass. It was a long time before I tracked down the origin of this, but one day I came across a cork stuck into about an inch of the neck of a bottle. This was a long time later, but I mention it here because it provided some valuable evidence. It was the cork and neck of a bottle of Irish whiskey, which Jack Tyrrell of Arklow, who built *Gipsy Moth III*, had sent me as a present at the start of this voyage. I knew exactly where this bottle had been standing, in a hole cut in a sheet of plywood to take the bottle in the wine locker on the starboard side of the cabin. This locker had a flap-down lid. So I knew exactly where the bottle had come from. I also knew exactly where it had gone to; it had hit a deck beam in the ceiling of the cabin, making a bruise a quarter of an inch deep in the wood. Here it had shattered into a thousand fragments, and it was not till even later in the voyage that I found out where most of these were. At the foot of Sheila's bunk on the port side of the cabin there was a shelf, of which half was boxed in with a flap-down lid. In this case also the lid had flown open when the boat went over, the pieces of glass had shot in, and the lid had closed down again. As I write this, the glass is still there. The last fragment of glass I found was one that had dropped onto the cabin floor from somewhere and lodged in the sole of my foot when I was going barefoot. The point about this glass is that it enabled me to measure the exact path of the bottle, which showed that the boat had turned through 131° when the bottle flew out of its niche; in other words, the mast would have then been 41° below the horizontal. I wondered if the shock of a wave hitting the boat had shot the bottle out of its locker, but there was other evidence which convinced me that this was not the case. On the roof of the doghouse the paintwork was spattered all over with particles of dirt up to a line just like a highwater mark on a beach. This dirt must have come from the floor of the cabin when the hatches above the bilge flew off. The particles were so small they would not have any momentum if a wave had hit the boat with a shock; they would have got on to the roof only by dropping there through gravity. What I have described and other little bits of evidence which I came across during the succeeding months convince me that the yacht rolled over until the mast was between 45 and 60° below the horizontal, and I couldn't believe it would have made much difference if she had come up the other side after completely rolling over.

But this detective work came later. I must return to the state of things at the time. There was butter everywhere and over everything, for 2 lb of butter had landed at the foot of my bunk, and splashed and spread. Coat hangers in the hanging locker were broken, and the basin was full of my clothes. Also in the basin was a Tupperware box containing my first aid equipment. Both cabin bunks had collapsed, spilling the contents of Tupperware containers on top of the contents of the drop lockers. Tins of food, fruit and milk were jumbled up on the cabin floor with shackles, sextants, biscuits and cushions. All the floor boards had taken to the air when *Gipsy Moth* went over, so everything that could find its way to the bilges had duly got there. My camera stand had broken in two, but the loose half was still lying on deck, up to windward. The main halliard was tangled with the burgee halliard.

Gipsy Moth capsized on the night of Monday, January 30. My log notes briefly: "About 22.30. Capsize." Heavy weather continued throughout Tuesday, January 31, and I spent the day lying ahull, doing what I could to clear up. The electric bilge pump would not work, so I had to pump by hand, trying to repair the electric pump in the intervals of hand pumping. After I had cleaned the impeller the electric pump worked for a few minutes, but then sucked at an air lock. The bilge was still half-full, but gradually I got the water down. I streamed my remaining green warp in the hope that it would keep the yacht headed downwind, but without any sails up the warp seemed to have no effect. So I hauled it back inboard and coiled it. The socket for the vane shaft of the self-steering gear was nearly off, so that had to be repaired, a dirty job which put me under water now and again. Thank God the water was warm! As I dealt with these various jobs one after another, my spirits began to pick up. I had been unbelievably lucky. The masts and rigging were all intact, which I attributed largely to Warwick's rigging. I felt a sense of loss that one of the big genoas had gone overboard, but I could get on without it. I was upset at losing one of my drogues and the 700 feet of drogue warp that went with it, for I had intended to stream a drogue at the end of a long warp to slow down *Gipsy Moth* and to keep her stern to the seas in Cape Horner storms. Later, after I had pondered the details of my capsize for many hours, I completely discarded the warp and drogue idea. So the loss of those items was not as serious as I thought at the time.

As the day wore on I began to feel a little hungry, and I lunched on three slices of bread and butter and marmalade. The bread was pretty mouldy, but it was solid food, and went down well. My log for that day notes cheerfully: "18.20. Called Sydney Radio. Told Sheila the tale."

That radio talk with Sheila meant much to me. She was as calm and confident as always, and never for a moment questioned my decision to carry on. I said again that I did not want any help. She was distressed as I was about the mess in our beautifully tidy boat. I could tell her about everything, because she knew exactly where everything was. I remember telling her about the horrible smell like stale, spilled beer, from wet vitamin tablets sticking to the cabin roof. I told her that I had spares on board for most things, and that in time I should be able to tidy up. I drew strength from her.

SEA BATTLES

The Battle of Salamis

by HERODOTUS,
translated by ISAAC LITTLEBURY

When the naval forces of Xerxes had viewed the dead bodies of the Lacedemonians, they passed over from Trachis to Histiaea; and after three days' stay, sailed through the Euripus, and in three days more arrived at Phaleron. Their numbers, in my opinion, were not less, both by land and by sea, when they came to Athens, than when they arrived at Sepias and at Thermopyle. For I balance the loss of those that perished in the storm, and at Thermopyle, as well as of those that were killed in the sea-fight at Artemisium, with the additional forces they received from the Melians, the Dorians, the Locrians, and generally from all the Boeotians except the Thespians and the Plataeans; none of these people having before joined the king's army. To this number I must also add the Carystians, the Andrians, and the Tenians, with all the rest of the Islanders, except the five cities I mentioned before. For the farther the Persian penetrated into Greece, the more was his army increased, by the nations that followed his fortune. When they were all arrived at Phaleron and at Athens, except only the Parians, who stayed at Cythnus in expectation of the event, Xerxes himself went on board the fleet to confer with the commanders, and to know their opinions: where, after he had taken his seat, and the kings of the several nations, with the other generals of his marine-forces, were assembled by his direction, they sat down likewise in the order appointed by him; the king of Sidon first; next to him the king of Tyre; then the rest in their respective ranks; and when they were all placed, Xerxes sent Mardonius to put the question to every one in particular, whether they should venture an engagement by sea, or not. Accordingly Mardonius beginning at the king of Sidon, collected the opinions of the whole assembly; which were unanimous for fighting, except only that of Artemisia, who said, "Mardonius, tell the king I give my opinion in these words: Sir, since I have not behaved myself worse, nor done less, than others, in the actions upon the coast of Euboea, I may with reason speak my thoughts freely, and let you know what I think most advantageous to your affairs. I advise you then to save your ships, and not to come to an engagement against those, who, by sea, are as much superior to your forces, as men are to women. Besides, what need have you to hazard another battle at sea? Is not Athens in your possession, for which you undertook the war? And you are master of the rest of Greece; for no man now opposes you, since those who ventured to resist, met with the fate they deserved. But, to tell you what I think will be the fortune of the enemy. If you abstain from hazarding a sea-fight, and order the fleet to continue here, you will easily compass the design you came about; whether you stay ashore in this place, or advance to Peloponnesus in person. For the Grecians cannot be long in a condition to resist; but must separate, and fly to their own cities; because, as I am informed, they have no provisions in this island. Neither can we with any reason believe, that, when you have marched your land-forces into Peloponnesus, those who came hither from thence, will continue here, and fight a battle by sea, in order to defend the territories of the Athenians. But if you determine to engage the enemy at this time, I fear the defeat of your naval-forces will cause the destruction of your land-army. Consider, Sir, that good men have sometimes bad servants, and bad men good. You are the best of men; but you have bad servants, who yet go under the name of your confederates; and such are the Egyptians, the Cyprians, the Cilicians, and the Pamphylians, all utterly insignificant.'' When Artemisia had said these words to Mardonius, her friends were not a little disturbed; fearing she might fall under the king's displeasure, for dissuading him from a battle at sea. But those who envied her, because she was no less honoured than the most considerable among the confederates, were glad she had delivered such an opinion, as they thought must certainly ruin her. Yet when the report was made to Xerxes, he shewed himself extremely pleased with the opinion of Artemisia; and having always esteemed her zealous for his interests, he now honoured her with greater praises than before. Nevertheless he determined to comply with the majority; and thinking his forces had not done their best at Euboea, because he was not present, he resolved to be spectator of the engagement. To that end orders were given out for sailing, and the whole fleet stood towards Salamis, drawing up into national squadrons at leisure: but because night was coming on, and the remaining light not sufficient for a battle, they prepared themselves to fight the next day. In the mean time the Grecians were under much fear and apprehensions, of which the Peloponnesians had the greatest share; reflecting with astonishment, that they were then at Salamis, ready to fight for a place belonging to the Athenians; and that if they were beaten, they should be besieged, and prevented from retiring to their own country, which they had left without defence.

In that same night the land-army of the Barbarians marched towards Peloponnesus; where the Grecians had done all they could to prevent an eruption by the way of the continent. For so soon as they had heard of the slaughter of the Peloponnesians with Leonidas, they drew together from their cities to the isthmus, and put themselves under the conduct of Cleombrotus the son of Anaxandrides, and brother to Leonidas. Being encamped there, they first fortified the passage of Sciron; and afterwards having resolved to erect a wall upon the isthmus, they brought that work to perfection; every man, of so many thousands that were in the army, performing his part, without exception: for they were all employed in carrying stones, bricks, timber, or hods of sand; working without intermission, both by night and by day. The Grecians who came to succour the common cause at the isthmus were, the Lacedemonians, the Arcadians, the Eleans, the Corinthians, the Sicyonians, the Epidaurians, the Phliasians, the Troezenians, and the Hermionians; all highly concerned for the danger of Greece. But the rest of the Peloponnesians took no care of any thing, though the Olympian and Carnian solemnities were past.

Peloponnesus is inhabited by seven nations; two of which are the Arcadians and the Cynurians; who being originally of that country, have always dwelt in the same places they now possess. After these, the Achaians; who, though they never abandoned Peloponnesus, yet left their ancient seat, and settled themselves in another. The remaining four are strangers; and consist of Dorians, AEtolians, Dryopians, and Lemnians. The cities of the Dorians are many and of great fame; the AEtolians have only Elis; the Dryopians, Hermione and Asina situate near Cardamyla, a city of Laconia; and the Lemnians are masters of all the places that lie at the foot of the mountains. Among these, the Cynurians alone appear to have been Ionians; but were accounted Dorians after they fell under the power of the Argians, as were also the Orneates and their neighbours. Now, except those nations I mentioned before, the rest of the seven sat still; or rather, if I may speak with freedom, absented themselves, because they favoured the Medes. Nevertheless the Grecians at the isthmus concurred with all possible diligence to finish the work they had undertaken, expecting no success from their navy. On the other hand, those at Salamis were much disturbed when they heard these things; as being more concerned for Peloponnesus than for themselves. They first began to whisper to one another, and to wonder at the imprudence of Eurybiades; till at last breaking out into open murmurings, a council of war was called, and a long debate arose. Some said they ought to sail for Peloponnesus, and hazard a battle for that country, rather than to stay and fight for a place already in the power of the enemy. But the Athenians, the AEginetes, and the Megareans, voted to stay and fight at Salamis. Then Themistocles seeing his opinion set aside by the Peloponnesians, went privately out of the council, and sent away a man to the enemy's fleet, in a small vessel, with such orders as he thought necessary. The name of the man was Sicinus: he lived in his family; had the care of instructing his sons; and in succeeding time, when the Thespians augmented the number of their citizens, Themistocles procured him to be made a citizen of Thespia, and gave him considerable riches. This person arriving in the fleet, delivered his message to the Barbarian generals in these words; "The captain of the Athenians, who is in the interest of the king, and desires your affairs may prosper, rather than those of Greece, has sent me privately away, with orders to let you know, that the Grecians in great consternation have determined to betake themselves to flight; and that you have now an opportunity of achieving the most glorious of all enterprises, unless your negligence opens a way to their escape. For being divided in their opinions, they will not oppose your forces; but you will see those who are your friends, fighting against those who are not of your party." Sicinus having thus delivered his message, departed immediately; and the enemy believing what he said, landed a considerable number of Persians in Psyttalea, an island lying between Salamis and the continent; and about midnight stretching the westwardly point of their fleet towards Salamis, whilst those who were about Ceos and Cynosura extended the other to Munychia, they shut up the whole coast with their ships. In this manner they disposed their fleet, that the Grecians finding no way to escape, might be all taken at Salamis, to compensate the loss of the Barbarians in the action of Artemisium; and landed the Persians in Psyttalea, to the end that, as they expected the most part of the disabled ships and distressed men would be driven thither, because that island is situate near the place where the battle was like to be fought, they might be ready to save whatever they thought fit, and to destroy the rest. But these things they endeavoured to conceal from the Grecians, and passed the whole night without sleep in making all necessary preparations. Considering the event of this war, I have nothing to say against the truth of oracles; resolving not to attempt to invalidate so manifest a prediction.

When circling ships shall join the sacred shore
Of Artemis to Cynosura's coast,
Just vengeance then shall reach the furious youth,
True son of violence, who vainly proud
Of ravag'd Athens, insolently thought
That all must stoop to his audacious rage.
For clashing swords shall meet, and Mars shall stain
The foaming billows with a purple gore.
Then Saturn's son and victory shall bring
A glorious day of liberty to Greece.

These words of Bacis are so clear, that I dare not dispute the veracity of oracles, nor shall admit the objections of others.

In the mean time the generals at Salamis continued their debates with great animosity, not knowing that they were surrounded by the ships of the Barbarians. But when day was come, they saw the enemy so disposed, as if they designed to make towards the shore: and whilst they were still in council, Aristides the son of Lysimachus arrived from AEgina. He was an Athenian; but voted into exile by the people; and yet, for as much as I have learnt of his manners, he was the best and justest man in Athens. This person coming to the place where the council sat, sent for Themistocles out, who was not his friend, but rather the fiercest of his enemies; yet the greatness of the impending danger made him forget their former enmity, and resolved to confer with him; because he had heard that the Peloponnesians were determined to retire with the fleet to the isthmus. When Themistocles came out, Aristides said, "We ought at this time, and on all occasions, to contend, who shall do the greatest service to our country. I assure you, that to say little or much to the Peloponnesians about their departure, is the same thing: for I tell you as an eye-witness, that neither Eurybiades himself nor the Corinthians can now retire, if they would; because we are on all sides inclosed by the enemy's fleet. Go in again therefore, and acquaint the council with our condition." Themistocles answered, "Your admonition is exceedingly grateful, and the news you bring most acceptable. For you tell me you have seen that, which I desired should come to pass above all things. Know then, that what the Medes have done, proceeds from me. For necessity required, that those Grecians who would not fight voluntarily, should be compelled to an engagement against their will. But since you have brought so good news, let the council hear it from yourself: because if I should be the reporter, they would think it a fiction, and I shall not persuade them that the Barbarians are doing such a thing. Go in therefore, and inform them of the fact: if they believe you, nothing better can happen: if not, we are still in the same condition: for they have no way open to escape by flight, if, as you say, we are already encompassed on all sides." Accordingly Aristides going in, gave the same account to the council, acquainting them that he came from AEgina, after he had with great difficulty made his passage, and eluded the vigilance of the enemy, who with the whole navy of Xerxes had entirely encompassed the Grecian ships. He counselled them therefore to prepare themselves with all diligence for their defence; and when he had said this, he retired. But yet, the dissension continued among the generals, and the greater part gave no credit to the report, till a Tenian sip commanded by Panaetius the son of Sosimenes, arriving from the enemy to join the Grecians, discovered the whole truth; and for that action the name of the Tenians was engraved upon the tripos consecrated at Delphi, among those who defeated the Barbarian. By the addition of this ship, and that of Lemnos, which came over at Artemisium, the Grecian fleet now amounted to three hundred and eighty sail; for before they wanted two of that number.

The Grecians believing the account they received from the Tenians, prepared for an engagement; and at day-break called a general assembly of the men at arms; in which Themistocles having first declared the hopes he had of a prosperous event, framed all his discourse to shew the difference between actions of the greatest glory, and those of less importance; animating them to choose the most noble, as far as the nature and condition of man permit. When he had finished his speech, he encouraged them to return on board; which they had no sooner done, than the ship they had sent to AEgina with orders touching the AEacides, returned to Salamis; and at the same time the Grecians weighed all their anchors. The Barbarians seeing them coming out, advanced with diligence; but the Grecians continued luffing, and bearing upon the stern; when Aminias an Athenian of the Pallenian tribe breaking out of the line, fell in among the enemy, and fastened the grappling iron to one of their ships; which the rest perceiving, and that there was no other way to bring him off, they made up to his assistance; and thus the Athenians say the fight began. But the AEginetes affirm that the ship which went to AEgina with the instructions about the AEacides, was the first engaged. There is also a report that a phantom appeared in the shape of a woman, encouraging the Grecians with so loud a voice, that she was heard by all the fleet, after she had first reproached them in these words; "Infatuated men! how long will you rest upon your oars, and forbear to advance?" In the order of battle, the Phoenicians were placed on that wing which fronted the Athenians, and extended westward towards Eleusis. The Ionians were ranged on the other point, facing the Lacedemonians,

and stretching towards the east and the Piraeeus. Of these some few, persuaded by the admonition of Themistocles, voluntarily omitted to perform
their part. Yet the greatest number did their best: and I could give the names of
many captains who took ships from the Grecians, though I shall mention no
more than Theomestor the son of Androdamas, and Phylacus the son of His-
tiaeus, both Samians. I name these two, because Theomestor was afterwards
made Tyrant of Samos by the Persians, for his service on this occasion; and
Phylacus was not only admitted into the number of those, who by deserving
well of the king, are called among the Persians Orosanges; but rewarded with
large possessions in land. And such were the recompences of these two commanders. Nevertheless this numerous fleet was defeated at Salamis, and received a terrible blow, principally from the Athenians and the AEginetes. For
the Grecians observed so good order, and such a steady conduct in the fight,
whilst the Barbarians fought in a disorderly manner, and without judgment,
that no other event could be expected. Yet the enemy shewed far more courage
that day, than they had done before on the coast of Euboea, or at any other
time; every one exerting himself vigorously, in fear of the king's displeasure,
because they all imagined that their actions were observed by him. I cannot
exactly relate, how each particular person, either of the Grecians or Barbarians, behaved himself in this engagement: but an adventure happened to Artemisia, which served to augment her credit with Xerxes. For when the king's
fleet was in the utmost confusion, Artemisia finding she was chased by an
Athenian ship, and not knowing whither to fly, because she had those of her
own party in front, and the enemy in the rear, contrived to do a thing which
turned to her great advantage. As she fled from the Athenian, she drove directly upon a ship of her own side, belonging to the Calyndians, and having
their king Damasithymus on board: but whether, on account of a contestation
they had together at the Hellespont, she purposely run down his ship, or
whether the Calyndians were in her way by accident, I cannot affirm: however,
the ship went down to rights, and Artemisia had the good fortune to reap a
double advantage by that blow. For the captain of the Athenian ship, when he
saw the Barbarian sunk, concluding Artemisia's ship to be a Grecian, or at
least one that had abandoned the enemy to join with the Grecians, gave over
the chace, and left her: by which means Artemisia not only escaped the danger, but advanced her reputation with Xerxes by a bad action. For they say,
that when the king, who was spectator of the exploit, had taken notice of the
ship which gave the shock, one of those about him said, "Sir, you see with
what courage Artemisia fights, and has sunk one of the enemy's ships." Then
the king asking, if indeed Artemisia had done that action? they answered, that
they knew the flag perfectly well; still imagining the lost ship to be an enemy.
For to the rest of her good fortune, which I mentioned before, this also was
added, that one of the company belonging to the Calyndian ship survived to
accuse her. So that when Xerxes heard their answer, he is reported to have
said, "My men have fought like women, and my women like men." In this
battle Ariabignes, the son of Darius and brother of Xerxes, was killed, with

great numbers of illustrious men, as well Persians and Medes as their confederates. On the part of the Grecians the slaughter was not great; because those who lost their ships, and survived the fate of war, saved themselves by their skill in swimming, and got ashore at Salamis; whereas most of the Barbarians, being ignorant of that art, perished in the sea. The greatest loss the enemy sustained, began after their headmost ships were put to flight; for those who lay astern, endeavouring to come up into the van, that they might shew the king some proof of their courage, fell foul upon their own flying ships. In this confusion, some Phoenicians, whose ships were destroyed, going to the king, told him the Ionians had betrayed all, and been the cause of their disaster: but contrary to their expectation, the punishment they designed to bring upon the Ionian commanders, fell upon the accusers themselves. For whilst they were yet speaking, a Samothracian ship attacking one of Attica, sunk the Athenian; and a ship of AEgina coming up in that instant, sunk the Samothracian. But the Samothracians being armed with javelins, poured in such a shower from the sinking vessel upon the AEginetes, that venturing to board the conquering ship, they carried her. This success saved the Ionians: for Xerxes having seen them perform so great an action, turned about to the Phoenicians; and being above measure troubled, and ready to fling the blame every where, commanded their heads to be struck off; that they might no more accuse those, who had fought better than themselves. He sat upon the descent of a hill called AEgaleos, over against Salamis; and whenever he saw a remarkable action done in the fight by any one of his officers, he made enquiry touching the man, and caused his secretaries to write down his name, his family, and his country. But not satisfied with the slaughter of the Phoenicians, he added that of Ariaramnes, a Persian and his favourite, who had been present at their death. In the end the Barbarians betaking themselves to open flight, made the best of their way towards Phaleron. But the AEginetes waiting for them in their passage through the straits, gave memorable proof of their valour; and as the Athenians destroyed those flying ships, which ventured to resist in the confusion; the AEginetes did no less execution upon those, which escaped out of the battle. So that for the most part, when any ship happened to avoid the Athenians, they fell into the hands of the AEginetes. In this rout the ship of Themistocles giving chace to one of the enemy, came up with another commanded by Polycritus of AEgina the son of Crius, as he was ready to attack a Sidonian ship, which proved to be the same that took the guard-ship of the AEginetes near Scyathus, with Pytheas the son of Ischenous on board; who being covered with wounds, was exempted from death by the Persians in admiration of his valour, and kept prisoner in the ship. In this action the Sidonian ship was taken with all the men on board, and by that means Pytheas returned safe to AEgina. But when Polycritus saw the Athenian ship, which he knew to be the admiral by the flag she carried, he called aloud to Themistocles, and in a jesting manner bid him take notice how the AEginetes favoured the Medes. In the mean time the Barbarians, with the ships they had left, fled in great disorder towards their land-forces, and arrived at Phaleron. Among the Gre-

cians that fought this battle, the AEginetes were most commended; and next to
these, the Athenians: among the captains, Polycritus of AEgina; and among
the Athenians, Eumenes of the Anagyrasian, with Aminias of the Pallenian
tribe; who gave chace to Artemisia; and if he had known she had been in the
ship, would not have given over the pursuit, till either he had taken her, or she
him. For the Athenians had given orders to that purpose to all their captains,
and promised a reward of ten thousand drachmas to the person who should
take her alive; resenting with great indignation, that a woman should make
war against Athens. But, as I said before, she made her escape, and with
divers other ships arrived at Phaleron. The Athenians say, that Adimantus the
Corinthian general, struck with a panic fear in the beginning of the fight, put
up all his sails, and betook himself to flight; that the Corinthians, seeing their
leader run, bore away after him; and when they had reached the temple of
Minerva at Sciras in Salamis, a frigate magnificently adorned fell in with their
squadron: that when they found she made no discovery whence she came, nor
had brought any message to the Corinthians from the army, they concluded the
thing to be divine; for as soon as the frigate came up with their ships, those on
board cried out, "Adimantus, thou hast by thy flight deprived the Grecians of
the assistance of these ships, and are a traitor to Greece; yet know, they shall
conquer their enemies, as completely as they desire." That finding Adimantus
gave no credit to their words, they added, that they would be contented to
remain as hostages, and be put to death, if the Grecians were not victorious:
upon which, Adimantus with the rest of the Corinthians returned to the fleet,
but came not in till the work was done. This report is current among the
Athenians; yet the Corinthians deny the fact, and affirm, they fought no less
valiantly than the best; all the rest of Greece concurring to confirm their assertion. Whilst things were in this confusion on the coast of Salamis, Aristides
the son of Lysimachus, the Athenian, mentioned by me a little before as a
most excellent person, taking with him a considerable number of men, all of
Athenian blood, who were drawn up along that shore in their arms, passed
over to Psyttalea, and put to the sword all the Persians he found in the island.
The Grecians, after the engagement by sea was over, brought to Salamis all the
wreck that continued floating about that coast, and prepared for another battle,
expecting the king would make use of his remaining ships to that end. But the
greater part of the broken vessels were carried by a south-wind to the shore of
Colias in Attica; that not only those predictions of Bacis and Musaeus touching the success of the sea-fight might be verified; but that also relating to the
shattered remains rolling to that coast, which many years before had been
delivered in these terms to Lysistratus, an Athenian augur, and concealed from
all the Grecians: "The Colian dames shall shake to see the oars." This was to
happen in the time of the king's expedition.

Ben-Hur Escapes from the *Astroea*

by LEWIS WALLACE

Every soul aboard, even the ship, awoke. Officers went to their quarters. The marines took arms, and were led out, looking in all respects like legionaries. Sheaves of arrows and armfuls of javelins were carried on deck. By the central stairs the oil-tanks and fire-balls were set ready for use. Additional lanterns were lighted. Buckets were filled with water. The rowers in relief assembled under guard in front of the chief. As Providence would have it, Ben-Hur was one of the latter. Overhead he heard the muffled noise of the final preparations—of the sailors furling sail, spreading the nettings, unslinging the machines, and hanging the armor of bull-hide over the side. Presently quiet settled about the galley again; quite full of vague dread and expectation, which, interpreted, means *ready*.

At a signal passed down from the deck, and communicated to the hortator by a petty officer stationed on the stairs, all at once the oars stopped.

What did it mean?

Of the hundred and twenty slaves chained to the benches, not one but asked himself the question. They were without incentive. Patriotism, love of honor, sense of duty, brought them no inspiration. They felt the thrill common to men rushed helpless and blind into danger. It may be supposed the dullest of them, poising his oar, thought of all that might happen, yet could promise himself nothing; for victory would but rivet his chains the firmer, while the chances of the ship were his; sinking or on fire, he was doomed to her fate.

Of the situation without they might not ask. And who were the enemy? And what if they were friends, brethren, countrymen? The reader, carrying the suggestion forward, will see the necessity which governed the Roman when, in such emergencies, he locked the hapless wretches to their seats.

There was little time, however, for such thought with them. A sound like the rowing of galleys astern attracted Ben-Hur, and the *Astroea* rocked as if in the midst of countering waves. The idea of a fleet at hand broke upon him—a fleet in manoeuvre—forming probably for attack. His blood started with the fancy.

Another signal order came down from deck. The oars dipped, and the galley started imperceptibly. No sound from without, none from within, yet each man in the cabin instinctively poised himself for a shock; the very ship seemed to catch the sense, and hold its breath, and go crouched tiger-like.

In such a situation time is inappreciable; so that Ben-Hur could form no judgment of distance gone. At last there was a sound of trumpets on deck, full, clear, long blown. The chief beat the sounding-board until it rang; the rowers reached forward full length, and, deepening the dip of their oars, pulled suddenly with all their united force. The galley, quivering in every timber, answered with a leap. Other trumpets joined in the clamor—all from the rear, none forward—from the latter quarter only a rising sound of voices in tumult heard briefly. There was a mighty blow; the rowers in front of the chief's platform reeled, some of them fell; the ship bounded back, recovered, and rushed on more irresistibly than before. Shrill and high arose the shrieks of men in terror; over the blare of trumpets, and the grind and crash of the collision, they arose; then under his feet, under the keel, pounding, rumbling, breaking to pieces, drowning, Ben-Hur felt something overridden. The men about him looked at each other afraid. A shout of triumph from the deck—the beak of the Roman had won! But who were they whom the sea had drunk? Of what tongue, from what land were they?

No pause, no stay! Forward rushed the *Astroea;* and, as it went, some sailors ran down, and, plunging the cotton balls into the oil-tanks, tossed them dripping to comrades at the head of the stairs: fire was to be added to other horrors of the combat.

Directly the galley heeled over so far that the oarsmen on the uppermost side with difficulty kept their benches. Again the hearty Roman cheer, and with it despairing shrieks. An opposing vessel, caught by the grappling-hooks of the great crane swinging from the prow, was being lifted into the air that it might be dropped and sunk.

The shouting increased on the right hand and on the left; before, behind, swelled an indescribable clamor. Occasionally there was a crash, followed by sudden peals of fright, telling of other ships ridden down, and their crews drowned in the vortexes.

Nor was the fight all on one side. Now and then a Roman in armor was borne down the hatchway, and laid bleeding, sometimes dying, on the floor.

Sometimes, also, puffs of smoke, blended with steam, and foul with the scent of roasting human flesh, poured into the cabin, turning the dimming light into yellow murk. Gasping for breath the while, Ben-Hur knew they were passing through the cloud of a ship on fire, and burning up with the rowers chained to the benches.

The *Astroea* all this time was in motion. Suddenly she stopped. The oars forward were dashed from the hands of the rowers, and the rowers from their benches. On deck, then, a furious trampling, and on the sides a grinding of ships afoul of each other. For the first time the beating of the gavel was lost in the uproar. Men sank on the floor in fear or looked about seeking a hiding-place. In the midst of the panic a body plunged or was pitched headlong down the hatchway, falling near Ben-Hur. He beheld the half-naked carcass, a mass of hair blackening the face, and under it a shield of bull-hide and wicker-work—a barbarian from the white-skinned nations of the North whom earth had robbed of plunder and revenge. How came he there? An iron hand had snatched him from the opposing deck—no, the *Astroea* had been boarded! The Romans were fighting on their own deck? A chill smote the young Jew:

Arrius was hard pressed—he might be defending his own life. If he should be slain! God of Abraham forefend! The hopes and dreams so lately come, were they only hopes and dreams? Mother and sister—house—home—Holy Land—was he not to see them, after all? The tumult thundered above him; he looked around; in the cabin all was confusion—the rowers on the benches paralyzed; men running blindly hither and thither; only the chief on his seat imperturbable, vainly beating the sounding-board, and waiting the order of the tribune—in the red murk illustrating the matchless discipline which had won the world.

The example had a good effect upon Ben-Hur. He controlled himself enough to think. Honor and duty bound the Roman to the platform; but what had he to do with such motives then? The bench was a thing to run from; while, if he were to die a slave, who would be the better of the sacrifice? With him living was duty, if not honor. His life belonged to his people. They arose before him never more real: he saw them, their arms outstretched; he heard them imploring him. And he would go to them. He started—stopped. Alas! a Roman judgment held him in doom. While it endured, escape would be profitless. In the wide, wide earth there was no place in which he would be safe from the imperial demand; upon the land none, nor upon the sea. Whereas he required freedom according to the forms of law, so only could he abide in Judea and execute the filial purpose to which he would devote himself: in other land he would not live. Dear God! How he had waited and watched and prayed for such a release! And how it had been delayed! But at last he had seen it in the promise of the tribune. What else the great man's meaning? And if the benefactor so belated should now be slain! The dead come not back to redeem the pledges of the living. It should not be—Arrius should not die. At least, better perish with him than survive a galley-slave.

Once more Ben-Hur looked around. Upon the roof of the cabin the battle yet beat; against the sides the hostile vessels yet crushed and grinded. On the benches, the slaves struggled to tear loose from their chains, and, finding their efforts vain, howled like madmen; the guards had gone up stairs; discipline was out, panic in. No, the chief kept his chair, unchanged, calm as ever— except the gavel, weaponless. Vainly with his clangor he filled the lulls in the din. Ben-Hur gave him a last look, then broke away—not in flight, but to seek the tribune.

A very short space lay between him and the stairs of the hatchway aft. He took it with a leap, and was half-way up the steps—up far enough to catch a glimpse of the sky blood-red with fire, of the ships alongside, of the sea covered with ships and wrecks, of the fight closed in about the pilot's quarter, the assailants many, the defenders few—when suddenly his foothold was knocked away, and he pitched backward. The floor, when he reached it, seemed to be lifting itself and breaking to pieces; then, in a twinkling, the whole after-part of the hull broke asunder, and, as if it had all the time been lying in wait, the sea, hissing and foaming, leaped in, and all became darkness and surging water to Ben-Hur.

It cannot be said that the young Jew helped himself in this stress. Besides his usual strength, he had the indefinite extra force which nature keeps in reserve for just such perils to life; yet the darkness, and the whirl and roar of water, stupefied him. Even the holding of his breath was involuntary.

The influx of the flood tossed him like a log forward into the cabin, where he would have drowned but for the refluence of the sinking motion. As it was, fathoms under the surface the hollow mass vomited him forth, and he arose along with the loosed debris. In the act of rising, he clutched something, and held to it. The time he was under seemed an age longer than it really was; at last he gained the top; with a great gasp he filled his lungs afresh, and, tossing the water from his hair and eyes, climbed higher upon the plank he held, and looked about him.

Death had pursued him closely under the waves; he found it waiting for him when he was risen—waiting multiform.

Smoke lay upon the sea like a semitransparent fog, through which here and there shone cores of intense brilliance. A quick intelligence told him that they were ships on fire. The battle was yet on; nor could he say who was victor. Within the radius of his vision now and then ships passed, shooting shadows athwart lights. Out of the dun clouds farther on he caught the crash of other ships colliding. The danger, however, was closer at hand. When the *Astroea* went down, her deck, it will be recollected, held her own crew, and the crews of the two galleys which had attacked her at the same time, all of whom were engulfed. Many of them came to the surface together, and on the same plank or support of whatever kind continued the combat, begun possibly in the vortex fathoms down. Writhing and twisting in deadly embrace, sometimes striking with sword or javelin, they kept the sea around them in agitation, at one place inky-black, at another aflame with fiery reflections. With their struggles he had nothing to do; they were all his enemies: not one of them but would kill him for the plank upon which he floated. He made haste to get away.

About that time he heard oars in quickest movement, and beheld a galley coming down upon him. The tall prow seemed doubly tall, and the red light playing upon its gilt and carving gave it an appearance of snaky life. Under its foot the water churned to flying foam.

He struck out, pushing the plank, which was very broad and unmanageable. Seconds were precious—half a second might save or lose him. In the crisis of the effort, up from the sea, within arm's reach, a helmet shot like a gleam of gold. Next came two hands with fingers extended—large hands were they, and strong—their hold once fixed, might not be loosed. Ben-Hur swerved from them appalled. Up rose the helmet and the head it encased—then two arms, which began to beat the water wildly—the head turned back, and gave the face to the light. The mouth gaping wide; the eyes open, but sightless, and the bloodless pallor of a drowning man—never anything more ghastly! Yet he gave a cry of joy at the sight, and as the face was going under again, he caught the sufferer by the chain which passed from the helmet beneath the chin, and drew him to the plank.

The man was Arrius, the tribune.

For a while the water foamed and eddied violently about Ben-Hur, taxing all his strength to hold to the support and at the same time keep the Roman's head above the surface. The galley had passed, leaving the two barely outside the stroke of its oars. Right through the floating men, over heads helmeted as well as heads bare, she drove, in her wake nothing but the sea sparkling with fire. A muffled crash, succeeded by a great outcry, made the rescuer look again from his charge. A certain savage pleasure touched his heart—the *Astroea* was avenged.

After that the battle moved on. Resistance turned to flight. But who were the victors? Ben-Hur was sensible how much his freedom and the life of the tribune depended upon that event. He pushed the plank under the latter until it floated him, after which all his care was to keep him there. The dawn came slowly. He watched its growing hopefully, yet sometimes afraid. Would it bring the Romans or the pirates? If the pirates, his charge was lost.

At last morning broke in full, the air without a breath. Off to the left he saw the land, too far to think of attempting to make it. Here and there men were adrift like himself. In spots the sea was blackened by charred and sometimes smoking fragments. A galley up a long way was lying to with a torn sail hanging from the tilted yard, and the oars all idle. Still farther away he could discern moving specks, which he thought might be ships in flight or pursuit, or they might be white birds a-wing.

An hour passed thus. His anxiety increased. If relief came not speedily, Arrius would die. Sometimes he seemed already dead, he lay so still. He took the helmet off, and then, with greater difficulty, the cuirass; the heart he found fluttering. He took hope at the sign, and held on. There was nothing to do but wait, and, after the manner of his people, pray.

The Escape of the *Primrose*

by RICHARD HAKLUYT

The escape of the *Primrose* a tall ship of London, from before the towne of
Bilbao in Biscay: which ship the Corrigidor of the same province,
accompanied with 97 Spaniards, offered violently to arrest, and was defeated
of his purpose, and brought prisoner into England.
Whereunto is added the Kings Commission for a generall imbargment or
arrest of all English, Netherlandish, and Easterlings ships, written in
Barcelona the 19 of May 1585.

It is not unknowen unto the world what danger our English shippes have lately
escaped, how sharpely they have beene intreated, and howe hardly they have
beene assaulted: so that the valiancie of those that mannaged them is worthy
remembrance. And therefore in respect of the couragious attempt and valiant
enterprise of the ship called the *Primrose* of London, which hath obteined
renowne, I have taken in hande to publish the trueth thereof, to the intent that
it may be generally knowen to the rest of the English ships, that by the good
example of this the rest may in time of extremitie adventure to doe the like: to
the honour of the Realme, and the perpetuall remembrance of themselves: The
maner whereof was as followeth.

Upon Wednesday being the sixe and twentieth day of May 1585, the shippe
called the *Primrose* being of one hundred and fiftie tunnes, lying without the
bay of Bilbao, having beene there two dayes, there came a Spanish pinnesse to
them, wherein was the Corrigidor and sixe others with him: these came aboord
the *Primrose*, seeming to be Marchantes of Biscay, or such like, bringing
Cherries with them, and spake very friendly to the Maister of the ship, whose
name was Foster, and he in courteous wise bad them welcome, making them
the best cheere that he could with beere, beefe, and bisket, wherewith that
ship was well furnished: and while they were thus in banquetting with the
Maister, foure of the seven departed in the sayd Pinnesse, and went backe
againe to Bilbao: the other three stayed, and were very pleasant for the time.
But Master Foster misdoubting some danger secretly gave speech that he was
doubtfull of these men what their intent was; neverthelesse he sayd nothing,
nor seemed in any outward wise to mistrust them at all. Foorthwith there came
a ship-boate wherein were seventie persons being Marchants and such like of
Biscay: and besides this boate, there came also the Pinnesse which before had
brought the other three, in which Pinnesse there came foure and twentie, as
the Spaniards themselves since confessed. These made towards the *Primrose*,
and being come thither, there came aboord the Corrigidor with three or foure
of his men: but Master Foster seeing this great multitude desired that there
might no more come aboord, but that the rest should stay in their boates,
which was granted: neverthelesse they tooke small heede of these wordes; for
on a suddaine they came foorth of the boate, entring the shippe, every Span-
iarde taking him to his Rapier which they brought in the boate, with other

weapons, and a drumme wherewith to triumph over them. Thus did the Spaniards enter the shippe, plunging in fiercely upon them, some planting themselves under the decke, some entring the Cabbens, and a multitude attending their pray. Then the Corrigidor having an officer with him which bare a white wand in his hand, sayd to the master of the ship: Yeeld your selfe, for you are the kings prisoner: whereat the Maister sayd to his men, We are betrayed. Then some of them set daggers to his breast, and seemed in furious manner as though they would have slaine him, meaning nothing lesse then to doe any such act, for all that they sought was to bring him and his men safe alive to shore. Whereat the Maister was amazed, and his men greatly discomfited to see themselves readie to be conveyed even to the slaughter: notwithstanding some of them respecting the daunger of the Maister, and seeing how with themselves there was no way but present death if they were once landed among the Spaniards, they resolved themselves eyther to defend the Maister, and generally to shunne that daunger, or else to die and be buried in the middest of the sea, rather than to suffer themselves to come into the tormentors hands: and therefore in very bold and manly sort some tooke them to their javelings, lances, bore-speares, and shot, which they had set in readinesse before, and having five Calievers readie charged, which was all the small shot they had, those that were under the hatches or the grate did shoote up at the Spaniards that were over their heads, which shot so amazed the Spaniards on the suddaine, as they could hardly tell which way to escape the daunger, fearing this their small shot to be of greater number then it was: others in very manlike sort dealt about among them, shewing themselves of that courage with bore-speares and lances, that they dismayed at every stroke two or three Spaniards. Then some of them desired the Maister to commaund his men to cease and holde their handes, but hee answered that such was the courage of the English Nation in defence of their owne lives, that they would slay them and him also: and therefore it lay not in him to doe it. Now did their blood runne about the ship in great quantitie, some of them being shot in betweene the legges, the bullets issuing foorth at their breasts, some cut in the head, some thrust into the bodie, and many of them very sore wounded, so that they came not so fast in on the one side, but now they tumbled as fast over boord on both sides with their weapons in their handes, some falling into the sea, and some getting into their boates, making haste towardes the Citie. And this is to be noted, that although they came very thicke thither, there returned but a small companie of them, neither is it knowen as yet how many of them were slaine or drowned, onely one English man was then slaine, whose name was John Tristram, and sixe other hurt. It was great pitie to behold how the Spaniards lay swimming in the sea, and were not able to save their lives. Foure of them taking holde of the shippe were for pities sake taken up againe by Maister Foster and his men, not knowing what they were: all the Spaniards bosomes were stuft with paper, to defend them from the shot, and these foure having some wounds were drest by the surgion of the shippe. One of them was the Corrigidor himselfe, who is governour of a hundred Townes and Cities in Spaine, his living by his office being better than sixe hundred pound yerely. This skirmish happened in the evening about sixe of the clocke, after they had laden twentie Tunne of goods and better out of the sayd ship: which goods were delivered by two of the same ship, whose names were John Burrell, and John Brodbanke, who being on shore were apprehended and stayed.

After this valiant enterprise of eight and twentie English men against 97 Spaniardes, they saw it was in vaine for them to stay and therefore set up sayles, and by Gods providence avoyded all danger, brought home the rest of their goods, and came thence with all expedition: and (God be thanked) arrived safely in England neere London on Wednesday being the 8 day of June, 1585. In which their returne to England the Spaniards that they brought with them offered five hundred crownes to be set on shore in any place: which, seeing the Maister would not doe, they were content to be ruled by him and his companie, and craved mercie at their hands. And after Master Foster demaunded why they came in such sort to betray and destroy them, the Corrigidor answered, that it was not done onely of themselves, but by the commandement of the king himselfe; and calling for his hose which were wet, did plucke foorth the kings Commission, by which he was authorized to doe all that he did: The Copie whereof followeth, being translated out of Spanish.

The Spanish kings commission for the generall imbargment or arrest of the English, &c.

Licentiat de Escober, my Corrigidor of my Signorie of Biskay, I have caused a great fleete to be put in readinesse in the haven of Lisbone, and the river of Sivill. There is required for the Souldiers, armour, victuals, and munition, that are to bee imployed in the same great store of shipping of all sortes against the time of service, and to the end there may be choise made of the best, upon knowledge of their burden and goodnesse; I doe therefore require you, that presently upon the arrival of this carrier, and with as much dissimulation as may be (that the matter may not be knowen untill it be put in execution) you take order for the staying and arresting (with great foresight) of all the shipping that may be found upon the coast, and in the portes of the sayd Signorie, excepting none of Holand, Zeland, Easterland, Germanie, England, and other Provinces that are in rebellion against mee, saving those of France which being little, and of small burden and weake, are thought unfit to serve the turne. And the stay being thus made, you shall have a speciall care that such marchandize as the sayd shippes or hulkes have brought, whether they be all or part unladen, may bee taken out, and that the armour, munition, tackels, sayles, and victuals may be safely bestowed, as also that it may be well foreseene, that none of the shippes or men may escape away. Which things being thus executed, you shall advertise me by an expresse messenger, of your proceeding therein: And send me a plaine and distinct declaration of the number of ships that you shall have so stayed in that coast and partes, whence every one of them is, which belong to my Rebels, what burthen & goods there are, and what number of men is in every of them, and what quantitie they have of armour, ordinance, munition, victuals, tacklings and other necessaries, to the end that upon sight hereof, having made choise of such as shall be fit for the service, we may further direct you what ye shall do. In the meane time you shall presently see this my commandement put in execution, and if there come thither any more ships, you shall also cause them to be stayed and arrested after the same order, using therein such care and diligence, as may answere the trust that I repose in you, wherein you shall doe me great service. Dated at Barcelona the 29 of May, 1585.

And thus have you heard the trueth and manner thereof, wherein is to be noted the great courage of the maister, and the loving hearts of the servants to save their master from the daunger of death: yea, and the care which the master had to save so much of the owners goods as hee might, although by the same the greatest is his owne losse in that he may never travell to those parts any more without the losse of his owne life, nor yet any of his servantes: for if hereafter they should, being knowen they are like to taste of the sharpe torments which are there accustomed in their Holy-house. And as for their terming English shippes to be in rebellion against them, it is sufficiently knowen by themselves, and their owne consciences can not denie it, but that with love, unitie, and concord, our shippes have ever beene favourable unto them, and as willing to pleasure their King, as his subjectes any way willing to pleasure English passengers.

The Great Armada

by CHARLES KINGSLEY

Britannia needs no bulwarks,
No towers along the steep,
Her march is o'er the mountain wave,
Her home is on the deep.
Campbell, *Ye Mariners of England.*

And now began that great sea-fight which was to determine whether Popery and despotism, or Protestantism and freedom, were the law which God had appointed for the half of Europe, and the whole of future America. It is a twelve days' epic, worthy, as I said in the beginning of this book, not of dull prose, but of the thunder-roll of Homer's verse: but having to tell it, I must do my best, rather using, where I can, the words of contemporary authors than my own.

"The Lord High Admirall of England, sending a pinnace before, called the *Defiance*, denounced war by discharging her ordnance; and presently approaching within musquet-shot, with much thundering out of his own ship, called the *Arkroyall* (alias the *Triumph*), first set upon the admirall's, as he thought, of the Spaniards (but it was Alfonso de Leon's ship). Soon after, Drake, Hawkins, and Frobisher played stoutly with their ordnance on the hindmost squadron, which was commanded by Recalde." The Spaniards soon discover the superior "nimbleness of the English ships;" and Recalde's squadron, finding that they are getting more than they give, in spite of his endeavours, hurry forward to join the rest of the fleet. Medina the Admiral, finding his ships scattering fast, gathers them into a half-moon; and the Armada tries to keep solemn way forward, like a stately herd of buffaloes, who march on across the prairie, disdaining to notice the wolves which snarl around their track. But in vain. These are no wolves, but cunning hunters, swiftly horsed, and keenly armed, and who will "shamefully shuffle" (to use Drake's own expression) that vast herd from the Lizard to Portland, from Portland to Calais Roads; and who, even in this short two hours' fight, have made many a Spaniard question the boasted invincibleness of this Armada.

One of the four great galliasses is already riddled with shot, to the great disarrangement of her "pulpits, chapels," and friars therein assistant. The fleet has to close round her, or Drake and Hawkins will sink her; in effecting which manoeuvre, the "principal galleon of Seville," in which are Pedro de Valdez and a host of blue-blooded Dons, runs foul of her neighbour, carries away her foremast, and is, in spite of Spanish chivalry, left to her fate. This does not look like victory, certainly. But courage! though Valdez be left behind, "our Lady," and the saints, and the *Bull Coenâ Domini* (dictated by one whom I dare not name here), are with them still, and it was blasphemous to doubt. But in the meanwhile, if they have fared no better than this against a

104

third of the Plymouth fleet, how will they fare when those forty belated ships, which are already whitening the blue between them and the Mewstone, enter the scene to play their part?

So ends the first day; not an English ship, hardly a man, is hurt. It has destroyed for ever, in English minds, the prestige of boastful Spain. It has justified utterly the policy which the good Lord Howard had adopted by Raleigh's and Drake's advice, of keeping up a running fight, instead of "clapping ships together without consideration," in which case, says Raleigh, "he had been lost, if he had not been better advised than a great many malignant fools were, who found fault with his demeanour."

Be that as it may, so ends the first day, in which Amyas and the other Bideford ships have been right busy for two hours, knocking holes in a huge galleon, which carries on her poop a maiden with a wheel, and bears the name of *Sta. Catharina*. She had a coat of arms on the flag at her sprit; probably those of the commandant of soldiers; but they were shot away early in the fight, so Amyas cannot tell whether they were De Soto's or not. Nevertheless, there is plenty of time for private revenge; and Amyas, called off at last by the Admiral's signal, goes to bed and sleeps soundly.

But ere he has been in his hammock an hour, he is awakened by Cary's coming down to ask for orders.

"We were to follow Drake's lantern, Amyas; but where it is, I can't see, unless he has been taken up aloft there among the stars for a new Drakium Sidus."

Amyas turns out grumbling: but no lantern is to be seen; only a sudden explosion and a great fire on board some Spaniard, which is gradually got under, while they have to lie-to the whole night long, with nearly the whole fleet.

The next morning finds them off Torbay; and Amyas is hailed by a pinnace, bringing a letter from Drake, which (saving the spelling, which was somewhat arbitrary, like most men's in those days) ran somewhat thus:—

DEAR LAD,

I have been wool-gathering all night after five great hulks, which the Pixies transfigured overnight into galleons, and this morning again into German merchantmen. I let them go with my blessing; and coming back, fell in (God be thanked!) with Valdez' great galleon; and in it good booty, which the Dons his fellows had left behind, like faithful and valiant comrades, and the Lord Howard had let slip past him, thinking her deserted by her crew. I have sent to Dartmouth a sight of noblemen and gentlemen, maybe a half-hundred; and Valdez himself, who when I sent my pinnace aboard must needs stand on his punctilios, and propound conditions. I answered him, I had no time to tell with him; if he would needs die, then I was the very man for him; if he would live, then, buena querra. He sends again, boasting that he was Don Pedro Valdez and that it stood not with his honour, and that of the Dons in his company. I replied, that for my part, I was Francis Drake, and my matches burning. Whereon he finds in my name salve for the wounds of his own, and comes aboard, kissing my fist, with Spanish lies of holding himself fortunate that he had fallen into the hands of fortunate Drake, and much more, which he might have kept to cool his porridge. But I have much news from him (for he is a leaky tub); and among others, this, that your Don Guzman is aboard of the *Sta. Catharina*, commandant of her soldiery, and has his arms flying at her sprit, beside *Sta. Catharina* at the poop, which is a maiden with a wheel, and is a lofty built ship of 3 tier of ordnance, from which God preserve you, and send you like luck with

> Your deare Friend and Admirall,
>
> F. DRAKE.

"She sails in this squadron of Recalde. The Armada was minded to smoke us out of Plymouth; and God's grace it was they tried not: but their orders from home are too strait, and so the slaves fight like a bull in a tether, no farther than their rope, finding thus the devil a hard master, as do most in the end. They cannot compass our quick handling and tacking, and take us for very witches. So far so good, and better to come. You and I know the length of their foot of old. Time and light will kill any hare, and they will find it a long way from Start to Dunkirk."

"The Admiral is in a gracious humour, Leigh, to have vouchsafed you so long a letter."

"*Sta. Catharina*! why, that was the galleon we hammered all yesterday!" said Amyas, stamping on the deck.

"Of course it was. Well, we shall find her again, doubt not. That cunning old Drake! how he has contrived to line his own pockets, even though he had to keep the whole fleet waiting for him."

"He has given the Lord High Admiral the door, at all events."

"Lord Howard is too high-hearted to stop and plunder, Papist though he is, Amyas."

Amyas answered by a growl, for he worshipped Drake, and was not too just to Papists.

The fleet did not find Lord Howard till nightfall; he and Lord Sheffield had been holding on steadfastly the whole night after the Spanish lanterns, with two ships only. At least there was no doubt now of the loyalty of English Roman Catholics, and, indeed, throughout the fight, the Howards showed (as if to wipe out the slurs which had been cast on their loyalty by fanatics) a desperate courage, which might have thrust less prudent men into destruction, but led them only to victory. Soon a large Spaniard drifts by, deserted and partly burnt. Some of the men are for leaving their place to board her; but Amyas stoutly refuses. He had "come out to fight, and not to plunder; so let the nearest ship to her have her luck without grudging." They pass on, and the men pull long faces when they see the galleon snapped up by their next neighbour, and towed off to Weymouth, where she proves to be the ship of Miguel d'Oquenda, the Vice-Admiral, which they saw last night, all but blown up by some desperate Netherland gunner, who, being "misused," was minded to pay off old scores on his tyrants.

And so ends the second day; while the Portland rises higher and clearer every hour. The next morning finds them off the island. Will they try Portsmouth, though they have spared Plymouth? The wind has shifted to the north, and blows clear and cool off the white-walled downs of Weymouth Bay. The Spaniards turn and face the English. They must mean to stand off and on until the wind shall change, and then to try for the Needles. At least, they shall have some work to do before they round Purbeck Isle.

The English go to the westward again: but it is only to return on the opposite tack; and now begin a series of manoeuvres, each fleet trying to get the wind of the other; but the struggle does not last long, and ere noon the English fleet have slipped close-hauled between the Armada and the land, and are coming down upon them right before the wind.

And now begins a fight most fierce and fell. "And fight they did confusedly, and with variable fortunes; while, on the one hand, the English manfully rescued the ships of London, which were hemmed in by the Spaniards; and, on the other side, the Spaniards as stoutly delivered Recalde being in danger." "Never was heard such thundering of ordnance on both sides, which not withstanding from the Spaniards flew for the most part over the English without harm. Only Cock, an Englishman" (whom Prince claims, I hope rightfully, as a worthy of Devon), "died with honour in the midst of the enemies in a small ship of his. For the English ships, being far the lesser, charged the enemy with marvellous agility; and having discharged their broadsides, flew forth presently into the deep, and levelled their shot directly, without missing, at those great and unwieldy Spanish ships." "This was the most furious and bloody skirmish of all" (though ending only, it seems, in the capture of a great Venetian and some small craft), "in which the Lord Admiral fighting amidst his enemies' fleet, and seeing one of his captains afar off (Fenner by name, he who fought the seven Portugals at the Azores), cried, 'O George, what doest thou? Wilt thou now frustrate my hope and opinion conceived of thee? Wilt thou forsake me now?' With which words he being enflamed, approached, and did the part of a most valiant captain;" as, indeed, did all the rest.

Night falls upon the floating volcano; and morning finds them far past Purbeck, with the white peak of Freshwater ahead; and pouring out past the Needles, ship after ship, to join the gallant chase. For now from all havens, in vessels fitted out at their own expense, flock the chivalry of England; the Lords Oxford, Northumberland, and Cumberland, Pallavicin, Brooke, Carew, Raleigh, and Blunt, and many another honourable name, "as to a set field, where immortal fame and honour was to be attained." Spain has staked her chivalry in that mighty cast; not a noble house of Arragon or Castile but has lent a brother or a son—and shall mourn the loss of one: and England's gentlemen will measure their strength once for all against the Cavaliers of Spain. Lord Howard has sent forward light craft into Portsmouth for ammunition: but they will scarce return to-night, for the wind falls dead, and all the evening the two fleets drift helpless with the tide, and shout idle defiance at each other with trumpet, fife, and drum.

The sun goes down upon a glassy sea, and rises on a glassy sea again. But what day is this? The twenty-fifth, St. James's-day, sacred to the patron saint of Spain. Shall nothing be attempted in his honour by those whose forefathers have so often seen him with their bodily eyes, charging in their van upon his snow-white steed, and scattering Paynims with celestial lance? He might have sent them, certainly, a favouring breeze; perhaps, he only means to try their faith; at least the galleys shall attack; and in their van three of the great galliasses (the fourth lies half-crippled among the fleet) thrash the sea to foam with three hundred oars apiece; and see, not St. James leading them to victory, but Lord Howard's *Triumph*, his brother's *Lion*, Southwell's *Elizabeth Jonas*, Lord Sheffield's *Bear*, Barker's *Victory*, and George Fenner's *Leicester*, towed stoutly out, to meet them with such salvoes of chain-shot, smashing oars, and cutting rigging, that had not the wind sprung up again toward noon, and the Spanish fleet come up to rescue them, they had shared the fate of Valdez and the Biscayan. And now the fight becomes general. Frobisher beats down the Spanish Admiral's mainmast; and, attacked himself by Mexia and Recalde, is rescued by Lord Howard; who, himself endangered in his turn, is rescued in his turn; "while after that day" (so sickened were they of the English gunnery), "no galliasse would adventure to fight."

And so, with variable fortune, the fight thunders on the livelong afternoon, beneath the virgin cliffs of Freshwater; while myriad sea-fowl rise screaming up from every ledge, and spot with their black wings the snow-white wall of chalk; and the lone shepherd hurries down the slopes above to peer over the dizzy edge, and forgets the wheatear fluttering in his snare, while he gazes trembling upon glimpses of tall masts and gorgeous flags, piercing at times the league-broad veil of sulphur-smoke which welters far below.

So fares St. James's-day, as Baal's did on Carmel in old time, "Either he is talking, or he is pursuing, or he is on a journey; or peradventure he sleepeth, and must be awaked." At least, the only fire by which he has answered his votaries, has been that of English cannon: and the Armada, "gathering itself into a roundel," will fight no more, but make the best of its way to Calais, where perhaps the Guises' faction may have a French force ready to assist them, and then to Dunkirk, to join with Parma and the great flotilla of the Netherlands.

So on, before "a fair Etesian gale," which follows clear and bright out of the south-south-west, glide forward the two great fleets, past Brighton Cliffs and Beachy Head, Hastings and Dungeness. Is it a battle or a triumph? For by sea Lord Howard, instead of fighting is rewarding; and after Lord Thomas Howard, Lord Sheffield, Townsend, and Frobisher have received at his hands that knighthood, which was then more honourable than a peerage, old Admiral Hawkins kneels and rises up Sir John, and shaking his shoulders after the accolade, observes to the representative of majesty, that his "old woman will hardly know herself again, when folks call her My Lady."

And meanwhile the cliffs are lined with pikemen and musketeers, and by every countryman and groom who can bear arms, led by their squires and sheriffs, marching eastward as fast as their weapons let them, towards the Dover shore. And not with them alone. From many a mile inland come down women and children, and aged folk in wagons, to join their feeble shouts, and prayers which are not feeble, to that great cry of mingled faith and fear which ascends to the throne of God from the spectators of Britain's Salamis.

Let them pray on. The danger is not over yet, though Lord Howard has had news from Newhaven that the Guises will not stir against England, and Seymour and Winter have left their post of observation on the Flemish shores, to make up the number of the fleet to an hundred and forty sail—larger, slightly, than that of the Spanish fleet, but of not more than half the tonnage, or one third the number of men. The Spaniards are dispirited and battered, but unbroken still; and as they slide to their anchorage in Calais Roads on the Saturday evening of that most memorable week, all prudent men know well that England's hour is come, and that the bells which will call all Christendom to church upon the morrow morn, will be either the death-knell or the triumphal peal of the Reformed faith throughout the world.

A solemn day that Sabbath must have been in country and in town. And many a light-hearted coward, doubtless, who had scoffed (as many did) at the notion of the Armada's coming, because he dare not face the thought, gave himself up to abject fear, "as he now plainly saw and heard that of which before he would not be persuaded." And many a brave man, too, as he knelt beside his wife and daughters, felt his heart sink to the very pavement, at the thought of what those beloved ones might be enduring a few short days hence, from a profligate and fanatical soldiery, or from the more deliberate fiendishness of the Inquisition. The massacre of St. Bartholomew, the fires of Smithfield, the immolation of the Moors, the extermination of the West Indians, the fantastic horrors of the Piedmontese persecution, which make unreadable the two truthful pages of Morland,—these were the spectres, which, not as now, dim and distant through the mist of centuries, but recent, bleeding from still gaping wounds, flitted before the eyes of every Englishman, and filled his brain and heart with fire.

He knew full well the fate in store for him and his. One false step, and the unspeakable doom which, not two generations afterwards, befell the Lutherans of Magdeburg, would have befallen every town from London to Carlisle. All knew the hazard, as they prayed that day, and many a day before and after, throughout England and the Netherlands. And none knew it better than she who was the guiding spirit of that devoted land, and the especial mark of the invaders' fury; and who, by some Divine inspiration (as men then not unwisely held), devised herself the daring stroke which was to anticipate the coming blow.

But where is Amyas Leigh all this while? Day after day he has been seeking the *Sta. Catharina* in the thickest of the press, and cannot come at her, cannot even hear of her: one moment he dreads that she has sunk by night, and balked him of his prey; the next, that she has repaired her damages, and will escape him after all. He is moody, discontented, restless, even (for the first time in his life) peevish with his men. He can talk of nothing but Don Guzman; he can find no better employment, at every spare moment, than taking his sword out of the sheath, and handling it, fondling it, talking to it even, bidding it not to fail him in the day of vengeance. At last, he has sent to Squire, the armourer, for a whetstone, and, half-ashamed of his own folly, whets and polishes it in bye-corners, muttering to himself. That one fixed thought of selfish vengeance has possessed his whole mind; he forgets England's present need, her past triumph, his own safety, everything but his brother's blood. And yet this is the day for which he has been longing ever since he brought home that magic horn as a fifteen years boy; the day when he should find himself face to face with an invader, and that invader Antichrist himself. He has believed for years with Drake, Hawkins, Grenvile, and Raleigh, that he was called and sent into the world only to fight the Spaniard: and he is fighting him now, in such a cause, for such a stake, within such battle-lists, as he will never see again: and yet he is not content; and while throughout that gallant fleet, whole crews are receiving the Communion side by side, and rising with cheerful faces to shake hands, and to rejoice that they are sharers in Britain's Salamis, Amyas turns away from the holy elements.

"I cannot communicate, Sir John. Charity with all men? I hate, if ever man hated on earth."

"You hate the Lord's foes only, Captain Leigh."

"No, Jack, I hate my own as well."

"But no one in the fleet, sir?"

"Don't try to put me off with the same Jesuit's quibble which that false knave Parson Fletcher invented for one of Doughty's men, to drug his conscience withal when he was plotting against his own admiral. No, Jack, I hate one of whom you know; and somehow that hatred of him keeps me from loving any human being. I am in love and charity with no man, Sir John Brimblecombe—not even with you! Go your ways in God's name, sir! and leave me and the devil alone together, or you'll find my words are true."

Jack departed with a sigh, and while the crew were receiving the Communion on deck, Amyas sate below in the cabin sharpening his sword, and after it, called for a boat and went on board Drake's ship to ask news of the *Sta. Catharina*, and listened scowling to the loud chants and tinkling bells, which came across the water from the Spanish fleet. At last, Drake was summoned by the Lord Admiral, and returned with a secret commission, which ought to bear fruit that night; and Amyas, who had gone with him, helped him till nightfall, and then returned to his own ship as Sir Amyas Leigh, Knight, to the joy and glory of every soul on board, except his moody self.

So there, the livelong summer Sabbath-day, before the little high-walled town and the long range of yellow sandhills, lie those two mighty armaments, scowling at each other, hardly out of gunshot. Messenger after messenger is hurrying towards Bruges to the Duke of Parma, for light craft which can follow these nimble English somewhat better than their own floating castles; and, above all, entreating him to put to sea at once with all his force. The duke is not with his forces at Dunkirk, but on the future field of Waterloo, paying his devotions to St. Mary of Halle in Hainault, in order to make all sure in his Pantheon, and already sees in visions of the night that gentle-souled and pure-lipped saint, Cardinal Allen, placing the crown of England on his head. He returns for answer; first, that his victual is not ready; next, that his Dutch sailors, who have been kept at their post for many a week at the sword's point, have run away like water; and thirdly, that over and above all, he cannot come, so "strangely provided of great ordnance and musketeers" are those five-and-thirty Dutch ships, in which round-sterned and stubborn-hearted heretics watch, like terriers at a rat's hole, the entrance of Nieuwport and Dunkirk. Having ensured the private patronage of St. Mary of Halle, he will return to-morrow to make experience of its effects: but only hear across the flats of Dixmude the thunder of the fleets, and at Dunkirk the open curses of his officers. For while he has been praying and nothing more, the English have been praying, and something more; and all that is left for the Prince of Parma is, to hang a few purveyors, as peace offerings to his sulking army, and then "chafe," as Drake says of him, "like a bear robbed of her whelps."

For Lord Henry Seymour has brought Lord Howard a letter of command from Elizabeth's self; and Drake has been carrying it out so busily all that Sunday long, that by two o'clock on the Monday morning, eight fire-ships "besmeared with wild-fire, brimstone, pitch, and resin, and all their ordnance charged with bullets and with stones," are stealing down the wind straight for the Spanish fleet, guided by two valiant men of Devon, Young and Prowse. (Let their names live long in the land!) The ships are fired, the men of Devon steal back, and in a moment more, the heaven is red with glare from Dover Cliffs to Gravelines Tower; and weary-hearted Belgian boors far away inland, plundered and dragooned for many a hideous year, leap from their beds, and fancy (and not so far wrongly either) that the day of judgment is come at last, to end their woes, and hurl down vengeance on their tyrants.

And then breaks forth one of those disgraceful panics, which so often follow overweening presumption; and shrieks, oaths, prayers, and reproaches, make night hideous. There are those too on board who recollect well enough Jenebelli's fire-ships at Antwerp three years before, and the wreck which they made of Parma's bridge across the Scheldt. If these should be like them! And cutting all cables, hoisting any sails, the Invincible Armada goes lumbering wildly out to sea, every ship foul of her neighbour.

The largest of the four galliasses loses her rudder, and drifts helpless to and fro, hindering and confusing. The duke, having (so the Spaniards say) weighed his anchor deliberately instead of leaving it behind him, runs in again after awhile, and fires a signal for return: but his truant sheep are deaf to the shepherd's pipe, and swearing and praying by turns, he runs up Channel towards Gravelines picking up stragglers on his way, who are struggling as they best can among the flats and shallows: but Drake and Fenner have arrived as soon as he. When Monday's sun rises on the quaint old castle and muddy dykes of Gravelines town, the thunder of the cannon recommences, and is not hushed till night. Drake can hang coolly enough in the rear to plunder when he thinks fit; but when the battle needs it, none can fight more fiercely, among the foremost; and there is need now, if ever. That Armada must never be allowed to re-form. If it does, its left wing may yet keep the English at bay, while its right drives off the blockading Hollanders from Dunkirk port, and sets Parma and his flotilla free to join them, and to sail in doubled strength across to the mouth of Thames.

So Drake has weighed anchor, and away up Channel with all his squadron, the moment that he saw the Spanish fleet come up; and with him Fenner burning to redeem the honour which, indeed, he had never lost; and ere Fenton, Beeston, Crosse, Ryman, and Lord Southwell can join them, the Devon ships have been worrying the Spaniards for two full hours into confusion worse confounded.

But what is that heavy firing behind them? Alas for the great galliasse! She lies, like a huge stranded whale, upon the sands where now stands Calais pier; and Amyas Preston, the future hero of La Guayra, is pounding her into submission, while a fleet of hoys and drumblers look on and help, as jackals might the lion.

Soon, on the south-west horizon, loom up larger and larger two mighty ships, and behind them sail on sail. As they near a shout greets the *Triumph* and the *Bear*; and on and in the Lord High Admiral glides stately into the thickest of the fight.

True, we have still but some three-and-twenty ships which can cope at all with some ninety of the Spaniards: but we have dash, and daring, and the inspiration of utter need. Now, or never, must the mighty struggle be ended. We worried them off Portland; we must rend them in pieces now; and in rushes ship after ship, to smash her broadsides through and through the wooden castles, "sometimes not a pike's length asunder," and then out again to re-load, and give place meanwhile to another. The smaller are fighting with all sails set; the few larger, who, once in, are careless about coming out again, fight with topsails loose, and their main and foreyards close down on deck, to prevent being boarded. The Duke, Oquenda, and Recalde, having with much ado got clear of the shallows, bear the brunt of the fight to seaward; but in vain. The day goes against them more and more, as it runs on. Seymour and Winter have battered the great *San Philip* into a wreck; her masts are gone by the board; Pimentelli in the *San Matthew* comes up to take the mastiffs off the fainting bull, and finds them fasten on him instead; but the *Evangelist*, though smaller, is stouter than the *Deacon*, and of all the shot poured into him, not twenty "lackt him thorough." His masts are tottering; but sink or strike he will not.

"Go ahead, and pound his tough hide, Leigh," roars Drake off the poop of his ship, while he hammers away at one of the great galliasses. "What right has he to keep us all waiting?"

Amyas slips in as best he can between Drake and Winter; as he passes he shouts to his ancient enemy,—

"We are with you, sir; all friends to-day!" and slipping round Winter's bows, he pours his broadside into those of the *San Matthew*, and then glides on to re-load; but not to return. For not a pistol shot to leeward, worried by three or four small craft, lies an immense galleon; and on her poop—can he believe his eyes for joy?—the maiden and the wheel which he has sought so long!

"There he is!" shouts Amyas, springing to the starboard side of the ship. The men, too, have already caught sight of that hated sign; a cheer of fury bursts from every throat.

"Steady, men!" says Amyas in a suppressed voice. "Not a shot! Re-load, and be ready; I must speak with him first;" and silent as the grave, amid the infernal din, the *Vengeance* glides up to the Spaniard's quarter.

"Don Guzman Maria Magdalena Sotomayor de Soto!" shouts Amyas from the mizzen rigging, loud and clear amid the roar.

He has not called in vain. Fearless and graceful as ever, the tall, mail-clad figure of his foe leaps up upon the poop-railing, twenty feet above Amyas's head, and shouts through his vizor,—

"At your service, sir! whosoever you may be."

A dozen muskets and arrows are levelled at him; but Amyas frowns them down. "No man strikes him but I. Spare him, if you kill every other soul on board. Don Guzman! I am Captain Sir Amyas Leigh; I proclaim you a traitor and a ravisher, and challenge you once more to single combat, when and where you will."

"You are welcome to come on board me, sir," answers the Spaniard in a clear, quiet tone; "bringing with you this answer, that you lie in your throat;" and lingering a moment out of bravado, to arrange his scarf, he steps slowly down again behind the bulwarks.

"Coward!" shouts Amyas at the top of his voice.

The Spaniard re-appears instantly. "Why that name, señor, of all others?" asks he in a cool, stern voice.

"Because we call men cowards in England, who leave their wives to be burnt alive by priests."

The moment the words had passed Amyas's lips, he felt that they were cruel and unjust. But it was too late to recall them. The Spaniard started, clutched his sword-hilt, and then hissed back through his closed vizor, —

"For that word, sirrah, you hang at my yard-arm, if Saint Mary give me grace."

"See that your halter be a silken one, then," laughed Amyas, "for I am just dubbed knight." And he stepped down as a storm of bullets rang through the rigging round his head; the Spaniards are not as punctilious as he.

"Fire!" His ordnance crash through the stern-works of the Spaniard: and then he sails onward, while her balls go humming harmlessly through his rigging.

Half-an-hour has passed of wild noise and fury; three times has the Vengeance, as a dolphin might, sailed clean round and round the *Sta. Catharina*, pouring in broadside after broadside, till the guns are leaping to the deck-beams with their own heat, and the Spaniard's sides are slit and spotted in a hundred places. And yet, so high has been his fire in return, and so strong the deck defences of the *Vengeance*, that a few spars broken, and two or three men wounded by musketry, are all her loss. But still the Spaniard endures, magnificent as ever; it is the battle of the thresher and the whale; the end is certain, but the work is long.

"Can I help you, Captain Leigh?" asked Lord Henry Seymour, as he passes within oar's length of him, to attack a ship ahead. "The *San Matthew* has had his dinner, and is gone on to Medina to ask for a digestive to it."

"I thank your Lordship: but this is my private quarrel, of which I spoke. But if your Lordship could lend me powder—"

"Would that I could! But so, I fear, says every other gentleman in the fleet."

A puff of wind clears away the sulphurous veil for a moment; the sea is clear of ships towards the land; the Spanish fleet are moving again up Channel, Medina bringing up the rear; only some two miles to their right hand, the vast hull of the *San Philip* is drifting up the shore with the tide, and somewhat nearer the *San Matthew* is hard at work at her pumps. They can see the white stream of water pouring down her side.

"Go in, my Lord, and have the pair," shouts Amyas.

"No, sir! Forward is a Seymour's cry. We will leave them to pay the Flushingers' expenses." And on went Lord Henry, and, on shore went the *San Philip* at Ostend, to be plundered by the Flushingers; while the *San Matthew*, whose captain, "on a hault courage," had refused to save himself and his gentlemen on board Medina's ship, went blundering miserably into the hungry mouths of Captain Peter Vanderduess and four other valiant Dutchmen, who, like prudent men of Holland, contrived to keep the galleon afloat till they had emptied her, and then "hung up her banner in the great church of Leyden, being of such a length, that being fastened to the roof, it reached unto the very ground."

But in the meanwhile, long ere the sun had set, comes down the darkness of the thunder-storm, attracted, as to a volcano's mouth, to that vast mass of sulphur-smoke which cloaks the sea for many a mile; and heaven's artillery above makes answer to man's below. But still, through smoke and rain, Amyas clings to his prey. She too has seen the northward movement of the Spanish fleet, and sets her topsails; Amyas calls to the men to fire high, and cripple her rigging: but in vain: for three or four belated galleys, having forced their way at last over the shallows, come flashing and sputtering up to the combatants, and take his fire off the galleon. Amyas grinds his teeth, and would fain hustle into the tick of the press once more, in spite of the galley's beaks.

"Most heroical captain," says Cary, pulling a long face; "if we do, we are stove and sunk in five minutes; not to mention that Yeo says he has not twenty rounds of great cartridge left."

So, surely and silent, the *Vengeance* sheers off, but keeps as near as she can to the little squadron, all through the night of rain and thunder which follows. Next morning the sun rises on a clear sky, with a strong west-north-west breeze, and all hearts are asking what the day will bring forth.

They are long past Dunkirk now; the German Ocean is opening before them. The Spaniards, sorely battered, and lessened in numbers, have, during the night, regained some sort of order. The English hang on their skirts a mile or two behind. They have no ammunition, and must wait for more. To Amyas's great disgust, the *Sta. Catharina* has rejoined her fellows during the night.

"Never mind," says Cary; "she can neither dive nor fly, and as long as she is above water, we— What is the Admiral about?"

He is signalling Lord Henry Seymour and his squadron. Soon they tack, and come down the wind for the coast of Flanders. Parma must be blockaded still; and the Hollanders are likely to be too busy with their plunder to do it effectually. Suddenly there is a stir in the Spanish fleet. Medina and the rearmost ships turn upon the English. What can it mean? Will they offer battle once more? If so, it were best to get out of their way, for we have nothing wherewith to fight them. So the English lie close to the wind. They will let them pass, and return to their old tactic of following and harassing.

"Good-bye to Seymour," says Cary, "if he is caught between them and Parma's flotilla. They are going to Dunkirk."

"Impossible! They will not have water enough to reach his light craft. Here comes a big ship right upon us! Give him all you have left, lads; and if he will fight us, lay him alongside, and die boarding."

They gave him what they had, and hulled him with every shot; but his huge side stood silent as the grave. He had not wherewithal to return the compliment.

"As I live, he is cutting loose the foot of his main sail! the villain means to run."

"There go the rest of them! Victoria!" shouted Cary, as one after another, every Spaniard set all the sail he could.

There was silence for a few minutes throughout the English fleet; and then cheer upon cheer of triumph rent the skies. It was over. The Spaniard had refused battle, and thinking only of safety, was pressing downward toward the Straits again. The Invincible Armada had cast away its name, and England was saved.

"But he will never get there, sir," said old Yeo, who had come upon deck to murmur his *Nunc Domine*, and gaze upon that sight beyond all human faith or hope: "Never, never will he weather the Flanders shore, against such a breeze as is coming up. Look to the eye of the wind, sir, and see how the Lord is fighting for His people!"

Yes, down it came, fresher and stiffer every minute out of the grey north-west, as it does so often after a thunder-storm; and the sea began to rise high and white under the "Claro Aquilone," till the Spaniards were fain to take in all spare canvas, and lie-to as best they could; while the English fleet, lying-to also, awaited an event which was in God's hands and not in theirs.

"They will be all ashore on Zealand before the afternoon," murmured Amyas; "and I have lost my labour! Oh, for powder, powder, powder! to go in and finish it at once!"

"Oh, sir," said Yeo, "don't murmur against the Lord in the very day of His mercies. It is hard, to be sure; but His will be done."

"Could we not borrow powder from Drake there?"

"Look at the sea, sir!"

And, indeed, the sea was far too rough for any such attempt. The Spaniards neared and neared the fatal dunes, which fringed the shore for many a dreary mile; and Amyas had to wait weary hours, growling like a dog who has had the bone snatched out of his mouth, till the day wore on; when behold, the wind began to fall as rapidly as it had risen. A savage joy rose in Amyas's heart.

"They are safe! safe for us! Who will go and beg us powder? A cartridge here and a cartridge there?—anything to set to work again!"

Cary volunteered, and returned in a couple of hours with some quantity: but he was on board again only just in time, for the south-wester had recovered the mastery of the skies, and Spaniards and English were moving away; but this time northward. Whither now? To Scotland? Amyas knew not, and cared not, provided he was in the company of Don Guzman de Soto.

The Armada was defeated, and England saved. But such great undertakings seldom end in one grand melodramatic explosion of fireworks, through which the devil arises in full roar to drag Dr. Faustus for ever into the flaming pit. On the contrary, the devil stands by his servants to the last, and tries to bring off his shattered forces with drums beating and colours flying; and, if possible, to lull his enemies into supposing that the fight is ended, long before it really is half over. All which the good Lord Howard of Effingham knew well, and knew, too, that Medina had one last card to play, and that was the filial affection of that dutiful and chivalrous son, James of Scotland. True, he had promised faith to Elizabeth: but that was no reason why he should keep it. He had been hankering and dabbling after Spain for years past, for its absolutism was dear to his inmost soul; and Queen Elizabeth had had to warn him, scold him, call him a liar, for so doing; so the Armada might still find shelter and provision in the Firth of Forth. But whether Lord Howard knew or not, Medina did not know, that Elizabeth had played her card cunningly, in the shape of one of those appeals to the purse, which, to James's dying day, overweighed all others save appeals to his vanity. "The title of a dukedom in England, a yearly pension of £5000, a guard at the queen's charge, and other matters" (probably more hounds and deer), had steeled the heart of the King of Scots, and sealed the Firth of Forth. Nevertheless, as I say, Lord Howard, like the rest of Elizabeth's heroes, trusted James just as much as James trusted others; and therefore thought good to escort the Armada until it was safely past the domains as of that most chivalrous and truthful Solomon. But on the 4th of August, his fears, such as they were, were laid to rest. The Spaniards left the Scottish coast and sailed away for Norway; and the game was played out, and the end was come, as the end of such matters generally come, by gradual decay, petty disaster, and mistake; till the snow-mountain, instead of being blown tragically and heroically to atoms, melts helplessly and pitiably away.

The *Ariel* Defeats the *Alacrity*

by JAMES FENIMORE COOPER

Thus guided on their course they bore,
Until they neared the main-land shore;
When frequent on the hollow blast
Wild shouts of merriment were cast.
Lord of the Isles.

The joyful shouts and hearty cheers of the *Ariel*'s crew continued for some time after her commander had reached her deck. Barnstable answered the congratulations of his officers by cordial shakes of the hand; and, after waiting for the ebullition of delight among the seamen to subside a little, he beckoned with an air of authority for silence.

"I thank you, my lads, for your good will," he said, when all were gathered around him in deep attention; "they have given us a tough chase, and, if you had left us another mile to go, we had been lost. That fellow is a king's cutter; and, though his disposition to run to leeward is a good deal mollified, yet he shows signs of fight. At any rate, he is stripping off some of his clothes, which looks as if he were game. Luckily for us, Captain Manual has taken all the marines ashore with him (though what he has done with them, or himself, is a mystery), or we should have had our decks lumbered with live cattle; but, as it is, we have a good working breeze, tolerably smooth water, and a dead match! There is a sort of national obligation on us to whip that fellow; and therefore, without more words about the matter, let us turn to and do it, that we may get our breakfasts."

To this specimen of marine eloquence the crew cheered as usual, the young men burning for the combat, and the few old sailors who belonged to the schooner shaking their heads with infinite satisfaction, and swearing by sundry strange oaths that their captain "could talk, when there was need of such thing, like the best dictionary that ever was launched."

During this short harangue, and the subsequent comments, the *Ariel* had been kept, under a cloud of canvas, as near to the wind as she could lie; and, as this was her best sailing, she had stretched swiftly out from the land to a distance whence the cliffs and the soldiers, who were spread along their summits, were plainly visible. Barnstable turned his glass repeatedly, from the cutter to the shore, as different feeling predominated in his breast, before he again spoke.

"If Mr. Griffith is stowed away among those rocks," he at length said, "he shall see as pretty an argument discussed, in as few words, as he ever listened to, provided the gentlemen in yonder cutter have not changed their minds as to the road they intend to journey. What think you, Mr. Merry?"

"I wish with all my heart and soul, sir," returned the fearless boy, "that Mr. Griffith was safe aboard us; it seems the country is alarmed, and God knows

118

what will happen if he is taken! As to the fellow to windward, he'll find it easier to deal with the *Ariel*'s boat than with her mother; but he carries a broad sail; I question if he means to show play."

"Never doubt him, boy," said Barnstable; "he is working off the shore, like a man of sense, and, besides, he has his spectacles on, trying to make out what tribe of Yankee Indians we belong to. You'll see him come to the wind presently, and send a few pieces of iron down this way, by way of letting us know where to find him. Much as I like your first lieutenant, Mr. Merry, I would rather leave him on the land this day than see him on my decks. I want no fighting captain to work this boat for me! But tell the drummer, sir, to beat to quarters."

The boy, who was staggering under the weight of his melodious instrument, had been expecting this command, and, without waiting for the midshipman to communicate the order, he commenced that short rub-a-dub air that will at any time rouse a thousand men from the deepest sleep, and cause them to fly to their means of offence with a common soul. The crew of the *Ariel* had been collected in groups studying the appearance of the enemy, cracking their jokes, and waiting only for this usual order to repair to the guns; and, at the first tap of the drum, they spread with steadiness to the different parts of the little vessel, where their various duties called them. The cannon were surrounded by small parties of vigorous and athletic young men; the few marines were drawn up in array with muskets; the officers appeared in their boarding-caps, with pistols stuck in their belts, and naked sabres in their hands. Barnstable paced his little quarter-deck with a firm tread, dangling a speaking-trumpet by its lanyard on his forefinger, or occasionally applying the glass to his eye, which, when not in use, was placed under one arm, while his sword was resting against the foot of the mainmast; a pair of heavy ship's pistols were thrust into his belt also; and piles of muskets, boarding-pikes, and naked sabres, were placed on different parts of the deck. The laugh of the seamen was heard no longer; and those who spoke uttered their thoughts only in low and indistinct whispers.

The English cutter held her way from the land, until she got an offing of more than two miles, when she reduced her sails to a yet smaller number; and, heaving into the wind, she fired a gun in a direction opposite to that which pointed to the *Ariel*.

"Now I would wager a quintal of codfish, Master Coffin," said Barnstable, "against the best cask of porter that was ever brewed in England, that fellow believes a Yankee schooner can fly in the wind's eye! If he wishes to speak to us, why don't he give his cutter a little sheet and come down?"

The cockswain had made his arrangements for the combat with much more method and philosophy than any other man in the vessel. When the drum beat to quarters, he threw aside his jacket, vest, and shirt, with as little hesitation as if he stood under an American sun, and with all the discretion of a man who had engaged in an undertaking that required the free use of his utmost powers. As he was known to be a privileged individual in the *Ariel*, and one whose opinions, in all matters of seamanship, were regarded as oracles by the crew, and were listened to by his commander with no little demonstration of respect, the question excited no surprise. He was standing at the breech of his long gun with his brawny arms folded on a breast that had been turned to the color of blood by long exposure, his grizzled locks fluttering in the breeze, and his tall form towering far above the heads of all near him.

"He hugs the wind, sir, as if it was his sweetheart," was his answer; "but he'll let go his hold soon; and, if he don't we can find a way to make him fall to leeward."

"Keep a good full!" cried the commander in a stern voice; "and let the vessel go through the water.—That fellow walks well, Long Tom; but we are too much for him on a bowling; though, if he continue to draw ahead in this manner, it will be night before we can get alongside him."

"Ay, ay, sir," returned the cockswain; "them cutters carries a press of canvas when they seem to have but little; their gaffs are all the same as young booms, and spread a broad head to their mainsails. But it's no hard matter to knock a few cloths out of their bolt-ropes, when she will both drop astern and to leeward."

"I believe there is good sense in your scheme this time," said Barnstable; "for I am anxious about the frigate's people—though I hate a noisy chase. Speak to him, Tom, and let us see if he will answer."

"Ay, ay, sir," cried the cockswain, sinking his body in such a manner as to let his head fall to a level with the cannon that he controlled, when, after divers orders, and sundry movements to govern the direction of the piece, he applied a match, with a rapid motion, to the priming. An immense body of white smoke rushed from the muzzle of the cannon, followed by a sheet of vivid fire, until, losing its power, it yielded to the wind, and, as it rose from the water, spread like a cloud, and, passing through the masts of the schooner, was driven far to leeward, and soon blended in the mists which were swiftly scudding before the fresh breezes of the ocean.

Although many curious eyes were watching this beautiful sight from the cliffs, there was too little of novelty in the exhibition to attract a single look of the crew of the schooner from the more important examination of the effect of the shot on their enemy. Barnstable sprang lightly on a gun, and watched the instant when the ball would strike, with keen interest, while Long Tom threw himself aside from the line of the smoke with similar intention; holding one of his long arms extended toward his namesake, with a finger on the vent, and supporting his frame by placing the hand of the other on the deck, as his eyes glanced through an opposite port-hole, in an attitude that most men might have despaired of imitating with success.

"There go the chips!" cried Barnstable. "Bravo! Master Coffin, you never planted iron in the ribs of an Englishman with more judgment. Let him have another piece of it; and, if he likes the sport, we'll play a game of long bowls with him!"

"Ay, ay, sir," returned the cockswain, who, the instant he witnessed the effects of his shot, had returned to superintend the reloading of his gun; "if he holds on half an hour longer, I'll dub him down to our own size, when we can close and make an even fight of it."

The drum of the Englishman was now, for the first time, heard rattling across the waters, and echoing the call to quarters, that had already proceeded from the *Ariel*.

"Ah! you have sent him to his guns!" said Barnstable; "we shall now hear more of it; wake him up, Tom—wake him up."

"We shall start him on end, or put him to sleep altogether, shortly," said the deliberate cockswain, who never allowed himself to be at all hurried, even by his commander. "My shot are pretty much like a shoal of porpoises, and commonly sail in each other's wake. Stand by—heave her breech forward—so; get out of that, you damned young reprobate, and let my harpoon alone!"

"What are you at there, Master Coffin?" cried Barnstable; "are you tongue-tied?"

"Here's one of the boys skylarking with my harpoon in the lee-scuppers, and by-and-by, when I shall want it most, there'll be a no-man's land to hunt for it in."

"Never mind the boy, Tom; send him aft here to me, and I'll polish his behavior; give the Englishman some more iron."

"I want the little villain to pass up my cartridges," returned the angry old seaman; "but if you'll be so good, sir, as to hit him a crack or two, now and then, as he goes by you to the magazine, the monkey will learn his manners, and the schooner's work will be all the better done for it.—A young herring-faced monkey! to meddle with a tool ye don't know the use of. If your parents had spent more of their money on your education, and less on your outfit, you'd ha' been a gentleman to what ye are now."

"Hurrah! Tom, hurrah!" cried Barnstable, a little impatiently; "is your namesake never to open his throat again?"

"Ay, ay, sir; all ready," grumbled the cockswain; "depress a little; so—so; a damned young baboon-behaved curmudgeon; overhaul that forward fall more; stand by with your match—but I'll pay him!—fire!" This was the actual commencement of the fight; for as the shot of Tom Coffin travelled, as he had intimated, very much in the same direction, their enemy found the sport becoming too hot to be endured in silence, and the report of the second gun from the *Ariel* was instantly followed by that of the whole broadside of the *Alacrity*. The shot of the cutter flew in a very good direction, but her guns were too light to give them efficiency at that distance; and as one or two were heard to strike against the bend of the schooner, and fall back innocuously, into the water, the cockswain, whose good humor became gradually restored as the combat thickened, remarked with his customary apathy:

"Them count for no more than love-taps—does the Englishman think that we are firing salutes?"

"Stir him up, Tom! every blow you give him will help to open his eyes," cried Barnstable, rubbing his hands with glee, as he witnessed the success of his efforts to close.

Thus far the cockswain and his crew had the fight, on the part of the *Ariel*, altogether to themselves, the men who were stationed at the smaller and shorter guns standing in perfect idleness by their sides; but in ten or fifteen minutes the commander of the *Alacrity*, who had been staggered by the weight of the shot that had struck him, found that it was no longer in his power to retreat, if he wished it; when he decided on the only course that was left for a brave man to pursue, and steered boldly in such a direction as would soonest bring him in contact with his enemy, without exposing his vessel to be raked by his fire. Barnstable watched each movement of his foe with eagle eyes, and when the vessel had got within a lessened distance, he gave the order for a general fire to be opened. The action now grew warm and spirited on both sides. The power of the wind was counteracted by the constant explosion of the cannon; and, instead of driving rapidly to leeward, a white canopy of curling smoke hung above the *Ariel*, or rested on the water, lingering in her wake, so as to mark the path by which she was approaching to a closer and still deadlier struggle. The shouts of the young sailors as they handled their instruments of death, became more animated and fierce, while the cockswain pursued his occupation with the silence and skill of one who labored in a regular vocation. Barnstable was unusually composed and quiet, maintaining the grave deportment of a commander on whom rested the fortunes of the contest, at the same time that his dark eyes were dancing with the fire of suppressed animation.

"Give it them!" he occasionally cried, in a voice that might be heard amid the bellowing of the cannon; "never mind their cordage, my lads; drive home their bolts, and make your marks below their ridge-ropes."

In the meantime the Englishman played a manful game.

He had suffered a heavy loss by the distant cannonade, which no metal he possessed could retort upon his enemy; but he struggled nobly to repair the error in judgment with which he had begun the contest. The two vessels gradually drew nigher to each other, until they both entered into the common cloud created by their fire, which thickened and spread around them in such a manner as to conceal their dark hulls from the gaze of the curious and interested spectators on the cliffs. The heavy reports of the cannon were now mingled with the rattling of muskets and pistols, and streaks of fire might be seen glancing like flashes of lightning through the white cloud which enshrouded the combatants; and many minutes of painful uncertainty followed, before the deeply-interested soldiers, who were gazing at the scene, discovered on whose banners victory had alighted.

We shall follow the combatants into their misty wreath, and display to the reader the events as they occurred.

The fire of the *Ariel* was much the most quick and deadly, both because she had suffered less, and her men were less exhausted; and the cutter stood desperately on to decide the combat, after grappling, hand to hand. Barnstable anticipated her intention, and well understood her commander's reason for adopting this course; but he was not a man to calculate coolly his advantages, when pride and daring invited him to a more severe trial. Accordingly, he met the enemy half-way, and, as the vessels rushed together, the stern of the schooner was secured to the bows of the cutter, by the joint efforts of both parties. The voice of the English commander was now plainly to be heard, in the uproar, calling to his men to follow him.

"Away there, boarders! repel boarders on the starboard quarter!" shouted Barnstable through his trumpet.

This was the last order that the gallant young sailor gave with this instrument; for, as he spoke, he cast it from him, and, seizing his sabre, flew to the spot where the enemy was about to make his most desperate effort. The shouts, execrations, and tauntings of the combatants now succeeded to the roar of the cannon, which could be used no longer with effect, though the fight was still maintained with spirited discharges of the small-arms.

"Sweep him from his decks!" cried the English commander, as he appeared on his own bulwarks, surrounded by a dozen of his bravest men, "drive the rebellious dogs into the sea!"

"Away there, marines!" retorted Barnstable, firing his pistol at the advancing enemy, "leave not a man of them to sup his grog again."

The tremendous and close volley that succeeded this order nearly accomplished the command of Barnstable to the letter, and the commander of the *Alacrity*, perceiving that he stood alone, reluctantly fell back on the deck of his own vessel, in order to bring on his men once more.

"Board her! graybeards and boys, idlers and all!" shouted Barnstable, springing in advance of his crew—a powerful arm arrested the movement of the dauntless seaman, and before he had time to recover himself, he was drawn violently back to his own vessel by the irresistible grasp of his cockswain.

"The fellow's in his flurry," said Tom, "and it wouldn't be wise to go within reach of his flukes; but I'll just step ahead and give him a set with my harpoon."

Without waiting for a reply, the cockswain reared his tall frame on the bulwarks, and was in the act of stepping on board of his enemy, when a sea separated the vessels, and he fell with a heavy dash of the waters into the ocean. As twenty muskets and pistols were discharged at the instant he appeared, the crew of the *Ariel* supposed his fall to be occasioned by his wounds, and were rendered doubly fierce by the sight, and the cry of their commander to—

"Revenge Long Tom! board her! Long Tom or death!"

They threw themselves forward in irresistible numbers, and forced a passage, with much bloodshed, to the forecastle of the *Alacrity*. The Englishman was overpowered, but still remained undaunted—he rallied his crew, and bore up most gallantly to the fray. Thrusts of pikes and blows of sabres were becoming close and deadly, while muskets and pistols were constantly discharged by those who were kept at a distance by the pressure of the throng of closer combatants.

Barnstable led his men in advance, and became a mark of peculiar vengeance to his enemies, as they slowly yielded before his vigorous assaults. Chance had placed the two commanders on opposite sides of the cutter's deck, and the victory seemed to incline toward either party, wherever these daring officers directed the struggle in person. But the Englishman, perceiving that the ground he maintained in person was lost elsewhere, made an effort to restore the battle, by changing his position, followed by one or two of his best men. A marine, who preceded him, levelled his musket within a few feet of the American commander, and was about to fire, when Merry glided among the combatants, and passed his dirk into the body of the man, who fell at the blow; shaking his piece with horrid imprecations, the wounded soldier prepared to deal his vengeance on his youthful assailant, when the fearless boy leaped within its muzzle, and buried his own keen weapon in his heart.

"Hurrah!" shouted the unconscious Barnstable, from the edge of the quarter-deck, where, attended by a few men, he was driving all before him. "Revenge!—Long Tom and victory!"

"We have them!" exclaimed the Englishman; "handle your pikes! we have them between two fires."

The battle would probably have terminated very differently from what previous circumstances had indicated, had not a wild-looking figure appeared in the cutter's channels at that moment, issuing from the sea, and gaining the deck at the same instant. It was Long Tom, with his iron visage rendered fierce by his previous discomfiture, and his grizzled locks drenched with the briny element from which he had risen, looking like Neptune with his trident. Without speaking he poised his harpoon, and, with a powerful effort, pinned the unfortunate Englishman to the mast of his own vessel.

"Starn all!" cried Tom, by a sort of instinct, when the blow was struck; and, catching up the musket of the fallen marine, he dealt out terrible and fatal blows with its butt on all who approached him, utterly disregarding the use of the bayonet on its muzzle. The unfortunate commander of the *Alacrity* brandished his sword with frantic gestures, while his eyes rolled in horrid wildness, when he writhed for an instant in his passing agonies, and then, as his head dropped lifeless upon his gored breast, he hung against the spar, a spectacle of dismay to his crew. A few of the Englishmen stood chained to the spot in silent horror at the sight, but most of them fled to their lower deck, or hastened to conceal themselves in the secret parts of the vessel, leaving to the Americans the undisputed possession of the *Alacrity*.

Two-thirds of the cutter's crew suffered either in life or limbs by this short struggle; nor was the victory obtained by Barnstable without paying the price of several valuable lives. The first burst of conquest was not, however, the moment to appreciate the sacrifice, and loud and reiterated shouts proclaimed the exultation of the conquerors. As the flush of victory subsided, however, recollection returned, and Barnstable issued such orders as humanity and his duty rendered necessary. While the vessels were separating, and the bodies of the dead and wounded were removing, the conqueror paced the deck of his prize, as if lost in deep reflection. He passed his hand frequently across his blackened and blood-stained brow, while his eyes would rise to examine the vast canopy of smoke that was hovering above the vessels like a dense fog exhaling from the ocean. The result of his deliberations was soon announced to the crew.

"Haul down all your flags," he cried; "set the Englishman's colors again, and show the enemy's jack above our ensign in the *Ariel*."

The appearance of the whole channel-fleet within half gun-shot would not have occasioned more astonishment among the victors than this extraordinary mandate. The wondering seamen suspended their several employments to gaze at the singular change that was making in the flags, those symbols that were viewed with a sort of reverence; but none presumed to comment openly on the procedure except Long Tom, who stood on the quarter-deck of the prize, straightening the pliable iron of the harpoon which he had recovered with as much care and diligence as if it were necessary to the maintenance of their conquest. Like the others, however, he suspended his employment when he heard this order, and manifested no reluctance to express his dissatisfaction at the measure.

"If the Englishmen grumble at the fight, and think it not fair play," muttered the cockswain, "let us try it over again, sir; as they are somewhat short of hands they can send a boat to the land, and get off a gang of them lazy riptyles, the soldiers, who stand looking at us like so many red lizards crawling on a beach, and we'll give them another chance; but damme, if I see the use of whipping them, if this is to be the better end of the matter."

"What's that you're grumbling there, like a dead northeaster, you horse-mackerel?" said Barnstable; "where are our friends and countrymen who are on the land? are we to leave them to swing on gibbets or rot in dungeons?"

The cockswain listened with great earnestness, and, when his commander had spoken, he struck the palm of his broad hand against his brawny thigh, with a report like a pistol, and answered:

"I see how it is, sir; you reckon the red-coats have Mr. Griffith in tow. Just run the schooner into shoal water, Captain Barnstable, and drop an anchor, where we can get the long gun to bear on them, and give me the whale-boat with five or six men to back me—they must have long legs if they get an offing before I run them aboard!"

"Fool! do you think a boat's crew could contend with fifty armed soldiers?"

"Soldiers!" echoed Tom, whose spirits had been strongly excited by the conflict, snapping his fingers with ineffable disdain; "that for all the soldiers that were ever rigged, one whale could kill a thousand of them; and here stands the man that has killed his round hundred of whales!"

"Pshaw! you grampus, do you turn braggart in your old age?"

"It's no bragging, sir, to speak a log-book truth; but if Captain Barnstable thinks that old Tom Coffin carries a speaking-trumpet for a figure-head, let him pass the word forward to man the boats."

"No, no, my old master at the marlinspike," said Barnstable, kindly; "I know thee too well, thou brother of Neptune! but shall we not throw the bread-room dust in those Englishmen's eyes by wearing their bunting awhile till something may offer to help our captured countrymen?"

The cockswain shook his head and cogitated a moment, as if struck with sundry new ideas, when he answered:

"Ay, ay, sir; that's blue-water philosophy—as deep as the sea. Let the rip-tyles clew up the corners of their mouths to their eyebrows now; when they come to hear the raal Yankee truth of the matter, they will sheet them down to their leather neckcloths!"

With this reflection the cockswain was much consoled, and the business of repairing damages and securing the prize proceeded without further interruption on his part. The few prisoners who were unhurt were rapidly transferred to the *Ariel*. While Barnstable was attending to this duty, an unusual bustle drew his eyes to one of the hatchways, where he beheld a couple of his marines dragging forward a gentlemen, whose demeanor and appearance indicated the most abject terror. After examining the extraordinary appearance of this individual for a moment, in silent amazement, the lieutenant exclaimed:

"Who have we here? some amateur in fights! an inquisitive wonder-seeking noncombatant, who has volunteered to serve his king, and perhaps draw a picture, or write a book, to serve himself! Pray, sir, in what capacity did you serve in this vessel?"

The captive ventured a sidelong glance at his interrogator, in whom he expected to encounter Griffith, but, perceiving that it was a face he did not know, he felt a revival of confidence that enabled him to reply:

"I came by accident; being on board the cutter at the time her late commander determined to engage you. It was not in his power to land me, as I trust you will not hesitate to do; your conjecture of my being a noncombatant—"

"Is perfectly true," interrupted Barnstable; "it requires no spy-glass to read that name written on you from stem to stern; but for certain weighty reasons—"

He paused to turn at a signal given him by young Merry, who whispered eagerly in his ear:

"'Tis Mr. Dillon, kinsman of Colonel Howard; I've seen him often, sailing in the wake of my cousin Cicely."

"Dillon!" exclaimed Barnstable, rubbing his hands with pleasure; "what, Kit of that name! he with 'the Savannah face, eyes of black, and skin of the same color?' He's grown a little whiter with fear; but he's a prize, at this moment, worth twenty *Alacritys*!"

These exclamations were made in a low voice, and at some little distance from the prisoner, whom he now approached and addressed.

"Policy, and consequently duty, require that I should detain you for a short time, sir; but you shall have a sailor's welcome to whatever we possess, to lessen the weight of captivity."

Barnstable precluded any reply, by bowing to his captive, and turning away to superintend the management of his vessels. In a short time it was announced that they were ready to make sail, when the *Ariel* and her prize were brought close to the wind, and commenced beating slowly along the land, as if intending to return to the bay whence the latter had sailed that morning. As they stretched in to the shore on the first tack, the soldiers on the cliffs rent the air with their shouts and acclamations, to which Barnstable, pointing to the assumed symbols that were fluttering in the breeze from his masts, directed his crew to respond in the most cordial manner. As the distance, and the want of boats, prevented any further communication, the soldiers, after gazing at the receding vessels for a time, disappeared from the cliffs, and were soon lost from the sight of the adventurous mariners. Hour after hour was consumed in the tedious navigation, against an adverse tide, and the short day was drawing to a close, before they approached the mouth of their destined haven. While making one of their numerous stretches, to and from the land, the cutter, in which Barnstable continued, passed the victim of their morning's sport, riding on the water, the waves curling over his huge carcass, as on some rounded rock, and already surrounded by the sharks, who were preying on his defenceless body.

"See! Master Coffin," cried the lieutenant, pointing out the object to his cockswain as they glided by it, "the shovel-nosed gentleman are regaling daintily; you have neglected the Christian's duty of burying your dead."

The old seaman cast a melancholy look at the dead whale, and replied:

"If I had the creature in Boston Bay, or on the Sandy Point of Munny Moy, 'twould be the making of me! But riches and honor are for the great and the larned, and there's nothing left for poor Tom Coffin to do, but to veer and haul on his own rolling tackle, that he may ride out the rest of the gale of life without springing any of his old spars."

"How now, Long Tom!" cried the officer; "these rocks and cliffs will shipwreck you on the shoals of poetry yet; you grow sentimental!"

"Them rocks might wrack any vessel that struck them," said the literal cockswain; "and as for poetry, I wants none better than the good old song of Captain Kidd; but it's enough to raise solemn thoughts in a Cape Poge Indian, to see an eighty-barrel whale devoured by sharks—'tis an awful waste of property! I've seen the death of two hundred of the creaters, though it seems to keep the rations of poor old Tom as short as ever."

The cockswain walked aft, while the vessel was passing the whale, and seating himself on the taffrail, with his face resting gloomily on his bony hand, he fastened his eyes on the object of his solicitude, and continued to gaze at it with melancholy regret, while it was to be seen glistening in the sunbeams, as it rolled its glittering side of white into the air, or the rays fell unreflected on the black and rougher coat of the back of the monster. In the meantime, the navigators diligently pursued their way for the haven we have mentioned, into which they steered with every appearance of the fearlessness of friends, and the exultation of conquerors.

A few eager and gratified spectators lined the edges of the small bay, and Barnstable concluded his arrangement for deceiving the enemy, by admonishing his crew that they were now about to enter on a service that would require their utmost intrepidity and sagacity.

The Battle of *Bonhomme Richard* and *Serapis*

by VALENTINE THOMSON

"Sail ho! Dead ahead." The cry pealed down from the maintop of the *Bonhomme Richard*. A sailor was pointing excitedly to the northwest. Jones stared at the horizon. A speck appeared . . . another. In the glowing sunlight reflected by the double mirror of the skies and sea, sails floated, transparent, unreal. At last! this was the expected fleet from the Baltic.

After the failure at Leith, the ships of the squadron had separated to hunt the enemy alone or in twos. Days passed all alike—monotony . . . The ship's log was uneventful. "Pleasant weather . . . came up with a ship . . . found her to be from Leith . . . from Hull . . . loaded with coal . . . with woods . . . hoisted out the pinnace and boarded her . . . brought the prisoners on board." Tedious work like this had gone on day after day; prisoners crowded all the ships.

Having been as far as Hull, Jones found himself back at Flamborough Head on the 21st of September for an appointed meeting with the *Alliance*. The point of Flamborough was perfect for an ambuscade. It jutted out from the shore at a salient angle which all ships coming from Norway and the Baltic Sea had to reconnoiter.

Jones felt discouraged. With the month of September drawing to a close, it was time to go to the Texel and accomplish the last part of his mission—try to bring back the cargoes destined for the King of France. But the apparition of this fleet, expected for days, revived his ambitions. Here was a real prize: All these vessels were loaded with wood and cordage for the English navy.

As the fleet neared, Jones could count more than thirty sails, convoyed by two men-of-war watching over them like shepherd dogs guarding helpless sheep. Jones immediately gave the order to clear the decks for action, to sling the yards with chains and haul up the courses. The sea glittered like a spangled carpet. The weather was clear without the slightest breeze. Jones paced the quarter deck of the *Bonhomme Richard* with confidence in his steps.

Now he could clearly distinguish the ships. Every man on the *Richard* was at his post. An officer with his glass made out the names of the two frigates: "The *Serapis*." Men laughed. "What sort of a name is that?" "The *Countess of Scarborough*." "Well at least that's dignified."

Captain Pearson, one of the most distinguished officers of the English navy and in command of the fine new frigate *Serapis*, had been informed only that morning that the "Damned pirate, Paul Jones" had been seen roving about.

But according to the reports he was now supposed to be in the vicinity of Hull. At the first sight of the squadron, however, the English commander decided that "this must be Jones" and calling all hands on deck, he proudly nailed his ensign to the mast with his own hands, swearing before God that he would never strike his colors to John Paul Jones. His men cheered wildly.

Pearson ordered the merchant ships to sail at large, but at the very mention of the name of Paul Jones, disregarding all signals, they fled like a stampeded flock toward the shore, seeking protection under the batteries of the fortress of Flamborough. In the meanwhile the two men-of-war came boldly forward putting themselves between the convoy and Paul Jones.

On the ramparts of the town, all along the shore, crowds had gathered to follow the manoeuvres of the new *Serapis*, pride of the Royal Navy, advancing toward the sombre mass of the *Bonhomme Richard*, huddled on the shining seas. "At last, the American will be taught his lesson." "It won't take long either." "Watch his stars fall in the 'wash.'" The crowds waited breathlessly for the first clash.

Obeying orders, the *Pallas* was making for the *Countess of Scarborough*. But Captain Landais, ordered by Jones to engage the *Serapis* in conjunction with the flagship, showing himself as recalcitrant as ever, tacked and sailed off.

On the *Richard*, the men lying flat at their posts, tense, nervous, laughed and jested. "Look men," yelled a voice, "here comes the *Sea Raper*." "Don't worry, we'll be trying long shots at her before night falls . . ." Startled laughs arose here and there as if to overcome any signs of emotion at the sight of this impressive British man-of-war at such close range.

The *Serapis* tacked and bore directly down upon the American ship.

The *Bonhomme Richard*'s bells struck the hour for the last time in her career: Seven o'clock. Silence fell, broken only by the sound of water lapping against the sides of the ships. Suddenly a voice hailed from the English frigate:

"What ship is that?"

The answer rang out from the *Richard*:

"Come a little closer and we'll tell you."

The next question from the enemy brought an explosion of laughter from the Americans.

"What are you laden with?"

And with true American humor came the answer:

"Round grape and double-headed shot." At the same moment, a lad named Jack Robinson leaned out of a port and shouted at the top of his lungs:

"Fire and be damned to you!"

Instantly the *Serapis* at close range poured a whole broadside of upper and quarterdeck guns into the *Richard*. Simultaneously came the *Richard*'s thunderous reply.

A terrible crash rocked the *Richard* crazily. Smoke belched from the interior of the ship. "What's happened?" Men came rushing from the hold. Three starboard guns had burst at the first firing. The ten men stationed at each of them had been killed or mortally wounded. The ship had a gaping hole in her hull. Immediately Jones gave orders not to fire the other three eighteen-pounders mounted on that deck and to close the ports.

Deprived of six heavy guns in the very beginning of the battle, with the water already pouring into the hold, Jones was badly handicapped. He ordered the best sharp-shooters to the tops to clear the enemy's decks.

The *Serapis* had now started shooting from her lower batteries, thus revealing that she was a double decker—more than a match for the *Richard*. The eighteen-pounders, handled by the perfectly trained British crew, were striking home with fearful accuracy, enlarging the terrible wound in the flank of the poor *Richard*. Splintering crashes told of the shots which were tearing the vitals of the ship and turning it into an inferno of arrows and slivers searing the flesh of the fighters. Men fell where they stood, pierced and torn, or ran blindly screaming with pain, the blood running between their fingers as they held their hands over their cut faces. Others were left with no hands to hold their bleeding wounds, and they stared stupidly at the stump of an arm. The bloody nightmare of those first terrible minutes took a heavy toll on the *Richard*. The *Serapis* was out-sailing her, two feet to one, and thus out-maneuvering her at every turn. Jones hardly dared think of the possible outcome. Only an unparalleled stroke of luck or genius could save the Americans from utter destruction.

In spite of the withering fire, the well-groomed French marines, commanded by Lieutenant-Colonel Chamillard, were aligned in perfect file on the poop of the *Richard*. Loading and unloading their muskets with automatic gestures, they aimed and fired with consummate skill and perfect complacency, all as if they were practicing at the royal barracks in Versailles.

Several eighteen-pound shots had already gone clean through the carcass of the *Richard*. The *Serapis* was hardly injured. Jones had used all his skill and art to get the advantage in position but Captain Pearson, a good sailor himself, balked this design and time after time gave the American ship terrific, raking fire.

"If this lasts an hour longer, the enemy will have slain nearly all our officers," decided Nathaniel Fanning, the Puritan fighter, who, in spite of the hurricane of fire, was steadily at work encouraging his men.

The ship was slowly but surely sinking, most of the guns were silent; Jones had to turn to the strategy of the old privateers: "get muzzel to muzzel and hand to hand and fight it through." He rushed to the deck where Richard Dale was standing. "Dick," he cried, "their metal is too heavy for us, they'll hammer us to pieces. We must close with them. Bring your men on the spar deck and pass out the small arms."

Without a thought for the death whirring on every side Jones ran back to the quarterdeck and calling the sailing master, Stacy, Jones ordered him to lay the enemy's ship on board. Stacy gave the order. The enemy was now ahead of them. It was wind they needed. Suddenly the capricious breeze which had so often forsaken him came to his aid, and as if to make up for past errors, filled the sails and shot the *Richard* quickly ahead and into the *Serapis*, which had been attempting to cut across their bow.

"She ran her jib-boom between the enemy's starboard mizzen shrouds and mizzen vane," called Fanning.

"Well done, my brave lads," cried Jones. "We've got her now. Throw on board the grappling irons and stand by for boarding." The order was promptly executed but just as promptly the enemy cut away the irons, in spite of a dangerous hail of fire from the tops of the *Richard*. Three times the manoeuvre was defeated before the enemy ship was finally snug alongside the *Richard*.

In the midst of the arduous work of tying them together, the enemy's jib-sail was cut away and fell upon the poop where Jones was assisting Stacy to make fast the end of the jib-stay to the *Richard*'s mast. Stacy, a hot-blooded Yankee, couldn't repress dutiful swearing. With a quick gesture, Jones stopped him. "Mr. Stacy," he said, "it is not time for swearing now, you may by the next moment be in eternity, but let us do our duty." Together they steadily and securely bound the ships one to the other.

Now, there was no way for the English ship to extricate herself from the tenacious grip of the *Richard*, which like a monstrous crow with iron claws clung to her prey with the fury of a last hope. In a supreme effort to rid herself of this clutch, the *Serapis* suddenly let go an anchor expecting that the current would pull the *Richard* away. They would then be able to train their deadly guns on her once more. But the effort failed and left the fighting ships locked in a death grip and securely anchored to the bottom of the sea where one or other of them was sure to end.

The enemy now made an attempt to board the *Richard* but men were waiting for them and drove them quickly back. Taking the offensive themselves, the Americans then tried to board the *Serapis* but they were killed as fast as they set foot on the enemy ship.

With his guns silent except for two nine-pounders on the enemy's side, Jones himself now rallied a few men to move another nine-pounder to that side of the ship and the battle was carried on with these three guns. Unable to board the enemy, Jones then sent every available man to the tops, which were now locked securely to the tops of the enemy.

The ships were now so close to each other that the heaviest cannon amidships were useless. The same fire seemed to devour both of them. Sparks flew like fire-flies among the riggings. The moment fire died down on the *Richard* it would blaze up on the *Serapis*.

Breathless, the crowds on the shore watched the fire threatening to consume English and Americans indiscriminately.

A screen of smoke which had risen between the two ships reflected the dancing flames, sparks and flashes, and threw a lurid and fantastic light upon the decks; a diabolic cortège of shadows passed and repassed before the red screen, rising to gigantic heights only to shrink and fade from the scene as in

some infernal nightmare. Here and there were red inhuman masses and fragments of once living people, gory shreds of flesh. From the riggings distorted
bodies fell heavily to the deck as if eager to join their fallen comrades.

Jones was everywhere—now taking the place of a man behind a nine-
pounder, while he bound his wound; now helping another to stop the blood
flowing from his armless sleeve; watching over all, finding the right word to
hearten these men; to give each of them the feeling that he held the destiny of
the ship in his own hands.

Decimated by the accurate fire of the English, the volunteers of Count de
Chamillard wavered. The unprotected poop deck was becoming unbearable.
Their colonel was wounded. Finally, as they started to retreat over the dead
bodies of their fallen fellows, Jones rushed to them and yelled: "Frenchmen,
are you going to give in under the eyes of Americans and English?" He
snatched a musket from the nearest man, mounted the rail and fired as fast as
the guns could be handed to him. With a cheer the Frenchmen followed his
electrifying example and started firing again with their usual precision.

From the hold to the topmast of the *Richard* one will animated all the
men—the captain's will—victory! Unceasing effort was driving the enemy
out of the riggings and down on to the deck to seek cover of any sort. But still
their between-deck guns poured demolishing fire into the *Richard*. Four guns
in the foremost bow were annihilating the American ship. The ensign of the
Richard had already been shot into the sea.

Suddenly one of those flashes of terror, which make the bravest crowd
shiver hysterically, bolted through the men. "Captain Jones and most of his
officers are dead." "The ship is ready to sink." A group of impassioned
fellows told the gunners they had to act as officers, "ask the enemy for quarters." There was no time to waste. They would all lose their lives. The gunner,
carpenter and master-at-arms scrambled to the deck, bawling at the top of their
lungs: *"Quarters! Quarters!* For God's sake, *quarters,* our ship is sinking!"
Disorder spread throughout the ship. Nathaniel Fanning thought the cries
came from the *Serapis.* All at once Jones's well-known voice pierced the
clamor like a trumpet:

"What damned rascals are those—shoot them—kill them!"

At the sound of his voice, the carpenter and master-at-arms wheeled about
and left the deck. The gunner was doing his best to follow them when he
caught a blow on the back of the head which sent him spinning to the foot of
the gangway ladder. Paul Jones, beside himself with rage, had thrown his
empty pistol and hit the man squarely on the skull.

Now, Captain Pearson came to the rail and his words could be heard
throughout the whole *Richard.*

"Do I understand that you have struck?"

In answer came the cry which thundered on to the *Serapis* and beyond, to
roll sonorously down the centuries.

"No, I have just begun to fight!" Such a man could not be defeated.

The battle went on, against the rising water, the consuming fire and the enemy who was securely tied to them. Jones turned to his men: "Yankees never haul down their colors until they are fairly beaten!" Cheers answered him, even from the wounded men.

As if he had not already enough difficulties on hand, Jones was now faced with a danger worse than fire and water, as an uproarious mob surged to the deck from the very bowels of the ship. The English prisoners, threatened by the fire inching its way toward them and by the water rising in the hold where they had been crammed, had somehow been released and were struggling to the open air in panic, yelling at the top of their lungs that the ship was sinking. Instantly they were faced with the figure of Paul Jones. Mastering them with a gesture, "It is the *Serapis* which is sinking," he cried, and then persuading them that their one chance to save their lives was to keep the *Richard* afloat, he gave them but one order: "Man the pumps." One man refused. He fell with a bullet in his head from the pistol of an officer. The rest went sheep-like to the pumps. In a second Jones had turned a threat of destruction into providential advantage, for having all the prisoners at the pumps working for their very lives he could recall all hands to the deck.

Then, as Jones described it, "The battle went on with double fury." Only a few minutes had passed when the cry of "FIRE!" was heard again in both ships. Cannons and muskets became silent while both crews frantically fought the flames. Only the monotonous clank of the pumps could be heard, throbbing like the heart of a monster in its last agony. Suddenly with distant clearness, the bells of a country church chimed across the water telling the poor devils fighting for their lives, that nearby in the countryside all was peace and quiet. The fire mastered, the men returned to the fight, carrying on with the few cannons left on the *Richard*, stink-bombs, hand-grenades, boarding pikes and pistols.

Advised by the bravest of his officers to yield, once more Captain Jones flatly refused. He had "other objectives in view," he said. Other objectives? There could be but one objective—victory—the victory he had promised to America, to France.

As if in answer to a prayer, the dark sails of a ship loomed in the blue of the night. The *Alliance*. What a miracle that Landais should come to the rescue.

But without warning, fresh, well-directed fire from the uninjured *Alliance* brutally swept the decks of the *Richard* and the *Serapis*. Horror rose in desperate cries from the throat of every man on the deck of the American ship. So perfect was the aim that the officers, believing her to be an English man-of-war, stared into the night unwilling to believe their eyes. As if ashamed to behold any longer such a bloody and treacherous scene, the moon hid behind a dark cloud. In vain did the cry go out that they were firing at the wrong ship; that the enemy was beaten and must give over in a moment. Taking a position at the head and then at the stern of the *Richard*, the *Alliance* continued firing indiscriminately into both ships. In frantic haste Jones ordered the signal of recognizance displayed. Three lighted lanterns in a horizontal line, at a height of fifteen feet, on the fore, main, and mizzen shrouds on the starboard side were quickly rigged up. But then instead of directing her fire at the unmistakable enemy, the *Alliance* disappeared into the night followed by the maledictions which swelled up from the breasts of the desperate crew.

Perched in the riggings, Jones's men were effectively keeping the enemy from consummating their only hope—severing the *Serapis* from the *Richard*. Systematically every man who ventured within sight was felled by the concentrated fire of muskets. During the confusion of the previous minutes, an American lad had crept out on the main yard with a basket of hand-grenades on his arm. Unconcernedly he was throwing his bombs for the hatchway, hoping that one would fall between the gun decks where the men of the *Serapis* were collected.

With a terrifying hole in her hull, her rigging in flames, masts weaving, ready to fall overboard, and the sails hanging in tatters, the *Bonhomme Richard* was no more than a monstrous wreck clinging desperately to her prey. But still alive among the flames and wreckage was the indomitable John Paul Jones. His gestures, his words galvanized the men into action. Stains of death were on every side; torn bodies, splashes of blood covered the splintered ship from one end to the other, but one thing remained flamingly alive, undamaged, invulnerable—the ardent will of the man standing there hardened as if built of steel. The defeat of the *Bonhomme Richard* would, in his eyes, have been the wreck of his honor. He must oblige the enemy to bring down their colors first; he had to hold out for a minute more than the *Serapis*, the minute which would mean victory.

The two vessels were now burning in the night like one torch. As though unavoidably drawn to the holocaust, the *Alliance* came once more out of the night to pour destructive fire into both ships, killing men on the *Bonhomme Richard*—Frenchmen, Americans. The curses of the crew followed the *Alliance* as she circled the ships like a wolf waiting for her prey. Landais was awaiting the moment when the *Richard* would sink and he would be able to step in and man the *Serapis* without difficulty.

Detecting the arming of boarders on the American ship, the English made an immediate assault. Jones dropped his musket and grabbed a pike to lead the defense. Both sides repelled the other and a new party of boarders were gathered.

Jones called out: "Are you ready, boarders?"

"Ay, ay, sir."

"Then now is your time. Go in," shouted the captain.

The boarders went and this time reached the deck of the other ship. Jones was seeking victory. His trained ear and eye told him what it told few others—the enemy was weakening.

Meeting the impatient Jack Robinson, the bo'sun, Jones asked him if he thought they should surrender. Robinson replied, "No, sir, I think we've still got a shot in the locker."

High above the decks there was another man who wouldn't have given up: the lad astride the mainyard with a basket of hand-grenades. With careful aim he was obstinately throwing his bombs at the open hatchway on the enemy's deck. A determined youngster—he was finally rewarded. After crazily glancing this way and that, a hand-grenade had ricocheted from the cover of the hatchway and disappeared between the decks.

A volcanic explosion rent the air and the hole into which the grenade had disappeared spewed forth wreckage and human remains. The grenade had struck powder and open cartridges in the place where the powder monkeys were gathered. Men were burned, killed and fearfully torn. Panic seized the enemy and the cry, "QUARTERS!" went up from the English ship. Pearson had but one alternative. Strike his colors. With his own hands he tore down the ensign which he had shortly before nailed to the mast.

In a second Richard Dale was on the enemy's deck, followed by Mayrant with a party of men. Mayrant was hurt, for the end had come so quickly that the crew of the *Serapis* continued shooting, not aware that their ship had struck. Dale found Captain Pearson sitting beside the mast from which he had just torn his flag. His head was in his hands; he was the picture of utter dejection.

With drooping shoulders, Pearson came across the deck to the place where Jones was standing. Bracing himself by straightening his shoulders, he said with a touch of arrogance as he handed over his sword: "It is painful to me that I must resign this to a man who fought with a halter around his neck." Ignoring the personal insult, Jones simply accepted the sword. "Sir," he answered, "you have fought like a hero and I have no doubt but that your sovereign will reward you in a most ample manner." Startled at such gallantry from "a pirate," Pearson then inquired about the nationality of the men of Jones's crew. When told they were mostly Americans, he said: "It has been diamond cut by diamond." Then the two commanders retired to a cabin to drink a glass of wine together.

The officers of the *Serapis* delivered up their sidearms to Lieutenant Dale as they filed aboard the *Bonhomme Richard*. The ships were now separated and the masts of the *Serapis*, with nothing to support them, fell overboard into the sea with a hideous splash.

On the shore a few scattered people remained for hours more watching the still burning ships. Their champion had lost.

The *Pallas* had captured the *Countess of Scarborough* after an hour's hard fighting and now came to the aid of the *Richard* and the *Serapis*. The latter having been pierced several times in vital spots by shots from the *Richard*, was thought ready to sink, so members of the other crews were called on board to keep the pumps working all night until the carpenters could plug the holes.

The *Richard* was in a worse condition but the pumps were kept going incessantly. Finally, the carpenters reported that they could do nothing to save her. She was sinking lower and lower. All the next day men were feverishly busy getting the wounded onto the other ships of the squadron.

Unwilling to give up his victorious ship, Jones still kept the men at the pumps the next day, but finally he knew that she would sink with the slightest wind. Fire still flared occasionally from the battered hulk. The powder had been thrown overboard, and most of the men were by this time transferred to the *Serapis,* but in spite of everything the hold was full of water and the mangled hulk was settling.

Broken-hearted at the thought of abandoning the good old ship, Jones made a last full survey of the *Bonhomme Richard.* Between decks the light showed through gaping holes, and illuminated a horribly bloody scene. The dead were lying in heaps. It was a sight to touch the heart of the most callous of men. Such was the swift toll of war. Returning from his rounds of the ship, Jones realized that she could not be saved and gave the order to abandon the *Bonhomme Richard.*

The transfer of the last of the men was now made rapidly with the help of the *Pallas.* A slight wind had arisen and Jones knew that the end would come quickly.

Once he was on the *Serapis,* Jones drifted along for a time, remaining on deck watching the dark mass of the *Bonhomme Richard,* which, with one charred mast standing straight upright supporting one cross bar, looked like a gigantic pedestal supporting a cross; a monument marking the spot of a tremendous tomb.

The old ship struggled no more. Her days of battle were over and she was ready to surrender to her destiny. Almost imperceptibly she was going . . . a slight eddy of wind caught her. For a second her nose came up and then went down into the water, the whole ship slid forward without effort and disappeared into the grey-green depths no tempest ever reached.

Trafalgar

by ROBERT SOUTHEY

The station which Nelson had chosen was some fifty or sixty miles to the west of Cadiz, near Cape St. Mary's. At this distance he hoped to decoy the enemy out, while he guarded against the danger of being caught with a westerly wind near Cadiz, and driven within the Straits. The blockade of the port was rigorously enforced, in hopes that the Combined fleet might be forced to sea by want. The Danish vessels, therefore, which were carrying provisions from the French ports in the bay, under the name of Danish property, to all the little ports from Ayamonte to Algeziras, from whence they were conveyed in coasting boats to Cadiz, were seized. Without this proper exertion of power, the blockade would have been rendered nugatory, by the advantage thus taken of the neutral flag. The supplies from France were thus effectually cut off. There was now every indication that the enemy would speedily venture out: officers and men were in the highest spirits at the prospect of giving them a decisive blow; such, indeed, as would put an end to all further contest upon the seas. Theatrical amusements were performed every evening in most of the ships: and "God Save the King" was the hymn with which the sports concluded. "I verily believe," said Nelson, writing on the 6th of October, "that the country will soon be put to some expense on my account; either a monument or a new pension and honours; for I have not the smallest doubt but that a very few days, almost hours, will put us in battle. The success no man can insure; but for the fighting them, if they can be got at, I pledge myself. The sooner the better: I don't like to have these things upon my mind."

At this time he was not without cause of anxiety; he was in want of frigates—the eyes of the fleet, as he always called them: to the want of which the enemy before were indebted for their escape, and Bonaparte for his arrival in Egypt. He had only twenty-three ships—others were on the way—but they might come too late; and, though Nelson never doubted of victory, mere victory was not what he looked to, he wanted to annihilate the enemy's fleet. The Carthagena squadron might effect a junction with this fleet on the one side; and, on the other, it was to be expected that a similar attempt would be made by the French from Brest; in either case a formidable contingency to be apprehended by the blockading force. The Rochefort squadron did push out, and had nearly caught the *Agamemnon* and *L'Aimable* in their way to reinforce the British Admiral. Yet Nelson at this time weakened his own fleet. He had the unpleasant task to perform of sending home Sir Robert Calder, whose conduct was to be made the subject of a court-martial, in consequence of the general dissatisfaction which had been felt and expressed at his imperfect victory. Sir Robert Calder, and Sir John Orde, Nelson believed to be the only two enemies whom he had ever had in his profession; and, from that sensitive delicacy which distinguished him, this made him the more scrupulously anxious to show every possible mark of respect and kindness to Sir Robert. He wished to detain him till after the expected action; when the services which he might perform, and the triumphant joy which would be excited, would leave nothing to be apprehended from an inquiry into the previous engagement. Sir Robert, however, whose situation was very painful, did not choose to delay a trial, from the result of which he confidently expected a complete justification: and Nelson, instead of sending him home in a frigate, insisted on his returning in his own ninety-gun ship; ill as such a ship could at that time be spared. Nothing could be more honourable than the feeling by which Nelson was influenced; but, at such a crisis, it ought not to have been indulged.

On the 9th, Nelson sent Collingwood what he called, in his Diary, the *Nelson-touch*. "I send you," said he, "my plan of attack, as far as a man dare venture to guess at the very uncertain position the enemy may be found in: but it is to place you perfectly at ease respecting my intentions, and to give full scope to your judgment for carrying them into effect. We can, my dear Coll., have no little jealousies. We have only one great object in view, that of annihilating our enemies, and getting a glorious peace for our country. No man has more confidence in another than I have in you; and no man will render your services more justice than your very old friend—Nelson and Bronte." The order of sailing was to be the order of battle; the fleet in two lines, with an advanced squadron of eight of the fastest-sailing two-deckers. The second in command, having the entire direction of his line, was to break through the enemy, about the twelfth ship from their rear; he would lead through the centre, and the advanced squadron was to cut off three or four ahead of the centre. This plan was to be adapted to the strength of the enemy, so that they should always be one-fourth superior to those whom they cut off. Nelson said, "That his Admirals and captains, knowing his precise object to be that of a close and decisive action, would supply any deficiency of signals, and act accordingly. In case signals cannot be seen or clearly understood, no captain can do wrong if he places his ship alongside that of an enemy." One of the last orders of this admirable man was, that the name and family of every officer, seaman, and marine, who might be killed or wounded in action, should be, as soon as possible, returned to him, in order to be transmitted to the Chairman of the Patriotic Fund, that the case might be taken into consideration, for the benefit of the sufferer or his family.

About half-past nine in the morning of the 19th, the *Mars*, being the nearest to the fleet of the ships which formed the line of communication with the frigates in-shore, repeated the signal, that the enemy were coming out of port.

The wind was at this time very light, with partial breezes, mostly from the S.S.W. Nelson ordered the signal to be made for a chase in the south-east quarter. About two, the repeating-ships announced that the enemy were at sea. All night the British fleet continued under all sail, steering to the south-east. At daybreak they were in the entrance of the Straits, but the enemy were not in sight. About seven, one of the frigates made signal that the enemy were bearing north. Upon this the *Victory* hove-to; and shortly afterwards Nelson made sail again to the northward. In the afternoon the wind blew fresh from the south-west, and the English began to fear that the foe might be forced to return to port. A little before sunset, however, Blackwood, in the *Euryalus*, telegraphed that they appeared determined to go to the westward. "And that," said the Admiral in his Diary, "they shall not do, if it is in the power of Nelson and Bronte to prevent them." Nelson had signified to Blackwood that he depended upon him to keep sight of the enemy. They were observed so well, that all their motions were made known to him; and, as they wore twice, he inferred that they were aiming to keep the port of Cadiz open, and would retreat there as soon as they saw the British fleet; for this reason he was very careful not to approach near enough to be seen by them during the night. At daybreak the Combined fleets were distinctly seen from the *Victory's* deck, formed in a close line of battle ahead, on the starboard tack, about twelve miles to leeward, and standing to the south. Our fleet consisted of twenty-seven sail of the line and four frigates; theirs of thirty-three and seven large frigates. Their superiority was greater in size and weight of metal than in numbers. They had four thousand troops on board; and the best riflemen who could be procured, many of them Tyrolese, were dispersed through the ships. Little did the Tyrolese, and little did the Spaniards, at that day, imagine what horrors the wicked tyrant whom they served was preparing for their country.

Soon after daylight Nelson came upon deck. The 21st of October was a festival in his family, because on that day his uncle, Captain Suckling, in the *Dreadnought*, with two other line-of-battle ships, had beaten off a French squadron of four sail of the line and three frigates. Nelson, with that sort of superstition from which few persons are entirely exempt, had more than once expressed his persuasion that this was to be the day of his battle also; and he was well pleased at seeing his prediction about to be verified. The wind was now from the west, light breezes, with a long heavy swell. Signal was made to bear down upon the enemy in two lines; and the fleet set all sail. Collingwood, in the *Royal Sovereign*, led the lee line of thirteen ships; the *Victory* led the weather line of fourteen. Having seen that all was as it should be, Nelson retired to his cabin, and wrote the following prayer:—

May the great God, whom I worship, grant to my country, and for the benefit of Europe in general, a great and glorious victory; and may no misconduct in any one tarnish it! and may humanity after victory be the predominant feature in the British fleet! For myself individually, I commit my life to Him that made me; and may His blessing alight on my endeavours for serving my country faithfully! To Him I resign myself, and the just cause which is entrusted to me to defend. Amen, Amen, Amen.

Having thus discharged his devotional duties, he annexed, in the same Diary, the following remarkable writing:—

October 21st, 1805.—Then in sight of the Combined fleets of France and Spain, distant about ten miles.

Whereas the eminent services of Emma Hamilton, widow of the Right Honourable Sir William Hamilton, have been of the very greatest service to my King and my country, to my knowledge, without ever receiving any reward from either our King or country.

First: That she obtained the king of Spain's letter in 1796, to his brother, the King of Naples, acquainting him of his intention to declare war against England; from which letter the ministry sent out orders to the then Sir John Jervis, to strike a stroke, if opportunity offered, against either the arsenals of Spain or her fleets. That neither of these was done is not the fault of Lady Hamilton; the opportunity might have been offered.

Secondly: The British fleet under my command could never have returned the second time to Egypt, had not Lady Hamilton's influence with the Queen of Naples caused letters to be wrote to the Governor of Syracuse, that he was to encourage the fleet's being supplied with everything, should they put into any port in Sicily. We put into Syracuse, and received every supply; went to Egypt, and destroyed the French fleet.

Could I have rewarded these services, I would not now call upon my country; but as that has not been in my power, I leave Emma Lady Hamilton therefore a legacy to my King and country, that they will give her an ample provision to maintain her rank in life.

I also leave to the beneficence of my country my adopted daughter, Horatia Nelson Thompson; and I desire she will use in future the name of Nelson only.

These are the only favours I ask of my King and country, at this moment when I am going to fight their battle. May God bless my King and country, and all those I hold dear! My relations it is needless to mention: they will, of course, be amply provided for.

NELSON AND BRONTE

Witness {(HENRY BLACKWOOD.
        {(T. M. HARDY.

The child of whom this writing speaks was believed to be his daughter, and so, indeed, he called her the last time that he pronounced her name. She was then about five years old, living at Merton, under Lady Hamilton's care. The last minutes which Nelson passed at Merton were employed in praying over this child, as she lay sleeping. A portrait of Lady Hamilton hung in his cabin; and no Catholic ever beheld the picture of his patron saint with devouter reverence. The undisguised and romantic passion with which he regarded it amounted almost to superstition; and when the portrait was now taken down, in clearing for action, he desired the men who removed it to "take care of his guardian angel." In this manner he frequently spoke of it, as if he believed there were a virtue in the image. He wore a miniature of her, also, next his heart.

Blackwood went on board the *Victory* about six. He found him in good spirits, but very calm; not in that exhilaration which he had felt upon entering into battle at Aboukir and Copenhagen: he knew that his own life would be particularly aimed at, and seems to have looked for death with almost as sure an expectation as for victory. His whole attention was fixed upon the enemy. They attacked to the northward, and formed their line on the larboard tack; thus bringing the shoals of Trafalgar and St. Pedro under the lee of the British, keeping the port of Cadiz open for themselves. This was judiciously done; and Nelson, aware of all the advantages which it gave them, made signal to prepare to anchor.

Villeneuve was a skilful seaman; worthy of serving a better master, and a better cause. His plan of defence was as well conceived, and as original, as the plan of attack. He formed the fleet in a double line; every alternate ship being about a cable's length to windward of her second ahead and astern. Nelson, certain of a triumphant issue to the day, asked Blackwood what he should consider as a victory. That officer answered, that, considering the handsome way in which battle was offered by the enemy, their apparent determination for a fair trial of strength, and the situation of the land, he thought it would be a glorious result if fourteen were captured. He replied: "I shall not be satisfied with less than twenty." Soon afterwards he asked him, if he did not think there was a signal wanting. Captain Blackwood made answer, that he thought the whole fleet seemed very clearly to understand what they were about. These words were scarcely spoken before that signal was made, which will be remembered as long as the language, or even the memory, of England shall endure—Nelson's last signal:—"ENGLAND EXPECTS EVERY MAN WILL DO HIS DUTY!" It was received throughout the fleet with a shout of answering acclamation, made sublime by the spirit which it breathed, and the feeling which it expressed. "Now," said Lord Nelson, "I can do no more. We must trust to the great Disposer of all events, and the justice of our cause. I thank God for this great opportunity of doing my duty."

He wore that day, as usual, his Admiral's frockcoat, bearing on the left breast four stars, of the different orders with which he was invested. Ornaments which rendered him so conspicuous a mark for the enemy were beheld with ominous apprehensions by his officers. It was known that there were riflemen on board the French ships; and it could not be doubted but that his life would be particularly aimed at. They communicated their fears to each other;

and the surgeon, Mr. Beatty, spoke to the chaplain, Dr. Scott, and to Mr. Scott, the public secretary, desiring that some person would entreat him to change his dress, or cover the stars; but they knew that such a request would highly displease him. "In honour I gained them," he had said, when such a thing had been hinted to him formerly, "and in honour I will die with them." Mr. Beatty, however, would not have been deterred by any fear of exciting displeasure, from speaking to him himself upon a subject in which the weal of England, as well as the life of Nelson, was concerned—but he was ordered from the deck before he could find an opportunity. This was a point upon which Nelson's officers knew that it was hopeless to remonstrate or reason with him; but both Blackwood and his own captain, Hardy, represented to him how advantageous to the fleet it would be for him to keep out of action as long as possible; and he consented at last to let the *Leviathan* and the *Téméraire*, which were sailing abreast of the *Victory*, be ordered to pass ahead. Yet even here the last infirmity of this noble mind was indulged; for these ships could not pass ahead if the *Victory* continued to carry all her sail; and so far was Nelson from shortening sail, that it was evident he took pleasure in pressing on, and rendering it impossible for them to obey his own orders. A long swell was setting into the Bay of Cadiz: our ships, crowding all sail, moved majestically before it, with light winds from the southwest. The sun shone on the sails of the enemy; and their well-formed line, with their numerous three-deckers, made an appearance which any other assailants would have thought formidable; but the British sailors only admired the beauty and the splendour of the spectacle; and, in full confidence of winning what they saw, remarked to each other, what a fine sight yonder ships would make at Spithead!

The French Admiral, from the *Bucentaure*, beheld the new manner in which his enemy was advancing—Nelson and Collingwood each leading his line; and pointing them out to his officers, he is said to have exclaimed, that such conduct could not fail to be successful. Yet Villeneuve had made his own dispositions with the utmost skill, and the fleets under his command waited for the attack with perfect coolness. Ten minutes before twelve they opened their fire. Eight or nine of the ships immediately ahead of the *Victory* and across her bows, fired single guns at her, to ascertain whether she was yet within their range. As soon as Nelson perceived that their shot passed over him, he desired Blackwood, and Captain Prowse, of the *Sirius*, to repair to their respective frigates; and, on their way, to tell all the captains of the line-of-battle ships that he depended on their exertions; and that, if by the prescribed mode of attack they found it impracticable to get into action immediately, they might adopt whatever they thought best, provided it led them quickly and closely alongside an enemy. As they were standing on the front poop, Blackwood took him by the hand, saying he hoped soon to return and find him in possession of twenty prizes. He replied, "God bless you, Blackwood; I shall never see you again!"

Nelson's column was steered about two points more to the north than Collingwood's, in order to cut off the enemy's escape into Cadiz: the lee line, therefore, was first engaged. "See," cried Nelson, pointing to the *Royal Sov-*

ereign, as she steered right for the centre of the enemy's line, cut through it astern of the *Santa Ana*, three-decker, and engaged her at the muzzle of her guns on the starboard side; "see how that noble fellow, Collingwood, carries his ship into action!" Collingwood, delighted at being first in the heat of the fire, and knowing the feelings of his Commander and old friend, turned to his captain, and exclaimed: "Rotherham, what would Nelson give to be here?" Both these brave officers, perhaps, at this moment, thought of Nelson with gratitude, for a circumstance which had occurred on the preceding day. Admiral Collingwood, with some of the captains, having gone on board the *Victory* to receive instructions, Nelson inquired of him where his captain was: and was told, in reply, that they were not upon good terms with each other. "Terms!" said Nelson, "good terms with each other!" Immediately he sent a boat for Captain Rotherham; led him, as soon as he arrived, to Collingwood, and saying: "Look; yonder are the enemy!" bade them shake hands like Englishmen.

The enemy continued to fire a gun at a time at the *Victory*, till they saw that a shot had passed through her main-top-gallant sail; then they opened their broadsides, aiming chiefly at her rigging, in the hope of disabling her before she could close with them. Nelson, as usual, had hoisted several flags, lest one should be shot away. The enemy showed no colours till late in the action, when they began to feel the necessity of having them to strike. For this reason, the *Santissima Trinidad*, Nelson's old acquaintance, as he used to call her, was distinguishable only by her four decks; and to the bow of this opponent he ordered the *Victory* to be steered. Meantime, an incessant raking fire was kept up upon the *Victory*. The Admiral's secretary was one of the first who fell; he was killed by a cannon-shot while conversing with Hardy. Captain Adair of the marines, with the help of a sailor, endeavoured to remove the body from Nelson's sight, who had a great regard for Mr. Scott; but he anxiously asked, "Is that poor Scott that's gone?" and being informed that it was indeed so, exclaimed, "Poor fellow!" Presently, a double-headed shot struck a party of marines, who were drawn up on the poop, and killed eight of them: upon which Nelson immediately desired Captain Adair to disperse his men round the ship, that they might not suffer so much from being together. A few minutes afterwards a shot struck the fore-brace bits on the quarter-deck, and passed between Nelson and Hardy, a splinter from the bit tearing off Hardy's buckle, and bruising his foot. Both stopped, and looked anxiously at each other: each supposed the other to be wounded. Nelson then smiled, and said: "This is too warm work, Hardy, to last long."

The *Victory* had not yet returned a single gun; fifty of her men had been by this time killed or wounded, and her main-top-mast with all her studding-sails and their booms shot away. Nelson declared, that, in all his battles, he had seen nothing which surpassed the cool courage of his crew on this occasion. At four minutes after twelve, she opened her fire from both sides of her deck. It was not possible to break the enemy's line without running on board one of their ships; Hardy informed him of this, and asked him which he would prefer. Nelson replied: "Take your choice, Hardy, it does signify much." The master was ordered to put the helm to port, and the *Victory* ran on board the *Redoutable*, just as her tiller ropes were shot away. The French ship received her with a broadside: then instantly let down her lower-deck ports, for fear of being boarded through them, and never afterwards fired a great gun during the action. Her tops, like those of all the enemy's ships, were filled with riflemen. Nelson never placed musketry in his tops; he had a strong dislike to the practice: not merely because it endangers setting fire to the sails, but also because it is a murderous sort of warfare, by which individuals may suffer, and a commander now and then be picked off, but which never can decide the fate of a general engagement.

Captain Harvey, in the *Téméraire*, fell on board the *Redoutable* on the other side. Another enemy was in like manner on board the *Téméraire*, so that these four ships formed as compact a tier as if they had been moored together, their heads lying all the same way. The lieutenants of the *Victory*, seeing this, depressed their guns of the middle and lower decks, and fired with a diminished charge, lest the shot should pass through and injure the *Téméraire*. And because there was danger that the *Redoutable* might take fire from the lower-deck guns, the muzzles of which touched her side when they were run out, the fireman of each gun stood ready with a bucket of water; which, as soon as the gun was discharged, he dashed into the hole made by the shot. An incessant fire was kept up from the *Victory* from both sides; her larboard guns playing upon the *Bucentaure*, and the huge *Santissima Trinidad*.

It had been part of Nelson's prayer, that the British fleet might be distinguished by humanity in the victory he expected. Setting an example himself, he twice gave orders to cease firing upon the *Redoutable*, supposing that she had struck, because her great guns were silent; for, as she carried no flag, there was no means of instantly ascertaining the fact. From this ship, which he had thus twice spared, he received his death. A ball fired from her mizzen-top, which, in the then situation of the two vessels, was not more than fifteen yards from that part of the deck where he was standing, struck the epaulette on his left shoulder, about a quarter after one, just in the heat of action. He fell upon his face, on the spot which was covered with his poor secretary's blood. Hardy, who was a few steps from him, turning round, saw three men raising him up. "They have done for me at last, Hardy!" said he. "I hope not!" cried Hardy. "Yes," he replied; "my backbone is shot through!" Yet even now, not for a moment losing his presence of mind, he observed, as they were carrying him down the ladder, that the tiller-ropes, which had been shot away, were not yet replaced, and ordered that new ones should be rove immediately. Then, that he might not be seen by the crew, he took out his handkerchief, and covered his face and his stars. Had he but concealed these badges of honour from the enemy, England, perhaps, would not have had cause to receive with sorrow the news of the battle of Trafalgar. The cockpit was crowded with wounded and dying men; over whose bodies he was with some difficulty conveyed, and laid upon a pallet in the midshipmen's berth. It was soon perceived, upon examination, that the wound was mortal. This, however, was concealed from all except Captain Hardy, the chaplain and the medical attendants. He himself being certain, from the sensation in his back, and the gush of blood he felt momently within his breast, that no human care could avail him, insisted that the surgeon should leave him, and attend to those to whom he might be useful. "For," said he, "you can do nothing for me." All that could be done was to fan him with paper and frequently to give him lemonade to alleviate his intense thirst. He was in great pain, and expressed much anxiety for the event of the action, which now began to declare itself. As often as a ship struck, the crew of the *Victory* hurrahed; and at every hurrah, a visible expression of joy gleamed in the eyes, and marked the countenance, of the dying hero. But he became impatient to see Captain Hardy; and as that officer, though often sent for, could not leave the deck, Nelson feared that some fatal cause prevented him, and repeatedly cried: "Will no one bring Hardy to me? He must be killed! He is surely dead!" An hour and ten minutes elapsed from the time when Nelson received his wound, before Hardy could come to him. They shook hands in silence; Hardy in vain struggling to suppress the feelings of that most painful and yet sublimest moment. "Well, Hardy," said Nelson; "How goes the day with us?" "Very well," replied Hardy; "ten ships have struck, but five of the van have tacked, and show an intention to bear down upon the *Victory.* I have called two or three of our fresh ships round, and have no doubt of giving them a drubbing." "I hope," said Nelson, "none of our ships have struck?" Hardy answered, "There was no fear of that." Then, and not till then, Nelson spoke of himself. "I am a dead man, Hardy," said he: "I am going fast; it will be all over with me soon. Come nearer to me. Let my dear Lady Hamilton have my hair, and all other things belonging to me." Hardy observed, that he hoped Mr. Beatty could yet hold out some prospect of life. "Oh no!" he replied; "it is impossible; my back is shot through. Beatty will tell you so." Captain Hardy then, once more, shook hands with him; and with a heart almost bursting, hastened upon deck.

By this time all feeling below the breast was gone; and Nelson, having made the surgeon ascertain this, said to him: "You know I am gone. I know it. I feel something rising in my breast" (putting his hand on his left side) "which tells me so." And upon Beatty's inquiring whether his pain was very great? he replied, "So great that he wished he was dead. Yet," said he, in a lower voice, "one would like to live a little longer too!" And after a few minutes, in the same undertone, he added: "What would become of poor Lady Hamilton if she knew my situation!" Next to his country, she occupied his thoughts. Captain Hardy, some fifty minutes after he had left the cockpit, returned, and again taking the hand of his dying friend and Commander, congratulated him on having gained a complete victory. How many of the enemy were taken he did not know, as it was impossible to perceive them distinctly, but fourteen or fifteen at least. "That's well!" cried Nelson; "but I bargained for twenty." And then, in a stronger voice, he said: "Anchor, Hardy; anchor." Hardy, upon this, hinted that Admiral Collingwood would take upon himself the direction of affairs. "Not while I live, Hardy," said the dying Nelson, ineffectually endeavouring to raise himself from the bed; "do you anchor." His previous order for preparing to anchor had shown how clearly he foresaw the necessity of this. Presently, calling Hardy back, he said to him, in a low voice: "Don't throw me overboard;" and he desired that he might be buried by his parents, unless it should please the King to order otherwise. Then reverting to private feelings,—"Take care of my dear Lady Hamilton, Hardy; take care of poor Lady Hamilton. Kiss me, Hardy," said he. Hardy knelt down and kissed his cheek; and Nelson said: "Now I am satisfied. Thank God, I have done my duty!" Hardy stood over him in silence for a moment or two, then knelt again, and kissed his forehead. "Who is that?" asked Nelson; and being informed, he replied: "God bless you, Hardy!" And Hardy then left him, for ever.

Nelson now desired to be turned upon his right side, and said: "I wish I had not left the deck; for I shall soon be gone." Death was, indeed, rapidly approaching. He said to the chaplain: "Doctor, I have *not* been a *great* sinner;" and after a short pause, "Remember that I leave Lady Hamilton, and my daughter Horatia as a legacy to my country." His articulation now became difficult; but he was distinctly heard to say: "Thank God, I have done my duty!" These words he repeatedly pronounced; and they were the last words which he uttered. He expired at thirty minutes after four, three hours and a quarter after he had received his wound.

The *Constitution* Captures
the *Guerrière*

by THEODORE ROOSEVELT

On August 2d the *Constitution* made sail from Boston and stood to the eastward, in hopes of falling in with some of the British cruisers. She was unsuccessful, however, and met nothing. Then she ran down to the Bay of Fundy, steered along the coast of Nova Scotia, and thence toward Newfoundland, and finally took her station off Cape Race in the Gulf of St. Lawrence, where she took and burned two brigs of little value. On the 15th she recaptured an American brig from the British ship-sloop *Avenger*, though the latter escaped; Captain Hull manned his prize and sent her in. He then sailed southward, and on the night of the 18th spoke a Salem privateer which gave him news of a British frigate to the south; thither he stood, and at 2 P.M. on the 19th, in lat. 41° 30′ N. and 55° W., made out a large sail bearing E.S.E. and to leeward, which proved to be his old acquaintance, the frigate *Guerrière* Captain Dacres. It was a cloudy day and the wind was blowing fresh from the northwest. The *Guerrière* was standing by the wind on the starboard tack, under easy canvas; she hauled up her courses, took in her top-gallant sails, and at 4.30 backed her main-top sail. Hull then very deliberately began to shorten sail, taking in topgallant sails, stay-sails, and flying jib, sending down the royal yards and putting another reef in the top-sails. Soon the Englishman hoisted three ensigns, when the American also set his colors, one at each mast-head, and one at the mizzen peak.

The *Constitution* now ran down with the wind nearly aft. The *Guerrière* was on the starboard tack, and at five o'clock opened with her weather-guns, the shot falling short, then wore round and fired her port broadside, of which two shot struck her opponent, the rest passing over and through her rigging. As the British frigate again wore to open with her starboard battery, the *Constitution* yawed a little and fired two or three of her port bow guns. Three or four times the *Guerrière* repeated this manoeuvre, wearing and firing alternate broadsides, but with little or no effect, while the *Constitution* yawed as often to avoid being raked, and occasionally fired one of her bow guns. This continued nearly an hour, as the vessels were very far apart when the action began, hardly any loss or damage being inflicted by either party. At 6.00 the *Guerrière* bore up and ran off under her top-sails and jib, with the wind almost astern, a little on her port quarter; when the *Constitution* set her main-topgallant sail and foresail, and at 6:05 closed within half pistol-shot distance on her adversary's port beam. Immediately a furious cannonade opened, each ship firing as the guns bore. By the time the ships were fairly abreast, at 6.20, the *Constitution* shot away the *Guerrière's* mizzen-mast, which fell over the starboard quarter, knocking a large hole in the counter, and bringing the ship round against her helm. Hitherto she had suffered very greatly and the *Constitution* hardly at all. The latter, finding that she was ranging ahead, put her helm aport and then luffed short round her enemy's bows, delivering a heavy raking fire with the starboard guns and shooting away the *Guerrière's* main-yard. Then she wore and again passed her adversary's bows, raking with her port guns. The mizzen-mast of the *Guerrière*, dragging in the water, had by this time pulled her bow round till the wind came on her starboard quarter; and so near were the two ships that the Englishman's bowsprit passed diagonally over the *Constitution's* quarter-deck, and as the latter ship fell off it got foul of her mizzen-rigging, and the vessels then lay with the *Guerrière's* starboard bow against the *Constitution's* port, or lee quarter-gallery. The Englishman's bow guns played havoc with Captain Hull's cabin, setting fire to it; but the flames were soon extinguished by Lieutenant Hoffmann. On both sides the boarders were called away; the British ran forward, but Captain Dacres relinquished the idea of attacking when he saw the crowds of men on the American's decks. Meanwhile, on the *Constitution*, the boarders and marines gathered aft, but such a heavy sea was running that they could not get on the *Guerrière*. Both sides suffered heavily from the closeness of the musketry fire; indeed, almost the entire loss on the *Constitution* occurred at this juncture. As Lieutenant Bush, of the marines, sprang upon the taffrail to leap on the enemy's decks, a British marine shot him dead; Mr. Morris, the first Lieutenant, and Mr. Alwyn, the master, had also both leaped on the taffrail, and both were at the same moment wounded by the musketry fire. On the *Guerrière* the loss was far heavier, almost all the men on the forecastle being picked off. Captain Dacres himself was shot in the back and severely wounded by one of the American mizzen topmen, while he was standing on the starboard forecastle hammocks cheering on his crew; two of the lieutenants and the master were also shot down. The ships gradually worked round till the wind was again on the port quarter, when they separated, and the *Guerrière's* foremast and main-mast at once went by the board, and fell over on the starboard side, leaving her a defenseless hulk, rolling her main-deck guns into the water. At 6.30 the *Constitution* hauled aboard her tacks, ran off a little distance to the eastward, and lay to. Her braces and standing and running rigging were much cut up and some of the spars wounded, but a few minutes sufficed to repair damages, when Captain Hull stood under his adversary's lee, and the latter at once struck, at 7.00 P.M., just two hours after she had fired the first shot. On the part of the *Constitution*, however, the actual fighting, exclusive of six or eight guns fired during the first hour, while closing, occupied less than 30 minutes.

The tonnage and metal of the combatants have already been referred to. The *Constitution* had, as already said, about 456 men aboard, while of the *Guerrière's* crew, 267 prisoners were received aboard the *Constitution;* deducting 10 who were Americans and would not fight, and adding the 15 killed outright, we get 272; 28 men were absent in prizes.

COMPARATIVE FORCE

	Tons.	Guns.	Broad-side.	Men.	Loss.	Comparative Force.	Comparative loss Inflicted.
Constitution	1576	27	684	456	14	1.00	1.00
Guerrière	1338	25	556	272	79	.70	.18

The loss of the *Constitution* includes Lieutenant William S. Bush, of the marines, and six seamen killed, and her first lieutenant, Charles Morris, Master, John C. Alwyn, four seamen, and one marine, wounded. Total, seven killed and seven wounded. Almost all this loss occurred when the ships came foul, and was due to the *Guerrière's* musketry and the two guns in her bridle-ports.

The *Guerrière* lost 23 killed and mortally wounded, including her second lieutenant, Henry Ready, and 56 wounded severely and slightly, including Captain Dacres himself, the first lieutenant, Bartholomew Kent, Master, Robert Scott, two master's mates, and one midshipman.

The third lieutenant of the *Constitution,* Mr. George Campbell Read, was sent on board the prize, and the *Constitution* remained by her during the night; but at daylight it was found that she was in danger of sinking. Captain Hull at once began removing the prisoners, and at three o'clock in the afternoon set the *Guerrière* on fire, and in a quarter of an hour she blew up. He then set sail for Boston, where he arrived on August 30th. "Captain Hull and his officers," writes Captain Dacres in his official letter, "have treated us like brave and generous enemies; the greatest care has been taken that we should not lose the smallest trifle."

The British laid very great stress on the rotten and decayed condition of the *Guerrière;* mentioning in particular that the main-mast fell solely because of the weight of the falling foremast. But it must be remembered that until the action occurred she considered a very fine ship. Thus, in Brighton's "Memoir of Admiral Broke," it is declared that Dacres freely expressed the opinion that she could take a ship in half the time the *Shannon* could. The fall of the main-mast occurred when the fight was practically over; it had no influence whatever on the conflict. It was also asserted that her powder was bad, but on no authority; her first broadside fell short, but so, under similar circumstances, did the first broadside of the *United States.* None of these causes account for the fact that her shot did not hit. Her opponent was of such superior force—nearly in the proportion of 3 to 2—that success would have been very difficult in any event, and no one can doubt the gallantry and pluck with which the British ship was fought; but the execution was very greatly disproportioned to the force. The gunnery of the *Guerrière* was very poor, and that of the *Constitution* excellent; during the few minutes the ships were yard-arm and yard-arm, the latter was not hulled once, while no less than 30 shot took effect on the former's engaged side, five sheets of copper beneath the bends. The *Guerrière,* moreover, was out-manoeuvred; "in wearing several

times and exchanging broadsides in such rapid and continual changes of position, her fire was much more harmless than it would have been if she had kept
more steady." The *Constitution* was handled faultlessly; Captain Hull displayed the coolness and skill of a veteran in the way in which he managed, first
to avoid being raked, and then to improve the advantage which the precision
and rapidity of his fire had gained. "After making every allowance claimed by
the enemy, the character of this victory is not essentially altered. Its pecu-
liarities were a fine display of seamanship in the approach, extraordinary efficiency in the attack, and great readiness in repairing damages; all of which
denote cool and capable officers, with an expert and trained crew; in a word, a
disciplined man-of-war." The disparity of force, 10 to 7, is not enough to
account for the disparity of execution, 10 to 2. Of course, something must be
allowed for the decayed state of the Englishman's masts, although I really do
not think it had any influence on the battle, for he was beaten when the main-
mast fell; and it must be remembered, on the other hand, that the American
crew was absolutely new, while the *Guerrière* was manned by old hands. So
that, while admitting and admiring the gallantry, and, on the whole, the seamanship of Captain Dacres and his crew, and acknowledging that he fought at
a great disadvantage, especially in being short-handed, yet all must acknowledge that the combat showed a marked superiority, particularly in gunnery, on
the part of the Americans. Had the ships not come foul, Captain Hull would
probably not have lost more than three or four men; as it was, he suffered but
slightly. That the *Guerrière* was not so weak as she was represented to be can
be gathered from the fact that she mounted two more main-deck guns than the
rest of her class; thus carrying on her main-deck 30 long 18-pounders in battery, to oppose to the 30 long 24's, or rather (allowing for the short weight of
shot) long 22's, of the *Constitution*. Characteristically enough, James, though
he carefully reckons in the long bow-chasers in the bridle-ports of the *Argus*
and *Enterprise*, yet refuses to count the two long eighteens mounted through
the bridle-ports on the *Guerrière*'s main-deck. Now, as it turned out, these
two bow guns were used very effectively, when the ships got foul, and caused
more damage and loss than all of the other main-deck guns put together.

Captain Dacres, very much to his credit, allowed the ten Americans on
board to go below, so as not to fight against their flag; and in his address to the
court-martial mentions, among the reasons for his defeat, "that he was very
much weakened by permitting the Americans on board to quit their quarters."
Coupling this with the assertion made by James and most other British writers
that the *Constitution* was largely manned by Englishmen, we reach the somewhat remarkable conclusion, that the British ship was defeated because the
Americans on board would *not* fight against their country, and that the American was victorious because the British on board *would*. However, as I have
shown, in reality there were probably not a score of British on board the
Constitution.

The Blow-up of the *Mohawk*

by WILLIAM ROBINSON

"The vessel flew
Towards the land, and then the billows grew
  Larger and whiter, and roar'd as triumphing,
Scattering on far and wide the heavy spray
  That shone like loose snow as it passed away."
Barry Cornwall.

We left the *Mohawk* rattling along under reefed topsails, and plunging her bows every now and then under water, as though about to explore the wonders of the deep. This she continued to do until about four bells; when the wind suddenly chopped round to the north, and commenced blowing "great guns" in earnest.

All the sails were now taken in, save close-reefed fore and main topsails, to keep her steady; and under those two sails only she scudded along at the rate of twelve knots.

All traces of the seventy-four and the frigate had now been lost sight of for above three hours; Captain Manly therefore congratulated himself on his providential escape; and felt a species of gratitude to the storm, for its opportune appearance.

About noon, land was seen on the lee bow; apparently at the distance of about two miles. It was concluded to be Cape Porpoise; and the bows of the ship were therefore hauled up some three points or so, in order to make Kennebunk-port, if possible.

The weather had been gradually thickening for the last quarter of an hour, and now, any object at the distance of a few hundred yards could not have been distinguished. The wind, too, at times came in such tornado-like puffs, that the ship more than once was nearly laid on her beam-ends; but the gallant craft behaved herself bravely; and though every timber and spar about her reaked and groaned, as though about to part asunder, she was all "right and tight" as yet.

Midshipman Weston, who had the command of the maintop, and where he had been, too, throughout nearly the whole gale, now descended to the deck, and coming aft, informed the captain that, instead of being as they thought near Cape Porpoise, they were within less than a quarter of a mile of the dangerous rocky islet, known as Boon Island; and not only that, but the ship was now, (through the influence of the current running between the island and the main coast) being driven directly on an immense line of breakers, but little more than five hundred yards off; and which, the thickness of the atmosphere, had prevented the forward watch on deck from seeing.

"Mr. Weston," said Captain Manly, anxiously, "are you sure you are right about our position?"

151

"Yes, sir," answered our hero. "I will stake my life on it that I am right. My father lives on the main coast nearly opposite to the island, therefore I ought to know."

"So you should," said the captain, "and I doubt not but what you are right. Monroe," continued he, turning to his lieutenant, "do you think she would carry any more canvas? If we could only edge her a point or two more to wind'ard, we might yet clear the reef."

"I don't think she would carry a rag more," answered Monroe; "even with the reefed topsail she has on her, you see the mast bends like a willow."

"It's our only chance, however," said the captain, "and we'll try it. Up, there, my lads," he shouted through his trumpet; "lively, lively—up with you, topmen—shake a reef out of that topsail."

"Aye, aye, sir," shouted the men, springing from the main-chains, and laying aloft to execute the order; and it was the last one they ever did execute for an earthly commander; for the whole volume of the sail was no sooner displayed to the blast, than a sharp, splitting sound was heard, and then crack went the topmast close by the cap head; and the five or six poor fellows who had gone aloft to take the reefs out of the top-sail, were hurled far away clear of the ship, beyond all reach of aid, where they sank to rise no more, beneath the furious waves.

The ship was now in a fearful position; for the breakers were not twenty yards from her bow; destruction seemed inevitable, and nothing, little short of a miracle, could save them. It was a moment to try the nerves of any commander; but Captain Manly was equal to it; his coolness never for a single moment deserted him; but calmly, clearly, and distinctly, as though working the ship into port, did he stand on the quarter deck, and issue forth his orders.

"Stand by there, men," he suddenly shouted in his trumpetlike voice; "stand by there to cut away the masts; and see the two hawsers and best bower cleared for dropping; if they'll hold, we may ride it out yet."

Luckily, this scheme, at the moment it was going to be put into effect, was rendered abortive by an almost miraculous event; this was no other than a gigantic and mountainous wave, which, striking the ship near the stern-sheets, hurled her completely clear of the low reef on which she was hurrying; so near, however, was she unto it, that a biscuit might with ease have been pitched upon it. In a few minutes more she had passed the dangerous ledge, and was again in deep water.

The gale had now evidently spent its fury; and though the sea was still fearfully high, and the breeze anything but a zephyr, it was plainly apparent to all now, that their chances of visiting the "coral halls" of David Jones, Esq., this cruise, were decidedly lessened.

All hands were now busily employed in clearing away the wreck of the topmast, rigging up a jury one, pumping out the water she had shipped, and refastening the spars, casks, and deck guns, that had been washed loose during the gale.

"Sail-ho!" sung out the look-out forward.

"Where away?"

"Three points on the weather-beam, sir; she is little more than a mile from us."

"What does she show like?" demanded Captain Manly.

"A large frigate, or seventy-four, sir," was the answer. "She is bearing down upon us under a heavy press of canvas."

Owing to the crippled state of the *Mohawk*, their chances of escaping their formidable opponent were anything but flattering; but it was not in the nature of Yankee tars to give up while there was hope.

All the sails that could be were now hoisted on board the *Mohawk*, and her bows turned directly on to the Maine coast; her commander determining, if possible, to run her ashore and blow her up, sooner than that she should fall into the hands of John Bull. As the land was only about three-quarters of a mile distant, this project seemed feasible enough.

The Englishman had now hoisted his colors, and was fast lessening the distance between him and his intended prize; and having opened a heavy fire from his bow chasers, was beginning to make terrible havoc among the spars and rigging of the *Mohawk*.

Captain Manly would fain have played a game at long bowls with his enemy, but he was afraid if he did so, it would impede the speed of his ship so much, as to materially endanger their chance of escape.

A thirty-two pound ball now struck the mizzen boom of the *Mohawk*, causing her to yaw so much, that she presented her full broadside to the seventy-four; a circumstance that no sooner took place, than, placing his trumpet to his mouth, Captain Manly bawled out:

"Give it to them, my lads! let us have one round with him before we take to the boats; point carefully, watch the roll of the sea, then show him what Yankee gunners can do."

Giving a stentorian hurra, the men applied their matches, and in another moment the eighteen barkers of the *Mohawk* opened on their enemy with such telling effect, that, had their ship been in good sailing trim, the Americans might have escaped with ease.

Sweeping heavily from the wind, the Englishman now presented his whole broadside to his opponent; while his three tiers of 32 pounders hurled forth their terrible and death-dealing contents.

"Out with the boats, men, lively; lively," cried Captain Manly, as the fearful execution of the last broadside now showed him the useless waste of life it would occasion by prolonging the fight with their gigantic opponent. "Out with them, and tumble in as quickly as possible; Monroe, see that the wounded are properly distributed among the boats, and that they are made as comfortable as possible; Mr. Drew," continued he, turning to the second lieutenant, "you go and lay an eight-minute train of powder to the magazine; we shall be all clear of the ship, by the time it burns up."

"Aye, aye, sir," answered Drew, hastening below to execute his perilous task.

About five minutes after the wounded had been lowered into the boats, and all hands in, Lieutenant Monroe called out—

"Captain Manly, we are all ready for starting; endanger not yourself by stopping too long aboard."

"Aye, aye, Monroe," replied the captain; "in a minute. Well," he added, as Lieutenant Drew now appeared, "is all right?"

"Yes, sir," answered Drew; "we shall barely have time to get a respectable distance, before the explosion takes place."

As Captain Manly, who was the last to leave the deck, placed his foot on the ladder to descend into the boat, Lieutenant Monroe suddenly exclaimed—

"Midshipman Weston is on board yet; I saw him go below about five minutes ago, and he has not come on deck since."

As the captain was about to spring on deck again, our hero appeared, dragging after him the traitor, Broom; and as he passed the guilty wretch down into the boat, he said—

"A shot from the enemy has sent the other one to his last account."

"It will save the Court Martial a job," exclaimed Captain Manly.

The boats now pulled off; and they had got but a little more than two hundred years, before "There came a burst of thunder sound," then a wide, lurid sheet of flame shot upwards, high and bright; the sky was darkened for a minute or two with the immense quantity of uphurled fragments; and, in another minute, all that remained of one of the tautest little frigates that ever ploughed old Neptune's broad domains, was a mass of charred and blackened fragments.

The Sinking of the
Confederate Steamer *Alabama*

by JOHN McINTOSH KELL

Soon after our arrival at Cherbourg an officer was sent on shore to ask permission of the port admiral to land our prisoners of the two captured ships. This being obtained without trouble or delay, Captain Semmes went on shore to see to the docking of the ship for repairs. Cherbourg being a naval station and the dock belonging to the government, permission had to be obtained of the emperor before we could do anything. The port admiral told us "we had better have gone into Havre, as the government might not give permission for repairs to a belligerent ship." The emperor was absent from Paris at some watering place on the coast, and would not return for some days. Here was an impediment to our plans which gave us time for thought, and the result of such thought was the unfortunate combat between the *Alabama* and the *Kearsarge*. The latter ship was lying at Flushing when we entered Cherbourg. Two or three days after our arrival she steamed into the harbor, sent a boat on shore to communicate, steamed outside and stationed off the breakwater. While Captain Semmes had not singled her out as an antagonist, and would never have done so had he known her to be chain-clad (an armored ship), he had about this time made up his mind that he would cease fleeing before the foe, and meet an equal in battle when the opportunity presented itself. Our cause was weakening daily, and our ship so disabled it really seemed to us our work was almost done! We might end her career gloriously by being victorious in battle, and defeat against an equal foe we would never have allowed ourselves to anticipate.

As soon as the *Kearsarge* came into the harbor Captain Semmes sent for me to come to his cabin, and abruptly said to me: "Kell, I am going out to fight the *Kearsarge*. What do you think of it?" We then quietly talked it all over. We discussed the batteries, especially the *Kearsarge's* advantage in 11-inch guns. I reminded him of our defective powder, how our long cruise had deteriorated everything, as proven in our target-practice off the coast of Brazil on the ship *Rockingham*, when certainly every third shot was a failure even to explode. I saw his mind was fully made up, so I simply stated these facts for myself. I had always felt ready for a fight, and I also knew that the brave young officers of the ship would not object, and the men would be not only willing, but anxious, to meet the enemy! To all outward seeming the disparity was not great between the two ships, barring the unknown (because concealed) chain armor. The *Kearsarge* communicated with the authorities to request that our prisoners be turned over to them. Captain Semmes made an objection to her increasing her crew. He addressed our agent, Mr. Bonfils, a communication requesting him to inform Captain Winslow, through the United States Consul, that "if he would wait till the *Alabama* could coal ship he would give him battle." We began to coal and at the same time to make preparation for battle. We overhauled the magazine and shell rooms, gun equipments, etc.

The *Kearsarge* was really in the fullest sense of the word a man-of-war, stanch and well built; the *Alabama* was made for flight and speed and was much more lightly constructed than her chosen antagonist. The *Alabama* had one more gun, but the *Kearsarge* carried more metal at a broadside. The seven guns of the *Kearsarge* were two 11-inch Dahlgrens, four 32-pounders, and one rifled 28-pounder. The *Alabama's* eight guns were six 32-pounders, one 8-inch and one rifled 100-pounder. The crew of the *Alabama* all told was 149 men, while that of the *Kearsarge* was 162 men. By Saturday night, June 18th, our preparations were completed. Captain Semmes notified the admiral of the port that he would be ready to go out and meet the *Kearsarge* the following morning. Early Sunday morning the admiral sent an officer to say to us that "the ironclad Frigate *Couronne* would accompany us to protect the neutrality of French waters."

Many offered to join us. William C. Whittle, Jr., Grimball, and others; also George Sinclair and Adolphe Marmelstein, officers of the *Tuscaloosa*, and others who were in Paris came down to join us, but the French authorities objected, and they were not allowed to do so. Between 9 and 10 o'clock, June 19th, everything being in readiness, we got under way and proceeded to sea. We took the western entrance of the harbor. The *Couronne* accompanied us, also some French pilot-boats and an English steam yacht, the *Deerhound*, owned by a rich Englishman (as we afterward learned), who, with his wife and children, was enjoying life and leisure in his pleasure yacht. The walls and fortifications of the harbor, the heights above the town, the buildings, everything that looked seaward, was crowded with people. About seven miles from the land the *Kearsarge* was quietly awaiting our arrival.

Officers in uniforms, men at their best, Captain Semmes ordered them sent aft, and mounting a gun-carriage made them a brief address: "Officers and seamen of the *Alabama:* You have at length another opportunity to meet the enemy, the first that has presented to you since you sank the *Hatteras*. In the meantime you have been all over the world, and it is not too much to say that you have destroyed and driven for protection under neutral flags one-half of the enemy's commerce, which at the beginning of the war covered every sea. This is an achievement of which you may well be proud, and a grateful country will not be unmindful of it. The name of your ship has become a household word wherever civilization extends. Shall that name be tarnished by defeat? [An outburst of Never! Never!] The thing is impossible. Remember that you are in the English Channel, the theatre of so much of the naval glory of our race. The eyes of all Europe are at this moment upon you! The flag that floats over you is that of a young Republic that bids defiance to her enemies, whenever and wherever found! Show the world that you know how to uphold it. Go to your quarters!"

We now prepared our guns to engage the enemy on our starboard side. When within a mile and a-quarter he wheeled, presenting his starboard battery to us. We opened on him with solid shot, to which he soon replied, and the action became active. To keep our respective broadsides bearing we were obliged to fight in a circle around a common center, preserving a distance of three quarters of a mile. When within distance of shell range we opened on him with shell. The spanker gaff was shot away and our ensign came down. We replaced it immediately at the mizzen masthead. The firing now became very hot and heavy. Captain Semmes, who was watching the battle from the horse block, called out to me, "Mr. Kell, our shell strike the enemy's side, doing little damage, and fall off in the water; try solid shot." From this time we alternated shot and shell. The battle lasted an hour and ten minutes. Captain Semmes said to me at this time (seeing the great apertures made in the side of the ship from their 11-inch shell, and the water rushing in rapidly), "Mr. Kell, as soon as our head points to the French coast in our circuit of action, shift your guns to port and make all sail for the coast." This evolution was beautifully performed; righting the helm, hauling aft the fore-trysail sheet, and pivoting to port, the action continuing all the time without cessation,—but it was useless, nothing could avail us. Before doing this, and pivoting the gun, it became necessary to clear the deck of parts of the dead bodies that had been torn to pieces by the 11-inch shells of the enemy. The captain of our 8-inch gun and most of the gun's crew were killed. It became necessary to take the crew from young Anderson's gun to make up the vacancies, which I did, and placed him in command. Though a mere youth, he managed it like an old veteran. Going to the hatchway, I called out to Brooks (one of our efficient engineers) to give the ship more steam, or we would be whipped. He replied she "had every inch of steam that was safe to carry without being blown up!" Young Matt O'Brien, assistant engineer, called out, "Let her have the steam; we had better blow her to hell than to let the Yankees whip us!" The chief engineer now came on deck and reported "the furnace fires put out," whereupon Captain Semmes ordered me to go below and "see how long the ship could float." I did so, and returning said, "Perhaps ten minutes." "Then, sir," said Captain Semmes, "cease firing, shorten sail, and haul down the colors. It will never do in this nineteenth century for us to go down and the decks covered with our gallant wounded." This order was promptly executed, after which the *Kearsarge* deliberately fired into us five shots! In Captain Winslow's report to the Secretary of the Navy he admits this, saying, "Uncertain whether Captain Semmes was not making some ruse, the *Kearsarge* was stopped."

Was this a time,—when disaster, defeat and death looked us in the face,—for a ship to use a ruse, a Yankee trick? I ordered the men to "stand to their quarters," and they did it heroically; not even flinching, they stood every man to his post. As soon as we got the first of these shot I told the quartermaster to show the white flag from the stern. It was done. Captain Semmes said to me, "Dispatch an officer to the *Kearsarge* and ask that they send boats to save our wounded—ours are disabled." Our little dingey was not injured, so I sent Master's Mate Fulham with the request. No boats coming, I had one of our quarter boats (the least damaged one) lowered and had the wounded put in her. Dr. Galt came on deck at this time, and was put in charge of her, with orders to take the wounded to the *Kearsarge*. They shoved off in time to save the wounded. When I went below to inspect the sight was appalling! Assistant Surgeon Llewellyn was at his post, but the table and the patient on it had been swept away from him by an 11-inch shell, which made an aperture that was fast filling with water. This was the last time I saw Dr. Llewellyn in life. As I passed the deck to go down below a stalwart seaman with death's signet on his brow called to me. For an instant I stood beside him. He caught my hand and kissed it with such reverence and loyalty,—the look, the act, it lingers in my memory still! I reached the deck and gave the order for "every man to save himself, to jump overboard with a spar, an oar, or a grating, and get out of the vortex of the sinking ship."

As soon as all were overboard but Captain Semmes and I, his steward, Bartelli, and two of the men—the sailmaker, Alcott, and Michael Mars—we began to strip off all superfluous clothing for our battle with the waves for our lives. Poor, faithful-hearted Bartelli, we did not know he could not swim, or he might have been sent to shore—he was drowned. The men disrobed us, I to my shirt and drawers, but Captain Semmes kept on his heavy pants and vest. We together gave our swords to the briny deep and the ship we loved so well! The sad farewell look at the ship would have wrung the stoutest heart! The dead were lying on her decks, the surging, roaring waters rising through the death-wound in her side. The ship agonizing like a living thing and going down in her brave beauty, settling lower and lower, she sank fathoms deep— lost to all save love, and fame, and memory!

After undressing with the assistance of our men we plunged into the sea. It was a mass of living heads, striving, struggling, battling for life. On the wild waste of waters there came no boats, at first, from the *Kearsarge* to our rescue. Had victory struck them dumb, or helpless—or had it frozen the milk of human kindness in their veins? The water was like ice, and after the excitement of battle it seemed doubly cold. I saw a float of empty shell boxes near me, and called out to one of the men (an expert swimmer) to examine the float. He said: "It is the doctor, sir, and he is dead." Poor Llewellyn! Almost within sight of home, the air blowing across the channel from it into the dead face that had given up the struggle for life and liberty. I felt my strength giving out, but strange to say I never thought of giving up, though the white caps were breaking wildly over my head and the sea foam from the billows blinding my eyes. Midshipman Maffitt swam to my side and said, "Mr. Kell, you are so exhausted, take this life-preserver" (endeavoring to disengage it). I refused, seeing in his own pallid young face that heroism had risen superior to self or bodily suffering! But "what can a man do more than give his life for his friend?" The next thing that I remember, a voice called out, "Here's our first lieutenant," and I was pulled into a boat, in the stern sheets of which lay Captain Semmes as if dead. He had received a slight wound in the hand, which with the struggle in the water had exhausted his strength, long worn by sleeplessness, anxiety and fatigue. There were several of our crew in the boat. In a few moments we were alongside a steam yacht, which received us on her deck, and we learned it was the *Deerhound,* owned by an English gentleman, Mr. John Lancaster, who used it for the pleasure of himself and family, who were with him at this time, his sons having preferred going out with him to witness the fight to going to church with their mother, as he afterwards told us.

In looking about us I saw two French pilot boats rescuing the crew, and finally two boats from the *Kearsarge.* I was much surprised to find Mr. Fulham on the *Deerhound,* as I had dispatched him in the little dingey to ask the *Kearsarge* for boats to save our wounded. Mr. Fulham told me that "our shot had torn the casing from the chain armor of the *Keararge,* indenting the chain in many places." This now explained Captain Semmes' observation to me during the battle—"our shell strike the enemy's side and fall into the water." Had we been in possession of this knowledge the unequal battle between the *Alabama* and the *Kearsarge* would never have been fought, and the gallant little *Alabama* have been lost by an error. She fought valiantly as long as there was a plank to stand upon. History has failed to explain, unless there were secret orders forbidding it, why the *Kearsarge* did not steam into the midst of the fallen foe and generously save life! The *Kearsarge* fought the battle beautifully, but she tarnished her glory when she fired on a fallen foe and made no immediate effort to save brave living men from watery graves! Both heroic commanders are now gone—before the great tribunal where "the deeds done in the body", are to be accounted for but history is history and truth is truth!

Mr. Lancaster came to Captain Semmes and said: "I think every man is saved, where shall I land you?" He replied, "I am under English colors; the sooner you land me on English soil the better." The little yacht, under a press of steam, moved away for Southampton. Our loss was nine killed, twenty-one wounded and ten drowned. That afternoon, the 19th of June, we were landed in Southampton and received with every demonstration of kindness and sympathy.

The Battle of Manila Bay

by GEORGE DEWEY

With the coming of broad daylight we finally sighted the Spanish vessels formed in an irregular crescent in front of Cavite. The *Olympia* headed toward them, and in answer to her signal to close up, the distance between our ships was reduced to two hundred yards. The western flank of the Spanish squadron was protected by Cavite peninsula and the Sangley Point battery, while its eastern flank rested in the shoal water off Las Pinas.

The Spanish line of battle was formed by the *Reina Cristina* (flag), *Castilla, Don Juan de Austria, Don Antonio de Ulloa, Isla de Luzón, Isla de Cuba,* and *Marqués del Duero.*

The *Velasco* and *Lezo* were on the other (southern) side of Cavite point, and it is claimed by the Spaniards that they took no part in the action. Some of the vessels in the Spanish battle-line were under way, and others were moored so as to bring their broadside batteries to bear to the best advantage. The *Castilla* was protected by heavy iron lighters filled with stone.

Before me now was the object for which we had made our arduous preparations, and which, indeed, must ever be the supreme test of a naval officer's career. I felt confident of the outcome, though I had no thought that victory would be won at so slight a cost to our side. Confidence was expressed in the very precision with which the dun, war-colored hulls of the squadron followed in column behind the flag-ship, keeping their distance excellently. All the guns were pointed constantly at the enemy, while the men were at their stations waiting the word. There was no break in the monotone of the engines save the mechanical voice of the leadsman or an occasional low-toned command by the quartermaster at the conn, or the roar of a Spanish shell. The Manila batteries continued their inaccurate fire, to which we paid no attention.

The misty haze of the tropical dawn had hardly risen when at 5.15, at long range, the Cavite forts and Spanish squadron opened fire. Our course was not one leading directly toward the enemy, but a converging one, keeping him on our starboard bow. Our speed was eight knots and our converging course and ever-varying position must have confused the Spanish gunners. My assumption that the Spanish fire would be hasty and inaccurate proved correct.

So far as I could see, none of our ships was suffering any damage, while, in view of my limited ammunition supply, it was my plan not to open fire until we were within effective range, and then to fire as rapidly as possible with all of our guns.

At 5.40, when we were within a distance of 5,000 yards (two and one-half miles), I turned to Captain Gridley and said:

"You may fire when you are ready, Gridley."

While I remained on the bridge with Lamberton, Brumby, and Stickney, Gridley took his station in the conning-tower and gave the order to the battery. The very first gun to speak was an 8-inch from the forward turret of the *Olympia*, and this was the signal for all the other ships to join the action.

At about the time that the Spanish ships were first sighted, 5.06, two submarine mines were exploded between our squadron and Cavite, some two miles ahead of our column. On account of the distance, I remarked to Lamberton:

"Evidently the Spaniards are already rattled."

However, they explained afterward that the premature explosions were due to a desire to clear a space in which their ships might manoeuvre.

At one time a torpedo-launch made an attempt to reach the *Olympia*, but she was sunk by the guns of the secondary battery and went down bow first, and another yellow-colored launch flying the Spanish colors ran out, heading for the *Olympia*, but after being disabled she was beached to prevent her sinking.

When the flag-ship neared the five-fathom curve off Cavite she turned to the westward, bringing her port batteries to bear on the enemy, and, followed by the squadron, passed along the Spanish line until north of and only some fifteen hundred yards distant from the Sangley Point battery, when she again turned and headed back to the eastward, thus giving the squadron an opportunity to use their port and starboard batteries alternately and to cover with their fire all the Spanish ships, as well as the Cavite and Sangley Point batteries. While I was regulating the course of the squadron, Lieutenant Calkins was verifying our position by crossbearing and by the lead.

Three runs were thus made from the eastward and two from the westward, the length of each run averaging two miles and the ships being turned each time with port helm. Calkins found that there was in reality deeper water than shown on the chart, and when he reported the fact to me, inasmuch as my object was to get as near as possible to the enemy without grounding our own vessels, the fifth run past the Spaniards was farther inshore than any preceding run. At the nearest point to the enemy our range was only two thousand yards.

There had been no cessation in the rapidity of fire maintained by our whole squadron, and the effect of its concentration, owing to the fact that our ships were kept so close together, was smothering, particularly upon the two largest ships, the *Reina Cristina* and *Castilla*. The *Don Juan de Austria* first and then the *Reina Cristina* made brave and desperate attempts to charge the *Olympia*, but becoming the target for all our batteries they turned and ran back. In this sortie the *Reina Cristina* was raked by an 8-inch shell, which is said to have put out of action some twenty men and to have completely destroyed her steering-gear. Another shell in her forecastle killed or wounded all the members of the crews of four rapid-fire guns; another set fire to her after orlop; another killed or disabled nine men on her poop; another carried away her mizzen-mast, bringing down the ensign and the admiral's flag, both of which were replaced; another exploded in the after ammunition-room; and still another exploded in the sick-bay, which was already filled with wounded.

When she was raised from her muddy bed, five years later, eighty skeletons were found in the sick-bay and fifteen shot holes in the hull; while the many hits mentioned in Admiral Montojo's report, and his harrowing description of the shambles that his flag-ship had become when he was finally obliged to leave her, shows what execution was done to her upper works. Her loss was one hundred and fifty killed and ninety wounded, seven of these being officers. Among the killed was her valiant captain, Don Luis Cadarso, who, already wounded, finally met his death while bravely directing the rescue of his men from the burning and sinking vessel.

Though in the early part of the action our firing was not what I should have liked it to be, it soon steadied down, and by the time the *Reina Cristina* steamed toward us it was satisfactorily accurate. The *Castilla* fared little better than the *Reina Cristina*. All except one of her guns was disabled, she was set on fire by our shells, and finally abandoned by her crew after they had sustained a loss of twenty-three killed and eighty wounded. The *Don Juan de Austria* was badly damaged and on fire, the *Isla de Luzón* had three guns dismounted, and the *Marqués del Duero* was also in a bad way. Admiral Montojo, finding his flag-ship no longer manageable, half her people dead or wounded, her guns useless and the ship on fire, gave the order to abandon and sink her, and transferred his flag to the *Isla de Cuba* shortly after even o'clock.

Victory was already ours, though we did not know it. Owing to the smoke over the Spanish squadron there were no visible signs of the execution wrought by our guns when we started upon our fifth run past the enemy. We were keeping up our rapid fire, and the flag-ship was opposite the centre of the Spanish line, when, at 7.35, the captain of the *Olympia* made a report to me which was as startling as it was unexpected. This was to the effect that on board the *Olympia* there remained only fifteen rounds per gun for the 5-inch battery.

It was a most anxious moment for me. So far as I could see, the Spanish squadron was as intact as ours. I had reason to believe that their supply of ammunition was as ample as ours was limited.

Therefore, I decided to withdraw temporarily from action for a redistribution of ammunition if necessary. For I knew that fifteen rounds of 5-inch ammunition could be shot away in five minutes. But even as we were steaming out of range the distress of the Spanish ships became evident. Some of them were perceived to be on fire and others were seeking protection behind Cavite Point. The *Don Antonio de Ulloa*, however, still retained her position at Sangly Point, where she had been moored. Moreover, the Spanish fire, with the exception of the Manila batteries, to which we had paid little attention, had ceased entirely. It was clear that we did not need a very large supply of ammunition to finish our morning's task; and happily it was found that the report about the *Olympia's* 5-inch ammunition had been incorrectly transmitted. It was that fifteen rounds had been fired per gun, not that only fifteen rounds remained.

Feeling confident of the outcome, I now signalled that the crews, who had had only a cup of coffee at 4 A.M., should have their breakfast. The public at home, on account of this signal, to which was attributed a nonchalance that had never occurred to me, reasoned that breakfast was the real reason for our withdrawing from action. Meanwhile, I improved the opportunity to have the commanding officers report on board the flag-ship.

There had been such a heavy flight of shells over us that each captain, when he arrived, was convinced that no other ship had had such good luck as his own in being missed by the enemy's fire, and expected the others to have both casualties and damages to their ships to report. But fortune was as pronouncedly in our favor at Manila as it was later at Santiago. To my gratification not a single life had been lost, and considering that we would rather measure the importance of an action by the scale of its conduct than by the number of casualties we were immensely happy. The concentration of our fire immediately we were within telling range had given us an early advantage in demoralizing the enemy, which has ever been the prime factor in naval battles. In the War of 1812 the losses of the *Constitution* were slight when she overwhelmed the *Guerrière* and in the Civil War the losses of the *Kearsarge* were slight when she made a shambles of the *Alabama*. On the *Baltimore* two officers (Lieutenant F. W. Kellogg and Ensign N. E. Irwin) and six men were slightly wounded. None of our ships had been seriously hit, and every one was still ready for immediate action.

In detail the injuries which we had received from the Spanish fire were as follows:

The *Olympia* was hulled five times and her rigging was cut in several places. One six-pound projectile struck immediately under the position where I was standing. The *Baltimore* was hit five times. The projectile which wounded two officers and six men pursued a most erratic course. It entered the ship's side forward of the starboard gangway, and just above the line of the main deck, passed through the hammock-netting, down through the deck planks and steel deck, bending the deck beam in a ward-room state-room, thence upward through the after engine-room coaming, over against the cylinder of a 6-inch gun, disabling the gun, struck and exploded a box of three-pounder ammunition, hit an iron ladder, and finally, spent, dropped on deck. The *Boston* had four unimportant hits, one causing a fire which was soon extinguished, and the *Petrel* was struck once.

At 11.16 A.M. we stood in to complete our work. There remained to oppose us, however, only the batteries and the gallant little *Ulloa*. Both opened fire as we advanced. But the contest was too unequal to last more than a few minutes.

Soon the *Ulloa*, under our concentrated fire, went down valiantly with her colors flying.

The battery at Sangley Point was well served, and several times reopened fire before being finally silenced. Had this battery possessed its four other 6-inch guns which Admiral Montojo had found uselessly lying on the beach at Subig, our ships would have had many more casualties to report. Happily for us, the guns of this battery had been so mounted that they could be laid only for objects beyond the range of two thousand yards. As the course of our ships led each time within this range, the shots passed over and beyond them. Evidently the artillerists, who had so constructed their carriages that the muzzles of the guns took against the sill of the embrasure for any range under two thousand yards, thought it out of the question that an enemy would venture within this distance.

The *Concord* was sent to destroy a large transport, the *Mindanao*, which had been beached near Bacoor, and the *Petrel*, whose light draught would permit her to move in shallower water than the other vessels of the squadron, was sent into the harbor of Cavite to destroy any ships that had taken refuge there. The *Mindanao* was set on fire and her valuable cargo destroyed. Meanwhile, the *Petrel* gallantly performed her duty, and after a few shots from her 6-inch guns the Spanish flag on the government buildings was hauled down and a white flag hoisted. Admiral Montojo had been wounded, and had taken refuge on shore with his remaining officers and men; his loss was three hundred and eighty-one of his officers and crew, and there was no possibility of further resistance.

At 12.30 the *Petrel* signalled the fact of the surrender, and the firing ceased. But the Spanish vessels were not yet fully destroyed. Therefore, the executive officer of the *Petrel*, Lieutenant E. M. Hughes, with a whale-boat and a crew of only seven men, boarded and set fire to the *Don Juan de Austria*, *Isla de Cuba*, *Isla de Luzón*, *General Lezo*, *Coreo*, and *Marqués del Duero*, all of which had been abandoned in shallow water and left scuttled by their deserting crews. This was a courageous undertaking, as these vessels were supposed to have been left with trains to their magazines and were not far from the shore, where there were hundreds of Spanish soldiers and sailors, all armed and greatly excited. The *Manila*, an armed transport, which was found uninjured after having been beached by the Spaniards, was therefore spared. Two days later she was easily floated, and for many years did good service as a gun-boat. The little *Petrel* continued her work until 5.20 P.M., when she rejoined the squadron, towing a long string of tugs and launches, to be greeted by volleys of cheers from every ship.

The order to capture or destroy the Spanish squadron had been executed to the letter. Not one of its fighting-vessels remained afloat. That night I wrote in my diary: "Reached Manila at daylight. Immediately engaged the Spanish ships and batteries at Cavite. Destroyed eight of the former, including the *Reina Cristina* and *Castilla*. Anchored at noon off Manila."

As soon as we had sunk the *Ulloa* and silenced the batteries at Sangley

Point, the *Olympia*, followed by the *Baltimore* and *Raleigh*, while the *Concord* and *Petrel* were carrying out their orders, started for the anchorage off the city. The Manila batteries, which had kept up such a persistent though impotent firing all the early part of the day, were now silent and made no attempt to reopen as our ships approached the city.

The Battle of Jutland

by JACQUES MORDAL, translated by LEN ORTZEN

The Grand Fleet was alerted, and at half past nine that evening Admiral Jellicoe sailed from Scapa Flow in the *Iron Duke*, with sixteen battleships and three battle-cruisers. Vice-Admiral Sir D. Beatty, in the *Lion*, put to sea from Rosyth with six battle-cruisers and four fast battleships. Six more battleships left Invergordon under the command of Vice-Admiral Sir Martyn Jerram to join Jellicoe at sea. All made course to be off the entrance to the Skagerrak by morning. At 14.00 hours Beatty was to reach the position 56 degrees 40 North, 5 degrees East, and if the enemy had not been sighted was then to turn towards Jellicoe, who would be about seventy miles to the north. The twenty-six battleships and the nine battle-cruisers would then together extend their reconnaissance towards the Horns Reef, off the west coast of Jutland, which could be said to mark the northern limit of the German Bight.

Beatty's force* reached the position and, not having sighted the enemy, turned north; and everyone began to think another sally had been made without result. After all, the mysterious message "31 Gg 2490" might be no more than a routine signal of no interest, especially as a misleading telegram from the Admiralty had informed Jellicoe that directional wireless signals placed the German fleet flagship, the *Friedrich der Grosse*, in the Jade river. But for all the Intelligence reports, the Admiralty was not aware of Scheer's latest ruse—when his flag-ship put to sea, he exchanged radio recognition signals with a shore transmitting station.

In fact, the mysterious message was a signal to all units of the German Fleet that Top Secret Order No. 2490 was to be put into effect on May 31st. This meant a reconnaissance in force towards the Norwegian coast by Admiral Hipper's battle group,** with the main body of the High Sea Fleet in support some fifty miles to the south. Scheer was hoping that Hipper's presence would

---

*Beatty had under his command the battle-cruisers *Lion*, *Princess Royal*, *Queen Mary*, *Tiger*, *New Zealand*, and *Indefatigable;* the Fifth Battle Squadron (Rear-Admiral Evan-Thomas) consisting of the battleships *Barham*, *Valiant*, *Warspite*, and *Malaya;* the First Light Cruiser Squadron (Commodore Alexander Sinclair), the Second (Commodore Goodenough), and the Third (Commodore Napier); and four destroyer flotillas.

**Hipper had under his command the five battle-cruisers *Lützow* (his flagship), *Derfflinger*, *Moltke*, *Seydlitz*, and *Von der Tann;* the four light cruisers *Frankfurt*, *Wiesbaden*, *Pillau*, and *Elbing*, commanded by Rear-Admiral Boedicker; and three destroyer flotillas under Commodore Heinrich in the *Regensburg*.

provoke a hurried sally by various elements of the Grand Fleet, and that he would be able to snap up some before being confronted by the whole force. He was far from suspecting that the entire Grand Fleet had put to sea four to five hours before he had himself.

Jellicoe's appreciation of the enemy intentions was correct, and with a little luck his dispositions would have proved perfect. Hipper had almost reached the same latitude as Beatty by 14.00 hours, but was to the east of him and below the horizon. If Hipper continued on course, in compliance with his orders, he would be caught between two fires; and Scheer, speeding towards the sound of the guns, would come up against the combined Fleet—which was not at all what he wanted.

But luck brought an old Danish tramp into the picture. The *N.J. Fjord* was sailing on a course that took her between the forces of Beatty and Hipper, at about equal distance from both. She was sighted by light cruisers on the wing of each force, which were out of sight of each other. The *Galatea*, on the eastern wing of the light cruiser screen, stood on to the south-east to examine her. Simultaneously, the *Elbing*, on the western wing of the German scouting force, made towards her. The Danish ship was thus the unwitting cause of the *Elbing* and the *Galatea* sighting each other and exchanging salvos, at the same time as their aerials began to crackle with the all-important news. The *Galatea* had opened fire first but the *Elbing* was on target the quicker, though the first shell that hit the British cruiser failed to explode. A sailor went to throw it overside. "Hell—the blasted thing's hot!" he exclaimed, snatching his hand away.

Such was the opening shot in the greatest naval battle the world has ever known.

It can be seen that the new means of reconnaissance adopted by either side—under water and by air—had not produced any results. The U-boats sent to patrol off the Scottish naval bases had only sent back fragmentary or incomplete reports; the Zeppelins had provided no information at all. Beatty had sent off one of the seaplanes carried in the *Engadine*, as soon as the *Galatea* reported sighting the enemy. The seaplane was forced down by engine trouble, but took off again, found Hipper's battle-cruisers and reported their position and course. Unfortunately, no one picked up the message. So that each commander-in-chief had to rely on what he himself could see and what his subordinates reported to him as well as possible—which was not very well, on the whole. In fact, the entire action took place in considerable confusion.

To begin with, the commander of the light cruiser squadron to which the *Galatea* belonged, Commodore Sinclair, turned away to the north in the hope of drawing the enemy after him and so towards Beatty, whose battle-cruisers would then be able to cut Hipper's line of retreat; but because Commodore Sinclair had not continued towards the enemy, the information he had of Hipper's strength and disposition was far from complete. While on the German side, the signals made by the *Elbing* were badly interpreted and gave the impression that twenty-four or twenty-six battleships had been sighted!

Nevertheless, the courses of the rival forces were swiftly converging. But the signals made by Beatty's flagship, the *Lion*, had not been at once understood by the Fifth Battle Squadron (Rear-Admiral Evan-Thomas), which continued for about ten minutes on a course that was taking it away from the battle-cruisers. And as Evan-Thomas's big ships needed more time to get up to their maximum speed—which was only twenty-four knots—they eventually found themselves about ten miles astern. Although Evan-Thomas managed to decrease the distance, he was still six miles astern and to port of the *Lion* when the action began, a little after three-thirty.

Beatty was then trying to pass astern of the German battle-cruisers and cut off their line of retreat; but Hipper was aware of the danger, recalled his light cruisers, and did a right-about turn to bring his force on a south-easterly course almost parallel to that of the British.

The sky is never very clear in the North Sea; and the billows of smoke from the destroyers as they circled the big ships did not help matters. The gun-control officers were not having an easy time on either side.

At 15.48 the *Lützow* (Hipper's flagship) opened fire on the *Lion* at 18,000 yards. Twenty seconds passed before the British battle-cruisers replied, and then they were more than a thousand yards over target. The Germans were easily the first to find their mark. After three minutes they had made eight hits on the *Lion*, the *Tiger*, and the *Princess Royal*, whereas it was seven minutes before the British registered a hit, when the *Queen Mary* put one of the *Seydlitz*'s gun-turrets out of action. In fact, it almost caused the end of the *Seydlitz;* the ammunition caught fire and, as at the battle of the Dogger Bank, the ship was saved only through her magazines being quickly flooded.

Meanwhile, the range had decreased to 12,000 yards; but for five minutes the British did not register a single hit. Moreover, due to some confusion in the distribution of fire, no ship was engaging the third battle-cruiser in the German line, the *Derfflinger*. "They've jumped over us," the gun-control officer, Lieutenant-Commander von Hase, said over the communications system. This was welcome news to the gun-crews, who applied themselves to their task as though on manoeuvres. Eventually, at 15.58 hours, the *Queen Mary* turned her guns on the *Derfflinger* and soon had her under accurate fire.

At 16.00 hours, the *Lion* and the *Lützow* obtained a hit on each other; the German flagship was not seriously damaged, but the *Lion* had her midship turret knocked out, the shell exploding near the magazine. But for the presence of mind and devotion to duty of Major F. W. Harvey of the Royal Marines (awarded a posthumous V.C.) who, when mortally wounded, saw to the flooding of the magazine, the flagship would doubtless have been destroyed. However, in the next few minutes the *Lion* was hit six times and had to draw out of the battle-line; there were fires raging everywhere, and several compartments were taking water. The *Princess Royal* had her after-turret put out of action. And then, at 16.05 hours, three shells from the *Von der Tann* crashed into the *Indefatigable* and exploded in her magazines. Another salvo burst all round the ship, which blew up and quickly sank. A German destroyer picked up two of her crew; they were the only survivors from the ship's company of one thousand and seventeen.

Matters were going badly for Beatty. But Evan-Thomas was coming up with his four powerful battleships, which could be expected to turn the balance in favour of the British. For the past hour they had been steaming at high speed to reach the scene of action. The *Von der Tann* had barely time to rejoice over the sinking of the *Indefatigable* before a 15-inch shell crashed into her on the water-line; six hundred tons of water poured into her, but she managed to stay in the battle-line.

The British battleships were firing much more accurately than the battle-cruisers, except the *Queen Mary*. But owing to the poor quality, their 15-inch shells were bursting without penetrating the enemy's armour. Hipper thus escaped disaster. Not only that; the *Derfflinger* and the *Seydlitz* concentrated their fire on the *Queen Mary*, and an explosion rent her asunder. She went down so rapidly that the *Tiger*, astern of her, had to turn sharply to avoid running on to the sinking ship. Only eight of her crew of 1,274 were saved.

"There seems to be something wrong with our damned ships, Chatfield," remarked Beatty to his flag-captain. No comment was necessary. There was indeed something wrong with the battle-cruisers—their magazines were insufficiently protected against fire spreading from the gun-turrets. The Admiralty endeavoured to remedy this fault when new battle-cruisers were built, but twenty-five years later the *Hood* met with disaster through the same weakness.

There were still eight British ships against five Germans, and they had great superiority in fire-power. Hipper had plenty to worry about, yet he was expected to hold the enemy until the arrival of Scheer—whose ships were only just beginning to show their topmasts above the horizon. So the German destroyers dashed in to attack without even waiting for the order. The British destroyers counter-attacked and, with the big ships firing their secondary armament, there was a great, confused mêlée over the churned-up, shell-spattered sea, and many brave deeds were performed on both sides. Not one torpedo struck, but the British destroyers under Commander Bingham in the *Nestor* sank two of the German destroyers. Then the *Nomad* and the *Nestor* herself were mortally hit, the latter by the concentrated fire of the *Regensburg*, the German flotilla-leader, and all the battle-cruisers. A second wave of British destroyers was about to go in, when the *Lion* signalled their recall and turned to run north.

It so happened that Commodore Goodenough, commanding the Second Light Cruiser Squadron in the *Southampton*, had been far enough south to sight the enemy battleships—whose presence at sea was still unknown to the British—and had made a signal direct to Beatty. The *Southampton* stood on to the south, followed by the rest of the squadron, until within 12,000 yards of the German battleships. They had not opened fire on the British squadron, which was well within their range, as the cruisers were difficult to identify while in line ahead. But when they began to wheel round, having seen that Scheer was out in full force, the shells started to fall all around them and they needed all their speed and dodging tactics to escape the hail of murderous steel.

The first part of the battle was now over, and Beatty's idea was to draw Scheer's battleships towards Jellicoe, whose presence was still unknown to the Germans. That was the reason for him suddenly turning to run north, a move which had seemed surprising at first, and which was not accomplished without a further exchange of broadsides with the German battle-cruisers as the rival forces passed on opposite courses. Hipper was heading south towards Scheer as Beatty steered north towards Jellicoe. Between the two, Even-Thomas continued on his easterly course, covering Beatty's withdrawal with his big ships until receiving the order to follow the movement. His four battleships then had to wheel in succession round the same point—a dangerous moment, for the German line was drawing ever nearer to it and could concentrate fire upon it. Evan-Thomas's squadron thus came under the combined force of Hipper's battle-cruisers and of Scheer's leading battleships. The *Barham* was the first to be hit, sustaining considerable casualties; and then the *Malaya* was straddled almost continuously for a good half-hour, being twice hit below the water-line. The enemy did not escape hurt, though; the *Lützow* and the *Derfflinger* were hit, and the *Seydlitz* in particular was damaged still further, while hits were also registered on two of the leading battleships, the *Grosser Kurfürst* and the *Markgraf*.

The time had come for the opposing commanders-in-chief to take control of the battle, after this prologue directed by their subordinates.

Scheer, in the High Sea Fleet flagship *Friedrich der Grosse*, was highly satisfied. He had no idea that the Grand Fleet was at sea, and certainly not that it was so near, but thought he had a portion of it at his mercy. Everything appeared to be going according to plan, and the information he had just received of the presence of the Fifth Battle Squadron only increased his satisfaction. His own three battle squadrons made a splendid spectacle as they sailed majestically north-west. In the van went the Third Squadron commanded by Rear-Admiral Behncke, the seven battleships *König, Grosser Kurfürst, Kronprinz, Markgraf, Kaiser, Kaiserin,* and *Prinzregent Luitpold*. Then came the First Squadron led by Vice-Admiral Schmidt in the *Osfriesland,* astern of the Fleet flagship, and comprising the *Thüringen, Heligoland, Oldenburg, Posen, Rheinland, Nassau,* and *Westfalen*. Astern of them was the Second Squadron under Rear-Admiral Mauve—the five battleships *Hessen, Pommern, Hannover, Schlesien,* and *Schleswig-Holstein*. The battleships had a screen of four destroyer flotillas commanded by Kommodore Michelsen in the *Rostock*. The only annoying fact was that the slowness of Mauve's older-class ships prevented the Fleet from exceeding fifteen knots. To gain time, Scheer had swung dead north when the battle-cruisers were engaged; and then, confident in his superiority over this enemy force, had ordered a general pursuit.

Hipper, whose ships had been badly battered, was not so convinced as his commander-in-chief. He endeavored to communicate his impressions, but the signalling was ineffective; so he resigned himself to join in the pursuit, although for the moment he was still under heavy fire from Evan-Thomas's battleships, which had closed to 11,000 yards. The *Derfflinger* was in a bad way; while the *Seydlitz* was down by the bows and only keeping afloat because of her watertight compartments. Hipper was forced to stand off a little to the east.

Meanwhile, in the *Iron Duke*, Jellicoe had learnt very little since receiving the *Galatea*'s signal "enemy battle-cruisers sighted." He had shaped course for the Horns Reef, increasing speed from eighteen to twenty knots, his twenty-four battleships sailing in six columns; he was waiting for further reports before deploying in the requisite battle formation. Some of the most glorious episodes in British history were evoked by the names of his battleships, which were in three Battle Squadrons:

Second Battle Squadron: First Division (Vice-Admiral Sir Martyn Jerram), *King George V, Ajax, Centurion, Erin;* Second Division (Rear-Admiral Leveson), *Monarch, Conqueror, Thunderer.*

Fourth Battle Squadron: Third Division (Admiral Sir John Jellicoe), *Iron Duke, Royal Oak, Superb, Canada;* Fourth Division (Vice-Admiral Sir Doveton Sturdee), *Benbow, Bellerophon, Temeraire, Vanguard.*

First Battle Squadron: Sixth Division (Vice-Admiral Sir Cecil Bruney), *Marlborough, Revenge, Hercules, Agincourt;* Fifth Division (Rear-Admiral Gavot), *Colossus, Collingwood, Neptune, St. Vincent.*

The Fourth Light Cruiser Squadron was giving close protection against U-boat attacks. The First and Second Armoured Cruiser Squadrons formed a screen eight miles ahead of the Battle Fleet. While some miles to the east the Third Battle Squadron (the *Invincible, Inflexible,* and *Indomitable)* under Rear-Admiral Horace Hood was speeding at twenty-two knots to cut off the enemy's line of retreat into the Skagerrak; but when Jellicoe was informed that Beatty was in action he ordered Hood to make at full speed towards the sounds of gunfire.

Jellicoe was receiving little information from his squadron commanders to the south, with the exception of Goodenough; he was the only one during the whole of the battle to give importance to the mission of sending back reports. His signal from the *Southampton* at 16.38 hours that Scheer was in sight and proceeding north had caused great surprise in the *Iron Duke*. The news had been at once transmitted to the Admiralty, with the announcement that battle was imminent and the request for all dockyards and arsenals along the East Coast to be put on the alert.

The leading battleship of the starboard column, the *Marlborough*, first reported gun-flashes ahead—at 17.30 hours—and then that she had sighted the battle-cruisers. Jellicoe at last knew the exact position of the forces engaged; at the same time he became aware that he was eleven miles nearer the High Sea

Fleet than he had believed, and that consequently battle would be joined twenty minutes sooner than foreseen. It was high time to deploy his fleet for action.

After due consideration, the commander-in-chief ordered the fleet to deploy on the port (or easterly) column, on a course south-east by south. The manoeuvre was a vital one. It delayed making contact with the enemy, but it effectively barred him from entering the Skagerrak. Moreover, had Jellicoe followed his natural inclination to deploy to starboard—on the side towards the enemy—the ships on that wing would have found themselves at grave disadvantage.

It was then 18.16 hours, and Scheer was alarmed at the dangerous situation he was in, as he saw that interminable line of battleships stretching back into the mist that shrouded the end of it. . . . This was a case of the biter bit, and the High Sea Fleet would undoubtedly have been swallowed altogether were it not for "magnificent tactical skill and the perfect firing-discipline of its ships."

And now the great confused mêlée was beginning.

Hipper's battered ships had retired towards Scheer. The *Lützow*, hit for the twentieth time, was completely disabled; and Hipper was obliged to leave her and go aboard a destroyer. For the next three hours his battle-cruisers were commanded by Captain Hartog in the *Derfflinger*. But the Germans soon sank another enemy ship—the *Invincible*, which had her midship-turret shattered. A violent explosion followed, and the ship broke in two. Rear-Admiral Hood, who had just complimented the gunnery officer, and the crew of nearly a thousand went down with the ship. There were only five survivors.

At almost the same instant British light cruisers had attacked and disabled the *Wiesbaden*. Two armoured cruisers, the *Warrior* and the *Defence*, approached to finish her off, but came under heavy fire themselves from the *Derfflinger* and four of the most powerful battleships. The *Defence* blew up, and the *Warrior* only escaped complete destruction because the enemy guns were turned on the *Warspite*, one of the battleships of the Fifth Battle Squadron.

In spite of these isolated successes, Scheer's situation was becoming more dangerous with every minute that passed. Jellicoe was about to "cross the T" to the enemy, and in a more perfect manner than any squadron commander would have dared imagine. In a short while, heavy fire from his battleships was being concentrated on the German van, and only one or two of Scheer's ships were in a position to reply. Two hits were made on the *König*, which was soon listing badly; the *Markgraf* had her speed reduced by a hit in the engine-room. But visibility was worsening all the time. As Jellicoe wrote in his report, "the ships were firing on what they could see, when they could see."

Scheer took advantage to extricate his fleet from the dangerous situation. At 18.35 hours he made the signal for the *Gefechtskehrwendung nach Steuerbord*—an emergency retirement which had been practised dozens of times during manoeuvres. The German destroyers dashed out, fired their torpedoes "into the brown," and put up a smoke-screen while each battleship did a right-about turn, beginning with the rear ship and followed in succession by those ahead. The manoeuvre was executed with perfect precision, and by 18.45 the German battleships had pulled out of range of the British, who ceased firing. None had thought to warn Jellicoe of the enemy manoeuvre, and he had continued on his easterly course, thus increasing still more the distance between the opposing fleets; he might well have lost contact completely if the vigilant Commodore Goodenough had not headed towards the retreating enemy in spite of the great risk to his light cruisers. It was not until 18.50 that Jellicoe altered course to the south; while Scheer, who was then twelve miles to the south-west of the Grand Fleet, also altered course—but it brought him nearer the enemy. This was a most surprising manoeuvre; it not only placed his hard-pressed battle-cruisers in the van, within 10,000 yards of the enemy, but it also enabled Jellicoe to "cross the T" for a second time.

One should remember that the German commander-in-chief was not in the best position, in the centre of his formation. Nevertheless, his manoeuvre was difficult to explain, and as the Official History of the German Navy has it, "went against all the rules." Scheer soon realized the fact. At 19.15 he ordered another right-about turn, this time leaving his battle-cruisers to protect the withdrawal, making a signal which has remained as celebrated in the annals of the German Navy as the order to charge given to the Light Brigade in the annals of the British Army. "Order to the battle-cruisers to make straight for the enemy. Charge and ram!"

Make for the enemy . . . but the battle-scarred ships were already under his fire. The *Derfflinger* had her two after-turrets knocked out; while in the *Von der Tann* the control-turret had been hit and everyone killed, and only one gun was still firing. Jellicoe was closing the range, bearing to starboard in order to concentrate the fire from his most powerful ships. The retirement of the German battleships—more hurried on this occasion, though the manoeuvre was miraculously executed without accident—was again aided by the destroyers dashing out to fire their torpedoes, from 7,000 yards, and then making a smoke-screen. Six of the destroyers were put out of action, and a seventh was sunk by a direct hit. The torpedoes—twenty-eight in all—either ran clear or fell short of their mark; but the attack saved the High Sea Fleet.

The best means of evading a torpedo is for the ship being attacked to turn on to a course parallel with the running torpedo; but obviously the ship has a choice between turning towards or away from the attacker. Jellicoe had turned his battleships two points and then again two points—45 degrees in all, which a rapid calculation showed to be sufficient—but 45 degrees *away* from the enemy. He thus widened the distance from an adversary who was in his power. "Twenty-eight torpedoes, and the firm determination to run no risk with his fleet, had robbed Jellicoe of the chance of gaining a decisive victory."

Actually, Jellicoe was unaware that his enemy had turned about. Several of his subordinates had seen Scheer's manoeuvre, but none of them had thought it necessary to inform his commander-in-chief. In the circumstances, Jellicoe had reckoned that with Scheer remaining on course he would lose about 1,600 yards, which could easily be regained. But, Scheer having turned about, the opposing forces were moving away from each other to a speed of twenty knots; so that, when Jellicoe returned to his south-westerly course at 19.45, he had lost some 4,000 yards.

The Germans began to breathe again. The damage had been restricted to three battleships, the *Markgraf, Grosser Kurfürst,* and *König;* and they were still able to maintain their stations in the line, with all their guns serviceable. The last two, though, had shipped 800 and 1,600 tons of water respectively. Scheer had no thought of seeking to renew the action; instead, he shaped course for the Horns Reef, trying to avoid being driven westwards by the enemy, the bulk of whose forces were to the east of him. The sun was sinking swiftly to the horizon; in half an hour it would disappear, and in an hour darkness would have fallen. The British, coming from the east, now had the light in their favour; it was high time to take advantage of the fact. Jellicoe ordered a course converging on the enemy's; contact could be made in twenty-five minutes, and there would be thirty left in which to deal with the Germans.

Beatty had only just lost sight of the enemy battle-cruisers, and a little before eight o'clock he asked Jellicoe to detach the leading battle-ships, affirming that he would then be able to cut the line of retreat of the enemy fleet. And it was not impossible for Beatty, if he had been joined by a squadron of battleships, to have "crossed the T" for a third time. But his request was impossible to give effect to, for the leading battle squadron (the Second, under Jerram) was not even in sight of Beatty and would have taken two hours to join him. So the action was renewed, at 20.00 hours, by Beatty's force alone. The *Derfflinger*'s remaining turret was put out of action, and more damage was inflicted on the *Seydlitz.* Mauve went to their assistance with his old battleships, but these could not withstand even the now reduced firing-power of the British battle-cruisers. The *Schleswig-Holstein,* the *Pommern,* and then the *Schlesien* were damaged, and Mauve was forced to break away to the west. Scheer regretfully altered course a few points to the west, too, realizing that he would be confronted with the whole of the Grand Fleet if he stood on to the south. Firing ceased at 20.45. Once again, Jellicoe had known nothing of it; but this time Beatty had a good excuse—the *Lion*'s wireless was out of action. As for the faithful Goodenough, he had been too busily occupied in the rear, beating off the destroyers attempting to make torpedo attacks on Evan-Thomas's squadron.

At nine o'clock Jellicoe altered course to the south, and twenty-five minutes later Beatty did the same, thinking he would thus head off the Germans from the west. So the three forces were speeding through the night on almost parallel courses, Beatty ahead and about eight miles in advance of Scheer, and Jellicoe about nine miles to the east of Scheer and abeam of him. But with none of the three very sure of his position in relation to the others.

The night was short; first light would be soon after three. Jellicoe decided, rightly, that Scheer was making for his base through the swept passage just west of the Horns Reef, and he sent the fast minelayer *Abdiel* on ahead to bottle it up. Scheer, too, had made a correct appreciation of his enemy's intentions. But he had no choice. There was no question of renewing the action in the morning; he had to make for his base during the night, come what may. And at 21.30 hours he ordered his fleet to steer south-east by south.

He did succeed in reaching his base; but to describe in detail how he managed it would require many pages. In short, his course converged on Jellicoe's, but he was astern of the British battleships; he smashed through their light cruiser screen when Jellicoe was less than six miles ahead.

It was a sharp, running action, with losses on both sides. The *Castor* was hit about ten times, the *Southampton* and the *Dublin* were both severely damaged, and the *Tipperary* was set on fire. Three British destroyers ran into each other at full speed, and one of them sank shortly afterwards. The Germans lost the *Frauenlob* and the *Rostock*, both being torpedoed; and the *Elbing* crashed into the *Posen*, damaging herself so badly that she had to be sunk.

The latter incidents occurred within sight of the two rear battleships of the Grand Fleet, the *Malaya* and the *Valiant*. But both captains seemed to think that it would be more appropriate for their Divisional commander to signal the incidents, and so Jellicoe remained unaware of what was happening!

At about midnight Scheer's battleships sank three destroyers—the *Ardent*, *Fortune*, and *Turbulent*—and a little later the armoured cruiser *Black Prince* was brought under concentrated fire and blew up, with the loss of all her crew. Just before dawn the British retaliated by sinking the *Pommern*, the attack being carried out by destroyers of the Twelfth Flotilla; she was the last ship to be sunk at the Battle of Jutland. There was a brief exchange between the light cruiser *Champion* and four German destroyers at 03.30 hours; but the destroyers soon made off, being hampered by having survivors from the *Lützow* on board—she had been scuttled earlier, being much too crippled to make port.

The mines laid by the *Abdiel* did no harm to the German ships, but the *Ostfriesland* struck a mine farther south and only just managed to limp into port. The battered *Seydlitz*, weighed down by 5,000 tons of water in her hold, went aground not far from the Horns Reef lightship but a salvage vessel from Wilhelmshaven got her away by eleven in the morning.

When Jellicoe turned north at 02.20 hours, in order to be off the Horns Reef at dawn, the sea ahead of him was empty of the enemy. His destroyer flotillas were scattered; fearing an attack by U-boats, he remained well out—missing the chance of finishing off the *Seydlitz*—and cruised until midday, when he set course to return to base. At that moment, Scheer's flagship was dropping anchor in the Jade estuary.

The wind got up, the sea was running high. . . . The damaged British ships struggled to make port, some still fighting fires or taking water. The *Warrior* never managed it. . . .

The losses were heavy on both sides, but the British had lost twice as much tonnage as the Germans, and had three times as many casualties. The German ships, better built and skilfully handled, had proved themselves individually to be more effective and the stouter. They had also been very fortunate in twice escaping the dire consequences of the crossing of the T, to which Scheer had deliberately exposed himself on the second occasion. But the withdrawal during the night, when the battleships had smashed their way through the British screen, was undoubtedly a triumph for the Germans; and the German newspapers had some reason for their headlines on the evening of June 1st—"Great Naval Victory." Although fighting five against eight—roughly the proportionate strength of the opposing fleets—the Germans had inflicted losses of eight to their five. On the other hand, it was the British who had remained in command of the scene of the action.

But the result of the battle should be measured in its after effects, rather than by its momentary losses. After Jutland, the High Sea Fleet hardly ever put to sea again.

The Sinking of the *Bismarck*

by C. S. FORESTER

In the *Bismarck,* Lutjens and Lindemann were looking at the gray sky.

"They should have attacked two hours ago," said Lindemann.

"One of the unpredictable accidents of war, I expect," said Lutjens. "One more hour of daylight . . . That's all."

At this moment came the yell of "Plane on the starboard bow!" followed by the roar of the alarm. The AA guns turned and began to fire, but the deafening racket was pierced by further cries: "Plane on the port beam. Plane on the starboard quarter."

Lindemann was giving rapid helm orders, which, transmitted down the voice-pipe, were translated into violent action by the helmsman at the wheel. The ship turned and twisted, to leave behind her a boiling, curved wake. There was a crash and a great jet of water at the bow as one torpedo exploded there; but the ship fought on without apparent damage. Then came a Swordfish, swooping at the stern as she swung; the wake of her dropped torpedo was clearly visible. On the wing of the bridge, Lutjens was shaking his fists at the plane.

"Hard a-port. Hard a-port!" shouted Lindemann, but there was not time to check the turn. The torpedo hit on her swinging stern, bursting close by the rudder in a shower of spray. A frightful vibration made itself felt throughout the ship, as if the whole vast structure would shake itself to pieces, and she heeled over madly as she continued in a tight turn.

"Starboard! Starboard!" shouted Lindemann.

Down below, the helmsman was struggling with the wheel while the compass before him still went swinging round over the card.

"I can't move the wheel, sir!" he said. "Rudder's jammed!"

On the bridge the vibration still continued and the ship still circled. A telephone squawked and the officer of the watch answered it.

"Engine room, sir," he said to the captain.

"Captain," said Lindemann calmly into the telephone. "Yes. . . . Yes. . . . Very well."

The shattering vibration ceased as he hung up, and some of the speed of the ship fell away.

"Portside engines stopped, sir," he said to the admiral. "Portside propellers were thrashing against some obstruction."

"Yes," said Lutjens.

Another telephone was squawking.

"Damage Control, sir," said the officer of the watch.

"Captain," said Lindemann into the telephone. "Yes. . . . Yes. . . . Very well, get going on that."

Then he turned to Lutjens.

"Steering flat is flooded, sir. Steering engine out of action."

"What about the hand steering?"

"They've just been trying it, sir, but the rudder's jammed right over. They're trying to clear it now."

"The fate of the Reich depends on getting that rudder clear," said Lutjens.

In the War Room in London the senior officers were gathered round a chart of a different sort. This was on a scale so large that it showed mostly blank ocean, with only a hint of the coast of France and Spain on the righthand side. But pinned upon the blank area were several tabs, marked, conspicuously, *Bismarck, King George V, Rodney,* FORCE H, VIAN'S DESTROYERS; and leading up to each tab were the black lines of the tracks of those ships during the last several hours. The only other feature of the map was a wide arc of a circle marking the limit of air cover from France.

A junior officer came over with a message in his hand.

"*Sheffield* has *Bismarck* in sight now, sir," he said, making an adjustment to *Bismarck*'s position. "She's reporting position, course and speed."

"How long before she's under air cover now?" demanded the admiral.

Someone swept with his dividers from *Bismarck*'s position to the arc. "A hundred and seventy-two miles, sir."

"Less than seven hours before she's safe!" said the rear admiral.

"And only an hour of daylight. What the devil's *Ark Royal* up to?"

"Here's a most immediate signal coming through now, sir," said an officer, "from *Sheffield:* HAVE SIGHTED SWORDFISH ATTACKING. *Bismarck* FIRING."

"That's *Ark Royal*'s planes," said the admiral.

"Come on, men! Come on!" said the air vice marshal.

"Most immediate from *Sheffield* again: *Bismarck* CIRCLING."

"That's something gained, anyway," said the rear admiral.

"Not enough to matter," said the admiral.

"Most immediate from *Sheffield:* ATTACK APPARENTLY COMPLETED. SWORDFISH RETURNING."

The rear admiral began to speak, but the admiral checked him, as the officer was still speaking.

"*Bismarck* STILL CIRCLING."

"Then the attack's not over," said the rear admiral.

"There's something odd," said the admiral.

The signals were clattering down the tubes to be opened hastily, but they were all, clearly, merely confirmations of what the young officer was announcing from his telephone.

"*Bismarck* HEADING NORTH."

"Heading north? Heading *north?* That's straight for *Rodney,*" said the admiral.

"Perhaps she's still avoiding a plane *Sheffield* can't see," said the rear admiral.

"I wonder . . ." said the admiral.

"ESTIMATE *Bismarck*'s SPEED AT 10 KNOTS."

"That hardly sounds likely," said the admiral.

"It must be pretty well dark there now."

Another young officer at the telephones spoke:

"Most immediate signal coming through from *Ark Royal,* sir."

"It's time we heard from her."

"FIRST FIVE AIRCRAFT RETURNING REPORT NO HITS."

The air vice marshal struck his fist into his hand, but the message went on.

"SHADOWING AIRCRAFT REPORTS *Bismarck* COURSE NORTH, SPEED 9 KNOTS."

"Something's happened to her, for sure," said the admiral.

"AIRCRAFT REPORTS HIT ON *Bismarck*'s STARBOARD BOW."

"Good! Good!" said the air vice marshal.

"But that wouldn't account for it," said the rear admiral.

"Sheffield reporting, sir," said the first young officer: *"Bismarck* COURSE NORTH, SPEED 9 KNOTS."

"There's no doubt about it, then," said the rear admiral.

"Ark Royal reporting, sir," said the second officer: "AIRCRAFT REPORTS HIT ON *Bismarck* RIGHT AFT."

"That's it, then!" said the rear admiral.

"Yes, that's it. Propellers or rudder, or both," said the admiral.

"Bismarck COURSE NORTH, SPEED 10 KNOTS."

"There's a heavy sea running and she can't turn her stern to it," said the admiral.

"Vian'll be up to her in an hour," said the rear admiral. "He'll keep her busy during the night."

"And *King George V* and *Rodney* will be up to her by daylight," said the admiral. "I think we've got her. I think we have."

"Hooray!" said the air vice marshal.

"Sheffield reporting, sir: HAVE SIGHTED VIAN'S DESTROYERS PREPARING TO ATTACK."

"Hooray!" said the air vice marshal again.

"Many men are going to die very soon," said the admiral.

"Any orders for Captain Vian, sir?"

There was only a moment's pause before that question was answered.

"No," said the admiral. "We all know Vian, and he knows his business. He won't lose touch with her. If she stays crippled he won't have to force the pace too much—he can bring in the battleships to get her at dawn. If she manages to repair herself he'll have to attack all-out."

"Not so easy with that sea running," said the rear admiral. "And *Bismarck*'s got a good radar, apparently. The darkness will hamper him and won't hamper her."

"That won't stop Vian from attacking," said the rear admiral. *"Bismarck* is certainly going to have a lively night."

"All the better for our battleships tomorrow, then. Her crew must be worn out already, and another sleepless night . . . But I'm not going to count our chickens before they're hatched. We don't know *all* that's going on."

Deep down in the stern of the *Bismarck* all was dark except for the beams of electric hand-lamps. There was the sound of water washing back and forth, and the gleam of it, reflected from the lamps, came and went. The working party there was faintly visible. For a few seconds could be seen a man in emergency diving kit disappearing into the surging water. A little farther forward a seaman was stringing an emergency wire which brought light to the dark spaces, so that now the dark water was illuminated as the sea surged backward and forward, roaring through the incredible confusion of twisted steel. There were pumps at work as the diver emerged, blood streaming from his lacerated shoulders. He made his report to the officer there, who went back to use the telephone against a dark bulkhead; to reach these a watertight door was opened for him and shut behind him, although, before it closed, the water came pouring in over the coaming with the movement of the ship. A working party was laboring to shore up the bulkhead, and he had to sign to the men to cease their deafening labor before he could make himself understood at the telephone switchboard.

In the chartroom of the *Bismarck* the captain was receiving the message.

"Yes," he said. "Yes. Very well."

Then when he replaced the telephone he addressed Lutjens and the staff officers gathered there.

"They don't think any repair can be effected," he went on. "Furthermore, unless we keep our bows to the sea they think the bulkhead will give way, and flood the next series of compartments. So we must hold this course as best we can."

"That means we go forward to meet our fate instead of trying to run away from it," said Lutjens. "That is what our Führer would like."

The chief of staff came forward with a bunch of signal forms in his hand.

"Berlin has just sent in a long message, a résumé of all the intelligence they can gather," he said. "The *King George V* is some fifty miles from us now, bearing northwesterly."

The assistant chief of staff opened the reference book to display a series of pictures.

"Fourteen-inch guns, speed 28 knots, 35,000 tons. Completed last year. Admiral Tovey's flagship; Captain Patterson."

"Renown and *Ark Royal—"*

"That's Force H," said Lutjens. "We know about them."

"And there's a force of destroyers, probably under Captain Vian—the man who captured the *Altmark*—close to us to the northward. From the position Berlin gives, they ought to be in sight now."

"No doubt they soon will be," said Lutjens. "I was hoping we might have a quiet night before our battle tomorrow."

"The men are falling asleep at their posts, as you know, sir," said Lindemann.

"Yes," said Lutjens.

"And there's the *Rodney*," went on the chief of staff. "She's in touch with the *King George V*, and may even have joined her by now."

The assistant chief of staff opened the reference book at another page. "Sixteen-inch guns, speed 24 knots, 35,000 tons, completed soon after the last war. Captain Dalrymple Hamilton."

"Twenty years old," said Lutjens. "And I know her well. I lunched on board her in '24 at Malta when I was a young lieutenant."

It called for no effort on the part of Lutjens to conjure up the memory before his mind's eye. The heat and the dazzling sunshine and the smooth water of the harbor—all so different from this bitter cold and tossing sea and gray sky—and the spotless battleship, glittering with fresh paint and polished brasswork; the white hand-ropes, the white uniforms, the dazzling gold lace; the bosun's mates lined up with their calls to their lips; the welcoming group of officers on the quarterdeck as Lutjens followed his captain on board; the salutes and the handshakes, the introductions and the formalities, before the English captain led the way below to a wide airy cabin, the armchairs gay with chintz, the table covered with white linen, the glassware sparkling.

"That was the peacetime Navy," said Lutjens.

If Lutjens could have seen the *Rodney* now, as she plowed over the sea towards him, he would hardly have recognized her. A British lieutenant and an American naval lieutenant were at that moment on the boat deck of the *Rodney* looking around them at the ship.

"A battle's the last thing we expected," said the Englishman.

"That's what it looks like," said the American.

His eyes traveled over the boat deck and the upper deck. They were piled with wooden cases secured in every available space.

"This Lend-Lease of yours," said the Englishman. "Very kind of you to refit us, I know. We couldn't do without it. But we have to bring half our refitting stores with us, the things you can't supply because of our different standards."

"I know about that," said the American.

"Those are pom-pom mountings," said the Englishman.

"They look more like the Pyramids," said the American. They were eyeing at the moment two enormous wooden cases that towered up beside them on the boat deck.

"We've five hundred invalids on board for Canada," went on the Englishman. "They'll see another battle before they see Canada, anyway, and their wishes haven't been consulted about it."

"Me too," replied the American mildly. "I'm only supposed to be quietly showing you the way to Boston."

"That's the old *Rodney* for you," said the Englishman. "She can't even start off on a quiet trip to America without crossing the bows of a German battleship. We always try to do our guests well—entertainment regardless of expense. You'll see fireworks tomorrow."

"Very kind of you," said the American.

"Mind you," went on the Englishman, "it may not be quite as lavish as we'd like. We haven't had time for a refit for two years. We're old and we're dingy. But we'll show you something good tomorrow, all the same. When those fellows talk—"

He pointed down to the turrets where the main armament crews were exercising. It was a moment of indescribable menace, as the sixteen-inch guns trained and elevated.

That was the same moment that Admiral Lutjens looked round at the rather depressed faces all round him, and went on: "Now, gentlemen, there's no need to despair. Three days ago we fought two battleships and won a tremendous victory. Now we face two battleships again. Our fighting capacity is unimpaired. We can sink this *King George V* and this Admiral Tovey. We can make this *Rodney* run away like the *Prince of Wales*. By noon tomorrow there'll be such an assembly of U-boats around us that no one will dare to attack us. We aren't fighting a battle of despair. We're fighting for victory. And for the Germany Navy, the Reich, and the Führer!"

It appeared as if his fighting words had some effect. Heads were raised higher again, and there was animation in the faces of those he addressed. Lindemann looked at the clock.

"Another half-hour of daylight," he said. "I'll have food issued to the men while there's time, before we darken ship."

"Always the thoughtful officer, Lindemann," said Lutjens.

And so the last meal was served out and carried round to the men at their posts during the last minutes of daylight. There were men who went on sleeping—men of that half of the crew who were allowed to sleep after the alarm of the attack by the Swordfish had ended, who flung themselves down on the steel decks in their aching longing for sleep. There were men who took a few mouthfuls of food. There were men who ate eagerly, with appetite. And there were the men struggling with damage repair below, who had no chance either to eat or sleep.

But darkness closed down from the gray sky so abruptly that even the half-hour of which Lutjens had spoken was cut short. The alarm roared through the ship. The sleepers whom even the alarm could not now rouse were shaken or kicked awake.

The voice-pipe spoke abruptly to the group in the chartroom: *"Destroyer on the starboard bow"*—and directly afterwards: *"Destroyer on the port bow."*

Outside, the darkened ship was suddenly illuminated by the flash of the secondary armament. The guns bellowed. That was the beginning of a dreadful night. As the hands of the clock crept slowly round, alarm followed alarm. *"Destroyer to port!" "Destroyer to starboard!"*

In the outer blackness, Vian's five destroyers—four British and one Polish—had made their way to shadowing positions encircling the *Bismarck*. It was not so easy to do in that howling wind and over that rough sea. The destroyers that made their way to *Bismarck*'s port side had to head directly into the waves.

The captain and navigating officer on the bridge of the leading destroyer felt the frightful impact as the successive seas crashed upon the forecastle, and the spray that flew aft was so solid that it was impossible to see anything as they looked forward.

"We can't keep it up," said the captain. "Slow to 18 knots."

At that speed the destroyer could just withstand the battering of the seas—although the plight of the men in exposed situations was horrible—and she could go heaving and plunging forward. The lookouts straining their eyes through the darkness could see nothing, could not pick out the smallest hint of the vast bulk of the *Bismarck* battling the waves. The lookout peering over the starboard bow was conscious of nothing—strive as he would—except roaring darkness and hurtling spray. Yet as he watched, the darkness was suddenly rent by the long vivid flashes of gunfire—pointed, as it seemed to him, directly into his eyes. Four seconds later—no more—the howl of the wind was augmented by the scream of shells overhead; the sea all about the destroyer was torn into wilder confusion still by a hail of splashes, and plainly through the lurching and staggering of the ship could be felt the sharper impact of shell fragments against the frail hull.

"Port fifteen," said the captain, and the destroyer swung away abruptly. Before her turn was completed the long flashes of the *Bismarck*'s guns appeared again in the darkness, and close under the destroyer's stern the salvo plunged into the sea to raise splashes brief-lived in the brisk wind.

"Good shooting in the dark," said the captain.

"That's their radar."

The destroyer's turn had taken her into the trough of the sea, and now she was rolling fantastically, far over, first on one side and then on the other, as the steep waves heaved her over.

"We'll try again," said the captain. "Starboard fifteen."

Another series of long flames, but longer and brighter than the preceding ones, stabbed into the darkness over there, yet no salvo splashed about them.

"One of the others is getting it," remarked the navigator.

"That's their fifteen-inch," said the captain. "They're using their secondary armament for us and the main battery on the other side."

The destroyer put her nose into a sea and something much solider than spray came hurtling aft to cascade against the bridge.

"We can't take that," said the captain. "Turn two points to port and slow to 15 knots."

A few seconds after the order had been given the gun flashes lit the sky to starboard again, and close beside the starboard bow the salvo hit the water.

"Just as well we made that turn," said the captain. "That's good shooting."

"And we haven't even seen her yet!" marveled the navigator.

"They haven't seen us either," said the captain. "This is modern warfare."

It was modern warfare. Far down below decks in the *Bismarck*, walled in by armor plate, a group of officers and men sat at tables and switchboards. Despite the vile weather outside, despite the winds and the waves, it was almost silent in here; in addition to the quiet orders and announcements of the radar fire-control team there could only be heard the low purring of the costly instruments they handled. Centered in the room was the yellow-green eye of the radar, echoing the impressions received by the aerial at the masthead a hundred feet above; the room was half dark to enable the screen to be seen clearly. And in accordance with what that screen showed, dials were turned and pointers were set and reports were spoken into telephones; save for the uniforms, it might have been a gathering of medieval wizards performing some secret rite—but it was not the feeble magic of trying to cause an enemy to waste away by sticking pins into his waxen image or of attempting to summon up fiends from the underworld. These incantations let loose a thousand foot tons of energy from the *Bismarck*'s guns and hurled instant death across ten miles of raging sea. It was as a result of what that eye saw that the exhausted men of the *Bismarck* forced themselves into renewed activity to serve the guns, although there were actually men who fell asleep with the guns bellowing in their very ears. Now and then, with a wink and then a dazzling flash, star shells soared up from the destroyers and hung over the doomed battleship, lighting her up as if it were day. Sometimes there would be a shadowy glimpse of the destroyers racing to get into position, their bow-waves gleaming except when the heavy seas burst over their bows. Even Lutjens himself was overtaken by sleep as he sat in the control room, nodding off in his chair while the guns fired, and pulling himself up with a jerk. Once when he roused himself he called a staff officer to his side.

"Send this to Berlin at once. WE SHALL FIGHT TO THE LAST SHELL. LONG LIVE THE FÜHRER!"

In the War Room in London the rear admiral entered after an absence.

"Vian's still engaging her," explained one of the officers.

"*Bismarck*'s still transmitting," said another.

"What's the weather report?"

"No change, sir. Wind force 8, westerly. High sea running, low cloud, visibility poor."

"King George V will sight her soon enough."

Back in the control room of the *Bismarck,* Lutjens was nodding off again in his chair. His head sank lower and lower, and after a while he gave up the struggle and settled back into a sound sleep. It lasted very little time, however, because the chief of staff came to him and laid a hand on his shoulder.

"Sunrise in half an hour, sir."

"I shall go on the bridge," said Lutjens. "I think a breath of fresh air will do me good."

"Your overcoat, sir," said his flag lieutenant as he went out.

"Do you think I shall need it?" asked Lutjens, but he put it on nevertheless.

Outside, the faint light was increasing. As ever, the wind was shrieking round them; the ship was rolling heavily in the waves, with the spray flying in sheets.

"Good morning, Admiral," said Lindemann.

"Good morning, Captain," said Lutjens.

"Destroyers out of range on the starboard bow, sir," said Lindemann. "And there's a cruiser somewhere to the northward of us. I'm sure she's the *Norfolk.*"

"That was the ship that sighted us in Denmark Strait," said Lutjens. "Still with us, is she?"

One of the lookouts blinked himself awake and stared forward through his binoculars. "Ship right ahead! Two ships right ahead!"

Lutjens and Lindemann trained their glasses forward.

"Battleships?" asked Lutjens.

"I think so, sir. Battleships."

The lookout in *King George V* was staring through his glasses.

"Ship right ahead!"

The lookout in *Rodney* reported.

"Ship bearing green 5!"

"That's *Bismarck!*" said an officer on the bridge of *Rodney.*

Down the voice-pipe, over the head of the quartermaster at the wheel of the *Rodney,* came a quiet order.

"Port ten."

"Port ten, sir," repeated the quartermaster, turning his wheel.

Up in the gunnery control tower the captain's voice made itself heard in the gunnery officer's earphones.

"We are turning to port. Open fire when your guns bear."

The gunnery officer looked down at the GUN READY lights. He looked through his glasses with the pointer fixed upon the silhouette of the *Bismarck.*

"Fire!" he said.

Out on the wing of the bridge stood the American officer and the British lieutenant, glasses to their eyes. Below them, just as on the evening before, the sixteen-inch guns were training round and reaching upwards towards extreme elevation. Then came the incredible roar and concussion of the salvo. The brown cordite smoke spurted out from the muzzles, to be borne rapidly away by the wind as the shells took their unseen way on their mission of death.

"Short but close. Damned close," said the Englishman; the last words were drowned by the din of the second salvo, and he did not speak again during the brief time of flight. But when he spoke it was in a voice high-pitched with excitement. "A hit! A hit! At the second salvo! I told you the old *Rodney*—"

Again his words were drowned by the roar of the guns, and he forced himself to keep his glasses steady on the target. Next it was the American who spoke.

"Another hit," he said. "She doesn't stand a chance now."

Down in the radar room of the *Bismarck* the same disciplined team was still at work.

"Range seventeen thousand meters," said the rating at the screen.

There was a roar like thunder then, all about them, as the first salvo hit the *Bismarck*. The lights went out and came on, went out and came on, and the yellow-green eye of the radar screen abruptly went lifeless. The rating there reached for other switches, clicked them on and off; he tried another combination.

"Radar not functioning, sir," he announced.

"You've tried the after aerial?" asked the officer.

"Yes, sir. No result."

"No connection with gunnery control, sir," announced another rating.

"No connection with—" began another rating, but another rolling peal of thunder cut off his words, and again the lights flickered. "No connection with the bridge, sir."

"Very well."

"No connection with the charthouse, sir."

"Very well."

The first wisps of smoke had begun to enter the radar room through the ventilating system. Wisp after wisp it came, seeping in thicker and thicker, swirling in, while the lights burned duller and duller. And peal after peal of thunder shook the whole structure, the shock waves causing the wreaths of smoke to eddy abruptly with each impact, and a section of paneling fell from the bulkhead with a sudden clatter. It was as if the witches' Sabbath in which they had been engaged had now roused the infernal forces for their own destruction. Throughout the doomed ship the lights were burning low and smoke was creeping in thicker and thicker.

In the War Room the young officer was repeating the messages heard on the telephone.

"Most immediate from *Norfolk*. *Rodney* HAS OPENED FIRE. . . . *King George V* HAS OPENED FIRE. . . . *Bismarck* IS RETURNING THE FIRE. . . . *Bismarck* HIT. . . . *Bismarck* HIT AGAIN."

It was almost possible for the men listening in the War Room to visualize what was actually going on. As the *Bismarck* trained her guns round, she was surrounded by a forest of splashes from *Rodney*'s salvo, and before she could fire, the splashes from *King George V*'s salvo surrounded her. Hardly had her guns spoken before a shell hit the second turret from forward and burst with a roar and a billow of smoke. The blast and the fragments swept everywhere about the bridge. The fabric was left a twisted litter of stanchions, and lying huddled and contorted in it were a number of corpses, among them those of Lindemann—conspicuous by its Knight's Cross—and of Lutjens.

The voice of the officer at the telephone went on describing what was going on. "*Bismarck* ON FIRE AFT. . . . *Bismarck* HIT. . . . *Bismarck* HIT. . . . *Bismarck*'s FORE TURRET OUT OF ACTION." Another officer broke in.

"*Ark Royal* signaling, sir: ALL PLANES AWAY."

"*Ark Royal?* I can't believe her planes will find anything to do. But quite right to send them in."

On the flight deck of the *Ark Royal* the sound of the gunfire was plainly to be heard, loudly, in the intervals of the Swordfish revving up their engines and taking off. Conditions were as bad as ever as the ship heaved and plunged in the rough sea under a lowering gray sky, yet somehow the lumbering aircraft managed to get away, and circle, and get into formation, and head northwards, low over the heaving sea and close under the dripping clouds. It was only a few seconds before the leader saw what he was looking for. There was a long bank of black smoke lying on the surface of the water, spreading and expanding from the denser and narrower nucleus to the northward, and it was towards that nucleus that he headed his plane.

"My God!" said the leader.

The smoke was pouring from the battered, almost shapeless hull of the *Bismarck*, stripped of her upper works, mast, funnels, bridge and all. Yet under the smoke, plainly in the dull gray light, he could see a forest—a small grove, rather—of tall red flames roaring upward from within the hull. But it was not the smoke nor the flames that held the eye, strangely enough, but the ceaseless dance of tall jets of water all about her. Two battleships were flinging shells at her both from their main and from their secondary armaments; and from the cruisers twenty eight-inch guns were joining in. There was never a moment when she was not ringed in by the splashes of the near-misses, but when the leader forced his eye to ignore the distraction of this wild water dance he saw something else: from bow to stern along the tortured hull he could see a continual coming and going of shellbursts, volcanoes of flame and smoke. From that low height, as the Swordfish closed in, he could see everything. He could see the two fore-turrets useless, one of them with the roof blown clean off and the guns pointing over side at extreme elevation, the other with the guns fore and aft drooping at extreme depression. Yet the aftermost turret was still in action; even as he watched, he saw one of the guns in it fling out a jet of smoke towards the shadowy form of the *King George V;* down there in the steel turret, nestling among the flames, some heroes were still contriving to load and train and fire. And he saw something else at the last moment of his approach. There were a few tiny, foreshortened figures visible here and there, scrambling over the wreckage, incredibly alive amid the flames and the explosions, leaping down from the fiery hull into the boiling sea.

He swung the Swordfish away from the horrible sight, to lead the way back to the *Ark Royal*. While that bombardment was going on there was no chance of a frail plane delivering a successful torpedo attack. He had seen the climax of the manifestation of sea power, the lone challenger overwhelmed by a colossal concentration of force. He was not aware of the narrowness of the margin of time and space, of how in the British battleships the last few tons of oil fuel were being pumped towards the furnaces, of German U-boats hastening, just too late, from all points in the North Atlantic to try to intervene in the struggle, of German air power chafing at the bit unable to take part in a battle only a few miles beyond their maximum range.

While the squadron was being led back to the *Ark Royal*, the officer at the telephone in the War Room was continuing to announce the signals coming through.

"*Bismarck* HIT AGAIN. . . . SHE IS ONLY A WRECK NOW. . . . *King George V* and *Rodney* TURNING AWAY."

In the War Room people looked sharply at each other at that piece of news. The admiral looked at the clock.

"That's the last minute they could stay. They'll only have just enough oil fuel to get them home. Not five minutes to spare."

"Here's a signal from the flag, sir," interposed another young officer. "SHIPS WITH TORPEDOES GO IN AND SINK HER."

"And there's *Norfolk* again," said the first young officer. "*Dorsetshire* GOING IN."

Bismarck lay, a shattered, burning, sinking hulk, as *Dorsetshire* approached. At two miles she fired two torpedoes which burst on *Bismarck*'s starboard side. At a mile and a half she fired another which burst on the port side of the wreck. *Bismarck* rolled over and sank, leaving the surface covered with debris and struggling men.

"*Bismarck* SUNK," said the young officer in the War Room. "*Bismarck* SUNK."

Those words of the young officer were spoken in a hushed voice, and yet their echoes were heard all over the world. In a hundred countries radio announcers hastened to repeat those words to their audiences. In a hundred languages, newspaper headlines proclaimed *Bismarck* SUNK to a thousand million readers. Frivolous women heard those words unhearing; unlettered peasants heard them uncomprehending, even though the destinies of all of them were changed in that moment. Stock exchange speculators revised their plans. Prime ministers and chiefs of state took grim note of those words. The admirals of a score of navies prepared to compose memoranda advising their governments regarding the political and technical conclusions to be drawn from them. And there were wives and mothers and children who heard those words as well, just as Nobby's mother had heard about the loss of the *Hood*.

Hospital Ship Rams U-Boat

by ALISTAIR MacLEAN

It was little more than half-light when the U-boat, in broken camouflage paint of various shades of gray and at a distance of less than half a mile, suddenly appeared from behind a passing snow squall. It was running fully on the surface with three figures clearly distinguishable on the conning tower and another three manning the deck gun just for'ard of that. The submarine was on a course exactly paralleling that of the *San Andreas* and could well have been for many hours. The U-boat was on their starboard hand, so that the *San Andreas* lay between it and the gradually lightening sky to the south. Both bridge wing doors were latched back in the fully open position. McKinnon reached for the phone, called the engine room for full power, nudged the wheel to starboard and began to edge imperceptibly closer to the U-boat.

He and Nasby were alone on the bridge. They were, in fact, the only two people left in the superstructure because McKinnon had ordered everyone, including a bitterly protesting Lieutenant Ulbricht, to go below to the hospital only ten minutes previously. Naseby he required and for two reasons. Naseby, unlike himself, was an adept Morse signaler and had a signaling lamp ready at hand; more important, McKinnon was more than reasonably certain that the bridge would be coming under attack in a short time, and he wanted a competent helmsman there in case he himself was incapacitated.

"Keep out of sight, George," McKinnon said. "But try to keep an eye on them. They're bound to start sending any minute now."

"They can see you," Naseby said.

"Maybe they can see my head and shoulders over the wing of the bridge. Maybe not. It doesn't matter. The point is that they will believe that I can't see them. Don't forget that they're in the dark quadrant of the sea and have no reason to believe that we're expecting trouble. Besides, a helmsman's job is to keep an eye on the compass and look ahead—no reason on earth why I should be scanning the seas around." He felt the superstructure begin to shudder as Patterson increased the engine revolutions, gave the wheel another nudge to starboard, picked up a tin mug from the shattered binnacle and pretended to drink from it. "It's a law of nature, George. Nothing more reassuring than the sight of an unsuspecting innocent enjoying a morning cup of tea."

For a full minute, which seemed like a large number of full minutes, nothing happened. The superstructure was beginning to vibrate quite strongly now, and McKinnon knew that the *San Andreas* was under maximum power. They were now at least a hundred yards closer to the U-boat than they had been when it had first been sighted, but the U-boat captain gave no indication that he was aware of this. Had McKinnon maintained his earlier speed, his acute angling in toward the U-boat would have caused him to drop slightly astern of the submarine, but the increase in speed had enabled him to maintain his relative position. The U-boat captain had no cause to be suspicious—and no one in his right mind was going to harbor suspicions about a harmless and defenseless hospital ship.

"He's sending, George," McKinnon said.

"I see him. 'Stop,' he says. 'Stop engines or I will sink you.' What do I send, Archie?"

"Nothing." McKinnon edged the *San Andreas* another three degrees to starboard, reached again for his tin mug and pretended to drink from it. "Ignore him."

"Ignore him?" Naseby sounded aggrieved. "You heard what the man said. He's going to sink us."

"He's lying. He hasn't stalked us all this way just to send us to the bottom. He wants us alive. Not only is he not going to torpedo us, he can't, not unless they've invented torpedoes that can turn corners. So how else is he going to stop us? With that little itsy-bitsy gun he's got on the fore-deck? It's not all that much bigger than a pompom."

"I have to warn you, Archie, the man's going to be very annoyed."

"He's got nothing to be annoyed about. We haven't seen his signal."

Naseby lowered his binoculars. "I also have to warn you that he's about to use that little itsy-bitsy gun."

"Sure he is. The classic warning shot over the bows to attract our attention. If he *really* wants to attract our attention, it may be into the bows for all I know."

The two shells, when they came, entered the sea just yards ahead of the *San Andreas,* one disappearing silently below the waves, the other exploding on impact. The sound of the explosion and the sharp flat crack of the U-boat's gun made it impossible any longer to ignore the submarine's existence.

"Show yourself, George," McKinnon said. "Tell him to stop firing and ask him what he wants."

Naseby moved out on the starboard wing and transmitted the message; the reply came immediately.

"One-track mind," Naseby said. "Message reads STOP OR BE SUNK."

"One of those laconic characters. Tell him we're a hospital ship."

"You think he's blind, perhaps?"

"It's still only half-light and the starboard side is our dark side. Maybe he'll think that we think he can't see. Tell him we're a neutral, mention Geneva conventions. Maybe he's got a better side to *his* nature."

Naseby clacked out his message, waited for the reply, then turned gloomily to McKinnon. "He hasn't got a better side to his nature."

"Not many U-boat captains have. What does he say?"

"Geneva conventions do not apply in the Norwegian Sea."

"There's little decency left on the high seas these days. Let's try for his sense of patriotism. Tell him we have German survivors aboard."

While Naseby sent the message, McKinnon rang down for slow ahead. Naseby turned in the doorway and shook his head sadly.

"His patriotism is on a par with his decency. He says: 'Will check nationals when we board. We commence firing in twenty seconds.' "

"Send: 'No need to fire. We are stopping. Check wake.' "

Naseby sent the message, then said: "Well, he got that all right. He's already got his glasses trained on our stern. You know, I do believe he's angling in toward us. Very little, mind you, but it's there."

"I do believe you're right." McKinnon gave the wheel another slight nudge to starboard. "If he notices anything he'll probably think it's because he's closing in on us and not vice versa. Is he still examining our wake?"

"Yes."

"Turbulence aft must have died away quite a lot by this time. That should make him happy."

"He's lowered his glasses," Naseby said. "Message coming."

The message didn't say whether the U-boat captain was happy or not, but it did hold a certain degree of satisfaction. "Man says we are very wise," Naseby said. "Also orders us to lower our gangway immediately."

"Acknowledge. Tell Ferguson to start lowering the gangway immediately but to stop it about, say, eight feet above the water. Then tell Curran and Trent to swing out the lifeboat and lower it to the same height."

Naseby relayed both messages then said: "You think we're going to need the lifeboat?"

"I quite honestly have no idea. But if we do, we're going to need it in a hurry." He called the engine room and asked for Patterson.

"Chief? Bosun here. We're slowing a bit, as you know, but that's only for the moment. The U-boat is closing in on us. We're lowering both the gangway and the lifeboat, the gangway on the U-boat's instructions, the lifeboat on mine. . . . No, they can't see the lifeboat—it's on our port side, their blind side. As soon as they are in position I'm going to ask for full power. A request, sir. If I do have to use the boat I'd appreciate it if you'd permit Mr. Jamieson to come with me. With your gun." He listened for a few moments while the receiver crackled in his ear then said: "Two things, sir. I want Mr. Jamieson because apart from yourself and Naseby he's the only member of the crew I can trust. Show him where the safety catch is. And no, sir, you know damn well you can't come along instead of Mr. Jamieson. You're the officer commanding and you can't leave the *San Andreas*." McKinnon replaced the receiver and Naseby said, plaintive reproach in his voice: "You might have asked me."

McKinnon looked at him coldly. "And who's going to steer this damned ship when I'm gone?"

Naseby sighed. "There's that, of course, there's that. They seem to be preparing some kind of boarding party across there, Archie. Three more men on the conning tower now. They've armed with submachine guns or machine pistols or whatever you call those things. Something nasty, anyway."

"We didn't expect roses. How's Ferguson coming long? If that gangway doesn't start moving soon, the U-boat captain is going to start getting suspicious. Worse, he's going to start getting impatient."

"I don't think so. At least, not yet awhile. I can see Ferguson, so I'm certain the U-boat captain can too. Ferguson's having difficulty of some kind, he's banging away at the lowering drum with a hammer. Icing trouble for a certainty."

"See how the boat's getting on, will you?"

Naseby crossed the bridge, moved out onto the port wing and was back in seconds. "It's down. About eight feet above the water, as you asked." He crossed to the starboard wing, examining the U-boat through his binoculars, lowered them and turned back to McKinnon.

"That's bloody funny. All those characters seem to be wearing some kind of gas masks."

"Gas masks? Are you all right?"

"Certainly I'm all right. They're all wearing a horseshoe-shaped kind of life jacket around their necks with a corrugated hose attached to the top. They're not wearing it at the moment, it's dangling down in front, but there's a mouthpiece and goggles attached to the end of the tube. When did German submariners start using gas?"

"They don't. What good on earth would gas be to a U-boat?" He took Naseby's binoculars, examined the U-boat briefly and handed the glasses back. "Tauchretter, George, Tauchretter. Otherwise known as the Dräger Lung. It's fitted with an oxygen cylinder and a carbon dioxide canister, and its sole purpose is to help people escape from a sunken submarine."

"No gas?" Naseby sounded vaguely disappointed.

"No gas."

"That doesn't look like a sunken submarine to me."

"Some U-boat commanders make their crews wear them all the time they're submerged. Bit pointless in these waters, I would have thought. At least six hundred feet deep here, maybe a thousand. There's no way you can escape from those depths, Dräger set or not. How's Ferguson coming along?"

"As far as I can tell, he's not. Still hammering away. No, wait a minute. He's put the hammer down and is trying the release lever. It's moving, Archie. It's coming down."

"Ah!" McKinnon rang for full power.

Some seconds passed, then Naseby said: "Halfway." A similar length of time elapsed then Naseby said in the same matter-of-fact voice: "It's down, Archie. Eight feet, give or take. Ferguson's secured it."

McKinnon nodded and spun the wheel to starboard until he had maximum rudder on. Slowly, ponderously at first, then with increasing speed, the *San Andreas* began to come round.

"Do you want to get your head blown off, George?"

"Well, no." Naseby stepped inside, closed the wing door behind him and peered out through the little window in the door. The *San Andreas*, no longer riding with the sea, was beginning to corkscrew, although gently; but the entire superstructure was beginning to vibrate as the engines built up to maximum power.

"And don't you think you ought to lie down?"

"In a minute, Archie, in a minute. Do you think they've gone to sleep aboard that U-boat?"

"Some trouble with their eyes, that's for sure. I think they're rubbing them and not believing what they're seeing."

Except that there was no actual eye-rubbing going on aboard the U-boat, McKinnon's guess was very close to the mark. The reactions of both the submarine commander and his crew were extraordinarily slow. Extraordinarily, but in the circumstances, understandably. The U-boat's crew had made both the forgivable and unforgivable mistake of relaxing, of lowering their guard at the precise moment when their alertness and sense of danger should have been honed at its edge. But the sight of the gangway being lowered in strict compliance with their orders must have convinced them that there was no thought or possibility of any resistance being offered and that the taking over of the *San Andreas* was no more than a token formality. Besides, no one in the history of warfare had ever heard of a hospital ship being used as . . . as an offensive weapon. It was unthinkable. It takes time to rethink the unthinkable.

The *San Andreas* was so far round now that the U-boat was no more than 45 degrees off the starboard bow. Naseby moved from the starboard wing door to the nearest small window let into the front of the bridge.

"They're lining up what you call that itsy-bitsy gun, Archie."

"Then maybe we'd both better be getting down."

"No. They're not lining up on the bridge, they're lining up on the hull aft. I don't know what they intend to—" He broke off and shouted: "No! No! Get down, get down!" and flung himself at McKinnon, bringing both men crashing heavily to the deck of the bridge. Even as they landed, hundreds of bullets, to the accompaniment of the staccato chattering of several machine guns, smashed into the fore end and starboard side of the bridge. None of the bullets succeeded in penetrating the metal, but all four windows were smashed. The fusillade lasted no more than three seconds and had no sooner ceased when the U-boat's deck gun fired three times in rapid succession, on each occasion causing the *San Andreas* to shudder as the shells exploded somewhere in the after hull.

McKinnon hauled himself to his feet and took the wheel. "If I'd been standing there I'd have been very much the late Archie McKinnon. I'll thank you tomorrow." He looked at the central window before him. It was holed, cracked, starred, abraded and completely opaque. "George?"

But Naseby needed no telling. Fire extinguisher in hand, he smashed away the entire window in just two blows. He hitched a cautious eye over the bottom of where the window had been, saw that the *San Andreas* was arrowing in on the bows of the U-boat, then abruptly straightened in the instinctive reaction of a man who realizes that all danger is past.

"Conning tower's empty, Archie. They've all gone. Bloody funny."

"Nothing funny about it." The bosun's tone was dry. If he was in any way moved or shaken by the narrowness of his recent escape he showed no sign. "It's customary, George, to go below and pull down the hatch after you when you're going to dive. In this case, crash dive."

"Crash dive?"

"Captain has no option. He knows she hasn't the fire-power to stop us and he can't possibly bring his torpedoes to bear. Right now he's blowing all main ballast. See those bubbles? That's water being blown from the ballast tanks by high-pressure air—something like three thousand pounds per square inch."

"But—but he's left his gun crew on deck."

"Indeed he has. Again, no choice. A U-boat is much more valuable than the lives of three men. See those valves they're twisting on the right-hand side of their suits? Oxygen valves. They're turning their Dräger lungs into life jackets. Much good it will do them if they run into a propellor. Will you go out on the wings, George, and see if there's any flame or smoke aft?"

"You could phone."

McKinnon pointed to the shredded phone in front of the wheel, shattered by a machine gun bullet. Naseby nodded and went out on both wings in turn.

"Nothing. Nothing you can see from the outside." Naseby looked ahead toward the U-boat, not much more than a hundred yards distant. "She's going down, Archie. Fore and aft decks are awash."

"I can see that."

"And she's turning away to her starboard."

"I can see that, too. Counsel of desperation. He's hoping that if he can turn his sub at an acute enough angle to us he'll be struck only a glancing blow. A glancing blow he could survive. I think."

"Hull's submerged now. Is he going to make it?"

"He's left it too late." McKinnon rang down for full astern and eased the wheel slightly to port. Five seconds later, with the top of the conning tower barely awash, the forefoot of the *San Andreas* tore into the hull of the U-boat some thirty feet for'ard of the tower. The *San Andreas* shook throughout its length but the overall effect of the impact was curiously small. For a period of not more than three seconds they felt rather than heard the sensation of steel grinding over steel. Then all contact was abruptly lost.

"Well," Naseby said, "so that's how it's done, is it?" He paused. "There's going to be a lot of jagged metal on that U-boat. If one of our props hits that—"

"No chance. The U-boat's been driven down, deep down—and they'll still be blowing main ballast. Let's just hope we haven't damaged ourselves too badly."

"You said the U-boat captain had no option. We didn't either. You think there'll be any survivors?"

"I don't know. If there are any, we'll find out soon enough. I question very much whether they would even have had time to close watertight doors. If they didn't, then that U-boat is on its way to the bottom. If anyone is going to escape, they're going to have to do it before it reaches the two-hundred-and-fifty-foot mark—I've never heard of anyone escaping from a submarine at a depth greater than that."

"They'd have to use the conning tower?"

"I suppose. There is a for'ard escape hatch—it's really an access hatch to the deck gun. But the chances are high that the fore part of the U-boat is completely flooded, so that's useless. There may be an after escape hatch, I don't know. The conning tower is probably their best bet, or would have been if we hadn't rammed them."

"We didn't hit the conning tower."

"We didn't have to. The compressive power of something like ten thousand tons deadweight has to be pretty fierce. The conning-tower hatch may have been jammed solid. Whether it would be possible to ease it or not I wouldn't know. Worse still, it may have sprung open and with a hundred gallons of water a second pouring down into the controlroom, there is no way anyone is going to get out. They'd probably be battered unconscious in the first few seconds. I'm going down on deck now. Keep going round to starboard and keep her astern till you stop, then heave to. I'll take the motorboat out as soon as you've lost enough way."

"What's the point in taking the boat if there are going to be no survivors?"

McKinnon led him out onto the port wing and astern to where three men were floundering about in the water. "Those three characters. The gun crew. As far as I could tell they were only wearing overalls and oilskins. Maybe the odd jersey or two, but that would make no difference. Leave them out there another few minutes and they'll just freeze to death."

"Let them. Those three bastards hit us aft three times. For all we can tell, some of those shells may have exploded inside the hospital."

"I know, George, I know. But I daresay there's something in the Geneva conventions about it." McKinnon clapped him lightly on the shoulder and went below.

Just outside the deck entrance to the hospital McKinnon found half a dozen people waiting for him—Patterson, Jamieson, Curran, Trent, McCrimmon and Stephen. Patterson said: "I believe we've been in some sort of collision, Bosun."

"Yes, sir. U-boat."

"And?"

McCrimmon pointed downward. "I just hope we don't go the same way. For'ard watertight bulkheads, sir?"

"Of course. At once." He looked at McCrimmon and Stephen, who left without a word. "And next, Bosun?"

"We were hit three times aft, sir. Any damage in the hospital?"

"Some. All three hit the hospital area. One appears to have exploded when it passed through the bulkhead between A and B Wards. Some injuries, no fatalities. Dr. Sinclair is attending to them."

"Not Dr. Singh?"

"He was in the recovery room with two injured seamen from the *Argos*. Door's jammed and we can't get inside."

"Shell explode in there?"

"Nobody seems to know."

"Nobody seems—but that's the next compartment to A Ward. Are they all deaf in there?"

"Yes. It was the first shell that exploded between the two wards. That deafened them all right."

"Ah. Well, the recovery room will just have to wait. What happened to the third shell?"

"Didn't explode."

"Where is it?"

"In the dining area. Rolling about quite a bit."

"Rolling about quite a bit . . ." McKinnon repeated slowly. "That's handy. Just because it didn't go off on impact—" He broke off and said to Curran: "A couple of heaving lines in the motorboat. Don't forget your knives." He went inside and reappeared within twenty seconds, carrying a very small, very innocuous-looking shell, threw it over the side and said to Jamieson: "You have your gun, sir?"

"I have my gun. What do you want the heaving lines for, Bosun?"

"Same reason as your gun, sir. To discourage people. Tie them up if we have to. If there are any survivors, they're not going to feel very kindly disposed because of what we've done to their boat and their shipmates."

"But those people aren't armed. They're submariners."

"Don't you believe it, sir. Many officers carry hand guns. Petty officers, too, for all I know."

"Even if they had guns, what could they do?"

"Take us hostage, that's what they could do. And if they could take us hostage they could still take over the ship."

Jamieson said, almost admiringly: "You don't trust many people, do you?"

"Some. I just don't believe in taking chances."

The motorboat was less than fifty yards away from the spot where the U-boat's gun crew were still floundering in the water when Jamieson touched McKinnon on the arm and pointed out over the starboard side.

"Bubbles. Lots of little bubbles."

"I see them. Could be there's someone coming up."

"I thought they always came up in a great big air bubble."

"Never. Big air bubble when they leave the submarine, perhaps. But that collapses at once." McKinnon eased back on the throttle as he approached the group in the water.

"Someone's just broken the surface," Jamieson said. "No, by God, two of them."

"Yes. They've got inflatable life jackets on. They'll keep." McKinnon stopped the engines and waited while Curran, Trent and Jamieson literally hauled the gun crew aboard—they seemed incapable of helping themselves. The trio were young, hardly more than boys, teeth chattering, shivering violently and trying hard not to look terrified.

"We search this lot?" Jamieson said. "Tie them up?"

"Good lord, no. Look at their hands—they're blue and frozen stiff. If they couldn't even hang on to the gunwale, and they couldn't, how could they press the trigger of a gun? Even if they could unbutton their oilskins, which they can't?"

McKinnon opened the throttle and headed for the two men who surfaced from the submarine. As he did, a third figure bobbed to the surface some two hundred yards beyond.

The two they hauled aboard seemed well enough. One of them was a dark-haired, dark-eyed man in his late twenties; his face was lean, intelligent and watchful. The other was very young, very blond and very apprehensive. McKinnon addressed the older man in German.

"What is your name and rank?"

"Obersteuermann Doenitz."

"Doenitz? Very appropriate." Admiral Doenitz was the brilliant Commander in Chief of the German submarine fleet. "Do you have a gun, Doenitz? If you say you haven't and I find one I shall have to shoot you because you are not to be trusted. Do you have a gun?"

Doenitz shrugged, reached under his blouse and produced a rubber-wrapped pistol.

"Your friend here?"

"Hans is an assistant cook." Doenitz spoke in fluent English. He sighed. "Young Hans is not to be trusted with a frying pan, far less a gun."

McKinnon decided to believe him for the moment and headed for the third survivor. As they approached, McKinnon could see that the man was at least unconscious, for his neck was bent forward and he was face down in the water. The reason for this was apparent: his Dräger apparatus was only partially inflated and the excess oxygen had gone to the highest point of the bag at the back of the neck, forcing his head down. McKinnon drew alongside, caught the man by his life jacket, put his hand under his chin and lifted the head from the water.

He studied the face for only a second or two then said to Doenitz: "You know him, of course."

"Heissmann, our first lieutenant."

McKinnon let the face fall back into the water. Doenitz looked at him with a mixture of astonishment and anger.

"Aren't you going to bring him aboard? He may just be unconscious, just half drowned perhaps."

"Your first lieutenant is dead," McKinnon's voice carried total conviction. "His mouth is full of blood. Ruptured lungs. He forgot to breathe out oxygen on the way up."

Doenitz nodded. "Perhaps he didn't know that he had to do that. I didn't know. I'm afraid we don't have much time for escape training these days."

He looked curiously at McKinnon. "How did you know? You're not a submariner."

"I was. Twelve years."

Curran called from the bows. "There's one more, Bosun. Just surfaced. Dead ahead."

McKinnon had the motorboat alongside the struggling man in less than a minute and had him brought aboard and laid on the thwarts. He lay there in a peculiar position, knees against his chest, his hands hugging both knees and trying to roll from side to side. He was in considerable pain. McKinnon forced open the mouth, glanced briefly inside, then gently closed it again.

"Well, this man knew enough to exhale oxygen on the way up." He looked at Doenitz. "You know this man, of course."

"Of course. Oberleutnant Klaussen."

"Your captain?" Doenitz nodded. "Well, he's in pain, but I wouldn't think he's in any danger. You can see he's been cut on the forehead—possibly banged his head on the escape hatch on the way out. But that's not enough to account for his condition, for he must have been conscious all the way up or he wouldn't have got rid of the oxygen in his lungs. Were you traveling underwater or on the surface during the night?"

"On the surface. All the time."

"That rules out carbon dioxide, which can be poisonous but you can't build up carbon dioxide when the conning tower is open. From the way he's holding his chest and legs it would seem to be caisson disease; that's where the effects hurt most. But it can't be that either."

"Caisson disease?" Jamieson said.

"Diver's bends. When there's too rapid a build-up of nitrogen bubbles in the blood when you're making a fast ascent." McKinnon, with the motorboat under full throttle, was heading directly for the *San Andreas,* which was stopped in the water at not much more than half a mile's distance. "But for that you have to be breathing in a high-pressure atmosphere for quite some time. Your captain certainly wasn't below long enough for that. Perhaps he escaped from a very great depth, perhaps a greater depth than anyone has ever escaped from a submarine. Then I wouldn't know what the effects might be. We have a doctor aboard. I don't suppose he'll know either—the average doctor can spend a lifetime and not come across a case like this. But at least he can stop the pain."

The motorboat passed close by the bows of the *San Andreas* which, remarkably, appeared to be quite undamaged. But that damage had been done was unquestionable—the *San Andreas* was at least six inches down by the head, which was no more than was to be expected if the for'ard compartments had been flooded.

McKinnon secured alongside and half helped, half carried the semi-conscious U-boat captain to the head of the gangway. Patterson was waiting for him there, as was Dr. Sinclair and three other members of the engine-room staff.

"This is the U-boat captain," McKinnon said to Dr. Sinclair. "He may be suffering from the bends, you know, nitrogen poisoning."

"Alas, Bosun, we have no decompression chamber aboard."

"I know, sir. He may just be suffering from the effects of having surfaced from a great depth. I don't know, all I know is he's suffering pretty badly. The rest are well enough, all they need is dry clothing and a little lesson in alertness." He turned to Jamieson, who had just joined him on deck. "Perhaps, sir, you would be kind enough to supervise their change of clothing?"

"You mean to make sure that they're not carrying anything they shouldn't be carrying?"

McKinnon smiled and turned to Patterson. "How are the for'ard watertight bulkheads, sir?"

"Holding. I've had a look myself. Bent and buckled but holding."

"With your permission, sir, I'll get a diving suit and have a look."

"Now? Couldn't that wait a bit?"

"I'm afraid waiting is the one thing we can't afford. We can be reasonably certain that the U-boat was in contact with Trondheim right up to the moment that he signed us to stop—I think it would be very silly of us to assume otherwise. Flannelfoot is still with us. The Germans know exactly where we are. Till now, for reasons best known to themselves, they have been treating us with kid gloves. Maybe now they'll be feeling like taking those gloves off, I shouldn't imagine that Admiral Doenitz will take too kindly to the idea of one of his U-boats being sunk by a hospital ship. I think it behooves us, sir, to get out of here and with all speed. Trouble, is we've got to make up our minds whether to go full speed ahead or full speed astern."

"Ah, yes. I see, You have a point."

"Yes, sir. If the hole in our bows is big enough, then if we make any speed at all I don't see the watertight bulkheads standing up to the pressure for very long. In that case we'd have to go astern. I don't much fancy that. It not only slows us down but it makes steering damn difficult. But it can be done. I knew of a tanker that hit a German U-boat about seven hundred miles from its port of destination. It made it—going astern all the way. But I don't much care for the idea of going stern first all the way to Aberdeen, especially if the weather breaks up."

"You make me feel downright nervous, Bosun. With all speed, Bosun, as you say, with all speed. How long will this take?"

"Just as long as it takes me to collect a rubber suit, mask and flashlight, then get there and back again. At the most, twenty minutes."

McKinnon was back in fifteen. Mask in one hand, flashlight in the other, he climbed up the gangway to where Patterson was awaiting him at the top.

"We can go ahead, sir," McKinnon said. "Full ahead, I should think."

"Good, good, good. Damage relatively slight, I take it. How small is the hole?"

"It's not a small hole. It's a bloody great hole, big as a barn door."

Patterson stared at him.

"There's a ragged piece of that U-boat, about eight foot by six, imbedded in our bows. Seems to be forming a pretty secure plug, and I should imagine that the faster we go the more securely it will be lodged."

"And if we stop, or have to go astern, or run into heavy weather—I mean, what if the plug falls off?"

"I'd be glad, sir, if you didn't talk about such things."

The Defeat of the *Yorktown*

by WALTER LORD

Signalman Peter Karetka let out a loud, long cheer. Stationed on the signal bridge of the destroyer Hughes, he was watching the motionless *Yorktown* when at 2:02 her yellow breakdown flag came down; up instead went a new hoist—"My speed 5."

On the *Yorktown* it meant that the battle of the boiler rooms had been won. Lieutenant Cundiff's diagnosis was correct. By cutting No. 1 down to a bare minimum, Lieutenant Commander Jack Delaney was able to get Nos. 4, 5 and 6 going again by 1:40, and 20 minutes later the ship was under way. With a little time Delaney thought he could work her up to 20 knots—enough to launch planes and get back into action.

Meanwhile there were other welcome developments. The cruisers *Pensacola* and *Vincennes,* the destroyers *Balch* and *Benham,* had appeared from the southeast—sent over by Spruance to beef up the screen. On the *Yorktown,* Commander Aldrich had the fires under control; by 1:50 it was safe enough to start refueling the fighters then on deck.

Solid evidence of recovery, but what gave the men their biggest lift was something less tangible. Captain Buckmaster—as good a psychologist as he was a sailor—chose this moment to break out a huge new American flag from the *Yorktown*'s foremast. No man who saw it will ever forget. To Ensign John d'Arc Lorenz, who had just been through the carnage at the 1.1 guns, it was an incalculable inspiration: "I shall always remember seeing it flutter in the breeze and what it meant to me at this critical time. It was new . . . bright colors, beautiful in the sunlight. For the first time I realized what the flag meant: all of us—a million faces—all our effort—a whisper of encouragement."

They needed it at 2:10 when the radar first picked up a new wave of bogeys to the northwest. "Stand by to repel air attack," the TBS intership radio blared. The screen moved in close, forming "disposition Victor" in a tight, protective circle. The *Yorktown* strained to build up her speed; by 2:18 she was making eight knots.

Then 10 knots . . . 12 knots . . . 15 knots by 2:28. But the *Balch* radar reported the bogeys were now only 37 miles away. Once again Worth Hare felt fear burning inside, and Signalman Donat Houle wondered what he was doing out here. On the *Benham* an Ivy League ensign nervously chattered about debutantes he had known in better times.

Captain Buckmaster watched the streaks of white foam race toward the *Yorktown*—and yearned for just a little more steam. At Coral Sea he had dodged other Japanese torpedoes—manipulating his 19,000 tons of steel with a grace that filled the crew with admiration—but then he had 30 knots to work with. Now he had only 19, and that was quite different. Still, he managed to dodge the first two streaks.

As the planes dropped, they veered away close alongside the ship. Watching from his searchlight platform, Signalman Martin wondered about the two flickering orange lights he could see in the rear cockpit. Suddenly he realized this was machine gun fire. He ducked behind a canvas wind screen and felt entirely different about the war. Bombs and torpedoes were impersonal, but this strafing was aimed at *him*. For the first time he felt really angry with the Japanese.

There were angry Japanese too. After dropping, one plane turned and flew along the *Yorktown*'s port side not 50 yards from the ship. As it went by, the rear-seat man stood up in his cockpit and shook his fist in defiance. The plane disintegrated in a hail of fire—everybody claimed it. For Gunner's Mate Jefferson Vick it was "the only time I smiled during the battle."

At 2:44 another streak of white foam appeared in the water, this time heading directly for the port side, just forward of amidships. Standing on the port catwalk, Yeoman Joseph Adams watched it come right at him. He grabbed a door and braced himself.

The jolt was appalling. Like a cat shaking a rat, like shaking out a rug—the men searched their peacetime memories for something similar . . . and found nothing to compare. Paint flew off the deck and into their faces; the catwalk rolled up like fencing; fuel oil gushed out; a yellow haze settled over the port side.

For 30 seconds Captain Buckmaster felt they just might pull through. The ship was listing 6° to port, but she still had headway. In damage control, CWT George Vavrek talked over his headphones, telling the men in the forward generator room where to transfer oil to correct the list.

Then a second torpedo hit—killing the man Vavreck was talking to . . . killing everybody in the generator room . . . knocking out all power, communications, even emergency lighting. The rudder jammed at 15° to port; a mushroom of gray-white smoke billowed up; the *Yorktown* stopped, listing 17° to port.

A sickening feeling came over Ensign Walter Beckham as he watched from the cruiser *Portland*. All antiaircraft guns were firing; 5-inch bursts blackened the sky; tracers criss-crossed in crazy patterns. Even the cruiser's 8-inch batteries were firing, in hopes that the splash would bring somebody down. The noise and clouds of smoke were bewildering, and there was something terrifying about those planes—the way they hung there in spite of all efforts to blot them out. Nothing worked, and they swept in "looking like some giant birds who were not to be foiled in their search for prey."

More planes kept coming. The *Astoria*'s gunners were again yelling like wild men. On the *Benham* a sailor named Lytells loaded 54 5-inch projectiles in a minute and 45 seconds—and each shell weighed 57 pounds. A 20 mm. crew on the *Russell* kept firing even after another destroyer fouled the range; skipper Roy Hartwig had to throw his tin hat at the gun to stop it. When the *Portland*'s 8-inchers let go, Marine Captain Donohoo—still recovering from the mumps—was knocked clear out of his bunk. Mumps or no, he rushed top-side to his station. On the *Hughes* Signalman Houle no longer wondered what the hell he was doing here. He now stood on a corner of the bridge, blazing away with a Thompson .45 submachine gun.

Occasionally they got one. There was the plane that never had a chance to make a run at all. As it broke through the screen, a freak shot (probably from the *Pensacola)* struck its torpedo. A blinding flash, and it simply vanished. Another made its drop, pulled across the *Yorktown*'s bow, and headed straight for the *Vincennes*. Captain F. L. Riefkohl saw it just in time, put his rudder hard right. Riddled from gunfire, the plane crashed 50 yards off the cruiser's bow, catapulting the pilot out of his cockpit. Still another—crowded out of position during its run—circled wide to the left and tried again. Second time around, it also opened up on the destroyer *Balch,* which happened to be in its line of sight. The *Balch* replied with everything it had; the plane disintegrated into the sea.

The U.S. fighters were there too, braving their own fleet's fire in a desperate effort to ward off the blow. Planes from the *Enterprise* and *Hornet* pitched in, but the greatest contribution came from the *Yorktown* herself. Even as the alarm sounded, she began launching the ten fighters refueling on deck; she was still at it when the Japanese began their final runs. Eighth and last man off was Ensign Milton Tootle, Jr., who had been on carrier duty just six days. Making his first nontraining flight, Tootle took off, turned hard left, tangled with a Japanese plane, shot it down, got hit himself by "friendly" fire, baled out, took a swim and was picked up by the *Anderson*—all within 15 minutes.

While the battle raged above, the men deep inside the ships waited and listened and sweated it out. In the glow of red battle lights, the members of Repair II on the *Pensacola* crouched in the darkened mess hall. They could feel the ship lurch heavily as the torpedoes slammed into the *Yorktown*—but at the time no one knew what had happened. Wondering—and not being able to shoot back—often made it harder to be below decks than above.

In the engine room of the *Astoria* Lieutenant Commander John Hayes developed a sort of ascending scale, based on the sound of gunfire, that he felt kept him pretty well informed. The dull boom of the 5-inchers meant "Maybe they're not after us"; the surging rhythm of the 1.1 mounts meant "Here they come"; the steady, angry clatter of the 50-caliber machine guns meant "Hit the floor plates!" Now he heard it all at once.

Then silence. As quickly as the Japanese appeared, they were gone again. At 2:52 the *Portland* was the last ship to cease fire—just 12 minutes after she was the first to open up. It was incredible that it all happened so quickly—and equally incredible that it all seemed so long. The men slumped by their guns in exhaustion. The elation of battle vanished; now there was utter weariness. Tears, too, as the gunners looked over at the *Yorktown*. She lay there, listing more than 20° now, wallowing in the gentle swell.

They had only one consolation. They had made the enemy pay a stiff price. Most were sure that none of the Japanese planes escaped.

"Head for the bow!" Lieutenant Hashimoto yelled as his torpedo sped on its way. Petty Officer Takahashi dropped even lower and skidded across the sea directly in front of the U.S. carrier. They drew little fire; Hashimoto thought the antiaircraft guns just couldn't get down that low.

"Did we get a hit?" Takahashi called. Hashimoto turned, but saw no sign of an explosion for a long, long time. Then suddenly a great geyser shot up so high he could see it clearly from the far side of the carrier. Without really meaning to, he let out a yelp of joy.

But his joy was interrupted. Looking around, he caught sight of CPO Nakane's plane and was horrified to see it still had its torpedo. Nakane was the "orphan" from the *Akagi*—maybe he was confused—but nothing excused this. "You fool," Hashimoto said to himself, "what did you come here for anyhow?"

He yanked back his canopy, attracted the attention of Nakane's rear-seat man, and pointed violently at the torpedo. The rear-seat man waved—yes, he understood—and jettisoned it into the sea. Hashimoto could only curse harder than ever.

Now he was back at the rendezvous point, waiting for Lieutenant Tomonaga's section to join up, but none of them ever appeared. Perhaps they were thrown off by the carrier's last-second maneuvering; perhaps Tomonaga took impossible risks. After all, he did know he could never get home on one gas tank. In any case, he and his five planes were gone.

But all five of Hashimoto's planes came through, and so did three of Lieutenant Mori's six fighters, and together they limped back toward the *Hiryu*, three of the torpedo planes too badly riddled ever to fly again. But they had done their job. Hashimoto was absolutely certain he had got a different carrier from the one hit by the dive bombers. As he neared home, he radioed ahead the glad tidings: "Two certain torpedo hits on an *Enterprise* class carrier. Not the same one as reported bombed."

Watching the *Enterprise* and *Hornet* untouched on the horizon was too much for Seaman Ed Forbes. "When are those two over there going to get into the fight?" he asked aloud to anyone who would listen. It was small of him and he knew it, but he was scared. As a gunner on the *Anderson*, desperately trying to protect the *Yorktown*, all he wanted at the moment was another big target to attract the Japs' attention.

Certainly the *Yorktown* had taken her share. Five minutes after the attack the clinometer on the bridge showed she was listing 26°. Captain Buckmaster checked below over the sound-powered phone, but heard only bad news. Lieutenant Commander Delaney reported from the engine room that all fires were out—no hope for any power. The auxiliary generator snapped on, but with all circuits out, it made no difference. Lieutenant Commander Aldrich, down in central station, said that without power there was no way he could pump, counterflood, shift fuel, or do anything else to correct the list. On the bridge, it looked as though the *Yorktown* might roll over.

Captain Buckmaster paced up and down in agony for several minutes. To no one in particular, he remarked aloud that he hated to give the order to abandon ship. The officers standing around gaped at him mutely. It was one of those moments that give true meaning to the loneliness of command.

Finally he said there was nothing else to do—they must abandon. The *Yorktown* seemed doomed, and as he later put it, "I didn't see any sense in drowning 2,000 men just to stick with the ship."

At 2:55 the order went out—by flag hoist to the screen, by word of mouth and sound-powered phone to the men below. From the engine room, the sick bay, the repair stations, the message center, a stream of men stumbled through darkened passageways, up oil-slick ladders, working their way clumsily topside.

The list, the darkness, the oil all made it difficult. No abandon-ship drill was ever like this. In the confusion most of the men ignored or forgot the usual procedures. The rough log was left on the bridge. The code room personnel left the safe open, code books and secret message files lying around. The airmen were just as hurried: some 70 sets of air contact codes lay scattered about the squadron ready rooms.

Down in the sick bay the doctors and corpsmen worked with flashlights, trying to get some 50-60 wounded men to the flight deck. Nothing was tougher than carrying those stretchers up the swinging ladders, across the oil-smeared deck plates. In the operating room the senior medical officer, Captain W. D. Davis, and his chief surgeon, Lieutenant Commander French, continued treating a wounded sailor. No one even told them the ship was being abandoned.

Hundreds of men milled around the flight deck, not knowing quite what to do. Some waited patiently at their regular stations by the motor launches—forgetting there was no power to lower the boats. Others were throwing life rafts overboard—sometimes still bundled together. Some walked sadly up and down the slanting deck, heart-heavy at the thought of leaving the ship. Others laughed and joked, and if the laughter seemed a little forced—well, everybody understood that.

Not that there weren't sour notes. One commander—obviously in a state of shock, his face dirty and tear-streaked—found out that Radioman James Patterson was in the last SBD that landed before the attack. "You led them here!" he screamed, trying to hit Patterson.

Now it was after 3:00. The destroyers moved in reassuringly close, and the men finally began to go. Commander Ralph Arnold knew just how to do it; he had talked with survivors from the *Lexington*. He carried a knife, took some gloves, and he was especially careful to keep on his shoes: when picked up, he'd have something to wear.

Most of the crew were more like Machinist's Mate George Bateman. He carefully arranged a neat pile on the deck consisting of his shoes, shirt, gloves, hat and flashlight. Gradually, in fact, pairs of shoes lined the whole deck, all meticulously placed with the toes pointing out.

At first a trickle, soon a steady stream of men were pouring down the starboard side. Dozens of knotted ropes hung from the rails, and Lieutenant William Crenshaw felt this would be the perfect time to use the knowledge he gained at the Naval Academy on climbing and descending ropes. One should go down carefully hand over hand, the instructor said, but when Crenshaw tried it, he plummeted straight down into the sea. The difference between this rope and the one at Annapolis was oil—it was everywhere, making a good grip next to impossible.

Others had the same trouble. Worth Hare burned his hands sliding down. Seaman Melvin Frantz was making it all right; then the man above slipped, came down on Frantz's shoulders, and they both plunged into the sea. Boatswain C. E. Briggs lost his grip too, and felt it took forever to come to the surface. He forgot he had given his life jacket away and was wearing shoes, sweater, pistol, two clips of ammunition, plus all his regular clothing. The wonder was he ever came up at all.

Occasionally a man did it right. Yeoman William Lancaster put on a turtleneck sweater, tightened his life jacket, and carefully lowered himself down one of the lines. When he reached the end, he did not let go. To his own great surprise, he stopped, held on to the line, and instinctively stuck his foot down to test the temperature of the water.

Some added a dash all their own. Commander "Jug" Ray went down clenching his inevitable brier pipe. Chief Radioman Grew gave his famous waxed mustache a farewell twirl. A young fireman asked Radio Electrician Bennett's permission to dive from the flight deck—he had wanted to do it ever since coming on board. Permission granted.

For the swimmers there was now a new hazard. The oil from the ripped port side had worked around to starboard, making a thick film that gradually spread out from the ship. Men retched and vomited as they struggled toward the clear water farther off. Watching from the flight deck, it reminded Yeoman Adams of a large group of turtles or crawfish swimming in a half-dried pond of mud and muck.

The nonswimmers posed a special problem. The more knowledgeable men gave up their own life jackets to help, but few took as decisive action as Radioman Patterson. As he pushed away from the ship, a sailor grabbed his shoulder, saying he couldn't swim. Patterson gave the man a 30-second course in dogpaddling—not a word wasted—and the two moved off together.

Another special problem was the sailor trapped when the torpedo struck and curled up the port catwalk. The wire mesh pinned him against the side of the *Yorktown* in his own private prison. It was on the low side of the ship, leading to all sorts of unpleasant possibilities if she rolled over. His buddies worked on anyhow, trying to pry him out. They finally succeeded, but all the time he was there he kept begging his friends to leave him and save themselves.

Down in the operating room, Captain Davis and Lieutenant Commander French still worked over their wounded man, oblivious of everything else. Finally finished, Davis went out and called for a corpsman to move the patient. Nobody answered the call. He asked some sailor with a walkie-talkie where the corpsman was.

"Oh," explained the sailor, "they passed the word some time ago for all hands to abandon ship." He added he was about to leave himself.

Davis and French carried their man to the flight deck; then Davis went down to check again. He looked around and called, but couldn't hear any one. Finally satisfied, he climbed back to the deck.

By now most of the swimmers, boats and rafts were all clear of the *Yorktown*. Looking around, Davis couldn't see any one else still aboard—just a vast, empty stretch of flight deck. He hung his gun on the lifeline and like so many before him, carefully placed his shoes at the edge of the deck. Then he inflated his life jacket and climbed down a rope ladder into the sea, feeling sure he was the last man off.

Captain Buckmaster watched him go, as did his executive officer Dixie Kiefer. Both men were standing on the starboard wing of the bridge—Buckmaster waiting to play out the old tradition that the captain be the last to leave his ship. Now it was Kiefer's turn to go. He swung over the side and started down a line toward the water. But he had burned his hands earlier and, like so many others, he lost his grip. Falling, he caromed off the ship's armor belt, breaking his ankle in the process. It took more than that to stop the ebullient Kiefer; he bobbed to the surface and swam for the rescue ships in the distance.

Buckmaster began a final tour of the *Yorktown* alone. First along the starboard catwalk all the way to the 5-inch gun platforms. Then back to the flight deck by No. 1 crane . . . down through Dressing Station No. 1 . . . forward through Flag Country and to the captain's cabin . . . across to the port side . . . down the ladder to the hangar deck.

Now it was really dark. There were a few emergency lamps in the island structure, but absolutely nothing down here—just yards and yards of empty blackness. He didn't even have a flashlight—someone had swiped that long ago.

He groped through a labyrinth of passageways and compartments, trying to walk with the list, keep his footing on the oil-slick deck. He banged into hatches, stumbled over bodies, slashed his leg on some jagged piece of steel.

On he went—always searching for any sign of life, shouting from time to time into the darkness.

No answer, except great belching sounds of air bursting out of compartments as one more bulkhead gave way and the water rushed in. Or sometimes a clanking door or a grating of steel, as the ship rose and fell in the gentle swell.

He went as deep as he dared. Finding no one, he felt his way topside again and walked aft to the very stern. A brief pause for a last look at his ship; then Elliot Buckmaster swung over the taffrail, caught a line, and dropped to the sea.

"Well, there goes 20 years' sermon notes," sighed one of the *Yorktown*'s chaplains as his raft moved clear of the ship. Captain Buckmaster also found a raft, loaded with wounded, and hung onto the ratlines. A launch came up, tossed over a line and began to pull. As the line jerked taut, a mess attendant lost his grip and drifted astern. He went under twice, yelling for help. A figure darted over and saved him. It was Buckmaster.

Dr. Davis had nothing to cling to. He was still swimming by himself, which perhaps made him all the more apprehensive when he glanced around and thought he saw the snout of a large fish. He turned the other way, but it followed him. Steeling his nerve, he made a grab—and came up with his own wallet.

Lieutenant Commander Hartwig could hardly believe his eyes. His destroyer *Russell* had been picking up scores of men—they came aboard in every conceivable way—but never anything like this. One of his launches was approaching the ship crowded to the gunwales with perhaps three times its supposed capacity; it was towing a life raft so loaded with men it was invisible; and the raft in turn was towing a long manila line to which scores of men were clinging like bees. And as if all this wasn't enough, at the very end of the line was the *Yorktown*'s supply officer, Commander Ralph Arnold, holding aloft his hat. Arnold, it later turned out, had just made commander; his wife had sent him a brand-new scrambled-eggs cap, and he wasn't about to ruin it in the oily water. At the moment Hartwig simply yelled down to him that no *Yorktown* sailor would ever have to tip his hat to get aboard the *Russell*.

Off to port Lieutenant Commander Harold Tiemroth on the *Balch* was putting into practice all the rescue plans he had so carefully made after Coral Sea. His men tossed over the specially prepared cargo nets and were soon hauling in scores of oil-soaked men. His hand-picked rescue swimmers Seaman Lewis and Fireman Prideaux went after those too exhausted to reach the ship. Ensign Weber took the motor whaleboat on trip after trip, sometimes gathering in 50 men at a time.

It was much the same on all seven destroyers. The *Benham* alone picked up 721. By 4:46, when the *Balch* completed a final swing around the scene, the little flotilla had rescued a grand total of 2,270 men. But the real meaning of this lay not in statistics, but in the human beings themselves. There was the *Yorktown* cook who gave up his life jacket, swam a thousand yards to the

Benham, then asked as he scrambled aboard, "Where's the galley? The cooks are going to need all the help they can get tonight." There was Commander Laing, Royal Navy; now dripping with oil, he reached the deck of the *Morris,* put on his British cap, saluted the colors and said, "God bless the King; God bless the U.S. Navy." There was the injured seaman—also on the *Morris*— who climbed aboard unassisted saying, "Help some of those other poor guys that are really hurt." He had lost his own leg at the knee.

Looking back at the *Yorktown,* listing heavily and silhouetted alone in the twilight, Commander Hartwig could barely stand the sight. For two years his destroyer *Russell* had been the carrier's guard ship. He felt almost a part of her. Now he was steaming away. With the survivors rescued, Admiral Fletcher had ordered the ships in the screen to head east and join up with Admiral Spruance. Orders were orders, but it wasn't easy to leave that sagging, lonely hulk. One thought, paraphrased from *Hamlet,* kept running through Hartwig's mind: "Alas, poor Yorick, I knew her well."

There were many others who felt, as they left the scene, that "it didn't seem right" to abandon the *Yorktown.* She was holding her own—the fires were contained, her list was no greater—and the *Portland* stood rigged to give her a tow. But there were other factors too, and Frank Jack Fletcher had to consider them all. It was getting dark . . . Japanese snoopers were about . . . Yamamoto's heavy ships were somewhere . . . enemy subs might turn up . . . a task force guarding a derelict carrier made an ideal target.

Once again war turned into a matter of "groping around." Fletcher weighed his chances, finally decided the odds were too dangerous. At 5:38 he issued his orders sending everybody east. For the next 35 minutes the *Yorktown* wallowed alone in the dusk; then at 6:13 new orders went out, detaching the destroyer *Hughes* to stand by her.

At sea the destroyer *Hughes* stood lonely guard on the deserted *Yorktown.* As Commander Ramsey saw the situation, he could expect the Japs to send one or two surface ships to finish her off during the night. He could also expect submarines, and perhaps an air attack after dawn. He had orders to sink the carrier to prevent capture or if serious fires developed—in any case, sink her before he got sunk.

All through the night he steamed an unpredictable course around the hulk. In the dark the *Yorktown* was an eerie sight. There were what appeared to be flickering lights, and members of the crew thought they could even hear voices and strange noises when the destroyer was close. Ramsey considered boarding to check—then thought better of it. That would mean stopping, lowering a boat, using lights. He would be just inviting trouble on a night like this. So the *Hughes* continued her nervous vigil.

No one on the destroyer *Hughes* actually saw the Japanese search plane. It was just a blip on the radar, picked up at 6:26 A.M. as the ship continued her lonely job of guarding the *Yorktown*. Commander Ramsey ordered the crew to stand by to repel air attack, but no one ever came. The blip just hovered there, 20 miles to the west, for about ten minutes. Then it gradually faded away.

The incident made the men all the more nervous when at 7:41 machine-gun bullets began cutting the water off the port side of the *Yorktown*. At first Signalman Peter Karetka was sure some Jap had sneaked in for a strafing run, but when no plane appeared, he knew it couldn't be that. Commander Ramsey thought it might be a gun going off, overheated by a smoldering fire somewhere.

More splashes, and the men suddenly realized it could only be somebody still alive on the *Yorktown*, trying to attract attention. The *Hughes* stood in close. There, sure enough, was a man waving from the port side of the hangar deck. Ramsey lowered his motor whaleboat, and the boarding party soon found Seaman Norman Pichette, now slumped unconscious beside his gun. He had a bad stomach wound and was wrapped in a sheet. They were all back on the *Hughes* by 8:35, and moments later the ship's doctor was cutting away the sheet. This seemed to rouse Pichette, who came to long enough to mumble there was still another man alive, lying in the *Yorktown*'s sick bay.

Again the whaleboat chugged over. This time it returned with Seaman George Weise, who had fractured his skull when blown off the smokestack. Weise never knew how he got to sick bay; he just remembered dimly hearing the alarm and the call to abandon ship. It was dark; the *Yorktown* was listing heavily; the ladder topside hung loose at a crazy angle. In the blur of shapes and shadows trying to get the wounded out, he recalled someone coming over to help him. Then he heard, or thought he heard, a voice say, "Leave him and let's go—he's done for anyway."

The last thing he remembered was sitting up in his bunk and swearing a blue streak . . . but by then everyone was gone. For hours he lay helpless in the dark, semiconscious and never able to move. Finally he became vaguely aware that Pichette was in the room too, also left behind in some fashion. Pichette was very badly off, but at least he could move. In the end it was he who found the strength to get up, wrap himself in his sheet, and stagger up three decks for help.

Were there any others? The men in the motor whaleboat thought so. They reported strange tapping sounds from deep inside the carrier, suggesting men trapped below. Ramsey sent the boat back again—this time with orders to explore everywhere. They found important code materials but no human beings. The tapping, it turned out, was just the sound of creaking steel as the *Yorktown* wallowed in the swell. No one else was alive on the ship.

But someone was very much alive in the water. While the whaleboat was off exploring the *Yorktown*, the men on the *Hughes* were amazed to see a man in a yellow rubber raft paddling furiously toward them. He turned out to be Ensign Harry Gibbs of Fighting 3. Gibbs had been shot down defending the *Yorktown* the day before. He spent a long night in his raft, then sighted the carrier at sunrise. He paddled six miles to get back to his ship.

Around 10:00 the mine sweeper *Vireo* turned up, and Ramsey arranged for a tow. A line was rigged, and by early afternoon they were under way, heading east at about two knots. The *Yorktown* yawed dreadfully. She seemed unwilling to leave the scene of battle. At times, in fact, she appeared to be pulling the *Vireo* backward.

Other destroyers began turning up—the *Gwin*, the *Monaghan*. With more muscle on hand, a jettisoning party went over to the *Yorktown*, began dropping loose gear overboard to help straighten her up. During the afternoon Ramsey also sent a message to CINCPAC, urging the organization of a salvage party. The carrier was holding her own; he was sure she could be saved.

Admiral Fletcher and Captain Buckmaster needed no prodding from CINCPAC. They were working hard on their own to save the *Yorktown*. But it wasn't a simple matter. By the morning of the 5th, Task Force 17 was 150 miles east of the carrier, and over 2,000 survivors were scattered among six different destroyers. It would take time to cull out the specialists needed for a proper salvage party and then get them back to the scene. One by one the destroyers came alongside the *Astoria,* and the men needed were transferred by breeches buoy to the cruiser. Here they were organized, briefed, and transferred again to the destroyer *Hammann,* which would take them back. They were mostly engineers and technicians, but there was no lack of volunteers among the cooks and yeomen. Everybody wanted to go. Finally guards had to be placed at the highlines to keep useless personnel from sneaking over in their determination to get back to the "Old Lady."

Midafternoon, and the *Hammann* started off. On board were Captain Buckmaster and a crack salvage team which, with the addition of a few from the *Hughes,* totaled 29 officers and 141 men. Escorted by the destroyers *Balch* and *Benham,* they reached the *Yorktown* shortly after 2:00 A.M. on the 6th.

Safety for the *Yorktown* meant Pearl Harbor, and by the dawn of June 6 the chances seemed better than ever of getting her there. Sunrise found the battered carrier still holding her own in a calm and dazzling sea.

Captain Buckmaster led the salvage party aboard. With a small burial party he first climbed to the sharply canted flight deck, where many of the dead still lay at their posts. Chief Pharmacist's Mate James Wilson turned to give some instructions, but the Captain silenced him with a wave of the hand. Uncovering, he addressed himself in prayer, gave thanks for the victory, and recited verbatim the beautiful but seldom-used service for Burial of the Dead at Sea.

This moment of reverie soon gave way to the clatter of hammers and the sputter of acetylene torches. Working parties started cutting away loose gear to lighten the ship. Others pitched two stranded planes, all live bombs and torpedoes into the sea. Lieutenant Greenbacker began collecting the classified papers strewn about.

The *Hammann* nudged up to the starboard side to provide power, portable pumps and fire hoses. Down below, men attacked the blaze still smoldering in the rag locker and began the important work of counterflooding. A high moment came when the first 5-inch gun on the port side was cut loose and dropped overboard. Free of the weight, the whole ship shook . . . and seemed to straighten up a little in relief.

By 1:00 P.M. they had worked 2° off the *Yorktown*'s list. It was time for a break, and the *Hammann* sent over fruit and sandwiches. Some distance out, the other five destroyers slowly circled the carrier. They were listening for submarines, but it was hard to tell. Echo-ranging conditions were poor due to what destroyer men call a "thermal barrier." Yet this was often the case on calm days, and there was no hint of real trouble. It was just 1:30, and on the *Yorktown* the men were about to go back to work. . . .

Lieutenant Tanabe raised his periscope for a last look. The carrier was now about 1,300 yards away. She was still under tow, but barely moving. The destroyer was still alongside. The others were still circling slowly—no sign they suspected. The hydrophone man said he couldn't even hear the enemy's sound detection system working. Tanabe made a mild joke about the Americans all being out to lunch.

The *I-168* had worked hard for this perfect chance. Nearly eight hours had passed since the lookout's cry of a "black object" on the horizon. It was, of course, the crippled U.S. carrier, just where Tanabe expected to find her at dawn.

It was only 5:30, and for the first 10 or 20 minutes he stayed on the surface. Approaching from the west, he was still sheltered by darkness. Then it got too light for that, and he submerged, poking up his periscope every 15 minutes.

By 7:00 the *I-168* was about six miles off, and Tanabe had a much better picture of the situation. For the first time he could see the destroyers guarding the carrier. To make detection harder, he now cut his speed to three knots and raised his periscope only once or twice an hour.

Ever so carefully, he stole closer. To get a sure kill, he decided to fire his four torpedoes with a spread of only 2°, instead of the usual 6°. This meant a bigger punch amidships, but it also required getting as near as possible.

He dived still lower, hoping to get through the destroyer screen. Next time he looked he was safely through, but now he was too close. The carrier loomed like a mountain only 700 yards away. He needed that much for the torpedo to run true. Slowly he curled in a wide circle to starboard, coming around to try again. This time everything was perfect. . . .

"Hey, look, porpoises!" CPO Joseph Kisela heard somebody call, pointing off the starboard side of the *Yorktown*. A couple of men stared out to sea. "Porpoises, hell!" a sailor snorted.

A machine gun on the bridge began firing. This was the prearranged signal in case of danger. There was a wild scramble topside. Coming up from the engine room, Lieutenant Cundiff looked to starboard and saw four white torpedo streaks heading straight for the ship. An avid photographer, he gasped. "What a once-in-a-lifetime shot, and no camera!"

Lieutenant Greenbacker, about to transfer some files to the *Hammann*, fled "downhill" to the port side of the quarterdeck. Then the thought occurred that torpedoes might be coming from that side too. He worked his way back "uphill" to the center of the ship—as close to neutral ground as he could get. Here he waited for the torpedoes to hit, and that seemed to take forever.

One missed . . . one struck the *Hammann* . . . the other two passed under the destroyer and crashed into the *Yorktown* amidships. Once again there was that teeth-rattling jar that came only from torpedoes. It whipped the tripod mast, shearing off most of the rivets at the base. It knocked down the ship's bell, shattering it completely. It bowled over the damage control officer, Commander Aldrich, breaking his left arm. It hurled Commander Davis, cutting loose the 5-inchers, right into the sea. It almost made Commander Ray bite off the stem of his pipe.

Seeing it was about to happen, Chief Electrician W. E. Wright made a wild leap to the deck of the *Hammann*. But this was no solution, for she was hit at almost the same instant. Wright was blown high in the air, landing in the water.

Commander Arnold True was desperately trying to back the *Hammann* clear when the torpedoes hit. To the end his gunners were firing at the streaks, hoping to explode the warheads. The crash hurled True across the bridge and into a chart desk, breaking two ribs and knocking out his wind. He couldn't speak for several minutes.

Few words were needed. The *Hammann*'s fate was clearly sealed. The concussion from the two hits on the *Yorktown* stove in her plates, and the direct hit snapped her almost in two. She looked like a toy ship that had been dropped from a great height—upright but broken.

Within two minutes the foredeck was awash, and the executive officer Lieutenant Ralph Elden ordered abandon ship. As the bow bent under, most of the crew swam off. Chief Torpedoman Berlyn Kimbrell, however, remained on the rising stern, trying to put the depth carges on "safe" and handing out life jackets. When Boilermaker Raymond Fitzgibbon went over the side, Kimbrell shook hands with him and gave him the Churchill "Victory" sign.

Then she was gone, but the worst was yet to come. The depth charges— though presumably set on "safe"—went off anyhow. (There are a dozen theories.) An immense explosion erupted under the water, right where everyone was swimming. The concussion was fantastic: one sailor's metal cigarette lighter was mashed absolutely flat in his pocket. The effect on a man's body could be far worse than that.

The destroyers *Benham* and *Balch* left the screen, rescuing the lucky ones who escaped, plus several from the *Yorktown* too. One man swam up to the *Benham* and climbed aboard unassisted. It was the same ship's cook they had saved on the 4th, who wanted only to help in the galley. This time he simply said, "I know where the galley is, I'll go get to work."

Long after everyone else was picked up, the *Balch* spotted a lone swimmer among the debris. He was desperately trying to hold the faces of two other men out of the water. It was the *Hammann*'s skipper Commander True. Barely conscious himself, he had struggled alone for nearly three hours to keep two of his dying men alive.

On the *Yorktown* it was time to leave again. The two new hits on the starboard side had the effect of straightening her up, but that was deceiving. She was definitely lower in the water. The *Vireo* pulled along the starboard side, and the salvage party swung down the lines to safety.

When everyone else seemed to be off, Captain Buckmaster came down hand over hand. Then at the last minute Commander Delaney and one of his engineers appeared from a final inspection below and also left the ship. Deprived of the privilege of being the last to leave, Buckmaster was enormously upset. He even wanted to swing back up the line and touch the *Yorktown* again, but the *Vireo* cast off before he could make it.

"My God, she's going right on over, isn't she?" Boatswain Forest Lunsford gasped to Ensign J. T. Andrews, as they stood on the *Benham* watching the *Yorktown* in the first light of day, June 7. For the men in the destroyer screen, the sight of the carrier at dawn ended any hope they still had of saving her.

Some time during the night the *Yorktown* had heeled back heavily to port, and by 4:30 her flight deck slanted into the water. Great bubbles were foaming up, and loud cracking noises came from somewhere inside her. From the halyards her last signal hoist hung straight down—"My speed, 15." Captain Buckmaster's American flag was still flying, but it almost touched the sea.

At 4:43 she lay on her port side, revealing a huge hole in her starboard bilge—the result of yesterday's submarine attack. The end was near, and at 4:54 all ships half-masted their colors; all hands uncovered and came to attention. Two patrolling PBYs appeared overhead and dipped their wings in salute.

At 5:01, well down at the stern, the *Yorktown* slowly sank from sight. There were the usual noises, the veil of smoke and steam, but to most of the men she went quietly and with enormous dignity—"like the great lady she was," as one of them put it.

On the *Hughes* Signalman Karetka fought to hold back his tears. He was very young and wanted to appear grown up. Then he saw that even the old-timers were crying, so he didn't feel too badly when he wept too.

Sea Disasters

A Wild Cannon Dooms
the *Claymore*

by VICTOR HUGO

One of the carronades of the battery, a twenty-four pound cannon, had become loose.

This is perhaps the most dreadful thing that can take place at sea. Nothing more terrible can happen to a man-of-war under full sail.

A cannon that breaks loose from its fastenings is suddenly transformed into a supernatural beast. It is a monster developed from a machine. This mass runs along on its wheels as easily as a billiard ball; it rolls with the rolling, pitches with the pitching, comes and goes, stops, seems to meditate, begins anew, darts like an arrow from one end of the ship to the other, whirls around, turns aside, evades, rears, hits out, crushes, kills, exterminates. It is a ram battering a wall at its own pleasure. Moreover, the battering-ram is iron, the wall is wood. It is matter set free; one might say that this eternal slave is wreaking its vengeance; it would seem as though the evil in what we call inanimate objects had found vent and suddenly burst forth; it has the air of having lost its patience, and of taking a mysterious, dull revenge; nothing is so inexorable as the rage of the inanimate. The mad mass leaps like a panther; it has the weight of an elephant, the agility of a mouse, the obstinacy of the axe; it takes one by surprise, like the surge of the sea; it flashes like lightning; it is deaf as the tomb; it weighs ten thousand pounds, and it bounds like a child's ball; it whirls as it advances, and the circles it describes are intersected by right angles. And what help is there? How can it be overcome? A calm succeeds the tempest, a cyclone passes over, a wind dies away, we replace the broken mass, we check the leak, we extinguish the fire; but what is to be done with this enormous bronze beast? How can it be subdued? You can reason with a mastiff, take a bull by surprise, fascinate a snake, frighten a tiger, mollify a lion; but there is no resource with the monster known as a loosened gun. You cannot kill it,—it is already dead; and yet it lives. It breathes a sinister life bestowed on it by the Infinite. The plank beneath sways it to and fro; it is moved by the ship; the sea lifts the ship, and the wind keeps the sea in motion. This destroyer is a toy. Its terrible vitality is fed by the ship, the waves, and the wind, each lending its aid. What is to be done with this complication? How fetter this monstrous mechanism of shipwreck? How forsee its comings and goings, its recoils, its halts, its shocks? Any one of those blows may stave in the side of the vessel. How can one guard against these terrible gyrations? One has to do with a projectile that reflects, that has ideas, and changes its direction at any moment. How can one arrest an object in its course, whose onslaught must be avoided? The dreadful cannon rushes about, advances, recedes, strikes to right and to left, flies here and there, baffles their attempts at capture, sweeps away obstacles, crushing men like flies.

The extreme danger of the situation comes from the unsteadiness of the deck. How is one to cope with the caprices of an inclined plane? The ship had within its depths, so to speak, imprisoned lightning struggling for escape; something like the rumbling of thunder during an earthquake. In an instant the crew was on its feet. It was the chief gunner's fault, who had neglected to fasten the screw-nut of the breeching chain, and had not thoroughly chocked the four trucks of the carronade, which allowed play to the frame and bottom of the gun-carriage, thereby disarranging the two platforms and parting the breeching. The lashings were broken, so that the gun was no longer firm on its carriage. The stationary breeching which prevents the recoil was not in use at that time. As a wave struck the ship's side the cannon, insufficiently secured, had receded, and having broken its chain, began to wander threateningly over the deck. In order to get an idea of this strange sliding, fancy a drop of water sliding down a pane of glass.

When the fastening broke, the gunners were in the battery, singly and in groups, clearing the ship for action. The carronade, thrown forward by the pitching, dashed into a group of men, killing four of them at the first blow; then, hurled back by the rolling, it cut in two an unfortunate fifth man, and struck and dismounted one of the guns of the larboard battery. Hence the cry of distress which had been heard. All the men rushed to the ladder. The gun-deck was empty in the twinkling of an eye.

The monstrous gun was left to itself. It was its own mistress, and mistress of the ship. It could do with it whatsoever it wished. This crew, accustomed to laugh in battle, now trembled. It would be impossible to describe their terror.

Captain Boisberthelot and Lieutenant la Vieuville, brave men though they were, paused at the top of the ladder, silent, pale, and undecided, looking down on the deck. Some one pushed them aside with his elbow, and descended. It was their passenger, the peasant, the man about whom they were talking a moment ago.

Having reached the bottom of the ladder he halted.

The cannon was rolling to and fro on the deck. It might have been called the living chariot of the Apocalypse. A dim wavering of lights and shadows was added to this spectacle by the marine lantern, swinging under the deck. The outlines of the cannon were indistinguishable, by reason of the rapidity of its motion; sometimes it looked black when the light shone upon it, then again it would cast pale, glimmering reflections in the darkness.

It was still pursuing its work of destruction. It had already shattered four other pieces, and made two breaches in the ship's side, fortunately above the water-line, but which would leak in case of rough weather. It rushed frantically against the timbers; the stout riders resisted,—curved timbers have great strength; but one could hear them crack under this tremendous assault brought to bear simultaneously on every side, with a certain omnipresence truly appalling.

A bullet shaken in a bottle could not produce sharper or more rapid sounds. The four wheels were passing and repassing over the dead bodies, cutting and tearing them to pieces, and the five corpses had become five trunks rolling hither and thither; the heads seemed to cry out; streams of blood flowed over the deck, following the motion of the ship. The ceiling, damaged in several places, had begun to give way. The whole ship was filled with a dreadful tumult.

The captain, who had rapidly recovered his self-possession, had given orders to throw down the hatchway all that could abate the rage and check the mad onslaught of this infuriated gun; mattresses, hammocks, spare sails, coils of rope, the bags of the crew, and bales of false assignats, with which the corvette was laden,—that infamous stratagem of English origin being considered a fair trick in war.

But what availed these rags? No one dared to go down to arrange them, and in a few moments they were reduced to lint.

There was just sea enough to render this accident as complete as possible. A tempest would have been welcome. It might have upset the cannon, and with its four wheels once in the air, it could easily have been mastered. Meanwhile the havoc increased. There were even incisions and fractures in the masts, that stood like pillars grounded firmly in the keel, and piercing the several decks of the vessel. The mizzen-mast was split, and even the main-mast was damaged by the convulsive blows of the cannon. The destruction of the battery still went on. Ten out of the thirty pieces were useless. The fractures in the side increased, and the corvette began to leak.

The old passenger, who had descended to the gun-deck, looked like one carved in stone as he stood motionless at the foot of the stairs and glanced sternly over the devastation. It would have been impossible to move a step upon the deck.

Each bound of the liberated carronade seemed to threaten the destruction of the ship. But a few moments longer, and shipwreck would be inevitable.

They must either overcome this calamity or perish; some decisive action must be taken. But what?

What a combatant was this carronade!

Here was this mad creature to be arrested, this flash of lightning to be seized, this thunderbolt to be crushed. Boisberthelot said to Vieuville:—

"Do you believe in God, Chevalier?"

"Yes and no, sometimes I do!" replied La Vieuville.

"In a tempest?"

"Yes, and in moments like these."

"Truly God alone can save us," said Boisberthelot.

All were silent, leaving the carronade to its horrible uproar.

The waves beating the ship from without answered the blows of the cannon within, very much like a couple of hammers striking in turn.

Suddenly in the midst of this inaccessible circus, where the escaped cannon was tossing from side to side, a man appeared, grasping an iron bar. It was the author of the catastrophe, the chief gunner, whose criminal negligence had caused the accident,—the captain of the gun. Having brought about the evil, his intention was to repair it. Holding a handspike in one hand, and in the other a tiller rope with the slip-noose in it, he had jumped through the hatch-way to the deck below.

Then began a terrible struggle; a titanic spectacle; a combat between cannon and cannoneer; a contest between mind and matter; a duel between man and the inanimate. The man stood in one corner in an attitude of expectancy, leaning on the rider and holding in his hands the bar and the rope; calm, livid, and tragic, he stood firmly on his legs, that were like two pillars of steel.

He was waiting for the cannon to approach him.

The gunner knew his piece, and he felt as though it must know him. They had lived together a long time. How often had he put his hand in its mouth. It was his domestic monster. He began to talk to it as he would a dog. "Come," said he. Possibly he loved it.

He seemed to wish for its coming, and yet its approach meant sure destruction for him. How to avoid being crushed was the question. All looked on in terror.

Not a breath was drawn freely, except perhaps by the old man, who remained on the gun-deck gazing sternly on the two combatants.

He himself was in danger of being crushed by the piece; still he did not move.

Beneath them the blind sea had command of the battle. When, in the act of accepting this awful hand-to-hand struggle, the gunner approached to challenge the cannon, it happened that the surging sea held the gun motionless for an instant, as though stupefied. "Come on!" said the man. It seemed to listen.

Suddenly it leaped towards him. The man dodged. Then the struggle began,—a contest unheard of; the fragile wrestling with the invulnerable; the human warrior attacking the brazen beast; blind force on the one side, soul on the other.

All this was in the shadow. It was like an indistinct vision of a miracle.

A soul!—strangely enough it seemed as if a soul existed within the cannon, but one consumed with hate and rage. The blind thing seemed to have eyes. It appeared as though the monster were watching the man. There was, or at least one might have supposed it, cunning in this mass. It also chose its opportunity. It was as though a gigantic insect of iron was endowed with the will of a demon. Now and then this colossal grasshopper would strike the low ceiling of the gun-deck, then falling back on its four wheels, like a tiger on all fours, rush upon the man. He—supple, agile, adroit—writhed like a serpent before these lightning movements. He avoided encounters; but the blows from which he escaped fell with destructive force upon the vessel. A piece of broken chain remained attached to the carronade. This bit of chain had twisted in some incomprehensible way around the breech-button.

One end of the chain was fastened to the gun-carriage; the other end thrashed wildly around, aggravating the danger with every bound of the cannon. The screw held it as in a clenched hand, and this chain, multiplying the strokes of the battering-ram by those of the thong, made a terrible whirlwind around the gun,—a lash of iron in a fist of brass. This chain complicate the combat.

Despite all this, the man fought. He even attacked the cannon at times, crawling along by the side of the ship and clutching his handspike and the rope; the cannon seemed to understand his movements, and fled as though suspecting a trap. The man, nothing daunted, pursued his chase.

Such a struggle must necessarily be brief. Suddenly the cannon seemed to say to itself: Now, then, there must be an end to this. And it stopped. A crisis was felt to be at hand. The cannon, as if in suspense, seemed to meditate, or— for to all intents and purposes it was a living creature—it really did meditate, some furious design. All at once it rushed on the gunner, who sprang aside with a laugh, crying out, "Try it again!" as the cannon passed him. The gun in its fury smashed one of the larboard carronades; then, by the invisible sling in which it seemed to be held, it was thrown to the starboard, towards the man, who escaped. Three carronades were crushed by its onslaught; then, as though blind and beside itself, it turned from the man, and rolled from stern to stem, splintering the latter, and causing a breach in the walls of the prow. The gunner took refuge at the foot of the ladder, a short distance from the old man, who stood watching. He held his handspike in readiness. The cannon seemed aware of it, and without taking the trouble to turn, it rushed backward on the man, as swift as the blow of an axe. The gunner, if driven up against the side of the ship, would be lost.

One cry arose from the crew.

The old passenger—who until this moment had stood motionless—sprang forward more swiftly than all those mad whirls. He had seized a bale of the false assignats, and at the risk of being crushed succeeded in throwing it between the wheels of the carronade. This decisive and perilous manoeuvre could not have been executed with more precision and adroitness by an adept in all the exercises given in the work of Durosel's "Manual of Naval Gunnery."

The bale had the effect of a plug. A pebble may block a log; a branch sometimes changes the course of an avalanche. The carronade stumbled, and the gunner, availing himself of the perilous opportunity, thrust his iron bar between the spokes of the back wheels. Pitching forward, the cannon stopped; and the man, using his bar for a lever, rocked it backward and forward. The heavy mass upset, with the resonant sound of a bell that crashes in its fall. The man, reeking with perspiration, threw himself upon it, and passed the slip-noose of the tiller-rope around the neck of the defeated monster.

The combat was ended. The man had conquered. The ant had overcome the mastodon; the pygmy had imprisoned the thunderbolt.

The soldiers and sailors applauded.

The crew rushed forward with chains and cables, and in an instant the cannon was secured.

Saluting the passenger, the gunner exclaimed,—

"Sir, you have saved my life!"

The old man had resumed his impassible attitude, and made no reply.

The man had conquered; but it might be affirmed that the cannon also had gained a victory. Immediate shipwreck was averted; but the corvette was still in danger. The injuries the ship had sustained seemed irreparable. There were five breaches in the sides, one of them—a very large one—in the bow, and twenty carronades out of thirty lay shattered in their frames. The recaptured gun, which had been secured by a chain, was itself disabled. The screw of the breech-button being wrenched, it would consequently be impossible to level the cannon. The battery was reduced to nine guns; there was a leakage in the hold. All these damages must be repaired without loss of time, and the pumps set in operation. Now that the gun-deck had become visible, it was frightful to look upon. The interior of a mad elephant's cage could not have been more thoroughly devastated. However important it might be for the corvette to avoid observation, the care for its immediate safety was still more imperative. They were obliged to light the deck with lanterns placed at intervals along the sides.

In the mean time, while this tragic entertainment had lasted, the crew, entirely absorbed by a question of life and death, had not noticed what was going on outside of the ship. The fog had thickened, the weather had changed, the wind had driven the vessel at will; they were out of their course, in full sight of Jersey and Guernsey, much farther to the south than they ought to have been, and confronting a tumultuous sea. The big waves kissed the wounded sides of the corvette with kisses that savored of danger. The heaving of the sea grew threatening; the wind had risen to a gale; a squall, perhaps a tempest, was brewing. One could not see four oars' length before one.

While the crew made haste with their temporary repairs on the gun-deck, stopping the leaks and setting up the cannons that had escaped uninjured, the old passenger returned to the deck.

He stood leaning against the main-mast.

He had taken no notice of what was going on in the ship. The Chevalier de la Vieuville had drawn up the marines on either side of the main-mast, and at a signal-whistle of the boatswain the sailors, who had been busy in the rigging, stood up on the yards. Count Boisberthelot approached the passenger. The captain was followed by a man, who, haggard and panting, with his dress in disorder, still wore on his countenance an expression of content.

It was the gunner who had so opportunely displayed his power as a tamer of monsters, and gained the victory over the cannon.

The count made a military salute to the old man in the peasant garb, and said to him:—

"Here is the man, General."

The gunner, with downcast eyes, stood erect in a military attitude.

"General," resumed Count Boisberthelot, "considering what this man has done, do you not think that his superiors have a duty to perform?"

"I think so," replied the old man.

"Be so good as to give your orders," resumed Boisberthelot.

"It is for you to give them; you are the captain."

"But you are the general," answered Boisberthelot.

The old man looked at the gunner.

"Step forward," he said.

The gunner advanced a step.

Turning to Count Boisberthelot, the old man removed the cross of Saint Louis from the captain's breast, and fastened it on the jacket of the gunner. The sailors cheered, and the marines presented arms.

Then pointing to the bewildered gunner he added:

"Now let the man be shot!"

Stupor took the place of applause.

Then, amid a tomb-like silence, the old man, raising his voice, said:—

"The ship has been endangered by an act of carelessness, and may even yet be lost. It is all the same whether one be at sea or face to face with the enemy. A ship at sea is like an army in battle. The tempest, though unseen, is ever present; the sea is an ambush. Death is the fit penalty for every fault committed when facing the enemy. There is no fault that can be retrieved. Courage must be rewarded and negligence punished."

These words fell one after the other slowly and gravely, with a certain implacable rhythm, like the strokes of the axe upon an oak-tree. Looking at the soldiers, the old man added,—

"Do your duty!"

The man on whose breast shone the cross of Saint Louis bowed his head, and at a sign of Count Boisberthelot two sailors went down to the gun-deck, and presently returned bringing the hammock-shroud; the two sailors were accompanied by the ship's chaplain, who since the departure had been engaged in saying prayers in the officers' quarters. A sergeant detached from the ranks twelve soldiers, whom he arranged in two rows, six men in a row. The gunner placed himself between the two lines. The chaplain, holding a crucifix, advanced and took his place beside the man. "March!" came from the lips of the sergeant; and the platoon slowly moved towards the bow, followed by two sailors carrying the shroud.

A gloomy silence fell on the corvette. In the distance a hurricane was blowing. A few moments later, a report echoed through the gloom; one flash, and all was still. Then came the splash of a body falling into the water. The old passenger, still leaning against the main-mast, his hands crossed on his breast, seemed lost in thought. Boisberthelot, pointing towards him with the fore-finger of his left hand, remarked in an undertone to La Vieuville,—

"The Vendée had found a leader."

But what was to become of the corvette? The clouds that had mingled all night with the waves had now fallen so low that they overspread the sea like a mantle, and completely shut out the horizon. Nothing but fog,—always a dangerous situation, even for a seaworthy vessel.

A heavy swell was added to the mist.

They had improved their time; the corvette had been lightened by throwing into the sea everything that they had been able to clear away after the havoc caused by the carronade,—dismantled cannons, gun-carriages, twisted or loosened timbers, splintered pieces of wood and iron; the portholes were opened, and the corpses and parts of human bodies, wrapped in tarpaulin, were slid down on planks into the sea.

The sea was running high. Not that the tempest was imminent. On the other hand, it seemed as if the hurricane, that was rumbling afar off on the horizon, and the wind were both decreasing and moving northward; but the waves were still high, showing an angry sea, and the corvette in its disabled condition could with difficulty resist the shocks, so that the high waves might prove fatal to it. Gacquoil, absorbed in thought, remained at the helm. To show a bold front in the presence of danger is the habit of commanders.

La Vieuville, whose spirits rose in time of trouble, addressed Gacquoil.

"Well, Pilot," he said, "the squall has subsided. Its sneezing-fit came to naught. We shall pull through. We shall get some wind, and nothing more."

"We can't have wind without waves."

A true sailor, neither gay nor sad; and his reply was charged with an anxious significance. For a leaking ship a high sea means a rapid sinking. Gacquoil had emphasized this prediction by frowning. Perhaps he thought that after the catastrophe with the cannon and the gunner, La Vieuville had been too quick to use light-hearted, almost cheerful, words. Certain things bring ill-luck at sea. The sea is reticent; one never knows its intentions, and it is well to be on one's guard.

La Vieuville felt obliged to resume his gravity.

"Where are we, Pilot?" he asked.

"In the hands of God," replied the pilot.

A pilot is a master; he must always be allowed to do what pleases him, and often to say what he chooses. That kind of man is not apt to be loquacious. La Vieuville left him, after asking a question to which the horizon soon replied.

The sea had suddenly cleared.

The trailing fogs were rent; the dusky heaving waves stretched as far as the eye could penetrate into the dim twilight, and this was the sight that lay before them.

The sky was shut in by clouds, although they no longer touched the water. The dawn had begun to illumine the east, while in the west the setting moon still cast a pale glimmering light. These two pallid presences in opposite quarters of the sky outlined the horizon in two narrow bands of light between the dark sea and the gloomy sky. Black silhouettes were sketched against them, upright and motionless.

In the west, against the moonlit sky, three high cliffs stood forth, like Celtic cromlechs.

In the east, against the pale horizon of the morning, eight sails drawn up in a row in formidable array came in view. The three cliffs were a reef, the eight sails a squadron. Behind them was Minquiers, a cliff of ill-repute, and in front were the French cruisers. With an abyss on the left hand, and carnage on the right, they had to choose between shipwreck and a battle. The corvette must either encounter the cliffs with a damaged hull, a shattered rigging, and broken masts, or face a battle, knowing that twenty out of the thirty cannons of which her artillery consisted were disabled, and the best of her gunners dead.

The dawn was still faint, and the night not yet ended. This darkness might possibly last for quite a long time, as it was caused mostly by the clouds that hung high in the air, thick and dense, looking like a solid vault.

The wind had scattered the sea-fog, driving the corvette on Minquiers.

In her extreme weakness, and dilapidated as she was, she hardly obeyed the helm as she rolled helplessly along, lashed onward by the force of the waves.

The Minquiers—that tragic reef!—was more dangerous at that time than it is now. Several of the turrets of this marine fortress have been worn away by the incessant action of the sea. The form of reefs changes; waves are fitly likened unto swords; each tide is like the stroke of a saw. At that time, to be stranded on the Minquiers meant certain death. The cruisers composed the squadron of Cancale,—the one that afterwards became so famous under the command of Captain Duchesne, called by Lequinio "Père Duchesne."

The situation was critical. During the struggle with the carronade the ship had wandered unconsciously from her course, sailing more in the direction of Granville than of St. Malo. Even had her sailing power been unimpaired, the Minquiers would have barred her return to Jersey, while the cruisers hindered her passage towards France. Although there was no storm, yet, as the pilot had said, the sea was rough. Rolled by the heavy wind over a rocky bottom, it had grown savage.

The sea never tells what it wants at the first onset. Everything lies concealed in its abyss, even trickery. One might almost affirm that it has a scheme. It advances and recedes; it offers and refuses; it arranges for a storm, and suddenly gives up its intention; it promises an abyss, and fails to keep its agreement; it threatens the north, and strikes the south. All night long the corvette

Claymore labored with the fog and feared the storm; the sea had disappointed them in a savage sort of way. It had drawn a storm in outline, and filled in the picture with a reef.

It was to be a shipwreck in any event, but it had assumed another form, and with one enemy to supplement the work of the other, it was to combine a wreck on the surf with destruction by battle.

"A shipwreck on the one hand and a fight on the other!" exclaimed Vieuville amid his gallant laughter. "We have thrown double-fives on both sides!"

The corvette was little better than a wreck.

A sepulchral solemnity pervaded the dim twilight, the darkness of the clouds, the confused changes of the horizon, and the mysterious sullenness of the waves. There was no sound except the hostile blasts of the wind. The catastrophe rose majestic from the abyss. It looked more like an apparition than an attack. No stir on the rocks, no stir on the ships. The silence was overpowering beyond description. Were they dealing with reality? It was like a dream passing over the sea. There are legends that tell of such visions. The corvette lay, so to speak, between a demon reef and a phantom fleet.

Count Boisberthelot in a low voice gave orders to La Vieuville, who went down to the gun-deck, while the captain, seizing his telescope, stationed himself behind the pilot. Gacquoil's sole effort was to keep up the corvette to the wind; for if struck on her side by the sea and the wind, she would inevitably capsize.

"Pilot, where are we?" said the captain.

"On the Minquiers."

"On which side?"

"On the worst one."

"What kind of bottom?"

"Small rocks."

"Can we turn broadside on?"

"We can always die."

The captain turned his spy-glass towards the west and examined the Minquiers; then turning it to the east he watched the sails that were in sight.

The pilot went on, as though speaking to himself:

"Yonder is the Minquiers. That is where the laughing sea-mew and the great black-hooded gull stop to rest when they migrate from Holland."

Meanwhile the captain had counted the sails.

There were, indeed, eight ships drawn up in line, their warlike profiles rising above the water. In the centre was seen the stately outline of a three-decker.

The captain questioned the pilot.

"Do you know those ships?"

"Of course I do."

"What are they?"

"That's the squadron."

"Of the French?"

"Of the Devil."

A silence ensued; and again the captain resumed his questions.

"Are all the cruisers there?"

"No, not all."

In fact, on the 2d of April, Valazé had reported to the Convention that ten frigates and six ships of the line were cruising in the Channel. The captain remembered this.

"You are right," he said; "the squadron numbers sixteen ships, and only eight are here."

"The others are straggling along the coast down below, on the lookout," said Gacquoil.

Still gazing through his spy-glass the captain murmured,—

"One three-decker, two first-class and five second-class frigates."

"I too have seen them close at hand," muttered Gacquoil. "I knew them too well to mistake one for the other."

The captain passed his glass to the pilot.

"Pilot, can you make out distinctly the largest ship?"

"Yes, Commander. It is the *Côte-d'Or.*"

"They have given it a new name. It used to be the *États de Bourgogne,*—a new ship of a hundred and twenty-eight cannon."

He took a memorandum-book and pencil from his pocket, and wrote down the number "128."

"Pilot, what is the first ship on the port?"

"The *Expérimentée.*"

"A frigate of the first class; fifty-two guns. She was fitting out at Brest two months ago."

The captain put down on his note-book the number "52."

"What is the second ship to port, Pilot?"

"The *Dryade.*"

"A frigate of the first class; forty eighteen-pounders. She has been in India, and has a glorious military record."

And below the "52" he wrote the number "40." Then, raising his head, he said,—

"Now, on the starboard?"

"They are all second-class frigates, Commander; there are five of them."

"Which is the first one from the ship?"

"The *Résolue.*"

"Thirty-two eighteen-pounders. The second?"

"The *Richmond.*"

"Same. Next?"

"The *Athée.*"

"A queer name to sail under. Next?"

"The *Calypso.*"

"Next?"

"The *Preneuse.*"

"Five frigates, each of thirty-two guns."

The captain wrote "160" under the first numbers.

"You are sure you recognize them, Pilot?" he asked.

"You also know them well, Commander. It is something to recognize them; but it is better to know them."

The captain, with his eyes on the note-book, was adding up the column to himself.

"One hundred and twenty-eight, fifty-two, forty, one hundred and sixty."

Just then La Vieuville came up on deck.

"Chevalier," exclaimed the captain, "we are facing three hundred and eighty cannon."

"So be it," replied La Vieuville.

"You have just been making an inspection, La Vieuville: how many guns have we fit for service?"

"Nine."

"So be it," responded Boisberthelot in his turn; and taking the telescope from the pilot, he scanned the horizon.

The eight black and silent ships, though they appeared immovable, continued to increase in size.

They were gradually drawing nearer.

La Vieuville saluted the captain.

"Commander," he said, "here is my report. I mistrusted this corvette *Claymore*. It is never pleasant to be suddenly ordered on board a ship that neither knows nor loves you. An English ship is a traitor to the French. That slut of a carronade proved this. I have made the inspection. The anchors are good; they are not made of inferior iron, but hammered out of solid bars; the flukes are solid; the cables are excellent, easy to pay out, and have the requisite length of one hundred and twenty fathoms. Plenty of ammunition; six gunners dead; each gun has one hundred and seventy-one rounds."

"Because there are only nine cannon left," grumbled the captain.

Boisberthelot levelled his glass to the horizon. The squadron continued its slow approach. Carronades have one advantage: three men are sufficient to man them. But they also have a disadvantage: they do not carry as far, and shoot with less precision than cannon. It was therefore necessary to let the squadron approach within the range of the carronades.

The captain gave his orders in a low voice. Silence reigned on the ship. No signal to clear the decks for action had been given, but still it had been done. The corvette was as helpless to cope with men as with the sea. They did their best with this remnant of a war-ship. Near the tiller-ropes on the gangway were piled spare hawsers and cables, to strengthen the mast in case of need. The quarters for the wounded were put in order. According to the naval practice of those days, they barricaded the deck,—which is a protection against balls, but not against bullets. The ball-gauges were brought, although it was rather late to ascertain the caliber; but they had not anticipated so many incidents. Cartridge-boxes were distributed among the sailors, and each one secured a pair of pistols and a dirk in his belt. Hammocks were stowed away, guns were pointed, and muskets, axes, and grapplings prepared. The cartridge and bullet stores were put in readiness; the powder-magazine was opened; every man stood at his post. Not a word was spoken while these preparations went on amid haste and gloom; and it seemed like the room of a dying person.

Then the corvette was turned broadside on. She carried six anchors, like a frigate, and all of them were cast,—the spare anchor forward, the kedger aft, the sea-anchor towards the open, the ebb-anchor towards the breakers, the bower-anchor to starboard, and the sheet-anchor to port. The nine uninjured carronades were placed as a battery on the side towards the enemy.

The squadron, equally silent, had also finished its evolutions. The eight ships now stood in a semi-circle, of which Minquiers formed the chord. The *Claymore* enclosed within this semicircle, and held furthermore by its own anchors, was backed by the reef,—signifying shipwreck. It was like a pack of hounds surrounding a wild boar, not giving tongue, but showing its teeth.

It seemed as if each side were waiting for something.

The gunners of the *Claymore* stood to their guns.

Boisberthelot said to La Vieuville,—

"I should like to be the first to open fire."

"A coquette's fancy," replied La Vieuville.

The passenger had not left the deck; he watched all that was going on with his customary impassibility.

Boisberthelot went up to him.

"Sir," he said, "the preparations are completed. We are now clinging to our grave; we shall not relax our hold. We must succumb either to the squadron or to the reef. The alternative is before us: either shipwreck among the breakers or surrender to the enemy. But the resource of death is still left; better to fight than be wrecked. I would rather be shot than drowned; fire before water, if the choice be left to me. But where it is our duty to die it is not yours. You are the man chosen by princes. You have an important mission,—that of directing the Vendean war. Your death might result in the failure of monarchy; therefore you must live. While honor requires us to stand by the ship, it calls on you to escape. You must leave us, General; I will provide you with a boat and a man. You may succeed in reaching the shore, by making a détour. It is not yet daylight; the waves are high and the sea dark. You will probably escape. There are occasions when to flee means to conquer."

The old man bent his stately head in token of acquiescence.

Count Boisberthelot raised his voice.

"Soldiers and sailors!" he called.

Every movement ceased, and from all sides faces were turned in the direction of the captain.

He continued:—

"This man who is among us represents the king. He has been intrusted to our care; we must save him. He is needed for the throne of France. As we have no prince, he is to be,—at least we hope so,—the leader of the Vendée. He is a great general. He was to land with us in France; now he must land without us. If we save the head we save all."

"Yes, yes, yes!" cried the voices of all the crew.

The captain went on:—

"He too is about to face a serious danger. It is not easy to reach the coast. The boat must be large enough to live in this sea, and small enough to escape the cruisers. He must land at some safe point, and it will be better to do so nearer Fougères than Coutances. We want a hardy sailor, a good oarsman and a strong swimmer, a man from that neighborhood, and one who knows the straits. It is still so dark that a boat can put off from the corvette without attracting attention; and later there will be smoke enough to hide it from view. Its size will be an advantage in the shallows. Where the panther is caught, the weasel escapes. Although there is no outlet for us, there may be for a small rowboat; the enemy's ships will not see it, and, what is more, about that time we shall be giving them plenty of diversion. It is decided?"

"Yes, yes, yes!" cried the crew.

"Then there is not a moment to be lost," continued the captain. "Is there a man among you willing to undertake the business?"

In the darkness, a sailor stepped out of the ranks and said,—

"I am the man."

A few minutes later, one of those small boats called a gig, which are always devoted to the use of the captain, pushed off from the ship. There were two men in this boat,—the passenger in the stern, and the volunteer sailor in the bow. The night was still very dark. The sailor, according to the captain's instructions, rowed energetically towards the Minquiers. For that matter, it was the only direction in which he could row. Some provisions had been placed in the bottom of the boat,—a bag of biscuits, a smoked tongue, and a barrel of water.

Just as they were lowering the gig, La Vieuville, a very scoffer in the presence of destruction, leaning over the stern-post of the corvette, cried out in his cool sneering voice a parting word:—

"Very good for escaping, and still better for drowning."

"Sir, let us joke no more," said the pilot.

They pushed off rapidly, and soon left the corvette far behind. Both wind and tide were in the oarsman's favor, and the small skiff flew rapidly along, wavering to and fro in the twilight, and hidden by the high crests of the waves.

A gloomy sense of expectation brooded over the sea.

Suddenly amid this illimitable, tumultuous silence a voice was heard; exaggerated by the speaking-trumpet, as by the brazen mask of ancient tragedy, it seemed almost superhuman.

It was Captain Boisberthelot speaking.

"Royal marines," he exclaimed, "nail the white flag to the mizzen-mast! We are about to look upon our last sunrise!"

And the corvette fired a shot.

"Long live the King!" shouted the crew.

Then from the verge of the horizon was heard another shout, stupendous, remote, confused, and yet distinct,—

"Long live the Republic!"

And a din like unto the roar of three hundred thunderbolts exploded in the depths of the sea.

The conflict began. The sea was covered with fire and smoke.

Jets of spray thrown up by the balls as they struck the water rose from the sea on all sides.

The *Claymore* was pouring forth flame on the eight vessels; the squadron, ranged in a semicircle around her, opened fire from all its batteries. The horizon was in a blaze. A volcano seemed to have sprung from the sea. The wind swept to and fro this stupendous crimson drapery of battle through which the vessels appeared and disappeared like phantoms. Against the red sky in the foreground were sketched the outlines of the corvette.

The fleur-de-lis flag could be seen floating from the main-mast.

The two men in the boat were silent. The triangular shoal of the Minquiers, a kind of submarine Trinacrium, is larger than the isle of Jersey. The sea covers it. Its culminating point is a plateau that is never submerged, even at the highest tide, and from which rise, towards the northeast, six mighty rocks standing in a line, producing the effect of a massive wall which has crumbled here and there. The strait between the plateau and the six reefs is accessible only to vessels drawing very little water. Beyond this strait is the open sea.

The sailor who had volunteered to manage the boat headed for the strait. Thus he had put Minquiers between the boat and the battle. He navigated skilfully in the narrow channel, avoiding rocks to starboard and port. The cliff now hid the battle from their view. The flaming horizon and the furious din of the cannonade were growing less distinct, by reason of the increased distance; but judging from the continued explosions one could guess that the corvette still held its own, and that it meant to use its hundred and ninety-one rounds to the very last. The boat soon found itself in smooth waters beyond the cliffs and the battle, and out of the reach of missiles. Gradually the surface of the sea lost something of its gloom; the rays of light that had been swallowed up in the shadows began to widen; the curling foam leaped forth in jets of light, and the broken waves sent back their pale reflections. Daylight appeared.

The boat was beyond reach of the enemy, but the principal difficulty still remained to be overcome. It was safe from grape-shot, but the danger of shipwreck was not yet past. It was on the open sea, a mere shell, with neither deck, sail, mast, nor compass, entirely dependent on its oars, face to face with the ocean and the hurricane,—a pygmy at the mercy of giants.

Then amid this infinite solitude, his face whitened by the morning light, the man in the bow of the boat raised his head and gazed steadily at the man in the stern as he said,—

"I am the brother of him whom you ordered to be shot."

The Loss of the *Endurance*

by SIR ERNEST SHACKLETON

The ice did not seriously trouble us again until the end of September, though during the whole month the floes were seldom entirely without movement. The routine of work and play on the *Endurance* steadily proceeded. Our plans and preparations for any contingency which might arise during the approaching summer had been made, but there was always plenty to do in and about our prisoned ship. Runs with the dogs and vigorous games of hockey and football on the rough, snow-covered floe kept all hands in good condition.

By the middle of September we were running short of fresh meat for the dogs. Nearly five months had passed since we had killed a seal, and penguins had seldom been seen. But on the 23rd we got an emperor penguin, and on the following day we secured a crab-eater seal. The return of seal-life was most opportune, as we wished to feed the dogs on meat, and seals also meant a supply of blubber to supplement our small remaining stock of coal.

During the last days of September the roar of the pressure grew louder, and I could see that the area of disturbance was rapidly approaching the ship. Stupendous forces were at work, and the fields of firm ice around the *Endurance* were steadily diminishing.

September 30th was a bad day, for at 3 P.M. cracks, which had opened during the night alongside the ship, began to work in a lateral direction. The ship sustained terrific pressure. The decks shuddered and jumped, beams arched, and stanchions buckled and shook. I ordered all hands to stand by in readiness for any emergency. But the ship resisted valiantly, and just when it seemed that the limit of her strength was being reached, one huge floe which was pressing down upon us cracked across and so gave relief.

"The behaviour of our ship in the ice," Worsley wrote, "has been magnificent. Since we have been beset her staunchness and endurance have been almost past belief again and again. . . . It will be sad if such a brave little craft should be finally crushed in the remorseless, slowly strangling grip of the Weddell pack, after ten months of the bravest and most gallant fight ever put up by a ship."

Indeed, the *Endurance* deserved all that could be said in praise of her. Shipwrights had never done sounder or better work. But how long could she continue the fight under such conditions? The vital question for us was whether the ice would open sufficiently to release us before the drift carried us into the dangerous area which we were approaching? With anxious hearts we faced the month of October.

On the first day of that month two bull crab-eaters climbed on to the floe close to the ship and were shot by Wild. They were both big animals in prime condition, and all anxiety as to the supply of fresh meat for the dogs was removed. Seal-liver also made a welcome change in our own diet.

Two or three days later we had no doubt that the movement of the ice was increasing. Frost-smoke from opening cracks was showing in all directions during October 6th. In one place it looked like a great prairie fire, at another it resembled a train running before the wind, the smoke rising from the engine straight upward; elsewhere the smoke columns gave the effect of warships steaming in line ahead.

Conditions did not change materially during the next two or three days, but on the 10th a thaw made things uncomfortable for us, and the dogs, who hated wet, looked most unhappy. The thaw indicated that winter was over, and we began preparations to re-occupy the cabins on the main deck. I also made several preparations for working the ship as soon as she was clear.

For several days the temperature remained relatively high, and all hands— amid much noise and laughter—moved on the 12th to their summer quarters in the upper cabins. On the 13th the ship broke free of the floe on which she rested to starboard sufficiently to come upright. The rudder freed itself and, the water being very clear, we could see that it had only suffered a slight twist to port at the water-line. It moved quite freely. The propeller, however, was found to be athwartship, and I did not think it advisable to try to deal with it at that stage.

The south-westerly breeze freshened to a gale on the 14th, and the temperature fell from +31° Fahr. to −1° Fahr. The wind died down during the day and the pack opened for five or six miles to the north. Our efforts, however, to force the ship out of the lead failed, and heavy pressure developed late on Sunday, the 17th. The two floes between which the ship was lying began to close, and the *Endurance* was subjected to a series of tremendously heavy strains. In the engine-room, the weakest point, loud groans, crashes and hammering sounds were heard. For nearly an hour the ship valiantly stood the strain, and then, to my great relief, she began to rise with heavy jerks and jars. The ice was getting below us and the immediate danger was past. Our position was lat. 69° 19' S., long. 50° 40' W.

The next attack of the ice came during the afternoon of October 19th. The two floes began to move laterally and exerted great pressure on the ship. Suddenly the floe on the port side cracked and huge pieces of ice shot up from under the port bilge. Within a few seconds the ship heeled over until she had a list of 30 degrees to port, being held under the starboard bilge by the opposing floe. Everything movable on deck and below fell to the lee side, and for a few minutes it looked as if the ship would be thrown upon her beam ends. The midship dog-kennels broke away and crashed down on to the lee kennels, and the howls and barks of the frightened dogs helped to create a perfect pandemonium. Order, however, was soon restored.

If the ship had heeled any farther it would have been necessary to release the lee boats and pull them clear, and Worsley was watching to give the alarm. Dinner in the wardroom that evening was a curious affair, for most of the diners had to sit on the deck, their feet against battens and their plates on their knees. At 8 P.M. the floes opened, and within a few minutes the *Endurance* was again nearly upright.

Although the ship was still securely imprisoned in the pool, it was obvious that our chance might come at any moment, and watches were set so as to be ready for working ship. At 11 A.M. on October 20th we gave the engines a gentle trial astern. Everything worked well after eight months of frozen inactivity, except that the bilge-pump and the discharge proved to be frozen up; with some little difficulty they were cleared.

The next two days brought low temperatures with them, and the open leads again froze over. The pack was working, and the roar of pressure ever and anon was heard. We waited for the next move of the gigantic forces arrayed against us, and on Sunday, October 24th, the beginning of the end for the *Endurance* came. The position was lat. 69° 11' S., long. 51° 5' W.

We now had twenty-two and a half hours of daylight, and throughout the day we watched the threatening advance of the floes. At 6.45 P.M. the ship sustained heavy pressure in a dangerous position. The onslaught was almost irresistible. The ship groaned and quivered as her starboard quarter was forced against the floe, twisting the stern-post and starting the heads and ends of planking. The ice had lateral as well as forward movement, and the ship was twisted and actually bent by the stresses. She began to leak dangerously at once.

I had the pumps rigged, got up steam, and started the bilge pumps by 8 P.M. By that time the pressure had relaxed. The ship was making water rapidly aft, and all hands worked, watch and watch, during the night, pumping ship and helping the carpenter. By morning the leak was being kept in check.

On Monday, October 25th, the leak was kept under fairly easily, but the outlook was bad. Heavy pressure-ridges were forming in all directions, and I realised that our respite from pressure could not be prolonged. The pressure-ridges, massive and menacing, testified to the overwhelming nature of the forces at work. Huge blocks of ice, weighing many tons, were lifted into the air and tossed aside as other masses rose beneath them.

I scarcely dared to hope any longer that the *Endurance* would live, and during that anxious day I reviewed all my plans for the sledging journey which we should have to make if we had to take to the ice. As far as forethought could make us we were ready for any contingency. Stores, dogs, sledges and equipment were ready to be moved from the ship at a moment's notice.

The following day was bright and clear, and the sunshine was inspiring. But the roar of pressure continued, new ridges were rising, and as the day wore on

I could see the lines of major disturbance were drawing nearer to the ship. The day passed slowly. At 7 P.M. very heavy pressure developed, with twisting strains which racked the ship fore and aft. The butts of planking were opened 4 or 5 inches on the starboard side, and at the same time we could see the ship bending like a bow under titanic pressure. Almost like a living creature she resisted the forces which would crush her; but it was a one-sided battle. Millions of tons of ice pressed inexorably upon the gallant little ship which had dared the challenge of the Antarctic. She was now leaking badly, and at 9 P.M. I gave the order to lower boats, gear, provisions and sledges to the floe, and move them to the flat ice a little way from the ship.

Then came a fateful day—Wednesday, October 27th. The position was lat. 69° 5′ S., long. 51° 30′ W. The temperature was −8.5° Fahr., a gentle southerly breeze was blowing and the sun shone in a clear sky.

"After long months of ceaseless anxiety and strain," I wrote, "after times when hope beat high and times when the outlook was black indeed, the end of the *Endurance* has come. But though we have been compelled to abandon the ship, which is crushed beyond all hope of ever being righted, we are alive and well, and we have stores and equipment for the task that lies before us. The task is to reach land with all the members of the Expedition. It is hard to write what I feel. To a sailor his ship is more than a floating home, and in the *Endurance* I had centred ambitions, hopes and desires. And now she is slowly giving up her sentient life at the very outset of her career. . . . The distance from the point where she became beset to the place where she now rests mortally hurt in the grip of the floes is 573 miles, but the total drift through all observed positions has been 1,186 miles, and we probably covered more than 1,500 miles.

"We are now 346 miles from Paulet Island, the nearest point where there is any possibility of finding food and shelter. A small hut built there by the Swedish Expedition in 1902 is filled with stores left by the Argentine relief ship. . . . The distance to the nearest barrier west of us is about 180 miles, but a party going there would still be about 360 miles from Paulet Island, and there would be no means of sustaining life on the barrier. We could not take food enough from here for the whole journey; the weight would be too great. . . .

"The attack of the ice reached its climax at 4 P.M. The ship was hove stern up by the pressure, and the driving floe, moving laterally across the stern, split the rudder and tore out the rudder-post and stern-post. Then, while we watched, the ice loosened and the *Endurance* sank a little. The decks were breaking upwards and the water was pouring in below. Again the pressure began, and at 5 P.M. I ordered all hands on to the ice.

"At last the twisting, grinding floes were working their will on the ship. It was a sickening sensation to feel the decks breaking up under one's feet, the great beams bending and then snapping with a noise like heavy gun-fire. The water was overmastering the pumps, and to avoid an explosion when it reached the boilers I ordered the fires to be drawn and the steam let down. The plans for abandoning the ship in case of emergency had been well made, and men and dogs made their way to an unbroken portion of the floe without a hitch.

"Just before leaving I looked down the engine-room skylight as I stood on the quivering deck, and saw the engines dropping sideways as the stays and bed-plates gave way. I cannot describe the impression of relentless destruction which was forced upon me as I looked down and around. The floes, with the force of millions of tons of moving ice behind them, were simply annihilating the ship."

Essential supplies had been placed on the floe about 100 yards from the ship, but after we had begun to pitch our camp there the ice started to split and smash beneath our feet. Then I had the camp moved to a bigger floe, and boats, stores and camp equipment had to be conveyed across a working pressure-ridge. A pioneer party, with picks and shovels, had to build a snow-causeway before we could get all our possessions across. By 8 P.M. the camp had been pitched again.

We had two pole tents, and three hoop tents which are easily shifted and set up. I took charge of the small pole tent, No. 1, with Hudson, Hurley and James as companions; Wild had the small hoop tent, No. 2, with Wordie, McNeish and McIlroy. The eight forward hands had the large hoop tent, No. 3; Crean had charge of No. 4 hoop tent, with Hussey, Marston and Cheetham; and Worsley had the other pole tent, No. 5, with Greenstreet, Lees, Clark, Kerr, Rickenson, Macklin, and Blackborrow, the last-named being the youngest of the forward hands.

After the tents had been pitched I mustered all hands and explained the position as briefly and clearly as I could. I told them the distance to the Barrier and the distance to Paulet Island, and stated that I proposed to try to march with equipment across the ice in the direction of Paulet Island. I thanked the men for the steadiness they had shown under trying circumstances, and told them I did not doubt that we should all eventually reach safety provided that they continued to work their utmost and to trust me. Then we had supper, and all hands except the watch turned in.

But, for myself, I could not sleep, and the thoughts which came to me as I walked up and down in the darkness were not particularly cheerful. At midnight I was pacing the ice, listening to the grinding floe and the groans and crashes that told of the death-agony of the *Endurance*, when I noticed suddenly a crack running across our floe right through the camp. The alarm-whistle brought all hands tumbling out, and we moved everything from what was now the smaller portion of the floe to the larger portion. Nothing more could be done then, and the men turned in again; but there was little sleep.

Morning came in chill and cheerless, and all hands were stiff and weary after their first disturbed night on the floe. Just at daybreak I went over to the *Endurance* with Wild and Hurley to retrieve some tins of petrol, which could be used to boil up milk for the rest of the men. The ship presented a painful spectacle of chaos and wreck, but with some difficulty we secured two tins of petrol, and postponed the further examination of the ship until after breakfast, when I went over to the *Endurance* again and examined the wreck more fully.

Only six of the cabins had not been pierced by floes and blocks of ice. All the starboard cabins had been crushed, and the whole of the aft part of the ship had been crushed concertina fashion. The forecastle and "The Ritz" were submerged, and the wardroom was three-quarters full of ice. The motor-engine forward had been driven through the galley. In short, scenes of devastation met me on every side. The ship was being crushed remorselessly.

Under a dull, overcast sky I returned to the camp, and, having examined the situation, I thought it wise to move to a larger and apparently stronger floe about 200 yards away. This camp became known as Dump Camp, owing to the amount of stuff that was thrown away there. I decided to issue a complete new set of Burberrys and underclothing to each man, and also a supply of socks. The camp was quickly transferred to the new floe, and there I began to direct the preparations for the long journey across the floes to Paulet Island or Snow Hill.

Meanwhile Hurley had rigged his kinematograph camera, and was getting pictures of the *Endurance* in her death-throes. While he was thus engaged, the foretop and top-gallant mast came down with a run and hung in wreckage on the fore-mast, with the foreyard vertical. The mainmast followed immediately, snapping off about 10 feet above the main deck. The crow's-nest fell within 10 feet of where Hurley was turning the handle of his camera, but he did not stop the machine and so secured a unique, though sad, picture.

The Torpedoing of the *Lusitania*

by DAVID BUTLER

On the wing of the bridge, Captain Turner was also watching the large prom-ontory to starboard. He was easier in his mind now that he knew where he was. The three-mile peninsula with its lighthouse could only be the Old Head of Kinsale, with the small fishing harbor of Kinsale tucked round out of sight on its other side. He wished he had a guinea for every landfall he had made at the Old Head. From here it was less than thirty miles to Queenstown and safety, if it was needed.

He had done what he had planned to do, used up some time and found out his position. Yet they were still some eighteen miles off shore and it was one thing to be satisfied himself, and another to be exact enough to satisfy the ship's log and the records. Besides, the deep-water lane in St. George's Chan-nel, at its narrowest between Wexford in Ireland and St. David's in Wales, was not much more than twenty miles wide, bordered by shoals and rocky shores. He had no intention of running the *Lusitania* through it in the dark by dead reckoning, without a definite starting position. He went back inside.

Bestwick was stifling a yawn. It was almost the end of his spell of duty and he was looking forward to a couple of hours with his feet up. He came to attention as Turner made for him.

"Ah—Bisset," Turner said. "You know how to take a four-point bearing?"

"Yes, sir," Bestwick told him.

"Good lad," Turner approved. "Then kindly take one on that light-house there."

Bestwick nearly opened his mouth to protest. To take a four-point bearing required a minimum of half an hour, with the ship kept to a fixed course and speed. The Captain was waiting. "Aye, aye, sir," Bestwick said.

Turner smiled slightly and moved away. He knew just what Bestwick was thinking, but scrupulous attention to tasks like that could one day change a junior officer into a master. He gave the order for the *Lusitania* to be brought round to starboard onto her earlier course, south 87 degrees east. "Eighteen knots," he said. "And hold her steady."

Copying the slow rise of Schwieger's right hand, Scherb slid the U 20's main periscope up very cautiously. He stopped abruptly when the hand cut to the side.

The hooded eye was just breasting the low waves and Schwieger rotated it very gently to cause as little disturbance of the surface as possible. The U-boat was crawling now, after almost an hour's blind dash underwater. Schwieger could not prevent himself from holding his breath as he searched. Nothing . . . nothing . . . then he had it!

He swore softly to himself. It was big, bigger than anything he had ever seen through the lens. But it was still over four miles away to port. And still heading for the shore.

He felt a bitter disappointment after the mounting excitement of the race. The *Lusitania* was still too far away, out of range of anything but the most desperate and rash shot. Yet in spite of his frustration, he could not help but admire her grace. He had leisure to appreciate her now and saw that she was beautiful, a masterpiece of construction and design. He had to remind himself of Lanz's description of her armament and of the stories he had read in newspapers at home of the deadly cargo of contraband she carried, with the connivance of the Americans, the same arrogant and selfish race whose presence on board had always protected her.

As he watched her, he noticed the long wave curling back from her bows leap higher. Surely she was not putting on more speed so close to land? Slowly he became aware of a shift in the perspective of her giant funnels. Almost imperceptibly the gap between them was growing narrower. She was not increasing speed, she was turning! Turning toward him. . . . In a few minutes, her bow waves had equalized and the funnels had merged into one. She was coming straight for him.

He glanced up and saw the others intent on him, trying to work out the reason for his silence, prepared for the cruelest disappointment. "She's ours," he said quietly.

Junior Third Officer Bestwick had taken the second of his four bearings and was preparing for the third. He put his tongue out at the lighthouse as Third Officer Lewis came toward him. "Yes, I know," Lewis smiled. "You should be off duty. All right, I'll relieve you. You get along and I'll finish off for you." Bestwick could hardly believe what he had heard. "Beat it," Lewis said. "Before I change my mind." Bestwick handed over gratefully and hurried for his cabin.

Jay Brooks, stripped to his shirt and flannel pants, had trotted up the ladder to the Marconi deck and began his run round it, which would be the end of his exercise. Bestwick smiled and saluted him as he went by.

Livvy was moving forward along the boat deck. She had promised to wait for Matt on this side, but with the *Lusitania* sailing parallel to the shore, she could no longer see the land from starboard.

Alice Scott and Arthur had finished their lunch. He was impatient to see the Irish coast and could not sit still while they waited for Elizabeth Duckworth to get through her ice cream. "I don't like to hurry it," Elizabeth said. "Just you go on up, Mrs. Scott. I'll find you on the shelter deck."

In their cabin, Beattie drew the coverlet up over her as she lay on the bed.

She was breathless, and felt as though she were floating. "It will never, ever be so good again," she whispered. Lying beside her, Lee smiled and pulled her gently to him to prove her wrong.

The weather was so charming that Charles Frohman had decided against returning to his suite after lunch. As he strolled on the promenade deck with Rita Jolivet and George Vernon, her brother-in-law, he was not listening to them, but composing a cable he would send to Maude the minute they docked. They passed Alfred Vanderbilt, who was smoking a cigar and reading the ship's newssheet. "Justus—Mr. Forman—said something very interesting this morning," Rita was saying. "He's seen most of the things I've been in. And he thinks it was in *Kismet* that I first showed my true potential."

"You certainly did, my dear," Frohman murmured. "That costume was very revealing."

Will Turner had come down to his day room, where his steward had laid out a light lunch. Turner did not want to eat, for it would keep him away from the bridge too long, but he was glad to be able to light up his pipe at last. Just a minute or two, he told himself. You've certainly earned your money this trip, Will. As Commodore, he had a salary of two thousand pounds a year now. That was something he would never have thought possible when he was Bestwick's age. He stretched his back. Something odder than that. Only two hours ago, he had never thought it possible for him to relax again.

In the second-class smoke room near the stern on the promenade deck, Matt was facing a muster of nearly all the Canadian volunteers. A group of civilians at one of the tables had stopped their poker game to listen. "Those of you who have units to go to," Matt was saying, "report to the military authorities in Liverpool and you'll be provided with travel warrants and instructions. Those of you for the Canadian Division, get on the London train with me. I'll telephone ahead and have someone meet us at the London terminal." He paused. "I want to wish each of you good luck, and say I'm happy we're all going to be serving together. Tomorrow's when it all begins."

"Three cheers for Captain Fletcher!" the temporary lieutenant from Toronto called. To the astonishment of the poker players, the volunteers crowded round Matt, cheering and shaking his hand.

Scherb came hurrying back through central control. He was proud, though self-conscious, knowing that everyone was looking at him as he hurried to rejoin Commander Schwieger. There had never been such a silence in the U 20. The only sound was the faint hum of the motors. The whole crew from Hirsch to the cook's mate was motionless, waiting.

"Forward torpedoes adjusted for depth of nine feet," Scherb reported. "Forward tubes ready."

"Thank you," Schwieger acknowledged. He watched as Scherb unscrewed the caps protecting the red firing buttons from accidental discharge. Haupert had taken over the periscope elevating lever. Lanz was standing at the side, next to Kurtz. He was sweating profusely.

Schwieger stepped to his place at the eyepiece and signed to Haupert. As the periscope rose, Schwieger tried to blot everything from his mind except the image in the lens. He had run the U 20 as far forward as he dared, considering the *Lusitania*'s powerful guns. He had maneuvered carefully and her bows were now pointing as straight as the helmsman could hold her at the line of the *Lusitania*'s path. For the next four or five minutes Schwieger needed total concentration.

The identity of the ship he was preparing to attack had ceased to have any relevance, like her size and gracefulness and passengers. To him she had become simply another target. He had angled the U-boat's position to give himself the chance of an ideal bowshot, calculated on the relative speeds of the target and of the torpedo, at a range of seven hundred yards. His only concern was the liner's construction, the watertight compartments and the cavernous coal bunkers along her side which could absorb shellfire without harm. With only three torpedoes left, two G-type in the two forward tubes and one older bronze model in the stern, he wondered if he had enough for the job. He had had them set with delayed fuses to explode after maximum penetration. It would be highly dangerous after the first shot. When the U 20 showed her asparagus again, it could be met by a full broadside.

The *Lusitania* was approaching on her straight course, still parallel to the shore, her speed unchanged. Her stark funnels stood out against the eggshell-blue sky. He could see her masts and radio antennae clearly now. And every detail of her white superstructure, even the tiny figures of people moving on her decks. He could not spot the guns, but she was so huge they might be easily concealed.

"Steady!" he called to the helmsman. "Stand by forward tubes!"

The target's prow was about to enter the hair-thin calibrations on the lens. *Lieber Herr Gott . . .* It was enormous! A towering black cliff. The closer the target came, the more Schwieger was staggered by its sheer size. Its side, a vast black wall studded with portholes. How could he even hope to make a pinprick in such a leviathan? Until now he had had no real conception of its bulk and was almost unnerved. He fought to control himself, readjusting the angles in his mind. In a moment it would be too late. He counted slowly to himself. Now! "Fire Number One!"

Livvy had moved forward on the boat deck until she was under the overhang of the starboard wing of the bridge. Ahead of her, she saw Marie Depage walking with the American doctor and two of the young volunteer nurses traveling out to work in her husband's hospital. They were talking earnestly and Livvy stopped, not wishing to intrude.

Beyond was the Irish coast. They were just opposite the point of the rocky promontory with its lighthouse and the smaller buildings, which Matt had reckoned might be a signal station, but already it was drawing away. Somehow the thought that they were leaving the land behind again was depressing, and Livvy felt the need of company. Passing the outside companionway ladder, she had heard Elbert Hubbard's chuckle and had glanced down to see him strolling toward the rear of the promenade deck with his wife, Alice, and Charles Lauriat, the bookseller. If she hurried, she could catch them up, but it might mean missing Matt. It was better to stay on this deck. She turned and began to walk slowly back.

There were just over two hours until the time they had arranged to meet the Allans for tea, and she hoped that Matt would really not be too long. They had still not had their serious talk. This afternoon they had a chance to go into everything calmly, where he expected to be billeted, whether she and the children were to remain in England and so on, to settle the practical details, so that their last evening on board would not be wasted in discussing them.

Two girls and a young man came chasing toward her, tossing a medicine ball from one to the other. The man threw the ball to Livvy, who smiled and bounced it back to the slim redheaded girl beside him. The girl missed it and scrambled for it, laughing, before following the other two who had started back toward the stern. Livvy had paused by the gap between the first and second starboard lifeboats. Something through the gap caught her eye, a frothy white line running across the surface of the sea. It ran so straight that it puzzled her.

Forward, in the very bows of the ship, Les Morton was stationed as starboard fo'c'sle lookout. He had come on duty ten minutes earlier, one minute after the older seaman with him, who had chosen the port side for their two-hour watch. The sea seemed as motionless as a pond. Although there was little wind, the *Lusitania* at her cruising speed of eighteen knots created her own and Les blinked against it. As his friends had predicted, the last week of constant hard slog had been very tiring and, because of the warmth of the day, he welcomed the breeze to prevent his nodding off to sleep.

At the same moment as Livvy he caught sight of the line in the water, a frothy, bubbling white streak heading at an angle for a point ahead of the *Lusitania*'s prow. It had not been there a few seconds before and, although he knew instinctively what caused it, it was another second before his eyes traced quickly back along the line to a V-shaped disturbance in the water and the periscope which projected about three feet at its apex.

He leaped up and leaned out dangerously over the bulwark, gazing at the approaching white streak. Ahead of it, he could just make out the long dark cigar shape driven at high speed by whirling propellers which threw back its foaming wake. He had thought it would shoot past some distance in front of the bows, but all at once he realized that the *Lusitania*'s own speed was carrying her inevitably into the torpedo's path. It could not fail to strike somewhere along her 785-foot length.

He dropped to the deck and snatched up the megaphone, shouting to the bridge, "Torpedo coming! Starboard side—torpedo coming!"

Second Officer Hefford was on duty on the upper bridge and heard Les's shout. He could not believe it, yet even as he turned to Chief Officer Piper, it was confirmed by a frantic message from one of the able seamen on lookout in the crow's nest halfway up the towering foremast.

Will Turner was watching the Old Head, about eighteen miles away. To be in charge of a lighthouse would be an almost ideal life for a retired skipper, he was thinking, to be snug on land in fair or foul weather, and watch the ships go by. He thought of his money in the safe in his day cabin. He had never greatly trusted banks and always carried his savings with him, not much to show for a lifetime of work, yet over the three or four years remaining he could add to it out of his commodore's pay and, with his pension, have enough to live out the rest of his days quite comfortably. He was not sure, however, that after this trip it mightn't be wiser to lodge his savings somewhere ashore. He agreed with Archie Bryce. For all who went down to the sea in ships in these uncertain times, things were going to get worse before they got better.

He was roused from his reverie by Hefford calling for him urgently. "A torpedo coming on the starboard side!" the second officer shouted down. Turner's mind reeled, but he recovered instantly and whirled round, beginning to hurry across the lower bridge. There was no dismissing the report as a false alarm. Over the far bulwark he could make out the torpedo's white trajectory. It seemed to be rushing straight toward him. In the next split second, the tip was out of sight below the bulwark and he braced himself instinctively.

The eighteen-foot-long torpedo slammed into the *Lusitania*'s starboard side at a speed of over forty knots, ten feet below the waterline and slightly behind the bridge, smashing through her steel plating into the cavernous coal bunker behind. The great liner quivered all along her length and Turner staggered, then was thrown to his knees as her bows bucked violently and water spouted up her side when the torpedo's delayed fuse detonated its warhead packed with 290 pounds of TNT.

The sound of the explosion was oddly muffled, but Turner knew a gaping hole must have been blown in her hull. Already she was heeling over, slewing to starboard as tons of water poured in. He pushed himself to his feet and made for the ladder to the navigating bridge. He sprinted up it and had just reached the door when a second, even more savage explosion shook her convulsively with a tremendous roar. He had grabbed the doorjamb and the force of the eruption spun him round, hurling him into the wheelhouse.

Livvy had stepped back quickly the moment she recognized the wake of the torpedo for what it was. She had wanted to run, but her legs seemed leaden. She was directly above the point of impact and the first explosion flung her against the bulkhead of the cabin behind her, drenching her with water. The second lifted her up and sent her toppling and rolling across the deck to fetch up against one of the collapsible boats. She lay crumpled and dazed, her arms clasped round her head to shut out the ear-splitting, screeching thunder of the blast.

The deck steadied under her and she looked up, wide-eyed with shock. Just then, a hideous cloud of coal dust, debris and steam, forced up by the detonation, spewed from the giant ventilators by the forward funnels and fountained twice as high as the masts before dropping back. The entire bridge was enveloped in smoke and steam lit by random flashes of fire as the vapors from the coal bunkers ignited. Livvy choked in the thick suffocating air as she cowered for protection against the side of the collapsible boat with wooden debris and jagged pieces of metal falling and ricocheting from the deck and bulkheads around her. With a jarring crash, something landed on the wildly swinging lifeboat beyond her, smashing it to pieces.

In the U 20, Walter Schwieger watched through the periscope incredulously. It had been a perfect bow shot from a range of 700 yards, angle of incidence 90 degrees. Technically it could not be faulted, although he now suspected the liner had been traveling at three or four knots less than the twenty-two which Lanz had estimated. For moments it had even seemed likely that the torpedo would shoot past ahead of its target. What held him so silent, intent on the eyepiece, was its devastating effect. He had hoped at the most to slow the liner down and prevent it taking evasive action, but the first explosion had been much more extensive than he anticipated. While the crew was still cheering, thirty seconds later had come the second detonation, so strong that, until the cloud of smoke dispersed, he half thought the entire forward section had been blown away. As it was, the superstructure by the bridge was badly damaged, and whatever had caused the second explosion—bursting boilers, coal or gunpowder—the huge liner was already settling noticeably by the bows. .

Of the five people on the *Lusitania*'s bridge, Will Turner was the first to recover. From the angle of the deck he knew the situation was serious and he hurried to the binnacle to check the spirit level. The indicator oscillated sharply between 15 and 18 points of list. Already the surface of the water was much closer to the forecastle deck.

Quartermaster Johnston had taken over the helm and Turner called to him, "Bring her round to port! Steer for the lighthouse!" Johnston fought the helm round against the starboard drag of the bows. He had realized at once that, however unthinkable, the liner was in danger of foundering and that the captain had decided to try to beach her in the shallower water off Kinsale. It all depended on her maintaining sufficient speed to cover the distance, and already it had been reduced by several knots.

Turner had snatched up the telephone linking him to the engine room, but the wires must have been severed and the line was dead. He stepped quickly to the voice tubes. "Engine room, this is the Captain! Report. Engine room?"

After a pause, they heard the hesitant voice of the Senior Second Engineer. "Cockburn, sir. I don't know what's become of Mr. Bryce. He was up forward in Number One boiler room. What was it, sir?"

"Torpedo," Turner told him tersely. He could not let himself think of Archie. If he had been working in one of the forward boiler rooms. . . . "Report. How are things down there?"

In the vast engine room the explosions had been magnified. After the first, the lights had gone out, plunging them into darkness, and Cockburn had clung to the high grating on which he stood while it bounced like a trampoline at the second mammoth thunderclap. In the pitch blackness, there was the hiss of steam and the smell of coal dust. He had known moments of sheer terror, then some of the lights began to flicker back on. Coal dust was billowing in through the door to No. 4 boiler room, the one that was shut down. He suspected that the engineers, firemen and Chief Engineer who were further forward were done for, and he shouted to the men on the lowest level to close the watertight door while he started down the suddenly inclined ladder for the level with the pressure gauges. "We—we're all right here, sir, for the time being," he reported. "But the pressure's falling. We've lost a lot of steam."

It was a hard thing to order men to remain in a metal prison below the waterline. "Stay with it," Turner said. "We need as much as you can give us for as long as you can." He called to Chief Officer Piper to check on the telltale board that all watertight doors were closed. Speed, buoyancy. . . . He bent to the end voice tube. "Crow's nest? Are you all right up there?"

The massive foremast, soaring to 170 feet above the water, had quivered like a wand at the convulsion of the bows, and in the open-topped crow's nest the two able seamen on watch, Quinn and Hennessy, had been whipped backward and forward, then enveloped by the choking cloud of steam and coal dust. It had taken them until now to recover and the backs of their hands, with which they had protected their faces, were beginning to blister. "Shaken about a bit, Captain," Quinn coughed, "but we're all right."

"Any sign of that submarine?"

". . . Still there, sir. Keeping pace with us."

"Very well," Turner said. "You'd better get down."

Now that she could breathe again, Livvy pulled herself up to her knees. Her throat felt raw and her ears were ringing. Her clothes were wet through and her arms and suit spattered with oily coal dust, but she knew she was lucky the steam had cooled before it reached her. All she could think of was Matt. Matt and the children, where were they?

As she began to stumble forward, she saw the pretty redheaded girl who had been playing with the ball. She was lying on her face on the deck beside some broken pieces of timber from the shattered lifeboat. The girl was unconscious and her hair had come loose. Livvy hurried to her, but as she crouched to help her up, she became aware that the girl's hair was still neatly waved, matching in color the pool of bright blood spreading round her head. Livvy started to turn her over gently and recoiled in horror. One of the heavy timber spars had crushed the girl's face beyond recognition. Splintered bone and teeth protruded through the pulped skin and one eye dangled obscenely on her cheek. Her neck was broken.

In the second-class dining saloon, toward the stern on D deck, the noise of the explosions had been much fainter, scarcely audible, although everyone had felt the jolt, which sent bottles and glasses spinning. There were many passengers for the late lunch sitting and, when the glasses smashed on the deck, an excited babble broke out. Robert Leith, the Marconi operator, was the first to react. The moment the jolt came, he dropped his coffee cup, pushed the table aside and ran for the door.

Elizabeth Duckworth had been on her way out. She was thrown off balance and fell sideways, catching at a large-mustached foreign man in a chair and nearly bringing him down with her. He managed to hold her. As she stammered her apologies and thanks, the lights went out.

In the darkness there was a surge of movement as everyone rose. Women were screaming and voices began shouting that the boat was sinking. The man was still holding Elizabeth and jabbering to her in Russian and she felt bodies blunder past them, seeking for the exit. The lights came on again and immediately there was a panic rush for the door, which was soon jammed with people pushing and falling on the strangely tilted deck.

Everyone was hurrying up the gangways to the shelter deck and Elizabeth was nearly carried with them. She drew aside, however, thinking of Alice Scott and Arthur. Alice had decided to return to their cabin for a coat before going up on deck. She would be there now with Arthur, two levels below and further forward, much nearer where the explosion must have come from. Unlike the others, Elizabeth turned and went down. The long passageways were sloping forward and to the side and made walking difficult. She heard voices, children crying, and had to lean against the bulkhead when three stewardesses helped a frightened group of elderly passengers toward a companionway beyond her.

When she reached her own corridor at last, it was strangely dark and she stopped in horror. Normally it was lit by two small portholes at either end, nine or ten feet above the water. The ones on the starboard side were completely obscured, the sea pressing against them outside like a dark green curtain.

As she inched herself up the sloping deck, she thought what a fool she would be if the Scotts had already gone. But when she opened the door, there was Alice sitting on the lower bunk with her folded coat over her knees and her arm round Arthur. "What are you doing?" Elizabeth asked.

"I tried to find a steward," Alice said, wide-eyed. "We heard a terrible noise and everything shook. I didn't know what to do."

"We get out of here, for a start," Elizabeth told her. "And bloody quick about it."

Leith had raced up a series of companionways to the boat deck. Here the list was more evident. The huge funnels seemed to hang over him and it was an effort to climb the outward-slanting ladder to the Marconi deck. There was a man clinging to a stayrope, breathing raggedly as though he had nearly drowned. He was plastered with greasy soot and Leith had difficulty recognizing him as Mr. Brooks, the passenger who often used this deck for exercise. "Are you all right, sir?" he asked.

Brooks could only nod. He had almost suffocated. He let go of the rope and stumbled off toward the opposite side of the deck.

Leith hurried into the radio shack. His assistant operator, McCormick, was at the transmitter, just waiting. "There's been no orders," he explained.

From what he had seen, Leith knew there was no need for orders and, if anyone had survived on the bridge, they would be too busy. He shoved McCormick away and, as he took over the chair, was already tapping out the *Lusitania*'s call sign and the beginning of the message: "Come at once, big list, ten miles south Old Head Kinsale."

Above deck in the second-class smoke room, the sound of the explosions had been unmistakable and there was a shocked silence when the liner shuddered and a pyramid of glasses cascaded from the bar. Someone shouted, "They've got us! Torpedo!" The men at the tables and standing at the bar scrambled for the door.

"She's going over!" Dan Connally gasped.

The angle of the deck was shifting under their feet and the party of volunteers round Matt nearly scattered, but when he did not move, they stood firm. His hand was half raised and, after long seconds, when he lowered it, they realized the angle was steady.

"Was it torpedoes?" Barney asked.

"Most likely," Matt said. "But you know this ship. It's unsinkable unless the hull's breached in a number of places. We'll have to trust the captain to take us out of range."

"What do we do?" Dan asked.

"First, get your life belts," Matt said. He was thinking, Livvy's alone up there! Where are the kids? They could hear from outside the sound of confused shouting. "There may be some panic. Do what you can to keep it down—and to assist the ship's officers." He turned and led the way to the door, forcing himself not to run until he was outside.

Will Turner had no doubt in his mind about what had happened. His first thought had been that the second blast had been caused by part of his lethal cargo of ammunition, but it was all stowed over a hundred feet further forward than the site of the explosion. The explanation was much simpler, if he read the belching cloud of steam and dust and the instant loss of power rightly. Archie Bryce had maintained the nineteen enormous boilers in the three forward boiler rooms at full steam. The *Lusitania* had used up nearly half of the coal stored in the compartments of her longitudinal shell. The torpedo, detonating inside one of those immense half-filled compartments and aided by the combustion of its gases, must have fractured the inner bulkhead of one of the two most forward boiler rooms. Water flooding in had collapsed the furnaces and cracked two or more of the boilers, or jammed them together. All along he had worried needlessly about the ammunition, although he had been assured it could not be set off by impact. The colossal boilers, maintained at a pressure of 195 pounds to the square inch, had exploded and jack-knifed upward, a more destructive force than any bomb yet invented.

It was only four minutes since the torpedo had struck. All on the bridge were watching him, waiting for orders. He was silent, calculating rapidly. The list was acute but steady at just over 15 degrees, which meant most of the watertight bulkheads were holding. She was settling slowly by the bows but should have several hours before it became fatal—if the U-boat left her alone. With reduced speed and difficulty in steering, he could not escape or even attempt to ram it. Cork Harbour was thirty miles to the east, too far to reach. His order to turn toward land had been instinct, yet it was right. Already the Old Head was nearer and in less than an hour he would run aground in shallower water. His passengers and cargo would be safe. Provided the *Lusitania*'s remaining power kept up. And that damned U-boat did not blow more holes in her. He tensed, hearing a popping rattle like irregular gunfire.

Hefford was helping First Officer Piper to lift the quartermaster who had been on starboard watch and been knocked unconscious. "It's—it's the ammunition!" he stammered. "I knew it! That's shells going off."

"No, Mr. Hefford," Turner said. "It's the high-pressure pipes."

Now the others could also make out that the noises were coming from the ventilators. Far below, the banks of steam pipes were bursting. In confirmation, the *Lusitania* all at once lost more headway and Quartermaster Johnston had to fight to control the steering.

Third Officer Lewis, gray-faced, had come in from the port side of the wing. "My compliments to Captain Anderson, Mr. Lewis," Turner said. "And would he kindly lower the boats in preparation to abandon ship." It was an order which Turner had never expected to hear himself issue. The others stared at him, still unable to face the terrible reality. "Jump to it!" Turner barked.

The Burning of the
Morro Castle
by THOMAS GALLAGHER

Out on the weather side of the bridge, Captain Warms could not focus his eyes on Alagna, much less listen to him. The gale was whirring against the ship, supplying all the oxygen the fire needed, and he was shouting at the top of his lungs to the deck hands below on A deck, "Don't break those windows!"

Didn't they realize that breaking them would make flues of the very corridors the passengers were escaping through? He brushed Alagna aside and shouted until his very lungs pained from the effort. "Don't—break—those—windows! Close all doors—on this—side!"

But the wind unmercifully censored him, and the men, hearing or thinking they heard, not orders but cries for help, went on breaking windows and opening doors so as not to trap people trying to get through them to the boats. And though they played tons of water into the openings they made, the gale found the fire first and sent it racing everywhere.

This tragedy was repeated all over the ship. Shouted orders full of urgency and good sense were given no better treatment by the wind than the hysterical cries of women. Indeed, it was hard in the tumult to distinguish between an authoritative voice, necessarily straining itself to be heard, and one pleading for instructions from someone in authority. "Help those passengers to get to the boats," became indistinguishable from just plain "Help!" No one knew to whom to listen or where to go, so that the captain, from whose vantage point everything could be seen—the confusion, the growth of the fire, the helplessness of seasick passengers and the bungling of an uninstructed crew—felt that his very brain was turning on a skewer.

"Captain, what about—Are there any instructions?" Alagna began, cursing himself for not wearing his radio officer's cap. Didn't Warms even know who he was?

What Alagna didn't know was that Captain Wilmott had suspected him of trying to sabotage the ship and that perhaps Warms, pursued as much by Wilmott's suspicions as by Alagna himself (hadn't he suggested locking Alagna up?), did not *want* to listen to him.

Warms pushed him away and stood seething with fury and frustration as the ship, as if persisting in being a ship to the very end, started on a series of rolls and the seamen on A deck began playing one leg against the other in an effort to hold their balance. It was obvious that they hadn't heard him, and their flame-lit movements, the hair flying straight off from their scalps, the pugnacity of wind against their trousered legs, were things that Warms would never forget as long as he lived. There was an unbearable poignancy in the sight of them that he would always associate with the loss of the ship, and with his one abortive day as master of it.

It was at this moment that Alagna made a most unusual request: "Captain, what about Wilmott's body? Can I put it in one of the boats?"

This suggestion from Alagna detained Warms for a moment, for if there was anything suspicious about Wilmott's death, why would the man most likely to be suspected of murdering him want to preserve the evidence? If Wilmott's body were left aboard and cremated, almost any unprovable charge could be made against Alagna. Did he know he was suspected of sabotage and already foresee his arrest? If so, he must have realized what an important part an autopsy of Wilmott's body would play in the proceedings.

But Clarence Hackney had rushed to the bridge, overheard Alagna's suggestion, and, after telling Warms, "I can't control it!", turned to Alagna and said, "The living are more important than the dead."

"Lower the boats to the rail," Warms said to Hackney and, as Hackney left, ran to the starboard wing of the bridge. "My God [the hoses were turning to syringes in the men's hands], what's happened to the water pressure?"

He shoved Alagna out of the way and started on the run in search of Chief Engineer Abbott—with Alagna right behind.

"Abbott! Where are you?" Warms shouted, ignoring Alagna's attempts to get through to him. "Chief—God damn it, where *are* you?"

They found Abbott hunched in a secure place outside the wheelhouse on the weather side, where the wind would naturally protect him from the fire—a limp witness of the fact that others were still trying. He was wringing his hands and crying, "What are we going to do? What are we going to do?"

Alagna had been struck by the sight of him before because Abbott had no business on the bridge, and by the fact that he was all dressed up in full uniform as though he were going to the captain's ball. He was coughing and looked a little decomposed already, shorter and smaller than he was because all tension was gone from his spine, the middle vertebrae of which were against the wheelhouse.

"What's happened to the water pressure?" Warms shouted at him.

"It's too late—" Abbott began. "Hundred hoses couldn't hold this fire now."

Abbott, who had been consulted throughout the *Morro Castle's* construction in 1930 at Newport News, knew that the steam fire pump at 100 pounds pressure had a capacity of 1000 gallons a minute, and that the 2 electric sanitary pumps added another 300 gallons a minute to the ship's fire-fighting capacity. He knew also that all 3 pumps discharged water into the same main and that though there were 42 hydrants situated throughout the ship, only 6 could be supplied with full pressure (30 pounds at each nozzle) at any one given time. With 12 hydrants open, the pressure at each nozzle would drop to at least one third of normal.

Now John Kempf, the New York City fireman, and young Phelps and Kendall, the two Harvard boys, were not the only passengers to use hoses in the corridors below. Several others, in different corridors and on different decks, had done the same thing, only unlike John Kempf, who naturally realized the importance of turning a hydrant off before abandoning it, these passengers had dropped the nozzles of their hoses and run for their lives. These hoses were thereupon burned off the hydrants, which meant that the wide-open valves, devoid of even the smaller nozzle openings to slow down the flow of water, were releasing pressure (ineffectually) as fast as the pumps could supply it. To make matters worse, these abandoned hydrants were closer to the source of supply, in both a distance and a gravity sense, than the hydrants on the higher decks to which Warms referred, so that while the unmanned hydrants were being supplied with water, the manned hydrants were being robbed of it.

All Abbott would have had to do to prevent this tragedy of a growing fire with less and less water to fight it (it was too late now, but he had been doing absolutely nothing for twenty minutes) was go down through the superstructure, or delegate one of his men to go down (and his men were all about, uninstructed by any superior) and turn the other hydrants off.

"Answer me!" Warms shouted at him. "What's happened to it?" But before Abbott could answer, the man at the wheel sang out, "Captain, she's not holding!" and Warms, more interested in hearing what a man still doing his duty had to say, ran into the wheelhouse to find Quartermaster Hoffman flying the wheel around as though it were attached to his own failing brain.

Hoffman had swung the wheel hard over in response to Warms's "Hard left," and though the ship had responded (the course now was almost due west—273 degrees), the gyrocompass, electrically controlled, and the electric steering apparatus, seemed to have burned out.

"She's not holding, sir," Hoffman said.

"Try the magnetic. Hard left."

Warms wanted the stern of the ship to the wind so the smoke and flame would be blown forward, away from the passengers who had found refuge aft. The ship, however, was now broadside to the wind, with all her windward glass broken, thus allowing an endless supply of oxygen into lobbies veneered with mahogany and rosewood and extending through four decks.

These lobbies, one forward and one aft, and each with a hardwood stairway built around an elevator shaft, communicated directly with the two main passageways on each deck, so that if the wind, as the ship swung, stopped feeding the fire from one direction, it immediately started feeding it from another. To confine such a fire as the present one, there were steel bulkheads fitted with sliding steel doors not more than 13 feet apart on each passenger deck, but these had not been closed at the first report of the fire at 2:50, and were not closed now for fear of trapping passengers trying to escape. Indeed, as the fire grew, and things that might have been done were not done, as one effort canceled out another and ignorance succeeded where negligence failed, the ship itself, from other shipping lanes, appeared out of control or piloted by madmen.

"Swing her as far as she'll go," Warms was saying. "Turn her south, one hundred and eighty degrees."

But when Hoffman swung the magnetic-compass wheel, operated hydraulically, it remained slack, which meant that the oil was not being put under pressure. He turned it to the right, then to the left again, and it still remained slack, which meant that the ship, still broadside to the wind, now had a powerless rudder.

The only thing left for Warms to do was to back and fill on the engines, that is, go ahead on one, astern on the other, and keep the ship's stern to the wind that way. This meant running out to the wing of the bridge to see how fast the stern was swinging, calling in to Hoffman for a compass reading, running in and reversing the engines again in the event the stern started either way too far, and running out again to direct the men fighting the fire and to delegate other men to help passengers into the boats.

Meanwhile, Ivan Freeman had returned to the bridge, black and coughing, to report the fire out of control. In the darkness and smoke he brushed against Quartermaster Fleischman and said, "Wasn't Warms in a position to see the full extent of the fire?"

Just then Warms, rushing out of the wheelhouse, saw Freeman and cried, "For God's sake, get forward and prepare to let go the anchor. We have a powerless ship!"

They both started on the run, Freeman toward the bow, Warms after Abbott, with Alagna, still trying desperately to get orders to send an S O S, right behind.

"Too late—" Abbott kept saying, "Too late. Hundred hoses. . . ."

Warms appeared on the verge of becoming someone else: that the fire *was* out of control had fastened upon his mind at last, and now, like the absurdity at the heart of all tragedy, a passenger was grabbing him around the waist from behind.

"You've got to save my girlfriend!" he kept screaming. "She's trapped in one of those cabins!" He began trying to push Warms aft toward her cabin. "You've got to save her!"

Fleischman and Hoffman grabbed the hysterical man and tried to explain to him that the captain was trying to save everybody and could not leave the bridge.

"Put him in a boat," Warms said. "Take him down and put him in a boat."

"There's nothing more we can do in the engine room without choking to death," Abbott was saying. "So we're going to shut off everything." He used the plural "we" and yet had not been to the engine room once since the fire started. "Keep the men there by all means," he had told First Engineer Bujia. "Don't let them leave until they have to."

He had heard Warms tell Hackney to lower the boats to the rail, and now, as Warms ran into the wheelhouse to swing the telegraph to Stop All Engines, called after him, "I'm going to leave now."

And he did leave, going right down the bridge ladder on the starboard side to the boat deck, where he got into number three boat. There were only 8 people in it and its capacity was 70 persons, but he shouted, "Lower away!"

"Don't lower that boat!" Warms suddenly began shouting from above. "Keep it at the rail for passengers."

The pelican hook holding it to the deck was jammed and Abbott kept shouting to the seaman, "Kick it! Kick it!"

The seaman finally freed it, but then one of the cables got fouled, making the bow higher than the stern. "This boat is never going down," Abbott said. Then, to Seaman Thomas Charles, as if to spur him on, "We better get away from here or we'll all be burned alive!"

He saw that number one boat, a motor lifeboat with a 58-person capacity, was in operating condition, and so got out of number three and into it.

"Warms, you coming?" Abbott kept shouting to the bridge from number one boat. When he received no answer, he turned to the seamen. "Lower away! For God's sake, lower away!"

Waiting in the boat for over ten minutes, and knowing that he could not remain in it and lower it into the water, too, he'd become half crazed with fear and frustration. The Melin-Macklachlan gravity davits were designed to prevent the premature lowering of a boat by the panic-stricken: they could be operated only from the deck of the ship. Abbott knew all about the idea behind that design and the knowledge only added to his panic. "Lower away!" he kept shouting. "Will someone, for God's sake, lower away?"

Warms, on the bridge, was distracted from Abbott's wailing by a tremendous blast on the portside of the ship. It was the ship's Lyle gun, falling through the gutted deck into the heart of the fire below. In the confusion no one had remembered to throw the pretzel can of gunpowder overboard.

"It fell through the deck into the middle of the fire," Howard Hansen said, "and twenty pounds of powder went off, blowing everything apart, all the windows and some doors and walls, and putting an end to the fire-fighting. I saw three of the crew killed and four passengers jump over the side, so I decided it was about time to abandon ship."

Warms heard the growing tumult and screams for help, and experienced an anguish such as he had never known. He was not only losing his ship, not only unable to get his passengers off safely, but they, in turn, were beginning to fight one another. Nothing seemed left of the world's goodness but the buoyancy of this horror ship, and only an hour before he'd felt his pleasure running like the very water fore and aft.

He had reached the point where he was no longer concentrating on how to extinguish the fire but on the fire itself. There were so many flames, all of them so hopelessly out of control, that no one flame demanded his special attention. His fear of the ship's destruction had grown to sheer, naked anxiety, so that just getting back to fear would have been an accomplishment—a spur to action. But there was nothing to be done; the maniacal flames had captured the ship.

A man was shouting in his ear, "Captain, listen to me. What about a distress signal?" It was Alagna, standing in the glow of the fire so Warms could see his radio officer's hat. He had been shouting against the wind and crackling flames until his teeth had almost bitten into the lobe of Warms's ear. "Rogers is *dying* in there! He can't hold out much longer. What do you want us to do?"

Warms turned and looked at him, but it was as if nothing could be of consequence any more.

"A ship has sighted us from a long distance!" Alagna went on.

The first mate aboard the *Luckenback,* Frank Magruder, said afterward that when he first looked through glasses at the burning ship (shortly after three), "the vessel, aflame from the fore part of her superstructure all the way aft to the break of the superstructure, was still traveling in a northerly direction." This contradicted Warms's claim that he turned the ship away from the wind immediately on being told that there was a fire in the writing room. If Magruder's eyes were not deceiving him, the *Morro Castle* traveled into a head wind for almost fifteen minutes after the fire was discovered.

"A ship has sighted us!" Alagna repeated.

It was at this point, he said later, that an inspiration seemed to cross Warms's face. There was one last hope to hurl at despair. "Is there still time to send an S O S?"

"Yes!"

"Send it!"

The Sinking of the *Squalus*

by NAT A. BARROWS

The *Squalus* moved ahead and the throb of the Diesels gave her men a healthy sense of well-being. There was a rhythm there that they could understand and appreciate. The engines, they could tell by the sound, were working themselves in nicely. The good old *Squalus* was finding herself, they felt. Those of the enlisted men still off watch idled about the crew's quarters in the after battery room and talked of the approaching dive as they drank coffee. There was plenty of elbow room. None of those jam-packed messrooms of the outdated R and S boats for these *Squalus* men. There was no wasted space, of course. Every inch of bulkhead and much of the compartment deck space held one kind of gadget or another, but the men had none of the feeling of claustrophobia so many of them had known in other, smaller submarines.

Preble, at coffee in the officers' wardroom, used the spare time to glance through his notes of the eighteen previous dives of the *Squalus*. He had them with him in a little book. He recalled the nature of those dives as he checked on the times. The first dive had been on April 8, a slow dive, little more than flooding down the tanks until she sank at her dock. It was a precaution to determine if the hull was watertight.

Flipping the pages, Preble studied the other dives . . . the first submerged builders' trials on April 20, off Portsmouth harbor, when the *Squalus* made a dive from her motors and then submerged again in the step-by-step trimming method of the first dive . . . the several running dives of May 15, again from the motors . . . the "quick dives" on May 16, "riding the vents," his notes said . . . the high-speed "single bank" dives of the following day . . . the submerged torpedo firing dives on May 18.

Preble remembered that he had described the "single bank" dives of May 17 as "extra good." He remembered, too, how Naquin had praised the performance of his diving officer, who actually handled the ship during the dive. In submarines, the diving officer, generally the second-in-command, executes the orders for diving, leaving the skipper free to plan his maneuvers. Naquin had said, speaking of his diving officer's performance:

"I can truthfully say I never saw a submarine so well trimmed and so well handled at such low speed."

The notebook reminded Preble of the three dives of the preceding day— May 22—when the *Squalus* had fired dummy "fish" from the forward tubes, then surfaced to assist in recovering the torpedoes before diving to fire from the stern.

He looked at his watch. A few minutes to go. He studied a sheet of orders hanging in the wardroom. One, dated back in January, always interested him. It was Naquin's first detail order to his men—the requirement that each of the officers and enlisted members prepare a notebook covering the general characteristics of the vessel and of the operating gear, and submit this book each Saturday morning for correction and discussion. That order came out five days after Naquin reported to the *Squalus* as commanding officer.

Preble reflected that the notebook system had been a good one. By the time the *Squalus* went into commission in March, all were at home below decks. The men certainly knew their ship, he could testify.

He recalled that the boat had suffered fewer minor technical troubles than any submarine he had ever tested. On her first dive, he remembered, the main induction valve failed to open all the way after the surfacing and the gear had been overhauled by Yard workmen. It was not considered a serious fault.

Books in a bulkhead rack caught Preble's eye as he idled in the wardroom. Most of them were standard naval references, highly technical, interesting only to the expert. The jackets of two books were bright enough to bring Preble over for a better look.

One title read: *The Importance of Living*.

The other was: *The Land Is Bright*.

Then he glanced at a list of the men aboard ship for this dive—59 of them: five officers, three civilian observers, 51 enlisted men. He read his own name, close to the bottom. Yes, it was spelled correctly: Harold C. Preble. He was listed under the heading, "Navy Yard Representatives," as a naval architect. Four other names were carried under this heading—Lieutenant (jg) Malcolm M. Garrison, John R. Curran, machinist, Jesse A. Thomas, machinist, and Charles M. Woods, electrician—but only one of this group, Woods, was aboard, Preble knew. The presence of the others had not been deemed necessary. They were back ashore. Preble and Woods, with Don Smith, representing the General Motors Corporation, were the civilian observers with the *Squalus* for that trip of May 23.

Preble left the "officers' country" in the forward battery room and strolled toward the control room, walking aft through a narrow corridor past partitions that made full use of every inch of space. He had to step over an opening in the deck of the battery room and he glanced down as he passed. It was a cramped area, full of batteries. An electrician's mate was in the pit, drawn up almost double as he wormed his way about. The place was dank and eerie. It reminded Preble of the pendulum pit of Edgar Allan Poe.

The throb of the Diesels, driving the boat at 16 knots, resounded even more loudly to Preble when he reached the control room, separated by one compartment from the engine rooms. He made himself comfortable to await the pleasure of the skipper.

Topside, Lieutenant Naquin guided his command nearer the selected diving area. He mulled over the prospects of the dive and was not displeased. The vessel's performance thus far gave him confidence that this next dive—the nineteenth—would be worthy of credit. It was going to be an exact rehearsal of the first official trial dive the *Squalus* would make in a fortnight or so for the Naval Board of Inspection and Survey, and, therefore, would be a major submergence, going down at 16 knots from the main engines under conditions similar to a quick dive in time of war when a protective covering of water was needed against the enemy.

He noted his wristwatch. It was time to get the ship ready for the training maneuver. The hatches had to be closed; the battle telephones had to be manned in each compartment; the men had to be called to their stations; the intricate gear had to be set in readiness.

"Rig for diving!"

The order rang through the boat. Forward and aft, the trial crew snapped into action. Preble, in the control room under the conning tower, passed out the trial board data books to those on data stations. Smith and Woods took their positions in the engine rooms. The ship's clock chimed out 8 A.M. in nautical couplets.

At his usual stand at the diving station in the control room, Lieutenant William T. Doyle, Jr., the second-in-command of the *Squalus*, studied the gauges that revealed the vessel's trim. To the surface mariner, he faced an incredible maze—kingston, vent and hull opening indicator boards, diving rudder indicators, trim indicators, manometer, pitometer log indicator, shaft revolution indicators. Everywhere were levers, gauges, indicators, all shining from elbow-grease.

Compartment by compartment, the reports came back to him that the boat was rigging for the dive. He tagged each report on the rigging board placed at the diving station to give a visual check on the changing conditions. Doyle had the responsibility of actually sending the *Squalus* underwater.

In the forward section, Lieutenant (jg) John C. Nichols carried out the "rig for diving" order, checking the position of the men and preparing for the final move. He had two compartments—the forward battery room and the forward torpedo room.

Aft, Ensign Joseph H. Patterson duplicated the check for his section—the after battery room, the two engine rooms and the after torpedo room.

The reports came to the control room first over the battle telephones now rigged in each compartment, a submarine version of the multiple-party line, and, later, by the personal reports of Nichols and Patterson. Doyle gave them an affirmation; then Nichols went forward; Patterson, aft.

Ensign Patterson, blond, stocky, nodded at Preble as he turned back to the engine rooms. That's a husky lad, thought Preble. The young ensign, soon to receive his promotion to junior grade, looked the part of the Annapolis track man who had placed fourth in the Olympics.

Doyle reported to the bridge the rigging of the ship. The time was 8:25 o'clock.

"Very good," replied Naquin. "Submerged trial crew take stations!"

The order went through the boat over the party phone line.

Next: "Observers take stations!"

Both orders were formalities. The men already were close to their diving positions.

Preble pulled out two stop watches, one for each hand, and prepared for his timing of the dive down to the 50-foot mark. A wiry, slight man, Preble always stood on a tool box placed close to the chart desk especially for him. It gave him increased height to see the indicator boards clearly. With Doyle's relay of the skipper's order, he took his customary left-footed stand at the after end of the chart desk, leaning against the desk, facing forward with the right foot on the bottom round of the ladder leading straight up to the conning tower. He had full visibility in the compartment, but it was a precarious perch.

Every nerve aboard ship was tense. All knew the importance of this rehearsal. On the previous dives they had tried various things to discover the true capabilities of the particular design of the *Squalus*. It was the training procedure scheduled by the Chief of Naval Operations. Now they were preparing to meet the specific requirements of the Secretary of the Navy.

Lieutenant Doyle called for a check of all the main ballast kingstons or flood valves. The sea would pour up through these valves when the air inside was vented out. Next, he ordered the operation of all the main ballast tank vents, both to test them and to ease the pressure.

Two high pressure air banks were cut in on the air manifold. The stern planes, protruding from the sides like large fins, received a test by power and by hand. The indicator lights were checked.

All were working properly, Doyle saw.

It was 8:30 when the word went up to the bridge:

"Ship rigged for diving except main engine exhaust valves, engine and hull inductions, radio antenna trunk, bow planes and conning tower hatch."

Lieutenant Naquin spoke to a lanky young junior lieutenant at his side. "Let's have a bearing, Robbie," he said.

Sighting over the bridge rail, the junior officer took a true bearing on Great Boar's Head stack, on the mainland.

"We've got about 1½ miles to go, I make it, sir," reported the JG, Robert N. Robertson, in a Texan accent.

The commanding officer passed the word below:

"Rig out the bow planes!"

It was done. A test was made.

"Send out the diving message!"

A radio operator, tucked away in a tiny hole off the control room, tapped out word to the Navy Yard that the *Squalus* was diving. He gave her position, course and speed. The dive was expected to last an hour, he told Portsmouth.

Through an error in transmission or in receipt, the longitude was sent out as 70:31. Actually, it was 70:36, almost 70:37. The radioman closed off his key and secured the antenna trunk in its valve through the hull. That now was watertight—another of the score of openings closed against the sea.

"Stand by to dive!" Naquin ordered, moving down into the conning tower.

"Sound the alarm!"

A klaxon whined the first diving alarm. It sounded like a fire siren.

At this point, Doyle took over the actual job of diving the boat. His rapid orders shot through the control room.

"Open all main ballast kingstons!"

"Open vents on bow buoyancy!"

"Open vents on No. 1 main ballast . . . No. 2 main ballast . . . Safety tanks!"

"Bow planes at hard dive!"

Lieutenant Naquin and his quartermaster, Francis Murphy, Jr., closed and dogged tight the hatch leading into the conning tower.

"All ahead emergency!" ordered Doyle.

A red light flickered away and turned to green on the main indicator board—the "Christmas Tree." The men in the control room knew that Lieutenant Naquin and Murphy had closed the conning tower hatch. Other lights turned from red to green. The four main engine outboard exhaust valves were closed. Phone reports from the engine rooms announced that all engines were stopped. The "black gang" was ready to switch from the Diesels to the battery-fed motors.

"All engines stopped and valves closed, sir!" Doyle reported up to the conning tower over his head.

"Close hull and engine inductions!"

Here it came. The dive was almost under way. A few more seconds and the *Squalus* would start to plane below the surface, carrying the momentum built up by her Diesels, driving forward with the push of the motors.

The most important job now was the closing of those enormous openings for surface air. Until hull and engine induction valves were closed off against the sea, the ship was as vulnerable to water as if the hatches were open.

In front of the hydraulic manifold, his hands already on the lever, a machinist's mate, second class, watched the exhaust valve lights. This operator, Alfred G. Prien, 26 years old and a Navy man for six years, already had helped put the *Squalus* through eighteen successful dives. He knew full well what would happen if those valves did not snap shut and remain shut.

Prien heard the control room talker give the report from the engine rooms. Immediately, he saw the exhaust valve lights turn green. The engines were silent; it was time to close the inductions.

He thrust the lever to the closed position—a simple movement of the one lever that controlled both induction valves. His act started the hydraulic power used to pull the T-like roof over the openings up in the fairwater a man's height above the deck.

The induction lights switched from red to green. Every man in the control room glanced at the board, thinking the one thought:

"Is it closed?"

The "Christmas Tree" was green. It was closed.

With the closing of the main inductions, Pierce started bleeding pressure air into the boat. The aneroid barometer rose 2-10ths of an inch. All eyes compared the two needles of the barometer. Good . . . the hull was airtight from within; therefore, it was watertight from without. The *Squalus* could dive, safe from the ocean.

Pierce called out:

"Pressure in the boat, sir!"

"Secure the air," Doyle ordered.

He made his own inspection of the board, a precaution that had long experience behind it. The diving officer of the *Squalus* was qualified in his own right to command a submarine of the United States Navy.

He held up two fingers. In an instant, Chief Torpedoman Roy H. Campbell, the chief-of-the-boat, jabbed a push button. Again the klaxon alarm whined. This time it was a signal to all hands that the engines had been stopped and the main induction valves, engine exhaust, and conning tower hatch were closed.

Prien moved levers to the main ballast tanks, admitting sea water through the bottom valves, allowing air to escape from the top.

The *Squalus* had begun her dive. The clock read 8:40.

Lieutenant Naquin was now in the control room. When the second alarm sounded, he was nearing the bottom of the ladder from the conning tower. His stop watch, started with the first alarm, indicated normal time.

"Pressure in the boat, green board, sir!" Doyle reported as the captain approached him.

Naquin made his way over to the diving station so that he could check by his watch the time it took for the vessel to reach a depth of 50 feet. After the report of a tight hull, he concentrated his attention on the depth gauges and the bubble angle indicators. The *Squalus* had assumed an angle down by the bow of about eight degrees, with the main motors pushing her forward at 200 revolutions a minute.

The deck sank from sight . . . then the gun abaft the superstructure . . . then the jack staff. Soon Lieutenant Robertson, in the conning tower, could see a green film of sea water surging past the eyeports.

At 35 feet on the big depth gauge in the control room, Preble's face lighted up as he compared the two stop watches he held at eye level. He checked what he saw with the times of the other *Squalus* dives.

"We're going to make our time all right," he said to the skipper.

Naquin made his own calculations.

"This is going to be a beauty," he replied.

At 40 feet, Doyle ordered Prien to close off the safety tank vents and the bow buoyancy vents. At 45 feet, he ordered all vents closed and told the diving plane operators to ease up so that the submarine could level off at about

63 feet. When the depth gauge read 50 feet, both Naquin and Preble sang out: "Mark!"

The *Squalus* had reached the timing depth for the dive. Stop watches were compared.

"Nice job, Bill," Naquin complimented the depth control officer.

Doyle watched the depth gauge carefully, ready to blow the water out of the ballast tanks in case the high speed forced the vessel down too deep.

The *Squalus* began to level off as usual. She appeared to be acting perfectly.

Forward and aft, the crew settled down to their routine tasks for a submerged run. Electricians crawled down into the battery pits under the compartment decks, huddling over flashlights to check the battery performances. The ship's cook, always an important factor in keeping up the morale of a submarine crew, went back to preparing the noonday meal. A Filipino messboy, licking his chops over the good smell, asked the cook what kind of dessert would be served. Another Filipino prosaically washed out a dish rag. The pharmacist's mate listened to the cough of a seaman and prepared to pour out a swallow of medicine. The engine room crew eyed the motor control board, and up forward Lieutenant Nichols went back to his job of moving a dummy torpedo into place.

Naquin walked over to the station at No. 1 periscope. He was breathing more freely now; the dive was going through successfully. For the next hour his job would be at the periscope, peering at a natural-color image of the seas through which the *Squalus* moved, only a crest of breaking water behind the periscope top to mark her progress. He gripped both handles of the periscope with the ambidextrous skill at his command in everything but writing. He spread his legs a little apart to give him a better stance. It would be a wearying task, that hour of walking the periscope around in its long housing cylinder, and he wanted no additional strain from muscles binding.

Just then a fluttering pressure bit into his ears like a hard slap on the head.

Simultaneously, the telephone talker in the control room poured out an incredible message. The engine rooms were flooding!

The soft-voiced yeoman of the *Squalus*, Charles S. Kuney, went rigid as he relayed the message of terror from the engine rooms. He called it out with a forced pitch that cut into the orderly routine of the control room like an acetylene flame biting into metal. It was Naquin's first indication of something wrong with the *Squalus*.

The ship's typist-stenographer never had the chance to repeat the initial cry of disaster that tumbled from his earphones. His amazed brain had barely assimilated the first report, "After engine room flooding!" when another frenzied voice broke in, distorted with tenseness: "Forward engine room flooding!"

Kuney called it all out in one breath:

"The engine rooms are flooding, sir!"

Impulsively he clapped his palms against the headset with a violence that made his ears ring, straining to catch any further information from back aft.

Before the cry of disaster was out of Kuney's mouth, before it could echo from the steel walls of the control room, another message crackled over the party telephone—actually the last sign of life ever to come from the engine compartments.

It said:

"Take 'er up: the inductions are open!"

Kuney's report was a flash of lightning that struck everybody in the control room. For the briefest moment it left all hands stunned. Then the thunder roared.

"Blow the main ballast!"

As one man, Naquin and Doyle acted spontaneously, shouting out the order—the all-important order—to get the submarine back to the surface. They responded to the emergency so quickly that their voices meshed.

In the same breath, the depth control officer added other orders intended to surface the *Squalus:*

"Blow safety tanks! . . . Blow bow buoyancy!"

No one stopped then to analyze the trouble aft. No one attempted to question Kuney. Somehow, water was pouring into the ship. Somehow, the huge induction valves were open. No matter then what caused the crisis. The *Squalus* had to get back to the surface. Shoot air into the tanks. Pour it in. Blow the ballast water out. Get her up!

The men in the control room went into action automatically, instinctively following their training. They knew what a flood of water in the engine rooms meant. They knew the size of that maw of the induction system. There was not a second to lose.

At the key post on the air manifold, Pierce slammed everything wide open in the high pressure air pipes to the main ballast tanks. He had been waiting to put an air bubble in the bow buoyancy tank to help the bow level off for the prospective hour's run underwater. Now, he threw his weight down hard, driving the levers home with a desperate thrust.

Preble, at this moment, realized that more high pressure air than the two available banks was needed. A reserve supply must be cut in on the air manifold to replenish the amount shot into the tanks during this frantic effort to surface. The civilian wedged himself between the chart desk and the manifold, sitting squat on the deck. The wrench handle for opening the reserve air supply was nearby and he picked it up.

The orders to Pierce automatically called for action by the men operating the diving planes. Immediately, they threw their levers to "hard rise." None required individual orders; the emergency attempt to blow ballast followed a carefully prepared routine.

The high pressure air roared into the tanks with the force of a hurricane, expelling the sea water with a mad whirl. The ballast spurted away in a disorder that burst above the ocean surface with the spray of a geyser.

Like a balloon suddenly inflated and set adrift, the *Squalus* tried to rise. She labored stertorously from the inrush of pressure air, and her whole frame quivered with strain.

The vessel slowly brought her bow up to a level angle. Some of the men, watching the inclinometer and the depth gauge with anxious eyes, thought she was on the way up—to safety. Would she make it? Could she make it? Or was the water pouring in aft already too great a burden?

For several seconds the boat hung at nearly an even keel, the same angle intended for the training dive. While she hung there, some 70 feet below the surface, her forward movement through the water gradually slowed and she came to a full stop for lack of motive power.

Lieutenant Naquin, at his post by the periscopes, suddenly knew that his boat would not surface. His sense of equilibrium told him plainly that the ship already was waterlogged beyond her buoyancy.

With a sickening trim the *Squalus* began to drop rapidly by the stern. She fell backward so sharply, like an overbalanced tilting board, that many of the men lost their footing and went sprawling downhill.

The angle quickly reached 35 or 40 degrees. Books, navigating instruments, loose gear, crashed to the deck flooring.

Lieutenant Naquin felt a sodden, discouraged manner in the *Squalus* as she inched away from the surface, sliding backward down, down, bow reaching for the skies, stern pointed for the muddy bottom. He had a bitter realization of his utter helplessness at the moment, like a mountaineer slipping toward an unfathomable abyss, but his mind raced with possibilities for action as soon as the *Squalus* reached the bottom. It was obvious to him that the submarine would have her own way at least until the bottom was reached.

Seconds, not minutes, marked the time between the cry of disaster and the downhill lurch, and the skipper still remained at the periscopes. With the sudden, backward pitch, he clutched the handles of No. 1 periscope, bracing himself on the well of the other periscope to keep from falling over.

Naquin's predicament as he struggled to hold his balance was enough to prevent a study of the depth gauge, now moving steadily to higher numbers as the *Squalus* eased to the bottom, but he did make a quick survey of the "Christmas Tree." So did every other man in the control room. It was their first thought once the surfacing maneuvering orders had been carried through.

What color did it show? They stared at the board and it only added to their puzzlement and despair. It was green in every light. There was not a sign of red anywhere.

This was beyond all understanding. The board showed that the hull was tight and secure. Yet, from Kuney's telephone the cry had come that water was pouring into the after compartments—down the 31-inch opening for the Diesels, down the 18-inch opening for the ship's surface cruising air. They stared at the board and could not grasp it: the huge inductions had opened but the signal had remained unchanged.

The men had no time for rationalizing; they could not pause to wonder at this apparent mechanical deficiency.

A new menace rushed at them.

Water began to pour from the ventilation pipes leading through the bulkheads between compartments, sounding its approach with a splitting rush of increased air pressure inside the control room.

It showered with a gush, bouncing and splattering on the steel deck plates. The cascade struck Preble's head with enough force to drive his shoulders down to his knees. It struck Pierce, too, and knocked him tumbling on top of Preble. The two sprawled crazily on the deck, doused to the skin with the bitterly cold salt water.

Lieutenant Naquin needed little more than the sound of water to tell him what was happening: sea water was coming down the ship's air induction system and the pipes that normally carried fresh air to the surfaced vessel were now alive with the ocean.

Grimly he snapped out:

"Close watertight doors and ventilation flappers!"

The order was superfluous. Already the men in the control room were desperately at work executing the duties so patiently absorbed during the emergency training drills back at Portsmouth. They needed no formal orders when faced with water in the air supply lines. The first sign of the incoming water told them the compartment pipe lines had to be sealed, and even the greenest "submariner" could do it on his first day aboard a submarine. It was elementary routine: shut the doors: close off the valves in the walls: make the compartment an isolated steel box. And hurry!

Swiftly but without panic, men threw themselves across the steel flooring and grasped turn-handles. Several lost their footing on the slippery floor, now as steep as a hill, but they came up quickly, knowing they were doomed unless the water could be stopped.

The work on the handles and valves was skillful, the product of trained fingers and alert minds. Soon the leaks stopped.

Pierce sputtered out a noseful and picked up the wrench where it had fallen from Preble's hand. He opened No. 1 air bank reserve, adding more pressure to the manifold outlets.

The mountainous slope of the deck gave the men an awkward stance. All had to lean forward, clinging for support to whatever was handy. The seconds flashed by and the *Squalus* continued her gradual drop to the bottom.

So many terrifying experiences flashed before the trapped men in the control room that they were hardly conscious of any time element. The nightmare of their own situation was heightened by their realization of what must be happening aft—men wallowing in deep water, trying to flee, struggling, crying out with terror. Subconsciously, the men in the control room envisioned the after torpedo room as a refuge against the torrent. They needed only the angle under their feet to show them that the *Squalus* was too far off balance for the engine rooms detail to have any real chance of reaching safety by climbing forward against the waterfall that must be pouring into the two engine compartments.

Could they reach the after compartment in time? Could they shut the door against the force of the water? And what about the men in the after battery room, next to the control room?

There still was a chance for those men, if they were lucky. The door between the two compartments was still open, a gaping hole in the wall. So brief had been the elapsed time since Kuney's cry of distress that the bulkhead guard, charged with the duty of closing this door in an emergency, was still struggling with it, trying to pull it uphill against the force of gravity.

Appreciation of their own serious plight returned to the control room men when the ship's lighting system began to fail. The overhead lights dimmed, flickered, brightened an instant, then went out, halting Prien's astonished survey of the green "Christmas Tree."

The darkness lasted only a few seconds. Someone groped to a switch and turned on the emergency lights, fed by batteries.

On his hands and knees, soaked with water, Preble wormed into the open. His head came up as he sought to get his feet under him and he saw men—seven of them—scramble in single file through the narrow steel door from the after battery room. They were knee deep in water before they leaped the doorstoop hurdle.

Preble saw that the bulkhead door guard was having a hard battle to close the door in the face of the rising water of the battery room.

The door finally came shut. The handles were dogged tight to keep it from reopening.

The sight of the men bursting into the control room one jump ahead of certain drowning shook Preble like a blow to the chest. These men were safe for the moment, but the margin of their escape, pursued by rising water that even now covered the glass eyeports in the door, told of the fate of those left behind. He needed no more proof of what had happened to the others.

Shaking from the chill of wet clothes, Preble got to his feet. At once he discovered that the steep angle had lessened. The *Squalus* had slowly poked her stern deep into the mud and just as slowly dropped her uplifted bow. No one was certain when the actual grounding came. It was a gentle descent, Preble thought, something like an elevator coming to a stop.

Soon he and the others in the control room could stand upright without leaning. The angle was down to 10 or 11 degrees.

The hand of the depth gauge held steady. There was no question about it then: the *Squalus* was hard and fast on the bottom in 240 feet of cold water.

The Fog

by WILLIAM HOFFER

At three o'clock on the afternoon of Wednesday, July 25, 1956, Captain Piero Calamai stood on the bridge of the great Italian luxury liner, the *Andrea Doria*, staring to the west. The afternoon sun was headed toward a nebulous haze on the western horizon, the unmistakable precursor of a July fog off the Massachusetts coast.

Fog. The quiet killer of the sea. It enshrouds a ship like a dark blanket, robbing a navigator of his single most treasured tool: vision. The *Andrea Doria* was equipped with the latest radar—two scopes, in fact—but Calamai was a traditional captain who preferred the evidence of his eyesight. He would rely on the radar when he had to, but he would keep his own senses vigilant. Fog destroyed more ships than storm winds, coral reefs, or icebergs.

Calamai was confident, if cautious. Dressed in his daytime whites emblazoned with the proud insignia of the Italian Merchant Marine, he felt at ease on the bridge of the *Andrea Doria* as no one else could. The ship and her master were almost a single personality, having traveled the North Atlantic together for three and one-half years. He was the only captain the ship had ever known.

Calamai stood six feet tall on the bridge, his uniform covering more muscle than would be found on most fifty-eight-year-olds. His bulbous nose overlooked a weathered face that testified that he had been at sea almost constantly since the age of eighteen, when he graduated from the Nautical Institute at Genoa. He came from a seafaring lineage, his father, Oreste, having founded a magazine called *La Marina Mercantile* and his brother Marco ranking as an admiral in the Italian navy. Piero himself served with distinction during both world wars. As master of the thirteenth largest passenger vessel in the world, Piero Calamai earned a salary of $625 per month.

He stared into the haze, trying to gauge its depth, contemplating the orders he would issue to protect his ship against this respected antagonist. When Calamai gave an order he rarely, if ever, raised his voice.

Calamai was a mild-mannered, almost antisocial master. He seemed happier on the bridge scanning the open sea than socializing with passengers. He never drank. Although he often dined with fellow officers at a special table in the first-class Dining Saloon, he never invited a passenger to join him. As Senior Chief Officer Luigi Oneto described him, Calamai was "dignified but distant."

He was secretive by nature, particularly toward the passengers. Once, early in the voyage, the ship made a ninety-degree turn in order to raise the starboard side slightly to repair a leaking drainpipe. A passenger visiting the bridge asked the captain why the ship was swinging. Calamai answered, "We saw a big whale in front and turned to avoid it." Perhaps the captain felt the layman would not understand a technical explanation, especially when delivered in his patchy English. This tendency to keep passengers uninformed would later be the source of intense controversy.

Calamai knew this would be his last voyage on the *Andrea Doria*. After his round-trip crossing he was due for his annual vacation, then was in line to take command of the *Doria's* younger sister, the *Cristoforo Colombo*. Calamai was sometimes saddened at the thought, for a master develops a sense of union with his ship that few others can ever know. Piero Calamai and the *Andrea Doria* had been through so much together. Leaving her for another ship would feel like an act of infidelity.

There was that troublesome maiden voyage in January 1953, when in these same waters near the eastern coast of the United States the *Andrea Doria* encountered a vigorous storm. A swell caught the ship broadside and she took a sudden twenty-eight-degree roll that sent passengers and crew tumbling to the decks. Twenty persons were injured. Since that time, however, the *Andrea Doria* had successfully crossed the Atlantic Ocean an even hundred times. On this voyage, the hundred and first, the ship left Genoa on July 17, stopped at Cannes, then Naples, and Gibraltar before heading out past the Azores and across a sunny summer route toward New York. She was estimated to arrive at her pier the next morning, Thursday, July 26, at 9:00 A.M.

Like every ship's captain, Calamai had issued standing orders that he was always to be summoned in the event of fog. This Wednesday afternoon he appeared on the bridge before he was called, perhaps sensing an impending haze. The suspicion was based more on experience than on mysticism, for the area off Nantucket Island is often foggy, particularly in July, when warm currents from the Gulf Stream collide with icy northern waters.

The captain walked out on one of the bridge wings, observation platforms that extended out on either side of the Sun Deck beyond the edges of the hull. Here, some eighty feet above the surface, he could view the horizon best. There was no mistake. A bank of fog stretched ahead of the bow. Calamai turned, strode back to the wheelhouse, and issued his orders.

He called to the engine room, relaying the information that they were in fog. "Reduce the speed," he said.

The engineers knew their duty. They reduced pressure in the boilers from 40 to 37 kilos per square centimeter, which dropped the speed of the ship from its cruising velocity of 23 knots to 21.8 knots. This was only a token reduction. In theory, a ship should be able to come to a stop in half the distance of its visibility. But in practice few captains choose to lose time that way. Every extra minute spent at sea burns up additional fuel oil, and every hour late into harbor produces more disgruntled passengers. A ship's captain is evaluated partly on his ability to meet schedules. At its slightly reduced speed the *Andrea Doria* would reach the Ambrose lightship, the last major checkpoint before New York Harbor, at 7:00 A.M., only one hour behind schedule.

Reinforcements arrived in the engine room to stand by in the event that fast maneuvering became necessary. Stopping, or even slowing, a great ship is a difficult job requiring many sets of muscles to twist cumbersome valve wheels. Even with extra manpower the task cannot be done quickly.

Calamai, alert on the bridge, was confident that he could guide the ship safely through despite the excessive speed.

"Close the watertight doors," he ordered, and an officer pressed the switches that activate the safety partitions. Twelve green lights on a control panel changed to red, indicating that the massive steel doors had slammed shut locking the ship into eleven separate compartments below A Deck.

Watertight compartmentalization was the feature that gave the ship the label "unsinkable." The *Andrea Doria* theoretically could remain afloat if two adjacent compartments were flooded. The watertight doors would keep the remaining nine compartments dry. Only one of the passenger levels, C Deck, rode beneath the water line, but for safety the watertight doors stretched up past B Deck to the bottom of A Deck. The ship would have to list more than twenty degrees to either side in order for seawater to pour in above the sealed-off sections.

The theory of watertight integrity was a good one, but more useful on a cargo ship or a military vessel. On a passenger liner, designers must always consider the comforts of paying customers. The use of more, smaller compartments would have been safer, but they would inhibit the movement of people through the lower decks. Fewer stairways were also preferable in case water penetrated above the compartments, but passengers flowed up and down the ship in a constant restless dance. They were on vacation. Competition for tourist dollars was important; recreational luxuries must be accessible. Thus, safety was compromisable.

Unconcerned with such theoretical engineering issues at the moment, Calamai continued with his fog precautions.

"Sound the whistle," he ordered. The ships foghorn began to bellow its six-second blast every one minute and forty seconds, a necessary but always foreboding symbol of a blinded ship steaming through fog.

Calamai sent a seaman up front to the forecastle on the tip of the bow where there was a telephone for quick communication with the bridge should the man spot an approaching hazard.

"Radar," Calamai said. First Officer Carlo Kirn switched on one of the two radar screens and checked to make sure that it worked properly. A bright green line of light swept around the circular scope in synchronization with the antenna on top of the bridge. Serious-faced officers stood ready for critical actions. The *Andrea Doria* was rigged for running in fog.

The 29,082-ton ship had been launched in Genoa at the Ansaldo shipyards on June 16, 1951, after nine million man-hours of labor. Because she was built only three years after the 1948 International Convention for the Safety of Life at Sea, she was equipped with the most modern safety devices available. The *Andrea Doria* had magnetic and gyrocompasses, an automatic pilot, a new device known as loran (*long-range navigational* instrument) for determining position at sea, radio direction finder equipment, two radar screens, and a complete meteorological station.

The 697-foot hull had a double bottom for extra strength. Various tanks in the deep holds could store nearly four thousand tons of fuel oil, three hundred tons of lighter-grade diesel oil, and four thousand tons of fresh water, all of which could be shifted around to maintain stability.

Throughout the ship, interiors were lined with nonflammable materials. A special fire-resistant insulation separated the steel hull from the cabin paneling. The decks were divided into thirty-three fire safety zones that could be sealed off by automatic doors. The ship had its own automatic sprinkler system, numerous fire extinguishers, a special carbon-dioxide fire smothering system, and its own hook and ladder company.

The 572-person crew was schooled in emergency procedures. When the *Andrea Doria* had stopped at Naples to embark passengers, the crew had conducted an abandon ship drill. Small groups of crew members received additional safety instructions daily, and every crewman was issued a booklet of regulations that included a personal emergency assignment.

In the event of a catastrophe, the *Andrea Doria* carried sixteen aluminum lifeboats with a capacity of two thousand persons, more than enough to accommodate a full load of passengers and crew. Two of the boats had marine engines and two-way radios.

All of the equipment was inspected and certified by the Registro Navale Italiano and the U.S. Coast Guard.

Thus, when the *Andrea Doria* slid silently into the wall of fog, Calamai and his officers exhibited no special concern. They and their ship were prepared.

She was on a heading of 267 degrees, aiming directly for the Nantucket lightship, a small, red-hulled Coast Guard vessel anchored off the hidden shoals near the coast. The lightship served as the first point of contact with North America for ships approaching from Europe at this critical juncture of shipping lanes some two hundred miles east of New York. So many ships converged in this area that some veteran seamen referred to the Nantucket coast as "The Times Square of the Atlantic." In 1934, the Greek liner *Olympic*, running in a heavy fog, crashed directly into the lightship, killing all hands on the Coast Guard vessel.

After an hour or so of hushed tension, the officers saw the fog lift suddenly. Calamai relaxed, stopped the foghorn, and allowed the ship to regain speed. He left the bridge to go to his cabin one deck below and write up the logbooks. But the respite was short. The fog rolled in again as rapidly as it had lifted, and Calamai was called back to the bridge.

As he prepared for his duty as a waiter in the cabin-class Dining Room, Giovanni Rovelli saw the fog close in on the ship once more, and it brought with it a premonition. Rovelli remembered similar fog conditions when he had been working on the *San Miguel*. Sailing through a Norwegian fjord, the *San Miguel* had rammed the *Binna*, which sank in fifteen minutes.

The shroud seemed to grow even thicker as evening approached. Sometimes the bow of the ship, two hundred feet forward, was not visible from the bridge. The atmosphere at the command headquarters was still one of professional vigilance, however, rather than alarm. The fog was a challenge these men had met many times in the past, and Calamai's officers considered him one of the best at handling a ship in delicate situations.

There were, in fact, four licensed masters on the bridge that evening. In addition to Calamai, Senior Second Officer Curzio Franchini, thirty-six, stood watch over the radar screen, which was set to a range of twenty miles. He also checked the ship's position frequently with loran. Tall, with heavy black hair, Franchini had graduated from the Italian Naval Academy as a reserve officer, finishing sixteenth in a class of eighty. Tonight he felt the usual excitement generated by the approach to New York.

Third Officer Eugenio Giannini, twenty-eight, assisted Franchini at the radar and frequently went out onto the wings of the bridge to keep watch with Calamai. A stocky man with wavy brown locks and energetic eyes, Giannini knew his role that night was to help wherever needed.

The fourth master present on the bridge was the second in command, Staff Captain Osvaldo Magagnini, who offered to relieve Calamai after his hours of anxious command.

At 8:00 P.M., just as the sun was setting as an undefined glow in the haze, Calamai allowed himself a short break. He left the bridge briefly to change from white into a fresh blue nighttime uniform with gold epaulets on the shoulders, topped by a natty beret. He stopped for a moment in the Belvedere Lounge, located just beneath the bridge, where the first-class passengers gathered nightly for drinks and dancing, and said hello to a few acquaintances. It was a rare social gesture for the shy captain.

He ate his dinner that night on the bridge. Despite the presence of the other officers, Calamai knew it was properly his job to command.

The evening was punctuated by moments of excitement as the *Andrea Doria* encountered and overtook several other ships. Franchini or Giannini kept them under radar observation until they steamed safely past. The ships were crossing north or south, or they were slower westbound ships that the speedy *Andrea Doria* overtook from the rear. None of them was eastbound, heading directly toward the *Andrea Doria*, and no one on the bridge expected to discover such a ship. Captains sailing to the east near Nantucket were supposed to take a route twenty miles to the south, thus reducing the hazard of meeting other ships head to head.

About 9:30 P.M., Giannini spotted a pip on the radar, seventeen miles distant from the ship. Franchini took a loran fix of the *Andrea Doria's* position, then listened with the radio direction finder for the signal sent out by the Nantucket lightship. He plotted the bearing of the signal and then reported to Calamai, "We are headed directly toward the lightship."

"Change to two hundred and sixty-one degrees," Calamai ordered soon after. Giannini relayed the command to the helmsman, and watched as he shifted the spoked wheel slightly to the left until the compass needle rested on 261. The new course would take the ship safely to the south of the Nantucket lightship, with an estimated passage distance of one mile

At 10:20 P.M., the telephone rang on the bridge. The forecastle lookout reported that he could hear a foghorn off the starboard bow. At the same time Franchini tracked a pip on the radar screen. He followed its movement as revealed by the sweeping flasher. He told Calamai that they were passing the lightship at a distance of one mile.

"Steer two sixty-eight," Calamai commanded, and Giannini ordered the helmsman to swing seven degrees to the right. The *Andrea Doria* now headed almost due west, directly toward New York.

Calamai's feet traced a path on the bridge wing. He looked up at the ship's masthead lights, fuzzy and dim in the heavy fog. Periodically he caught glimpses of stars and the full moon, and he knew that the fog was patchy, rather than a continual dark haze. He shivered slightly in the cool breeze created by the ship's forward motion. The whoop of the foghorn lent an air of solemnity to the misty night. Calamai and Giannini remained out on the wings, their eyes alert for the lights of any approaching ship.

It was 10:45 P.M., Eastern daylight time, when Franchini yelled out to the others from the chartroom, where he was crouched over the dim radar screen.

"It's a ship. We can see a ship," he said.

Giannini went to look. The men watched as the bright green sweep line of the radar moved around the circular screen several times. Each time it revolved it illuminated the small, bean-shaped pip. Franchini noted the change of location with each sweep.

"What's the distance and bearing?" Calamai called out to Franchini.

"Seventeen miles distance and bearing, four degrees on the starboard bow." The unknown ship was almost directly in the line of the *Andrea Doria*'s course. The radar screen showed the pip to be off to the north by a matter of only a few millimeters.

Calamai joined Franchini at the radar while Giannini returned to keep watch on the wing. Franchini studied four indicators on the round cathode ray screen. The first, a series of concentric circles, with the *Andrea Doria* at the center, showed the distance of any foreign body from the ship. A luminous green sliver of light called the *flasher* rotated constantly with the antenna, and with each revolution illuminated the ominous pip in its new location. The *heading flasher* was a stationary line set on the course of the *Andrea Doria*. Another line, the *cursor,* could be manually adjusted. Franchini set the cursor on the position of the pip and could then read the bearing. By comparing the location of the cursor with each new pip, he could follow the progress of the other ship as it moved through the sea.

For his calculations to be valid, Franchini had to be sure that the heading flasher correctly reflected the exact course of his own ship. This was not the bearing ordered by the captain but the precise direction steered by the helmsman at the moment. Even the best helmsman allowed the ship to yaw back and forth slightly. To monitor the course, Franchini glanced at the gyro repeater attached to his radar screen, which reflected the actual compass bearing.

A few sweeps of the flasher told the officers that the ship was not merely a slower one moving west, such as others they had passed that evening. This ship was moving east, toward the *Andrea Doria*. It was disconcerting since the oncoming ship was twenty miles north of the recommended eastbound route.

"I think it is unusual for a ship to be coming eastbound in these waters," Franchini told Captain Calamai.

"Yes, it is very unusual," the captain replied.

Franchini knew his duty was to watch closely and keep track of the bearing of the pip. If the bearing continually increased to the north, it meant that the other ship was on a course that would allow it to pass safely on the starboard side of the *Andrea Doria*. If the bearing decreased, then the ships were on a dangerous course and would have to take evasive action.

Calamai, now back out on the starboard wing, called out, "How's the bearing?"

"It's increasing," Franchini reported. If both ships held their courses, they would pass safely starboard-to-starboard. When two ships meet head-on in the open sea, they are supposed to past port-to-port, unless that would force them into a crossing course. Since the other ship was already on the starboard side, to the north, there seemed to be no reason to swing to the right for the normal port-to-port passage. Franchini decided that a starboard-to-starboard passage would be equally safe. Several times Calamai returned to the radar screen to check the pip himself. It was a fast ship—not as speedy as the *Andrea Doria*, but fast nonetheless.

When the other ship was about seven miles ahead, Franchini switched the radar to a range of eight miles. Immediately the pip retreated toward the edge of the screen and grew to more than double its previous size. On the screen it was closing faster now, for the relatives size and distances had increased.

Franchini did not take the precaution of plotting the progress of the pip on the Marconi Locater Graph that sat nearby in the first drawer of the plotting table. Franchini had not used the device since the ship left Gibraltar five days earlier. To use the plotter, Franchini would have had to note the location of the pip each time the sweep revealed it, correct for any course error shown on the gyro repeater then transfer that location to the plotting board. By connecting the dots he would be able to monitor the course of the ship and would note any changes. Instead, he set the cursor each time the pip reappeared, so that he could follow the progress only from one reading to the next.

Each reading seemed to confirm his observation that the other ship would pass safely on his starboard, or right, side.

Calamai approached Franchini at the radar. "How close will she pass?" the captain asked.

"About one mile to starboard," Franchini replied.

The captain returned to the bridge wing and searched the horizon. Five minutes later from the wheelhouse, Franchini called the newest radar data. "Bearing fifteen degrees. Range three and a half miles."

Calamai responded with an immediate order. "Steer four degrees to port."

Calamai reasoned that the slight swing to the left would open the gap between the two ships and allow them to pass starboard-to-starboard even farther than the one mile estimated by Franchini. It was also his way of telling the helmsman not to allow the ship to yaw to the right. But the course change was not dramatic enough to be readily apparent to anyone who might be watching a radar screen on the other ship.

The change of course seemed to bring the *Andrea Doria* to an area where the fog was not quite so dense, but Calamai still estimated visibility at less than half a mile. The *Andrea Doria*'s fog whistle continued to send out its wail every hundred seconds.

Calamai and Giannini watched the horizon carefully on the starboard wing. It was important to make visual contact with the other ship at the earliest possible moment, for radar is at best an imprecise aid to navigation. Eyes are more trustworthy. Calamai did not expect to see the other vessel until it was close, because of the fog, but he was puzzled that he did not at least hear its foghorn.

"Why don't we hear her?" Giannini asked the captain. "Why doesn't she whistle?"

Calamai did not reply. His forehead furrowed as he stared into the night. It was a few minutes after 11:00 P.M.

Giannini left the wing to check the radar screen once more and fix in his mind the position where the other ship should appear. "We can't hear the fog whistle," he commented to Franchini. He quickly studied the radar and saw the other ship at a distance of one and a half miles and at a bearing of thirty to thirty-five degrees to the right. He came back outside and searched to starboard with his binoculars. Suddenly he saw a blur of lights some thirty-five degrees off to the right, just as the radar had indicated.

"Did you see?" Giannini said, pointing to the glow.

"Yes, I see," Calamai replied.

Franchini, hearing that the men had made visual contact, abandoned his radar screen and joined the other officers on the right wing of the bridge.

The ships were about one mile apart when the vague glow of the approaching vessel separated into visible masthead lights. The officers studied carefully to determine the course of the other ship. There are four signal lights that reveal the direction of an oncoming vessel. A bright green light glows from the starboard side of the bridge, indicating that the right side of the oncoming ship is visible; or a red light from the port, or left side, indicates the opposite. Two white masthead lights are also key indicators. The lower light is situated forward of the higher light. If the lights are aligned vertically, then the other ship is heading directly toward the observer. If the lower light is to the left or right of the higher light, then the ship is heading in that particular direction.

Giannini pointed his binoculars at the glow and strained to see the masthead lights. There were two white lights, the lower one slightly to the right of the other.

For an instant, Calamai thought the other ship would pass safely to the right. It was perhaps the last serene moment Captain Piero Calamai would ever experience.

Then Giannini focused his binoculars once more on the lights of the approaching ship. He was suddenly confronted with the ghastly realization that the lower masthead light of the other ship was rapidly swinging to the left of the higher masthead light, and the red light on the port side of the other ship was now visible for the first time. Incredibly, unbelievably, the other ship was turning directly toward the *Andrea Doria*.

"She is turning! She is turning!" Giannini exclaimed. "She is showing the red light. She is coming toward us."

Calamai looked anxiously at the approaching ship and verified Giannini's alarm. He had to act quickly, but there was little time. The master's decision was one of desperation. When collision is unavoidable, a ship should turn *toward* danger to minimize impact. A head-on collision of streamlined vessels is more likely to result in a glancing blow. But Calamai could not bring himself to concede the inevitable. His choice was made instantly, but it was the product more of his intense affection for his glorious ship than the hard judgment of years at sea.

"Hard left!" he yelled at Helmsman Giulio Visciano. Even the Italian word for "left," *sinistra,* was foreboding. It was a last daring attempt to outrun a disaster, by turning the *Andrea Doria* to the left faster than the unknown vessel was turning to the right. But in doing so Calamai risked turning the *Andrea Doria* broadside to the other ship.

Visciano swung the wheel to the left with all his strength, using both hands to maintain pressure on the rudder and accelerate the turn. Giannini jumped on the ledge of the middle window in the wheelhouse for a better view of the onrushing ship.

Calamai seemed suddenly immobilized. Franchini knew that they should signal their turn to the other ship.

"The two whistles?" Franchini reminded.

Calamai nodded, and Franchini disconnected the foghorn in order to blow two short blasts, indicating a left turn.

"The engines?" Franchini suggested, wondering whether they should be shut down to lessen impact.

"No," Calamai said. "Don't touch the engines. It turns more rapidly." Still he clung to the hope of outrunning his attacker.

Straining under the hard left rudder, the *Andrea Doria* slid forward for perhaps a half a mile before the turn took effect.

"Is she turning? Is she turning?" Giannini asked Visciano imploringly.

"Now," the helmsman replied, "she is beginning to turn." Giannini heard the click of the gyrocompass recording the change of direction. But instead of easing the *Andrea Doria* away from the menacing ship coming toward them, the turn exposed the broad mass of the *Doria*'s side, like a target, to the onrushing bow of the other vessel.

"She is coming against us!" Calamai yelled in amazement.

The captain instinctively drew back from the railing of the wing. The bow of the intruder seemed to point directly at him on the bridge, though he knew it would hit much lower, probably no higher than the Upper Deck, some forty feet below. For an instant Calamai wished he was down there where the impact would crush him. It would be an act of mercy, for the captain saw in the approaching bow a more horrible destiny. He was a captain! This was his ship! How could this happen to him?

Never in all his years at sea had Piero Calamai felt so alone.

At 9:15 Friday night, four-year-old Norma di Sandro died at the Brighton Marine Hospital in Boston without regaining consciousness.

Fifty-one people had died as a result of the collision of the two great ships: forty-six passengers from the *Andrea Doria* and five crewmen from the *Stockholm*.

It is a tragic statistic. But perhaps a more significant, and often overlooked, fact is that 1660 men, women, and children, many of whom never expected to survive, were taken safely off a ship that threatened to slide into the ocean at any moment.

SEA DIVERS

Captain Nemo's Revenge

by JULES VERNE

The way of describing this unlooked-for scene, the history of the patriotic ship, told at first so coldly, and the emotion with which this strange man pronounced the last words, the name of the *Avenger,* the significance of which could not escape me, all impressed itself deeply on my mind. My eyes did not leave the Captain; who, with his hand stretched out to sea, was watching with a glowing eye the glorious wreck. Perhaps I was never to know who he was, from whence he came, or where he was going to, but I saw the man move, and apart from the savant. It was no common misanthropy which had shut Captain Nemo and his companions within the *Nautilus,* but a hatred, either monstrous or sublime, which time could never weaken. Did this hatred still seek for vengeance? The future would soon teach me that. But the *Nautilus* was rising slowly to the surface of the sea, and the form of the *Avenger* disappeared by degrees from my sight. Soon a slight rolling told me that we were in the open air. At that moment a dull boom was heard. I looked at the Captain. He did not move.

"Captain?" said I.

He did not answer. I left him and mounted the platform. Conseil and the Canadian were already there.

"Where did that sound come from?" I asked.

"It was a gunshot," replied Ned Land.

I looked in the direction of the vessel I had already seen. It was nearing the *Nautilus,* and we could see that it was putting on steam. It was within six miles of us.

"What is that ship, Ned?"

"By its rigging, and the height of its lower masts," said the Canadian, "I bet she is a ship of war. May it reach us; and, if necessary, sink this cursed *Nautilus.*"

"Friend Ned," replied Conseil, "what harm can it do to the *Nautilus?* Can it attack it beneath the waves? Can it cannonade us at the bottom of the sea?"

"Tell me, Ned," said I, "can you recognize what country she belongs to?"

The Canadian knitted his eyebrows, dropped his eyelids, and screwed up the corners of his eyes, and for a few moments fixed a piercing look upon the vessel.

"No, sir," he replied; "I cannot tell what nation she belongs to, for she shows no colours. But I can declare she is a man-of-war, for a long pennant flutters from her main-mast."

For a quarter of an hour we watched the ship which was steaming towards us. I could not, however, believe that she could see the *Nautilus* from that distance; and still less, that she could know what this submarine engine was. Soon the Canadian informed me that she was a large armoured two-decker ram. A thick black smoke was pouring from her two funnels. Her closely-furled sails were stopped to her yards. She hoisted no flag at her mizzen-peak. The distance prevented us from distinguishing the colours of her pennant, which floated like a thin ribbon. She advanced rapidly. If Captain Nemo allowed her to approach, there was a chance of salvation for us.

"Sir," said Ned Land, "if that vessel passes within a mile of us I shall throw myself into the sea, and I should advise you to do the same."

I did not reply to the Canadian's suggestion, but continued watching the ship. Whether English, French, American, or Russian, she would be sure to take us in if we could only reach her. Presently a white smoke burst from the fore part of the vessel; some seconds after the water, agitated by the fall of a body, splashed the stern of the *Nautilus*, and shortly afterwards a loud explosion struck my ear.

"What! They are firing at us!" I exclaimed.

"So please you, sir," said Ned, "they have recognized the unicorn, and they are firing at us."

"But," I exclaimed, "surely they can see that there are men in the case?"

"It is, perhaps, because of that," replied Ned Land, looking at me.

A whole flood of light burst upon my mind. Doubtless they knew now how to believe the stories of the pretended monster. No doubt, on board the *Abraham Lincoln*, when the Canadian struck it with the harpoon, Commander Farragut had recognized in the supposed narwhal a submarine vessel, more dangerous than a supernatural cetacean. Yes, it must have been so; and on every sea they were now seeking this engine of destruction. Terrible indeed! if, as we supposed, Captain Nemo employed the *Nautilus* in works of vengeance. On the night when we were imprisoned in that cell, in the midst of the Indian Ocean, had he not attacked some vessel? The man buried in the coral cemetery, had he not been a victim to the shock caused by the *Nautilus?* Yes, I repeat it, it must be so. One part of the mysterious existence of Captain Nemo had been unveiled; and, if his identity had not been recognized, at least, the nations united against him were no longer hunting a chimerical creature, but a man who had vowed a deadly hatred against them. All the formidable past rose before me. Instead of meeting friends on board the approaching ship, we could only expect pitiless enemies. But the shot rattled above us. Some of them struck the sea and ricocheted, losing themselves in the distance. But none touched the *Nautilus*. The vessel was not more than three miles from us. In spite of the serious cannonade, Captain Nemo did not appear on the platform; but, if one of the conical projectiles had struck the shell of the *Nautilus*, it would have been fatal. The Canadian then said, "Sir, we must do all we can to get out of this dilemma. Let us signal them. They will then, perhaps, understand that we are honest folks."

Ned Land took his handkerchief to wave in the air; but he had scarcely displayed it, when he was struck down by an iron hand, and fell, in spite of his great strength, upon the deck.

"Fool!" exclaimed the Captain, "do you wish to be pierced by the spur of the *Nautilus* before it is hurled at this vessel?"

Captain Nemo was terrible to hear; he was still more terrible to see. His face was deadly pale, with a spasm at his heart. For an instant it must have ceased to beat. His pupils were fearfully contracted. He did not *speak*, he *roared*, as, with his body thrown forward, he wrung the Canadian's shoulders. Then, leaving him, and turning to the ship of war, whose shot was still raining around him, he exclaimed, with a powerful voice, "Ah, ship of an accursed nation, you know who I am! I do not want your colours to know you by! Look! and I will show you mine!"

And on the fore part of the platform Captain Nemo unfurled a black flag, similar to the one he had placed at the south pole. At that moment a shot struck the shell of the *Nautilus* obliquely, without piercing it; and, rebounding near the Captain, was lost in the sea. He shrugged his shoulders; and addressing me, said shortly, "Go down, you and your companions go down!"

"Sir," I exclaimed, "are you going to attack this vessel?"

"Sir, I am going to sink it."

"You will not do that?"

"I shall do it," he replied, coldly. "And I advise you not to judge me, sir. Fate has shown you what you ought not have seen. The attack has begun; go down."

"What is this vessel?"

"You do not know? Very well! so much the better! its nationality to you, at least, will be a secret. Go down!"

We could but obey. About fifteen of the sailors surrounded the Captain, looking with implacable hatred at the vessel nearing them. One could feel that the same desire of vengeance animated every soul. I went down at the moment another projectile struck the *Nautilus*, and I heard the Captain exclaim—

"Strike, mad vessel! Shower your useless shot! And then, you will not escape the spur of the *Nautilus*. But it is not here that you shall perish! I would not have your ruins mingle with those of the *Avenger!*"

I reached my room. The Captain and his second had remained on the platform. The screw was set in motion, and the *Nautilus*, moving with speed, was soon beyond the reach of the ship's guns. But the pursuit continued, and Captain Nemo contented himself with keeping his distance.

About four in the afternoon, being no longer able to contain my impatience, I went to the central staircase. The panel was open, and I ventured on to the platform. The Captain was still walking up and down with an agitated step. He was looking at the ship, which was five or six miles to leeward.

He was going round it like a wild beast, and drawing it eastward, he allowed them to pursue. But he did not attack. Perhaps he still hesitated? I wished to mediate once more. But I had scarcely spoken, when Captain Nemo imposed silence, saying—

"I am the law, and I am the judge! I am the oppressed, and there is the oppressor! Through him I have lost all that I loved, cherished, and venerated,—country, wife, children, father, and mother. I saw all perish! All that I hate is there! Say no more!"

I cast a last look at the man-of-war, which was putting on steam, and rejoined Ned and Conseil.

"We will fly!" I exclaimed.

"Good!" said Ned. "What is this vessel?"

"I do not know; but whatever it is, it will be sunk before night. In any case, it is better to perish with it, than be made accomplices in a retaliation, the justice of which we cannot judge."

"That is my opinion too," said Ned Land, coolly. "Let us wait for night."

Night arrived. Deep silence reigned on board. The compass showed that the *Nautilus* had not altered its course. It was on the surface, rolling slightly. My companions and I resolved to fly when the vessel should be near enough either to hear us or to see us; for the moon, which would be full in two or three days, shone brightly. Once on board the ship, if we could not prevent the blow which threatened it, we could, at least we would, do all that circumstances would allow. Several times I thought the *Nautilus* was preparing for attack; but Captain Nemo contented himself with allowing his adversary to approach, and then fled once more before it.

Part of the night passed without any incident. We watched the opportunity for action. We spoke little, for we were too much moved. Ned Land would have thrown himself into the sea, but I forced him to wait. According to my idea, the *Nautilus* would attack the ship at her waterline, and then it would not only be possible, but easy to fly.

At three in the morning, full of uneasiness, I mounted the platform. Captain Nemo had not left it. He was standing at the forepart near his flag, which a slight breeze displayed above his head. He did not take his eyes from the vessel. The intensity of his look seemed to attract, and fascinate, and draw it onward more purely than if he had been towing it. The moon was then passing the meridian. Jupiter was rising in the east. Amid this peaceful scene of nature, sky and ocean rivalled each other in tranquillity, the sea offering to the orbs of night the finest mirror they could ever have in which to reflect their image. As I thought of the deep calm of these elements, compared with all those passions brooding imperceptibly within the *Nautilus*, I shuddered.

The vessel was within two miles of us. It was ever nearing that phosphorescent light which showed the presence of the *Nautilus*. I could see its green and red lights, and its white lantern hanging from the large foremast. An indistinct vibration quivered through its rigging, showing that the furnaces were heated to the uttermost. Sheaves of sparks and red ashes flew from the funnels, shining in the atmosphere like stars.

I remained thus until six in the morning, without Captain Nemo noticing me. The ship stood about a mile and a half from us, and with the first dawn of day the firing began afresh. The moment could not be far off when, the *Nautilus* attacking its adversary, my companions and myself should for ever leave this man. I was preparing to go down to remind them, when the second mounted the platform, accompanied by several sailors. Captain Nemo either did not, or would not, see them. Some steps were taken which might be called the signal for action. They were very simple. The iron balustrade around the platform was lowered, and the lantern and pilot cages were pushed within the shell until they were flush with the deck. The long surface of the steel cigar no longer offered a single point to check its manoeuvres. I returned to the saloon. The *Nautilus* still floated; some streaks of light were filtering through the liquid beds. With the undulations of the waves the windows were brightened by the red streaks of the rising sun, and this dreadful day of the 2d of June had dawned.

At five o'clock the log showed that the speed of the *Nautilus* was slackening, and I knew that it was allowing them to draw nearer. Besides, the reports were heard more distinctly, and the projectiles, labouring through the ambient water, were extinguished with a strange hissing noise.

"My friends," said I, "the moment is come. One grasp of the hand, and may God protect us!"

Ned Land was resolute, Conseil calm, myself so nervous that I knew not how to contain myself. We all passed into the library; but the moment I pushed the door opening on to the central staircase, I heard the upper panel close sharply. The Canadian rushed on to the stairs, but I stopped him. A well-known hissing noise told me that the water was running into the reservoirs, and in a few minutes the *Nautilus* was some yards beneath the surface of the waves. I understood the maneuver. It was too late to act. The *Nautilus* did not wish to strike at the impenetrable cuirass, but below the waterline, where the metallic covering no longer protected it.

We were again imprisoned, unwilling witnesses of the dreadful drama that was preparing. We had scarcely time to reflect; taking refuge in my room, we looked at each other without speaking. A deep stupor had taken hold of my mind; thought seemed to stand still. I was in that painful state of expectation preceding a dreadful report. I waited, I listened, every sense was merged in that of hearing! The speed of the *Nautilus* was accelerated. It was preparing to rush. The whole ship trembled. Suddenly I screamed. I felt the shock, but comparatively light. I felt the penetrating power of the steel spur. I heard rattlings and scrapings. But the *Nautilus*, carried along by its propelling power, passed through the mass of the vessel, like a needle through sailcloth!

I could stand it no longer. Mad, out of my mind, I rushed from my room into the saloon. Captain Nemo was there, mute, gloomy, implacable; he was looking through the port panel. A large mass cast a shadow on the water; and that it might lose nothing of her agony, the *Nautilus* was going down into the abyss with her. Ten yards from me I saw the open shell through which the water was rushing with the noise of thunder, then the double line of guns and the netting. The bridge was covered with black agitated shadows.

The water was rising. The poor creatures were crowding the ratlines clinging to the masts, struggling under the water. It was a human ant-heap overtaken by the sea. Paralysed, stiffened with anguish, my hair standing on end, with eyes wide open, panting, without breath, and without voice, I too was watching! An irresistible attraction glued me to the glass! Suddenly an explosion took place. The compressed air blew up her decks, as if the magazines had caught fire. Then the unfortunate vessel sunk more rapidly. Her topmast, laden with victims, now appeared; then her spars, bending under the weight of men, and last of all, the top of her main mast. Then the dark mass disappeared, and with it the dead crew, drawn down by the strong eddy.

I turned to Captain Nemo. That terrible avenger, a perfect archangel of hatred, was still looking. When all was over, he turned to his room, opened the door, and entered. I followed him with my eyes. On the end wall beneath his heroes, I saw the portrait of a woman still young, and two little children. Captain Nemo looked at them for some moments, stretched his arms towards them, and kneeling down burst into deep sobs.

Teddy Tucker, Bermuda Diver

by ROBERT F. MARX

Of all the underwater explorers I have known over the years, few have even come close to having led as exciting and interesting a life as Edward "Teddy" Tucker. Tucker claims he would have liked to have lived several centuries ago and been a pirate and even today he would be the perfect person to play the pirate role in a Hollywood movie. In addition to being one of the best-known residents on Bermuda, he is also recognized as one of the most knowledgeable and successful underwater treasure hunters.

He comes from one of the island's oldest and most respected families. One of his ancestors was the first governor of Bermuda in the early seventeenth century. Born there in 1926 he was the black sheep of the family even as a young boy. He was expelled from almost every school on the island: once for smoking a pipe in school at the age of ten, and another time, when he was thirteen, for coming to school drunk.

In 1938, at the age of twelve, he convinced an old helmet diver working in Hamilton Harbor to teach him to dive. Tucker became so fascinated with the underwater environment that he fashioned a diving helmet from a small boiler tank, which was connected by a garden hose to a hand air pump on the surface. With several of his school chums, he explored miles and miles of the reefs which surround Bermuda and made ample spending money selling coral, sea fans and shells to the tourists. He loved the sea and hated school so much that his parents had to physically take him to school each day.

At fifteen he stowed away on a merchant ship and reached England, where he lied about his age and joined the Royal Navy during World War Two. He claims to have spent most of his navy years in numberless brigs and jails. Once, while stationed in Plymouth, England, he was ordered to clean up the base's mascot, a jackass. He was given methylated spirits to clean the animal's hoofs, but instead he mixed it with beer and drank it, ending up in the brig again for several weeks. While awaiting his discharge papers after the war ended in 1945, he was arrested and sent to prison in Singapore for selling weapons to a Chinese trader. After his release he set out on a hitchhiking tour of Asia and managed to sample several other prisons before returning to Bermuda in 1948. To support himself during these years, he worked as a commercial diver salvaging modern shipwrecks and other things, which gave him the opportunity of seeing the underwater world in exotic places like the Strait of

Malacca, the Gulf of Siam, the Bay of Bengal and many other places in the Indian Ocean.

Returning to Bermuda Tucker decided to forsake his swashbuckling past and become a respectable citizen of the community. He even gave up drinking, which he blames for many of his past problems. In 1949 with another diver, Bob Canton, who became his brother-in-law, he started a commercial salvage firm, chiefly recovering brass, lead and other metals from modern shipwrecks. Today he still makes a good living doing this type of work during the winter months. When the salvage business was slow, Canton and Tucker worked as commercial fishermen.

One day in 1950 while searching for one of his fish traps with a glass-bottom bucket, Tucker spotted two old iron cannon on the bottom. Several days later he returned to the spot, which was about ten miles offshore from Hamilton Harbor, and raised both cannon, as well as a large copper kettle full of lead musket balls. At first they were going to sell the cannon as scrap iron, but several members of the Bermuda Monuments Trust Commission heard of his discovery and offered him a great deal more than he would have received selling them for scrap. They went back to the wreck site again and recovered four more cannon, an anchor and a pewter plate. The wreck was interesting, but Tucker and Canton decided to stick to their regular type of salvage.

One day after a storm had passed the area, late in the summer of 1955, the two men stopped at the wreck site and Tucker jumped in with a face mask. The underwater visibility was excellent and he noticed that the storm had removed a great amount of sand in the area. Reaching the bottom he saw a piece of metal and pulled it out. It was a beautifully decorated bronze apothecary mortar, with a date of 1561 on it. Excited by the find, he returned to the boat, started the air compressor and then jumped back in wearing his DESCO shallow water diving mask. Using a small piece of board, he began fanning the sand away in the area where he had discovered the mortar and in five minutes he had a handful of blackened silver coins. He continued digging a trench about eighteen inches deep and soon after saw a bright object fall out the side of the trench: it was a gold cube weighing two ounces. Tucker was so intoxicated by this find that he bumped his head on the bottom of the boat while surfacing. Forgetting their bread-and-butter commercial salvage operation, Tucker and his brother-in-law decided on the spot to become full-time treasure hunters.

Having decided to systematically work the wreck, the following day they gathered a group of friends to serve as diving tenders and deck hands. There were ominous signs of a storm brewing, but nothing could have kept them off the wreck that day. Their first goal was to remove all visual signs of the shipwreck for fear that someone else might stumble on the site, particularly once word leaked out of their discoveries. The finds of the previous day were uncovered in a sandpocket of the reef, which was about fifty feet in diameter. The reef rose to within eight feet of the surface around the hole and they located dozens of iron cannon balls and several muskets embedded in the coral growth and chopped them out with axes. Attached to these objects they discovered more than two hundred silver Spanish and French coins, and the most recent date on any of them was 1592. Tucker realized that this probably meant that the ship had been lost before English colonists settled on the island in 1619 and that there was a possibility of its having more treasure. Tucker then began fanning away the sand using a Ping-pong paddle, in the same area where he had discovered the gold cube. Enlarging the trench he discovered three beautiful gold buttons, each studded with three large pearls. Just when things were getting exciting, the storm struck and they were forced to run for shelter.

The storm continued for three days and the minute it abated, Tucker and Canton got underway for the wreck site. During the first hour on the bottom, Tucker discovered a round gold disc, which weighed eighteen ounces, and contained the stamp mark of the Spanish Crown. The rest of the day only produced another of the gold and pearl buttons and a number of ceramic shards.

A strong northeaster was blowing the following day and it blew hard for two whole days, preventing them from returning to the site. All of Tucker's thoughts during the day and his dreams at night were of treasure. In one of the dreams he was working about twenty feet from the spot where he had stopped when the bad weather set in and above his head on the reef was a bright yellow brain coral formation. He began fanning directly under it and discovered a round gold ingot and two smaller pieces of gold. He awoke and told his wife, Edna, about his dream, and she was convinced that the dream was a premonition.

When Tucker got back to the wreck, he swam around until he located the brain coral and it looked just as he had seen it in his dream. He began fanning away in the spot he had remembered from the dream and in less than ten minutes he proved the dream was wrong. Instead of finding three pieces of gold, he only found two: a large ten-and-a-half-inch bar, of twenty-four-carat gold, weighing over two pounds; and another small gold cube. The bar was marked with the royal tax stamp and tally number, and the name "PINTO." He later learned the gold came from the Pinto gold mine in Colombia.

On the fifth day of diving on the wreck he discovered a number of interesting artifacts, and on the sixth, another small gold bar and a number of silver coins. Several days more of bad weather struck and it appeared for a while that he might not get back to the wreck until the following summer, since the hurricane season had started when large seas break on the reefs for months on end.

The seventh day on the wreck was the most exciting day of Tucker's life. He discovered the most valuable single item of treasure ever recovered from an old shipwreck. Fighting against time, he decided to use a water hose to blast away the sand on the bottom. After excavating a large hole, he turned the jet off to let the sediment settle. As soon as there was a few inches of visibility in the hole, he stuck his head in and saw a magnificent emerald-studded gold cross. There were seven emeralds and each was about the size of a musket ball. He surfaced with the cross and his wife and others aboard the boat dampened his spirits by saying they must be green glass and couldn't be real emeralds. Not until a year later when the cross was sent to the British Museum were the stones positively identified as emeralds. Tucker felt he had a valuable find, but had no idea that eventually the cross would be valued at $200,000.

Before the bad weather forced a halt to that year's work on the wreck, Tucker and Canton managed to put in three more days of diving. More gold and pearl buttons were recovered and an interesting array of artifacts which included: a ceremonial spear made by the Carib Indians, other Indian artifacts, several pewter plates and porringer bowls, hand grenades, swords, muskets, a breast plate, small brass weights used by the ship's surgeon, a pair of navigational dividers, timing glasses, a pottery cruet for oil or vinegar, buckles, buttons, and hundreds of cannon and musket balls. After removing all of the coral incrustation from the bronze mortar, they discovered the name Peter Van den Ghein engraved on it. He was a member of a prominent family of mortar founders in Mechelen, Belgium.

Tucker and Canton soon discovered that it was more difficult to keep a treasure than to find one. They had decided to keep their find a secret; however, they had been too casual in telling many of their friends about the wreck and soon rumors were flying all over the island. Some had them recovering several tons of gold. One of the island's newspapers ran a story about the rumors, but the government, which they had feared might seize the treasure, remained silent. Having no idea of the intrinsic value of their find, they contacted Mendel Peterson of the Smithsonian Institution and invited him to Bermuda to appraise the treasure.

Edwin Link came over with Peterson and their eyes almost popped out of their heads when they saw the treasure. After several days of study, Peterson evaluated the treasure and artifacts at $130,000, but later he admitted he had been too conservative and raised the value to $250,000.

Before leaving, Link offered to buy the long gold bar and although Peterson had placed a value of $25,000 on the round gold disc of eighteen ounces, he suggested a price of only $2000 for the long gold bar. A Bermuda government official appeared while the transaction was in progress and offered to buy it for the government at the same price. Tucker later realized that the bar was worth ten times the price he had sold it to the government for and Peterson later apologized for the rather low appraisal price he had placed on it. By purchasing the bar, Tucker and Canton felt that the government had officially recognized their ownership of the treasure and the wreck.

Life magazine ran a feature article on their find and then their real problems began. Every time they went to sea, they were followed by other boats trying to learn the location of the wreck. After a prowler attempted to break into his home, he moved the treasure to a safe deposit box in a bank. Then he was notified that the Bermuda Government had decided that the treasure was legally theirs because it had been discovered in their territorial waters. After an angry meeting with the Colonial secretary, who stated that the government planned to confiscate the treasure, Tucker quickly retrieved it from the bank and that night put it all in a potato sack and hid it under water in a cave several miles at sea.

Some weeks later he learned that the government had feared he would smuggle the treasure from the island and for that reason planned to confiscate it. Once the government officials discovered that he had hid the treasure, they began to ease their demands and another meeting was held. Tucker and Canton convinced them that they also wanted to have the treasure remain on the island and the government co-operated in helping them establish a museum. Tucker was not the type to be a museum curator, so he had his wife and several friends manage the museum. Although many experts assured him that he could sell the treasure for at least $250,000 in 1961, he sold the whole museum and all the treasure to the Bermuda Government for only $100,000. Tucker felt it would require too much of his time to sell the treasure in individual pieces, so he sold it at this low price.

After months of historical research, Peterson was able to identify the wreck as being a Spanish merchant vessel named *San Pedro*, which was lost in 1596, while sailing between Mexico and Spain. The documents did not indicate the type of cargo or the amount of treasure she carried, nor if any attempts had been made by the Spaniards to salvage her.

Most of the summer of 1956 was spent working on the *San Pedro* and hundreds of other interesting artifacts were recovered, but only a few small pieces of treasure. The following summer they were joined by Peterson, who has spent two months working with them each summer since. Most of their subsequent efforts were devoted to locating new wrecks and during the course of the summer they discovered more than thirty wreck sites, ranging in date from the early seventeenth to the late nineteenth century. Tucker estimates that more than 350 ships have been lost around Bermuda over the centuries and at the present time he has located more than 130 of them. That summer they used three methods of visual search; the waters are so clear around the island that Tucker has located many wrecks by standing on the bow of his boat and looking down at the sea floor. Some were located by towing divers behind the boat on a line and still others sighted from a light plane.

They continued searching the following summer and toward the end of the season made another important discovery. While searching from the bow of his boat, Tucker sighted an iron cannon barely visible on the sand bottom and ordered the boat stopped. There were only a few more hours of daylight left, but they decided to dig a few holes on the site with an airlift. In a short time they discovered two dozen silver coins, several fragments of gold chain, a pair of brass navigational dividers, lead musket shot and many ceramic shards. The finds indicated an old Spanish wreck lay buried there, so Tucker decided to devote the remainder of the season to the wreck. Each day they uncovered more of the ship's timbers and made more intriguing finds: a gold ring with a large emerald mounted on it, more silver coins, swords, pulley blocks, bits of rigging, leaf tobacco and many pieces of ceramic ware.

Research proved the wreck to be the *San Antonio*, a Spanish merchant vessel of 300 tons, which was lost in 1621. Colonists on the island at that time rescued all of the crew and passengers and salvaged most of the cargo.

Work continued intermittently on the *San Antonio* during the following three summers when Tucker and his team were not engaged in locating and salvaging other wrecks. A large part of the ship's main cargo was also discovered: indigo and cochineal dyes. Several thousand cowrie shells, undoubtedly to be used by the Spaniards to purchase slaves in Africa, where they were used as exchange, were also recovered.

The most important discovery in 1959 was the wreck *Vigo*, a small Spanish merchant vessel lost in 1639. During the two weeks remaining that season, they recovered hundreds of fascinating artifacts, a forty-inch gold chain, two large gold nuggets and fifty silver coins. The following season's efforts were divided up between the *Vigo* and *San Antonio*. At the end of the summer, Tucker gave Peterson several coral-incrusted iron objects for preservation and when one of Peterson's assistants began removing the coral growth, a beautiful gold ring with three stones—emerald, almandite and crystal—was discovered. On the inside of the ring was the inscription in Castilian: "Yours and Always Will Be." This ring turned out to be the most important find made that year and it had almost been overlooked.

During the summer of 1961, Tucker pioneered a new method of locating old shipwrecks, using a helium-filled balloon, which was towed behind a boat at an elevation of about two hundred feet. The first wreck located proved to be the *Virginia Merchant*, an English merchant vessel sailing between Plymouth, England, and Jamestown, Virginia, which was lost in 1660 with 179 persons aboard. Several weeks of excavation on the wreck produced thousands of artifacts: clay pipes, tools, weapons, house bricks, writing utensils, pieces of silverware, pewter plates and many fragments of chinaware and pottery.

The next wreck sighted from the balloon turned out to be a sister ship of the *Virginia Merchant*, the merchant vessel *Eagle*, which was also sailing between Plymouth and Jamestown with trade goods and passengers in 1659. A tremendous number of trade good artifacts were also discovered on this wreck, but while working on it Tucker and Donald Canton, Bob's brother, almost lost their lives. They were using the airlift in about thirty-six feet of water next to a massive coral ridge which almost rose to the surface. Digging right at the base of the coral formation, they uncovered a large wooden box containing several thousand clay pipes. Digging deeper they found a copper teapot, then a slate and stylus, which were probably used by the navigator in plotting the ship's position. Suddenly Tucker felt a strong tremor and the years of working under water had taught him to act fast. He grabbed Donald Canton and they scrambled out of the hole. Seconds later a huge piece of coral, weighing at least a ton, toppled right into the hole they had been working. After another close call with a large shark the following day, Tucker decided that the wreck was jinxed and determined to spend the rest of the season completing the salvage of the *San Antonio*.

Tucker found the cost of helium for his balloon too high, so he resorted to visual search from a boat during the summer of 1962. The first wreck located and worked was the French frigate *L'Hermoine,* lost in 1838. Large numbers of weapons, shot, copper powder cans, porcelain objects, glass bottles— many with their original contents—and uniform buttons were recovered. Nearby they located the remains of the English merchant ship *Caesar,* lost in 1819. This wreck yielded hundreds of grindstones of various sizes, kegs of white lead and bottles of many different descriptions.

Toward the close of the season, through Tucker's sighting of a few ballast rocks on a sandy bottom, the oldest ship yet discovered in Bermuda waters was located. Digging an exploratory hole on the site, a vast amount of ballast rock was uncovered buried about five feet in the sand and also a small clump of badly sulphated silver coins, which dated around the middle of the six-teenth century.

On the last diving day of the season, Tucker convinced everyone to "have a look" at the old *San Pedro.* It almost appeared that Tucker had planted trea-sure because he was only down a few minutes, before most of the others had time to come down, when he discovered a small gold bar, later valued at $16,000.

The summers of 1963 and 1964 were totally devoted to working the old sixteenth-century wreck discovered in 1962. Historical research indicates that it was probably the *Capitana* of the New Spain Fleet, commanded by Captain General Juan Menendez, lost in 1563. With the exception of the small clump of silver coins discovered in the exploratory hole, no other treasure was found on this wreck—in fact, it yielded very few important artifacts, which indicates that it was probably completely salvaged by the Spaniards. However, its early date and the fact that a large section of the lower hull of the ship was intact and in a remarkable state of preservation, convinced Peterson that the wreck should be excavated and he obtained a grant to hire Tucker and his team to do the work. A great amount of archaeological data was obtained from the wreck, and much was learned about the construction of ships from this histori-cal period.

I was fortunate in having the opportunity of spending most of the 1963 summer working with Tucker and rarely have I seen such a dedicated and hard-working individual on the bottom. Every day he would jump over the side with his airlift tube and stay down on the wreck for hours and hours. One day he stayed down for twelve hours before he finally surfaced—and then only because the rest of us were starving to death and the only way we could get him to come up was by turning off the air compressor.

Although Tucker is very serious about his work, he is also an irrepressible practical joker. I will never forget, nor forgive him, for one joke at my ex-pense. We had been working on the *Capitana* for several weeks, with negative results, and everyone was a bit disheartened by the lack of interesting finds, so he decided to give everyone a good laugh. Jumping overboard one morning, he had a replica of a gold coin hidden in his swimsuit and, remembering where I had stopped excavating the previous day, he placed the coin deep in some tar between two of the ship's ribs. I was only down a few minutes when I sighted the gleam of gold and surfaced with the coin and a big smirk on my face. Tucker was also back on board the boat, grinning from ear to ear. While I was climbing up the ladder, he grabbed the coin and shouted: "Marx found a gold coin, hot damn!" Then appearing to throw the coin to one of the others aboard, he threw it so hard that it flew overboard, and my heart almost stopped beating. Everyone jumped in to find the coin, but unknown to everyone, Tucker found it and hid it again. After a while everyone gave up searching for the coin except me, claiming they wanted to find some themselves on the wreck. I searched frantically for the coin for thirteen hours, until darkness came and we had to head back to port. When Tucker told us the truth on the way in, only my tiredness prevented me from throttling him.

During the summers of 1965 and 1966 he returned to some of the earlier wrecks he had discovered—*Virginia Merchant, Eagle, Caesar* and *L'Hermoine*—and recovered vast amounts of artifacts from them. In 1965 he also spent a few days on the *San Pedro* and discovered another gold bar weighing thirty-nine ounces, which Peterson valued at $50,000 and of which he declared: "It is the most valuable numismatic item yet discovered in the Western Hemisphere."

After many years of visually searching the waters around Bermuda, Tucker convinced Peterson that he had probably located all the wrecks which could be found by visual methods. Consequently, during the summer of 1967 they conducted a magnetometer search in various areas around the island. The Explorers Club of New York provided a sizable grant of money and a magnetometer was rented from Mel Fisher, the president of Treasure Salvors, Inc. A number of nineteenth-century wrecks were located and they also discovered a new area of material associated with the wreck of the *Virginia Merchant*. The area was excavated and they found a great deal of cannon shot, and in addition, objects of personal use such as ivory combs, brass buttons and clay pipes.

Their most important discovery was the English merchant brig *Warwick*, which arrived in Castle Harbor from England on October 20, 1619, bringing the first governor and badly needed supplies to the recently arrived settlers. A month later it sank in the harbor during a storm.

A preliminary survey of the wreck revealed extensive timber remains; and the wooden hull was found more complete than any other yet discovered in the Western Hemisphere. The ship had settled quickly in the harbor silt, which preserved her from keel to gunwale. Tucker and Peterson devoted the next two summers to excavating, and obtained invaluable archaeological data from the wreck.

Tucker has spent the past two summer seasons working secretly "somewhere in the Bahamas" on a wreck, which he refuses to talk about at the present. Eventually, Teddy Tucker will most likely announce another important discovery—perhaps even greater than the many he has had in the past two decades.

The Cannons of the *Atocha*

by ROBERT DALEY

The "final" year of the search for the *Atocha* had started.

The divers hovered in the craters. Sand abraded their flesh, collected inside their gloves, inside their fins, their ears, their swimsuits. By day it invaded their bodies and by night their dreams. Some, particularly the new divers, continued to stumble into the steely grip of the mailbox blast. Cannonading down, the high-velocity water rolled men into the bottom of the hole, bounced them, hurled them spinning and bounding out into the calm depths of the sea.

This always produced great mirth among onlookers, if any. Again this year the pretense was being kept up that this quest for gold was not really serious, much less dangerous, and no one would get hurt. Never mind that gold in the past had always imposed terrible sanctions on those who sought it.

The divers wore full wet suits all spring as the water warmed up, and usually half wet suits even in summer, though water temperature was over 80° F. by then. Human body temperature however is 98.6° F., and an hour's work in the bottom left even these strong eager boys chilled and fatigued. The sea drained away calories, as well as money and faith.

Fisher planned an all-out assault, and there were many new divers.

Jim Bradley, twenty-two, called Spaghetti, was from Buffalo. He had reached Key West with a beard, a guitar, a stash of grass, and a desire to catch a boat farther south into the Caribbean. But when Fisher hired him he stayed. Bradley was both a diver and a welder. Fisher always needed welders. Fisher's entire world was held together by welders.

Bruce Wisely, twenty-one, an Oklahoma University marine biology major, had never dived in anything except creeks, streams, and flooded mine shafts. He had nothing in common with the other divers, except his love of diving. "When you dive down 120 feet in a mine shaft it's pitch black. It feels kind of crazy. When you dive so deep that you can't see, it becomes a whole new world."

Tim March, twenty-three, was from York, Pennsylvania. He had curly red hair and the physique of a weight lifter, and he liked to lift anchors out of the water single-handed, muscles bulging. He loved diving. "Until this year I had never done anything in my life worthwhile. Diving is a whole new world. It's the nicest natural high I've ever experienced. At sea you can relax and get your head together." March's mother had died when he was three. The child was placed in a home and left there for six and a half years. A good many of Fisher's divers were what might be described as lost souls, waifs like March

295

wandering about the world. In Fisher such boys seemed to think that they had found something solid they could hang on to.

Joe Spangler, twenty-three, was a doctor's son from Columbus, Ohio, and he found gold almost at once. At a depth of about twenty-five feet, hovering with Pat Clyne on top of ten to fifteen feet of sand, he watched the mailboxes bore toward the bedrock. Visibility was so bad Spangler could barely see his own hands. How could anyone find treasure in murk like this? But suddenly Clyne scooped two pieces of gold chain off the bottom. When Clyne held this close to Spangler's face mask, Spangler was stunned. Finding gold must be easy.

They went up to change tanks. It was getting dark, but Spangler wanted to go down again and find his own gold. While Spangler swam along with his nose close to bedrock, Clyne illuminated the scene with a dive light.

Suddenly Spangler grabbed up what seemed to be a gold penknife. Clyne shone the dive light on it. It was a boatswain's whistle on a double-strand golden chain. But it was a kind of penknife, too, for it opened out into a fingernail cleaner, a toothpick, and an earwax scoop.

Spangler, on deck, had his hand wrung by everybody. He stood grinning, trying to blow his whistle. Out came seawater and sand. Finally it tweeted. The other boys began begging to blow his whistle, whose sound, all were aware, had not been heard by men's ears for more than three and a half centuries.

Fisher was fascinated by the boatswain's whistle, too, and for a while wore it around his neck to meetings that he addressed, piping on it from time to time. It made a mournful sound, and seemed to have a morbid fascination for everyone. Fisher was fond of saying, "The last guy who blew this was a sailor who's still down there."

The whistle would sell for $50,000 or more, for it was an exquisite piece of jewelry. It must have been extremely valuable in 1622 too, and doubtless had belonged to no ordinary sailor. An officer or wealthy passenger must have owned it, and probably the man went into the sea with the whistle around his neck.

Gold remained pure after being immersed for no matter how many centuries, but nearly everything else the divers found was burly with encrustations. However slim itself, each object had become as unrecognizable as a man in a heavy overcoat. One had to watch carefully. The older divers knew what to look for—principally any sort of geometric pattern that did not exist in nature, especially straight lines.

In theory new divers found nothing, though this spring the opposite seemed true. Soon after Spangler's whistle, Tom Ford, on only his second trip to sea, found a bar of gold bullion.

Ford represented another of Fisher's ingenious solutions to a vexing problem. Technically Ford worked not for Fisher but for the Key Security Agency. Technically he was not a diver but a security guard, and it was his job to catalogue and authenticate any recovered treasure. Later the Key Security

Agency would supply certificates (countersigned by Tom Ford) attesting to the authenticity of each item, and these apparently impeccable pedigrees would accompany the treasure when it went on sale. Certificates from an independent outside agency were vital. Buyers were not going to pay high prices for treasure unless convinced it was authentic.

The only trouble was that Ford was not really an independent outside agent. He was really a diver, just like the others.

Formerly the state agent on board had served to authenticate Fisher's treasure. Now that state agents rode his boats no longer, Fisher had had to find a substitute. Key Security had seemed the answer. When the agency had asked, "Which of our guards do you want?" Fisher had replied, "I want you to hire a fellow named Tom Ford, and assign him to me."

Ford had come to Fisher for a job as a diver. Seeing that he was a superb one, Fisher had sent him first to Key Security, and then to sea—as diver and authenticator both.

Almost the first treasure Ford had to authenticate was his own gold bar. The tip of one end was peeking out of the sand, twinkling at him and he grabbed it. He was not impressed by it or himself, thinking that finding gold was what he was there for. And he swam up and thumped the bar down on deck.

The reaction of everybody on board astonished him. Elation spilled over into hysteria—with a good deal of jealousy mixed in, he noted. He had never in his life observed such silliness and glee.

That was when he realized how rare gold was.

Few divers remained who had seen the first treasure come up almost four years before: Don Kincaid, John Brandon, Bouncy John Lewis, Pat Clyne, Hugh Spinney, Spencer Wickens, one or two others.

Of these Wickens, twenty-three, had never found any gold at all until suddenly he too, after three and a half years of diving, plucked an eight-inch-long bar of gold bullion out of the sand. It caused one of the biggest adrenaline rushes of his life, he said later. He thrust it so close to his face mask that he nearly broke the glass. He couldn't believe his eyes. He showed it to John Brandon who was in the hole with him. Wickens realized his bubbles were flying in all directions. So were Brandon's. Brandon clapped his hand to his face mask and pretended to swoon.

Instead of thumping the bar down on deck, Wickens stuffed it inside the sleeve of his wet suit, and started up the dive ladder. When the others came close he peeled the sleeve back slightly, letting the gold peek out, and letting himself grin at last as everyone began screaming and hugging him.

Then a reaction set in that Wickens was totally unprepared for. He began to tremble as if he had just had a car crash. He was sucking in fresh air as if through a regulator. It took him five minutes to calm down enough to go back under. But there was no other gold in that hole, or in any other he was to dive in that day or any day.

Treasure diving was a continual intellectual puzzle. One asked oneself why there was only one bar of gold in Ford's hole, or Wickens' hole. How did it get

there? Had some Spaniard had it in his pocket? Were these divers finding
nothing but corpses?

Similar questions could be applied to Fisher's entire search. It was now the
summer of 1975. Fisher had been searching this spot for more than five years.
A 600-ton, 100-foot long galleon had disappeared here, a massive thing. Fisher couldn't seem to find it. Where were the *Atocha*'s eighteen bronze cannons? Where were the 898 remaining silver bars? Assuming that Fisher had
found two chests of pieces of eight and that the *Atocha* had carried around
eighty chests in all, then where were the other seventy-eight chests? Why had
he found swords, but no pikes or armor? Why only one anchor, but not the
others? Why dyes, but no tobacco? Where were all the tons of copper? Fisher
was finding only bits and pieces of the *Atocha*, add widely scattered bits and
pieces at that. Where was the rest of it? The gold bars were far smaller and
fewer than the silver bars, yet he had found eight gold bars and only three
silver ones. Why? The whole thing was crazy.

Now, on a Sunday morning in July, Dirk dove deep under the *Northwind*.
Down, down he swam. Reaching the bottom, he began to kick his way along,
from time to time patting the ocean floor with his hand, testing its consis-
tency—it was crusted mud here. He was searching only for yesterday's half-
dug hole, but instead swam right into the most astonishing discovery of this or
any other treasure hunt.

About a hundred feet off the tug's starboard bow he exploded screaming to
the surface. He was screaming as loud as he could.

Aboard the *Northwind*, Angel rushed in panic to the rail. She thought he
was being attacked by sharks. Then she made out Dirk's words, "We're rich.
We're rich. Get a buoy quick!"

Then Dirk dove under again. Five of the *Atocha*'s cannons were down
there. Down to the bottom he swam. At first he couldn't find them again. The
water was murky. Visibility was about four feet. Then he saw them once
more—first one, then all five. Bronze cannons.

He swam to the surface again hollering, "Five bronze cannons."

Angel later wrote in the log, "The day we've been waiting for."

Everybody was screaming. Everybody was in the water, free diving down to
see the cannons. The cannons were great in themselves. But everybody was
convinced that Dirk had found much more than cannons. The main portion of
the galleon must be there too.

Angel, in the blue-and-white-striped bikini she always wore, geared up and
dove down with her Nikonos to photograph the cannons as they looked to
Dirk, all in a tumble and partially covered with sand, for soon the landscape
down there would be altered. Dirk wanted them dusted off so he could see
them better.

It took nearly an hour to maneuver the *Northwind* into position exactly over the cannons. The water depth was measured: thirty-nine feet. Then the *Northwind*'s engines were started up, the great props began to turn, and in a moment the mailboxes were thundering. For sixty seconds the Gulf of Mexico was turned against itself. The sea writhed as if being tortured, but at the end of that time, as if its resistence had at last been broken, this portion of the secret it had guarded so religiously for 353 years lay totally revealed: five bronze cannons. One by one, Angel and the nine divers all went down for another loving look.

Dirk couldn't get enough of his cannons. He had to touch each one. He swam around them in dazed circles. No treasure hunter had ever found five bronze cannons before. Bronze cannons in the past had hardly ever been found at all. They showed on no instrument. They had to be found with the eyes and the hands and the heart. In the treasure hunting business bronze cannons were legendary. Anybody could find gold, why not, there was so much of it down there. Bronze cannons were rarer than gold—the rarest prize of all. Bronze cannons were simply fabulous.

There was a good deal of ballast stone nearby, and Dirk, endlessly, happily circling, also found a copper ingot. His joy was indescribable. The entire galleon must be here. The cannons, the ballast stone, the copper—that's what it all added up to: the *Atocha*.

Angel had begun shouting the news into the radio.

"And guess who found them?" Dramatic pause. "Raddy!" Raddy was their pet name for each other, and the word was delivered in a kind of scream.

A crowd would be out from Key West soon, but in the meantime there was work to be done aboard the *Northwind*. One of the bow anchors was dragging. A new line had to be run out. A buoy had to be prepared and anchored firmly to those cannons.

This work progressed—except that every few minutes Dirk Fisher would stop what he was doing, stand up to his full height—he was six foot two—and let out a joyous yell. This yell Angel would answer by honking on the *Northwind*'s foghorn.

The grin on Dirk's face would not go away. He wore it all day. He wore it from ear to ear. So did Angel. Every once in a while Dirk would plunge over the side and swim down to look at his cannons again.

The speedboats arrived from Key West. Mel Fisher brought steaks and champagne—and, inevitably, reporters. Mel Fisher went down to see the cannons himself. All the rest of the day he took down any visitor who wanted to see them. Aboard all the boats that had congregated there was a great deal of saluting, yelling, screaming, and honking. Cheers erupted for no reason. Champagne corks popped. Dirk Fisher was walking around in a dream. A TV news crew from Channel 4 Miami arrived, and the footage they made of Dirk and Angel was a record of happiness such as had seldom been filmed.

Across that day's calm sea the *Northwind*'s celebration was audible for great distances. Shrimp boats came by to stare at all the crazy people aboard the old yellow tugboat. Pleasure boats came.

All day Angel kept announcing Dirk's cannons over the radio. She chirped and sang and wept.

Night came. The guests in their speedboats went back to port. Dirk and Angel were at last alone, but their happiness was as great as ever; and they got a dive light and swam down to look at the cannons one last time.

The next day everyone was up early. The seas were one to two feet. The wind blew at about fifteen knots, but it was steady. The water was exceptionally clear. Because they now lay totally exposed, and also because one now knew where to look, the cannons were visible from the surface. The *Northwind* had to be moved into a new position. But just after ten o'clock the mailboxes went down and the engines started a two-minute dig. A single cannonball was revealed and salvaged. Then came another two-minute dig. Dirk, Bouncy John, and a new diver named Rick Gage each found small bits of gold—buttons or beads. They were so small it seemed a miracle anyone had noticed them, but that day anything seemed possible, and divers on the bottom were all eyes. Rich Gage's piece of gold was about the size of a shirt button. He had only joined the crew a few days before, and for him too time was running out. He was as ecstatic as if he had found bullion. But as he climbed the dive ladder, the bit of gold fell from his grasp into the water. Dirk Fisher free dove down and found it immediately. Dirk was a superb free diver. He dove down thirty-nine feet, made a careful search, and emerged with a grin on his face, and the bit of gold between his fingers.

Digging soon stopped as the archaeologist Duncan Mathewson, who had been preparing his equipment, plunged over the side, together with Don Kincaid and his cameras. On the bottom Mathewson began to take measurements and compass bearings, and to make drawings of how the cannons lay. A steel grid was laid out by Mathewson in sections, and Kincaid photographed each of the cannons in relation to the grid. Mathewson had been collecting data for a year and a half; with today's new data he would begin to form some new theories as to what exactly had happened to the *Atocha* on September 6, 1622.

The following day, Tuesday, Mathewson and Kincaid were still down there. Above their heads, Dirk paced the deck restlessly. He wanted to dig. He still thought he had located the entire *Atocha*. A few blasts of the mailboxes would reveal it. The archaeologist and the photographer were simply holding him up.

At noon Mathewson and Kincaid at last surfaced. Immediately Dirk ordered divers Jim Solanick and Pat Clyne over the side, and he turned the mailboxes on for a one-minute dig. But that first dig revealed nothing. Dirk thought about it for a moment, then ordered the tugboat's stern winched slightly south. A three-minute dig followed.

Both divers immediately surfaced shouting "Two more cannons!" Another three-minute dig revealed them more clearly. The divers surfaced again, and the news was shouted topside.

"Definitely bronze!"

Another three-minute dig. And still another triumphant shout from the surfacing divers, "Two more cannons!"

The hysteria of the first day was not repeated. Dirk Fisher was all business now. Nine cannons had been found. They weighed a total, probably, of fifteen tons. They could not have floated very far from where the *Atocha* sank. Any second Dirk Fisher expected to reveal the remaining nine cannons, and the sunken galleon's entire carcass.

The rest of the day was a series of short blasts down the mailboxes. A three-minute dig just before 1:00 P.M. revealed a bar shot and a musket ball. At 1:05 Dirk started a fifteen-minute dig. But it revealed nothing. At 1:35 a ten-minute dig was begun. But this hole was empty too. At 1:50 another ten-minute dig. Nothing.

Fretting, Dirk ordered the *Northwind* winched thirty feet to the southeast. Where were those other nine cannons? Any shifting of the clumsy tug usually took considerable time. Not today. The boys had her position in thirteen minutes, and the mailboxes began drilling a new hole. Five minutes deep into the sand a heavy incrusted object was revealed, probably a marlin spike. The engines were stopped while it was brought up, then started again. At 2:20 the divers found some broken pottery.

The missing nine cannons were not found that day, nor were any of the missing chests of coins or the silver bars. Nothing more was found that day at all, though Dirk kept winching the *Northwind* this way and that, and the anxious Angel kept noting each blast into the log: 2:36—10 minutes; 2:56—5 minutes; 3:24—5 minutes; 3:45—8 minutes; 3:58—5 minutes; 4:25—5 minutes; 4:54—5 minutes; 5:09—5 minutes; 5:25—5 minutes; 5:42—5 minutes; 6:10—5 minutes.

At 7:30 the mailboxes were raised, and it was over for the day.

The next day, Wednesday, dawned sunny but windy. The seas were running two to three feet. The mailboxes went down at nine in the morning, and during the day there were eleven moves. Eleven craters were blasted. But nothing was found.

The following day, with TV cameramen filming topside and below, and with Mel Fisher directing operations personally, two cannons were lifted off the ocean floor and swung aboard the *Northwind*. It was a time-consuming and dangerous business, for each cannon weighed a ton and a half, and there was no way a secure line could be fastened to either of them. Instead, each had to be laid in a rope sling and guided up from the deep. If horizontal equilibrium were lost, the cannon would nosedive out of the sling back to the bottom again, and its great weight would surely crush any person or thing in its way.

But the raising of the two cannons, though it took most of the day, was accomplished without incident. There they lay on deck exposed to sunshine again for the first time in 353 years. They were green and only slightly encrusted with marine growth. One bore plainly visible numbers, including the year it was cast: 1607; and its weight: 3,110 pounds. It was eight feet long and bore a shield or coat of arms as well. A few oysters and barnacles were stuck to the butt end, and a half-inch-thick crust circled the middle of the barrel near two graceful bronze dolphins which, curled as if to dive, formed handle loops. Dirk Fisher stared down at it with quiet pride.

Duncan Mathewson, wearing blue denim shorts, his beard bleached by sun and salt, was crouched over this first cannon. He was comparing its numbers with those Lyon had found on the *Atocha*'s manifest. This cannon was the twelfth one down on Lyon's list. The jubilant Mathewson cried, "This is positive identification! This cannon came from the *Atocha!*"

The second cannon bore no markings at all. Indeed, half its muzzle had been worn away, and it resembled nothing as much as the nose of a shark. Fisher, jumping down to the fantail as it was lifted on board, had cried, "That's the shark! I've been hunting for a bronze cannon for thirty years. These are the first I've found, and this one's mine."

When the reporters who had congregated on the *Northwind*'s deck asked how much such cannons were worth, Fisher threw out a figure. "The going price for bronze cannons is $20,000 each."

Well, maybe. If he could find anyone who wanted one that badly.

Next a reporter wanted to know why one cannon was worn smooth.

Fisher's answer took its inspiration from the great sea turtle that the divers found nosing about the cannons that morning. Grabbing onto its carapace, Kim Fisher and Pat Clyne had ridden the panicked creature toward daylight. When all three heads broke the water simultaneously, the crowd aboard the *Northwind* had broken into gales of laughter.

It was turtles such as this one, Fisher now confided to the reporters, that were responsible for the highly polished condition of cannon number two. "The turtles have been scratching their bellies against it for 350 years," he said, nodding sagaciously.

In fact it was Mathewson's opinion—and also Dr. Lyon's opinion later—that the polishing had been done not by turtles but by the tides, the currents, and the shifting sands. But Fisher liked his own romantic story better and went on repeating it. There was something about Fisher that militantly resisted ordinary explanations of anything. Other people in order to live needed principally food and clothing. Fisher needed hope and dreams. He needed drama. He was sustained by fantasy.

With two cannons on board, Dirk Fisher started back toward Key West, but the *Northwind* was so slow that he had to anchor for the night off the Marquesas. He continued into port the following day, where he off-loaded the cannons onto the deck of the pirate galleon amidst a second champagne celebration.

Fisher had promised a bonus of $2,000 to whoever should find one of the *Atocha*'s bronze cannons, and Dirk had found five in one day, and once the cannons were safely obscured under the sopping old mattresses, the proud father, who happened to be temporarily flush, handed his son a check for $10,000. This was enough money to keep the vessels at sea for three weeks or more, and it just about cleaned Fisher out.

Dirk rushed straight to the bank to get the check cashed. Drunk with success, the boy stared with glazed eyes at the money. He had $10,000 in cash in his straw hat. Then he and Angel flew to Miami. They came back that same night driving a new car that had cost more than $5,000.

In the morning Angel Fisher went grocery shopping for ten day's provisions for ten divers and herself, and then the *Northwind* set sail again. Dirk couldn't wait to get back to his remaining cannons, and to the *Atocha*'s main treasure mass, which he was sure lay so close. Mel Fisher on the pier watched with a benevolent smile as Dirk backed the *Northwind* into the harbor. With father and son waving to each other across the increasing distance, the decrepit yellow tug steamed out of Key West on what was to be its final voyage—and the final voyage for a number of those aboard, too.

The *Northwind*'s crew was a confident and extremely happy one. The generous Fisher had distributed bonuses to everybody—$500 to each of the veteran divers, $100 to the new ones. A favored few, Bouncy John for one, had also received new wet suits.

At the wreck site forty miles away, the *Virgalona* was digging. The day's yield: a solid silver candlestick. No one knew it then, but this was the last treasure that would be recovered that year.

Sea Explorers

First Crossing of the Atlantic

by SAMUEL ELIOT MORISON

By the second day of August, 1492, everything at last was ready. That night every man and boy of the fleet confessed his sins, received absolution and made his communion at the church of Palos, which by happy coincidence was dedicated to Saint George, patron saint of Genoa. Columbus went on board his flagship in the small hours of Friday the third and gave the signal to get under way. Before the sun rose, all three vessels had anchors aweigh, and with sails hanging limp from their yards were floating down the Rio Tinto on the morning ebb, using their long sweeps to maintain steerageway. As they swung into the Saltés and passed La Rábida close aboard, they could hear the friars chanting the ancient hymn *Iam lucis orto sidere* with its haunting refrain *Et nunc et in perpetuum,* which we render "Evermore and evermore."

This fleet of good hope, whose achievements would radically alter world history, sailed parallel to another fleet of misery and woe. On the very same tide there dropped down the Saltés the last vessel carrying the Jews whom Ferdinand and Isabella had expelled from Spain. August 2 was their deadline; any who remained thereafter were to be executed unless they embraced Christianity. Thousands of pitiful refugees, carrying what few household goods they could stow in the crowded ships, were bound for the more tolerant lands of Islam, or for the only Christian country, the Netherlands, which would receive them. Columbus in all his writings dropped no word of pity for the fate of this persecuted race, and even expressed the wish to exclude them from the lands he discovered. But if there had been a new prophet among the Spanish Jews, he might have pointed out the Columbian fleet to his wretched compatriots on that August morning and said, "Behold the ships that in due time will carry the children of Israel to the ends of the earth."

Columbus's plan for the voyage was simple, and its simplicity insured his success. Not for him the boisterous head winds, the monstrous seas and the dark, unbridled waters of the North Atlantic, which had already baffled so many Portuguese. He would run south before the prevailing northerlies to the Canary Islands, and there make, as it were, a right-angle turn; for he had observed on his African voyages that the winter winds in the latitude of the Canaries blew from the east, and that the ocean around them, more often than not, was calm as a millpond. An even better reason to take his departure from the Canaries was their position astride latitude 28 degrees North, which, he believed, cut Japan, passing en route the mythical Isle of Antilia, which would make a good break in the westward passage. Until about a hundred years ago when chronometers became generally available to find longitude, sailors always tried to find the latitude of their destination and then would "run their westing" (or easting) down until they hit it. That is what Columbus proposed to do with respect to Japan, which he had figured out to be only 2400 nautical miles due west of the Canaries.

The first leg of the voyage was made in less than a week. Then, within sight of the Grand Canary, the fleet ran into a calm that lasted two or three days. Columbus decided to send *Pinta* into Las Palmas for some needed repairs while *Santa María* and *Niña* went to Gomera, westernmost of the Canaries that the Spaniards had wrested from their native inhabitants. At Gomera the Captain General (as we should call Columbus on this voyage before he made Admiral) sent men ashore to fill extra water casks, buy breadstuffs and cheese, and put a supply of native beef in pickle. He then sailed to Las Palmas to superintend *Pinta's* repairs and returned with her to Gomera.

On September 2 all three ships were anchored off San Sebastián, the port of that island. Columbus then met for the first time Doña Beatriz de Bobadilla, widow of the former captain of the island. Beatriz was a beautiful lady still under thirty, and Columbus is said to have fallen in love with her; but if that is true, he did not love her warmly enough to tarry to the next full moon. Additional ship's stores were quickly hoisted on board and struck below, and on September 6, 1492, the fleet weighed anchor for the last time in the Old World. They had still another island to pass, the lofty Ferro or Hierro. Owing to calms and variables Ferro and the 12,000-foot peak of Tenerife were in sight until the ninth, but by nightfall that day, every trace of land had sunk below the eastern horizon, and the three vessels were alone on an uncharted ocean. Columbus himself gave out the course: "West; nothing to the north, nothing to the south."

Before going into the details of the voyage, let us see how those vessels were navigated, and how a day was passed at sea. Celestial navigation was then in its infancy, but rough estimates of latitude could be made from the height of the North Star above the horizon and its relation to the two outer stars (the "Guards") of the Little Dipper. A meridian altitude of the sun, applied to available tables of the sun's declination, also gave latitude, by a simple formula. But the instruments of observation—a solid wood or brass quadrant and the seaman's astrolabe—were so crude, and the movement of a ship threw them off to such an extent, that most navigators took their latitude sights ashore. Columbus relied almost completely on "dead reckoning," which means plotting your course and position on a chart from the three elements of direction, time and distance.

The direction he had from one or more compasses which were similar to those used in small craft until recently—a circular card graduated to the 32 points (N, N by E, NNE, NE by N, NE, and so on), with a lodestone under the north point, mounted on a pin and enclosed in a binnacle with gimbals so it could swing freely with the motion of the ship. Columbus's standard compass was mounted on the poop deck where the officer of the watch could see it. The helmsman, who steered with a heavy tiller attached directly to the rudder head, was below decks and could see very little. He may have had another compass to steer by, but in the smaller vessels, at least, he was conned by the officer of the deck and kept a steady course by the feel of the helm. On a sailing vessel you can do that; it would be impossible in any power craft.

Time on the vessels of that day was measured by a half-hour glass which hung from a beam so the sand could flow freely from the upper to the lower half. As soon as the sand was all down, a ship's boy turned the glass and the officer of the deck recorded it by making a stroke on a slate. Eight glasses made a watch; the modern ship's bells were originally a means of marking the glasses. This half-hour-glass time could be corrected daily in fair weather by noting the moment when the sun lay due south, which was local noon.

Distance was the most variable of these three elements. Columbus had no chip log or other method of measuring the speed of his vessels. He and the watch officers merely estimated it and noted it down. By carefully checking Columbus's Journal of his First Voyage, Captain J. W. McElroy ascertained that he made an average 9 percent overestimate of his distance. This did not prevent his finding the way home, because the mistake was constant, and time and course were correct. It only resulted in Columbus placing the islands of his discovery farther west than they really were.

Even after making the proper reduction for this overestimate, the speed of his vessels is surprising. Ships of that day were expected to make 3 to 5 knots in a light breeze, up to 9½ in a strong, fair gale, and at times to be capable of 12 knots. In October 1492, on the outward passage, the Columbus fleet made an average of 142 miles per day for five consecutive days, and the best day's run, 182 miles, averaged 8 knots. On the homeward passage, in February 1493, Niña and Pinta covered 198 miles one day, and at times hit it up to 11 knots. Any yachtsman today would be proud to make the records that the great Admiral did on some of his transatlantic crossings in the fifteenth century. Improvements in sailing vessels since 1492 have been more in seaworthiness and comfort than in speed.

One reason Columbus always wanted two or more vessels was to have someone to rescue survivors in case of sinking. But he made an unusual record for that era by never losing a ship at sea, unless we count the Santa María, grounded without loss of life. Comforts and conveniences were almost totally lacking. Cooking was done on deck over a bed of sand in a wooden firebox protected from the wind by a hood. The diet was a monotonous one of salt meat, hardtack and dried peas. For drink they had wine, while it lasted, and water in casks, which often went bad. Only the Captain General and the ships' captains had cabins with bunks; the others slept where they could, in their clothes.

In those days, sailors were the most religious of laymen. On each vessel a boy was charged with singing a ditty at daybreak, which began:

Blessed be the light of day
And the Holy Cross, we say;

after which he recited the Lord's Prayer and the Ave Maria, and invoked a blessing on the ship's company. Every half hour a boy sang out when turning the glass. For instance, at what we would call five bells, he sang:

> Five is past and six floweth,
> More shall flow if God willeth,
> Count and pass make voyage fast.

After sunset, and before the first night watch was set, all hands were called to evening prayers. The service began with the boy whose duty it was to light the binnacle lamp singing:

> God give us a good night and good sailing;
> May our ship make a good passage,
> Sir Captain and Master and good company.

All hands then said the Lord's Prayer, the Creed and the Ave Maria, and concluded by singing the *Salve Regina*. Here are the correct words and music of the ancient Benedictine chant, but as Columbus himself said, "Seamen sing or say it after their own fashion," bawling it out in several keys at once and murdering the stately Latin words. But was it the less acceptable to the Virgin, under whose protection all sailors felt secure?

Now the boy who turns up the glass for the eighth time sings:

> The watch is called,
> The glass floweth.
> We shall make a good voyage
> If God willeth.

And as the vessels sail westward through the soft tropic night, rolling and pitching, sails bellying and slatting, cordage straining, bows throwing foam, every half hour is marked by this chantey:

> To our God let's pray
> To give us a good voyage,
> And through the Blessed Mother,
> Our advocate on high,
> Protect us from the waterspout
> And send no tempest nigh.

So much for the sea ritual that went on every day, whatever the weather. Now for the events of the voyage.

On September 9, the day he dropped the last land below the horizon, Columbus decided to keep a true reckoning of his course for his own use and a false one to give out to the people, so that they would not be frightened at sailing so far from land. But, owing to his overestimate of speed, the "false" reckoning was more nearly correct than the "true"!

During the first ten days (September 9 to 18), the easterly trade wind blew steadily, and the fleet made 1163 nautical miles' westing. This was the honeymoon of the voyage. *Que era plazer grande el gusto de las mañanas*—"What a delight was the savor of the mornings!" wrote Columbus in his Journal. That entry speaks to the heart of anyone who has sailed in the trades; it recalls the beauty of the dawn, kindling clouds and sails rose color, the smell of dew drying on a wooden deck, and, something Columbus didn't have, the first cup of coffee. Since his ships were at the northern edge of the northeast trades, where the wind first strikes the water, the sea was smooth, and the air, remarked the Captain General in his Journal, was "like April in Andalusia; the only thing wanting was to hear the song of the nightingale." But there were plenty of other birds following the ships: the little Mother Carey's chickens, dabbling for plankton in the bow waves and wakes; the boatswain bird, so called (as old seamen used to say) because it carries a marlinspike in its tail; the man-of-war or frigate bird, "thou ship of the air that never furl'st thy sails," as Walt Whitman wrote; and when the fleet passed beyond the range of these birds, the big Jaeger gulls gave it a call. During this period the fleet encountered its first field of sargassum or gulfweed and found that it was no hindrance to navigation. "Saw plenty weed" was an almost daily notation in the Captain General's log. The gulfweed bothered him much less than observing a westerly variation of the compass, for in European waters the variation is always easterly.

On September 19, only ten days out from Ferro, the fleet temporarily ran into an area of variable winds and rain. It was near the point on Columbus's chart where the fabled island of Antilia should have been, and all hands expected to sight land. The Captain General even had the deep-sea lead hove, and found no bottom at 200 fathoms; no wonder, since the ocean is about 2300 fathoms deep at the point he had reached. But the seamen who, on the tenth day of the northeast trades, were beginning to wonder whether they could ever beat back home were cheered by the change of wind.

During the next five days only 234 miles were made good. During this spell of moderate weather it was easy to converse from ship to ship and to talk about this or that island, St. Brendan's or Antilia, which they might pick up. In the middle of one of these colloquies, a seamen of *Pinta* gave the "Land Ho!" and everyone thought he saw an island against the setting sun. Columbus fell on his knees to thank God, ordered *Gloria in excelsis Deo* to be sung by all hands, and set a course for the island. But at dawn no island was visible; there was none. It was simply a cloud bank above the western horizon resembling land, a common phenomenon at sea. Martín Alonso Pinzón apparently wished to beat about and search for this island, but Columbus refused, because, he said, "his object was to reach the Indies, and if he delayed, it would not have made sense."

The trade wind now returned, but moderately, and during the six days September 26 to October 1, the fleet made only 382 miles. Under these circumstances the people began to mutter and grumble. Three weeks was probably more than they had ever been outside sight of land before. They were all getting on each other's nerves, as happens even nowadays on a long voyage to a known destination. There was nothing for the men to do in the light wind except to follow the ship's routine, and troll for fish. Grievances, real or imaginary, were blown up; cliques were formed; Spain was farther away every minute, and what lay ahead? Probably nothing, except in the eye of that cursed Genoese. Let's make him turn back, or throw him overboard!

On the first day of October the wind increased, and in five days (October 2 to 6) the fleet made 710 miles. On the sixth, when they had passed longitude 65 degrees West and actually lay directly north of Puerto Rico, Martín Alonso Pinzón shot his agile *Pinta* under the flagship's stern and shouted, "Alter course, sir, to southwest by west . . . Japan!" Columbus did not understand whether Martín Alonso meant that he thought they had missed Japan and should steer southwest by west for China, or that Japan lay in that direction; but he knew and Pinzón knew that the fleet had sailed more than the 2400 miles which, according to their calculations, lay between the Canaries and Japan. Naturally Columbus was uneasy, but he held to the west course magnetic, which, owing to the variation for which he did not allow, was about west by south, true.

On October 7, when there was another false landfall, great flocks of birds passed over the ships, flying westsouthwest; this was the autumn migration from eastern North America to the West Indies. Columbus decided that he had better follow the birds rather than his chart, and changed course accordingly that evening. That was "good joss"; it was his shortest course to the nearest land. Now, every night, the men were heartened by seeing against the moon (full on October 5) flocks of birds flying their way. But by the tenth, mutiny flared up again. No land for thirty-one days. Even by the phony reckoning which Columbus gave out they had sailed much farther west than anyone had expected. Enough of this nonsense, sailing west to nowhere; let the Captain General turn back or else—! Columbus, says the record, "cheered them as best he could, holding out good hope of the advantages they might gain; and, he added, it was useless to complain, *since he had come to go to the Indies, and so had to continue until he found them, with Our Lord's help.*"

That was typical of Columbus's determination. Yet even he, conscious of divine guidance, could not have kept on indefinitely without the support of his captains and officers. According to one account, it was Martín Alonso Pinzón who cheered him by shouting, *Adelante! Adelante!* which an American poet has translated, "Sail on! Sail on!" But, according to Oviedo, one of the earliest historians who talked with the participants, it was Columbus alone who persuaded the Pinzóns and La Cosa to sail on, with the promise that if land were not found within three days, he would turn back. If this version is correct, as I believe it is, the Captain General's promise to his captains was made on October 9. Next day the trade wind blew fresher, sending the fleet along at 7 knots; it so continued on the eleventh, with a heavy following sea. But signs of land, such as branches of trees with green leaves and flowers, became so frequent that the people were content with their Captain General's decision, and the mutinous mutterings died out in the keen anticipation of making a landfall in the Indies.

As the sun set under a clear horizon October 11, the northeast trade breezed up to gale force, and the three ships tore along at 9 knots. But Columbus refused to shorten sail, since his promised time was running out. He signaled everyone to keep a particularly sharp watch, and offered extra rewards for first landfall in addition to the year's pay promised by the Sovereigns. That night of destiny was clear and beautiful with a late rising moon, but the sea was the roughest of the entire passage. The men were tense and expectant, the officers testy and anxious, the Captain General serene in the confidence that presently God would reveal to him the promised Indies.

At 10 P.M., an hour before moonrise, Columbus and a seaman, almost simultaneously, thought they saw a light "like a little wax candle rising and falling." Others said they saw it too, but most did not; and after a few minutes it disappeared. Volumes have been written to explain what this light was or might have been. To a seaman it requires no explanation. It was an illusion, created by overtense watchfulness. When uncertain of your exact position, and straining to make a night landfall, you are apt to see imaginary lights and flashes and to hear nonexistent bells and breakers.

On rush the ships, pitching, rolling, throwing spray—white waves at their bows and white wakes reflecting the moon. *Pinta* is perhaps half a mile in the lead, *Santa María* on her port quarter, *Niña* on the other side. Now one, now another forges ahead, but they are all making the greatest speed of which they are capable. With the sixth glass of the night watch, the last sands are running out of an era that began with the dawn of history. A few minutes now and destiny will turn up a glass the flow of whose sands we are still watching. Not since the birth of Christ has there been a night so full of meaning for the human race.

At 2 A.M., October 12, Rodrigo de Triana, lookout on *Pinta*, sees something like a white cliff shining in the moonlight, and sings out, *Tierra! tierra!* "Land! land!" Captain Pinzón verifies the landfall, fires a gun as agreed, and shortens sail to allow the flagship to catch up. As *Santa María* approaches, the Captain General shouts across the rushing waters, "Señor Martín Alonso, you *did* find land! Five thousand maravedis for you as a bonus!"

Yes, land it was this time, a little island of the Bahamas group. The fleet was headed for the sand cliffs on its windward side and would have been wrecked had it held course. But these seamen were too expert to allow that to happen. The Captain General ordered sail to be shortened and the fleet to jog off and on until daylight, which was equivalent to a southwesterly drift clear of this island. At dawn they made full sail, passed the southern point of the island and sought an opening on the west coast, through the barrier reef. Before noon they found it, sailed into the shallow bay now called Long or Fernandez, and anchored in the lee of the land, in five fathoms.

Here on a gleaming beach of white coral occurred the famous first landing of Columbus. The Captain General (now by general consent called Admiral) went ashore in the flagship's boat with the royal standard of Castile displayed, the two Captains Pinzón in their boats, flying the banner of the Expedition— the green crowned cross on a white field. "And, all having rendered thanks to Our Lord, kneeling on the ground, embracing it with tears of joy for the immeasurable mercy of having reached it, the Admiral rose and gave this island the name *San Salvador*"—Holy Saviour.

The natives of Guanahaní, as they called this island, fled to the jungle when they saw three marine monsters approaching, but curiosity was too much for them, and when they peered out and saw strangely dressed human beings coming ashore, they approached timidly, with propitiatory gifts. Columbus, of course, had to believe that he was in the Indies, so he called these people "Indians," and Indians the native inhabitants of the Americas have become in all European languages.

Those first encountered were of the Taino branch of the Arawak language group. Coming from the mainland in dugout canoes, and with no better weapons than wooden spears, they had wrested the Bahamas and most of Cuba from the more primitive Siboney, within the previous century. The Tainos grew corn, yams and other roots for food; they knew how to make cassava bread, to spin and weave cotton and to make pottery. The Spaniards observed with wonder their fine build and almost complete nakedness, and noted with keen interest that some of them wore, suspended from the nose, little pendants of pure gold. The guilelessness and generosity of these children of nature—"they invite you to share anything that they possess, and show as much love as if their hearts went with it," wrote Columbus—their ignorance of money and of iron, and their nudity, suggested to every educated European that these people were holdovers from the Golden Age. Peter Martyr, first historian of the New World, wrote, "They seem to live in that golden world of the which old writers speak so much, wherein men lived simply and innocently without enforcement of laws, without quarreling, judges and libels, content only to satisfy nature." Columbus would much rather have encountered sophisticated orientals than "noble savages," but as usual he made the best of the situation. He observed "how easy it would be to convert these people—and to make them work for us." In other words, enslave them but save their souls. Indeed, it seems to have been from the sailors who returned from this voyage that every Spaniard got the idea that no white man need do a hand's turn of work in the New World—God had provided docile natives to labor for the lords of creation.

For two days Columbus explored San Salvador. It was a pretty island then, with a heavy covering of tropical hardwood, but the Admiral knew full well that, interesting as the discovery of a new island and Golden Age natives might be, he had to bring home certain evidence of Japan or China, or plenty of gold and spices, to prove his voyage a success. The natives of San Salvador indicated by sign language that scores of islands lay to the west and south; it seemed to Columbus that these must be the ones shown on his chart, lying south of Cipangu, and that if they did not lead him to golden Japan, they would prove to be steppingstones to China.

So, detaining six Indians as guides, Columbus shoved off on the afternoon of October 14. That day he discovered another island which he named Santa María de la Concepción—the English prosaically called it Rum Cay. The natives proved to be similar in every respect to those on San Salvador and were equally pleased with the Admiral's gifts of red caps, glass beads and hawks' bells. That standard trading truck for the African coast proved equally saleworthy in the Antilles, especially the hawks' bells. These were little spherical bells about the diameter of a quarter dollar or shilling, which were attached to the birds used in falconry; they had a pleasant little tinkle like a miniature sleighbell, and the natives loved them. Indians would paddle out to the flagship, waggling their fingers and saying *Chuq! chuq!* meaning, "More hawks' bells, please!" Lace points, the metal tips to the laces then used to fasten men's clothing, and brass tambourine jingles also were favorites.

The Admiral's native guides, eager to please, kept assuring him by signs that in the next island there would be plenty of gold, but each one in succession—Long Island, Crooked Island, Fortune Island—proved to be no different from San Salvador. Each was a flat, jungle-covered bit of land inhabited by friendly natives who had no gold except for a few ornaments which they had obtained elsewhere. Where they got them he could never make out, because of the language barrier; De Torres, the interpreter, found his Arabic no use whatsoever. Columbus saw the first maize or Indian corn ever observed by a European, the first hammocks, woven from native cotton, and the first yams and sweet potatoes; also, a tree that he estimated correctly would prove to be good dye wood. But no sign of gold except on the natives' persons.

As the Admiral and his Indian guides came to understand each other better, he heard about a big island that they called Colba (Cuba) and made up his mind that it must be either Japan or part of China. So to Colba he must go, and the Indians took him there by their usual canoe route, so laid out as to be the shortest possible jump over blue water. They sailed across Crooked Island Passage to the line of cays at the southeast edge of the Great Bahama Bank. From Ragged Island, on October 27, the fleet made a fast sail over the shoals now named Columbus Bank, with a fresh northeast wind, to where the Indians pointed out "Colba." And on the morning of October 28 they entered Bahía Bariay, in the Cuban Province of Oriente. Columbus observed in his Journal that he had never seen so beautiful a harbor—trees all fair and green and different from ours, some with bright flowers and some heavy with fruit, and the air full of birdsong. But where was the evidence of Japan? Where the golden-roofed temples, the dragon-mouthed bronze cannon, the lords and ladies in gold-stiffened brocade?

Poor Columbus! He tried so hard to find compensation in the strange new things he did see for the Oriental objects he so much wanted to see, but it was difficult to describe the scenery, flora and inhabitants of Cuba in such wise as to interest important people in Spain. Nor could he be hospitable to the teasing thought that this was not the Orient after all, but a new world.

Next day the three ships sailed westward along the many-harbored coast of Cuba, Columbus hoping every moment to meet a welcoming fleet of Chinese junks, and anchored in Puerto Gibara. There they remained for twelve days, except for a brief jaunt westward to Punta Cobarrubia and back.

As the San Salvador interpreters assured the local Indians that the strangers in the white-winged monsters were fine people, with piles of good trading truck, business for a time was brisk. Anxious to please, they told Columbus that there was gold in the interior, at a place called Cubanacan, which meant mid-Cuba. The Admiral, eager to present his letter of introduction to the Chinese Emperor, mistook this for *El Gran Can,* the Great Khan. So nothing would do but to send an embassy to Cubanacan. Luís de Torres, the Arabic scholar, was in charge and second in command was Rodrigo de Xeres, an able seaman who had once met a Negro king in Guinea and so was supposed to know the proper way to approach pagan royalty. Indians carried the diplomatic portfolio (Latin passport and royal letter of credence to the Grand Khan), a gift considered suitable for royalty, and strings of glass beads to buy food from the natives. The embassy tramped up the valley of the Cacoyuguin River, past fields cultivated with corn, beans and sweet potatoes, to what they hoped would be Cambaluk, the imperial city where the Great Khan resided. Alas, it was a village of about fifty palm-thatched huts, on the site of the present town of Holguín. The two Spaniards, regarded as having come from the sky, were feasted by the local cacique, while the populace swarmed up to kiss their feet and present simple gifts. Rodrigo the sailor loved it—he had never had it so good in Africa—but Torres was mortified that his Arabic was not understood, and, expecting a reception by mandarins in a stone-built capital of ten thousand houses, he felt very much let down.

Yet, on their way back to the harbor, the embassy made a discovery which (had they only known it) would have more far-reaching results in human happiness than any possible treaty with China. As Columbus records it, they met "many people who were going to their villages, with a firebrand in the hand, and herbs to drink the smoke thereof, as they are accustomed." You have guessed it, reader; this was the first European contact with tobacco. The Tainos used it in the form of cigars (which they called *tobacos*); a walking party, such as the embassy encountered, would carry a large cigar and at every halt light it from a firebrand; everyone then took three or four "drags" from it through his nostrils; and after all were refreshed, the march was resumed, small boys keeping the firebrand alight until the next stop. Not long after Spaniards settled in the New World, they tried smoking tobacco and liked it, and through them its use spread rapidly through Europe, Asia and Africa.

While the embassy was absent, Columbus totted up his dead reckoning and figured that he had made 90 degrees of westing. This, owing to his overestimate of the length of Asia, should put the ships right where China began. He decided that Cuba was the "Province of Mangi," a name which the more or less imaginative maps of China that he had seen placed on a peninsula at the southeast corner of the Empire. The Admiral also tried to shoot the North Star with his primitive quadrant. Unfortunately, he picked the wrong star, Alfirk of the constellation Cepheus, which on that November evening hung directly over Polaris, and so found Cuba to be in latitude 42 degrees North, the latitude of Cape Cod! Of course he knew that this was wrong, since he had sailed across on 28 degrees North, and in his Letter on this voyage he corrected that latitude of northern Cuba to 26 degrees, still 5 degrees too much.

The Admiral began a collection of specimens which he hoped would convince people at home that he was at least on the fringe of Asia. There was a shrub which smelled something like cinnamon, and so must be cinnamon; the gumbo-limbo, which he supposed to be an Asiatic form of gum mastic that he had seen in Chios; and the small, inedible *nogal del país,* which he identified as the coconut mentioned by Marco Polo. Coconut palms are such a feature of the Caribbean coast today that we forget that they, like the banana, were introduced by the Spaniards. The men dug up some roots which Maestro Sánchez, the surgeon, pronounced to be Chinese rhubarb, a valuable drug imported into Europe, but it turned out to be something different, not even as valuable as the humble pieplant.

And no gold as yet. When the Spaniards asked for gold, the Indians always waved them on to some other place. According to them, there was an island called Babeque where the people gathered gold on the beach by candlelight and hammered it into bars. This choice piece of misinformation brought about the first rift in the Spanish high command. Without asking the Admiral's permission, Martín Alonso Pinzón took off in *Pinta,* hoping to be the first to reach Babeque. He called at Great Inagua Island, which lay in the general direction indicated by the Indians, and, needless to say, found no gold by candle or any other light.

The Admiral in *Santa María,* with *Niña* (whose captain, Vicente Yáñez Pinzón, remained always loyal), sailed eastward along the superb coast of the Oriente Province. Noble mountains rise directly from the sea, but every few miles there is a river whose mouth makes a good landlocked harbor. He called at Bahía Tánamo with its bottle-neck entrance and, within, little wooded islands running up "like diamond points," and others flat-topped "like tables." Next, he put in at the beautiful Puerto Cayo Moa, where you have to pick an opening through the breakers and then find yourself, as Columbus said, in "a lagoon in which all the ships of Spain could lie and be safe." The peculiar charm of this placid harbor, so calm between lofty mountains and the barrier of foaming reefs, was noted by Columbus in words that are not in the least exaggerated. He had an eye, too, for practical matters, and when the men rowed him up the river mouth, he observed on the mountain slopes pine trees which he said would make timber for the Spanish Navy. The descendants of those pines are now being sawed at a mill run by the mountain stream whose distant roar Columbus heard on a Sunday in November, 1492.

On he sailed, with a breeze that fortunately came from the west, noting no less than nine little harbors, behind which leafy valleys ran up into the lofty sierra. He passed the anvil-shaped mountain El Yunque, landmark for Baracoa, a harbor which Columbus well described as round "like a little porringer." Here, a proper site for a colony, the first Spanish settlement in Cuba was pitched in 1512, but Baracoa afforded no gold, and the fleet passed on as soon as the wind turned fair. At sunrise December 5 it was off Cape Maisí, easternmost point of Cuba. In the hope that this was the extremity of Asia, corresponding to Cape St. Vincent in Europe, Columbus named it Cape Alpha and Omega, where East ends and West begins.

Now the fleet crossed the Windward Passage, and at nightfall arrived off the Haitian harbor of San Nicolás Môle, so named by Columbus because he entered it on the feast day of that favorite saint of children. His Indian guides had indicated that gold was to be found on this great island, the home of their ancestors, and this time they were right. It may be said that this island saved Columbus's reputation, for if he had returned home with no more "evidence" than he had yet obtained, people would have said, "This Genoese has found some interesting savage islands, inhabited by gentle natives of the Golden Age, but as for their being the Indies—pooh!"

Nimble *Niña* got into harbor that night, but *Santa María* sailed an offshore leg with the land breeze, in order to be in a good windward position to enter San Nicolás next morning. At daylight the Admiral took a four-point fix on Cape San Nicolás Môle, the Island of Tortuga and two Haitian capes to the eastward, so accurately that we can pinpoint his position on a modern chart.

A fair breeze took the two vessels to Moustique Bay, where they were detained five days by easterly winds and rain. It was here that the Admiral, "seeing the grandeur and beauty of this island, and its resemblance to the land of Spain," named it La Isla Española, The Spanish Isle. Three of his seamen captured a young and beautiful girl clad only in a golden nose plug, and brought her on board. The Admiral "sent her ashore very honorably," decently clad in slop-chest clothing and bedecked with jingles and hawks' bells, although she indicated that she would rather stay with the boys. This move proved to be useful for public relations, as the damsel was a cacique's daughter. Next day nine Spaniards who followed a trail were conducted to a big village of one or two thousand people and given everything they wanted— food, drink, parrots and girls.

On December 15 the two ships beat up the Tortuga Channel to the mouth of Trois Rivières, a clear mountain stream that flows through a valley that Columbus well named the Valley of Paradise. Next day, when the fleet lay off a beach, some five hundred people came down, accompanied by their youthful cacique, who made the Admiral a state visit. Columbus had not been much impressed by a cacique who came on board in Cuba, but this one was different. He had dinner alone with the Admiral in his cabin, and behaved himself with royal poise and dignity. Moreover, he and his suite were bedecked with solid-gold jewelry! Columbus had the cacique piped over the side in proper naval style and given a twenty-one-gun salute. Again the thought passed through his mind that these people were ripe for exploitation—"very cow-

ardly," and "fit to be ordered about and made to work, to sow and do aught
else that may be needed." A wonderful chance, he observed, for his Sovereigns, whose subjects were not notably fond of hard work!

At sunrise December 20, the ships were off Acul Bay, the beauty of which
was so striking that the Admiral ran out of adjectives describing it. Acul certainly is one of the most beautiful bays in the world. The high mountains part
to reveal a conical peak at the head of the valley, which for the last 150 years
has been crowned by the stone citadel of Henri Christophe, King of Haiti.
Here the natives, in 1492, were in an even more pristine state of innocence
than elsewhere; the women did not even wear a scanty cotton clout, and the
men did not mind exhibiting their wives and daughters to the strangers. Also,
they seemed to have plenty of gold. Every day the Spaniards' appetite for the
precious metal was being whetted.

During the night of December 22–23, and the following morning, about a
thousand people came out in canoes to visit *Santa María,* and some five hundred more swam out, although she was anchored over three miles from the
nearest shore. After Indians and white men had taken each others' measure,
any such promiscuous visiting would not have been allowed, lest the natives
capture the ships, but no such thought now crossed the minds of these gentle
Tainos.

A messenger arrived at Acul from Guacanagarí, the cacique of Marien, the
northwestern part of Haiti, and a more important potentate than the one entertained a few days earlier. Guacanagarí sent the Admiral a magnificent belt with
a solid-gold mask for buckle, and invited him to call. He needed no second
invitation, since everyone assured him the gold mines were in that direction,
and that the central part of the island was called Cibao, which suggested
Cipangu, Japan. So, before sunrise on December 24, *Santa María* and *Niña*
departed Acul Bay, all hands planning to spend a merry Christmas at the court
of Guacanagarí, who might even turn out to be the Emperor of Japan!

Fate decreed otherwise. With a contrary wind, the two vessels were unable
to cover the few miles between Acul and Guacanagarí's capital on Caracol Bay
in a day. By 11 P.M., when the watch was changed, *Niña* and *Santa María* were
becalmed east of Cape Haitien, inside the Limonade Pass to the barrier reef.
Everyone on board was exhausted from the previous all-night entertainment of
natives, and as the water was calm, with only a slight ground swell and no
wind, a feeling of complete security—the most dangerous delusion a seaman
can entertain—stole over the flagship. Even the Admiral retired to get his first
sleep in forty-eight hours; the helmsman gave the big tiller to a small boy and
joined the rest of the watch in slumber.

Just as midnight ushered in Christmas Day, *Santa María* settled on a coral
reef, so gently that nobody was awakened by the shock. The boy helmsman,
feeling the rudder ground, sang out; the Admiral was first on deck, followed
by Captain La Cosa and all hands. As the bow only had grounded, Columbus
saw a good chance to get her off stern first and ordered La Cosa and a boat's
crew to run an anchor out astern. Instead of obeying orders, they rowed to
Niña. Captain Vincente Pinzón refused to receive them and sent a boat of his

own to help. *Niña*, which was either more vigilant than the flagship or not on the same bearing, had passed the reef safely.

Owing to La Cosa's cowardice or insubordination, an hour was wasted, and that doomed *Santa María*. The ground swell had been driving her higher and higher on the reef, and coral heads were punching holes in her bottom. As the hull was filling with water, Columbus ordered abandon ship, hoping that daylight would make it easier to float her. And the tide, though only a few inches, might help.

Guacanagarí and his subjects worked hard with the Spaniards to get her off after daybreak, but it was too late. All they could salvage were the equipment, stores and trading truck, which the Indians faithfully guarded and (so the Admiral recorded) purloined not so much as a lace point.

Columbus, with his strong sense of divine guidance, tried to figure out what this strange and apparently disastrous accident meant. Presently he had it: God intended him to start a colony at that point, with *Santa María's* crew. Guacanagarí begged him to do so, as he wanted fire power to help him against enemies elsewhere on the island. The Spaniards fell over each other to volunteer, because signs of gold were now so plentiful that they were confident of making their fortunes. So Columbus gave orders to erect a fortified camp ashore and named it Villa de la Navidad (Christmas Town) in honor of the day of disaster, which he fondly thought had been turned to his advantage.

Navidad, the first attempt by Europeans since that of the Northmen to establish themselves in the New World, was soon built. It was probably located on the sandspit now called Limonade Bord-de-mer, off which there is good anchorage. The fort was constructed largely out of *Santa María's* timbers. Thirty-nine men, mostly from the flagship but some from *Niña*, were left behind under command of Columbus's Cordovan friend Diego de Harana. The Admiral gave them a good part of his provisions, most of the trading truck and the flagship's boat. They were instructed to explore the country with a view to finding a permanent settlement, to trade for gold and to treat the natives kindly.

Columbus was now certain that he had found the Indies. Hispaniola might not be Japan, but it was a great and rich island off the coast of China, with a population ripe both for conversion and exploitation. He now had enough gold artifacts to convince the most skeptical that a land of wealth and plenty had been discovered.

On the day after New Year's, 1493, Guacanagarí and Columbus held a farewell party. *Niña* fired gunshots through what was left of the hull of *Santa María* to impress the natives, and the cacique feasted all hands. After final expressions of mutual love and esteem, and warm embraces, the new allies parted, and the Admiral went on board *Niña*. He would return home in her, with *Pinta* if he could find her; otherwise, alone. After a wait for a favorable wind, and for shipmates who had overstayed their leave, she set sail at sunrise January 4, and the homeward passage began.

The Ambush and Death
of Magellan

by CHARLES McKEW PARR

The formal christening of *Datu* Humabon, Rajah of Cebu, whose conversion had just been made, now occupied the minds of the Christian enthusiasts. The last difficult problem was solved when Magellan tolerantly overlooked the doctrine of monogamy. He succeeded in prevailing upon Padre Valderrama not to press the point, but to baptize the ruler and his plural wives at the same time. The ceremony, according to Don Antonio, was made as impressive as possible. The costumes of the participants were breath-taking, and there was a parade, with banners and bands, and with the strictest protocol governing who went before whom. The pagan idols were destroyed in a supreme act of renunciation by the natives, and a Christian altar was erected. Finally occurred the solemn military Mass, followed by the baptism of the Rajah, of his queens, and of his relatives and courtiers.

After the main ceremony, the populace formed in long lines for baptism, mothers leading their children and carrying infants. At last the exhausted priest, weighed down by his heavy, stiff vestments, could no longer even mutter the holy ritual. He had no strength left to raise his arms in blessing, and in the late afternoon thousands of would-be converts had to be turned away. For the balance of the week, the devoted Padre worked every day administering the holy rites, until at last he triumphantly announced that most of the subjects of the Rajah had become duly accepted children of the Holy Church.

Magellan was filled with elation at the successful demonstration that civilized Christianity could be brought to the heathen in the manner prescribed by its founder, preaching love and charity and peaceful brotherhood. He well might feel triumphant, for he had gained the salvation of many souls, in addition to securing for Don Charles the willing fealty of a populous province whose very existence had hitherto been unknown to Europe. Padre Valderrama was in ecstasy with all the conversions. The proselytizing dream of Ferdinand Magellan did indeed take permanent form, for to this day the people of these islands number millions of Catholics and constitute the only Christian commonwealth in all Asia.

Magellan now concentrated upon consolidating his Christian kingdom. He learned that some of the caciques, or chiefs, of outlying villages, had failed to desert their idols, and he at once summoned them before him. In the presence of the Christian King, as he now styled the Rajah, he demanded the immediate surrender of the wooden idols for destruction. He threatened the caciques with death, and their villages with fire, should they persist in their idolatry. Despite Magellan's previous fair words, this amounted to forced conversion, a practice by no means uncommon even up to recent times, and certainly more the rule than the exception in the sixteenth century. He had several old women arrested and punished for concealing figures of their heathen gods, and he upbraided the Christian King for retaining some household images.

Ferdinand Magellan, Padre Valderrama, Cristóbal Rabelo, and Don Antonio were so engrossed in preaching the principles of upright Christian behavior that they were the last to know what was going on at the same time behind the Captain General's back. Magellan's two captains and many of their followers were, in fact, engaging in loose and drunken behavior ashore, even going so far as to raid the harems of the chiefs by force. Although the extent of their disgraceful nocturnal excesses was by tacit conspiracy hidden from Magellan, his native converts knew and were scandalized. It finally became impossible to keep Duarte Barbosa's absence on a spree from his knowledge, and, just as once before, he had to arrest and shackle his incorrigible friend in order to bring him back to sobriety. This time he felt himself forced to demote Barbosa from command and to entrust the captaincy of the Victoria to the dependable but inexperienced Cristóbal Rabelo.

The visit of the Christian armada to Cebu had now degenerated into a saturnalia completely incompatible with the high pretensions of its Christian commander. As we have seen, the armada was mostly manned by very youthful sailors, and the Captain General himself was only forty-one. The men had had no female companionship since leaving Brazil sixteen months before, and when they were given unlimited shore leave in the sensuous environment of polygamous Cebu, their reactions were inevitable. It was the native custom for only married women to wear clothing; the maidens' innocent nudity was a further cause of demoralization to the seamen. The young sailors had been reared in the prurient belief that human nakedness was sinful, and now they ran wild. Just as in Brazil, a lad who had a jack-knife or a few iron fishhooks to trade could obtain all the feminine companionship he wished.

Magellan attempted to curb this license by invoking the wrath of the Church. He had Padre Valderrama assemble the crew and denounce it as a mortal sin for any Christian man to hold intercourse with a pagan woman. The result of this sermon was paradoxical. The simple and forthright sailors became ardent apostles of Christianity and artlessly baptized any women with whom they proposed to have intercourse; they thereby joyously furthered the Christianizing of the populace. Don Antonio says that the native women preferred the white men to the native males as lovers. The women's preference for the more vigorous Europeans deeply wounded the pride of the Filipino chieftains, and quite naturally aroused their jealousy. Relations between the two races were rapidly reaching an explosive pitch, but Magellan, in his ecstatic state of religious fervor, remained oblivious of the imminent crisis.

The practical veterans of the fleet, Serrano, Barbosa, Carvalho, and others who had dealt at arms' length with dozens of native potentates, all were disturbed by the state of religious exaltation in which Magellan had become enveloped. They thought his indulgent and sympathetic attitude toward the Filipinos complete folly. This cynicism of the leaders was natural and reflected the viewpoint of their caste. They all had been trained in the Iberian school of colonial administration, and their attitude toward weaker populations was as pitiless as that of da Gama, Albuquerque, Cortes, and Pizarro. Had any one of them been Captain General at Cebu, slavery would have been the lot of the natives rather than the clasped hand of Christian brotherhood. They resented Magellan's altruistic attitude, his apostasy toward his own militant class, and also his neglect of mercantile considerations. Magellan was, perhaps, not wholly ahead of his own day in his kindliness toward the Filipinos, for his policy was that advocated by las Casas in the Spanish colonies and by Francis Xavier in the Portuguese territories; they, however, were priests, and he was a man of the sword. His captains considered that he was yielding to the influence of Padre Valderrama, and thought he would do better to listen to their own realistic counsel.

After the *Datu* Humabon had been baptized in the name of Rajah Charles, the Captain General thereafter formally referred to him as the Christian King. This was evidence of Magellan's far-reaching intention to establish him as ruler of the extensive Archipelago of St. Lazarus (as Magellan had named these islands) in the name of his suzerain, the Emperor Charles; Magellan had gone so far as to offer to sustain him in this hegemony. The Rajah now informed the Captain General that some of the chiefs on the Island of Cebu and many on the nearby islands had refused to accept his rule, saying they were as good as he. They also declined to abandon their old religion. The Captain General called a convocation of all the chiefs in Cebu and announced that any man who refused to acknowledge the sovereignty of the Christian King would be killed and his possessions confiscated. He also insisted again that all the chiefs should at once become Christians, destroy the old shrines, and burn their idols. His threat cowed the chiefs, and they all agreed to conform to his dictum.

There was, however, one powerful cacique who did not attend the meeting, but who sent word to the Christian King that he would not abandon the old religion and would wage war on any chief who did so. This rebel was Cacique Cilapulapu, whose district was on the Island of Mactan, directly across the channel from Cebu and forming one side of its harbor. On learning of his defiance, Magellan sent a detachment of marines under Espinosa to burn Cilapulapu's capital, the town of Bulaia. The town was sacked and the women all ravished before the torch was applied. The Captain General then sent a peremptory demand that Cilapulapu render homage to the Christian King, as ruling for the Emperor Charles. He also demanded that the rebel chief immediately pay a tribute, the amount of which was fixed in certain quantities of swine, goats, fowl, rice, and coconuts, in accordance with native precedents in such cases. The recalcitrant chieftain agreed to pay tribute, but offered to send only about two-thirds of the quantities demanded. Magellan thereupon decided to make an example of him, in order to establish the prestige of the Spaniards and support the authority of the Christian King.

He called a council of his officers and informed them of his intention. All his lieutenants, led by John Serrano, urged him not to intervene in civil wars nor to take on the responsibilities of the Rajah Humabon. They pointed out that not only was this contrary to the best colonial tradition of Spain and Portugal, but in their case they had been sent not to colonize, and not to do missionary work, but simply and solely to find the western route to Maluco and to bring back spices to Spain. They referred to the royal orders, which particularly forbade any deviation from the limited duties assigned to them. They strongly reminded the Captain General that, in the previous council, held on April 3, 1521, at Limassawa, they had unanimously presented the same facts and arguments, but that he himself had vetoed them. He had proposed that they cruise up as far as Cebu merely in order to acquaint themselves with the features of the archipelago, so that they might report back to Don Charles regarding its possibilities. They remarked that they had now been at Cebu three weeks and had accomplished many unforeseen things, but they all vigorously urged that the armada should disengage itself from any further commitments there and proceed at once to keep its rendezvous with Francisco Serrano at Ternate. They knew that they were less than a fortnight's easy sail from Ternate, for they had learned, presumably from the Siamese trader, Cristóbal the Moor, the route to the Spice Islands. Don Antonio writes, "We heard of Maluco while at Cebu."

Magellan stubbornly vetoed the proposal for an immediate departure, and he not only announced his intention of punishing Cacique Cilapulapu, but also his determination to command the punitive expedition himself. This statement was received with dismay. The officers immediately objected that the King's express command ordered the Captain General to stay with the fleet, rather than go ashore, and it was especially against orders that he should engage in any such hazardous enterprise. They brought out that it was a basic principle of both the Portuguese and Spanish governments that fleet commanders should not risk their persons ashore. Duarte Barbosa reminded Ferdinand of the loss in South Africa of his former chief, Viceroy Francisco de Almeida, who had incautiously exposed himself. He spoke of the massacre of Magellan's predecessor, Captain Juan Dias de Solis, who also had risked his person with a landing party.

The Captain General was practically convinced that it would be best for him not to accompany the landing party when someone, perhaps del Cano, insinuated with sly malice that he had reached the age when he should no longer participate in hand-to-hand combat. The Captain General, stung by the sneer, swung back to his original intention of leading the foray in person.

Although Magellan had proposed to discipline Cilapulapu as a policy measure, he now began to assume that the project was a religious one; he would punish the defiant pagan for having sacrilegiously denounced Christ and for having proclaimed his intention of persecuting the Christian converts.

The officers had hardly recovered from their first shock when the Captain General announced decisively that he would not permit any of them to accompany him in the attack on Cilapulapu, that he would not let Espinosa or the men-at-arms take part in it, and that he would allow only volunteers to share with him in the undertaking. In terms of religious exaltation, he affirmed that he would depend upon the Cross of Christ and the support of his Patroness, Our Lady of Victory, to win the battle for him. He then abruptly dismissed the council, leaving his associates dumbfounded at his condition, which they considered to be a state of religious hysteria.

Magellan's next steps are almost incredible for a veteran of so many amphibious raids in East Africa, India, Morocco, and Malaya. No one knew better than he the importance of the element of surprise and the need for painstaking preparation of the task force as well as close study of the terrain to be assaulted. Obsessed as he now was with his idea of being a soldier of Christ who would be made irresistible by Divine aid, Magellan not only neglected the most elementary precautions, but in fact took steps which would certainly insure defeat to any foray not counting upon a miracle to give it victory.

Instead of keeping his plan secret, he invited the people of the town of Cebu to be witnesses of the exploit. The Christian King offered to assist him with a thousand veteran warriors, but the Captain General not only loftily declined the offer, but explicitly forbade the Christian King to intervene in the fight. Crown Prince Cilumai then came to Magellan privately and disclosed that he planned to land secretly on Mactan with a contingent of his own, to take the enemy in the rear after the Spaniards had engaged them, but the Captain General dissuaded him from doing this and instead invited him to be a spectator of the battle.

That night, a son of the Cacique Zula, who ruled over half of Mactan and was an enemy of Cilapulapu, came in a canoe to the Trinidad, ostensibly to deliver two goats as part of his father's tribute. He brought a message to Magellan from Cacique Zula that he would cooperate by attacking Cilapulapu by land when Magellan invaded the island. Magellan rebuffed the offer, stating that he needed no help to punish the rebel, but would do so with his own men.

The Captain General then announced that he would make the attack that very night, but instead of instructing the *alguacil*, Gonzalo Gomes de Espinosa, to lead his disciplined marines under their sergeants, he reiterated that he did not desire any of the officers, but only wished to take volunteers from among the men, twenty from each ship.

Accordingly the *alguacil* and his fighters felt piqued and did not volunteer. At midnight, a motley contingent of stewards, grumetes, cabin boys, and *sobresalientes* assembled. They were armored with corselets and helmets, but were not supplied with greaves or leg armor. In addition to swords and lances, they were given harquebuses and crossbows, although many of them were not experts in the handling of these complicated arms. The sixty volunteers filled three batels. The row to the beach was very short, and they arrived three hours before dawn. Twenty or thirty *balanghais* bearing spectators, including the Christian King, the Crown Prince, and some of the Christianized chiefs, accompanied the three attacking boats and ranged themselves behind them, not to participate in the attack, but to observe the Christian victory.

Instead of attacking at once, Magellan sent Cristóbal the Moor ashore with a message to Cilapulapu that, if he would obey the Emperor Charles, recognize the Christian King as his Sovereign, and pay his tribute to the Captain General, he would consider him as a friend; but if he wished otherwise, he should see how the Spanish lances could wound. Cilapulapu replied defiantly that if the Spaniards had lances, his men also had lances of bamboo, as well as stakes hardened with fire. He naively requested that the Captain General not attack at once, but wait until morning, as he would then have more men to oppose him. Magellan took this as a ruse to get him to attack in the darkness, which would have been advantageous to the defenders because they had dug pitfalls in front of their positions. The Christian King counseled the Captain General to wait until daylight, he again asked permission to join him with a thousand men, and again his offer was declined.

The absence of planning began to make itself felt as the cramped volunteers were kept crowded and uncomfortable in the longboats for three long hours, shivering in the chill from the river and tortured by night insects. When dawn came, Magellan ordered the boats forward, but it was found that the entire distance between the batels and the shore was filled with coral reefs and the craft could not proceed. The tide was at ebb, and only with a full tide could the boats have got the men to shore. As it was, they had to leap overboard in their heavy armor and stumble waist-deep over concealed reefs for the distance of two good bowshots. Forty-eight men were led ashore, and eleven were left behind to serve the bombards, although it soon appeared that the range was too long for fire from the cannon to reach the shore. Consequently the landing party had no artillery coverage.

A preliminary heavy bombardment would have been feasible, for the three ships were anchored in the stream only three miles down and one of them could easily have moved up into position within half an hour; its broadsides could have given the attackers a protective barrage. However, Captains Serrano and Barbosa were sulking in their cabins, obeying orders that they were to have nothing to do with the operation, and faithful Espinosa and his men-at-arms stayed behind, having been told they were not needed.

When the already tired and partly dispirited volunteers landed, they found waiting to receive them a native army variously estimated at from fifteen hundred to six thousand trained warriors. These were divided into three divisions, drawn up in a crescent so that they could easily surround the little Spanish force from three sides. There were a series of three parallel trenches between the beach and the town. Cilapulapu and his bodyguard were posted behind these, so that they were not only beyond the range of the bombards, but also beyond effective reach of the small arms.

The Spaniards advanced to the edge of the first ditch and opened fire, but their bullets and crossbow bolts were so spent by the distance that they hardly penetrated the light shields of the Filipinos. The harquebuses were a novel weapon, still in an experimental stage of development, and to handle them required training which was lacking in this instance. The enemy had at first been frightened by the noise of their discharge, but when they found that the balls were harmless, they lost their fear. The firing of a crossbow in battle required skill, and these excellent combat weapons were of but little use to the untrained attackers. When Magellan realized the ineffectiveness of his fire and recognized that he was rapidly exhausting his store of powder and of arrows, Don Antonio says he called again and again, "Cease fire! Cease fire!" But the excited volunteers gave no heed to his command. The company had not been drilled, and there were no subalterns or noncommissioned officers to repeat the orders or to see that they were carried out. Magellan was almost alone in attempting to direct a mob of demoralized men. His only aides were Don Antonio, a foreigner, and Cristóbal Rabelo, an inexperienced youth, neither of whom had any prestige with the fighters. Had the *alguacil* and his *merinos* been there, they would undoubtedly have saved the day.

Magellan saw that it was useless to continue fighting at such long range. He ordered his men to close with the enemy, for, with their armor and superior steel weapons, he thought they could defeat them in combat. To carry out his order, it was necessary for them to cross the three lines of deep trenches, sliding down the bank of each trench and then clambering up the slippery opposite side, a difficult feat under the weight of heavy armor and carrying a lance and a bulky harquebus or crossbow. The enemy did not dispute the crossing of the trenches, since they were perfectly willing to have the Spaniards walk into their trap; the trenches would be serious barriers to a retreat. After the last trench had been traversed, Magellan arranged his muddy, tired men in battle formation and proceeded against the enemy, who had retreated to a position in the village. As the Spaniards advanced against them, the Filipinos retreated, and Magellan realized that they were trying to draw him inland away from the range of the ship artillery, should the fleet come to his support. Therefore he ordered Cristóbal Rabelo to take a squad and set fire to the village, while he drew back to the edge of the nearest trench.

When the Spaniards attempted to carry out this order, the Filipinos immediately rushed forward and cut off Cristóbal Rabelo and his young comrade Juan de la Torre, the son-in-law of John Serrano. Despite their armor and their brave defense, the mass of attackers overwhelmed the young Spaniards and quickly killed them with their spears.

Both these brave young men were favorites of Magellan, and both seem to have been related to him. To see them thus abruptly cut down by the massed enemy frightened the inexperienced soldiers, and the shock seems to have brought Magellan to his senses. For the first time he apparently realized his predicament in face of the large and effective native force. At all events, he ordered his men to withdraw to the boats.

The Filipinos were greatly encouraged by their success in the village, and, as soon as the Spaniards began to retreat, they charged them with spears, but were repulsed. Magellan handled the withdrawal through the ditches in his usual skillful manner. He divided his vastly outnumbered force into two lines; one line kept the enemy at bay until the other had slid, wallowed, and crawled across the ditch and taken a position on the opposite side. From there, the second line covered the retirement of the first with their arrows. This tactic was successfully repeated three times, although the enemy kept up an incessant attack throughout. When the entire body had finally extricated itself from the third trench and was retreating in good order toward the beach, the natives sent strong forces at a run around both their flanks with the intention of intercepting them before they could reach the boats. When the raw, undisciplined sailors saw they were in danger of being cut off from the sea, they broke ranks and raced in panic for the shore, every man for himself. Magellan tried to rally them, but they paid no attention to him. He was left with Don Antonio, Enrique, and six other men, including the supernumerary Anton de Escovar, the foreign *lombardero* Filiberto, two sailors, and two stewards. These devoted men stayed with him, instead of fleeing with the others.

While the nine Spaniards, fighting desperately, were holding their ground, a poisoned arrow struck Magellan in his unarmored leg. He plucked it out and continued to fight where he was, although for safety's sake he should then have retreated. Don Antonio says that the Captain General stayed back purposely in order to prevent the enemy from cutting off the fugitives, many of whom were wounded and could retreat but slowly through the water. Don Antonio wrote, "When they wounded him, he turned back many times to see if they were all in the boats. Had it not been for that unfortunate Captain, not a single one of us would have been saved, for while he was fighting, the others retired to the boats."

As soon as Magellan was satisfied that his men had escaped, he commenced to give ground, but his wounded leg was already very lame, and he was able to retreat but slowly. Those with him picked him up and, covering him as well as they could with their shields, carried him down the beach and into the sea. By this time they were beset by so many of the enemy that they could no longer continue their retreat, but had to put Magellan down and defend him there, standing up to their knees in water, hoping for help from the boats. The Filipinos in fury concentrated their attack on Magellan. Twice they knocked off his helmet, and twice his defenders were able to replace it. They now were under a shower of spears, and even of stones and sod. Don Antonio says that the Filipinos would pick up the same spear and throw it four or six times.

This terrible fight continued for a full hour, while forty armored Spaniards sat in the boats a hundred yards away. Our Lady of Victory had not intervened, and not one man dared come to Magellan's relief. Finally some of the Christianized natives could stand idly by no longer, and heroically advanced to attempt to bring him off. Just as the rescue party neared the little group, now cut down to five, the Spaniards in one of the boats discharged a culverin at the shore. They had aimed it so badly that, instead of reaching the enemy, the shrapnel charge of small stones and bullets struck the rescuing squad of friendly Filipinos in the rear, killing four of them and dispersing the others. The spectators looked on as if mesmerized.

At this juncture, Magellan was wounded in the face by a spear, but valiantly killed his attacker with his lance. As the Filipino fell, the lance remained in his body and was wrenched from Magellan's hands. His lance gone, Magellan tried to draw his sword, but could only get it half way out of the scabbard; he had been wounded in his sword arm with a bamboo spear, and he could not control his muscles.

When the natives saw that Magellan was defenseless, they rushed upon him. Only Don Antonio, Enrique, Filiberto, and Escobar were left to try to cover him with their shields. His other four defenders had already given their lives. The heavy onslaught pushed the wounded and weakened warriors to one side. A Filipino slashed beneath their shields with a long scimitar and cut Magellan on his unarmored left leg, so that he fell face downward into the water. Then Don Antonio says, "They all rushed upon him with iron and bamboo spears, and with their cutlasses, until they killed our mirror, our light and comfort, and our true guide." He continues: "Thereupon, beholding him dead, we, being wounded, retreated as best we could to the boats, which were already pulling off."

It was finished. The earthly destiny of Ferdinand Magellan had led him to voyage around the whole world to his death, and his last weeks of religious exaltation seem to have been almost premonitory. It was as if the reward of earthly riches he had striven for so hard and long was not worth the having to him; once it was in his grasp, his whole being turned away from it, toward the realms of the spirit.

A great career was over, but life went on. His little fleet had to carry on somehow. If, with the death of Ferdinand Magellan, Spain's chance of acquiring Maluco, of establishing an Empire in the Orient, and of making the Pacific Ocean a Castilian Lake also died, what of that? The Philippine Islands remained Christian, as Magellan had hoped. His name is immortalized by his *paso* and by the constellation that shines down upon the ocean which he opened up to the western world.

And we can but repeat Don Antonio's prayer uttered to the Grand Master of Rhodes: "I hope that the fame of so noble a Captain will not be effaced in our time."

The Voyage of the *Mayflower*

by WILLIAM BRADFORD

These troubles being over, and all being together in the one ship, they put to sea again on September 6th with a prosperous wind, which continued for several days and was some encouragement to them, though, as usual, many were afflicted with sea-sickness. I must not omit to mention here a special example of God's providence. There was an insolent and very profane young man,—one of the sailors, which made him the more overbearing,—who was always harassing the poor people in their sickness, and cursing them daily with grievous execrations, and did not hesitate to tell them that he hoped to help throw half of them overboard before they came to their journey's end. If he were gently reproved by any one, he would curse and swear most bitterly. But it pleased God, before they came half seas over, to smite the young man with a grievous disease, of which he died in a desperate manner, and so was himself the first to be thrown overboard. Thus his curses fell upon his own head, which astonished all his mates for they saw it was the just hand of God upon him.

After they had enjoyed fair winds and weather for some time, they encountered cross winds and many fierce storms by which the ship was much shaken and her upper works made very leaky. One of the main beams amid-ships was bent and cracked, which made them afraid that she might not be able to complete the voyage. So some of the chief of the voyagers, seeing that the sailors doubted the efficiency of the ship, entered into serious consultation with the captain and officers, to weigh the danger betimes, and rather to return than to cast themselves into desperate and inevitable peril. Indeed there was great difference of opinion amongst the crew themselves. They wished to dc whatever could be done for the sake of their wages, being now half way over; on the other hand they were loth to risk their lives too desperately. But at length all opinions, the captain's and others' included, agreed that the ship was sound under the water-line, and as for the buckling of the main beam, there was a great iron screw the passengers brought out of Holland, by which the beam could be raised into its place; and the carpenter affirmed that with a post put under it, set firm in the lower deck, and otherwise fastened, he could make it hold. As for the decks and upper works, they said they would calk them as well as they could; and though with the working of the ship they would not long keep stanch, yet there would otherwise be no great danger, if they did not overpress her with sail.

So they committed themselves to the will of God, and resolved to proceed. In several of these storms the wind was so strong and the seas so high that they could not carry a knot of sail, but were forced to hull for many days. Once, as they thus lay at hull in a terrible storm, a strong young man, called John Howland, coming on deck was thrown into the sea; but it pleased God that he caught hold of the top-sail halliards which hung overboard and ran out at length; but he kept his hold, though he was several fathoms under water, till he was hauled up by the rope and then with a boat-hook helped into the ship and saved; and though he was somewhat ill from it he lived many years and became a profitable member both of the church and commonwealth. In all the voyage only one of the passengers died, and that was William Button, a youth, servant to Samuel Fuller, when they were nearing the coast. But to be brief, after long beating at sea, on November 11th they fell in with a part of the land called Cape Cod, at which they were not a little joyful. After some deliberation among themselves and with the captain, they tacked about and resolved to stand for the southward, the wind and weather being fair, to find some place near Hudson's River for their habitation. But after they had kept that course about half a day, they met with dangerous shoals and roaring breakers, and as they conceived themselves in great danger,—the wind falling,—they resolved to bear up again for the Cape, and thought themselves happy to get out of danger before night overtook them, as by God's providence they did. Next day they got into the bay, where they rode in safety.

A word or two, by the way, of this Cape. It was first thus named by Captain Gosnold and his people in 1602, because they caught much of that fish there; and afterwards was called Cape James by Captain Smith; but it retains the former name among seamen. The point where they first met with those dangerous shoals they called Point Care, or Tucker's Terror; but the French and Dutch to this day call it Malabar.

Having found a good haven and being brought safely in sight of land, they fell upon their knees and blessed the God of Heaven who had brought them over the vast and furious ocean, and delivered them from all the perils and miseries of it, again to set their feet upon the firm and stable earth, their proper element. And no marvel that they were thus joyful, when the wise Seneca was so affected with sailing a few miles on the coast of his own Italy, that he affirmed he had rather take twenty years to make his way by land, than to go by sea to any place in however short a time,—so tedious and dreadful it was to him.

But here I cannot but make a pause, and stand half amazed at this poor people's present condition; and so I think will the reader, too, when he considers it well. Having thus passed the vast ocean, and that sea of troubles before while they were making their preparations, they now had no friends to welcome them, nor inns to entertain and refresh their weatherbeaten bodies, nor houses—much less towns—to repair to.

It is recorded in scripture (Acts. xxviii) as a mercy to the apostle and his shipwrecked crew, that the barbarians showed them no small kindness in refreshing them; but these savage barbarians when they met with them (as will appear) were readier to fill their sides full of arrows than otherwise! As for the season, it was winter, and those who have experienced the winters of the country know them to be sharp and severe, and subject to fierce storms, when it is dangerous to travel to known places,—much more to search an unknown coast. Besides, what could they see but a desolate wilderness, full of wild beasts and wild men; and what multitude there might be of them they knew not! Neither could they, as it were, go up to the top of Pisgah, to view from this wilderness a more goodly country to feed their hopes; for which way soever they turned their eyes (save upward to the Heavens!) they could gain little solace from any outward objects. Summer being done, all things turned upon them a weather-beaten face; and the whole country, full of woods and thickets, presented a wild and savage view.

If they looked behind them, there was the mighty ocean which they had passed, and was now a gulf separating them from all civilized parts of the world. If it be said that they had their ship to turn to, it is true; but what did they hear daily from the captain and crew? That they should quickly look out for a place with their shallop, where they would be not far off; for the season was such that the captain would not approach nearer to the shore till a harbour had been discovered which he could enter safely; and that the food was being consumed apace, but he must and would keep sufficient for the return voyage. It was even muttered by some of the crew that if they did not find a place in time, they would turn them and their goods ashore and leave them.

Let it be remembered, too, what small hope of further assistance from England they had left behind them, to support their courage in this sad condition and the trials they were under; for how the case stood between the settlers and the merchants at their departure has already been described. It is true, indeed, that the affection and love of their brethren at Leyden towards them was cordial and unbroken; but they had little power to help them or themselves.

What, then, could now sustain them but the spirit of God, and His grace? Ought not the children of their fathers rightly to say: Our fathers were Englishmen who came over the great ocean, and were ready to perish in this wilderness; but they cried unto the Lord, and He heard their voice, and looked on their adversity. . . . Let them therefore praise the Lord, because He is good, and His mercies endure forever. Yea, let them that have been redeemed of the Lord, show how He hath delivered them from the hand of the oppressor. When they wandered forth into the desert-wilderness, out of the way, and found no city to dwell in, both hungry and thirsty, their soul was overwhelmed in them. Let them confess before the Lord His loving kindness, and His wonderful works before the sons of men!

They thus arrived at Cape Cod on the 11th of November, and necessity called on them to look out for a place of habitation. Having brought a large shallop with them from England, stowed in quarters in the ship, they now got her out, and set their carpenters to work to trim her up; but being much bruised and battered in the foul weather they saw she would be long mending. So a few of them volunteered to go by land and explore the neighbouring parts, whilst the shallop was put in order; particularly since, as they entered the bay, there seemed to be an opening some two or three leagues off, which the captain thought was a river. It was conceived there might be some danger in the attempt; but seeing them resolute, sixteen of them, well-armed, were permitted to go, under charge of Captain Standish. They set forth on the 15th of November, being landed by the ship's boat, and when they had marched about the space of a mile by the sea-side, they espied five or six persons with a dog coming towards them. They were savages; but they fled back into the woods, followed by the English, who wished to see if they could speak with them, and to discover if there were more lying in ambush. But the Indians, seeing themselves followed, left the woods, and ran along the sands as hard as they could, so our men could not come up with them, but followed the track of their feet several miles. Night coming on, they made their rendezvous, and set sentinels, and rested in quiet. Next morning they again pursued the Indians' tracks, till they came to a great creek, where they had left the sands and turned into the woods. But they continued to follow them by guess, hoping to find their dwellings; but soon they lost both the Indians and themselves, and fell into such thickets that their clothes and armour were injured severely; but they suffered most from want of water. At length they found some, and refreshed themselves with the first New England water they had drunk; and in their great thirst they found it as pleasant as wine or beer had been before. Afterwards they directed their course towards the other shore, for they knew it was only a neck of land they had to cross over. At length they got to the sea-side, and marched to this supposed river, and by the way found a pond of fresh water, and shortly after a quantity of cleared ground where the Indians had formerly planted corn; and they found some of their graves. Proceeding further, they saw stubble where corn had been grown the same year, and also found a place where a house had lately been, with some planks, and a great kettle and heaps of sand newly banked, under which they found several large baskets filled with corn, some in the ear of various colours, which was a very goodly sight they having never seen any like it before. This was near the supposed river that they had come to seek. When they reached it, they found that it opened into two arms, with a high cliff of sand at the entrance, but more likely to be creeks of salt water than fresh, they thought. There was good harbourage for their shallop, so they left it to be further explored when she was ready. The time allowed them having expired, they returned to the ship, lest the others should be anxious about their safety. They took part of the corn and buried the rest; and so, like the men from Eshcol, carried with them of the fruits of the land, and showed their brethren; at which the rest were very glad, and greatly encouraged.

After this, the shallop being ready, they set out again for the better reconnoitering of the place. The captain of the ship desired to go himself, so there were some thirty men. However, they found it to be no harbour for ships, but only for boats. They also found two of the Indians' houses covered with mats, and some of their implements in them; but the people had run away and could not be seen. They also found more corn, and beans of various colours. These they brought away, intending to give them full satisfaction when they should meet with any of them,—as about six months afterwards they did.

And it is to be noted as a special providence of God, and a great mercy to this poor people, that they thus got seed to plant corn the next year, or they might have starved; for they had none, nor any likelihood of getting any, till too late for the planting season. Nor is it likely that they would have got it if this first voyage had not been made, for the ground was soon all covered with snow and frozen hard. But the Lord is never wanting unto His in their great need; let His holy name have all the praise.

The month of November being spent in these affairs, and foul weather coming on, on the sixth of December they sent out their shallop again with ten of their principal men and some sailors upon further discovery, intending to circumnavigate the deep bay of Cape Cod. The weather was very cold, and it froze so hard that the spray of the sea froze on their coats like glass. Early that night they got to the lower end of the bay, and as they drew near the shore they saw ten or twelve Indians very busy about something. They landed about a league or two from them; though they had much ado to put ashore anywhere, it was so full of flats. It was late when they landed, so they made themselves a barricade of logs and boughs as well as they could in the time, and set a sentinel and betook them to rest, and saw the smoke of the fire the savages made that night. When morning came they divided their party, some to coast along the shore in the boat, and the rest to march through the woods to see the land, and, if possible, to find a fit place for their settlement. They came to the place where they had seen the Indians the night before, and found they had been cutting up a great fish like a grampus, covered with almost two inches of fat, like a hog. The shallop found two more of the same kind of fish dead on the sands, a usual thing after storms there, because of the great flats of sand. They ranged up and down all that day, but found no people nor any place they liked. When the sun got low they hastened out of the woods to meet their shallop, making signs to it to come into a creek hard by, which it did at high water. They were very glad to meet, for they had not seen each other since the morning. They made a barricade, as they did every night, with logs, stakes, and thick pine boughs, the height of a man, leaving it open to leeward; partly to shelter them from the cold wind, making their fire in the middle and lying round it; and partly to defend them from any sudden assaults of the savages, if they should try to surround them. So being very weary, they betook them to rest. But about midnight they heard a hideous cry, and their sentinel called "Arm, arm!" So they bestirred themselves and stood to their arms, and shot a couple of muskets and then the noise ceased. They concluded it was a pack of wolves, or some such wild beasts; for one of the sailors told them he had often heard such noises in Newfoundland. So they rested till about five o'clock in the morning. After prayer they prepared for breakfast, and it being day dawning, it was thought best to be carrying things down to the boat. Some said it was not best to carry the guns down; others said they would be the readier, for they had wrapped them up in their coats to keep them from the dew. But some three or four would not carry their guns down to the boat till they went themselves. However, as the water was not high enough, the others laid theirs down on the bank of the creek, and came up to breakfast. But soon, all of a sudden, they heard a great and strange cry, which they knew to be the same as they had heard in the night, though with various notes. One of the company who was outside came running in and cried: "Men; Indians, Indians;" and at that their arrows came flying amongst them! The men ran down to the creek with all speed to recover their guns, which by the providence of God they succeeded in doing. In the meantime two of those who were still armed discharged their muskets at the Indians; and two more stood ready at the entrance of the rendezvous, but were commanded not to shoot till they could take fell aim at them; and the other two loaded again at full speed, there being only four guns there to defend the barricade when it was first assaulted.

The cry of the Indians was dreadful, especially when they saw the men run out of the rendezvous towards the shallop to recover their guns, the Indians wheeling about them. But some of the men, armed with coats of mail and with cutlasses in their hands, soon got their guns and let fly among them, which quickly stopped their violence. There was one big Indian, and no less valiant, who stood behind a tree, within half a musket-shot, and let his arrows fly at them. He was seen to shoot three arrows, which were all avoided. He stood three musket-shots, till one of them made the bark and splinters of the tree fly about his ears, at which he gave an extraordinary shriek, and away all of them went. The men left some of the party to guard the shallop, and followed the Indians about a quarter of a mile, shouting once or twice, and shooting off two or three guns, and then returned. They did this so that the natives might not think they were afraid of them.

Thus it pleased God to vanquish their enemies, and give them deliverance; and by His special providence so to dispose that not one of them was hit, though the arrows came close to them, on every side, and some of their coats which were hung up in the barricade were shot through and through. Afterwards they gave God solemn thanks and praise for their deliverance, and gathered up a bundle of the arrows, and later sent them to England by the captain of the ship. They called the place "The First Encounter."

Then they left, and coasted all along, but discovered no likely place for a harbour. So they made all speed to a spot which their pilot—a Mr. Coppin, who had been in the country before—assured them was a good harbour, which he had been in, and which they might fetch before night. Of this they were glad, for the weather began to be foul. After some hours' sailing, it began to snow and rain, and about the middle of the afternoon the wind increased, and the sea became very rough. They broke their rudder, and it was as much as two men could do to steer her with a couple of oars. But the pilot bade them be of good cheer, and said he saw the harbour; but the storm increasing and night drawing on, they carried all the sail they could to get in while they could see. Then their mast broke in three pieces, and the sail fell overboard in a very heavy sea, so that they were in danger of being wrecked; but by God's mercy they recovered themselves, and having the tide with them, struck in towards the harbour. But when they came to, the pilot found he had mistaken the place, and said the Lord be merciful to them, for he had never seen the place before; and he and the mate were about to run her ashore, in a cove full of breakers, before the wind. But one of the seamen, who steered, bade the rowers, if they were men, about with her, or they would all be cast away; which they did with speed. So he bid them be of good cheer and row lustily, for there was a fair sound before them, and he did not doubt but they would find a place where they could come to safely. Though it was very dark and rained hard, they ultimately got under the lee of a small island, and remained there safely all night; but they did not know it was an island till morning. They were divided in their minds; some wished to stay in the boat, for fear there would be more Indians; others were so weak and cold they could not endure it, but got ashore and with much ado made a fire—everything being wet,—and then the rest were glad enough to join them; for after midnight the wind shifted to the north-west and it froze hard.

But though this had been a night of much hardship and danger, God gave them a morning of comfort and refreshment, as He usually doth to His children; for the next day was a fair sun-shining day, and they found they were on an island secure from the Indians, where they could dry their stuff, fix their arms, and rest themselves and give God thanks for His mercies in their manifold deliverances. This being the last day of the week they prepared to keep the Sabbath there. On Monday they sounded the harbour and found it fit for shipping; and marching inland they found several cornfields and little running brooks,—a place, as they supposed, fit for a settlement; at least it was the best they could find, and considering the season of the year and their present necessity they were thankful for it. So they returned with this news to the rest of their people aboard the ship, which cheered them greatly.

On the 15th day of December they weighed anchor to go to the place they had discovered, and came within two leagues of it, but had to bear up again. On the 16th day the wind came fair, and they arrived safe in the harbour. Afterwards they took a better view of the place, and resolved where to pitch their dwellings; and on the 25th day they began to erect the first house for common use, to receive them and their goods.

The Death of Captain Cook

by ANDREW KIPPIS

Early on the 4th the ships sailed out of Karakakooa Bay, being followed by a large number of canoes. It was our commander's design, before he visited the other islands, to finish the survey of Owhyhee, in hopes of meeting with a road better sheltered than the bay he had just left. In case of not succeeding in this respect, he purposed to take a view of the south-east part of Mowee, where he was informed that he should find an excellent harbour.

The circumstances which brought Captain Cook back to Karakakooa Bay, and the unhappy consequences that followed, I shall give from Mr. Samwell's narrative of his death. This narrative was, in the most obliging manner, communicated to me in manuscript by Mr. Samwell, with entire liberty to make such use of it as I should judge proper. Upon a perusal of it, its importance struck me in so strong a light that I wished to have it separately laid before the world. Accordingly, with Mr. Samwell's concurrence, I procured its publication, that if any objections should be made to it, I might be able to notice them in my own work. As the narrative hath continued for more than two years unimpeached and uncontradicted, I esteem myself fully authorized to insert it in this place, as containing the most complete and authentic account of the melancholy catastrophe which, at Owhyhee, befell our illustrious navigator and commander.

"On the 6th we were overtaken by a gale of wind; and the next night the *Resolution* had the misfortune of springing the head of her foremast, in such a dangerous manner that Captain Cook was obliged to return to Keragegooah, in order to have it repaired; for we could find no other convenient harbour on the island. The same gale had occasioned much distress among some canoes that had paid us a visit from the shore. One of them, with two men and a child on board, was picked up by the *Resolution*, and rescued from destruction: the men, having toiled hard all night, in attempting to reach the land, were so much exhausted that they could hardly mount the ship's side. When they got upon the quarter-deck, they burst into tears, and seemed much affected with the dangerous situation from which they had escaped; but the little child appeared lively and cheerful. One of the *Resolution's* boats was also so fortunate as to save a man and two women, whose canoe had been upset by the violence of the waves. They were brought on board, and, with the others, partook of the kindness and humanity of Captain Cook.

"On the morning of Wednesday, the 10th, we were within a few miles of the

337

harbour, and were soon joined by several canoes, in which appeared many of our old acquaintance, who seemed to have come to welcome us back. Among them was Coo, aha, a priest: he had brought a small pig, and some cocoa-nuts in his hand, which, after having chanted a few sentences, he presented to Captain Clerke. He then left us, and hastened on board the *Resolution* to perform the same friendly ceremony before Captain Cook. Having but light winds all that day we could not gain the harbour. In the afternoon, a chief of the first rank, and nearly related to Kariopoo, paid us a visit on board the *Discovery*. His name was Ka, mea, mea: he was dressed in a very rich feathered cloak, which he seemed to have brought for sale, but would part with it for nothing except iron daggers. These the chiefs, some time before our departure, had preferred to every other article; for, having received a plentiful supply of hatchets and other tools, they began to collect a store of warlike instruments. Kameamea procured nine daggers for his cloak; and being pleased with his reception, he and his attendants slept on board that night.

"In the morning of February 11th, the ships anchored again in Keragegooah Bay, and preparation was immediately made for landing the *Resolution's* foremast. We were visited but by few of the Indians, because there were but few in the bay. On our departure, those belonging to other parts had repaired to their several habitations, and were again to collect from various quarters, before we could expect to be surrounded by such multitudes as we had once seen in that harbour. In the afternoon I walked about a mile into the country, to visit an Indian friend who had, a few days before, come near twenty miles, in a small canoe, to see me, while the ship lay becalmed. As the canoe had not left us long before a gale of wind came on, I was alarmed for the consequence: however, I had the pleasure to find that my friend had escaped unhurt, though not without some difficulties. I take notice of this short excursion merely because it afforded me an opportunity of observing that there appeared no change in the disposition or behavior of the inhabitants. I saw nothing that could induce me to think that they were displeased with our return, or jealous of the intention of our second visit. On the contrary, that abundant good nature which had always characterized them seemed still to glow in every bosom and to animate every countenance.

"The next day, February 12th, the ships were put under a taboo, by the chiefs: a solemnity, it seems, that was requisite to be observed before Kariopoo, the king, paid his first visit to Captain Cook, after his return. He waited upon him the same day, on board the *Resolution*, attended by a large train, some of which bore the presents designed for Captain Cook, who received him in his usual friendly manner, and gave him several articles in return. This amicable ceremony being settled, the taboo was dissolved; matters went on in the usual train; and the next day, February 13th, we were visited by the natives in great numbers; the *Resolution's* mast was landed, and the astronomical observatories erected on their former situation. I landed, with another gentlemen, at the town of Kavaroah, where we found a great number of canoes, just arrived from different parts of the island, and the Indians busy in constructing temporary huts on the beach for their residence during the stay of

THE DEATH OF CAPTAIN COOK

the ships. On our return on board the *Discovery*, we learned that an Indian had been detected in stealing the armourer's tongs from the forge, for which he received a pretty severe flogging, and was sent out of the ship. Notwithstanding the example made of this man, in the afternoon another had the audacity to snatch the tongs and a chisel from the same place, with which he jumped overboard and swam for the shore. The master and a midshipman were instantly despatched after him, in the small cutter. The Indian, seeing himself pursued, made for a canoe; his countrymen took him on board, and paddled as swift as they could towards the shore. We fired several muskets at them, but to no effect, for they soon got out of the reach of our shot. Pareah, one of the chiefs, who was at that time on board the *Discovery*, understanding what had happened, immediately went ashore, promising to bring back the stolen goods. Our boat was so far distanced, in chasing the canoe which had taken the thief on board, that he had time to make his escape into the country. Captain Cook, who was then ashore, endeavoured to intercept his landing; but it seems that he was led out of the way by some of the natives, who had officiously intruded themselves as guides. As the master was approaching near the landing-place, he was met by some of the Indians in a canoe. They had brought back the tongs and chisel, together with another article that we had not missed, which happened to be the lid of the water-cask. Having recovered these things, he was returning on board, when he was met by the *Resolution*'s pinnace with five men in her, who, without any orders, had come from the observatories to his assistance. Being thus unexpectedly reinforced, he thought himself strong enough to insist upon having the thief, or the canoe which took him in, delivered up as reprisals. With that view he turned back; and having found the canoe on the beach, he was preparing to launch it into the water when Pareah made his appearance, and insisted upon his not taking it away, as it was his property. The officer not regarding him, the chief seized upon him, pinioned his arms behind, and held him by the hair of his head; on which one of the sailors struck him with an oar. Pareah instantly quitted the officer, snatched the oar out of the man's hand, and snapped it in two across his knee. At length the multitude began to attack our people with stones. They made some resistance, but were soon overpowered, and obliged to swim for safety to the small cutter, which lay farther out than the pinnace. The officers, not being expert swimmers, retreated to a small rock in the water, where they were closely pursued by the Indians. One man darted a broken oar at the master; but his foot slipping at the time, he missed him, which fortunately saved that officer's life. At last Pareah interfered and put an end to their violence. The gentlemen, knowing that his presence was their only defence against the fury of the natives, entreated him to stay with them till they could get off in the boats; but that he refused, and left them. The master went to seek assistance from the party at the observatories; but the midshipman chose to remain in the pinnace. He was very rudely treated by the mob, who plundered the boat of everything that was loose on board, and then began to knock her to pieces for the sake of the iron-work; but Pareah fortunately returned in time to prevent her destruction. He had met the other gentlemen on his way to the observatories, and, suspecting his errand, had forced him to return. He dispersed the crowd again, and desired the gentlemen to return on board: they represented that all the oars had been taken out of the boat; on which he brought some of them back, and the gentlemen were glad to get off without farther molestation. They had not proceeded far, before they were overtaken by Pareah, in a canoe: he delivered the midshipman's cap, which had been taken from him in the scuffle, joined noses with them in token of reconciliation, and was anxious to know if Captain Cook would kill him for what had happened. They assured him of the contrary, and made signs of friendship to him in return. He then left them and paddled over to the town of Kavaroah, and that was the last time we ever saw him. Captain Cook returned on board soon after, much displeased with the whole of this disagreeable business, and the same night sent a lieutenant on board the *Discovery* to learn the particulars of it, as it had originated in that ship.

"It was remarkable that in the midst of the hurry and confusion attending this affair, Kanynah (a chief who had always been on terms particularly friendly with us) came from the spot where it happened, with a hog to sell on board the *Discovery*; it was of an extraordinary large size, and he demanded for it a pahowa, or dagger, of an unusual length. He pointed to us that it must be as long as his arm. Captain Clerke not having one of that length, told him he would get one made for him by the morning; with which being satisfied, he left the hog, and went ashore without making any stay with us. It will not be altogether foreign to the subject to mention a circumstance that happened today on board the *Resolution*. An Indian chief asked Captain Cook, at his table, if he was a *Tata Toa*; which means a fighting man, or a soldier. Being answered in the affirmative, he desired to see his wounds. Captain Cook held out his right hand, which had a scar upon it, dividing the thumb from the finger, the whole length of the metacarpal bones. The Indian, being thus convinced of his being a Toa, put the same question to another gentlemen present, but he happened to have none of those distinguishing marks; the chief then said that he himself was a Toa, and showed the scars of some wounds he had received in battle. Those who were on duty at the observatories were disturbed during the night with shrill and melancholy sounds, issuing from the adjacent villages, which they took to be the lamentations of the women. Perhaps the quarrel between us might have filled their minds with apprehensions for the safety of their husbands; but be that as it may, their mournful cries struck the sentinels with unusual awe and terror.

"To widen the breach between us, some of the Indians in the night took away the *Discovery's* large cutter, which lay swamped at the buoy of one of her anchors: they had carried her off so quietly that we did not miss her till the morning, Sunday, February 14th. Captain Clerke lost no time in waiting upon Captain Cook to acquaint him with the accident: he returned on board with orders for the launch and small cutter to go, under the command of the second lieutenant, and lie off the east point of the bay, in order to intercept all canoes that might attempt to get out; and, if he found it necessary, to fire upon them. At the same time the third lieutenant of the *Resolution*, with the launch and small cutter, was sent on the same service to the opposite point of the bay; and the master was despatched in the large cutter in pursuit of a double canoe, already under sail, making the best of her way out of the harbour. He soon came up with her, and by firing a few muskets drove her on shore, and the Indians left her: this happened to be the canoe of Omea, a man who bore the title of Orono. He was on board himself, and it would have been fortunate if our people had secured him, for his person was held as sacred as that of the king. During this time Captain Cook was preparing to go ashore himself, at the town of Kavaroah, in order to secure the person of Kariopoo, before he should have time to withdraw himself to another part of the island, out of our reach. This appeared the most effectual step that could be taken, on the present occasion, for the recovery of the boat. It was the measure he had invariably pursued, in similar cases, at other islands in these seas, and it had always been attended with the desired success: in fact, it would be difficult to point out any other mode of proceeding on these emergencies likely to attain the object in view. We had reason to suppose that the king and his attendants had fled when the alarm was first given: in that case, it was Captain Cook's intention to secure the large canoes which were hauled up on the beach. He left the ship about seven o'clock, attended by the lieutenant of marines, a sergeant, a corporal, and seven private men: the pinnace's crew were also armed, and under the command of Mr. Roberts. As they rowed towards the shore, Captain Cook ordered the launch to leave her station at the west point of the bay, in order to assist his own boat. This is a circumstance worthy of notice; for it clearly shows that he was not unapprehensive of meeting with resistance from the natives, or unmindful of the necessary preparation for the safety of himself and his people. I will venture to say that, from the appearance of things just at that time there was not one beside himself who judged that such precaution was absolutely requisite: so little did his conduct on the occasion bear the marks of rashness, or a precipitate self-confidence! He landed with the marines, at the upper end of the town of Kavaroah: the Indians immediately flocked round, as usual, and showed him the customary marks of respect, by prostrating themselves before him.— There were no signs of hostilities, or much alarm among them. Captain Cook, however, did not seem willing to trust to appearances; but was particularly attentive to the disposition of the marines, and to have them kept clear of the crowd. He first inquired for the king's sons, two youths who were much attached to him, and generally his companions on board. Messengers being sent for them, they soon came to him, and informing him that their father was asleep at a house not far from them, he accompanied them thither, and took the marines along with them. As he passed along the natives everywhere prostrated themselves before him, and seemed to have lost no part of that respect they had always shown to his person. He was joined by several chiefs, among whom was Kanynah, and his brother Koohowrooah. They kept the crowd in order, according to their usual custom; and, being ignorant of his intention in coming on shore, frequently asked him if he wanted any hogs, or other provisions: he told them that he did not, and that his business was to see the king. When he arrived at the house, he ordered some of the Indians to go in and inform Kariopoo that he waited without to speak with him. They came out two or three times, and instead of returning any answer from the king, presented some pieces of red cloth to him, which made Captain Cook suspect that he was not in the house; he therefore desired the lieutenant of marines to go in. The lieutenant found the old man just awaked from sleep, and seemingly alarmed at the message; but he came out without hesitation. Captain Cook took him by the hand, and in a friendly manner asked him to go on board, to which he very readily consented. Thus far matters appeared in a favorable train, and the natives did not seem much alarmed or apprehensive of hostility on our side: at which Captain Cook expressed himself a little surprised, saying that as the inhabitants of that town appeared innocent of stealing the cutter, he should not molest them, but that he must get the king on board. Kariopoo sat down before his door, and was surrounded by a great crowd: Kanynah and his brother were both very active in keeping order among them. In a little time, however, the Indians were observed arming themselves with long spears, clubs, and daggers, and putting on thick mats, which they used as armor. This hostile appearance increased, and became more alarming on the arrival of two men in a canoe from the opposite side of the bay, with the news of a chief called Kareemoo having been killed by one of the *Discovery's* boats. In their passage across they had also delivered this account to each of the ships. Upon that information the women, who were sitting upon the beach at their breakfasts, and conversing familiarly with our people in the boats, retired, and a confused murmur spread through the crowd. An old priest came to Captain Cook, with a cocoa-nut in his hand, which he held out to him as a present, at the same time singing very loud. He was often desired to be silent, but in vain: he continued importunate and troublesome, and there was no such thing as getting rid of him or his noise: it seemed as if he meant to divert their attention from his countrymen, who were growing more tumultuous, and arming themselves in every quarter. Captain Cook, being at the same time surrounded by a great crowd, thought his situation rather hazardous: he therefore ordered the lieutenant of marines to march his small party to the waterside, where the boats lay within a few yards of the shore: the Indians readily made a lane for them to pass, and did not offer to interrupt them. The distance they had to go might be about fifty or sixty yards; Captain Cook followed, having hold of Kariopoo's hand, who accompanied him very willingly: he was attended by his wife, two sons, and several chiefs. The troublesome old priest followed, making the same savage noise. Keowa, the younger son, went directly into the pinnace, expecting his father to follow; but just as he arrived at the waterside, his wife threw her arms about his neck, and, with the assistance of two chiefs, forced him to sit down by the side of a double canoe. Captain Cook expostulated with them, but to no purpose: they would not suffer the king to proceed, telling him that he would be put to death if he went on board the ship. Kariopoo, whose conduct seemed entirely resigned to the will of others, hung down his head, and appeared much distressed.

"While the king was in this situation, a chief, well known to us, of the name of Coho, was observed lurking near with an iron dagger, partly concealed under his cloak, seemingly with the intention of stabbing Captain Cook or the lieutenant of marines. The latter proposed to fire at him, but Captain Cook would not permit it. Coho closing upon them obliged the officer to strike him with his piece, which made him retire. Another Indian laid hold of the sergeant's musket and endeavoured to wrench it from him, but was prevented by the lieutenant's making a blow at him. Captain Cook, seeing the tumult increase and the Indians growing more daring and resolute, observed that if he were to take the king off by force he could not do it without sacrificing the lives of many of his people. He then paused a little, and was on the point of giving his order to re-embark, when a man threw a stone at him; which he returned with a discharge of small shot (with which one barrel of his double piece was loaded). The man, having a thick mat before him, received little or no hurt; he brandished his spear and threatened to dart it at Captain Cook, who, being still unwilling to take away his life, instead of firing with ball knocked him down with his musket. He expostulated strongly with the most forward of the crowd upon their turbulent behavior. He had given up all thoughts of getting the king on board, as it appeared impracticable; and his care was then only to act on the defensive, and to secure a safe embarkation for his small party, which was closely pressed by a body of several thousand people. Keowa, the king's son, who was in the pinnace, being alarmed on hearing the first firing, was, at his own entreaty, put on shore again; for even at that time Mr. Roberts, who commanded her, did not apprehend that Captain Cook's person was in any danger: otherwise he would have detained the prince, which, no doubt, would have been a great check on the Indians. One man was observed behind a double canoe, in the action of darting his spear at Captain Cook, who was forced to fire at him in his own defense, but happened to kill another close to him, equally forward in the tumult: the sergeant observing that he had missed the man he aimed at received orders to fire at him, which he did, and killed him. By this time the impetuosity of the Indians was somewhat repressed; they fell back in a body and seemed staggered: but being pushed on by those behind, they returned to the charge and poured a volley of stones among the marines, who, without waiting for orders, returned it with a general discharge of musketry, which was instantly followed by a fire from the boats. At this Captain Cook was heard to express his astonishment: he waved his hand to the boats, called to them to cease firing, and to come nearer in to receive the marines. Mr. Roberts immediately brought the pinnace as close to the shore as he could, without grounding, notwithstanding the showers of stones that fell among the people: but—, the lieutenant, who commanded in the launch, instead of pulling in to the assistance of Captain Cook, withdrew his boat farther off, at the moment that everything seems to have depended upon the timely exertions of those in the boats. By his own account he mistook the signal: but be that as it may, this circumstance appears to me to have decided the fatal turn of the affair, and to have removed every chance which remained with Captain Cook of escaping with his life. The business of saving the marines out of the water, in consequence of that, fell altogether upon the pinnace; which thereby became so much crowded that the crew were, in a great measure, prevented from using their fire-arms, or giving what assistance they otherwise might have done to Captain Cook; so that he seems, at the most critical point of time, to have wanted the assistance of both boats, owing to the removal of the launch. For notwithstanding that they kept up a fire on the crowd, from the situation to which they removed in that boat, the fatal confusion which ensued on her being withdrawn, to say the least of it, must have prevented the full effect that the prompt co-operation of the two boats, according to Captain Cook's orders, must have had towards the preservation of himself and his people. At that time it was to the boats alone that Captain Cook had to look for his safety; for when the marines had fired, the Indians rushed among them and forced them into the water, where four of them were killed: their lieutenant was wounded, but fortunately escaped and was taken up by the pinnace. Captain Cook was then the only one remaining on the rock: he was observed making for the pinnace, holding his left hand against the back of his head, to guard it from the stones, and carrying his musket under the other arm. An Indian was seen following him, but with caution and timidity; for he stopped once or twice, as if undetermined to proceed. At last he advanced upon him unawares, and with a large club, or common stake, gave him a blow on the back of the head, and then precipitately retreated. The stroke seemed to have stunned Captain Cook: he staggered a few paces, then fell on his hand and one knee, and dropped his musket. As he was rising, and before he could recover his feet, another Indian stabbed him in the back of the neck with an iron dagger. He then fell into a bite of water about knee deep, where others crowded upon him and endeavoured to keep him under: but struggling very strongly with them he got his head up, and casting his look towards the pinnace, seemed to solicit assistance. Though the boat was not above five or six yards distant from him, yet from the crowded and confused state of the crew, it seems it was not in their power to save him. The Indians got him under again, but in deeper water: he was, however, able to get his head up once more, and being almost spent in the struggle, he naturally turned to the rock, and was endeavoring to support himself by it, when a savage gave him a blow with a club, and he was seen alive no more. They hauled him up lifeless on the rocks, where they seemed to take a savage pleasure in using every barbarity to his dead body, snatching the daggers out of each other's hands, to have the horrid satisfaction of piercing the fallen victim of their barbarous rage.

"I need make no reflection on the great loss we suffered on this occasion, or attempt to describe what we felt. It is enough to say that no man was ever more beloved or admired: and it is truly painful to reflect that he seems to have fallen a sacrifice merely for want of being properly supported; a fate singularly to be lamented as having fallen to his lot, who had ever been conspicuous for his care of those under his command, and who seemed, to the last, to pay as much attention to their preservation as to that of his own life.

"If anything could have added to the shame and indignation universally felt on this occasion, it was to find that his remains had been deserted, and left exposed on the beach, although they might have been brought off. It appears, from the information of four or five midshipmen, who arrived on the spot at the conclusion of the fatal business, that the beach was then almost entirely deserted by the Indians, who at length had given way to the fire of the boats, and dispersed through the town: so that there seemed no great obstacle to prevent the recovery of Captain Cook's body; but the lieutenant returned on board without making the attempt. It is unnecessary to dwell longer on this painful subject, and to relate the complaints and censures that fell on the conduct of the lieutenant. It will be sufficient to observe that they were so loud as to oblige Captain Clerke publicly to notice them, and to take the depositions of his accusers down in writing. The captain's bad state of health and approaching dissolution, it is supposed, induced him to destroy these papers a short time before his death.

"It is a painful task to be obliged to notice circumstances which seem to reflect upon the character of any man. A strict regard to truth, however, compelled me to the insertion of these facts, which I have offered merely as facts, without presuming to connect with them any comment of my own: esteeming it the part of a faithful historian, 'to extenuate nothing, nor set down aught in malice.'

"The fatal accident happened at eight o'clock in the morning, about an hour after Captain Cook landed. It did not seem that the king, or his sons, were witnesses to it: but it is supposed that they withdrew in the midst of the tumult. The principal actors were the other chiefs, many of them the king's relations and attendants: the man who stabbed him with the dagger was called Nooah. I happened to be the only one who recollected his person, from having on a former occasion mentioned his name in the journal I kept. I was induced to take particular notice of him, more from his personal appearance than any other consideration, though he was of high rank, and a near relation of the king: he was stout and tall, with a fierce look and demeanor, and one who united in his figure the two qualities of strength and agility, in a greater degree than ever I remembered to have seen before in any other man. His age might be about thirty, and by the white scurf on his skin, and his sore eyes, he appeared to be a hard drinker of Kava. He was a constant companion of the king, with whom I first saw him, when he paid a visit to Captain Clerke. The chief who first struck Captain Cook with the club was called Karimano, craha, but I did not know him by his name. These circumstances I learned of honest Kaireekea, the priest; who added, that they were both held in great esteem on account of that action: neither of them came near us afterwards. When the boats left the shore, the Indians carried away the dead body of Captain Cook and those of the marines, to the rising ground at the back of the town, where we could plainly see them with our glasses from the ships.

"This most melancholy accident appears to have been altogether unexpected and unforeseen, as well on the part of the natives as ourselves. I never saw sufficient reason to induce me to believe that there was anything of design, or a preconcerted plan on their side, or that they purposely sought to quarrel with us: thieving, which gave rise to the whole, they were equally guilty of in our first and second visits. It was the cause of every misunderstanding that happened between us: their petty thefts were generally overlooked, but sometimes slightly punished; the boat which they at last ventured to take away was an object of no small magnitude to people in our situation, who could not possibly replace her, and therefore not slightly to be given up. We had no other chance of recovering her but by getting the person of the king into our possession: on our attempting to do that the natives became alarmed for his safety, and naturally opposed those whom they deemed his enemies. In the sudden conflict that ensued, we had the unspeakable misfortune of losing our excellent commander, in the manner already related. It is in this light the affair has always appeared to me, as entirely accidental, and not in the least owing to any previous offence received, or jealousy of our second visit entertained by the natives.

"Pareah seems to have been the principal instrument in bringing about this fatal disaster. We learned afterward that it was he who had employed some people to steal the boat: the king did not seem to be privy to it, or even apprised of what had happened, till Captain Cook landed.

"It was generally remarked that at first the Indians showed great resolution in facing our fire-arms; but it was entirely owing to ignorance of their effect. They thought that their thick mats would defend them from a ball as well as from a stone; but being soon convinced of their error, yet still at a loss to account how such execution was done among them, they had recourse to a stratagem which, though it answered no other purpose, served to show their ingenuity and quickness of invention. Observing the flashes of the muskets, they naturally concluded that water would counteract their effect, and therefore very sagaciously dipped their mats, or armor, in the sea, just as they came on to face our people: but finding this last resource to fail them, they soon dispersed, and left the beach entirely clear. It was an object they never neglected, even at the greatest hazard, to carry off their slain; a custom probably owing to the barbarity with which they treat the dead body of an enemy, and the trophies they make of his bones." *

In consequence of this barbarity of disposition, the whole remains of Captain Cook could not be recovered. For though every exertion was made for that purpose, though negotiations and threatenings were alternately employed, little more than the principal part of his bones (and that with great difficulty) could be procured. By the possession of them, our navigators were enabled to perform the last offices to their eminent and unfortunate commander. The bones having been put into a coffin, and the service being read over them, were committed to the deep, on the 21st, with the usual military honors. What were the feelings of the companies of both the ships, on this occasion, must be left to the world to conceive; for those who were present know that it is not in the power of any pen to express them.

---

* "Samwell's Narrative of the Death of Captain James Cook," p. 2-20.

Southward Ho to the Pole

by RICHARD EVELYN BYRD

It's a funny thing about a polar expedition, but no matter how much care is given to its organization, it will evoke more surprises than a grab-bag. At Wellington I had instructed the personnel officer to take on nine volunteers. They were to assist in the unloading of supplies in the Bay of Whales and to help work the ship back to Dunedin. Dunedin would again be the winter base for the ships. The first afternoon out all hands were summoned forward for a counting of heads. I discovered then that instead of nine, eighteen men had been signed on. The personnel officer wasn't quite sure how it happened. "Maybe I signed on twins," he said brightly. Nevertheless it was a serious matter. We had little food and clothing to spare beyond our fixed requirements. While I was canvassing this situation, Captain Verleger burst into the cabin.

"There's three more of 'em, Admiral!" he exclaimed.

"Three more what?"

"Stowaways," he said. "In No. 4 lifeboat. When we unshipped the tarpaulin, there they were, tucked in snug as bugs in a rug. What'll we do with 'em—keelhaul 'em on general principles, or throw 'em in the brig till we can think of somethin' better?"

We had no brig, and keelhauling is outlawed by civilized society; so a different procedure was in order. After thinking the matter over, I resolved to do what seemed to be the fair thing. I called all the new men together and explained to them the circumstances that made the meeting necessary. We were over-manned, I said, and this meant a shortage of food and clothing. Not a dangerous shortage; with careful husbanding and thrift we could get by; but it would mean discomfort. Quarters, too, would be crowded.

"You are in no wise to blame for this," I concluded. "The fault is largely ours. If you find this prospect displeasing and more than you bargained for—if you wish to be returned to Wellington, that action will be taken. Will those men who wish to return please step forward?"

Nobody stirred. If a man had moved one of our most successful operations would have been extinguished at the start. The time lost in returning to port would have ruined all hope of an extended operation in the Pacific quadrant.

"All right," I said. "That finishes it."

The incident had an amusing sequel. A couple of days later Captain English, who had just put out of Tahiti, radioed: "Have just found two stowaways

347

aboard. Please send instructions." I replied: "Suggest you return and try to recruit another. We're one up on you."

The ship's company now numbered ninety-five men, and with quarters originally intended for scarcely a third that number congestion was inevitable. Men alternated watches in order to share bunks. Later on, when the weather turned colder, I saw men coming off watch turn over heavy coats to their reliefs. A dozen new bunks, makeshift affairs, were hastily built on the shelter deck, across from the cows. There was little comfort and more than a little hardship, but the newcomers took it in a commendable spirit. It was a matter of share and share alike; and once the reasonableness of that philosophy permeated the crew all dissatisfaction disappeared. As for the stowaways, fairness compels me to say that the three of them—Pilcher, Christian and Wray—worked like dogs; instead of cursing them we were later to rejoice over the deception that brought them into the expedition.

Except for the discomfort involved, the increased man-power was really a blessing. With extra hands to work the ship it was possible, now, to relieve most of the prospective members of the Ice Party from routine ship's duties and turn them to the job of preparing for the problem of disembarkation in the Bay of Whales. The veterans of the first expedition, whose backs still ached with the memory of an earlier struggle, knew what the tenderfeet could never know without experience: that unloading would be a long, bitter nightmare, and that strategy and planning would save much grief later on.

The problem of organizing the disembarkation I turned over to "Vic" Czegka. This Marine warrant-officer, impatient, but with a gift for precision, knew what it was all about. He had been through the mill before. Czegka's job was to work out a practicable plan of unloading for any of several situations we were likely to meet in the Bay of Whales: and to supervise the reëstablishment of Little America as expeditiously as possible. Assigned to assist and cooperate with him were June, Haines and Innes-Taylor, all veterans of the first expedition, Executive Officer Noville and his assistant, Ken Rawson.

You see, we were devising means to overcome our problems thousands of miles before we came to them. Often we were wrong. Often, too, in this as in similar problems, we spent uncounted hours discussing contingencies that never arose and, in the casual run of things, were hardly likely to arise. But at least we always knew what we were up against and were prepared for the worst. If I have any philosophy at all about polar exploration it flows from this sense of empirical experimentation. A Micawber is soon brought up hard in the polar regions.

The readiness with which the ship shook down after putting out from Wellington was gratifying. Usually, after a long stay in port and especially after the infusion of new blood, a crew is backward about falling into a smooth routine. Instead, the life of the ship moved smartly from the first; and except for the clipped English accents and Cockney twang echoing unfamiliarly in the passageways and the "good-o's" and "right-o's" that responded to an order, the New Zealanders melted easily into the organization. We liked them, and I think they liked us. Two New Zealanders—First Officer Bayne and Second Officer Dempster—were on the bridge.

In the various reaches of the ship a great deal of work, apart from the routine activities of the ship's crew, was gathering speed. Czegka and Ronne were hurrying to finish the assembly of sledges required for unloading operations. On the shelter deck Tinglof was constructing from stock lumber a dozen heavy tractor sledges—heavy, rigid affairs intended to carry loads of several tons. Captain Innes-Taylor and his dog department were putting their gear in order for the punishing grind of hauling cargo into Little America. Cox was building a portable cow barn in No. 3 hold. Up forward in the fo'c's'le, "Sails" Kennedy and Dr. Shirey were busy over the sewing machines, turning out large quantities of windproof clothing, trail tents of various designs, and thousands of orange trail flags fitted to slender bamboo strips. Supply Officer Corey, who was responsible for all general expedition stores, and his assistants were segregating, checking and marking the supplies earmarked for Little America, to facilitate the movement from the ship. These and other related jobs left no time for idleness.

My diary reports:

Wed., Dec. 13, 9:50 P.M.

Noon position: Lat 45°05'S., Long. 177° 43'E. A heavy fog closed in during the middle watch this morning, and visibility was reduced to half a ship's length. Nevertheless, being well out of the steamer lanes, we are running at full speed. The air is calm and considerably colder. At noon mess Commodore Gjertsen remarked that it has the look of "iceberg weather." It's hardly likely that we should encounter bergs this far north, but to be on the safe side lookouts were stationed in the eyes of the ship. Supply officer Corey is issuing heavy clothing to all men on watch.

We lost our seventh dog today—Watch. He died of strangulation—fell, unobserved, over the side and strangled in his collar. Innes-Taylor, Dane and Moody worked over his body for an hour, but couldn't save him. It is always a tragedy to lose a good dog, but no blame attaches in a case like this. I can't praise the dog department too highly. The mortality rate among the dogs has been surprisingly low—only 7 out of 153. We had expected to lose upwards of twenty percent in the tropics.

Course was laid to fetch us up in the vicinity of the intersection of the Antarctic Circle and the 150th meridian west, where we planned to launch our first attack. Except for the fog the Roaring Forties were good to us. The sea was calm as a millpond. The more sensitive landlubbers began to take heart; at the mess tables there were sly speculations that the infamous reputation of these seas was just a conspiracy contrived by explorers.

"Didn't I promise you fellows a calm voyage!" Captain Verleger roared. "Eighteen years I've sailed the seas, and never had a storm. If you stick with me, you'll never have to feed the goldfish."

Bill Haines had been eyeing the barometer. He chuckled softly. "Maybe so, Captain. But I figure that before long you're going to miss a lot of familiar faces at this table."

On our second Thursday December 14th (having again crossed the 180th meridian, we recovered the day lost on December 3rd), the crew got a taste of the strength within these seas. A heaving sea, with an irregular beam swell, set the ship to rolling heavily. We took spray over the decks. Though the sun came through dimly for a few hours during the late afternoon, the fog still held, and during the night watches we were obliged to reduce speed to slow and half. In addition to the routine lookouts stationed on the bridge, two iceberg lookouts, one to port and one to starboard, were assigned to the fo'c's'le, with a bell at hand and certain signals for the bridge. One bell meant iceberg to starboard, two to port, and three dead ahead. As another precaution, the engine room now made hourly reports to the bridge on sea water temperature, an excellent indicator of the presence of the cold current bearing bergs northward.

Fri., Dec. 15, 11:40 P.M.

Noon position: Lat. 55° 91' S., Long. 172° 27' W. Day's run (noon to noon 243 miles, the best since leaving port. Moderate south-south-westerly swell: sky still overcast, with furred gray clouds. Light north-westerly winds, which are easing us along.

Again and again, it is impressed upon me that an especially indulgent Providence must watch over the destinies of a polar expedition. For a voyage toward the South Pole is paved with the good intentions of land-lubbers. Without a sense of humor I'd be a nervous wreck.

Last night Noville went forward to relieve Paige on iceberg lookout. "Where's the bell?" Noville asked, being unable to find it in the dark. "Right here, sir," said the artist, and promptly struck one bell. Up on the bridge the officer on watch slammed the telegraph to stop, and then bellowed for more information while Noville desperately tried to signal him with a flashlight that it was just a case of artistic license. It took a long time to get that straightened out.

Yesterday a new lookout on the bridge made the same sort of mistake. Toying with the cord, he accidentally struck one bell. Thinking quickly, he glanced at his watch, saw that it was nearly six-thirty, and brightly added four bells. But instead of striking them with nautical crispness and a right respect for spacing, he hammered them out in a way that sounded like a general alarm.

. . . Just now one of my most difficult jobs is to impress upon all hands the absolute need for economy. Men can't seem to get it into their heads that everything we have is limited; and that where we're going there'll be no chance for replacement. The stores allocated for the Ice Party have been segregated and plainly identified; the stern unwritten law of the expedition is that these stores shall not be touched, notwithstanding which I discovered today that several boxes had been broken into. It has been necessary to discipline one man for broaching cargo.

The other day a scientist tossed a piece of scrap lumber overboard. Czegka happened to see him do it. "Maybe you wouldn't have been so hasty," the veteran observed, "if you stopped to realize that it would take you a hundred thousand years to grow a piece of wood that size at Little America."

As we pressed southeast I was impressed anew by the profusion of pelagic life in higher southern latitudes, in contrast with the barrenness of the Pacific crossing. From the invisible reaches of these vast wastes of water the ship attracted a whole world of flying life, which it carried along with it. Black-browed albatross, Cape pigeons, white-faced storm petrels, Mother Carey's chickens and fulmars, darting and soaring like clouds of aircraft, hung about the ship, cheerfully joining their errand with its own. Occasionally we over-took small schools of blue penguins, which porpoised out of our path like frightened rabbits. And from time to time we sighted whales.

The fog was somewhat disquieting. We were still in it on the 16th, twelve hundred miles southeast of Wellington. Sometimes it would lift a bit for a few hours, then shut in again, thick as wool. The telegraph moved fretfully from full speed, to half, then slow, then back again to half and full. Commodore Gjertsen and Captain Verleger were constantly on the bridge. Decks, spars and rigging dripped with oozing moisture, and the dogs, hating wet, laid back their ears and whined, night and day.

Sat., Dec. 16, 9:10 P.M.

A bit of excitement last night—a flare-back in the fire box of the midships boiler. The ship trembled with the shock. Colombo, who was standing near the fire box, just escaped being caught by the mass of flame that gushed out. The worst thing was that a shower of sparks from the funnel fell about the *William Horlick*, and several small holes were burned in the fabric. I'm really afraid of the plane catching fire. At rather frequent intervals the engine room is obliged to blow tubes, and the plane consequently is doused with small sparks raining down from the stack. The officers on watch have been instructed to alter course while this is going on, if necessary, so as to bring the wind on the beam, and carry the sparks clear of the plane.

. . . The wind, still holding in the northwest, is rising, flicking spray from the waves. Barometer dropping fast—from a bulge of 29.84 inches at noon, yesterday, it had dropped to 28.82 inches this afternoon. It's still dropping. Though a drop of this magnitude would mean hurricane warnings in lower latitudes, it very often means nothing here.

However, the rising agitation of the sea points to dirty weather. Exclaiming that it was indecent to keep such a thing in plain view, the less tranquil diners tonight draped the barograph on the sideboard with a black cloth.

We're only several days' steaming from the Midnight Sun; so there are just a few hours of twilight now. This evening the air cleared with great suddenness, and we had a rare taste of sunlight.

Sun, Dec. 17, Midnight.

We're in for it now. Having blithely passed through the Forties and Fifties, we've poked our bow against a wind of close to hurricane force on the threshold of the Sixties. The log dismisses it as a gale, but the aviators tell me that gusts of wind registered a velocity of seventy knots on the Condor's air speed indicator. In all events, we've had our baptism in the elements for which these latitudes are celebrated, and tonight we're lucky to have the plane and dogs intact.

In the wake of the spectacular barometric dip, the storm built up rapidly. The first squalls hit us shortly after midnight. The wind rose violently in the northwest, almost dead astern. The ship made heavy going of it, with the propeller lifting clear and thrashing wildly as the seas tossed the stern. Were it not for the plane, we might have run before it: but being wholly unprotected from following winds, the plane took a bad beating.

Shortly after seven o'clock, after all hands were called, things started to happen fast. The plane, rising and falling on its timbered pedestal, was trembling under the lash of the wind and the strain of the pitch and roll. The ailerons and flippers, which had been set at neutral, were vibrating wildly. There was only one thing to do: to round the ship into the wind and give the plane what little lee the midships boat deck offered. This meant bringing her over into the trough of the seas, a risky and difficult maneuver.

As the ship started around the aviation gang fell to the task of securing the plane. By that time the aileron battens and lashings had been carried away and the control surfaces were all oscillating dangerously. Bowlin, Swan, Smith, McCormick, Schlossbach and Demas now swarmed aboard the plane and struggled to pass wide strips of canvas tape around the wings, to hold the ailerons fast. It was a mean job. Footing was insecure, hail and snow drove into their faces, wind tore at their clothing, and below them green water creamed over the deck. With one hand they clung on, and with the other worked the canvas and lashings around. Once Swan was spun off his feet by a stiff gust and for seconds hung by one hand from a wire before somebody hauled him onto the wing. Three times the deck force assisting them was caught by boarding seas, and sent flying across the deck, before they grabbed something handy.

One wave lifted a dozen dog crates on the starboard side and swept them, dogs and all, clear to the port rail. Innes-Taylor, Buckley, Wade, Paine and Russell, who were on watch, dived in and made them fast before a second wave carried them overboard. Herb, a big Manitoba, who was chained to the deck, was washed over the side. Somebody saw him just in time and hauled him back. The dogs really had a fearful day. I pitied them.

After a long struggle, we finally got the ship headed into the wind, and the danger abated. For two hours we had our bow pointed toward New Zealand. When, in the forenoon, the storm worked into the west, then into the southwest, we followed it round, holding the ship in the wind. This afternoon a short lull came, which was broken by savage squalls. Now the wind is rising again. The sea has a wild aspect. The wind is like a solid force, ripping spray from the waves before they break; and black wind shadows, like cats' paws, rake the sea where they strike. Above the crash of the seas the vibrating flying wires of the plane make a deep, sonorous, thrumming note, like the sound of a plane in flight.

The barometer, having touched a low of 28.26 inches this morning, is rising fast. . . .

Mon., Dec. 18, 10:30 P.M.

The gale blew itself out during the night, and at noon today we resumed our course, with the engines at full speed. The wind has dropped to a fresh breeze, and the seas have moderated. Our noon position was Lat. 61° 29' S., Long 162° 06'W., which put us only 439 miles from the intersection of the Antarctic Circle and the 150th meridian West.

It's getting colder. The air temperature has dropped to 31°, and the sea temperature to 33°. This morning all winches were started, and from now on they will turn slowly all day and all night. It's the best way to prevent them from freezing. Most of the asbestos lagging so patiently wound around the steam lines was washed away yesterday. Ice is already forming on the spars and rigging.

Blue sky this afternoon, and in the evening, the sun leapt through the cloud wrack. A good omen. Tomorrow, unless we are stopped by pack, we shall surpass Cook's southing. We're lucky not to have met ice before this.

Tuesday, December 19th, was a notable day. On this day we raised our first icebergs in the early watch; we broke past Cook's tracks for a new record southing; and we celebrated the arrival of Iceberg, Klondike's bull calf. The first event was an incident, the second a creditable achievement, and the third (though Messrs. Clark and Cox, who had Klondike's destiny in hand, were disinclined to see it that way) was an event over which we had no control.

Say what you will, but of all the natural beauties of the world there can be few lovelier and more stirring to the contemplative traveler than his first glimpse of true Antarctic tabular icebergs. They are something apart, something incredibly unreal, yet so perfectly and instinctively appropriate within their setting that you are moved to exclaim: here is an ultimate definition! It is so meaningless to call them sentinels. They are much more than that. They are mobile extensions of the Antarctic itself, stately white caravels afloat on a painted sea; a sky-filling architecture schemed and wrought by Nature from the marble quarries of the Ice Age. On some we saw the whole of Manhattan could have been disposed, even to its subways. Beyond the rose-flaming horizon lay the undiscovered coast from which the glacial pressures piling up from behind, and the tidal movements working from below, had wrenched these bergs. Now, in the persuasive sway of submarine currents, they drifted softly toward extinction. In these waste waters sailed a doomed fleet, the fairest that ever put to sea.

Dick Russell, on lookout, sighted the first iceberg. At 1:25 A.M., he raised the cry: "Berg on the port bow!" A moment later half a dozen more lifted frosted domes above the horizon. Soon the sea was crowded with them. Two hundred were counted in view at one time: and, at the speed we were making, we were raising a new horizon every hour. The largest was perhaps four miles long and three miles wide. Later on, in the Devil's graveyard, we were to steam past mountains of ice that would make these bergs seem mere cream puffs. But these claimed our awe now.

The day broke beautifully—a lovely golden panel of light pushing through softly furred, gray cumulus clouds. The air stirred under a light, variable westerly wind; the sea was choppy. In the fractured sides of the bergs, in the grottoes and caves worn at their water line, were strange, rich blues, pale delicate greens, and weathered yellows and grays. The sea surged over their submerged spurs, and exploded in shining puffs of surf. The scene was a study in magic. Wherever you looked it faithfully and uncannily reflected whatever phantasy with which you invested it. You could see white sailing ships, with towering canvas set, standing out to sea: you could see turreted castles of fabulous architecture, enormous battlements, steepled and gabled structures cunningly wrought by the weathering hands of wind and sea. One was like a battleship down by the stern, its bow tilted crazily toward the sky, its crumpled upper works strewn across the deck. Another was a breathless reproduction of the Colosseum, weathered and decaying, with three perfectly formed arches, two hundred feet high, through the portals of which the sea surged boisterously. There was beauty there of a rare and infinitely varied pattern.

But we had a job to do, and no time for thumbing Baedeker. We pressed past these shining structures at top speed, steering various courses to pass among them. At 8:30 P.M., at Lat. 65° S., Long. 153° 32'W, our observations indicated that we had surpassed Cook's southing: that we were at last on the rim of the unknown sea. One hundred and fifty years had passed since a keel had furrowed these blue waters. Instinctively my eyes sought the southern horizon for the yellow-white effulgence of ice blink. No, still a water sky. For a while at least the road south lay open.

But the significance of geographical discovery, I must confess, was largely lost upon the expedition. Almost to a man the crew waited with breathless expectancy for an event which has been common in Nature since the world began. Klondike, one of the Guernsey cows, was about to—well, let's go back to the beginning. When Klondike came aboard at Newport News, she was already in that state which columnists no longer describe as "an interesting condition." In fact, I suspect that this was her outstanding claim to preference, and I suspect, also, there had been some sly counting on the fingers, too.

Anyhow, Cox and Clark were unaccountably eager to have the calf born within the Antarctic Circle. It appears that they had a sublimely confident understanding to that effect with The Guernsey Cattle Club. A calf born in these frosty latitudes, they reasoned, would have a unique claim to immortality. December 19th had been fixed as the date, at which time Cox, Clark and the whole palpitating constituency of The Guernsey Cattle Club calculated the expedition would be well within the Circle. They made the fatal mistake of not reckoning on Klondike.

Nor on the fog, either. As the days wore on the countenances of Cox and Clark grew haggard; they studied the log, scanned the noon positions, checked the day's run, watched the sky for ice blink, consulted the skipper. On the 19th they were up all night. Captain Verleger came upon them on the shelter deck.

"How far from the Circle now?" Cox asked, huskily.

"Three hundred miles," said the skipper, "and if you want that calf born within the Circle, my advice is to borrow the plane and fly the cow across, because it looks to me as if Klondike ain't goin' to wait for mere latitude."

The hours passed, and Cox and Clark breathed easier. They tiptoed topside for a look at the bergs. Suddenly a shout flew over the ship.

Klondike had declined to wait for destiny.

With eleven thousand miles of voyaging behind her, the frost in the air assured her that her journey was about run; and not caring to quibble about a few degrees of latitude, she quietly and definitely achieved the everlasting duty of her sex.

An immediate dead reckoning placed the event just 247 nautical miles north of the Circle. A suggestion from the news correspondent that in view of the peculiar circumstances surrounding the event, the calf be named "Caught Short," was violently resisted. Iceberg it was named.

Shortly before midnight, just after the sun set for the last time, we marked the creamy glow of ice blink on the southern horizon. That meant pack ahead. The bergs were thinning out. The ship was running south-southeast. At 6:30 A.M., December 20th, Lat. 65° 55' S., Long. 151° 10'W., 35 miles north of the Circle, we fetched up against the northern rim of the pack. Great fields of loose, pancake ice curved irregularly to the east and west. Southward they extended to the limit of vision. It looked none too promising; neither did it look too bad.

With Commodore Gjertsen on the bridge, giving quick commands to the helmsman, we worked eastward through scattered floes, looking for a feasible passage. Remember, we had an old iron ship which for years had lain unused in a government graveyard. Her plates were only seven-eighths of an inch thick; they were rusty, and there was no telling how much of a strain her rivets could withstand. We went cautiously, side-stepping the heavier floes.

At 8:20 we paused for a manual sounding. A successful sounding would give us a hint of the nearness or remoteness of the undiscovered coast to the south. No bottom at 300 fathoms. We broke through patches of light, new ice. At 9:30 another sounding. No bottom at 300 fathoms. A ribbon of black water unrolled before our bow, and we took a southerly heading through the pack.

It was really exciting. Past the rim of geographical discovery, we felt our way forward, scanning the radiant horizon for the secrets it might at any moment yield. Above the gray flooring of the pack a white cliff, seeming without end, slowly emerged. "Barrier coast," sang out the man in the crow's nest. But he was wrong. Twenty minutes later we marked sky on either side: just a berg. About ten o'clock another monstrous ice structure tempted us. We altered course to approach it, crunching through fairly heavy ice at slow speed. This time I was taken in. For a long time that gleaming dome, with its sheer cliffs, held a tantalizing promise. But what was that odd peak sticking up behind it? Of course. Just two bergs, seven miles, maybe eight miles long.

Disappointed, we stood away. The ship zig-zagged down narrow leads, holding to the south. On a small floe the first Antarctic seal, a Crab-Eater, raised his head resentfully as the swell from the ship disturbed his sanctuary, stared hard with bloodshot eyes, then promptly rolled back on his belly. Flights of snowy petrels, white as the snow against which they flew, were precipitated out of the sky and flickered tirelessly about the ship. Still, it was wonderfully quiet. The pack heaved on a gentle swell, grating ever so slightly, with a sound like that of branches rubbing together in a forest. The ice yielded and parted before the ship's forefoot, and slipped, hissing, with soft protests, along the plates. Otherwise it was utterly peaceful.

By mid-afternoon it was evident that the ice massing in front of us was too heavy to be taken by assault. The ship inched through heavier, older ice. The shocks of impact came more frequently; several times, when we struck masses of hard, blue-green ice, the *Ruppert* trembled the length of her keel. Down in the engine room you could hear the hollow sound of the ice banging against the plates.

Commodore Gjertsen shook his head. "She's an old ship," he reminded us. "It's not as if you had a wooden ship, built for ice. Her plates won't stand much punishment. All we have to do is sheer off a couple of rivets. . . ."

The ship was virtually blocked, though we continued to struggle on for a few hours more. There is no sense battering your heads against a stone wall, not if you can vault it. Bill Haines, wise in the lore of Antarctic weather, was appraising the wind, studying the barometer. At six o'clock that evening he came into my cabin.

"The barometer has leveled off, and the wind is in the south," he said. "Looks as if it's going to be pretty good flying weather."

So we made ready to fit the second string to our bow.

Shortly after six, at Lat. 67° 09' S., Long. 148° 00' W., we turned. On her own hook the *Ruppert* had exceeded Cook's penetration by 148 statute miles. It was up to aviation to renew the assault.

U.S.S. *Skate* Surfaces at North Pole

by JAMES CALVERT

After supper we submerged and once more headed for the Pole, now less than 250 miles away. A night of travel under the ice covered the distance and on the morning of the seventeenth we were nearing our destination.

When we reached the Pole we would start a slow crisscrossing search of the immediate vicinity. If nothing showed up at first, we would be patient and keep searching. The ice cover was constantly shifting, and the new ice coming over might be better. Assuming the ice was moving at 2½ miles a day (an average speed), in twenty-four hours 5000 yards of ice would drift over the North Pole. In that stretch we might be able to find what we wanted.

The test would not be without military value. After we returned from the Arctic in the fall of 1958, many senior officers wanted to know what our chances were of surfacing at a given geographic location in the Arctic—not a place like Drift Station Alfa, which shifted with the ice, but an assigned latitude and longitude. Well, we would see.

At the breakfast table the talk was, as usual, of ice. We began discussing the clumsiness of our name for these areas of thin ice which were so vital to us. Actually they were newly frozen leads but that seemed an awkward way to put it. What we needed was a new name. Many were suggested but none seemed to convey the idea. Then Dr. Lyon, who had heard me discussing what they looked like through the periscope, said, "Why don't you just call them skylights?"

And that's what they resembled. They were like a stretch of blue-green translucent glass in an otherwise black ceiling. The places where the ice was thin enough to let in the light to the dark sea below were the places we were looking for to reach the light and air above. *Skylights* they would be.

But we found no skylights as we approached the Pole. We cruised slowly, adjusting our course carefully according to the instructions of Bill Layman. Zane Sandusky and Bob Wadell methodically plotted the readings from their green tubes on reams of orange graph paper. Slowly but surely, the submarine was delicately conned into the spot where every direction is south. The *Skate* had returned to the Pole.

I made a brief announcement to the crew, reminding them of something most of them already knew—that almost exactly fifty years ago (it had been April 6, 1909) Robert Peary had first reached the Pole. How different his circumstances from ours! Accompanied by four Eskimos and his steward,

Matt Henson, Peary had had no scientific marvels to guide him to his goal. He measured distance traveled with a crude wheel attached to one of the sledges. His determination of position was by observation of the sun—and this depended partially on a timepiece that had gone for weeks without an accurate check. But Peary had known what he was about. After he had reached the Pole, according to his best navigation, he spent thirty hours marching and countermarching around the general area to make certain he had achieved his goal. He had spent twenty years of his life in its quest and had no desire to miss it by a few miles through miscalculation. When he was certain he had located the Pole as well as his limited equipment would allow, he planted his flags and took his pictures. And then, in a few hours, the drifting ice of the Arctic had carried his flags away from the Pole. The shifting signs of fame!

Our task still lay ahead of us. Thanks to the marvels of inertial navigation, we had reached the Pole with little difficulty. Reaching the surface would be a different matter—that would be up to us.

There was not a sign of a skylight. With the ship stopped 200 feet under the sea directly at the North Pole, I raised the periscope in the hope of seeing something. But the sea was black—absolutely and completely. Not the faintest glimmer shone through the ice above; we were sealed in.

We began our crisscross search in the immediate area, proceeding at a very slow speed and using the periscope as well as the ice detector and the television. No luck.

Here at the Pole the sun would still be below the horizon; if the overcast were as heavy as the day before, there wouldn't be much light anyway. Well, I thought, we'd just have to wait and see. Several hours went by with no results.

And then we saw it. At first it was just a faint glimmer of emerald green, visible only through the periscope. It looked too small for the ship, but it was worth investigating. Carefully we maneuvered the *Skate* under it and looked at our ice detector. The trace showed thin ice.

This was a different game from that of last summer, when we made long leisurely loops under lakes, taking care to get ourselves safely in the middle of a relatively large piece of open water. Here, trying to surface at a pre-chosen spot in winter, we had to be satisfied with a patch of thin ice scarcely large enough to hold us. No need to maneuver the ship beneath it to plot its shape— it was so small we could see the whole area at a glance through the periscope, outlined sharply by the black floes around it. At the same time, we would simply not have had the courage or skill to try such a dangerous and delicate task without the confidence that had come of last summer's experience.

We drifted up to 100 feet. The skylight was dog-legged in shape and treacherously small; we had never attempted anything like this. However, I knew that if we could once break through the ice above us the *Skate* would be held as tightly as in a vise. There would be no danger of damage from drifting into the sides of the small opening.

"Stand by to hit the ice," I said. "Bring her up."

We had barely started up again when Al Kelln, standing at the ice detector, called out nervously, "Heavy ice overhead—better than twelve feet!"

I could see what had happened. The ice was moving, and the skylight was simply drifting away from the submarine.

"Flood her down, Guy!" I said. Reluctantly the three-thousand-ton ship reversed her course and began to sink slowly back into the black depths. Patiently we realigned the ship under the small opening, twisting first one way and then the other with the propellers.

The second try was no better than the first; again we drifted out from under the tiny skylight.

"We'd better try an offset," said Bill. He quickly calculated how far to the side we should position ourselves in order to come up from 100 feet and find ourselves in the right position. Painstakingly the *Skate* was maneuvered into position.

This time, as we started upward, Kelln told us that we had heavy ice overhead. Not a very comfortable feeling, with the top of the sail only 50 feet or so below the ice, but we could only count on the drift to carry us into position.

As we rose, I was forced to lower the periscope. Now we were blind except for the television camera, which showed only the fuzzy edge of the heavy ice.

Now the top of the sail was only 25 feet under the heavy ice. "Heavy ice, still heavy ice," Kelln reported, the strain apparent in his voice. How much longer can we wait?

"Flood her down—emergency!" I snapped. We could wait no longer. The wave of air pressure slapped into my ears as Shaffer opened the vent of the negative tank and sent tons of water cascading into the ship to bring her down. Quickly we fell away from the ominous ice cliffs.

"Blow negative to the mark," Shaffer ordered, trying to regain control of the now swiftly falling *Skate*. The roar of high-pressure air filled the room.

"Blow secured; negative at the mark," reported Chief Dornberg at his side.

"Shut the flood, vent negative, pump from auxiliaries to sea," said Guy, watching his gauges through narrowed eyes.

Slowly our downward momentum slackened and finally, far deeper than we had intended to go, we were once more motionless.

Beads of perspiration were standing out on my brow and I could sense the feeling of strain that ran through the ship. With grim determination, we started all over again.

"There are heavy pressure ridges on either side of this opening except at the dog-leg corner," reported Al Kelln. "I've had a chance to catch them on the ice detector."

Once more Bill Layman calculated the offset required, this time allowing for a little less drift.

I attempted to set the ship near the corner of the dog-leg to avoid the ridges Al had mentioned. The whir of the trimming pump announced our slow ascent.

"Heavy ice, still heavy ice," intoned Kelln like the voice of doom. Time for the periscope to go down.

"Thin ice! There she is! Looks good!" exclaimed Al.

The television screen showed us very close. We braced ourselves. With a sickening lurch we hit and broke through.

"Don't let her drop out, Guy," I warned. Again I had the feeling of having a tenuous foothold at the top of an impossible peak.

Shaffer put a puff of air into the ballast tanks; we seemed to be maintaining our position. I raised the periscope on the chance of seeing something; I was most reluctant to surface blind when I knew heavy pressure ridges were close by.

The periscope went up, but revealed nothing but a field of blank white. Frozen.

I glanced at the diving instruments; we were holding our position well. If we could break through, we would make history.

"Stand by to surface at the Pole," I announced over the speaker system.

Swiftly preparations were made, and Shaffer turned to me with a smile, "Ready to surface," he said, "at the Pole!"

Slowly we blew the tanks and the *Skate* moved reluctantly upward. It was apparent we were under heavier ice here than any we had experienced before. After what seemed an eternity of delay, the upper hatch was far enough above the ice to be opened. Our tenuous foothold was becoming more firm.

"Open the hatch!" I shouted, and raced up the ladder. The ice we had broken was so heavy that it had not fallen into the bridge but had split and fallen outside. I leaped to the bridge and was struck by the first heavy wind I had ever experienced in the Arctic. It howled and swirled across the open bridge, carrying stinging snow particles which cut like flying sand. Heavy gray clouds hung in the sky; the impression was of a dark and stormy twilight about to fade into night.

We had broken through almost exactly at the bend of the dog-leg. The lead was narrow and heavily hummocked on either side, wandering into the blowing snow like a meandering creek for the quarter of a mile or so I could see. These hummocks were the tallest we had yet seen in the Arctic—we later estimated their height at 18 feet.

Although we were closer to one side of the narrow lead than I would have liked, we seemed to have a clear path in which to surface the rest of the way. Only our sail protruded from the ice, but the ship was held tightly—there was no chance of drifting.

The phones were rigged and the tanks blown with high-pressure air. With loud cracks that sounded like gunshots, the deck began to break through. This lead had frozen with many large chunks of heavier ice floating in it. They were now caught in the matrix of the thinner ice like almonds in chocolate.

Finally the *Skate* lay on the surface—the first ship in history to sit at the very top of the world. In every direction—ahead, astern, to port, to starboard—was south. The planet turned ponderously beneath us. When the sun rose on March 19, just two days away, it would swing around the horizon for twenty-four hours in a perpetual sunrise.

The *Skate* had arrived at her goal. Last summer's attainment of the Pole had brought little satisfaction because we had been forced to remain submerged where, for all the difference it made to us, we could have been anywhere else in the oceans of the world. Only our instruments had told us we were there.

But this—with its blowing snow and lowering sky—this was the North Pole. The lodestone of the Arctic, which had lured brave men to their deaths for over a century and which had even been denied to the indomitable Nansen, had fallen to the modern submarine.

Sea Life

The Midshipman

by FREDERICK MARRYAT

The weather side of the quarter-deck of H.M. frigate Unicorn was occupied by two very great personages: Captain Plumbton, commanding the ship; who was very great in width if not in height, taking much more than his allowance of the deck, if it were not that he was the proprietor thereof, and entitled to the lion's share. Captain P. was not more than four feet ten inches in height; but then he was equal to that in girt: there was quite enough of him, if he had only been *rolled out*. He walked with his coat flying open, his thumbs stuck into the armholes of his waistcoat, so as to throw his shoulders back and increase his horizontal dimensions. He also held his head well aft, which threw his chest and stomach well forward. He was the prototype of pomposity and good-nature, and he strutted like an actor in a procession.

The other personage was the first lieutenant, whom nature had pleased to fashion in another mould. He was as tall as the captain was short—as thin as his superior was corpulent. His long, lanky legs were nearly up to the captain's shoulders; and he bowed down over the head of his superior as if he were the crane to hoist up, and the captain the bale of goods to be hoisted. He carried his hands behind his back, with two fingers twisted together: and his chief difficulty appeared to be to reduce his own stride to the parrot march of the captain. His features were sharp and lean as was his body, and wore every appearance of a crossgrained temper.

He had been making divers complaints of divers persons, and the captain had hitherto appeared imperturbable. Captain Plumbton was an even-tempered man, who was satisfied with a good dinner. Lieutenant Markitall was an odd-tempered man, who would quarrel with his bread and butter.

"Quite impossible, sir," continued the first lieutenant, "to carry on the duty without support."

This oracular observation, which, from the relative forms of the two parties, descended, as it were, from above, was replied to by the captain with a "Very true."

"Then, sir, I presume you will not object to my putting that man in the report for punishment."

"I'll think about it, Mr. Markitall." This, with Captain Plumbton, was as much as to say, no.

"The young gentlemen, sir, I am sorry to say, are very troublesome."

"Boys always are," replied the captain.

365

"Yes, sir; but the duty must be carried on, and I cannot do without them."

"Very true—midshipmen are very useful."

"But I'm sorry to say, sir, that they are not. Now, sir, there's Mr. Templemore; I can do nothing with him—he does nothing but laugh."

"Laugh!—Mr. Markitall, does he laugh at you?"

"Not exactly, sir; but he laughs at everything. If I send him to the masthead, he goes up laughing: if I call him down, he comes down laughing; if I find fault with him, he laughs the next minute: in fact, sir, he does nothing but laugh. I should particularly wish, sir, that you would speak to him, and see if any interference on your part—"

"Would make him cry—eh? Better to laugh than cry in this world. Does he never cry, Mr. Markitall?"

"Yes, sir, and very unseasonably. The other day, you may recollect, when you punished Wilson the marine, whom I appointed to take care of his chest and hammock, he was crying the whole time; almost tantamount—at least an indirect species of mutiny on his part, as it implied—"

"That the boy was sorry that his servant was punished; I never flog a man but I am sorry myself, Mr. Markitall."

"Well, I do not press the question of his crying—that I might look over; but his laughing, sir, I must beg that you will take notice of that. Here he is, sir, coming up the hatchway. Mr. Templemore, the captain wishes to speak to you."

Now, the captain did not wish to speak to him, but, forced upon him as it was by the first lieutenant, he could do no less. So Mr. Templemore touched his hat, and stood before the captain, we regret to say, with such a good-humored, sly, confiding smirk on his countenance, as at once established the proof of the accusation, and the enormity of the offence.

"So, sir," said Captain Plumbton, stopping in his perambulation, and squaring his shoulders still more, "I find that you laugh at the first lieutenant."

"I, sir?" replied the boy, the smirk expanding into a broad grin.

"Yes, you, sir," said the first lieutenant, now drawing up to his full height; "why, you're laughing now, sir."

"I can't help it, sir—it's not my fault; and I'm sure it's not yours, sir," added the boy, demurely.

"Are you aware, Edward—Mr. Templemore, I mean—of the impropriety of disrespect to your superior officer?"

"I never laughed at Mr. Markitall but once, sir, that I can recollect, and that was when he tumbled over the messenger."

"And why did you laugh at him then, sir?"

"I always do laugh when any one tumbles down," replied the lad; "I can't help it, sir."

"Then, sir, I suppose you would laugh if you saw me rolling in the lee scuppers?" said the captain.

"Oh!" replied the boy, no longer able to contain himself, "I'm sure I should burst myself with laughing—I think I see you now, sir."

"Do you, indeed! I'm very glad that you do not; though I'm afraid, young gentlemen, you stand convicted by your own confession."

"Yes, sir, of laughing, if that is any crime; but it's not in the articles of war."

"No, sir; but disrespect is. You laugh when you go to the mast-head."

"But I obey the order, sir, immediately—do I not, Mr. Markitall?"

"Yes, sir, you obey the order; but, at the same time, your laughing proves that you do not mind the punishment."

"No more I do, sir. I spend half my life at the mast-head, and I'm used to it now."

"But, Mr. Templemore, ought you not to feel the disgrace of the punishment?" inquired the captain, severely.

"Yes, sir, if I felt that I deserved it, I should. I should not laugh, sir, if *you* sent me to the mast-head," replied the boy, assuming a serious countenance.

"You see, Mr. Markitall, that he can be grave," observed the captain.

"I've tried all I can to make him so, sir," replied the first lieutenant; "but I wish to ask Mr. Templemore what he means to imply by saying, 'when he deserves it.' Does he mean to say that I have ever punished him unjustly?"

"Yes, sir," replied the boy, boldly; "five times out of six, I am mast-headed for nothing—and that's the reason why I do not mind it."

"For nothing, sir! Do you call laughing nothing?"

"I pay every attention that I can to my duty, sir; I always obey your orders; I try all I can to make you pleased with me—but you are always punishing me."

"Yes, sir, for laughing, and, what is worse, making the ship's company laugh."

"They 'haul and hold' just the same, sir—I think they work all the better for being merry."

"And pray, sir, what business have you to think?" replied the first lieutenant, now very angry. "Captain Plumbton, as this young gentleman thinks proper to interfere with me and the discipline of the ship, I beg you will see what effect your punishing may have upon him."

"Mr. Templemore," said the captain, "you are, in the first place, too free in your speech, and, in the next place, too fond of laughing. There is, Mr. Templemore, a time for all things—a time to be merry, and a time to be serious. The quarter-deck is not the fit place for mirth."

"I'm sure the gangway is not," shrewdly interrupted the boy.

"No—you are right, nor the gangway; but you may laugh on the forecastle, and when below with your messmates."

"No, sir, we may not; Mr. Markitall always sends out if he hears us laughing."

"Because, Mr. Templemore, you are always laughing."

"I believe I am, sir; and if it's wrong I'm sorry to displease you, but I mean no disrespect. I laugh in my sleep—I laugh when I awake—I laugh when the sun shines—I always feel so happy; but although you do mast-head me, Mr. Markitall, I should not laugh, but be very sorry, if any misfortune happened to you."

"I believe you would, boy—I do, indeed, Mr. Markitall," said the captain.

"Well, sir," replied the first lieutenant, "as Mr. Templemore appears to be aware of his error, I do not wish to press my complaint—I have only to request that he will never laugh again."

"You hear, boy, what the first lieutenant says; it's very reasonable, and I beg I may hear no more complaints. Mr. Markitall, let me know when the foot of that foretopsail will be repaired—I should like to shift it to-night."

Mr. Markitall went down under the half-deck to make the inquiry.

"And, Edward," said Captain Plumbton, as soon as the lieutenant was out of earshot, "I have a good deal more to say to you upon this subject, but I have no time now. So come and dine with me—at my table, you know, I allow laughing in moderation."

The boy touched his hat, and with a grateful, happy countenance, walked away.

We have introduced this little scene, that the reader may form some idea of the character of Edward Templemore. He was, indeed, the soul of mirth, good-humor, and kindly feelings towards others; he even felt kindly towards the first lieutenant, who persecuted him for his risible propensities. We do not say that the boy was right in laughing at all times, or that the first lieutenant was wrong in attempting to check it. As the captain said, there is a time for all things, and Edward's laugh was not always seasonable; but it was his nature, and he could not help it. He was joyous as the May morning; and thus he continued for years, laughing at everything—pleased with everybody—almost universally liked—and his bold, free, and happy spirit, unchecked by vicissitude or hardship.

He served his time—was nearly turned back, when he was passing his examination, for laughing, and then went laughing to sea again—was in command of a boat at the cutting-out of a French corvette, and, when on board, was so much amused by the little French captain skipping about with his rapier, which proved fatal to many, that, at last, he received a pink from the little gentleman himself, which laid him on the deck. For this affair, and in consideration of his wound, he obtained his promotion to the rank of lieutenant—was appointed to a line-of-battle ship in the West Indies—laughed at the yellow fever—was appointed to the tender of that ship, a fine schooner, and was sent to cruise for prize money for the admiral, and promotion for himself, if he could, by any fortunate encounter, be so lucky as to obtain it.

Life in the Forecastle

by WILLIAM McFEE

It was a pleasant life, trading the wide world round, and the scenes came so rapidly before him that Hannibal felt the need of a readjustment in his mental process. No longer was it possible (and the change from mess-room to forecastle made the process imperative) to brood over the rich phantasmagoria of sea-life as he had brooded over the easy monotony of youth. When you are going to and fro across the Seven Seas, carrying coal to the Islands, loading oil in the West, taking sugar from Java to Germany, and salt from Germany to New York, your attitude towards the eternal verities becomes strained. You begin to understand the men about you, why they say continually that these things are nothing, and revolve on your own pivot. The ship takes on an importance you could not conceive before: her very vilenesses are dear to you. You become a part of her. You hear, in the night watches, her voice as she labors onward, the little intimate complaints of her fabric. And then, when in the forecastle you hear the incredible clangours of the chain-locker as the anchor plunges headlong to the mud of the harbour, it is to you more than the fall of empires, and the first look through the port is like the discovery of a new world.

So he changed, this young man from London, and into his eyes came the look of those who have seen the great distances. He grew lean and wiry and tanned, and a small black moustache, like a charcoal smear, came into being on his upper lip. The refinements of urban life, such as he had, fell from him, and his speech became supple with the *lingua franca* of the sea. He took his meals seated on a soap box, with the platters on his knee, and he learned the wisdom of eating from the middle of the kid, where a man's thumb cannot reach. He became, as is necessary in the forecastle, primeval, contracting his visible personality to a canvas bag and the boards on which he slept. Day and night disappeared from his view and he judged men and things by the middle-watch. Each night and noon he took his way along the fore-deck, under the stars or beneath a furnace sky, and descended into his appointed place. Here again were conditions astonishingly inimical to the conventions of the "Little Brown Box." He never forgot his first day, leaving sunny Las Palmas, in the bunkers. The Second had taken him down through the stokehold, where men stabbed furiously at burned-down fires, and great heaps of glowing clinker spattered and stank as water was flung over them, through a small door and up, up into blackness and pungent odours to where small yellow flames burned

369

smokily in the fog of a coal slide. He saw yawning openings in the decks into which he was to tumble barrow after barrow, openings into which he nearly tumbled himself once or twice. And he had been left there, with instructions to get a move on and keep it running. He had set to work in feverish fashion, shedding first the blue dungaree coat, then the shirt, and finally stripped to the skin, shovelling, shovelling, eyes and nose and mouth full of the acrid impalpable dust and the sweat making rivulets of white skin on his chest. He had gone at it bald-headed at first, after the manner of the tyro, and at two o'clock lay panting on the coal, too exhausted to climb up or down. The Second, crawling cat-like over the hummocks, found him and diagnosed the disease. "You won't last a week if you slog at it like that, man," he had said, his eyes gleaming in his soot-darkened face. "Take it steady, pitch-and-pitch. Like this," and taking the great square-mouthed shovel he drove it deep into the coal, swung it back and out with a long measured lunge and shot the mass, clean and solid, into the hole ten feet beyond. Hannibal watched him attentively, saw the sense of slow-moving persistence, and tried again. He got into the way of it in a day or two, and kept her running easily enough. And when the agonizing stiffness of biceps and thighs had worn away he even enjoyed it. It was fierce, but it was nearer being a man than anything he had ever experienced before. At first he had regretted the flesh-pots, and sighed on Thursday for the ham-and-eggs of the mess-room, but he soon discovered that the most important part of a meal was the pipe that followed. He had discarded his short stumpy briar, and divided his affections between a thick clay and a thin-stemmed corncob. He learned to cut up the sweet Boreen, paring it into his hand, rolling it with a slow circular motion, and packing it away skilfully into the bowl, wasting none of it. He would take his corncob up on the forecastle head after tea, which was his favourite time, and with his back against the windlass drum look out from under the low awning at the opal and turquoise of sea and sky. It was quiet up there, and he discovered the sense of separation that this gives, far away from the immediate tumult of the engine-room. Even in the bunkers he heard them but faintly, muffled throbs mingling with the scoop and rattle of the shovel, the croon of the dry barrow wheel, or the thunder of heavy lumps against the bulkheads. Up there he would sit and sometimes watch for Tommy. Half-way up the foremast was the crow's-nest, and after tea, if it was his watch, Tommy would climb up to the ladder and ensconce himself there for an hour, peering out across the level floors. Sometimes he would look down and grin at the sedate Hannibal puffing luxuriously under the awning. It was in this way that Hannibal learned the beginning of a story that had its ending the day before they reached Japan. The brown-bearded man with the bloodshot blue eyes who trimmed on the four-to-eight watch, and who slept in the bunk over Hannibal's used to join him at eight bells, and sweeping the kid clean with a crust, discourse upon life as he had found it. He was bitter concerning life, apparently, blaming it for many things, and bitterer concerning women. It was difficult to discover exactly what his grievance against them was, for from his own telling they had been kind to him

in a casual way, helping him in divers trouble, giving him money, and asking
naught but love in return. He was very proud of his power over women. They
would do anything for him, he said. It was possible, for women are foolish,
and he had the mobile mouth and unabashed eye that lures them to folly. And
yet he spoke of them with bitterness. They were all no good, except one, and
she was dead. Perhaps this was his grievance. She had died while he was away,
and her mother, the old hag! had demanded money to keep the child. That was
years ago, when he was young, and might have settled down. He had had every
intention of settling down if she had only lived. Of course, he only told his
own side of the story. He said nothing of his desertion of the woman. How was
he to know she would have a child? And he never had any money, it seemed to
go somehow. But he had been thinking, and he was going to make a change;
he was going to save this trip's money, not get drunk at all, go back to Amster-
dam and get a boatman's job. He would put ten pounds in the bank at least,
and buy a boat and some clothes with the rest. Sailormen were fools, he
argued.

Hannibal would listen and nod, letting the brown-bearded man go on, and
in this way they grew friendly, exchanging tobacco and matches, pooling
things like butter and tea, and doing little kindnesses to one another. They
shared the bucket that the Second had given Hannibal, and took turns in washing clothes on the fore-hatch. Little as there is to steal in a forecastle, men will
steal it, and these two would guard each other's tiny belongings in the watch
below, taking one another's part in the wrangle over the tinned milk, and so
cultivating a certain humanity that makes for the soul's good. It was Jan who
took Hannibal ashore in New York, when they were loading there, and led him
across the Brooklyn Bridge into the unimaginable uproar of Manhattan. Hannibal's breath stopped as he stood there, that Saturday afternoon, among the
tangle of iron rods and flying trolley cars, and looked out at New York. It was
to his unaccustomed eyes the City of a Dream. He walked through the deep
streets, a pigmy among pigmies, dazed and frightened. The roar of it, and the
immensity of it, appalled him. But when they walked down to the Battery and
saw the great ferries sliding back and forth like shuttles on the bright water,
saw the blue sea shimmering beyond, he felt reassured. Jan laughed and said it
was nothing. He had worked there once for a time, got four dollars a day until
he went on the booze and lost his job. It had not been his fault. Some one had
put knock-out drops in his liquor and cleaned him up while he was unconscious. All his money gone, he had shipped away again on a German ship, and
tried to start afresh. But Hannibal's gaze returned again and again to the tremendous buildings with their innumerable windows, tier on tier to the sky,
their giant towers and stark outlines. It seemed to him that there was a personal
antagonism in this monstrous conglomeration of alien energy, and he felt
afraid. What would they think of it at home? How would Mr. Grober regard it?
It did not occur to him that he might find Mr. Grobers in New York as in
London. It seemed impossible. This was a place for men who had leaped the
quicksands of life, who were not to be sucked in like Mr. Grober. And yet as

his eyes took in the more immediate details, he saw old men and slatternly women on the seats around them dozing in the heat, very like people on seats at home. It was when they boarded a surface-car and went away uptown that he saw a difference. There was a brisk, unrelenting hardness in the faces, a ceaseless striving after smartness in the clothing, a disquieting lack of human-ity in the way the conductor pushed an old man off the step, that seemed in keeping with those prodigious structures among which they crept. Hannibal's uneasiness deepened. The atmosphere was charged with unrest. The brown-bearded man and his young companion in their rough and crinkled clothes seemed out of place. They got off and walked along aimlessly, suddenly tired. Hannibal felt that he was not equal to it. He wanted to get back to the ship. He remembered that he ought to write a letter.

So he saw the world in fugitive peeps, and began to comprehend why seamen in the fullness of their knowledge called it nothing. He felt that too; all those millions of people hurrying to and fro were nothing to him. He was but an alien, a haphazard atom of humanity dropped among them for an idle hour. A day or two, and he was on the sea again. He preferred it that way. As the weeks grew into months he became aware of a fuller and more passionate love of it. The cool wind at evening, when he sat by the windlass and thought of Nellie; the endlessly changing panorama of clouds, the sublime galaxies of the tropic sky, the friendly moon flooding the wide ocean with silver light, the lonely tramp passing a mile away—all these things touched him and filled his heart with peace.

He had had no letter yet from her, he remembered, as they drove southward toward the Cape. Of course, it was a difficult job to time a letter properly to catch a ship that was wandering hither and thither. Plenty of other men on the ship had missed letters they were sure had been mailed. Perhaps he would get one in Durban. He tried to feel worried but he did not succeed. He longed for the time when he would return, and yet he was very happy as he was. He liked it, this life of strenuous toil. He liked the monotony of it. It gave him time to think about things. He acquired a sort of spiritual stoicism often cultivated at sea. It is the ultimate good to be derived from the sea by those who dwell in the hot, unhealthy huddle of towns. In there among those roadways, in the clashing din of the market and the bawl of the money-changers, you cannot see mankind for the people, you cannot feel for your nerves. At sea, you behold the ignoble rabble in perspective, the black many-headed swarm lie on the fair earth like a blight, you perceive the contemptible insignificance of their pas-sions in comparison with the terrible passion of the sea, and if you have been living "according to your lights," you will have time and space to see the lights of eternity, to listen to the west wind, and to harken to the voice of the storm.

He had too much to reflect upon to become morbidly interested in himself. No man can be an egoist in the forecastle. The lack of privacy and the commu-nal discipline of toil precludes it. When the *Caryatid* pushed her blunt nose across the thirtieth parallel, and the cool rushing trade-wind poured down the ventilators and flapped the shirts bent to the forecastle rails, Hannibal would sit amongst his mates and listen to their vague maundering speech. They were scarcely to be called men, if you selected, say, Sir Anthony Gilfillan as a typical man. Rather were they dumb-driven cattle, capable nevertheless of turning, the red light of battle in the dull eye, and rushing upon their owners. They did this once—and it may happen again.

For the most they slept or read penny stories of true love and virtue triumphant. There were twelve of them there in that dark triangular cupboard. Three small ports admitted a dim twilight upon them as they sat about on boxes or lolled in their bunks. At night a single bulb of light behind a ground-glass screen burned like a relentless eye watching them. When they moved, vast shadows swept across bulkhead and ceiling with idiotic speed. Men hung pants and towels over their rails to obscure the light, while others read. Fritz, the German greaser, had fashioned a hinged tin box to cover it in the night-watches, and this box had a habit of working loose from its hook and, coming down with a bang in the middle of a desultory conversation, plunge them in darkness. The floor was littered with matches and soiled with black boot-tracks. Here and there some one had laid down a piece of sacking in an attempt to keep the place tidy. One or two bunks were neat and clean. Often you might see a half-naked figure rubbing with sweat-rag and soap at some unpremeditated soilure on his bunk-board, the petty motions of his arm repeated in gigantic grotesque across the wall. But these were exceptions. The great Greek, whose feet hung over the bunk-board near the door and tended to obtrude upon the incoming stranger, terrifying him with their very vastness, blackness, and sprawling articulation, was not a clean man. Hannibal would sit on his box and look up at this recumbent enigma, wondering what he thought about. It was his duty twice a day, at four o'clock, to arouse the man. Once—the day they left New York, to be precise—he had been unable to arouse him. Pinching, punching, shouting into the sooty orifice of his ear, was of no avail. Hannibal called the Second Engineer, and received some instruction in the art of turning out the watch. The Second placed his oil-smooth hands on the Greek's enormous abdomen and rolled him slowly from side to side. If you have a nervous temperament this will cause you to sit up, knocking your head against the bulb-iron of the ceiling, and shrieking with simple terror. But the Greek was fathoms deep in an aftermath of carouse, and he only sighed, flinging one great arm over his head. He lay there in magnificent pose for a sculptor, the eccentricities of the lighting throwing his profile into sharp relief. The Second was not a sculptor, and he merely scratched his hand and cast his eyes down at the bottom bunk. A tow-haired Norwegian lay there, wide-eyed, watching him. The Second crooked his finger. "Get out," he said shortly. The man came obediently, feet first, hitching his grey flannel under-clothes as he stood up. The Second got into the bunk, lay down and put his feet against the loose boards of the top bunk. What followed was almost too rapid for Hannibal to take in. The body of the Greek rose as though in some terrible physical convulsion, swayed, and fell over the board, belly first, clothes, mattress and all, in one tumultuous cascade upon the floor. Hannibal and the Norwegian stepped back to avoid the crash. For a moment the malodorous heap lay still. A man putting on his boots on the other side of the room muttered "Jesus Christ!" rose up and slouched away on deck. Slowly the Greek raised himself to his knees, coughed and spat, the saliva dribbling in discolored threads from his lips. He looked round as an ox looks round in the pen, suspicious, bewildered, the whites of his eyes rolling.

"Goin' to turn to?" asked the Second.

Once again the man spat, and struggled to his feet blindly.

"Serve you right," said the Second, looking down at the disarray of the bedding. "Too much whisky, Angelatos. Get busy now! There you are!"

High up in the crow's-nest the bell tanged sharply, eight strokes.

And Hannibal went down to wash himself in the stokehold.

It was somewhere in that interminable crawl across the Indian Ocean from Durban to Sabang that he got his first taste of the fever that seizes the Northerner by way of carelessness. Day after day they followed the long slant northeasterly, crossing the burning line at an angle of twenty degrees. Day after day the sun blazed down upon them, and night followed night in breathless succession. And then one evening there came a change. The light air that Hannibal sought so eagerly after tea on the forecastlehead, dropped entirely, the black smoke of the Natal coal rose in a spectral column from the funnel-top. Up on the bridge the white figures of the Captain and Mate showed against the teak wheel-house where they talked. Out of the ship's side a great tin wind-scoop could be seen sticking from the Steward's room, twisting round and round as he endeavoured vainly to catch the slightest draught. Late into the first watch Hannibal lay up there winking at the stars, turning in hot discomfort on his pallet, and watching a black line thicken and spread over the horizon. As the hours crept past it grew, a dense blackness like a smudge of charcoal on dark blue paper. When he was called at One Bell the blue dome was blotted out, and he had to feel his way to the ladder. It was about half-past one, as he stood under the ventilator in the stokehold dripping with sweat after cleaning the ashpits, that he heard the thin clear call of the Chief's whistle. As he climbed the ladders a heavy blob of warm greasy rain smote his cheek, another fell on his hand. The Chief, ghostly in his white sleeping-suit, was standing by the fiddle-top.

"Yessir?" asked Hannibal.

"It's goin' to be some shower," muttered the Chief, taking hold of his arm and pointing to the skylights. "Better get up and shut 'em. Turn the ventilators aft. Quick!"

Hannibal climbed quickly, but the rain was quicker. As he thrust the first skylight lift hard down, it came. Each great drop, as it struck his vest and pants, seemed to pin them to his body. He bowed his head to shield his eyes, and the rain poured down his neck in streams. The sound of it battering on the awnings and canvas covers of the lifeboats was deafening. He had to feel for each lift as he struggled round. He could see the Third, far down in the glittering radiance of the engine-room, looking up, wondering at the noise. In less than half a minute Hannibal was as wet as though he had been dipped in the sea. His boots were full, his pants clung to his limbs, and the rain ran from his hair into his eyes. He jumped down to the deck, felt for the rope ladder that was lashed in the bunker hatch, and disappeared, swaying, into the deeper darkness of the coal. Anywhere to get out of the rain!

"Gor lummy!" he muttered to himself, crouching on the coal, and wondering how long it would last. And as he sat there he began to shiver. He tore off his singlet and tried to wipe his body with his sweat-rag. He stripped and went on wiping, his teeth chattering. He hardly knew what to do. All his dry things were in the forecastle. He went to the ladder and looked up. The breeze was cooler now, a tear in the black canopy showed a strip of velvet blue sky studded with stars. He decided to chance it before it came on again, and climbing up, he ran swiftly forward, his white body gleaming in the darkness. He found a dry cotton vest and clean dungarees and put them on. Certainly it had been "some shower."

The next morning, when they called him for his breakfast, he lay on, shivering with cold and streaming with sweat. His stomach seemed tied into knots. The Second came along and looked at him, scratching his head. When he asked what was the matter, Hannibal turned over in utter weariness and said he was sick. There was something wrong with his inside. The Second went away and the Steward came, bringing the simple therapeutics of the sea. He put a slim glass tube in Hannibal's mouth and told him to keep it there for a minute. When the Steward took the thermometer out again and looked at the temperature he said "Sufferin' Moses!" and ran away to speak to the Old Man. They returned together, white figures overwhelmingly incongruous in the dim kennel. Captain Briscoe looked down at the youth lying motionless under the blanket. You would not have thought, to look at the Captain's immaculate drill suit with the gold shoulder-straps, the white-covered cap with its ornate badge and cord, his neatly-trimmed beard, his pipe-clayed shoes, that he had lived many years in the forecastles of sailing-ships. He stood looking down, his hands clasped behind him, while the Steward tried the temperature again.

"Hundred and one—hundred and two, now, sir! Better give him the fever-mixture, I should think."

"And a dose of salts," added the Captain. "What's his name?" he asked generally.

Nobody knew his name, Jan, lying in his bunk, leaned over and looked down at the young man.

"Hanny, what's your name?" he called. "Captain wants to know your name."

"Gooderich, sir," he whispered, and the Captain gave a scarcely perceptible start.

"What's he been doing?"

"In the rain, I expect, last night," said the Steward. "I felt it on me face. Had to shut the port, sir."

The Captain went out into the daylight and walked up and down the bridge for an hour, pulling at his beard. Mr. Cadoxton, in exceedingly fine raiment which he had got, at great expense, from a Liverpool tailor, surveyed the ocean with a satisfied smile. He was a nice-looking lad, with a complexion tending to ruddiness and freckles beneath the eyes. His teeth were white and regular and he used a manicure set. Captain Briscoe had not made up his mind about Mr. Cadoxton. Finding him playing cards one evening in the dog-watch, he had remarked that he would be better employed studying for his Master's ticket. This was excellent in its way, only Mr. Cadoxton, who was a little older than his clean-shaven and fresh-looking features betokened, already possessed an extra-master's certificate, and Captain Briscoe should have found it out before. He knew, and he knew that Mr. Cadoxton knew, that *he* himself would never get an extra-master's certificate if he lived to be a thousand years old. Mr. Cadoxton looked down even on "Conway boys." As he stepped jauntily to and fro, keeping his eyes with exasperating vigilance upon the empty horizon, Captain Briscoe, walking fore and aft alongside the wheel-house, reflected with some bitterness upon the puzzling tangle of existence. He would have given fifty pounds for someone to talk to. He dared not open his mouth to the Mate, the man's every movement implied his unappeasable hunger for promotion. The Second Mate was fat and secretive, and his record was clouded by that grotesque bigamy charge. With the curious contrariness of human proclivities, Captain Briscoe desired greatly the confidence of Mr. Cadoxton. He felt that the young man had the indefinable requisites of gentility; his voice betrayed him when he spoke of "my people." Captain Briscoe, with an effort, remembered to lay his knife and fork together before the Steward removed the plate. Mr. Cadoxton did it without remembering just as he took his soup from the further edge. Captain Briscoe had every reason to hate the young man, and did hate him at times, and yet he felt that if only they could gain one another's confidence in some trivial accidental way, he might derive comfort from the circumstance. They approached each other automatically in their walk, and Mr. Cadoxton withdrew his eyes from the ocean.

"The Steward tells me there's a trimmer sick, sir," he remarked in his small refined voice.

"A touch of fever," assented Captain Briscoe. "It's a very curious coincidence," he went on, "that young feller's name is the same as my wife's."

"Is that so, sir? It is curious, certainly. We all have poor relations somewhere."

Captain Briscoe thought this an excellent notion, and democratic.

"A matter we can't be held responsible for," he suggested.

"Of course. It may be only a coincidence though: I have heard the name before. That's the chap who was in the mess-room, I think."

"That's him."

"Very decent young chap, sir. I spoke to him about the boat-drill last Saturday and he was very civil. Most unusual in the firemen class."

"I can't say," said the Old Man—"I can't say as I'd like to have anybody belonging to me in the forecastle, nowadays. Still, I don't know anything against it, if the man's respectable."

"Not at all. A man isn't responsible for the others. But why don't you ask him, sir? Has Mrs. Briscoe mentioned any of her relations who follow the sea?"

"No," said the Captain, taking out a cigar. "She didn't."

"Perhaps he's one of the independent sort, quarrelled with his people, perhaps."

"Maybe. What is it, Chief?"

The Chief, in his suit of blotched khaki with the brass buttons enamelled with verdigris, stood looking up at them. He pointed to the forecastle.

"Oh, he'll be all right tomorrow, Chief. Put 'em on six-hour watches," and the Chief walked slowly back to the afterdeck.

"You think he's quarrelled, eh?"

"I had a cousin who went to Canada," remarked Mr. Cadoxton, reaching for the binoculars in the box by the telegraph. "And I believe he did something of the sort. Left the Army and went out for good."

"Fireman?" asked the Captain hopefully.

"Oh, much worse, sir. I believe he's a billiard-marker in a club."

Captain Briscoe resumed his walk. The long voyage was telling on his nerves. Fifty days out, and still they crawled in an unbroken circle of cobalt blue. They were making, according to orders, for Sabang, a new coaling station somewhere in the north of Sumatra. This was the second time they had crossed the line. Twice more they would have to pass that mystic circle ere they started northward up the China Sea. He reflected with impatience upon the absurd regulations of the Canal which made case-oil prohibitive if carried on that route. In Sabang he would get coal and fresh meat, and what was more important, letters. He had had a letter in Durban, a brief scribble without any of the luxuriant language of newly-wedded love and therefore unsatisfying. She said she was busy with her flat, had joined a women's club, would write more next time. He could not help being proud of the stylish handwriting, the embossed lettering of the address, the thick square envelope. She knew how to do things all right. But he longed for a little gush. Was it anyway possible she disliked being called his own dear darling little wife? A warm flush of vexation came over his face, and he went down to get a peg of whisky.

Two or three days of breathless inaction and semistarvation, racked by diarrhoea and headache, and Hannibal crawled out into the daylight again. The Second told him to take it easy, and gave him a stiff dose of whisky. It did him good, though he found the shovel strangely heavy, and often he would grow dizzy and have to lie on the hatch with his face on his arm, exhausted. Swansea seemed a long way off. Was she thinking of him? He hoped so. He found now, in his weakness, that tears came easily. He was sorry for himself. And one night as he sat in the cool breeze that blew from the Nicobars, he heard the mates and engineers in the Second Mate's room singing "Rolling Home":—

Rollin' home, rollin' home,
Rollin' home, rollin' home,
Rollin' home—across—the sea,
Rollin' home to dear old England,
Rollin' home—dear heart—to thee!

He felt a terrible pain in his chest, and the tears came unbidden to his eyes. He heard a growl from some one of them, overwrought.

"For the Lord's sake sing something else! I can't stand it!" And Hannibal understood perfectly.

Twenty-eight days after they had quitted Durban, the *Caryatid*, rounding Acheen Head, passed slowly into the land-locked harbour of Sabang and made fast to the white timbers of the jetty. Angelatos went to the door of the fore-castle as the Mate shouted, "Make fast!" and looked round, licking his lips. He had been this way before, had Angelatos, and he knew that gin was a shilling a bottle.

Aloft on the *Flying Cloud*

by MORLEY ROBERTS

There is something inexplicably spiritual in a ship, from whatever standpoint she be viewed, whether from the main-deck or from the taffrail under which the divided waters join and bubble joyfully, or from the end of the jibboom, which is nearest to her purpose, as one may say. She is a magnificent creature, a thing complete, visibly complete and austerely adequate (the austerity lying in the nothing beyond her purpose, her splendid economy of means), and her spirituality comes from her completeness; her finite and declared divisions; her lofty silences; her community with the winds and the sea and sky. It comes—ah! who shall say how it comes!—but it is up aloft among the fine tracery of her rigging and her gear that her soul is most manifest. Where, indeed, could it be more manifest than from the high places where one sees her gracious dependence on her winds, while her naked body is in the priestlike font of the sea? Oh, most blessed of created things, of the works of man working divinely! Every step of hers in the great waters is a baptism.

It were easy to make her material if, indeed, the vision which perceives her were material, for what is she but iron and timber and cordage? Yet iron is wrought out in fire, and timber sweetens in the great woods, and hemp grows in glory under the same skies as the ship. To go aloft is but to climb by ratlines and the shrouds, to hang in the futtock rigging, to clamber over the rim of the top, and then further by the topmast rigging; a mere catalogue if told in wooden words. But told as it should be (help me, oh, most divine sea and wind that speak together as in an organic psalm!), it becomes a pilgrimage, now of pleasure so sweet that nought can equal it, now of tremendous toil that's even sweeter. One leaves the little world of the deck whereon men tread, and the sounds of mankind grow dim, and ever dimmer, until they die away like the breaking of the foam about her bows, and so one ascends among the silent, very splendid machinery of the winds; one lies in the very plumage of her wings, thanking God and the divinity within one which with others wrought so lovely and strong a creature.

Now was the wind warm and gentle, but full and clean and steady as a river of crystal. It breathed upon the two that went aloft, on wan white cheek and ruddy, on the one who knew, and on him who was virgin as to his mind of ships, and the heart of the one was haughty pride and the heart of the other eager innocence.

They climb, and to old Mac looking up aloft are but two boys, young and

379

foolish. They were two material objects, two things objective, coloured and visible, tangible objects of the world of sense. They weighed so much, and could talk. But to us they are other than this, something akin to the ship herself on her most spiritual side: part of her very spirit, part of her power of achievement, and this though they chattered as boys will climbing a tree. Yet this was the greatest of all trees, where the very birds of God might nest. One saw their wings and named them as sails. They were vans and pinions, clouds of high Heaven.

By now they've reached the top of the mainrigging and stand under the top itself. Jack, the climber of the tree, this giant tree, this most magnificent Beanstalk into the Cloud Land, stood and breathed. Fear and pain of joy got hold of him and he stared about him open-eyed, open-mouthed, perceiving, without knowing it, that the greatest thing on earth or at sea, or up aloft, is to attain a new point of view. Let us drink to such as climb masts or high mountains, or scale the inmost inaccessible fastnesses of the spirit. The main thing is to climb.

You shall hear Jack say the most commonplace things, in the most natural manner. What of that? Even Dante's visions were strangely material, were they not? Yet had he not been there, been to hell and heaven? How would one expect a youngster devoid of beautiful words, barely furnished with necessary ones, to mouth full-organed the opening divinity of vision in him? It's absurd to ask a babe to describe the Apocalypse. Nevertheless, though he said, "Damn!" it might mean, "This is a real white rose of an hour in my life"; and that hour might remain in his soul's bosom as long as any rose given by Beatrice to an endowed poet and lover.

Indeed, the boy said "Damn" often. It helped; one knows it helped.

"Now, will you come over the rim of the top or go through there?" asked the rare devil the Professor.

"There" was a hole in the top.

"What is it?"

"The Lubber's Hole," said Bram.

The boy flushed and looked at it, and stared overhead and inspected the outward leaning futtock-shrouds and the rim of the top above him. His heart beat fast, but his spirit was monstrously perturbed at such a notion. How could he, on this his first ascent to heaven, go through any passage named the lubber's hole?

But he temporized.

"I'll go the way you go," he said, meekly, but still with a flush on his cheeks.

And he saw Bram climb above, leaning outward, saw him lift himself, grasp the unseen topmast rigging and draw himself over, and kick a haughty heel at conquered space. It was dramatic, very wonderful! No Col de Lion, no shoulder of the Matterhorn, no arête of windy Monte Rosa, no cornice of the Lyskamm, seemed half so awe-inspiring. For it was wholly new, and therein lay its wonder and its power to draw him.

"I'll come," he gasped, and launched himself into the task, feeling that he must necessarily and by all the laws of space and time and matter fall headlong and be converted into pulp. It took courage, and he drew on his youthful heart for it, and found, Heaven be thanked! sufficient at his godlike account, and so drawing, drew himself up and found himself proudly on the top with Bram, who said, "Well done, sonny!"

Now can you or anyone who understands as much as "a, b, c," of the great alphabet of all life, wonder that Jack felt bound with hooks of steel, and grapnels and cables and hawsers to such a man, though he was a debauched young ruffian who knew more Limericks than Latin, and had as little grace as Greek about him? Jack would have blacked his boots, and quite rightly would have blacked them, though they had been seven leagues from heel to toe.

"I say!" said Jack.

He said nothing, though on encouragement he could talk almost as ceaselessly as the spirits that cluster about a vessel's bows. They can be heard most delightfully at night, when the trade wind blows, if the hearer climbs over the head, and, perhaps, out upon the boom where the jibs sleep and work and dream. But now Jack, uplifted from the common ranks of men, had nothing to say, but everything to feel.

He saw the gigantic curve of the mainsail beneath him with the gear lying across its bosom. It was the king of sails, the monarch, the great doer. He inspected it curiously; noted the great spread of the yard, the jackstay to which the sail was made fast, the truss, the great chain slings. Sunlight poured on the sail; he saw shadows on the deck. The air seemed finer already; his lungs filled like big sails; he could go. He was in the middle of the machinery of things: the topsail was before him. Aye, and his hand was on the topmast rigging. Bram slung round and started climbing. Jack followed.

As he climbed he had a sense of losing the ship, of leaving her. There was a magical lightness in her tracery, for all the strength of her proved rigging and well-tried gear. It was the infinite lightness of beauty and simple adequacy that the beholder notes in the loveliest Gothic architecture. She seemed fragile, but was not. The great solidity of the ship lay beneath: the hull narrowed tremendously: aloft the sky opened, the sky still cut by stays, the mizzen t'gallant stay, the mizzen-royal, the sky so heavenly blue over the wrinkled blue sea. He passed the belly of the upper topsail, noting with anxious eyes the spilling lines, the bull's-eyes in the foot of the sail; the topsail-sheets of iron, and gear he could not name. The reef-points were a joy to him; they hung in a steady row; they looked like good workmen, like soldiers of manilla.

So they came to the cross-trees and sat astride them abaft the belly of the t'gallantsail.

"Well?" said Bram, casually. He sat without touching anything. It was a boast. He was a splendid braggart always. But Jack held tight to the mast and the royal-halliards going away down past him.

"Oh!" said Jack. To develop that "Oh!" were a task indeed. For it meant that this was a very wonderful world, a bright, light, splendid world, and that if a ship was a wonder, her lofty spars were astronomy compared with land surveying. She was sheer grace, magical adequacy, and her cross-trees a throne, a great observatory, a peak. It was a joy, a great terrible joy, to think that one might and could fall. It was a risk, and what's so good as that? Life is the more immense as one sees the chance of losing it. Death is the great adventure, after all.

Though the sea was calm and the wind light upon the cross-trees, the Greenhorn felt sweet motions, felt that calmness was but relative. There was a beautiful musical thrill about him; it was as if a far faint organ played, as if spiritual beings touched harps of magic. There was a delicious thrill under and around and in him. His heart responded; he felt the tonic of the open, high world. He looked down and clutched tightly.

That was Mr. Mackintosh! How strange it seemed that he should be so little when at his word strange things might happen. He had clothed the *Flying Cloud* in her majesty, had tended her in her trouble, had stood by her as she slept cradled in the lifting surges when she lay to but a little time ago. The decks looked warm, comfortable, earthlike. A pang went through the boy. This was fine, but it was dreadfully lonely. He desired to go down from aloft. And yet—there was the royal-yard above him and the skysail. Could he?

Bram dangled a careless leg over destruction. But his bright eyes of blue were brighter still.

"How do you like it, Jack?" he asked.

"I'm thinking—"

"What?"

"What it must be up here at night when it's blowing hard."

"Aye, my lad, that's the time!"

For Jack, who had the elements of imagination in him, the sun went down and the wind blew and the sea got up. He looked at the foot-ropes of the t'gallant-yard, and in his mind climbed out upon them, and with the Lascars picked up the sail. He was very much afraid, and still more fearful of showing it.

Then he came back to the cross-trees and saw Bram with a pipe in his mouth.

"Let's go on the royal-yard," said Bram.

Jack's mind, or body perhaps, said that he would much rather not. It was ridiculous to go up there, highly ridiculous. What good would it do? That was what his body wanted to know as he rose carefully and reluctantly and followed. Every step he took was forced now; his reason clamoured against him. He hated Bram very much.

And he found the royal-yard much more hazardously magnificent than the cross-trees. He quite loved Bram for saying "Let's go up to the royal-yard." He even imitated Bram after a moment's pause and sat down on the yard with his heels on the bellying quiet sail. He hugged the mast tightly.

Now he could see under the foot of the skysail. He looked down on the fore-royal and far over it across the open sea. The ship itself was lost; there was no ship, nothing but a little glimpse of the foc's'le head under the roached foot of the lower fore-topsail. A mannikin moved there. He heard a faint far voice speak. The thrill of the rigging was greater yet than it had been in the cross-trees; it was more musical, more vibrant, stronger. A musical ear would have heard subtle tones, overtones, harmonics, and some might have assigned them their stations in the great instrument of the winds.

There came a dissonance.

"Like to go on the skysail-yard, sonny?"

Insatiable beast, the trier of man! Jack looked at him malevolently and saw him staring aloft to where that white bird the lone main-skysail spread its vans to the most heavenly air. The mast itself seemed now but a pole, the yard a thin wand; the backstays and the stays but threads. Jack said he was a vulgarian to bellow there in heaven, at the foot of the great white throne, and yet he knew he was an angel saying "Come." The upward journey was not finished yet and only a recreant would pause now.

There were no more ratlines, but Bram grasped the mast and swarmed it, and said, when he straddled the yard, "Steady does it." It was a saint encouraging a catechumen struggling in faith for sight. Jack drew in his breath and took hold of his young courage and climbed. He swung his leg across the yard and sat shaking and triumphant. Oh, amazing—

Ye Gods of starry depths and the pathless wastes of sun-washed ocean, who shall stand upon the skysail-yard of any *Flying Cloud* and not declare your glory? There are untouched virgins of the rocks and snows who still baffle mankind's ardours and frown or smile in chastity; but still there's no such height in Alp or Himalaya or Cordillera as the summit that we stand on now. No Golden Throne nor Illimani, nor white Dom, nor Aconcagua, nor Tupungato, lone and glacier-bearing, has a majesty so overpowering as the amazing skysail-yard. Below lies the world itself, the ship, and the world is nothing; here on clouds equal in grace to those of the nigh heaven itself, we float up-borne, and advance into the celestial air that's crystal. We breathe God's air, drink divinest dews, sip from the very bowl of azure that holds the stars and sun, and look down as gods ourselves upon the banded emerald and amethystine pavement of old Ocean.

There's no such glory as the glory of the ship, and no such glory in the ship as when we lift our eyes and hearts upon her nearest reach to heaven. Would it were mine to sing the Swan Song of the great-sailed ships that soon shall be no more, and even now sail over the rim of the great seas to sink and be forever unknown!

The sacred neophyte and the unsacred white-faced wonderful devil who led him there, sat up aloft for an hour. There to my mind they sit yet, brown face and white, debauchee and innocent, half divine and half diabolic. In so pure and holy a spot, while the *Flying Cloud* moved before her attendant winds, let us leave them for a while. There should be a new page now. There is a great argument for leaving fair white pages at times in books. Thereon they who are capable should write the unwritten that's in their hearts, in their tears, their joys, their anguish, and their prayers.

The Fight with the Sharks

by ERNEST HEMINGWAY

They sailed well and the old man soaked his hands in the salt water and tried to keep his head clear. There were high cumulus clouds and enough cirrus above them so that the old man knew the breeze would last all night. The old man looked at the fish constantly to make sure it was true. It was an hour before the first shark hit him.

The shark was not an accident. He had come up from deep down in the water as the dark cloud of blood had settled and dispersed in the mile deep sea. He had come up so fast and absolutely without caution that he broke the surface of the blue water and was in the sun. Then he fell back into the sea and picked up the scent and started swimming on the course the skiff and the fish had taken.

Sometimes he lost the scent. But he would pick it up again, or have just a trace of it, and he swam fast and hard on the course. He was a very big Mako shark built to swim as fast as the fastest fish in the sea and everything about him was beautiful except his jaws. His back was as blue as a sword fish's and his belly was silver and his hide was smooth and handsome. He was built as a sword fish except for his huge jaws which were tight shut now as he swam fast, just under the surface with his high dorsal fin knifing through the water without wavering. Inside the closed double lip of his jaws all of his eight rows of teeth were slanted inward. They were not the ordinary pyramid-shaped teeth of most sharks. They were shaped like a man's fingers when they are crisped like claws. They were nearly as long as the fingers of the old man and they had razor-sharp cutting edges on both sides. This was a fish built to feed on all the fishes in the sea, that were so fast and strong and well armed that they had no other enemy. Now he speeded up as he smelled the fresher scent and his blue dorsal fin cut the water.

When the old man saw him coming he knew that this was a shark that had no fear at all and would do exactly what he wished. He prepared the harpoon and made the rope fast while he watched the shark come on. The rope was short as it lacked what he had cut away to lash the fish.

The old man's head was clear and good now and he was full of resolution but he had little hope. It was too good to last, he thought. He took one look at the great fish as he watched the shark close in. It might as well have been a dream, he thought. I cannot keep him from hitting me but maybe I can get him. *Dentuso*, he thought. Bad luck to your mother.

The shark closed fast astern and when he hit the fish the old man saw his mouth open and his strange eyes and the clicking chop of the teeth as he drove forward in the meat just above the tail. The shark's head was out of water and his back was coming out and the old man could hear the noise of skin and flesh ripping on the big fish when he rammed the harpoon down onto the shark's head at a spot where the line between his eyes intersected with the line that ran straight back from his nose. There were no such lines. There was only the heavy sharp blue head and the big eyes and the clicking, thrusting all-swallowing jaws. But that was the location of the brain and the old man hit it. He hit it with his blood mushed hands driving a good harpoon with all his strength. He hit it without hope but with resolution and complete malignancy.

The shark swung over and the old man saw his eye was not alive and then he swung over once again, wrapping himself in two loops of the rope. The old man knew that he was dead but the shark would not accept it. Then, on his back, with his tail lashing and his jaws clicking, the shark plowed over the water as a speedboat does. The water was white where his tail beat it and three-quarters of his body was clear above the water when the rope came taut, shivered, and then snapped. The shark lay quietly for a little while on the surface and the old man watched him. Then he went down very slowly.

"He took about forty pounds," the old man said aloud. He took my harpoon too and all the rope, he thought, and now my fish bleeds again and there will be others.

He did not like to look at the fish anymore since he had been mutilated. When the fish had been hit it was as though he himself were hit.

But I killed the shark that hit my fish, he thought. And he was the biggest *dentuso* that I have ever seen. And God knows that I have seen big ones.

It was too good to last, he thought. I wish it had been a dream now and that I had never hooked the fish and was alone in bed on the newspapers.

"But man is not made for defeat," he said. "A man can be destroyed but not defeated." I am sorry that I killed the fish though, he thought. Now the bad time is coming and I do not even have the harpoon. The *dentuso* is cruel and able and strong and intelligent. But I was more intelligent than he was. Perhaps not, he thought. Perhaps I was only better armed.

"Don't think, old man," he said aloud. "Sail on this course and take it when it comes."

But I must think, he thought. Because it is all I have left. That and baseball. I wonder how the great DiMaggio would have liked the way I hit him in the brain? It was no great thing, he thought. Any man could do it. But do you think my hands were as great a handicap as the bone spurs? I cannot know. I never had anything wrong with my heel except the time the sting ray stung it when I stepped on him when swimming and paralyzed the lower leg and made the unbearable pain.

"Think about something cheerful, old man," he said. "Every minute now you are closer to home. You sail lighter for the loss of forty pounds."

He knew quite well the pattern of what could happen when he reached the inner part of the current. But there was nothing to be done now.

"Yes there is," he said aloud. "I can lash my knife to the butt of one of the oars."

So he did that with the tiller under his arm and the sheet of the sail under his foot.

"Now," he said. "I am still an old man. But I am not unarmed."

The breeze was fresh now and he sailed on well. He watched only the forward part of the fish and some of his hope returned.

It is silly not to hope, he thought. Besides I believe it is a sin. Do not think about sin, he thought. There are enough problems now without sin. Also I have no understanding of it.

I have no understanding of it and I am not sure that I believe in it. Perhaps it was a sin to kill the fish. I suppose it was even though I did it to keep me alive and feed many people. But then everything is a sin. Do not think about sin. It is much too late for that and there are people who are paid to do it. Let them think about it. You were born to be a fisherman as the fish was born to be a fish. San Pedro was a fisherman as was the father of the great DiMaggio.

But he liked to think about all things that he was involved in and since there was nothing to read and he did not have a radio, he thought much and he kept on thinking about sin. You did not kill the fish only to keep alive and to sell for food, he thought. You killed him for pride and because you are a fisherman. You loved him when he was alive and you loved him after. If you love him, it is not a sin to kill him. Or is it more?

"You think too much, old man," he said aloud.

But you enjoyed killing the *dentuso*, he thought. He lives on the live fish as you do. He is not a scavenger nor just a moving appetite as some sharks are. He is beautiful and noble and knows no fear of anything.

"I killed him in self-defense," the old man said aloud. "And I killed him well."

Besides, he thought, everything kills everything else in some way. Fishing kills me exactly as it keeps me alive. The boy keeps me alive, he thought. I must not deceive myself too much.

He leaned over the side and pulled loose a piece of the meat of the fish where the shark had cut him. He chewed it and noted its quality and its good taste. It was firm and juicy, like meat, but it was not red. There was no stringiness in it and he knew that it would bring the highest price in the market. But there was no way to keep its scent out of the water and the old man knew that a very bad time was coming.

The breeze was steady. It had backed a little further into the north-east and he knew that meant that it would not fall off. The old man looked ahead of him but he could see no sails nor could he see the hull nor the smoke of any ship. There were only the flying fish that went up from his bow sailing away to either side and the yellow patches of gulf-weed. He could not even see a bird.

He had sailed for two hours, resting in the stern and sometimes chewing a bit of the meat from the marlin, trying to rest and to be strong, when he saw the first of the two sharks.

"*Ay,*" he said aloud. There is no translation for this word and perhaps it is just a noise such as a man might make, involuntarily, feeling the nail go through his hands and into the wood.

"*Galanos*," he said aloud. He had seen the second fin now coming up behind the first and had identified them as shovel-nosed sharks by the brown, triangular fin and the sweeping movements of the tail. They had the scent and were excited and in the stupidity of their great hunger they were losing and finding the scent in their excitement. But they were closing all the time.

The old man made the sheet fast and jammed the tiller. Then he took up the oar with the knife lashed to it. He lifted it as lightly as he could because his hands rebelled at the pain. Then he opened and closed them on it lightly to loosen them. He closed them firmly so they would take the pain now and would not flinch and watched the sharks come. He could see their wide, flattened, shovel-pointed heads now and their white-tipped wide pectoral fins. They were hateful sharks, bad smelling, scavengers as well as killers, and when they were hungry they would bite at an oar or the rudder of a boat. It was these sharks that would cut the turtles' legs and flippers off when the turtles were asleep on the surface, and they would hit a man in the water, if they were hungry, even if the man had no smell of fish blood nor of fish slime on him.

"*Ay*," the old man said. "*Galanos*. Come on *Galanos*."

They came. But they did not come as the Mako had come. One turned and went out of sight under the skiff and the old man could feel the skiff shake as he jerked and pulled on the fish. The other watched the old man with his slitted yellow eyes and then came in fast with his half circle of jaws wide to hit the fish where he had already been bitten. The line showed clearly on the top of his brown head and back where the brain joined the spinal cord and the old man drove the knife on the oar into the juncture, withdrew it, and drove it in again into the shark's yellow cat-like eyes. The shark let go of the fish and slid down, swallowing what he had taken as he died.

The skiff was still shaking with the destruction the other shark was doing to the fish and the old man let go the sheet so that the skiff would swing broadside and bring the shark out from under. When he saw the shark he leaned over the side and punched at him. He hit only meat and the hide was set hard and he barely got the knife in. The blow hurt not only his hands but his shoulder too. But the shark came up fast with his head out and the old man hit him squarely in the center of his flat-topped head as his nose came out of water and lay against the fish. The old man withdrew the blade and punched the shark exactly in the same spot again. He still hung to the fish with his jaws hooked and the old man stabbed him in his left eye. The shark still hung there.

"No?" the old man said and he drove the blade between the vertebrae and the brain. It was an easy shot now and he felt the cartilage sever. The old man reversed the oar and put the blade between the shark's jaws to open them. He twisted the blade and as the shark slid loose he said, "Go on, *galano*. Slide down a mile deep. Go see your friend, or maybe it's your mother."

The old man wiped the blade of his knife and laid down the oar. Then he found the sheet and the sail filled and he brought the skiff onto her course.

"They must have taken a quarter of him and of the best meat," he said aloud. "I wish it were a dream and that I had never hooked him. I'm sorry about it, fish. It makes everything wrong." He stopped and he did not want to look at the fish now. Drained of blood and awash he looked the colour of the silver backing of a mirror and his stripes still showed.

"I shouldn't have gone out so far, fish," he said. "Neither for you nor for me. I'm sorry, fish."

Now, he said to himself. Look to the lashing on the knife and see if it has been cut. Then get your hand in order because there still is more to come.

"I wish I had a stone for the knife," the old man said after he had checked the lashing on the oar butt. "I should have brought a stone." You should have brought many things, he thought. But you did not bring them, old man. Now is no time to think of what you do not have. Think of what you can do with what there is.

"You give me much good counsel," he said aloud. "I'm tired of it."

He held the tiller under his arm and soaked both his hands in the water as the skiff drove forward.

"God knows how much that last one took," he said. "But she's much lighter now." He did not want to think of the mutilated under-side of the fish. He knew that each of the jerking bumps of the shark had been meat torn away and that the fish now made a trail for all sharks as wide as a highway through the sea.

He was a fish to keep a man all winter, he thought. Don't think of that. Just rest and try to get your hands in shape to defend what is left of him. The blood smell from my hands means nothing now with all that scent in the water. Besides they do not bleed much. There is nothing cut that means anything. The bleeding may keep the left from cramping.

What can I think of now? he thought. Nothing. I must think of nothing and wait for the next ones. I wish it had really been a dream, he thought. But who knows? It might have turned out well.

The next shark that came was a single shovel-nose. He came like a pig to the trough if a pig had a mouth so wide that you could put your head in it. The old man let him hit the fish and then drove the knife on the oar down into his brain. But the shark jerked backwards as he rolled and the knife blade snapped.

The old man settled himself to steer. He did not even watch the big shark sinking slowly in the water, showing first life-size, then small, then tiny. That always fascinated the old man. But he did not even watch it now.

"I have the gaff now," he said. "But it will do no good. I have the two oars and the tiller and the short club."

Now they have beaten me, he thought. I am too old to club sharks to death. But I will try it as long as I have the oars and the short club and the tiller.

He put his hands in the water again to soak them. It was getting late in the afternoon and he saw nothing but the sea and the sky. There was more wind in the sky than there had been, and soon he hoped that he would see land.

"You're tired, old man," he said. "You're tired inside."

The sharks did not hit him again until just before sunset.

The old man saw the brown fins coming along the wide trail the fish must make in the water. They were not even quartering on the scent. They were headed straight for the skiff swimming side by side.

He jammed the tiller, made the sheet fast and reached under the stern for the club. It was an oar handle from a broken oar sawed off to about two and a half feet in length. He could only use it effectively with one hand because of the grip of the handle and he took good hold of it with his right hand, flexing his hand on it, as he watched the sharks come. They were both *galanos*.

I must let the first one get a good hold and hit him on the point of the nose or straight across the top of the head, he thought.

The two sharks closed together and as he saw the one nearest him open his jaws and sink them into the silver side of the fish, he raised the club high and brought it down heavy and slamming onto the top of the shark's broad head. He felt the rubbery solidity as the club came down. But he felt the rigidity of bone too and he struck the shark once more hard across the point of the nose as he slid down from the fish.

The other shark had been in and out and now came in again with his jaws wide. The old man could see pieces of the meat of the fish spilling white from the corner of his jaws as he bumped the fish and closed his jaws. He swung at him and hit only the head and the shark looked at him and wrenched the meat loose. The old man swung the club down on him again as he slipped away to swallow and hit only the heavy solid rubberiness.

"Come on, *galano*," the old man said. "Come in again."

The shark came in a rush and the old man hit him as he shut his jaws. He hit him solidly and from as high up as he could raise the club. This time he felt the bone at the base of the brain and he hit him again in the same place while the shark tore the meat loose sluggishly and slid down from the fish.

The old man watched for him to come again but neither shark showed. Then he saw one on the surface swimming in circles. He did not see the fin of the other.

I could not expect to kill him, he thought. I could have in my time. But I have hurt them both badly and neither one can feel very good. If I could have used a bat with two hands I could have killed the first one surely. Even now, he thought.

He did not want to look at the fish. He knew that half of him had been destroyed. The sun had gone down while he had been in the fight with the sharks.

"It will be dark soon," he said. "Then I should see the glow of Havana. If I am too far to the eastward I will see the lights of one of the new beaches."

I cannot be too far out now, he thought. I hope no one has been too worried. There is only the boy to worry, of course. But I am sure he would have confidence. Many of the older fishermen will worry. Many others too, he thought. I live in a good town.

He could not talk to the fish anymore because the fish had been ruined too badly. Then something came into his head.

"Half fish," he said. "Fish that you were. I am sorry that I went too far out. I ruined us both. But we have killed many sharks, you and I, and ruined many others. How many did you ever kill, old fish? You do not have that spear on your head for nothing."

He liked to think of the fish and what he could do to a shark if he were swimming free. I should have chopped the bill off to fight them with, he thought. But there was no hatchet and then there was no knife.

But if I had, and could have lashed it to an oar butt, what a weapon. Then we might have fought them together. What will you do now if they come in the night? What can you do?

"Fight them," he said. "I'll fight them until I die."

Reaching Marbella

by WILLIAM F. BUCKLEY, JR.

Well, tomorrow would be another day, as the saying goes. Certainly there were no indications of any change in weather. The barometer hadn't budged in days—hadn't tipped us off, as a matter of fact, to what we were in. Presumably we were still in the same Azores High, but in a part of it that was windy. I missed, also, our daily swims, though the rain and the waves kept us well laundered, besides which there is a splendid shower by the master stateroom. The sights have been irregular, and this afternoon we spotted a Portuguese warship and spoke it (*v.t.*). The reply: "We ahrr Portugal, you ahrr what?" I suppose if we had said we were Mozambique they'd have declined cooperation, but we gave our flag, and asked if they had a position, and after a few minutes' silence they gave us one. Either we were six miles south of where I had us, or they were six miles north of where they placed themselves. I had had a noon sight and was not lightly going to give ground on the subject, though those northerly winds were probably giving us considerable set and leeway, and I cranked our course north by three degrees. I'm not worried about where we are. As a matter of fact, I thought, turning off the reading light, I wasn't really worried about anything. The *Sealestial* was built without any notion of being overwhelmed by such seas as come at you with winds of forty miles per hour, and was proving it very nicely.

The next day was just as bad, but it was on the evening of it that Allen made his remarkable prediction. It is hard to describe the joy that comes to a sailor when after a particularly long blast, the weather clears. I swear, it's like V-J Day. You just want to go out and be happy. There were still swells at 6 P.M., but the wind was down to seven knots. For the first time since leaving the Azores, we ate in the cockpit. The moon was perfect, the stars were out. The music was on. Everyone had a snort, and wine besides. Tom was fully recovered, and once again was finding everything funny, including imitations of him during the preceding three days (Reggie's was superior. To do it right, you must lie flat on your back, and look straight up, and put your hand over your eyes. The tone of voice must be funereal. "I'll have one saltine. No! Make that *half* a saltine. Thank you"). And the whole of the next day was more of the same, with just enough wind to sail by.

I began to make calculations. As I've suggested, I don't like to end a big trip at anticlimactic hours. At the rate we were going, we'd pull into Marbella at about two in the afternoon, and that is no damn good for celebrating. Rather like being married at six in the morning. So, said I studying the charts, I have a proposal. Let's go into Gibraltar, get off the boat, have lunch there, look around for an hour or two, then reboard and sail up the thirty miles to Marbella. My proposal was greeted with cheers from all sides, and I knew how Magellan must have felt when he said, "What do you say we pop around the world?" That night was especially animated, we played poker followed by a little wild Red Dog, and when the chips were counted, the whole exercise resulted in an entirely tolerable redistribution of wealth, a modest amount of it in my direction.

You must not ever count on uneventful endings to ocean pasages. For every day I have finished a race or cruise in calm circumstances, I can think of two that have been turbulent.

The next morning the breeze was on the nose, and before I came on deck, Tony had hardened up the sails; and now, the wind having veered directly east, we had given way, heading about 110 degrees. We had run into what they call in those parts a "levanter," namely a tough wind that comes out of the Mediterranean from the east, and has a swooshing funnel effect in the Strait of Gibraltar, which after all is only nine miles wide at its closest point.

I took the helm, and hung on to it for six hours, enjoying it all, though it was fierce and salty. By now we could see the southern coast of Spain—and the northwestern tip of Africa. The navigation from this point would be visual. Consulting the Coast Pilot, I learned that after high water in Gibraltar, the current flows east to west beginning four hours after high tide in Gibraltar, until the next high tide. So, all we needed to do was find out what time was high tide in Gibraltar.

There ensured a search through every paper and document on board the *Sealestial*. We came up with stuff that would have permitted us to navigate up the Amazon, around Patagonia, into uncharted ports in Micronesia; but no tide tables for the Mediterranean.

So I asked Allen to try Radio Gibraltar, which he did. *This is Whiskey Oscar George 9842 Whiskey Oscar George 9842 calling Radio Gibraltar, calling Radio Gibraltar.* Nothing. By now we were coasting along the shore of Africa, with a good view of the wind-harried dunes, including a relatively new-looking tanker that had missed the turn by a mere quarter mile and was now abandoned, on its side on the rocks. There is a spectacular lighthouse there, at a point east of which the Barbary pirates took sanctuary for so many years. Now we were abeam of Tangier, and I suggested we try Tangier Radio, with which, however, we had no better results than with Gibraltar. Okay, I said, let's try the handheld radio with which we had successfully communicated with several vessels during our passage. There were great tankers and freighters of every nationality and size steaming east and west across the Strait. All we desired was the simplest datum—namely, What time was high water in Gibraltar?

We tried it in English, in French, and in Spanish: just the bare question.

There was a sullen muteness in all that traffic: hard, really, to understand, because ships at sea tend to be civil to one another. I tacked about again, to starboard, pointing now to the Spanish coast about ten miles west of Gibraltar, and thought: what the hell, we'll stay on this course. If the tide is favorable, it will waft us into Gibraltar. If it isn't it will blow us west with the wind, and worse fates are imaginable than spending a night in a southern Spanish bay, *reculer pour mieux sauter* and all that sort of thing.

The triple-reefed main was augmented by a storm jib, because we had blown out the staysail and topsail, so we added engine power and moved tight into the wind at a full nine knots.

Within one hour, we knew we had gambled—and won.

Two hours later, without tacking again, we were suddenly surrounded by hills—we were in the Bay of Gibraltar, and the time was four in the afternoon. Too late for our lunch plans, but not too late, I thought, for a little *tour d'horizon*, and so, with the binoculars, I got the lay of the land and brought the *Sealestial* through a crack in the breakwater, only to run into a frenzied harbor pilot on an armed launch, directing us away from the southern end we thought to tour. "Probably Limey off-limits naval forces," Allen commented. I was glad to experience the sinews of Western military strength: but thirty seconds later we heard the crack of a gun. It was not a fusillade, let alone the beginning of the third world war. It was a blank cartridge signaling the start of a children's dinghy race. We had been escorted out of an area in the bay reserved for ten-year-old kids on the days they race. Oh well.

So we took in other parts of Gibraltar, passing the fancy hotels serenely, looking up at the mountain where all the monkeys are cosseted, passing a dozen freighters tied up, loading and unloading. The girls were handing around some wine, and I took some and said, "Well, gentlemen, shall we proceed to Spain?" The consensus was affirmative, and so we moseyed out of Gibraltar and, to our surprise, found that the levanter had entirely dissipated, leaving us waters so placid, one would not have thought they had experienced wind in a week. We rounded, and I set the pilot on automatic, with a heading for Puerto Banús, whose light we would in any event pick up within a couple of hours. I don't remember ever seeing such pinks and blues as we saw that night, quietly proceeding at a mere thirteen hundred rpm so that there would be no noise to contend with. Every few moments, as the sun went down and the moon blared up, the color combinations changed, and we saw deep mauves, every color every painter ever used, when painting in a tranquil frame of mind; such a frame of mind as our own. Dinner was served slowly and consumed slowly, and there was barely time for coffee, brandy, and cigars before we saw the light and closed down on our destination.

I had seen it before, and remembered sending Danny in a dinghy to delineate absolutely the angular little channel by which you enter the huge facility at Marbella. I remembered it, and we crawled in, and instantly spotted two flashlights signaling us in a direction where, through the glasses, I could make out an unoccupied section of a dock, about the length of the *Sealestial*, and so I gave my last command: "Fenders, port side." I approached, did a figure eight to test the current, and we slid in. Betsy and a friend had just then (at midnight) arrived, expecting an all-night vigil. Betsy and Christopher had eloped only last November.

There was great commotion at the Immigration dock during which we all endeavored to place telephone calls to America, on the understanding that doing so would not interfere with our consumption of champagne, which Van had sent ahead in copious supply and Betsy had taken care to keep chilled. I don't know why, but suddenly I felt an impulse to pull out. I did so without ceremony, walking, champagne glass in hand, back along the lifeless dock, toward the boat. I stepped gingerly over the lifeline, grasping the shroud with my left hand: the other hand was not available, as there was still the champagne glass. The boat, mothballed in moonlight, was dead. Everyone was ashore, telephoning, reveling, roistering. There was no breeze, no sound. I walked aft to the stern cockpit and maneuvered down the stillness of the companionway to the master cabin, flicked on the reading light, dropped my pants, shoes, and socks with a single downward motion, and slid between the sheets. For the first time in seven days, no need to fasten the canvas leeboards that had kept me, during those screeching moments of heel, from being tossed onto the floorboards. I picked up my journal and began to write. The dozen words I managed I cannot, at this moment, decipher. They are illegible. But I know what they say. Know what they express. Gratitude.

Sea Mutinies

Slaver: The *Amistad*

by A.B.C. WHIPPLE

Despite the lackadaisical American efforts to patrol the African coast and the Middle Passage, it was too risky to take big shiploads of slaves straight into a U.S. port. So Havana became the clearing-house—Havana because it was near the American mainland and because the U.S. consul there, Nicholas P. Trist, was proslavery and could be counted on not to put any obstacles in the way of slaving transactions. Soon the *Tecora* was beating her way into Havana Harbor, while her captives, chained by the neck in groups of five, were led on deck and readied for swift debarkation. The vessel swung up to a dock. A crude gangplank went out. The long file of black bodies shuffled onto the dock and off down a waterfront street. That was the last they saw of the captain and crew of the *Tecora,* who were paid off at the then lavish amounts ranging from five thousand dollars for the captain to fifteen hundred dollars for a seaman. After a short and riotous shore leave, they would run back to the African coast, making as many as half a dozen round trips a year.

At the end of Havana's waterfront street the Africans found something that reminded them of home: more barracoons. Here their neck irons were taken off and they were permitted to flop on the soft ground where they liked, restrained only by chain hobbles on their ankles. Here too, in the next few days, they were helped to recuperate from their ordeal at sea. They were given nearly as much food as they could eat, and within a day or two the emaciated bodies began to fill out. They were given water to wash with and oil to rub on their clean bodies. Quickly they began to feel fit. With merciful swiftness they forgot the seasickness, the rolling, bruising deck, the stench, the bloody flux, the lashes and the searing pain of vinegar and gunpowder. What the future held for them they did not know. Their past occasionally swept over them in waves of homesickness. But the present was far better than what they had just endured in the barracoons of Sierra Leone and the Middle Passage. Little by little the human spirit reasserted itself, and the captives began to sing together and dance and even laugh.

Then an immaculately dressed Spaniard was shown into the barracoon. Walking among the black bodies, he appraised them carefully and ordered sixty of them to stand in line. From the sixty he chose forty-nine. With no further ado his selection was formed into another line at the door of the barracoon. A few papers were signed, payment of $450 per slave was made, and neck irons were clamped onto the forty-nine. They were now the property of a slave dealer, Don José Ruiz.

Down the streets of Havana they marched again, to the docks and onto the deck of a long, slim schooner. They were to go to sea again; this time their destination was one of the ports of the U.S. South. The schooner was the *Amistad*.

Don José Ruiz was joined by another slave dealer, Don Pedro Montez, with four black children he had purchased. All the slaves were quickly herded below, where their chains were locked to ringbolts in the deck. The oppressiveness of the slave ship settled on them again. The rocking of the schooner at her wharf made some of their stomachs queasy. The almost palpable stench crept over them. As darkness came and the slave deck turned to pitch black, the children began to cry. A few of the older slaves groaned. But from some of them came a sound that was new, increasing and ominous. It was the murmuring threat of revolt.

The schooner *Amistad* was commanded by Captain Ramon Ferrer. Ruiz and Montez were listed as passengers. Counting captain, passengers and a crew of four, there were seven whites aboard the *Amistad*—seven whites and forty-nine strong, well-fed adult blacks.

Smaller than the *Tecora*, the *Amistad* was about seventy-five feet long. Her black sides and green bottom were divided by a white water line, and she carried a golden eagle figurehead. Her masts were slim and raked, with a square topsail on her foremast. Her hold was cut up into slave decks, with a minimum of space aft for captain, passengers and crew. All available space was utilized to transport slaves. Little wonder—the bodies that cost $450 apiece in the Havana barracoon would bring at least a thousand dollars in Florida, Georgia or the Carolinas. The *Amistad* could carry many more than the forty-nine adults now chained in her hold; but this was a large enough number to make a handsome profit. It is possible also that Captain Ferrer intended to pick up more slaves at his next call, Puerto Príncipe. The schooner's papers mentioned a cargo of goods and fifty-three Negroes (including the children) bound for Puerto Príncipe, but the *Amistad* may well have been scheduled to increase the slave cargo there. Whatever the plan, on the morning of June 27, 1839, the schooner *Amistad* weighed anchor and sailed out of Havana Harbor into history.

Ordinarily the voyage to Puerto Príncipe, only three hundred miles along the Cuban coast, took a fast schooner like the *Amistad* about two days and nights. But as the schooner rounded the last Havana promontory and the captain set her course, the wind blew into their teeth. The schooner would have been able to point up close to the wind if she had not carried a square foretopsail. As it was, Captain Ferrer had to wear off at about seventy degrees and run down his true course on a gradual slant, hoping as he set the new course that the wind would haul about and that they would not have to beat against it all the way to Puerto Príncipe. But the wind stayed in this quarter and the *Amistad* plunged into the nearly head-on sea hour after hour all through the first day and night. Again seasickness turned the slave decks into a stinking hell, and again the pounding of the ship and the chafing irons rubbed raw sores on the captives' necks, wrists and ankles.

Next day the slaves were brought onto the schooner's narrow open deck, a few at a time, and marched back and forth for exercise. It was hot work under the tropical sun, and the water ration was meager; but the captain refused to issue any more. By next day, with the wind still unfavorable and the *Amistad* pounding into a quartering sea, the slaves were frantic with thirst. As they were being exercised, one of them snatched a cupful from the water cask on the deck. He was immediately grabbed and held while one of the crew lashed at him with the "cat." Still sobbing from the pain of the vinegar and gun- powder rubbed into the gashes across his back, he was chained below. And that night the slaves began plotting among themselves, reminding each other over and over again that the count was forty-nine to seven.

Next day the wind was still against them. The food and water were getting dangerously low, and rations were cut even more. The strain began to tell on the crew, and more of the slaves were lashed, for no apparent reason. But on the next morning came the break the slaves had been watching for.

The wind, still from the same quarter, had increased. Short, spitting squalls kept every crew member busy trimming sail. When the slaves were brought on deck, they milled about more freely than before. And one of them found a loose nail in the deck planking.

His name was Cinque. He was a strong, young man, the son of an African chief and the most intelligent of the group. He it was who had led the plotting in the conversations below. Now he quickly tucked the nail in his armpit and waited until he and his companions were locked in their chains again.

By nightfall the *Amistad* had worked to within a couple of miles of the Cuban shore. The sea slowly subsided. The clouds parted and the moon peeped through. The exhausted captain ordered mattresses brought on deck. With only the man at the helm on duty, captain and crew flopped down on the mattresses to recover from their battle with the head winds and squalls. As they slept, the captives below were quietly working on their locks with the nail Cinque had found on deck that morning.

It took many hours of patient flexing and picking at the locks, but the nail worked. One by one most of the chains were cast off, and by two hours after midnight the last of the slaves had broken free. But before they went on deck, Cinque led them into the cargo hold, where they found a case of sugar cane knives. Then, with each African wielding one of the flat-bladed, sharply honed machetes, Cinque led them up the hatchway and onto the quiet deck.

The moon was still out, with only a few ragged clouds sweeping off astern. The deck was bathed by the soft light, the only other illumination coming from the compass binnacle, which cast a yellow gleam on the face of the man nodding at the helm. There was no sound save the sloshing of the sea at the bow and the slow creak of a mast. Along the deck were scattered the mattresses, on which were sprawled the sleeping bodies of the crew. And nearest to the hatch was the form of Captain Ferrer.

With Cinque in the lead, the Africans padded softly across the deck toward the sleeping captain. But evidently, quiet as they were now, their ransacking of the cargo hold had awakened Don José Ruiz. For at this moment he came on deck from the after cabin.

For a moment he looked about the deck. Then he saw the dark movement of the approaching slaves and the flicker of the moonlight on the blade of a machete. By this time Cinque had reached the sleeping Captain Ferrer and raised his machete for the kill. The two cries, one from Ruiz and one from Cinque, came almost simultaneously.

"No! No!!"

"Kill the white man!"

And the night came alive with the shouts of the Africans, the screams of the sailors, and the whack of the machete blade.

Taken completely by surprise, still half asleep and nearly paralyzed by terror, the sailors were quickly overcome. The *Amistad*'s cook had tortured the captives by telling them they were to be eaten; now he was one of the first to die. Captain Ferrer, wounded but not killed by Cinque's misdirected machete blow, got to his feet and fought off a dozen blacks with his rapier. But he was quickly overwhelmed, in time for Cinque to step in again, this time connecting with one whistling swing that split open the captain's head like a pumpkin. Don José Ruiz, beaten into unconsciousness, lay on the deck. Two or three of the crew plunged over the side, preferring to take their chances with the sharks. Don Pedro Montez ran for the cargo hold to hide among the bales and barrels. But his trail of blood was easily followed. Cinque dragged him out of the hold and brought him on deck. Only he, Ruiz and Antonio, the cabin boy, remained, and Ruiz was still recovering consciousness. Cinque had them shackled together, with the chains that had been used on the Africans. In a matter of minutes the situation aboard the *Amistad* had been exactly reversed.

And now came the aftermath. For the rest of the night while the schooner wallowed about with scarcely a hand on the helm, the freed captives ran riot through the ship. Not a cask or chest in the hold went unopened. Crockery, yards of cloth, crates, everything was scattered through the hold and on deck as if a hurricane had gone through the schooner. The Africans concentrated on the food, strewing cases of beef and biscuit and fruits through the vessel as they gorged themselves. Digging into cases of wine and a shipment of medicine, they drank both wine and medicine, and this is what finally put an end to the orgy of looting and gorging, as the medicines made then sick to their stomachs and the wines put them to sleep. By morning the *Amistad* was like a shipwreck. But she was still afloat, and she was headed away from the coast of Cuba.

Cinque and his followers knew what they wanted to do with the schooner, but they did not know how. Their plan was to sail east. All Cinque knew was that east was the opposite of the direction the *Tecora* had come. So if he now took the *Amistad* east, he should eventually reach the coast of Africa and home. But how to make the ship sail in the direction they wanted? How to keep those yards of canvas from flapping about? How to make sense out of the maze of ropes hanging from the deck to the tops of the masts?

That was why Cinque had let Ruiz, Montez and Antonio live. He had seen Montez sail the ship when Captain Ferrer had tired after the long battle against the head winds. Presumably Ruiz could sail the schooner also. And Antonio spoke Mendi, Cinque's tongue, so he could serve as interpreter when Cinque's new English failed him, which it did most of the time.

For days after the mutiny Ruiz was only semiconscious. But Montez quickly recovered from his flesh wounds, and Cinque put him to work navigating the schooner. His orders were to keep her headed east day and night, and Cinque's threats of what would happen if he failed were enough to resign him to his humiliating new role. Montez had another reason for accepting the *Amistad*'s helm. By day, and whenever at night Cinque could see the moon, Montez kept the schooner on her easterly course. But on cloudy nights, and whenever Cinque was asleep, Montez gradually eased the schooner over onto a northerly course—north for Florida, the Carolinas, New York or New England. Whichever landfall they made, this would be his only salvation.

So the *Amistad* worked her way through the waters south of the Florida Keys, running east by day and north by night. Somehow she avoided the shoal areas of the Great Bahama Bank. They touched at Andros Island for wood and water, but broke and ran when they were spotted by some of the island's few inhabitants. They rounded the island and anchored off Green Cay, east of Andros, and filled the water casks. Cinque went below for a good sleep. A few hours later he was brought on the deck by the shouts of the Africans; they had sighted an island with houses. Montez was racing to take the *Amistad* into New Providence, the central island of the Bahamas, before Cinque awoke. Cinque grabbed the helm and headed her south and east. Then he had Montez thrashed with the "cat." Howling at the taste of his own medicine, Montez refused to navigate the schooner any longer. Cinque replied that in that case there was no further use for him, and drew his rapier. Montez changed his mind.

Next day the schooner anchored off Cape Sainte Maria, the northern tip of the Bahamas' Long Island. For three days they loaded the hold with water, fruit and wild vegetables. Then they hauled anchor. Montez guided the schooner eastward past Rum Cay, Conception Island and San Salvador—the island that nearly three centuries earlier had signified to Christopher Columbus that his westward voyage had ended. Beyond here was the open Atlantic, and Africa.

Don Pedro Montez, hanging on the helm and still recovering from his lashing, knew that his only chance lay in somehow working the schooner toward the American coast. So that night he took another chance, this time swinging the *Amistad* not to north but all the way around the west. Before dawn, when

Cinque came on deck, Montez had the vessel back on her easterly course. The Spaniard calculated that on this zigzag course he could fetch up near New England, if only the winds did not favor the daytime leg over the nighttime one.

The winds not only did not betray him, but favored him. For the next few days there were light breezes and they came out of the east. Montez had tried to teach the Africans how to handle the sails, but with no success. So the schooner made little headway, and the nighttime legs brought them closer to the mainland. For more than a week this went on. Cinque knew that they were not heading east, but he knew that they could not sail into the wind, so he was helpless to do anything but watch the *Amistad* tack north and south. And he was not surprised when, in mid-August, they sighted land.

It was a low-lying land, with wide strips of white sand at the water's edge and green fringes of trees beyond. There was little sign of habitation along the part of the coast they could see. The still, moist heat of the August day was reminiscent of Africa. But this obviously was not Africa. It had been more than a month since they had taken the ship; but Cinque knew that that was not enough time to reach Africa and home.

Slowly the schooner worked her way along the coast, which seemed to stretch interminably to the east. At the helm Montez watched and prayed for the ship he hoped would rescue him and Ruiz, and perhaps even restore their slaves to them. Soon one vessel, then another and then another appeared, far off on the horizon. But they were too far away to hail, even if Montez had taken the chance. In an agony of frustration he watched them sail away—when suddenly another came into view, headed straight across the course of the *Amistad*.

She was the schooner *Eveline*, Captain Sears, bound from New Bedford to Philadelphia. Studying the *Amistad*'s tattered, flapping sails and her erratic course, Captain Sears decided to investigate.

Aboard the *Amistad* Montez could scarcely contain himself. The schooner came closer and swung out a boat. Then Cinque ordered Montez dragged below. He and Ruiz were quickly locked in the main cabin, with a huge African wielding a machete. Cinque made it clear that one shout from either man would be his last.

The *Eveline*'s boat rowed across to the *Amistad*. Cinque greeted Captain Seers as he climbed aboard. Through Antonio Cinque announced that the captain of the *Amistad* was too sick to talk. They needed food and water, for which they could pay with doubloons. Seers tried to go below, but his way was blocked by stout blacks with machetes. He returned to the *Eveline* and sent over a keg of water and a message that food was on the way. Cinque decided not to take the chance of waiting. When the *Eveline*'s sailors returned, they were met by musket fire as the *Amistad* moved off east, still following the long coastline on the port side.

Next day came a repeat of the *Eveline* meeting. A boat sent across from the pilot boat *Blossom* traded some bread and water for doubloons. But when a sailor tried to climb aboard and discover the reason for the odd-appearing schooner and her black crew, more musket fire drove him off. The *Blossom* was joined by another pilot boat, but both fled to escape the musketry from the *Amistad*. Next day another approaching vessel was scared away. Then the *Amistad* reached the point of the long coastline running east.

They were at Montauk Point, at the end of Long Island, New York. Montez was at the helm again, and he brought the schooner around the tip of the island and into calm water off Culloden Point. Cinque decided that they would anchor and go ashore for water and whatever food they could find. There were two or three houses visible from the water, but he felt it was worth taking a chance. In fact, emboldened by his recent transactions at sea, he considered buying some food. In a money belt around his middle he carried more of the doubloons which he had found below. He ordered the boat lowered and climbed into it himself, taking along six of the Africans and Antonio to serve as interpreter.

The foraging expedition had been ashore only a short while, and Cinque was trying in vain to buy food from two hunters he had encountered near a marsh, when one of the men called the alarm from his lookout post down on the beach. Cinque ran to the beach in time to see a brig of war come sailing down on the *Amistad,* swing into the wind and drop anchor. Before he could even collect his men, a boat from the brig had swung down and, with military precision, was gliding swiftly across the water to the *Amistad*.

Lieutenant Meade of the U.S. surveying brig *Washington* led his men aboard the battered schooner, to be greeted by an onrush of blacks carrying machetes. Clubbing them off with his pistol, Meade advanced down the deck. His sailors, close behind him, aimed their pistols at the blacks as they bunched at one end of the schooner.

And, without a shot, they surrendered. Cinque was still halfway to the schooner, his excited men thrashing the water with their oars. But without him on hand, the *Amistad* Africans capitulated easily. Lieutenant Meade had just started to disarm them when Montez and Ruiz came running on deck. Cinque watched the scene and realized that his only hope was flight. He ordered his men to row for shore, but they were too slow for the brig's boat, which caught up with them quickly.

The triumphant expressions of Ruiz and Montez were too much for Cinque to bear as he was led aboard the *Amistad*. He avoided them, trying to grasp what the naval officer was saying. Then, suddenly, he made one more dash for freedom. Breaking loose, he ran the width of the *Amistad*'s deck, dived over the rail, and started swimming underwater toward shore. Surfacing for a gulp of air, he went under again. But when he came up for air again the *Washington*'s boat was almost upon him. Within a few more yards he was captured. Sitting in the stern of the boat, held firmly by two sailors, Cinque studied the long, low silhouette of the disheveled schooner that might have been his deliverance, as he was brought back alongside her familiar hull for the last time.

The *Amistad*'s mutineers became a nationwide *cause célèbre* before their story was done. In the battle that developed over their trial, abolitionists were pitted against powerful proslavery forces and most of America was divided into antagonistic camps before the mutineers were finally freed. Many of them eventually made it back to Africa, under the protection of church organizations. But the trial and other delays kept them in America for two years, and most of them, including Cinque, never found their families again. Cinque returned to his village as a missionary, but soon slipped back into his tribal ways.

As for the *Amistad,* she was sold by the District Court in New London, Connecticut. Her name was changed and she entered the busy stream of maritime commerce along the American coast. Still sharp and rakish, she probably made a fast and successful trading schooner. Whether she returned to her nefarious trade again, no one knows. Certainly, she was well adapted to it. Whether she did or not, never again did she experience a slaving voyage like the one that ended that moonlit night off the coast of Cuba and made the *Amistad* the most infamous slaver in history.

The Mutiny

by HERMAN WOUK

A steamship, not being a slave to the wind like a sailing vessel, is superior to any ordinary difficulties of storms. A warship is a special kind of steamship, built not for capaciousness and economy, but for power. Even the minesweeper *Caine* could oppose to the gale a force of some thirty thousand horsepower; energy enough to move a weight of half a million tons one foot in one minute. The ship itself weighed little more than a thousand tons. It was a gray old bantam bursting with strength for emergencies.

But surprising things happen when nature puts on a freak show like a typhoon, with wind gusts up to a hundred and fifty miles per hour or more. The rudder, for instance, can become useless. It works by dragging against the water through which it is passing; but if the wind is behind the ship, and blows hard enough, the water may start piling along as fast as the rudder so there is no drag at all. Then the ship will yaw or even broach to. Or the sea may push one way on the hull, and the wind another, and the rudder a third, so that the resultant of the forces is very erratic response of the ship to the helm, varying from minute to minute, or from second to second.

It is also theoretically possible that while the captain may want to turn his ship in one direction, the wind will be pushing so hard in the other direction that the full force of the engines will not suffice to bring the ship's head around. In that case the vessel will wallow, broadside to, in very bad shape indeed. But it is unlikely. A modern warship, functioning properly and handled with wisdom, can probably ride out any typhoon.

The storm's best recourse in the contest for the ship's life is old-fashioned bogeyman terror. It makes ghastly noises and horrible faces and shakes up the captain to distract him from doing the sensible thing in tight moments. If the wind can toss the ship sideways long enough it can probably damage the engines or kill them—and then it wins. Because above all the ship must be kept steaming under control. It suffers under one disadvantage as a drifting hulk, compared to the old wooden sailing ship: iron doesn't float. A destroyer deprived of its engines in a typhoon is almost certain to capsize, or else fill up and sink.

When things get really bad, the books say, the best idea is to turn the ship's head into the wind and sea and ride out the blow that way. But even on this the authorities are not all agreed. None of the authorities have experienced the worst of enough typhoons to make airtight generalizations. None of the authorities, moreover, are anxious to acquire the experience.

The TBS message was so muffled by static and the noise of wind and waves that Willie had to put his ear to the loudspeaker: *Chain Gang from Sunshine. Discontinue fueling. Execute to follow. New fleet course 180. Small Boys reorientate screen.*

"What? What was it?" said Queeg at Willie's elbow.

"Discontinue fueling, sir, and turning south. Execute to follow."

"Getting the hell out, hey? About time."

Maryk, squat and enormous in his life jacket, said, "I don't know how she'll ride, sir, with her stern to the wind. Quartering seas always murder us——"

"Any course that takes us out of here is the right course," said Queeg. He peered out at the ragged waves, rearing and tossing everywhere as high as the ship's mast. The flying spray was like a cloudburst. A few hundred yards beyond the ship the gray mountains of water faded into a white misty wall. The spray was beginning to rattle against the windows, sounding more like hail than water. "Kay, Willie. Call Paynter and tell him to stand by his engines for some fast action. Steve, I'm going to conn from the radar shack. You stay here."

The TBS scratched and whined. The voice came through gurgling, as though the loudspeaker were under water: *"Small Boys from Sunshine. Execute reorientation. Make best speed."*

"Kay. All engines ahead full. Right standard rudder. Steady on 180," said Queeg, and ran out of the wheelhouse. The *Caine* went plunging downhill into a foaming trough. Stilwell spun the helm, saying, "Christ, this wheel feels loose."

"Rudder's probably clear out of the water," Maryk said. The nose of the ship cut into the sea and came up slowly, shedding thick solid streams. The wheelhouse trembled.

"Rudder is right standard, sir," said Stilwell. "Jesus, she's getting shoved around fast. Heading 010, sir—020——" Like a kite taking the wind, the minesweeper heeled, and swept sharply to the right. Fear tingled in Willie's arms and legs as he was swung against the wet windows. "Heading 035, sir—040——"

Hanging increasingly to starboard, the *Caine* was rising and falling on the waves, blown sideways, riding more like flotsam again than a ship under control. Spray blew across the forecastle in clouds. Instinctively Willie looked to Maryk, and was deeply relieved to see the exec hanging with both arms to an overhead beam, his back planted against the bulkhead, calmly watching the swift veer of the forecastle across the water.

"Say, Willie!" The captain's voice was angry and shrill through the speaking tube. "Get your goddamn radio technician up here, will you? I can't see anything on this goddamn radar."

Willie roared, "Aye aye, sir," into the speaking tube and passed a call for the technician over the p.a. He was beginning to feel nauseous from the dizzy sidewise slipping of the *Caine* and the queer rise and fall of the slanted deck.

"Mr. Maryk," the helmsman said in a changed tone, "she's stopped coming around——"

"What's your head?"

"Zero nine three."

"We're broadside to. Wind's got her. She'll come slow."

"Still 093, sir," said Stilwell, after a minute of bad wallowing—heavy slow rolls upright and swift sickening drops to starboard. It was hard to tell whether the *Caine* was moving through the water at all, or simply being flung sidewise and forward. The sense of motion came entirely from the sea and the wind; yet the engines were making twenty knots.

"Bring your rudder hard right," said Maryk.

"Hard right, sir——Christ, sir, this goddamn wheel *feels like the wheel ropes are broken!* Just sloppy——" The hair of Willie's head prickled to see the looks of fright on the sailors. He felt the same expression forming on his own face.

"Shut your yap, Stilwell, the wheel ropes are okay," said Maryk. "Don't be such a baby. Haven't you ever had the wheel in a sea before——"

"Now God damn it, Steve," came the squeak of Queeg, "what the hell's going on out there? Why aren't we coming around?"

Maryk yelled into the speaking tube, "Wind and sea taking charge, sir. I've got the rudder at hard right——"

"Well, use the engines. *Get* her around. Christ on a crutch, do I have to do everything here? *Where's* that technician? There's nothing but grass on this radar——"

Maryk began to manipulate the engines. A combination of standard speed on the port screw and slow backing on the starboard started swinging the ship's head slowly to the south. "Steady on 180, sir," Stilwell said at last, turning his face to Maryk, his eyes glinting with relief.

The ship was tossing and heeling from side to side. But there was no alarm in the steepest rolls any more, so long as they were even dips both ways. Willie was getting used to the sight of the three rusty stacks lying apparently parallel to the sea, so that between them he saw nothing but foaming water. The whipping of the stacks back and forth like gigantic windshield wipers was no longer a frightening but a pleasant thing. It was the slow, slow dangling rolls to one side that he dreaded.

Queeg came in, mopping at his eyes with a handkerchief. "Damn spray stings. Well, you finally got her around, hey? Guess we're okay now."

"Are we on station, sir?"

"Well, pretty near, I guess. *I* can't tell. Technician says the spray is giving us this sea return that's fogging up the scope. I guess if we're too far out of line Sunshine will give us a growl——"

"Sir, I think maybe we ought to ballast," said the exec. "We're pretty light, sir. Thirty-five per cent on fuel. One reason we don't come around good is that we're riding so high——"

"Well, don't worry, we're not capsizing yet."

"It'll just give us that much more maneuverability, sir——"

"Yes, and contaminate our tanks with a lot of salt water, so we lose suction every fifteen minutes once we refuel. Sunshine has our fuel report. If he thought there was any danger he'd issue ballasting orders."

"I also think we ought to set the depth charges on safe, sir."

"What's the matter, Steve, are you panicky on account of a little bad weather?"

"I'm not panicky, sir——"

"We're still supposed to be an anti-submarine vessel, you know. What the hell good are depth charges set on safe if we pick up a sub in the next five minutes?"

Maryk glanced out of the blurred window at the colossal boiling waves. "Sir, we won't be making any sub runs in this——"

"How do we know?"

"Sir, the *Dietch* in our squadron got caught in a storm in the Aleutians, and got sunk by its own depth charges tearing loose. Blew off the stern. Skipper got a general court——"

"Hell's bells, if your heart is so set on putting the depth charges on safe go ahead. I don't care. Just be damn sure there's somebody standing by to arm them if we pick up a sub——"

"Mr. Maryk," spoke up Stilwell, "the depth charges are on safe, sir."

"They are!" exclaimed Queeg. "Who says so?"

"I—I set 'em myself, sir." The sailor's voice was shaky. He stood with legs spread, clutching the wheel, his eyes on the gyrocompass.

"And who told you to do that?"

"I got standing orders, sir, from Mr. Keefer. When the ship is in danger, I set 'em on safe——"

"And who said the ship was in danger, hey?" Queeg swung back and forth, clinging to a window handle, glaring at the helmsman's back.

"Well, sir, on that big roll around seven o'clock, I—I set 'em. The whole fantail was awash. Had to rig a life line——"

"God damn it, Mr. Maryk, why am I never informed of these things? Here I am, steaming around with a lot of dead depth charges——"

Stilwell said, "Sir, I told Mr. Keefer——"

"You speak when you're spoken to, you goddamned imbecile, and not otherwise!" shrieked Queeg. "Mr. Keith, place this man on report for insolence and neglect of duty! He told Mr. *Keefer!* I'll attend to Mr. Keefer! Now Steve, I want you to get another helmsman and keep this stupid idiot's ugly face out of my sight from now on——"

"Captain, pardon me," said the exec hurriedly, "the other helmsmen are still shot from last night. Stilwell's our best man and we need him——"

"Will you stop this back talk?" screamed the captain. "Great bloody Christ, is there one officer on this ship who takes orders from me? I said I want——"

Engstrand stumbled into the wallowing wheelhouse and grabbed at Willie to keep from falling. His dungarees ran with water. "Sorry, Mr. Keith. Captain, the barometer——"

"What about the barometer?"

"Twenty-eight ninety-four, sir—twenty-*eight*——"

"Who the hell's been watching the barometer? Why haven't I had a report for a half hour?" Queeg ran out on the wing, steadying himself from hand to hand on the windows, the engine-room telegraph, the doorway.

"Mr. Maryk," the helmsman said hoarsely, "I can't hold her on 180. She's falling off to port——"

"Give her more rudder——"

"I got her at emergency right, sir—heading 172, sir—falling off fast——"

"Why is the rudder emergency right?" Queeg bellowed, lurching through the doorway. "Who's giving rudder orders here? Is everybody on this bridge going crazy?"

"Captain, she's yawing to port," said Maryk. "Steersman can't hold her at 180——"

"One *six* zero, sir, now," said Stilwell, with a scared look at Maryk. It was the dreaded weather-vane effect, taking charge of the *Caine*. The rudder was not holding, and the ship was skidding sideways at the pleasure of the wind and waves. The head was dropping off from south to east.

Queeg grabbed at the helmsman and steadied himself to stare at the compass. He jumped to the telegraph and signaled "Flank Speed" with one handle and "Stop" with the other. The engine-room pointers answered instantly. The deck began to vibrate with the one-sided strain on the engines. "That'll bring her around," said the captain. "What's your head now?"

"Still falling off, sir, 152——148——"

Queeg muttered, "Needs a few seconds to take hold."

Once again the *Caine* took a sickening cant to starboard and hung there. Waves coming from the port side broke over the ship as though it were a floating log. It wallowed feebly under the tons of water, but did not right itself. It came halfway back to level and sagged further to starboard again. Willie's face was pushed against the window and he saw water no more than inches from his eyes. He could have counted little bubbles of foam. Stilwell, hanging to the wheel, with his feet sliding out from under him, stammered, "Still falling off, sir—heading 125——"

"Captain, we're broaching to," said Maryk, his voice lacking firmness for the first time. "Try backing the port engine, sir." The captain seemed not to hear. "Sir, sir, *back the port engine."*

Queeg, clinging to the telegraph with his knees and arms, threw him a frightened glance, his skin greenish, and obediently slid the handle backward.

The laboring ship shuddered fearfully; it continued to drift sidewise before the wind, rising and falling on each swell a distance equal to the height of a tall building. "What's your head?" The captain's voice was a muffled croak.

"Steady on 117, sir——"

"Think she'll grab, Steve?" murmured Willie.

"I hope so."

"Oh holy Mother of Christ, make this ship come around!" spoke a queer wailing voice. The tone made Willie shiver. Urban, the little signalman, had dropped to his knees and was hugging the binnacle, his eyes closed, his head thrown back.

"Shut up, Urban," Maryk said sharply. "Get on your feet——"

Stilwell exclaimed, "Sir, heading *120!* Coming right, sir!"

"Good," said Maryk. "Ease your rudder to standard."

Without so much as a glance at the captain, Stilwell obeyed. Willie noticed the omission, for all that he was terror-stricken; and he noticed, too, that Queeg, frozen to the telegraph stand, seemed oblivious.

"Rudder is eased to standard, sir—heading 124, sir——" The *Caine* stood erect slowly and wobbled a little to port before heeling deep to starboard again.

"We're okay," said Maryk. Urban got off his knees and looked around sheepishly.

"Heading 128—129—130——"

"Willie," said the exec, "take a look in the radar shack. See if you can tell where the hell we are in the formation."

"Aye aye, sir." Willie staggered out past the captain on to the open wing. The wind immediately smashed him against the bridgehouse, and spray pelted him like small wet stones. He was astounded and peculiarly exhilarated to realize that in the last fifteen minutes the wind had actually become much stronger than before, and would blow him over the side if he exposed himself in a clear space. He laughed aloud, his voice thin against the guttural "Whooeeee!" of the storm. He inched himself to the door of the radar shack, freed the dogs, and tried to pull the door open, but the wind held it tightly shut. He pounded on the wet steel with his knuckles, and kicked at it, and screamed, "Open up! Open up! It's the OOD!" A crack appeared and widened. He darted through, knocking down one of the radarmen who was pushing against the door. It snapped shut as though on a spring.

"What the hell!" exclaimed Willie.

There were perhaps twenty sailors jammed in the tiny space, all in life jackets with waterproof searchlights pinned to them, all with whistles dangling around their necks, all with the same round-eyed bristly white face of fear. "How are we doing, Mr. Keith?" spoke the voice of Meatball from the rear of the crush.

"We're doing fine——"

"We gonna have to abandon ship, sir?" said a filthy-faced fireman.

Willie suddenly realized what was so very strange about the shack beside the crowd. It was brightly lit. Nobody was paying any attention to the dim green scopes of the radars. He let loose a stream of obscenity that surprised him as it came out of his mouth. The sailors shrank a little from him. "Who turned on the lights in here? Who's got the watch?"

"Sir, there's nothing on the scopes but sea return," whined a radarman.

Willie cursed some more, and then said, "Douse the lights. Get your faces against these scopes and keep them there."

"Okay, Mr. Keith," said the radarman, in a friendly, respectful tone, "but it won't do no good." In the gloom Willie quickly saw that the sailor was right. There was no trace of the pips of the other ships, nothing but a blurry peppering and streaking of green all over the scopes. "You see, sir," said the voice of the technician, patiently, "our masthead ain't no higher than the water most of the time, and, anyway, all this spray, why, it's like a solid object, sir. These scopes are jammed out——"

"All the same," said Willie, "the watch will be maintained on these radars, and you'll keep trying till you do get something! And all the guys who don't belong in here—well—well, stay here, and keep your faces closed so the watch-standers can do their duty——"

"Sir, are we really okay?"

"Will we have to abandon ship?"

"I was ready to jump on that last roll——"

"Will the ship come through it, Mr. Keith?"

"We're okay," shouted Willie. "We're okay. Don't lose your heads. You'll be back chipping paint in a few hours——"

"I'll chip this rusty old bitch till doomsday if she just rides out this blow," said a voice, and there was a ripple of small laughs.

"I'm staying up here if I get a court-martial for it——"

"Me, too—"

"Hell, there are forty guys over on the lee of the bridge——"

"Mister Keith"—the gutter twang of Meatball again—"honest, does the old man know what the Christ he's doing? That's all we want to know."

"The old man's doing great. You bastards shut up and take it easy. Couple of you help me get this door open."

Wind and spray blasted in through the open crack. Willie pulled himself out and the door clanged. The wind blew him forward into the pilothouse. In the seconds that elapsed he was drenched as by buckets of water. "Radars are jammed, Steve. Nothing to see until this spray moderates——"

"Very well."

Despite the whining and crashing of the storm, Willie got the impression of silence in the wheelhouse. Queeg hung to the telegraph as before. Stilwell swayed at the wheel. Urban, wedged between the binnacle and the front window, clutched the quartermaster's log as if it were a Bible. Usually there were other sailors in the wheelhouse—telephone talkers, signalmen—but they were avoiding it now as though it were the sickroom of a cancer victim. Maryk stood with both hands clamped to the captain's chair. Willie staggered to the starboard side and glanced out at the wing. A crowd of sailors and officers pressed against the bridgehouse, hanging to each other, their clothes whipping in the wind. Willie saw Keefer, Jorgensen, and nearest him, Harding.

"Willie, are we going to be okay?" Harding said.

The OOD nodded, and fell back into the wheelhouse. He was vexed at not having a flashlight and whistle, like everyone else. "Just my luck to be on watch," he thought. He did not really believe yet that the ship was going to founder, but he resented being at a disadvantage. His own man-overboard gear was in his desk below. He thought of sending the boatswain's mate for it; and was ashamed to issue the order.

The *Caine* yawed shakily back and forth on heading 180 for a couple of minutes. Then suddenly it was flung almost on its beam-ends to port by a swell, a wave and a gust of wind hitting together. Willie reeled, brought up against Stilwell, and grabbed at the wheel spokes.

"Captain," Maryk said, "I still think we ought to ballast—at least the stern tanks, if we're going to steam before the wind."

Willie glanced at Queeg. The captain's face was screwed up as though he were looking at a bright light. He gave no sign of having heard. "I request permission to ballast stern tanks, sir," said the exec.

Queeg's lips moved. "Negative," he said calmly and faintly.

Stilwell twisted the wheel sharply, pulling the spokes out of Willie's hands. The OOD grasped an overhead beam.

"Falling off to *starboard* now. Heading 189—190—191——"

Maryk said, "Captain—hard left rudder?"

"Okay," murmured Queeg.

"Hard left rudder, sir," said Stilwell. "Heading 200——"

The exec stared at the captain for several seconds while the minesweeper careened heavily to port and began its nauseating sideslipping over the swells, the wind flipping it around now in the other direction. "Captain, we'll have to use engines again, she's not answering to the rudder. . . . Sir, how about heading up into the wind? She's going to keep broaching to with this stern wind—"

Queeg pushed the handles of the telegraph. "Fleet course is 180," he said.

"Sir, we have to maneuver for the safety of the ship——"

"Sunshine knows the weather conditions. We've received no orders to maneuver at discretion——" Queeg looked straight ahead, constantly clutching the telegraph amid the gyrations of the wheelhouse.

"Heading 225—falling away fast, sir——"

An unbelievably big gray wave loomed on the port side, high over the bridge. It came smashing down. Water spouted into the wheelhouse from the open window, flooding to Willie's knees. The water felt surprisingly warm and sticky, like blood. "Sir, we're shipping water on the goddamn *bridge!*" said Maryk shrilly. "We've *got* to come around into the wind!"

"Heading 245, sir." Stilwell's voice was sobbing. "She ain't answering to the engines at all, sir!"

The *Caine* rolled almost completely over on its port side. Everybody in the wheelhouse except Stilwell went sliding across the streaming deck and piled up against the windows. The sea was under their noses, dashing up against the glass. "Mr. Maryk, the light on this gyro just went out!" screamed Stilwell, clinging desperately to the wheel. The wind howled and shrieked in Willie's ears. He lay on his face on the deck, tumbling around in salt water, flailing for a grip at something solid.

"Oh Christ, Christ, Christ, Jesus Christ, save us!" squealed the voice of Urban.

"Reverse your rudder, Stilwell! Hard right! Hard right!" cried the exec harshly.

"Hard right, sir!"

Maryk crawled across the deck, threw himself on the engine-room telegraph, wrested the handles from Queeg's spasmodic grip, and reversed the settings. "Excuse me, Captain——" A horrible coughing rumble came from the stacks. "What's your head?" barked Maryk.

"Two seven five, sir!"

"Hold her at hard right!"

"Aye aye, sir!"

The old minesweeper rolled up a little from the surface of the water.

Willie Keith did not have any idea of what the executive officer was doing, though the maneuver was simple enough. The wind was turning the ship from south to west. Queeg had been trying to fight back to south. Maryk was doing just the opposite, now; seizing on the momentum of the twist to the right and assisting it with all the force of engines and rudder, to try to swing the ship's head completely northward, into the wind and sea. In a calmer moment Willie would easily have understood the logic of the act, but now he had lost his bearings. He sat on the deck, hanging stupidly to a telephone jack box, with water sloshing around his crotch, and looked to the exec as to a wizard, or an angel of God, to save him with magic passes. He had lost faith in the ship. He was overwhelmingly aware that he sat on a piece of iron in an angry dangerous sea. He could think of nothing but his yearning to be saved. Typhoon, *Caine*, Queeg, sea, Navy, duty, lieutenant's bars, all were forgotten. He was like a wet cat mewing on wreckage.

"Still coming around? What's your head? *Keep calling your head!*" yelled Maryk.

"Coming around hard, sir!" the helmsman screamed as though prodded with a knife. "Heading 310, heading 315, heading 320——"

"Ease your rudder to standard!"

"*Ease* the rudder, sir?"

"Yes, ease her, ease her!"

"Ru-rudder is eased, sir——"

"Very well."

Ease, ease, ease—the word penetrated into Willie's fogged mind. He pulled himself to his feet, and looked around. The *Caine* was riding upright. It rolled to one side, to the other, and back again. Outside the windows there was nothing but solid white spray. The sea was invisible. The forecastle was invisible. "You okay, Willie? I thought you were knocked cold." Maryk, braced on the captain's chair, gave him a brief side glance.

"I'm okay. Wha-what's happening, Steve?"

"Well, this is it. We ride it out for a half hour, we're okay—What's your head?" he called to Stilwell.

"Three two five, sir—coming around slower, now——"

"Well, sure, fighting the wind—she'll come around—we'll steady on 000——"

"Aye aye, sir——"

"We will not," said Queeg.

Willie had lost all awareness of the captain's presence. Maryk had filled his mind as father, leader, and savior. He looked now at the little pale man who stood with arms and legs entwined around the telegraph stand, and had the feeling that Queeg was a stranger. The captain, blinking and shaking his head as though he had just awakened, said, "Come left to 180."

"Sir, we can't ride stern to wind and save this ship," said the exec.

"Left to 180, helmsman."

"Hold it, Stilwell," said Maryk.

"Mr. Maryk, fleet course is 180." The captain's voice was faint, almost whispering. He was looking glassily ahead.

"Captain, we've lost contact with the formation—the radars are blacked out——"

"Well, then, we'll find them—I'm not disobeying orders on account of some bad weather——"

The helmsman said, "Steady on 000——"

Maryk said, "Sir, how do we know what the orders are now? The guide's antennas may be down—ours may be—call up Sunshine and tell him we're in trouble——"

Butting and plunging, the *Caine* was a riding ship again. Willie felt the normal vibration of the engines, the rhythm of seaworthiness in the pitching, coming up from the deck into the bones of his feet. Outside the pilothouse there was only the whitish darkness of the spray and the dismal whine of the wind, going up and down in shivery glissandos.

"We're not in trouble," said Queeg. "Come left to 180."

"Steady as you go!" Maryk said at the same instant. The helmsman looked around from one officer to the other, his eyes popping in panic. "Do as I say!" shouted the executive officer. He turned on the OOD. "Willie, note the time." He strode to the captain's side and saluted. "Captain, I'm sorry, sir, you're a sick man. I am temporarily relieving you of command of this ship, under Article 184 of *Navy Regulations.*"

"I don't know what you're talking about," said Queeg. "Left to 180, helmsman."

"Mr. Keith, *you're* the OOD here, what the hell should I do?" cried Stilwell.

Willie was looking at the clock. It was fifteen minutes to ten. He was dumbfounded to think he had had the deck less than two hours. The import of what was taking place between Maryk and Queeg penetrated his mind slowly. He could not believe it was happening. It was as incredible as his own death.

"Never you mind about Mr. Keith," said Queeg to Stilwell, a slight crankiness entering his voice, fantastically incongruous under the circumstances. It was a tone he might have used to complain of a chewing-gum wrapper on the deck. "I told you to come left. That's an order. Now you come left, and fast——"

"Commander Queeg, you aren't issuing orders on this bridge any more," said Maryk. "I have relieved you, sir. You're on the sick list. I'm taking responsibility. I know I'll be court-martialed. I've got the conn——"

"You're under arrest, Maryk. Get below to your room," said Queeg. "Left to 180, I say!"

"Christ, Mr. Keith!" exclaimed the helmsman, looking at Willie. Urban had backed into the farthest corner of the wheelhouse. He stared from the exec to Willie, his mouth open. Willie glanced at Queeg, glued to the telegraph, and at Maryk. He felt a surge of immense drunken gladness.

"Steady on 000, Stilwell," he said. "Mr. Maryk has the responsibility. Captain Queeg is sick."

"Call your relief, Mr. Keith," the captain said at the same instant, with something like real anger. "You're under arrest, too."

"You have no power to arrest me, Mr. Queeg," said Willie.

The shocking change of name caused a look of happy surprise to appear on Stilwell's face. He grinned at Queeg with contempt. "Steady on 000, Mr. Maryk," he said, and turned his back to the officers.

Queeg suddenly quit his grasp on the telegraph stand, and stumbled across the heaving wheelhouse to the starboard side. "Mr. Keefer! Mr. Harding! Aren't there *any* officers out there?" he called to the wing.

"Willie, phone Paynter and tell him to ballast all empty tanks on the double," Maryk said.

"Aye aye, sir." Willie seized the telephone and buzzed the fireroom. "Hello, Paynt? Listen, we're going to ballast. Flood all your empty tanks on the double——You're goddamn right it's about time——"

"Mr. Keith, I did *not* issue any orders to ballast," said Queeg. "You call that fireroom right back——"

Maryk stepped up to the public-address system. "Now, all officers, report to the bridge. All officers, report to the bridge." He said aside to Willie, "Call Paynter and tell him that word doesn't apply to him."

"Aye aye, sir." Willie pulled the phone from the bracket.

"I said once and I say again," Queeg exclaimed querulously, "both of you are under arrest! Leave the bridge, right now. Your conduct is disgraceful."

Queeg's protests gave Willie a growing sense of gladness and power. In this shadowy careening wet wheelhouse, in the twilit darkness of midmorning, with a murderous wind shrieking at the windows, he seemed to be living the happiest moment of his life. All fear had left him.

Maryk said, "Willie, think you can grab a look at the barometer without being blown over the side?"

"Sure, Steve." He went out on the port wing, clinging carefully to the bridge structure. As he crept up to the charthouse door it came open, and Harding, Keefer, and Jorgensen emerged, clasping each other's hands.

"What's the dope, Willie? What goes on?" yelled Keefer.

"Steve relieved the captain!"

"*What?*"

"Steve relieved the captain! He's got the conn! He's put the captain on the sick list!" The officers looked at each other and lunged for the wheelhouse. Willie edged to the rear bulkhead and peered around at the blurry barometer. He dropped to his hands and knees and crawled back to the pilothouse. "Steve, it's up," he cried, jumping to his feet as he came to the doorway. "It's up! Twenty-eight ninety-nine, almost 29.00!"

"Good, maybe we'll be through the worst of it in a while." Maryk stood beside the wheel, facing aft. All the officers except Paynter were grouped, dripping, against the bulkhead. Queeg was hanging to the telegraph again, glaring at the exec. "Well, that's the story, gentlemen," Maryk said, his voice pitched high over the roar of the wind and the rattle of spray on the windows. "The responsibility is entirely mine. Captain Queeg will continue to be treated with the utmost courtesy, but I will give all command orders——"

"Don't kid yourself that the responsibility is all yours," Queeg interposed sulkily. "Young Mr. Keith here supported you in your mutinous conduct from the start and he'll pay just as you will. And you officers"—he turned, shaking his finger at them—"if you know what's good for you, will advise Maryk and Keith to put themselves under arrest and restore command to me while the restoring is good. I may be induced to overlook what's happened in view of the circumstances, but——"

"It's out of the question, Captain," said Maryk. "You're sick, sir——"

"I'm no sicker than you are," exclaimed Queeg with all his old irritation. "You'll all hang for collusion in mutiny, I kid you not about that——"

"Nobody will hang but me," said Maryk to the officers. "This is my act, taken without anybody's advice, under Article 184, and if I've misapplied Article 184, I'll get hung for it. Meantime all of you take my orders. There's nothing else you can do. I've taken command, I've ballasted on my own re-sponsibility, the ship is on the course I ordered——"

"Mr. Maryk," Stilwell shouted. "Something up ahead, a ship or some-thing, close aboard, sir!"

Maryk whirled, squinted out through the windows, and grabbed at the tele-graph handles, hurling Queeg roughly aside. The captain staggered and grasped a window handle. "Hard right rudder!" the exec shouted, ringing up full astern on both engines.

Visibility had improved so that the sea was in sight through the driving spray some fifty yards beyond the bows. A vast dim red shape bobbed on the black swells, slightly to port.

The *Caine* veered quickly, shoved sideways by the wind as soon as it turned a little. The thing drifted closer. It was immense, long and narrow, longer than the *Caine* itself, bright red. Waves were breaking over it in showers of foam.

"Holy Mother of God," said Keefer. "It's the bottom of a ship."

Everybody stared in awe at the horror. It slipped slowly down the port side, endlessly long and red, rolling gently under the breaking waves. "Destroyer," Harding said in a choked voice.

The *Caine* was moving well clear of it. Part of the wreck was already gone in the gloom. "We'll circle," said Maryk. "All engines ahead full, Willie."

"Aye aye, sir." The OOD rang up the order. There was a hideous sickness at the pit of his stomach.

Maryk went to the p.a. box and pressed the lever. "Now all hands topside keep a sharp lookout for survivors. We will circle the capsized ship twice. Report anything you see to the bridge. Don't get excited. Don't anybody get blown overboard, we have enough trouble as it is."

Queeg, braced in a forward corner against the windows, said, "If you're so worried about the safety of this ship, how can you go monkeying around looking for survivors?"

"Sir, we can't just steam by and forget it——" said the exec.

"Oh, don't misunderstand me. I think we should look for survivors. In fact, I order you to do so. I'm simply pointing out your inconsistency for the record——"

"Left standard rudder," said Maryk.

"I should also like to point out," said Queeg, "that twenty minutes before you illegally relieved me I ordered you to get rid of that helmsman and you disobeyed me. He's the worst troublemaker on the ship. When he obeyed you instead of me he became a party to this mutiny, and he'll hang if it's——"

A roaring wave broke over the *Caine's* bridge and buffeted the ship far over to port, and Queeg tumbled to his hands and knees. The other officers slid and tottered about, clutching at each other. Once again the minesweeper labored in difficulties as the wind caught it and swept it sideways. Maryk went to the telegraph stand and manipulated the engines, altering the settings frequently, and shouting swift-changing rudder orders. He coaxed the ship around to the south, and steamed ahead until the hulk came vaguely in view again. Then he commenced a careful circling maneuver, keeping the *Caine* well clear of the foundering wreck. It was entirely awash now; only when a deep trough rode under it did the round red bottom break to the surface. The officers muttered among themselves. Queeg, his arm around the compass stand, stared out of the window.

It took forty minutes for the *Caine* to maneuver through a full circle around the lost ship against wind and waves, and all the time it wallowed and thrashed as badly as it had been doing since morning, and took several terrible rolls to leeward. Willie was scared each time. But he now knew the difference between honest fright and animal terror. One was bearable, human, not incapacitating; the other was moral castration. He was no longer terrorized, and felt he no longer could be, even if the ship went down, provided Maryk were in the water near him.

The exec was out on the wing, shielding his eyes from the hurtling spray with both hands, peering around at the heavy spires of black water, as the *Caine* steadied on north again. He came into the wheelhouse, trailing streams from his clothes. "We'll come around once more and then quit," he said. "I think it's gone under. I can't see it——Left standard rudder."

Willie groped to the barometer once more and saw that it had risen to 29.10. He crawled to Maryk's side and reported the reading, yelling into the exec's ear. Maryk nodded. Willie rubbed his hands over his face, fevered with the sting of the flailing spray. "Why the hell doesn't it let up, Steve, if the barometer's rising?"

"Oh, Jesus, Willie, we're thirty miles from a typhoon center. Anything can happen in here." The exec grinned into the wind, baring his teeth. "We may still catch all kinds of hell——Rudder amidships!" he shouted through the doorway.

"Rudder amidships, sir!"

"Getting tired, Stilwell?"

"No, sir. Wrestle with this son of a bitch all day if you want me to, sir."

"Very good."

The door of the radar shack pushed open, and the telephone talker, Grubnecker, poked out his whiskered face. "Something that looks like a raft on the starboard quarter, sir, Bellison reports."

Maryk, followed by Willie, went trampling through the wheelhouse to the other side of the bridge, shouting at Stilwell as he passed, "Hard right rudder!"

At first they saw nothing but peaks and troughs of water veiled by spray; then, broad on the beam, as the *Caine* rose to the top of a swell, they both spied a black dot sliding down the slant of a wave.

"I think there's three guys on it!" shrieked Willie. He danced aft to the flagbag rails for a better look. A stiff gust of wind sent him sprawling on his stomach on the canvas cover of the flagbag. As he gasped and clutched wildly at the halyards to keep from rolling over the side, swallowing salt water from the puddle on the canvas, the wind stripped his trousers clean off his legs, and they went flapping away over the bulwark into the sea. He pulled himself to his feet, paying no attention at all to the loss.

Queeg stood in the doorway, face to face with the executive officer. "Well, Mr. Maryk, what are you waiting for? How about rigging your cargo net to starboard and having your deck force stand by with life buoys?"

"Thank you, sir. I was about to give those orders, if you'll let me pass."

Queeg stepped aside. The exec went into the pilothouse, and passed the instructions over the loudspeaker. He began to maneuver the lurching ship toward the object, which soon showed clear, a gray balsam raft, with three men on it and two more heads bobbing beside it in the water.

"You'll be interested to know, gentlemen," Queeg said to the officers while Maryk manipulated engines and rudder, "that I was about to issue orders to ballast and head into the wind when Mr. Maryk committed his panic-stricken criminal act. I had previously determined in my own mind that if the fleet guide had given no orders by 1000 I would act at my own discretion——"

Maryk said, "All right, Stilwell, head over to the right some more. Hard right——"

Queeg went on, "And I saw no reason for confiding my command decisions to Mr. Maryk, who seemed to be treating me like a feeble-minded idiot, and I'll say as much over the green table, and there'll be plenty of witnesses to——"

"Don't run 'em down, Stilwell! Rudder amidships!" Maryk stopped the engines and went to the loudspeaker. "Now throw over your buoys!"

The survivors were pulled aboard. A white-faced, wild-eyed sailor, naked except for white drawers, streaked with broad smears of oil, with a bleeding gash in his cheek, was brought to the bridge by Bellison. The chief said, "It was the *George Black*, sir. This here is Morton, quartermaster third. The others are down in sick bay."

Morton stammered a brief, horrid tale. The *George Black* had been thrown broadside to the wind and all combinations of engine and rudder had failed to bring it around. Ventilators, ammunition boxes, and davits were ripped off the decks by the seas; water began flooding the engine rooms; power failed; the lights went out. The helpless ship drifted for ten minutes, rolling further and further to starboard, with all hands screaming or praying, and finally took a tremendous roll to starboard and never stopped rolling. His next recollection was being under water in complete blackness, and after that he was at the surface, being dashed against the red bottom of his ship.

"We'll keep circling," said Maryk. He peered out at the streaked sea, visible now for several hundred yards. "I think it's letting up some. Take him below, Bellison."

"I am resuming the conn, Mr. Maryk," said Queeg, "and we'll drop the matter entirely until the storm has abated."

Maryk turned wearily to the captain. "No, sir. I've got it. I respectfully ask you to lay below to your cabin. Contradictory orders will endanger the ship——"

"Are you putting me off my bridge, sir?"

"Yes, Captain."

Queeg looked to the officers. Their faces were scared and somber. "Do all you gentlemen concur in this act? . . . Do you, Mr. Keefer?"

The novelist gnawed at his lips, and turned his glance to Maryk. "Nobody is concurring. Nobody has to concur," the exec said quickly. "Please leave the bridge, Captain, or at least refrain from giving orders."

"I shall remain on the bridge," said Queeg. "The ship is still my responsibility. Mutiny doesn't relieve me of it. I shall not speak unless your acts appear to me to be endangering my ship. In that case I shall speak even at pistol point——"

"Nobody's pulling pistols on you, sir. What you say suits me." The exec nodded to the officers. "Okay, no need for you to hang around. We'll have a meeting as soon as weather permits."

The officers began straggling out of the wheelhouse. Keefer went up to Willie, saluted, and said with a pallid grin, "I am ready to relieve you, sir."

Willie looked at the clock in astonishment. Time had stopped running in his mind. It was a quarter to twelve. "Okay," he said. The formulas of the relieving ceremony came mechanically to his lips. "Steaming on various courses and speeds to look for survivors of the *George Black*. Steaming on boilers one, two, and three. Depth charges set on safe. Condition Able set throughout the ship. Last time I saw the barometer it had risen to 29.10. Fleet course is 180, but we've lost contact with formation due to jammed radars, and I don't know where we are. About one hundred and fifty miles east of Ulithi, I'd say. You can check our 0800 dead reckoning position. We're in the same place, more or less. The captain has been relieved under Article 184, and is still on the bridge. The executive officer has command and is at the conn. I guess that's all."

"Just a routine watch," said Keefer. Willie smiled ruefully.

Keefer saluted. "Okay, I've got it." He grasped Willie's hand, pressed it warmly, and whispered, "Good work."

"God help us all," murmured Willie.

Sea Phantoms

The Giant Ship

by WILLIAM BASSETT

Somewhere in the Western Ocean in those tossing leagues of sea that lie to the eastward of the fishing grounds upon the Grand Banks of Newfoundland the stout bark Etoile de Saint Malo rolled sullenly in a dark sea and shook from her idle sails enfolding masses of fog. Her hold was full of the shining cod, her heavy trawl boats stowed and lashed for a voyage, and up and down her decks strode her aged master impatient of the walls of fog, and of the listless air that would not lift her sheets. She was an ancient little ship with the stately bow of a medieval frigate. Her long bowsprit cocked high into the air and about her quarters was the scroll work of a false gallery, as though she had once been the pet of some admiral of France. From a distance she was a fair sight for any sailor eye, but once alongside one saw that whatever noble past she may have had she was now a fisherman. Her frayed ratlines drew down cracked and withered deadeyes, and rusty stains smouldered on her greasy and battered planks. The staysail and spanker that swung listlessly with her roll were stained a dull red and the rest of her canvas was tattered and patched. An old-style anchor with wooden stock hung by ring and fluke from her rail, and its rusty chain clanked idly in her hawse. Two long days she had thus whistled for a breeze and clanged her doleful bell against the curtains of fog. Sailors in wooden shoes, stout jerseys and round watch caps smoked by the forecastle hatch and pretended to keep a lookout. It was late summer and the keen flat smell of ice was in the air. Warm weather had broken the northern ice packs and their great masses were moving ponderously southward, their mailed fists masked in the velvet gauntlet of the mist.

Amidships a fresh foretopsail lay in stiff folds upon the deck and five sailors with palmthimbles and fids laboriously overhauled its leeches. Adrien Bort, the master, kept an eye upon them and an eye aloft for the first sign of a breeze.

Seven months the little ship had been away from the walled garden of St. Malo and the sweet waters of the Rance, and Adrien was impatient of the quiet sea, impatient of the drifting hull and idle sails. Never a close navigator he was now many days from his last observation and literally "at sea" as to his position. Fifty years he had followed the sea from cabin boy to master, but to-day he longed for the shore and burned with the petulance of inaction. It was bad enough, this fishing ground of the "New-worlders"; even when the sun shone, the ship lay hove to under try sails in bright sea, the trawl boats came merrily back with their silver treasures, and the tackles creaked to the glad chorus of the banks,

> La v'la pourtant finie,
> La maudite campagne du banc,

but this helpless floating on unknown currents with an idle wheel was insufferable. His memory went back to days in the roaring wilderness of the Horn,
to glorious nights under royals in the vast Pacific, to the noisy docks of Amoy
and the heat-browned banks of the Hoogli, and he shivered in the stark air of
the north.

Toward evening there was a change in the flat sounds about the ship. From
somewhere beyond the wall a long swell rolled toward the brig and heaved
itself under her quarters. Her yards swung drunkenly as she rolled away from
it, and a thousand protesting voices awoke aloft. Men scrambled on deck from
the forward hatch as Adrien Bart shouted, "It is finished; behold the fair
wind!" The fog seemed to harden and to roll up from its base; lanes and
shadings of light appeared in it; cloud shapes evolved themselves whose crests
toppled and rolled forward and in a moment the fog was flying away to leeward
before a fresh breeze. The spanker sheet was eased away, yards trimmed and
the topsail mastheaded to the cry of

> Ali, Alo, pour maschero.
> Il mange la viande et nous donnes les os.

The bitter drudgery of the north was done and St. Malo lay ahead, the fog and
ice, salt burns and gurry sores were forgotten and with gear coiled away and
made snug for the night, smoke pouring from the galley stack and the master
himself at the wheel the watch below went back joyfully to their forecastle as
night set in. Worn packs of cards were brought out, an accordion dragged out
of a sea chest and the dark little room resounded to the call of happy voices.
Here was Jules Bourbier, one time man-of-war's man, who knew the songs of
a hundred ports. Over there with the round red cap sat Alfonse the cook who
could and would improvise a bass to support any song. Anatole of Dol it was
who brought forth the accordion and no one had a better memory than he for
the endless songs of the sailor saints of Brittany. No man of the throngs that
journeyed to the Foire es Marins at Vieux Bourg, was better known. Jules
urged him to sing the rowing song of St. Malo, another called for the beautiful
"Er re goli," the Breton litany, but Anatole waved them aside and in a high
voice sang

> We were three sailors of Groix
> On board the Saint François.

All hands nodded their delight and joined loudly in the chorus:

> Embarqués sur le Saint François
> Et du vin à tous les repas
> Mon traderi, tra la la la.

In the after-cabin a sturdy lad of fifteen lit a swinging lamp and set out upon
a small table a decanter of wine and some biscuit. The light showed a cozy

cabin, a bunk neatly made up, a case of charts, three pictures of the saints. The boy set a plate-fiddle upon the table and made it fast and then went up the companionway to the deck. The wind had freshened, and the ship, rather deeply laden, tore heavily and noisily through the seas, shouldering the water from her lee bow and bobbing her head into the seas to her very eyes. The boy hurried aft to the wheel where the captain still stood, "Very well, grandfather, she hurries right back to St. Malo. I think we shall be out of the ice very soon." The old man shook his head. "We run too fast in the dark, little son. I am a happy man when I hand you back safely to your mother on the quai of St. Malo. The old ship makes too many groans to-night, and I feel the ice somewhere near." He threw his wheel up three spokes as a curling hurrying sea grasped at the weather rail, and steadied himself as the vessel heeled slowly before it. A snatch of song from the forecastle crept faintly aft as the ship's bow rose to the sea but was immediately lost in the clamor of her scuppers.

The captain swung his wheel down again and sent the lad forward to see if the lookout was at his post. Groping his way along the weather rail, past the dark bulks of the trawl boats, the lad found the lookout and was about to return when he heard the loud chorus from the forecastle, *"Mon traderi, tra la la la."* Quietly he slipped down through the hatch into the circle of sailors below. The song was ended and he joined in the applause for Anatole's singing.

"Sit down, little man," they cried. "Here's plenty of room. All the villagers will be here presently, and we shall dance and maybe have a play. There are no better times to be had on *La Grande Chasse Foudre* herself."

"What ship is that?" asked the boy. "Is she a new-worlder?"

"Ha, listen to the boy, the poor little farmer boy! You'll hear of that grand ship soon enough, but if you steal any more cakes from the cook you'll never get aboard her." A shout greeted the sally, and the lad covered with confusion edged away and ran up the ladder into the darkness of the forward deck. His eyes were blinded for a moment by the smoke and light of the forecastle and he felt his way carefully aft, groping along the rail.

He had taken but a step when a wild cry suddenly rent the air, "Bear away, bear away!" It was a cry of agony and fear from the lookout, and almost at the same moment and before the words had died away the rushing hull struck with shattering impact a great mass of submerged ice. The straining masts snapped short off and fell with a mighty roar upon the decks; planks ground and splintered, and the blasted hull groaning in dissolution slipped from the edge of its destroyer, and slowly and sullenly subsided into the icy waters. With the first shock, the aged master and the boy were thrown against the lee rail stunned and bleeding. In a moment they scrambled to their feet and grasping each other in the darkness they jumped into a trawl boat and with their sharp knives cut away the lashings that held it to its chocks upon the deck. They threw themselves into the bottom of the boat and as the ship slipped softly down into the deep they were lifted clear of the deck and tossed and whirled about in the eddies above her grave. Numbed by the cold and shocked by the suddenness of their disaster they lay quietly in the trawl boat.

Morning came slowly to the cold northern sea. A faint light crept into the
sky and gradually illuminated the heavy walls of mist that hung about the boat.
All night the old man and the boy had lain under the thin protection of a torn
boat cover which had barely served to keep the spray and dripping fog from
their aching bodies. With the first light the boy dragged himself painfully onto
the thwart and looked about him eagerly for some promise of rescue. A small
amount of water ran under the boat floor and this he carefully bailed out. For a
long time he sat huddled in the stern waiting for the dawn that should enable
him to see beyond the encircling curtains of morning mist. There were oars in
the boat but no sail, and without provisions or fresh water he realized that the
only hope to which he and the old man could look was that another ship might
see them during the coming day. He was reluctant to disturb his grandfather
and left him in his stupor of shock and cold until with the advancing morning
the sheer loneliness and hopelessness of his position got the better of him and
he shook the old man and aroused him from his sleep.

"Grandfather, what shall we do? I cannot see any of the others; we have no
water; we have nothing to eat."

The old man opened his eyes heavily and stared at the boy without comprehension for a time, until all of the events of their terrible last moment aboard
the brig reshaped themselves in his mind.

"Alas," he said at last, "she is gone—my good ship, and all my brave
boys, and all my fine cod, and Saint Anne D'Ouray has forgotten me."

"Yes, grandfather, but some one will see us and we shall get back to St.
Malo, but I wish we had something to eat."

The old man, with the help of the boy, tried to rise, but he fell back weakly
and gasped out that his ribs were broken, and so he lay there staring into the
misty sky—this old sailor, who, for half a century had laughed at the menace
of these cold, gray seas.

The boat tossed sullenly within her dull circle of sea, and the boy, cold,
hungry and dispirited, sat by the side of the old man, and thought over the
short years of his life. He recalled the little town of Miquelon where he was
born, and the broad fields that now spread their golden stubble in the late
summer sun. He saw again St. Malo with her ancient causeway and encom-
passing walls, and the bright roadstead where he had first seen the brig Etoile
lying proudly at anchor. He lived over again the day with the village boys
when they had stolen oranges from the open market, and the proud morning
when he had first donned sailor's cap and blouse and gone with his grandfather as part of the crew of the lost brig.

Small fry of the sea flashed out of the water alongside and dashed away
before an unseen pursuer. Bright sea cucumbers, the "punkins" of the Banks,
floated idly by, and the day wore on, bringing nearer another night of cold,
hunger and thirst with its possibilities even of rain or wind.

The old man's face was sunken and purple, and the youth found it more and
more difficult to arouse him or hold his attention. The loneliness of his position and the thought that if the old man again fell into a deep sleep he might

never awake, filled the boy with terror, and he strove by every means to keep him awake and to have the comfort of his voice.

"Last night," said the boy, "I was in the fo'castle and the lads were singing, and they said how happy it was and they said it was like *La Grande Chasse Foudre*. What ship is that, grandfather? Did she come from St. Malo?"

Day was fast going, and the chill of night creeping in from measureless ice-packs of the north fastened upon the sluggish frame of the old sailor with a grip of steel, as he lay upon the tossing floor, with his sea dimmed eyes staring up into the unfriendly sky of the north. He laid a massive hand on the boy's knee.

"Fifty years, little son, I have followed the sea, from Labrador to the Horn, and from Sydney to Amoy. In the little church at St. Malo hang many of my gifts, and I have never forgotten my duty to the church and to the saints. Now I am old and at last I am through with night watches and salt meat, with gurry-sores and chilblains. To-morrow the fog will clear, we'll have a brave breeze, and then you shall see *La Grande Chasse Foudre*, and her captain will send a boat and I will go aboard her.

"Aye, that's a fine ship, and I shall have all my good boys with me again, and meat every meal— the fine fat mutton that they keep on board, and never any beans any more, and Burgundy for breakfast, for dinner Madeira, and a glass or so of rum at night. She is a famous ship, lad, a big ship and plenty of room for a man to swing his hammock, for, of course, I shall be a sailor aboard, probably a maintop-man."

"Well, tell me, grandfather, how large is this ship and how fast can she sail?"

"Yes, you may well ask how large she is, but I cannot tell you, for no one knows how may thousand leagues long she is and everything about her is in the same proportion. Why, I have heard it said that her masts are so tall that if you, a mere boy, should start to her maintop to carry soup to the topman you would be a gray old man like me before you reached her futtock-shrouds.

"I don't say though that she is a fast sailor. You don't have to run her head-sheets when she goes about. She sails no faster than a buoy, but then she doesn't go about very often, and when she does it takes her a hundred years to go from full to full. The men take plenty of time for everything and indeed, my boy, it takes plenty of time. They say it takes two hundred years to raise her anchor."

Thus the old sailor, rising above the terror of the moment, beat down his fears with the vision of faith, and the lad, great-eyed and eager, caught from the words of this ancient oracle of the sea a vision of hope and salvation which stilled the pains of hunger and thirst, and shut out the spectre of the cold and menacing sea. In a corner of the boat-cover myriad beads of moisture had merged into a tiny pool and this the boy deftly emptied into his hand and poured it between the old sailor's lips. After a moment he went on:

"There is plenty of room for every one, lad, and she is a brave ship with plenty of arms aboard. There is space for an army to exercise with guns upon her main truck. Her mizzen royal is a nice little sail for a man to handle. It is larger than all Europe.

"I believe I shall know the captain when we see him. He is a great, large, fine man, and he is very old, so old that no one knows any one older, and, of course, he is a big man to hold that berth. He has a long white moustache, thick enough to make a cable for an eighty-gun ship, but that would not make the signal halliard for the *Chasse Foudre*, her signal halliards are as large as the great tower of Toulon, so you can well imagine the size of her cable. Perhaps you would like to be the boy aboard and have a silver pipe? Well, I can tell you, the pipes of her boys are as great as frigates!

"Plenty of good times aboard! Why, there is an inn in every block and plenty of country to hunt and fish and ride about in her tops, and you don't have to do any rigging for her. She was built by one man at the commencement of the world, and it took twenty-five years to build her and quite as long to rig her."

It was late afternoon by this time, and far off on the horizon to the westward, the boy's eyes caught a gathering of dark clouds brooding over a squall of rain.

"There's a rainbow, grandfather, isn't it a good sign?"

The old man seemed lost in his own thoughts. His eyes were shining and seemed to look through the sky into which he peered and to see there some vision of ineffable happiness. The plucky lad had knelt down at his side and slowly raised the master so that his eyes looked out over the edge of the gunwale toward the western sky.

"See there," cried the boy, "there is my rainbow." The light brightened again in the old sailor's eyes.

"That's no rainbow, lad; that must be the pennant of *La Grande Chasse Foudre*. All those colors that you see are the emblems of all nations for she is the ship of every country. She comes slowly, boy, but she will be here in the morning.

"When the master sees us he will blow his whistle and call away a boat. That is the sound you hear in the blocks when the wind blows like the devil. Then you will hear the officer of the watch call for the boat's crew with his trumpet and that is what you country boys call the thunder; and the tides, you think the moon attracts them, but that is only the captain entering the quarter-galleries, and the ebb, *bien!* that is the men pumping water to wash the decks in the morning."

The old man sank back and closed his eyes, with the smile of assured peace.

"I shall see there again all of my good and brave boys and we shall sail forever, for there is no dying aboard the *Chasse Foudre*."

The boy, straining his eyes to windward, saw a faint blackness on the horizon, which, as he watched, grew to a smudge of smoke. Struggling to his feet he stood shading his eyes in the fading light, seeing the faint blur lengthen and darken until it was unmistakably the breath of some high-powered ship. In a frenzy of glad excitement he strove in vain to arouse the old sailor, who had sunk again into a deep sleep. Hurriedly he tore the back from his blouse and lashed it to the blade of a long oar which he held aloft in the light breeze.

Slowly but surely a dark line appeared below the streamer of smoke and his heart raced with the hope that the approaching vessel would see his ragged signal before night set in. Like some pasteboard ship upon a painted drop she moved nearer and nearer until presently, in the dim light of the evening, she seemed gradually to expand. Brass rails and white cabin walls suddenly appeared and as the boy waved his tattered pennant to and fro he saw the long ship's side gradually swing away and the great bow, crowned with its lines of stacks, stood toward him.

He shouted wildly, "Grandfather, grandfather, she sees us! She's coming!"

But the old man gave him no sign. He dropped his oar as the great ship slowly approached him to windward and a boat dropped noisily into the water. The tense hours of fasting and fear were over, and the exhausted youth dropped his head upon the gunwale of the boat and sobbed in thankfulness and exhaustion. Strong arms lifted him up and gave him water and brandy, and he looked once more into the face of the living.

He turned to the old man, still lying upon the boat cover on the floor, and saw him there in the arms of a young ship's surgeon, in whose face he read the message that the old sailor had at last heard the call of the master of *La Grande Chasse Foudre*, and had gone to take his place with all those good and happy sailor mates of his past in the crew of the great ship which would sail forever more.

The Craft of Death

by R. T. ROSS

Night was upon the sea. Outstretched, sprawling, upon a little raft of barely sufficient buoyancy to support its burden, lay the form of a man. There was nothing, absolutely nothing else upon the raft, save a slight mast near one end, down which hung limply a shapeless piece of canvas. The sea heaved gently in slow and rhythmic pulses, the sodden raft rising heavily to each movement.

The dawn was near. The eastern sky changed from black to gray, and as quickly to blue; broad shafts of light shot upward toward the zenith, and abruptly the big white sun, instantly hot, sprang from out the glassy water.

The form stirred. Awakened by the light, the man raised his head, and, gripping the mast, got heavily and painfully to his feet. Clasping the mast closely, he turned his dim eyes slowly around the horizon, then slid down again into a formless heap at the mast's foot.

Hour by hour the sun climbed in the clear sky, merciless, gathering strength as it rose, pouring its pitiless heat upon the raft and its helpless burden, forsaken alike by man and God. At times the man crawled weakly to different parts of the raft, as the scant shadow of the mast shifted.

A sea-bird circled overhead, screaming curiously. A fish splashed the oily water. The man looked at them in turn, despairingly. He dipped his hands in the sea and wet his face and breast. The water dried upon him, and whitened him with its salt. The sun reached the meridian and began a lingering descent. Slowly it neared the western horizon and at last disappeared beneath the waste of waters. The stars blazed out, and there came a change.

A soft, cool breeze rippled the smooth surface of the water; it filled the shapeless sail, and the raft surged gently ahead. The coolness soothed the man and he slept. After a while he awakened; he sat up, got his back against the mast and sighed, even in his misery, with a comparative contentment.

The refreshing coolness increased as the night wore on. The raft bubbled softly through the water and the man presently found strength to look around him with some interest. A dark shape stole noiselessly out of the shrouding night. The man's eyes fastened themselves upon it. What was it? Was it but another vision? No, it was real—it was approaching—it was nearer—it was a boat, a large boat, with a mast and sail set,—a large, square sail!

The man opened his mouth and strove to call, but no sound issued from his dry lips save the hoarse whistling of his breath. The boat neared the raft; it touched; the man stretched forth his hand and clutched its edge with the grip of desperation, and soon the boat and the raft were brought to a common speed.

Gritting his teeth and holding fast with the tenacity of death, the man dragged himself to the boat, and, with a final desperate determination, tumbled himself over its edge, fell prostrate in its bottom and lay there exhausted.

The cool air revived him after awhile and he essayed to rise. Twice he tried, grasping the boat's gunwale, but he was too nearly spent. The third time he succeeded, and seated himself with a grunt of triumph upon a thwart, with the strain of his effort producing red flashes before his eyes.

When he could see and had caught his breath, he looked around him. He saw that his feet rested against a mingled heap of boxes, kegs and sacks, piled up in the boat's bow. On the thwart before him, lashed to the mast, was a large keg, with a dipper fastened to it by a cord. He filled the dipper from the spigot and put it to his lips; it was water! He drank; again and again he drank. He straightened his shoulders and drew a long breath. He opened one of the sacks; it was filled with ship's bread. He ate of it ravenously. He seized one of the smaller kegs. It was wine, and he drank deeply. The vigor of it shot through him; he stretched out his legs before him and breathed deeply.

The breeze had ceased, and the sail hung motionless across the boat in front of him. He looked at it inquiringly. Finally he got to his feet and stumblingly picked his way into the other part of the boat.

Lying there in the bottom of the boat, stretched out in various attitudes, he beheld the motionless forms of a number of men. Evidently they were sleeping and had not heard him enter the boat.

The man paused to collect himself and sank down upon a thwart as his weakness reasserted itself for the moment. How would they receive him—he, the stranger, who brought nothing, and would but draw the more upon their stores? Pshaw! was he not also shipwrecked and in the very extremity of suffering, and were they not also human beings?

He reached down and shook the nearest man. He lay as a log. He shook him again and yet again, and harder yet. The man lay as one dead. He kneeled and looked closer at him in the starlight, and as he did so his nostrils caught the unmistakable odor of putrefaction. He staggered to his feet, drawing long breaths, gazing at the dead man. He turned to the others, but the same discovery awaited him in each case. He sank upon a seat, his head in his hands. What was the meaning of this awful thing? Why could he not think? Was it all but another of those horrid dreams?

The sun was risen ere the man lifted his head and gazed upon the blotched and swollen faces of the dead. A book lying upon a seat caught his eye. He arose and seized it and on its open page read:

May 6, 18—. Ship *Glenora*, Calcutta to London, Peters master, abandoned to-day in latitude —, longitude —. All dead of black plague but ourselves,— John Small, second mate; Fellows, Smith, Lawson, and Gammet, seamen.

May 8. All dead but myself. I have the vomit. May God have mercy on my soul! John Small.

The book fell from the man's nerveless hands, and he stood there, gazing upon the dead. Then he laughed; loud and long his horrid laughter rang out o'er the silent sea; and then, throwing up his hands, he pitched headlong down into the bottom of the boat and lay still among the dead men there.

The Phantom Death

by W. CLARK RUSSELL

On the 24th of April, 1840, having finished the business that had carried me into the Brazils, I arrived at Rio de Janeiro, where I found a vessel lying nearly loaded, and sailing for the port of Bristol in four or five days. In those times, passenger traffic between Great Britain and the eastern coast of South America was almost entirely carried on in small ships, averaging from 200 to 500 tons. The funnel of the ocean mail steamer, with her gilded saloons and side wheels, which, to the great admiration of all beholders, slapped twelve knots an hour out of the composite fabric, had not yet hove into sight above the horizon of commerce, and folks were very well satisfied if they were no longer than three months in reaching the Brazilian coast out of the River Thames.

The little ship in which I took passage was a barque called the *Lord of the Isles;* her burden was something under four hundred tons. She was a round-bowed wagon of a vanished type, with a square, sawed-off stern, painted ports, heavy over-hanging channels, and as loftily rigged, I was going to say, as a line-of-battle ship, owing to her immense beam, which gave her the stability of a church. I applied to the agent and hired a cabin, and found myself, to my secret satisfaction, the only passenger in the ship. Yes, I was rejoiced to be the sole passenger; my passage out had been rendered memorably miserable by the society of as ill-conditioned, bad-tempered, sulky lot of wretches as ever turned in of a night into bunks, and cursed the captain in their gizzards in a calm for not being able to whistle a wind up over the sea-line.

The name of the skipper of the *Lord of the Isles* was Joyce. He was unlike the average run of the men in that trade. Instead of being beef-faced and bow-legged, humid of eye and gay with grog-blossoms, he was tall, pale, spare; he spoke low and in a melancholy key; he never swore; he drank wine and water, and there was little or nothing in his language to suggest the sailor. His berth was right aft on the starboard side; mine was right aft also, next his. Three cabins on either hand ran forward from these two after-berths. Two of them were occupied by the first and second mates. Between was a roomy "state-cabin," as the term then was: a plain interior furnished with an oblong table and fixed chairs, lighted by day by a large skylight, by night by a couple of brass lamps.

We sailed away on a Monday morning, as well as I recollect, out of the spacious and splendid scene of the harbor of Rio, and under full breasts of canvas, swelling to the height of a main-skysail big enough to serve as a mizzen topgallant-sail for a thousand-ton ship of to-day, and with taut bowlines and yearning jibs, and a heel of hull that washed a two-foot wide streak of greenish copper through the wool-white swirl of froth that broke from the bows, the *Lord of the Isles* headed on a straight course for the deep solitudes of the Atlantic.

All went well with us for several days. Our ship's company consisted of twelve men, including a boatswain and carpenter. The forecastle hands appeared very hearty, likely fellows, despite their pier-head raiment of Scotch cap and broken small clothes, and open flannel shirt, and greasy sheath-knife belted to the hip. They worked with a will, they sang out cheerily at the ropes, they went in and out of the galley at meal-time without faces of loathing, and but one complaint came aft before our wonderful, mysterious troubles began: the ship's bread crawled, they said, and, being found truly very bad, good white flour was served out in lieu.

We had been eight days at sea, and in that time had made fairly good way: it drew down a quiet, soft, black night with the young moon gone soon after sunset, a trembling flash of stars over the mastheads, a murky dimness of heat and of stagnation all round about the sea-line, and a frequent glance of sea-fire over the side when a dip of the barque's round bends drove the water from her in a swelling cloud of ebony. I walked the quarter-deck with the captain, and our talk was of England and of the Brazils, and of his experiences as a mariner of thirty years' standing.

"What of the weather?" said I, as we came to a pause at the binnacle, whose bright disc of illuminated card touched into phantom outlines the hairy features of the Jack who grasped the wheel.

"There's a spell of quiet before us, I fear," he answered, in his melancholy, monotonous voice. "No doubt a day will come, Mr. West, when the unhappy sea-captain upon whose forehead the shipowner would be glad to brand the words, 'Prompt Despatch' will be rendered by steam independent of that most capricious of all things—wind. The wind bloweth as it listeth—which is very well whilst it keeps all on blowing; for with our machinery of trusses, and parrels, and braces, we can snatch a sort of propulsion out of anything short of hurricane antagonism within six points of what we want to look up for. But of a dead night and of a dead day, with the wind up and down, and your ship showing her stern to the thirty-two points in a single watch, what's to be done with an owner's request of *look sharp?* Will you come below and have some grog?"

The second mate, a man named Bonner, was in charge of the deck. I followed the captain into the cabin, where he smoked a cigar; he drank a little wine and water, I drained a tumbler of cold brandy grog, then stepped above for an hour of fresh air, and afterwards to bed, six bells, eleven o'clock, striking as I turned in.

I slept soundly, awoke at seven o'clock, and shortly afterwards went on deck. The watch were at work washing down. The crystal brine flashed over the white plank to the swing of the bucket in the boatswain's powerful grasp, and the air was filled with the busy noise of scrubbing-brushes, and of the murmurs of some live-stock under the long boat. The morning was a wide radiant scene of tropic sky and sea—afar, right astern on the light blue verge, trembled the mother-o'-pearl canvas of a ship; a small breeze was blowing off the beam; from under the round bows of the slightly-leaning barque came a pleasant, brook-like sound of running waters—a soft shaling as of a foam over stones, sweet to the ear in that heat as the music of a fountain. Mr. Bonner, the second mate, was again in charge of the deck. When I passed through the companion hatch I saw him standing abreast of the skylight at the rail: the expression of his face was grave and full of concern, and he seemed to watch the movements of the men with an inattentive eye.

I bade him good morning; he made no reply for a little, but looked at me fixedly, and then said, "I'm afraid Captain Joyce is a dead man."

"What is wrong with him?" I exclaimed eagerly, and much startled.

"I don't know, sir. I wish there was a medical man on board. Perhaps you'd be able to tell what he's suffering from if you saw him."

I at once went below, and found the lad who waited upon us in the cabin preparing the table for breakfast. I asked him if the captain was alone. He answered that Mr. Stroud, the chief mate, was with him. On this, I went to the door of Captain Joyce's cabin and lightly knocked. The mate looked out, and, seeing who I was, told me in a soft voice to enter.

Captain Joyce lay in his bunk dressed in a flannel shirt and a pair of white drill trousers. All his throat and a considerable portion of his chest were exposed, and his feet were naked. I looked at him, scarcely crediting my sight: I did not know him as the man I had parted with a few hours before. He was swelled from head to foot as though drowned: the swelling contorted his countenance out of all resemblance to his familiar face; the flesh of him that was visible was a pale blue, as if rubbed with a powder of the stuff called "blue" which the laundresses use in getting up their linen. His eyes were open, but the pupils were rolled out of sight, and the "whites," as they are called, were covered with red blotches.

I had no knowledge of medicine, and could not imagine what had come to the poor man. He was unconscious, and evidently fast sinking. I said to Mr. Stroud, "What is this?"

The mate answered, "I'm afraid he's poisoned himself accidentally. It looks to me like poison. Don't it seem so to you, sir? See how his fingers and toes are curled."

I ran my eye over the cabin and exclaimed, "Have you searched for any bottles containing poison?"

"I did so when he sent for me at four o'clock, and complained of feeling sick and ill. He was then changing color, and his face was losing its proper looks. I asked him if he thought he had taken anything by mistake. He answered no, unless he had done so in his sleep. He awoke feeling very bad, and that's all he could tell me."

I touched the poor fellow's hand, and found it cold. His breathing was swift and thin. At moments a convulsion, like a wrenching shudder, passed through him.

"Is it," I asked, "some form of country sickness, do you think—some kind of illness that was lying latent in him when we sailed?"

"I never heard of any sort of sickness," he answered, "that made a man look like that—not cholera even. And what but poison would do its work so quickly? Depend upon it he's either been poisoned, or poisoned himself unawares."

"Poisoned!" I exclaimed. "Who's the man in this ship that's going to do such a thing?"

"It's no natural illness," he answered, looking at the livid, bloated face of the dying man; and he repeated with gloomy emphasis, "He's either been poisoned, or he's poisoned himself unawares."

I stood beside Mr. Stroud for about a quarter of an hour, watching the captain and speculating upon the cause of his mortal sickness; we talked in low voices, often pausing and starting, for the convulsions of the sufferer made us think that he had his mind and wished to sit up and speak; but the ghastly, horrid, vacant look of his face continued fixed by the stubborn burial of the pupils of his eyes; his lips moved only when his frame was convulsed. I put my finger upon his pulse and found the beat thread-like, terribly rapid, intermittent, and faint. Then, feeling sick and scared, I went on deck for some air.

The second mate asked me how the captain was and what I thought. I answered that he might be dead even now as I spoke; that I could not conceive the nature of the malady that was killing him, that had apparently fastened upon him in his sleep, and was threatening to kill him within the compass of four or five hours, but that Mr. Stroud believed he had been poisoned, or had poisoned himself accidentally.

"Poisoned!" echoed the second mate, and he sent a look in the direction of the ship's galley. "What's he eaten that we haven't partaken of? A regular case of poisoning, does the chief officer think it? Oh no—oh no—who's to do it? The captain's too well liked to allow of such a guess as that. If the food's been fouled by the cook in error, how's it that the others of us who ate at the cabin table aren't likewise seized?"

There was no more to be said about it then, but in less than half an hour's time the mate came up and told us the captain was gone.

"He never recovered his senses, never spoke except to talk in delirium," he said.

"You think he was poisoned, sir?" said the second mate.

"Not wilfully," answered Mr. Stroud, looking at me. "I never said that; nor is it a thing one wants to think of," he added, sending his gaze around the wide scene of flashing ocean.

He then abruptly quitted us and walked to the galley, where for some while he remained out of sight. When he returned he told the second mate with whom I had stood talking that he had spoken to the cook, and thoroughly overhauled the dressing utensils, and was satisfied that the galley had nothing to do with the murderous mischief which had befallen the skipper.

"But why be so cock-certain, Mr. Stroud," said I, "that the captain's dead of poisoning?"

"I *am* cock-certain," he answered shortly, and with some little passion. "Name me the illness that's going to kill man in three or four hours, and make such a corpse of him as lies in the captain's cabin."

He called to the second mate, and they paced the deck together deep in talk. The men had come up from breakfast, and the boatswain had set them to the various jobs of the morning; but the news of the captain's death had gone forward; it was shocking by reason of its suddenness. Then, again, the death of the master of a ship lies cold and heavy upon the spirits of a company at sea; 'tis the head gone, the thinking part. The mate may make as good a captain, but he's not the man the crew signed articles under. The seamen of the *Lord of the Isles* wore grave faces as they went about their work; they spoke softly, and the boatswain delivered his orders in subdued notes. After a bit the second mate walked forward and addressed the boatswain and some of the men, but what he said I did not catch.

I breakfasted and returned on deck; it was then ten o'clock. I found the main-topsail to the mast and a number of seamen standing in the gangway, whilst the two mates hung together on the quarter-deck, talking as though waiting. In a few minutes four seamen brought the body of the captain up through the companion hatch, and carried it to the gangway. The corpse was stitched up in a hammock and rested upon a plank, over which the English ensign was thrown. I thought this funeral very hurried, and dreaded to think that the poor man might be breathing and alive at the instant of his launch, for after all we had but the mate's assurance that the captain was dead; and what did Mr. Stroud know of death—that is, as it would be indicated by the body of a man who had died from some swift, subtle, nameless distemper, as Captain Joyce seemingly had?

When the funeral was over, the topsail swung, and the men returned to their work, I put the matter to the mate, who answered that the corpse had turned black, and that there could be no more question of his being dead than of his now being overboard.

The breeze freshened that morning. At noon it was blowing strong, with a dark, hard sky of compacted cloud, under which curls and shreds of yellow scud fled like a scattering of smoke, and the mates were unable to get an observation. Mr. Stroud seemed engrossed by the sudden responsibilities which had come upon him, and talked little. That afternoon he shifted into the captain's berth, being now, indeed, in command of the barque. It was convenient to him to live in that cabin, for the necessary nautical appliances for navigating the ship were there along with the facilities for their use. Mr. Bonner told me that he and the mate had thoroughly examined the cabin, overhauled the captain's boxes, lockers, shelves and the like for anything of a poisonous nature, but had met with nothing whatever. It was indeed an amazing mystery, he said, and he was no longer of opinion with Mr. Stroud that poison, accidentally or otherwise taken, had destroyed the captain. Indeed, he now leaned to my view, that Captain Joyce had fallen a victim to some disease which had lain latent in him since leaving Rio, something deadly quick and horribly transforming, well known, maybe, to physicians of the Brazils, if, indeed, it were peculiar to that country.

Well, three days passed, and nothing of any moment happened. The wind drew ahead and braced our yards fore and aft for us, and the tub of a barque went to leeward like an empty cask, shouldering the head seas into snowstorms off her heavy round bow, and furrowing a short scope of oil-smooth wake almost at right angles with her sternpost. Though Mr. Stroud had charge of the ship, he continued from this time to keep watch and watch with Mr. Bonner as in the captain's life, not choosing, I daresay, to entrust the charge of the deck to the boatswain. On the evening of this third day that I have come to, I was sitting in the cabin under the lamp writing down some memories of the past week in a diary, when the door of the captain's berth was opened, and my name was faintly called. I saw Mr. Stroud, and instantly went to him. His hands were clasped upon his brow, and he swayed violently as though in pain, with greater vehemence than the heave of the deck warranted; his eyes were starting, and, by the clear light of the brace of cabin lamps I easily saw that his complexion was unusually dusky, and darkening even, so it seemed to me, as I looked.

I cried out, "What is the matter, Mr. Stroud?"

"Oh, my God!" he exclaimed, "I am in terrible pain—I am horribly ill—I am dying."

I grasped him by the arm and conducted him to his bunk, into which he got, groaning and holding his head, with an occasional strange short plunge of his feet such as a swimmer makes when resting in the water on his back. I asked him if he was only just now seized. He answered that he was in a deep sleep, from which he was awakened by a burning sensation throughout his body. He lay quiet awhile, supposing it was a sudden heat of the blood; but the fire increased, and with it came torturing pains in the head, and attacks of convulsions; and even whilst he told me this the convulsive fits grew upon him, and he broke off to groan deeply as though in exquisite pain and distress of mind; then he'd set his teeth, and then presently scream out, "Oh, my God! I have been poisoned—I am dying!"

I was thunderstruck and terrified to the last degree. What was this dreadful thing—this phantom death that had come into the ship? Was it a contagious plague? But what distemper is there that, catching men in their sleep, swells and discolors them even as the gaze rests upon them, and dismisses their souls to God in the space of three or four hours?

I ran on deck, but waited until Mr. Bonner had finished bawling out some orders to the men before addressing him. The moon was young, but bright, and she sheared scythe-like through the pouring shadows, and the light of her made a marvelous brilliant whiteness of the foam as it burst in masses from the plunge of the barque's bows. When I gave the news to Mr. Bonner, he stared at me for some moments wildly and in silence, and then rushed below. I followed him as quick as he went, for I had often used the sea, and the giddiest dance of a deck-plank was all one with the solid earth to my accustomed feet. We entered the mate's berth, and Mr. Bonner lighted the bracket lamp and stood looking at his shipmate, and by the aid of the flame he had kindled, and the bright light flowing in through the open door I beheld a tragic and wonderful change in Mr. Stroud, though scarce ten minutes had passed since I was with him. His face was bloated, the features distorted, his eyes rolled continuously, and frequent heavy twitching shudders convulsed his body. But the most frightful part was the dusky hue of his skin, that was of a darker blue than I had observed in the captain.

He still had his senses, and repeated to the second mate what he had related to me. But he presently grew incoherent, then fell delirious, in about an hour's time was speechless and lay racked with convulsions; of a horrid blue, the features shockingly convulsed, and the whites of his eyes alone showing as in the captain's case.

He had called me at about nine o'clock, and he was a dead man at two in the morning, or four bells in the middle watch. Both the second mate and I were constantly in and out with the poor fellow; but we could do no good, only marvel, and murmur our astonishment and speculations. We put the captain's steward, a young fellow, to watch him—this was an hour before his death—and at four bells the lad came out with a white face, and said to me, who sat at the table, depressed and awed and overwhelmed by this second ghastly and indeterminable visitation, that the chief mate was dead, had ceased to breath, and was quickly turning black.

Mr. Bonner came into the cabin with the boatswain, and they went into the dead man's berth and stayed there about a quarter of an hour. When they came out the boatswain looked at me hard. I recollect that that man's name was Matthews. I asked some questions, but they had nothing to tell, except that the body had turned black.

"What manner of disease can it be that kills in this fashion?" said I. "If it's the plague, we may be all dead men in a week."

"It's no plague," said the boatswain, in a voice that trembled with its own volume of sound.

"What is it?" I cried.

"Poison!" he shouted, and he dropped his clenched fist with the weight of a cannon-ball upon the table.

I looked at the second mate, who exclaimed, "The boatswain swears to the signs. He's seen the like of that corpse in three English seamen who were poisoned up at Chusan."

"Do you want to make out that both men have committed suicide?" I exclaimed.

"I want to make out that both men have been poisoned!" shouted the boatswain, in his voice of thunder.

There was a significance in the insolence of the follow that confounded and alarmed me, and the meaning was deepened by the second mate allowing his companion to address me in this roaring, affronting way without reproof. I had hoped that the man had been drinking, and that the second mate was too stupid with horror to heed his behavior to me, and without giving either of them another word, I walked to my cabin and lay down.

I have no space here to describe the wild and terrifying fancies which ran in my head. For some while I heard the boatswain and the second mate conversing, but the cabin bulkhead was stout, the straining and washing noises all about the helm heavy and continuous, and I caught not a syllable of what they said. At what hour I fell asleep I cannot tell; when I awoke my cabin was full of sunshine that streamed in through the stern window. I dressed, and took hold of the handle of the door, and found myself a prisoner. Not doubting I was locked up in error, I shook the door, and beat upon it, and called out loudly to be released. After a few minutes the door opened, and the second mate stood in the threshold. He exclaimed—

"Mr. West, it's the wish of the men that you should be locked up. I'm no party to the job—but they're resolved. I'll tell you plainly what they think: they believe you've had a hand in the death of the captain and the chief mate— the bo'sun's put that into their heads; I'm the only navigator left, and they're afraid you'll try your hand on me if you have your liberty. You'll be regularly fed and properly seen to; but it's the crew's will that you stop here."

With that, and without giving me time to utter a word, he closed and secured the door. I leaned against the bulkhead and sought to rally my wits, but I own that for a long while I was as one whose mind comes slowly to him after he has been knocked down insensible. I never for an instant supposed that the crew really believed me guilty of poisoning the captain and chief mate: I concluded that the men had mutinied, and arranged with Mr. Bonner to run away with the ship, and that I should remain locked up in my cabin until they had decided what to do with me.

By-and-by the door was opened, and the young steward put a tray containing some breakfast upon the cabin deck. He was but a mule of a boy, and I guessed that nothing but what might stiil further imperil me could come of my questioning him, so in silence I watched him put down the tray and depart. The meal thus sent to me was plentiful, and I drew some small heart out of the attention. Whilst I ate and drank, I heard sounds in the adjoining berth, and presently gathered that they were preparing the body of the chief mate for its last toss over the side. After a bit they went on deck with the corpse, and then all was still in the cabin. I knew by the light of the sun that the vessel was still heading on her course for England. It was a bright morning, with a wild windy sparkle in as much of the weather as I could see through the cabin window. The plunge of the ship's stern brought the water in a roar of milky froth all about the counter close under me, and the frequent jar of rudder and jump of wheel assured me that the barque was travelling fast through the seas.

What, in God's name, did the men mean by keeping me a prisoner? Did they think me a madman? Or that I, whose life together with theirs depended upon the safe navigation of the barque, would destroy those who alone could promise me security? And what had slain the two men? If poison, who had administered it? One man might have died by his own hand, but not both. And since both had perished from the same cause, self-murder was not to be thought of. What was it, then, that had killed them, visiting them in their sleep, and discoloring, bloating, convulsing, and destroying them in a few hours? Was it some deadly malady subtly lurking in the atmosphere of the after part of the vessel? If so, then I might be the next to be taken. Or was there some devilish murderer lying secretly hidden? Or was one of the crew the doer of these things? I seemed to smell disease and death, and yearned for the freedom of the deck, and for the sweetness of the wide, strong rush of the wind.

The day passed. The second mate never visited me. The lad arrived with my meals, and when he came with my supper I asked him some questions, but obtained no more news than that the second mate had taken up his quarters in the adjoining berth as acting captain, and that the boatswain was keeping watch and watch with him.

I got but little rest that night. It blew hard, and the pitching of the vessel was unusually heavy. Then, again, I was profoundly agitated and in deep distress of mind; for, supposing the men in earnest, it was not only horrible to be thought capable of murder, there was the prospect of my being charged and of having to clear my character. Or, supposing the men's suspicion or accusation a villainous pretext, how would they serve me? Would they send me adrift, or set me ashore to perish on some barren coast, or destroy me out of hand? You will remember that I am writing of an age when seafaring was not as it now is. The pirate and the slaver were still afloat doing a brisk business. There often went a desperate spirit in ships' forecastles, and the maritime records of the time abound with the tragic narratives of revolt, seizure, cruelty of a ferocious sort.

Another day and another night went by, and I was still locked up in my cabin, and, saving the punctual arrival of the lad with my meals, no man visited me.

Some time about eight o'clock on the morning of the third day of my confinement, I was looking through the cabin window at the space of grey and foaming sea and sallow flying sky which came and went in the square of the aperture with the lift and fall of the barque's stern, when my cabin door was struck upon, and in a minute afterwards open, and the boatswain appeared.

"Mr. West," he said, after looking at me for a moment in silence with a face whose expression was made up of concern and fear and embarrassment, "I've come on my own part, and on the part of the men, sir, to ask your pardon for our treatment of you. We was mistook. And our fears made us too willing to believe that you had a hand in it. We dunno what it is now, but as Jesus is my God, Mr. West, the second mate he lies dead of the same thing in the next cabin!"

I went past him too stupefied to speak, and in a blind way sat down at the cabin table and leaned my head against my hand. Presently I looked up, and on lifting my eyes I caught sight of two or three sailors staring down with white faces through the skylight.

"You tell me that the second mate's dead?" said I.

"Yes, sir, dead of poison, too, so help me God!" cried the boatswain.

"Who remains to navigate the ship?" I said.

"That's it, sir!" he exclaimed. "Unless you can do it?"

"Not I. There's no man amongst you more ignorant. May I look at the body?"

He opened the door of the cabin in which the others had died, and there, in the bunk from which the bodies of Captain Joyce and Mr. Stroud had been removed, lay now the blackened corpse of the second mate. It was an awful sight and a passage of time horrible with the mystery which charged it. I felt no rage at the manner in which I had been used by that dead man there and the hurricane-lunged seaman alongside of me and the fellows forward; I could think of nothing but the mystery of the three men's deaths, the lamentable plight we were all in through our wanting a navigator, with the chance, more-over, that it *was* the plague, and not poison mysteriously given, that had killed the captain and mates, so that all the rest of us, as I have said, might be dead men in another week.

I returned to the cabin, and the boatswain joined me, and we stood beside the table conversing, anxiously watched by several men who had stationed themselves at the skylight.

"What we've got to do," said I, "is to keep a bright lookout for ships, and borrow someone to steer us home from the first vessel that would lend us a navigator. We're bound to fall in with something soon. Meanwhile, you're a smart seaman yourself, Matthews, as well qualified as any one of them who have died to sail the ship, and there's surely some intelligent sailor amongst the crew who would relieve you in taking charge of the deck. I'll do all I can."

"The question is, where's the vessel now?" said the boatswain.

"Fetch me the log-book," said I, "and see if you can find the chart they've been using to prick the courses off on. We should be able to find out where the ship was at noon yesterday. I can't enter that cabin. The sight of the poor fellow makes me sick."

He went to the berth and passed through the door, and might have left me about five minutes, evidently hunting for the chart, when he suddenly rushed out, roaring in his thunderous voice, "I've discovered it! I've discovered it!" and fled like a madman up the companion steps. I was startled almost to the very stopping of my heart by this sudden furious wild behavior in him: then wondering what he meant by shouting "he had discovered it!" I walked to the cabin door, and the very first thing my eye lighted upon was a small snake, leisurely coiling its way from the head to the feet of the corpse. Its middle was about the thickness of a rifle-barrel, and it then tapered to something like whipcord to its tail. It was about two feet long, snow white, and speckled with black and red spots.

This, then, was the phantom death! Yonder venomous reptile it was, then, that, creeping out of some secret hiding-place, and visiting the unhappy men one after another, had stung them in their sleep, in the darkness of the cabin, and vanished before they had struck a light and realized indeed that something desperate had come to them!

Whilst I stood looking at the snake, whose horror seemed to gain fresh accentuation from the very beauty of its snow-white speckled skin and diamond bright eyes, the boatswain, armed with a long handspike, and followed by a number of the crew, came headlong to the cabin. He thrust the end of the handspike under the belly of the creature, and hove it into the middle of the berth.

"Stand clear!" he roared, and with a blow or two smashed the reptile's head into a pulp. "Open that cabin window," said he. One of the men did so, and the boatswain with his boot scraped the mess of smashed snake on the handspike and shook it overboard.

"I told you they were poisoned," he cried, breathing deep; "and, oh my God, Mr. West—and I humbly ask your pardon again for having suspected ye—do you know, sir, whilst I was a-talking to you just now I was actually thinking of taking up my quarters in this here cabin this very night."

Thus much: and now to end this singular experience in a sentence or two. Three days after the discovery of the snake we sighted and signalled a large English merchantman bound to London from the Rio de la Plata. Her chief officer came aboard, and we related our story. He asked to see the snake. We told him we had thrown it overboard. On my describing it, he informed me that he guessed it was the little poisonous reptile known in certain districts of South America as the Ibiboboko. He returned to his ship, and shortly afterwards the commander sent us his third officer, with instructions to keep in company as long as possible.

Sea Pirates and Privateers

Agra Outwits Two Pirate Ships

by CHARLES READE

The way the pirate dropped the mask, showed his black teeth, and bore up in chase, was terrible: so dilates and bounds the sudden tiger on his unwary prey. There were stout hearts among the officers of the peaceable *Agra*; but danger in a new form shakes the brave; and this was their first pirate: their dismay broke out in ejaculations not loud but deep. "Hush!" said Dodd, doggedly; "the lady!"

Mrs. Beresford had just come on deck to enjoy the balmy morning.

"Sharpe," said Dodd, in a tone that conveyed no suspicion to the new-comer, "set the royals, and flying jib. Port!"

"Port it is," cried the man at the helm.

"Steer due south!" And, with these words in his mouth, Dodd dived to the gun-deck.

By this time elastic Sharpe had recovered the first shock; and the order to crowd sail on the ship galled his pride and his manhood; he muttered, indignantly, "The white feather!" This eased his mind, and he obeyed orders briskly as ever. While he and his hands were setting every rag the ship could carry on that tack, the other officers, having unluckily no orders to execute, stood gloomy and helpless, with their eyes glued by a sort of sombre fascination, on that coming fate: and they literally jumped and jarred, when Mrs. Beresford, her heart opened by the lovely day, broke in on their nerves with her light treble.

"What a sweet morning, gentlemen! After all, a voyage is a delightful thing; oh, what a splendid sea! and the very breeze is warm. Ah! and there's a little ship sailing along: here, Freddy, Freddy darling, leave off beating the sailor's legs, and come here and see this pretty ship. What a pity it is so far off! Ah, ah! what is that dreadful noise?"

For her horrible small talk, that grated on those anxious souls like the mockery of some infantine fiend, was cut short by ponderous blows and tremendous smashing below. It was the captain staving in water-casks: the water poured out at the scuppers.

"Clearing the lee guns," said a middy, off his guard.

Colonel Kenealy pricked up his ears, drew his cigar from his mouth, and smelt powder. "What, for action?" said he briskly. "Where's the enemy?"

Fullalove made him a signal, and they went below.

Mrs. Beresford had not heard, or not appreciated, the remark: she prattled on till she made the mates and midshipmen shudder.

Realize the situation, and the strange incongruity between the senses and the mind in these poor fellows! The day had ripened its beauty; beneath a purple heaven shone, sparkled, and laughed a blue sea, in whose waves the tropical sun seemed to have fused his beams; and beneath that fair, sinless, peaceful sky, wafted by a balmy breeze over those smiling, transparent golden waves, a bloodthirsty pirate bore down on them with a crew of human tigers; and a lady babble babble babble babble babble babble babbled in their quivering ears.

But now the captain came bustling on deck, eyed the loftier sails, saw they were drawing well, appointed four midshipmen a staff to convey his orders; gave Bayliss charge of the carronades, Grey of the cutlasses, and directed Mr. Tickell to break the bad news gently to Mrs. Beresford, and to take her below to the orlop deck; ordered the purser to serve out beef, biscuit, and grog to all hands, saying, "Men can't work on an empty stomach; and fighting is hard work;" then beckoned the officers to come round him. "Gentlemen," said he confidentially, "in crowding sail on this ship I had no hope of escaping that fellow on this tack, but I was, and am, most anxious to gain the open sea, where I can square my yards and run for it, if I see a chance. At present I shall carry on till he comes up within range; and then, to keep the company's canvas from being shot to rags, I shall shorten sail; and to save ship and cargo and all our lives, I shall fight while a plank of her swims. Better be killed in hot blood than walk the plank in cold."

The officers cheered faintly; the captain's dogged resolution stirred up theirs.

The pirate had gained another quarter of a mile and more. The ship's crew were hard at their beef and grog, and agreed among themselves it was a comfortable ship; they guessed what was coming, and woe to the ship in that hour if the captain had not won their respect. Strange to say, there were two gentlemen in the *Agra* to whom the pirate's approach was not altogether unwelcome. Colonel Kenealy and Mr. Fullalove were rival sportsmen and rival theorists. Kenealy stood out for a smooth bore, and a four-ounce ball: Fullalove for a rifle of his own construction. Many a doughty argument they had, and many a bragging match; neither could convert the other. At last Fullalove hinted that by going ashore at the Cape, and getting each behind a tree at one hundred yards, and popping at one another, one or other would be convinced.

"Well, but," said Kenealy, "if he is dead, he will be no wiser; besides, to a fellow like me, who has had the luxury of popping at his enemies, popping at a friend is poor insipid work."

"That is true," said the other regretfully. "But I reckon we shall never settle it by argument."

Theorists are amazing; and it was plain, by the alacrity with which these good creatures loaded the rival instruments, that to them the pirate came not so much a pirate as a solution. Indeed, Kenealy, in the act of charging his piece, was heard to mutter, "Now this is lucky." However, these theorists were no sooner loaded, than something occurred to make them more serious. They were sent for in haste to Dodd's cabin: they found him giving Sharpe a new order.

"Shorten sail to the taupsles and jib, get the colors ready on the halliards, and then send the men aft."

Sharpe ran out full of zeal, and tumbled over Ramgolam, who was stooping remarkably near the keyhole. Dodd hastily bolted the cabin-door, and looked with trembling lip and piteous earnestness in Kenealy's face and Fullalove's. They were mute with surprise at a gaze so eloquent yet mysterious.

He manned himself, and opened his mind to them with deep emotion, yet not without a certain simple dignity.

"Colonel," said he, "you are an old friend; *you*, sir, are a new one; but I esteem you highly, and what my young gentlemen chaff you about, you calling all men brothers, and making that poor negro love you, instead of fear you, that shows me you have a great heart. My dear friends, I have been unlucky enough to bring my children's fortune on board this ship: here it is, under my shirt. Fourteen thousand pounds. This weighs me down. Oh, if they should lose it after all! Do pray give me a hand apiece, and pledge your sacred words to take it home safe to my wife at Barkington, if you, or either of you, should see this bright sun set to-day, and I should not."

"Why, Dodd, old fellow," said Kenealy cheerfully, "this is not the way to go into action."

"Colonel," replied Dodd, "to save this ship and cargo I must be wherever the bullets are, and I will, too."

Fullalove, more sagacious than the worthy colonel, said earnestly, "Captain Dodd, may I never see Broadway again, and never see heaven at the end of my time, if I fail you. There's my hand."

"And mine," said Kenealy warmly.

They all three joined hands, and Dodd seemed to cling to them.

"God bless you both! God bless you! Oh, what a weight your true hands have pulled off my heart! Good-by for a few minutes. The time is short. I'll just offer a prayer to the Almighty for wisdom, and then I'll come up and say a word to the men, and fight the ship, according to my lights."

Sail was no sooner shortened, and the crew ranged, than the captain came briskly on deck, saluted, jumped on a carronade, and stood erect. He was not the man to show the crew his forebodings.

(Pipe.) "Silence fore and aft."

"My men, the schooner coming up on our weather quarter is a Portuguese pirate. His character is known: he scuttles all the ships he boards, dishonors the women, and murders the crew. We cracked on to get out of the narrows, and now we have shortened sail to fight this blackguard, and teach him to molest a British ship. I promise, in the Company's name, twenty pounds prize money to every man before the mast if we beat him off or out-manoeuvre him, thirty if we sink him, and forty if we tow him astern into a friendly port. Eight guns are clear below, three on the weather side, five on the lee; for, if he knows his business, he will come up on the lee quarter: if he doesn't, that is no fault of yours nor mine. The muskets are all loaded, the cutlasses ground like razors"—

"Hurrah!"

"We have got women to defend"—

"Hurrah!"

"A good ship under our feet, the God of justice overhead, British hearts in our bosoms, and British colors flying—run 'em up—over our heads." (The ship's colors flew up to the fore, and the Union Jack to the mizzen-peak.) "Now, lads, I mean to fight this ship while a plank of her" (stamping on the deck) "swims beneath my foot, and— What do you say?"

The reply was a fierce "Hurrah!" from a hundred throats, so loud, so deep, so full of volume, it made the ship vibrate, and rang in the creeping-on pirate's ears. Fierce, but cunning, he saw mischief in those shortened sails, and that Union Jack, the terror of his tribe, rising to a British cheer: he lowered his mainsail, and crawled up on the weather quarter. Arrived within a cable's length, he double-reefed his foresail to reduce his rate of sailing nearly to that of the ship; and the next moment a tongue of flame, and then a gush of smoke, issued from his lee bow, and the ball flew screaming like a sea-gull over the *Agra*'s mizzen-top. He then put his helm up, and fired his other bow-chaser, and sent the shot hissing and skipping on the water past the ship. This prologue made the novices wince. Bayliss wanted to reply with a carronade, but Dodd forbade him sternly, saying, "If we keep him aloof we are done for."

The pirate drew nearer, and fired both guns in succession, hulled the *Agra* amidships, and sent an eighteen-pound ball through her foresail. Most of the faces were pale on the quarter-deck: it was very trying to be shot at, and hit, and make no return. The next double discharge sent one shot smash through the stern cabin-window, and splintered the bulwark with another, wounding a seaman slightly.

"LIE DOWN FORWARD!" shouted Dodd. "Bayliss, give him a shot."

The carronade was fired with a tremendous report, but no visible effect. The pirate crept nearer, steering in and out like a snake to avoid the carronades, and firing those two heavy guns alternately into the devoted ship. He hulled the *Agra* now nearly every shot.

The two available carronades replied noisily, and jumped as usual: they sent one thirty-two-pound shot clean through the schooner's deck and side, but that was literally all they did worth speaking of.

"Curse them!" cried Dodd; "load them with grape! they are not to be trusted with ball. And all my eighteen-pounders dumb! The coward won't come alongside and give them a chance."

At the next discharge the pirate chipped the mizzen-mast, and knocked a sailor into dead pieces on the forecastle. Dodd put his helm down ere the smoke cleared, and got three carronades to bear, heavily laden with grape.

Several pirates fell, dead or wounded, on the crowded deck, and some holes appeared in the foresail; this one interchange was quite in favor of the ship.

But the lesson made the enemy more cautious: he crept nearer, but steered so adroitly, now right astern, now on the quarter, that the ship could seldom bring more than one carronade to bear, while he raked her fore and aft with grape and ball.

In this alarming situation Dodd kept as many of the men below as possible; but, for all he could do, four were killed and seven wounded.

Fullalove's word came too true: it was the sword-fish and the whale: it was a fight of hammer and anvil; one hit, the other made a noise. Cautious and cruel, the pirate hung on the poor hulking creature's quarters, and raked her at point-blank distance. He made her pass a bitter time. And her captain! To see the splintering hull, the parting shrouds, the shivered gear, and hear the shrieks and groans of his wounded, and he unable to reply in kind! The sweat of agony poured down his face. Oh, if he could but reach the open sea, and square his yards, and make a long chase of it; perhaps fall in with aid. Wincing under each heavy blow, he crept doggedly, patiently, on, towards that one visible hope.

At last, when the ship was cloved with shot, and peppered with grape, the channel opened; in five minutes more he could put her dead before the wind.

No. The pirate, on whose side luck had been from the first, got half a broadside to bear at long musket shot, killed a midshipman by Dodd's side, cut away two of the *Agra*'s mizzen shrouds, wounded the gaff, and cut the jib-stay: down fell that powerful sail into the water, and dragged across the ship's forefoot, stopping her way to the open sea she panted for. The mates groaned: the crew cheered stoutly, as British tars do in any great disaster. The pirates yelled with ferocious triumph, like the devils they looked.

But most human events, even calamities, have two sides. The *Agra* being brought almost to a standstill, the pirate forged ahead against his will, and the combat took a new and terrible form. The elephant gun popped, and the rifle cracked, in the *Agra*'s mizzen-top, and the man at the pirate's helm jumped into the air and fell dead; both theorists claimed him. Then the three car-ronades peppered him hotly, and he hurled an iron shower back with fatal effect. Then at last the long eighteen-pounders on the gun-deck got a word in. The old Niler was not the man to miss a vessel alongside in a quiet sea: he sent two round shot clean through him; the third splintered his bulwark, and swept across his deck.

"His masts! fire at his masts!" roared Dodd to Monk through his trumpet; he then got the jib clear, and made what sail he could without taking all the hands from the guns.

This kept the vessels nearly alongside a few minutes, and the fight was hot as fire. The pirate now for the first time hoisted his flag. It was black as ink. His crew yelled as it rose: the Britons, instead of quailing, cheered with fierce derision; the pirate's wild crew of yellow Malays, black chinless Papuans, and bronzed Portuguese, served their side guns, twelve-pounders, well and with ferocious cries; the white Britons, drunk with battle now, naked to the waist, grimed with powder, and spotted like leopards with blood, their own and their mates', replied with loud undaunted cheers, and deadly hail of grape from the quarter-deck; while the master-gunner and his mates, loading with a rapidity the mixed races opposed could not rival, hulled the schooner well between wind and water, and then fired chain shot at her masts, as ordered, and began to play the mischief with her shrouds and rigging. Meantime, Fullalove and Kenealy, aided by Vespasian, who loaded, were quietly butchering the pirate crew two a minute, and hoped to settle the question they were fighting for: smooth bore *v.* rifle; but unluckily neither fired once without killing; so "there was nothing proven."

The pirate, bold as he was, got sick of fair fighting first; he hoisted his mainsail and drew rapidly ahead, with a slight bearing to windward, and dismounted a carronade and stove in the ship's quarter-boat, by way of a parting kick.

The men hurled a contemptuous cheer after him; they thought they had beaten him off. But Dodd knew better. He was but retiring a little way to make a more deadly attack than ever: he would soon wear, and cross the *Agra*'s defenceless bows, to rake her fore and aft at pistol-shot distance: or grapple, and board the enfeebled ship two hundred strong.

Dodd flew to the helm, and with his own hands put it hard a-weather, to give the deck guns one more chance, the last, of sinking or disabling the destroyer. As the ship obeyed, and a deck gun bellowed below him, he saw a vessel running out from Long Island, and coming swiftly up on his lee quarter.

It was a schooner. Was she coming to his aid?

Horror! A black flag floated from her foremast head.

While Dodd's eyes were staring almost out of his head at this death-blow to hope, Monk fired again; and just then a pale face came close to Dodd's, and a solemn voice whispered in his ear: "Our ammunition is nearly done!"

Dodd seized Sharpe's hand convulsively, and pointed to the pirate's consort coming up to finish them; and said, with the calm of a brave man's despair, "Cutlasses! and die hard!"

At that moment the master-gunner fired his last gun. It sent a chain shot on board the retiring pirate, took off a Portuguese head and spun it clean into the sea ever so far to windward, and cut the schooner's foremast so nearly through that it trembled and nodded, and presently snapped with a loud crack, and came down like a broken tree, with the yard and sail; the latter overlapping the deck and burying itself, black flag and all, in the sea; and there, in one moment, lay the destroyer buffeting and wriggling—like a heron on the water with his long wing broken—an utter cripple.

The victorious crew raised a stunning cheer.

"Silence!" roared Dodd, with his trumpet. "All hands make sail!"

He set his courses, bent a new jib, and stood out to windward close hauled, in hopes to make a good offing, and then put his ship dead before the wind, which was now rising to a stiff breeze. In doing this, he crossed the crippled pirate's bows within eighty yards: and sore was the temptation to rake him; but his ammunition being short, and his danger being imminent from the other pirate, he had the self-command to resist the great temptation.

He hailed the mizzen-top: "Can you two hinder them from firing that gun?"

"I rather think we can," said Fullalove, "eh, Colonel?" and tapped his long rifle.

The ship no sooner crossed the schooner's bows * than a Malay ran forward with a linstock. Pop went the colonel's ready carbine, and the Malay fell over dead, and the linstock flew out of his hand. A tall Portuguese, with a movement of rage, snatched it up, and darted to the gun: the Yankee rifle cracked, but a moment too late. Bang! went the pirate's bow-chaser, and crashed into the *Agra*'s side, and passed nearly through her.

"Ye missed him! ye missed him!" cried the rival theorist, joyfully. He was mistaken: the smoke cleared, and there was the pirate captain leaning wounded against the mainmast with a Yankee bullet in his shoulder, and his crew uttering yells of dismay and vengeance. They jumped and raged and brandished their knives and made horrid gesticulations of revenge; and the white eyeballs of the Malays and Papuans glittered fiendishly; and the wounded captain raised his sound arm and had a signal hoisted to his consort, and she bore up in chase, and jamming her fore latine flat as a board, lay far nearer the wind than the *Agra* could, and sailed three feet to her two, besides. On this superiority being made clear, the situation of the merchant vessel, though not so utterly desperate as before Monk fired his lucky shot, became pitiable enough. If she ran before the wind, the fresh pirate would cut her off: if she lay to windward, she might postpone the inevitable and fatal collision with a foe as strong as that she had only escaped by a rare piece of luck; but this would give the crippled pirate time to refit and unite to destroy her. Add to this the failing ammunition and the thinned crew.

Dodd cast his eyes all around the horizon for help.

The sea was blank.

The bright sun was hidden now; drops of rain fell, and the wind was beginning to sing, and the sea to rise a little.

"Gentlemen," said he, "let us kneel down and pray for wisdom in this sore strait."

He and his officers kneeled on the quarter-deck. When they rose, Dodd stood rapt about a minute; his great thoughtful eye saw no more the enemy, the sea, nor anything external; it was turned inward. His officers looked at him in silence.

"Sharpe," said he, at last, "there *must* be a way out of them both with such a breeze as this is now, if we could but see it."

---

* Being disabled, the schooner's head had come round to windward, though she was drifting to leeward.

"Ay, *if,*" groaned Sharpe.

Dodd mused again.

"About ship!" said he, softly, like an absent man.

"Ay, ay, sir!"

"Steer due north!" said he, still like one whose mind was elsewhere.

While the ship was coming about, he gave minute orders to the mates and the gunner, to insure co-operation in the delicate and dangerous manoeuvres that were sure to be at hand.

The wind was west-north-west: he was standing north: one pirate lay on his lee beam stopping a leak between wind and water, and hacking the deck clear of his broken mast and yards. The other, fresh and thirsting for the easy prey, came up to weather on him and hang on his quarter, pirate fashion.

When they were distant about a cable's length, the fresh pirate, to meet the ship's change of tactics, changed his own, luffed up, and gave the ship a broadside, well aimed but not destructive, the guns being loaded with ball.

Dodd, instead of replying immediately, put his helm hard up and ran under the pirate's stern, while he was jammed up in the wind, and with his five eighteen-pounders raked him fore and aft, then paying off, gave him three carronades crammed with grape and canister; the rapid discharge of eight guns made the ship tremble, and enveloped her in thick smoke; loud shrieks and groans were heard from the schooner; the smoke cleared; the pirate's mainsail hung on deck, his jib-boom was cut off like a carrot and the sail struggling; his foresail looked lace, lanes of dead and wounded lay still or writhing on his deck, and his lee scuppers ran blood into the sea. Dodd squared his yards and bore away.

The ship rushed down the wind, leaving the schooner staggered and all aboard. But not for long; the pirate wore, and fired his bow-chasers at the now flying *Agra*, split one of the carronades in two, and killed a Lascar, and made a hole in the foresail; this done, he hoisted his mainsail again in a trice, sent his wounded below, flung his dead overboard, to the horror of their foes, and came after the flying ship, yawing and firing his bow-chasers. The ship was silent. She had no shot to throw away. Not only did she take these blows like a coward, but all signs of life disappeared on her, except two men at the wheel, and the captain on the main gangway.

Dodd had ordered the crew out of the rigging, armed them with cutlasses, and laid them flat on the forecastle. He also compelled Kenealy and Fullalove to come down out of harm's way, no wiser on the smooth bore question than they went up.

The great patient ship ran environed by her foes: one destroyer right in her course, another in her wake, following her with yells of vengeance, and pounding away at her—but no reply.

Suddenly the yells of the pirates on both sides ceased, and there was a moment of dead silence on the sea.

Yet nothing fresh had happened.

Yes, this had happened: the pirates to windward and the pirates to leeward of the *Agra* had found out, at one and the same moment, that the merchant captain they had lashed and bullied and tortured, was a patient but tremendous man. It was not only to rake the fresh schooner, he had put his ship before the wind, but also by a double, daring master-stroke to hurl his monster ship bodily on the other. Without a foresail she could never get out of her way. The pirate crew had stopped the leak, and cut away and unshipped the broken foremast, and were stepping a new one, when they saw the huge ship bearing down in full sail. Nothing easier than to slip out of her way could they get the foresail to draw; but the time was short, the deadly intention manifest, the coming destruction swift.

After that solemn silence came a storm of cries and curses, as their seamen went to work to fit the yard and raise the sail; while their fighting men seized their matchlocks and trained the guns. They were well commanded by an heroic, able villain. Astern the consort thundered; but the *Agra*'s response was a dead silence more awful than broadsides.

For then was seen with what majesty the enduring Anglo-Saxon fights.

One of that indomitable race on the gangway, one at the foremast, two at the wheel, conned and steered the great ship down on a hundred matchlocks and a grinning broadside, just as they would have conned and steered her into a British harbor.

"Starboard!" said Dodd, in a deep calm voice, with a motion of his hand.

"Starboard it is."

The pirate wriggled ahead a little. The man forward made a silent signal to Dodd.

"Port!" said Dodd, quietly.

"Port it is."

But at this critical moment the pirate astern sent a mischievous shot and knocked one of the men to atoms at the helm.

Dodd waved his hand without a word, and another man rose from the deck and took his place in silence, and laid his unshaking hand on the wheel stained with that man's warm blood whose place he took.

The high ship was now scarce sixty yards distant; *she seemed to know:* she reared her lofty figure-head with great awful shoots into the air.

But now the panting pirates got their new foresail hoisted with a joyful shout; it drew, the schooner gathered way, and their furious consort close on the *Agra*'s heels just then scourged her deck with grape.

"Port!" said Dodd, calmly.

"Port it is."

The giant prow darted at the escaping pirate. That acre of coming canvas took the wind out of the swift schooner's foresail; it flapped; oh, then she was doomed! That awful moment parted the races on board her: the Papuans and Sooloos, their black faces livid and blue with horror, leaped yelling into the sea, or crouched and whimpered; the yellow Malays and brown Portuguese, though blanched to one color now, turned on death like dying panthers, fired two cannon slap into the ship's bows, and snapped their muskets and matchlocks at their solitary executioner on the ship's gangway, and out flew their knives like crushed wasps' stings. CRASH! the Indiaman's cutwater in thick smoke beat in the schooner's broadside: down went her masts to leeward like fishing-rods whipping the water; there was a horrible shrieking yell; wild forms leaped off on the *Agra*, and were hacked to pieces almost ere they reached the deck—a surge, a chasm in the sea, filled with an instant rush of engulfing waves, a long, awful, grating, grinding noise never to be forgotten in this world, all along under the ship's keel—and the fearful majestic monster passed on over the blank she had made, with a pale crew standing silent and awe-struck on her deck; a cluster of wild heads and staring eyeballs bobbing like corks in her foaming wake, sole relic of the blotted-out destroyer; and a wounded man staggering on the gangway, with hands uplifted and staring eyes.

Shot in two places, the head and the breast.

With a loud cry of pity and dismay, Sharpe, Fullalove, Kenealy, and others rushed to catch him; but, ere they got near, the captain of the triumphant ship fell down on his hands and knees, his head sunk over the gangway, and his blood ran fast and pattered in the midst of them, on the deck he had defended so bravely.

They got to the wounded captain and raised him. He revived a little; and the moment he caught sight of Mr. Sharpe he clutched him, and cried, "Stunsels!"

"O captain!" said Sharpe, "let the ship go; it is you we are anxious for now."

At this Dodd lifted up his hands and beat the air impatiently, and cried again in the thin, querulous voice of a wounded man, but eagerly, "STUNSELS! STUNSELS!"

On this Sharpe gave the command:—

"Make sail! All hands set stunsels 'low and aloft!"

While the unwounded hands swarmed into the rigging, the surgeon came aft in all haste; but Dodd declined him till all his men should have been looked to; meantime he had himself carried to the poop, and laid on a mattress, his bleeding head bound tight with a wet cambric handkerchief, and his pale face turned towards the hostile schooner astern. She had hove to, and was picking up the survivors of her blotted-out consort. The group on the *Agra*'s quarter-deck watched her to see what she would do next; flushed with immediate success, the younger officers crowed their fears, she would not be game to attack them again; Dodd's fears ran the other way. He said, in the weak voice to which he was now reduced, "They are taking a wet blanket aboard; that crew of blackguards we swamped won't want any more of us; it all depends on the pirate captain; if he is not drowned, then blow wind, rise sea, or there's trouble ahead for us."

As soon as the schooner had picked up the last swimmer, she hoisted foresail, mainsail, and jib, with admirable rapidity, and bore down in chase.

The *Agra* had, meantime, got a start of more than a mile, and was now running before a stiff breeze with studding sails alow and aloft.

In an hour the vessels ran nearly twelve miles, and the pirate had gained half a mile.

At the end of the next hour they were out of sight of land; wind and sea rising, and the pirate only a quarter of a mile astern.

The schooner was now rising and falling on the waves; the ship only nodding, and firm as a rock.

"Blow wind, rise sea!" faltered Dodd.

Another half-hour passed without perceptibly altering the position of the vessels. Then suddenly the wounded captain laid aside his glass, after a long examination, and rose unaided to his feet in great excitement, and found his manly voice for a moment; he shook his fist at the now pitching schooner, and roared, "Good-bye, ye Portuguese lubber! out-fought—out-manoeuvred— AND OUTSAILED!"

It was a burst of exultation rare for him; he paid for it by sinking faint and helpless into his friend's arms; and the surgeon, returning soon after, insisted on his being taken to his cabin, and kept quite quiet.

As they were carrying him below, the pirate captain made the same discovery; that the ship was gaining on him. He hauled to the wind directly, and abandoned the chase.

The End of Black-Beard, the Pirate

by HOWARD PYLE

Captain Teach, alias Black-beard, passed three or four months in the river, sometimes lying at anchor in the coves, at other times sailing from one inlet to another, trading with such sloops as he met for the plunder he had taken, and would often give them presents for stores and provisions he took from them; that is, when he happened to be in a giving humour; at other times he made bold with them, and took what he liked, without saying "By your leave," knowing well they dared not send him a bill for the payment. He often diverted himself with going ashore among the planters, where he revelled night and day. By these he was well received, but whether out of love or fear I cannot say. Sometimes he used them courteously enough, and made them presents of rum and sugar in recompense of what he took from them; but, as for liberties, which it is said he and his companions often took with the wives and daughters of the planters, I cannot take upon me to say whether he paid them *ad valorem* or no. At other times he carried it in a lordly manner towards them, and would lay some of them under contribution; nay, he often proceeded to bully the governor, not that I can discover the least cause of quarrel between them, but it seemed only to be done to show he dared do it.

The sloops trading up and down this river being so frequently pillaged by Black-beard, consulted with the traders and some of the best of the planters what course to take. They saw plainly it would be in vain to make any application to the governor of North Carolina, to whom it properly belonged to find some redress; so that if they could not be relieved from some other quarter, Black-beard would be like to reign with impunity; therefore, with as much secrecy as possible, they sent a deputation to Virginia, to lay the affair before the governor of that colony, and to solicit an armed force from the men-of-war lying there to take or destroy this pirate.

This governor consulted with the captains of the two men-of-war, viz., the *Pearl* and *Lime*, who had lain in St. James's river about ten months. It was agreed that the governor should hire a couple of small sloops, and the men-of-war should man them. This was accordingly done, and the command of them given to Mr. Robert Maynard, first lieutenant of the *Pearl*, an experienced officer, and a gentleman of great bravery and resolution, as will appear by his gallant behaviour in this expedition. The sloops were well manned, and furnished with ammunition and small arms, but had no guns mounted.

About the time of their going out the governor called an assembly, in which it was resolved to publish a proclamation, offering certain rewards to any person or persons who, within a year after that time, should take or destroy any pirate. The original proclamation, being in our hands, is as follows:—

By his Majesty's Lieutenant- Governor and Commander-in-Chief of the Colony and Dominion of Virginia.

A PROCLAMATION,

Publishing the Rewards given for apprehending or killing Pirates.

WHEREAS, by an Act of Assembly, made at a Session of Assembly, begun at the capital in Williamsburg, the eleventh day of November, in the fifth year of his Majesty's reign, entitled, An Act to Encourage the Apprehending and Destroying of Pirates: It is, amongst other things, enacted, that all and every person, or persons, who, from and after the fourteenth day of November, in the Year of our Lord one thousand seven hundred and eighteen, and before the fourteenth day of November, which shall be in the Year of our Lord one thousand seven hundred and nineteen, shall take any pirate, or pirates, on the sea or land, or, in case of resistance, shall kill any such pirate, or pirates, between the degrees of thirty-four and thirty-nine of northern latitude, and within one hundred leagues of the continent of Virginia, or within the provinces of Virginia, or North Carolina, upon the conviction, or making due proof of the killing of all and every such pirate, and pirates, before the Governor and Council, shall be entitled to have, and receive out of the public money, in the hands of the Treasurer of this Colony, the several rewards following: that is to say, for Edward Teach, commonly called Captain Teach, or Black-beard, one hundred pounds; for every other commander of a pirate ship, sloop, or vessel, forty pounds; for every lieutenant, master, or quartermaster, boatswain, or carpenter, twenty pounds; for every other inferior officer, fifteen pounds; and for every private man taken on board such ship, sloop, or vessel, ten pounds; and that for every pirate which shall be taken by any ship, sloop, or vessel, belonging to this colony, or North Carolina, within the time aforesaid, in any place whatsoever, the like rewards shall be paid according to the quality and condition of such pirates. Wherefore, for the encouragement of all such persons as shall be willing to serve his Majesty, and their country, in so just and honourable an undertaking as the suppressing a sort of people who may be truly called enemies to mankind: I have thought fit, with the advice and consent of his Majesty's Council, to issue this Proclamation, hereby declaring the said rewards shall be punctually and justly paid, in current money of Virginia, according to the directions of the said Act. And I do order and appoint this proclamation to be published by the sheriffs at their respective country houses, and by all ministers and readers in the several churches and chapels throughout this colony.

Given at our Council-Chamber at Williamsburgh, this 24th day of November, 1718, in the fifth year of his Majesty's reign.

GOD SAVE THE KING.

A. SPOTSWOOD.

The 17th of November, 1718, the lieutenant sailed from Kicquetan, in James river in Virginia, and the 31st, in the evening, came to the mouth of Okerecock inlet, where he got sight of the pirate. This expedition was made with all imaginable secrecy, and the officer managed with all the prudence that was necessary, stopping all boats and vessels he met with in the river from going up, and thereby preventing any intelligence from reaching Black-beard, and receiving at the same time an account from them all of the place where the pirate was lurking. But notwithstanding this caution, Black-beard had information of the design from his Excellency of the province; and his secretary, Mr. Knight, wrote him a letter particularly concerning it, intimating "that he had sent him four of his men, which were all he could meet with in or about town, and so bid him be upon his guard." These men belonged to Black-beard, and were sent from Bath Town to Okerecock inlet, where the sloop lay, which is about twenty leagues.

Black-beard had heard several reports, which happened not to be true, and so gave the less credit to this advice; nor was he convinced till he saw the sloops. Then it was time to put his vessel in a posture of defence. He had no more than twenty-five men on board, though he gave out to all the vessels he spoke with that he had forty. When he had prepared for battle he sat down and spent the night in drinking with the master of a trading sloop, who, it was thought, had more business with Teach than he should have had.

Lieutenant Maynard came to an anchor, for the place being shoal, and the channel intricate, there was no getting in where Teach lay that night; but in the morning he weighed, and sent his boat ahead of the sloops to sound, and coming within gun-shot of the pirate, received his fire; whereupon Maynard hoisted the king's colours, and stood directly towards him with the best way that his sails and oars could make. Black-beard cut his cable, and endeavoured to make a running fight, keeping a continual fire at his enemies with his guns. Mr. Maynard, not having any, kept a constant fire with small arms, while some of his men laboured at their oars. In a little time Teach's sloop ran aground, and Mr. Maynard's, drawing more water than that of the pirate, he could not come near him; so he anchored within half gun-shot of the enemy, and, in order to lighten his vessel, that he might run him aboard, the lieutenant ordered all his ballast to be thrown overboard, and all the water to be staved, and then weighed and stood for him; upon which Black-beard hailed him in this rude manner: "Damn you for villains, who are you; and from whence came you?" The lieutenant made him answer, "You may see by our colours we are no pirates." Black-beard bid him send his boat on board that he might see who he was; but Mr. Maynard replied thus: "I cannot spare my boat, but I will come aboard of you as soon as I can with my sloop." Upon this Black-beard took a glass of liquor, and drank to him with these words: "Damnation seize my soul if I give you quarter, or take any from you." In answer to which Mr. Maynard told him "that he expected no quarter from him, nor should he give him any."

By this time Black-beard's sloop fleeted as Mr. Maynard's sloops were rowing towards him, which being not above a foot high in the waist, and consequently the men all exposed, as they came near together (there being hitherto little or no execution done on either side), the pirate fired a broadside charged with all manner of small shot. A fatal stroke to them!—the sloop the lieutenant was in having twenty men killed and wounded, and the other sloop nine. This could not be helped, for there being no wind, they were obliged to keep to their oars, otherwise the pirate would have got away from him, which, it seems, the lieutenant was resolute to prevent.

After this unlucky blow Black-beard's sloop fell broadside to the shore; Mr. Maynard's other sloop, which was called the *Ranger,* fell astern, being for the present disabled. So the lieutenant, finding his own sloop had way and would soon be on board of Teach, he ordered all his men down, for fear of another broadside, which must have been their destruction and the loss of their expedition. Mr. Maynard was the only person that kept the deck, except the man at the helm, whom he directed to lie down snug, and the men in the hold were ordered to get their pistols and their swords ready for close fighting, and to come up at his command; in order to which two ladders were placed in the hatchway for the more expedition. When the lieutenant's sloop boarded the other Captain Teach's men threw in several new-fashioned sort of grenades, viz., case-bottles filled with powder and small shot, slugs, and pieces of lead or iron, with a quick-match in the mouth of it, which, being lighted without side, presently runs into the bottle to the powder, and, as it is instantly thrown on board, generally does great execution, besides putting all the crew into a confusion. But, by good Providence, they had not that effect here, the men being in the hold. Black-beard, seeing few or no hands aboard, told his men "that they were all knocked to head, except three or four; and therefore," says he, "let's jump on board and cut them to pieces."

Whereupon, under the smoke of one of the bottles just mentioned, Black-beard enters with fourteen men over the bows of Maynard's sloop, and were not seen by him until the air cleared. However, he just then gave a signal to his men, who all rose in an instant, and attacked the pirates with as much bravery as ever was done upon such an occasion. Black-beard and the lieutenant fired the first shots at each other, by which the pirate received a wound, and then engaged with swords, till the lieutenant's unluckily broke, and stepping back to cock a pistol, Black-beard, with his cutlass, was striking at that instant that one of Maynard's men gave him a terrible wound in the neck and throat, by which the lieutenant came off with only a small cut over his fingers.

They were now closely and warmly engaged, the lieutenant and twelve men against Black-beard and fourteen, till the sea was tinctured with blood round the vessel. Black-beard received a shot into his body from the pistol that Lieutenant Maynard discharged, yet he stood his ground, and fought with great fury till he received five-and-twenty wounds, and five of them by shot. At length, as he was cocking another pistol, having fired several before, he fell down dead; by which time eight more out of the fourteen dropped, and all the rest, much wounded, jumped overboard and called out for quarter, which was granted, though it was only prolonging their lives a few days. The sloop *Ranger* came up and attacked the men that remained in Black-beard's sloop with equal bravery, till they likewise cried for quarter.

Here was an end of that courageous brute, who might have passed in the world for a hero had he been employed in a good cause. His destruction, which was of such consequence to the plantations, was entirely owing to the conduct and bravery of Lieutenant Maynard and his men, who might have destroyed him with much less loss had they had a vessel with great guns; but they were obliged to use small vessels, because the holes and place she lurked in would not admit of others of greater draught. And it was no small difficulty for this gentleman to get to him, having grounded his vessel at least a hundred times in getting up the river, beside other discouragements, enough to have turned back any gentleman without dishonour had he been less resolute and bold than this lieutenant. The broadside that did so much mischief before they boarded in all probability saved the rest from destruction; for, before that, Teach had little or no hopes of escaping, and therefore had posted a resolute fellow, a negro, whom he had bred up, with a lighted match in the powder-room, with commands to blow up when he should give him orders, which was as soon as the lieutenant and his men could have entered, that so he might have destroyed his conquerors with himself. And when the negro found how it went with Black-beard, he could hardly be persuaded from the rash action by two prisoners that were then in the hold of the sloop.

What seems a little odd is that some of these men, who behaved so bravely against Black-beard, went afterwards a-pirating themselves, and one of them was taken along with Roberts; but I do not find that any of them were provided for, except one that was hanged. But this is a digression.

The lieutenant caused Black-beard's head to be severed from his body, and hung up at the boltsprit end; then he sailed to Bath Town, to get relief for his wounded men.

It must be observed that, in rummaging the pirate's sloop, they found several letters and written papers, which discovered the correspondence between Governor Eden, the secretary and collector, and also some traders at New York, and Black-beard. It is likely he had regard enough for his friends to have destroyed these papers before the action, in order to hinder them from falling into such hands, where the discovery would be of no use either to the interest or reputation of these fine gentlemen, if it had not been his fixed resolution to have blown up together, when he found no possibility of escaping.

When the lieutenant came to Bath Town, he made bold to seize in the governor's storehouse the sixty hogsheads of sugar, and from honest Mr. Knight, twenty; which it seems was their dividend of the plunder taken in the French ship. The latter did not survive this shameful discovery, for, being apprehensive that he might be called to an account for these trifles, fell sick, it is thought, with the fright, and died in a few days.

After the wounded men were pretty well recovered, the lieutenant sailed back to the men-of-war in James River, in Virginia, with Black-beard's head still hanging at the boltsprit end, and fifteen prisoners, thirteen of whom were hanged.

Pirate Captain William Fly

by CHARLES JOHNSON

As to the birth of this pirate, we can discover nothing by the inquiries we have hitherto made; and indeed had we succeeded in our search, it would have been of no great consequence; for it is certain by the behaviour of the man, he must have have been of very obscure parents; and by his education, (as he was no artist) very unfit in all respects, except that of cruelty, for the villainous business he was in. We have been informed, that he had been in a pirate in a private capacity, and having escaped justice, had an opportunity of repenting his former crimes, and as a foremast man, or petty officer, of getting his bread in a warrantable way. But no—ignorant as he was of letters, he was ambitious of power, and capable of the most barbarous actions to acquire it.

Capt. Green, of Bristol, in April, 1726, shipped this Fly as boatswain, at Jamaica, being bound, in the Elizabeth snow, of Bristol, for the coast of Guinea. Fly, who had insinuated himself with some of the men, whom he found ripe for any villainy, resolved to seize the said snow, and murder the captain and mate, and taking the command on himself, turn pirate. He proposed this design to his brothers in iniquity, who approving it, he, having the watch at one o'clock in the morning, on the 27th day of May, went up to one Morrice Cundon, then at the helm, accompanied by Alexander Mitchel, Henry Hill, Samuel Cole, Thomas Winthrop, and other conspirators, and swore if he spoke one word, or stirred either hand or foot, he would blow his brains out; and tucking up his shirt above the elbows with a cutlass in his hand, he, with Mitchel, went into the captain's cabin, and told him he must turn out. The captain, asking what was the matter, was answered by Mitchel, they had no time to answer impertinent questions; that if he would turn out and go upon deck quietly, it would save them the trouble of scraping the cabin; if he would not, a few buckets of water and a scraper would take his blood out of the deck: that they had chosen Capt. Fly for commander, and would allow of no other, and would not waste their provisions to feed useless men.

The Captain replied, that since they had so resolved, he should make no resistance; but begged they would not murder him, since his living could be no obstacle to their designs; that he had never been harsh to either of them, and therefore they could not kill him out of revenge; and if it was only for their security, he desired, if they would not take his word to do nothing to obstruct the measures they had resolved on, they would secure him in irons, till he might be put somewhere on shore, *Ah*, says Fly, *to live and hang us, if we are ever taken: no, no, walk up, that bite won't take; it has hanged many an honest fellow already.* Mitchel and Fly then laying hold of him, pulled him out of his bed. The poor captain entreating them to spare his life for his soul's sake, told them he would bind himself down by the most solemn oaths, never to appear against them; that he was unfit to appear before the judgment seat of a just and pure God; that he was loaded with sins, and to take him off before he had washed those stains, which sullied his soul, by the tears of repentance, would be a cruelty beyond comparison greater than that of depriving him of life, were he prepared for death, since it would be, without any offence committed against them, dooming him to eternal misery. However, if they would not be persuaded that his life was consistent with their safety, he begged they would allow some time to prepare himself for the great change: that he begged no other mercy than what the justice and compassion of the laws would allow them, should they hereafter be taken. — *your blood,* said Mitchel, *no preaching. Be — a' you will, what's that to us? Let him look out who has the watch. Upon deck you dog, for we shall lose no more time about you.*

They hauled him into the steerage, and forced him upon deck, where one of the hell-hounds asked if he had rather take a leap like a brave fellow, or be tossed over like a sneaking rascal? The captain addressing himself to Fly, said, *Boatswain, for God's sake don't throw me overboard; if you do I am for ever lost; Hell's the portion of my crimes.* — *him,* answered Fly, *since he's so Godly, we'll give him time to say his prayers, and I'll be parson. Say after me,* Lord have mercy on me. *Short prayers are best, so no more words and over with him, my lads.* The captain still cried for mercy, and begged an hour's respite only, but all in vain; he was seized by the villains and thrown overboard. He caught, however, and hung by the main sheet, which Winthrop seeing, fetched the cooper's broad axe, and chopping off the unhappy master's hand, he was swallowed up by the sea.

The captain being thus dispatched, Thomas Jenkins, the mate, was secured and brought upon deck, to share the same cruel fate. His entreaties were as useless as the captain's; the sentence they had passed upon him was not to be reversed; they were deaf to his prayers and remonstrances, strangers to humanity and compassion. He was of the captain's mess, they said, and they should e'en drink together; it was a pity to part good company.

Thus they jested with his agonies. He, however, made some struggle, which irritating his murderers, one of them snatched up the axe, with which Winthrop had lopped off the captain's hand, and gave him a great cut on the shoulder, by missing his head, where the blow was aimed, and he was thrown into the sea. He swam notwithstanding, and called out to the doctor to throw him a rope, who, poor man, could not hear him, being secured, and laid in irons in his own cabin; and had he heard, and been able to have thrown the rope required, could it be expected that these hardened wretches would have relented, and shown him mercy? But the sinking man will catch at a straw, and hope, they say, is the last that deserts us. While we have life we are apt to flatter ourselves some lucky accident may favour us.

It was next debated what should be done with the doctor. Some were for sending him to look after the captain and mate; but the majority, as he was a useful man, thought it better to keep him. All obstacles being removed, Mitchel saluted Fly captain, and with the rest of the crew who had been in the conspiracy, with some ceremony, gave him possession of the great cabin.

Here a bowl of punch being made, Morrice Cundon was called down, and one John Fitzherbert, set to the helm in his place. At the same time the carpenter and Thomas Streaton were brought before the captain, who told them they were three rascals, and richly deserved to be sent after the captain and mate, but that they were willing to show them mercy, and not put them to death in cold blood and he would therefore only put them in irons, for the security of the ship's crew. They were accordingly ordered out, and ironed. Fly then told his comrades it was convenient to resolve on some course, when word was brought them, that a ship was very near them. The council broke up, and made a clear ship, when in a very little while after, they found it was the *Pompey*, which had left Jamaica in company with the snow. The *Pompey*, standing for the snow which did not make from her, soon hailed and asked how Capt. Green did, and was answered by Fly, that he was very well. They did not think fit to attack this ship, but returned to hold their consultation, it was resolved to steer for North Carolina.

Upon their arrival on that coast they spied a sloop at anchor within the bar. She was called the *John and Hannah*, and commanded by Capt. Fulker who thinking the snow might want a pilot, stepped into his boat with his mate, Mr. Atkinson, and Mr. Roan, two passengers, and a young lad, in order to bring her in. When they came on board, they were told, that the snow was from Jamaica, with a cargo. Capt. Fulker and Mr. Roan were desired to walk down to the captain, who was in the cabin. Fly received them very civilly, ordered a bowl of punch, and hearing Capt. Fulker had brought another passenger on board Mr. Atkinson was also invited down.

The punch being brought in, Capt. Fly told his guest, *that he was no man to mince matters; that he and his comrades were gentlemen of fortune, and should make bold to try if Capt. Fulker's sloop was a better sailer than the snow. If she was, she would prove much fitter for their business, and they must have her.* The snow came to an anchor about a league off the sloop, and Fly ordered Fulker, with six of his own hands, into the boat to bring her along side of the snow; but the wind proving contrary, their endeavours proved also vain, and they returned again in the boat, bringing Capt. Fulker back with them. As soon as they got on board the snow, Fly fell into a violent passion, cursing and abusing Fulker for not bringing off the sloop. He gave him his reason, and said it was impossible. *You lie you dog,* replied the pirate, *but your hide shall pay for your roguery, and if I can't bring her off, I'll burn her where she lies.* He then ordered Capt. Fulker to the geers; no reason, no arguments could prevail; he was stripped and lashed after a very inhuman manner; and the boat's crew being sent again, with much ado carried her off as far as the bar, where she bilged and sunk. The pirates then endeavoured to set what remained of her out of water on fire, but they could not burn her.

The snow getting under sail to look out for some booty, Fulker and the others desired they might be set at liberty, but it was denied them for the present, though not without a promise that they should be released the first vessel they took. On the 5th of June they left Carolina, and the next day spied a sail, which proved the *John and Betty*, commanded by Capt. Gale, bound from Barbadoes to Guinea. Fly gave chase, but finding the ship wronged him, he made a signal of distress, hoisting his jack at the main-top-mast head; but this decoy did not hinder the ship making the best of her way. Fly continued the chase all night, and the wind slackening, he came within shot of the ship, and fired several guns at her under his black ensign. The ship being of no force, and the pirates ready to board, the captain struck; and Fly, manning his long-boat, the crew being well armed with pistols and cutlasses, went on board the prize, and sent Capt. Gale, after having secured his men, prisoner on board the snow. This prize was of little value to the pirates, who took nothing but some sail-cloth and small arms, and after two days let her go, but took away six of his men, setting on board Capt. Fulker, a passenger, and Capt. Green's surgeon. They kept Mr. Atkinson, knowing he was a good artist, and lately master of the Boneta brigantine, as a pilot for the coast of New England, which they were satisfied he was well acquainted with.

Upon Mr. Atkinson's desiring to have his liberty with the others, Capt. Fly refused it with the most horrid oaths and imprecations, and insisted upon it that he should act as their pilot; assuring him at the same time, if he piloted them wrong, his life should be the forfeit.

Mr. Atkinson answered, it was very hard he should be forced to take upon himself the pilotage, when he did not pretend to know the coast, and that his life should answer for any mistake his ignorance of it might make him guilty of, and therefore begged he might be set on board Capt. Gale; and that they would trust their own knowledge, since he did not doubt there being better artist on board. *No no*, replied Fly, *that won't do—your palavering won't save your bacon; so either discharge your trust like an honest man, (for go you shan't) or I'll send you with my service to the d—l: so no more words about the matter.*

There was no reply made, and they stood for the coast of New England. Off Delaware Bay they made a sloop, commanded by one Harris, bound from New York to Pennsylvania. She had on board about fifty passengers. Fly gave chase, and coming up with her, hoisted his black ensign, and ordered her to strike, which she immediately did; and Fly sent Capt. Atkinson on board, to sail her, though he would not allow him (Atkinson) any arms. The pirates ransacked this prize, but not finding her of any use to them, after a detention of 24 hours, they let her go, with her men, excepting only a well made young fellow, whose name was James Benbrooke, whom they kept.

Fly, after having released the prize, ordered Capt. Atkinson to carry the snow into Martha's Vineyard, but he willfully missed this place. Fly, finding himself beyond Nantucket, and that his design was balked, called to Atkinson, and told him *he was a rascally scoundrel, and that it was a piece of cruelty to let such a villain live, who designed the death of so many honest fellows.* Atkinson, in his defence, said, he never pretended to know the coast, and that it was very hard he should die for being thought an abler man than he really was. Had he pretended to be their pilot, and did not know his business, he deserved punishment; but when he was forced upon a business which he before declared he did not understand, it would be certainly cruel to make him suffer for their mistake. *You are an obstinate villain*, replied Fly, *and your design is to hang us; but blood and wounds, you dog, you shan't live to see it*—and saying this, he ran into his cabin and brought a pistol, with design to shoot Atkinson; but by the interposition of Mitchel, who thought him innocent of any design, he escaped.

Atkinson, who perceived his life every minute in danger, began to ingratiate himself with the pirates and gave them hopes, that with good and gentle usage, he might be brought to join them. This he did not say in express terms, but by words he now and then let drop, as by accident. They were not a little rejoiced at the idea of having so good artist to join them; nay some of them hinted to him, that if he would take upon him the command, they were ready to dispossess Capt. Fly, who carried his command too high, and was known to all the crew to be no artist, and to understand nothing beyond the business of a boatswain. Atkinson thought it his interest to keep them in the opinion that he would join; but always declined hearing any thing as to the command.

This made him less severely used, and protected him from the insults of Fly, who imagined he would betray them the first opportunity, therefore, more than once proposed his being thrown overboard, which was never approved by the snow's company.

From Nantucket they stood to the eastward, and off Brown's Bank made a fishing schooner. Fly, coming up with her, fired a gun, and hoisting his black ensign, swore, *if they did not instantly bring to, and send their boat on board, he would sink her.* The schooner obeyed, and sent away her boat on board the snow. He examined the captain as to what vessels were to be met with, and promised, if he could put him in the way of meeting with a good sailer, to let him go, and give him his vessel, or he should otherwise keep her. The poor man told him he had a companion which would soon be in sight, and was a much better vessel. Accordingly about 12 at noon, the same day, which was the 23d of June, the other schooner hove in sight; upon which Fly manned this prize with six pirates and a prisoner named George Tasker and sent her in chase, having himself on board the snow, no more than three pirates, Capt. Atkinson, (who had worked himself into some favour with him) and fifteen forced men; but he took care to have his arms upon deck by him.

The men who had not taken on with Fly, were, Atkinson, Capt. Fulker's mate, and two youths belonging to him; the carpenter and gunner belonging to Capt. Green; six of Capt. Gale's men, and the aforesaid Benbrooke, who belonged to Capt. Harris, with three of the men out of the schooner. Atkinson, seeing the prisoners and forced men were five to one of the pirates, thought of delivering himself from the bondage he was in: and as by good luck several other fishing vessels hove in sight, right ahead of the snow, he called to Capt. Fly, and told him he spied several other vessels ahead, desiring he would come forward and bring his glass. Fly did so, and leaving his arms on the quarter deck, set on the windlass to see if he could make out what they were. Atkinson, who had concerted his measures with one Walker and the above mentioned Benbrooke, secured the arms on the quarter deck, and gave them a signal to seize Fly; which they did, with very little trouble, and afterwards made themselves masters of the other three pirates and the snow, the rest of the prisoners, not knowing any thing of, or what the design might be, remaining altogether inactive, and brought the snow and pirates to Great Brewster, where a guard was put on board, June 28, 1726.

Soon after, the said pirates were brought to their trial, that is, on the 4th of July following, before the Honourable William Dummer, Esq., Lieutenant Governor and commander in chief of the province of Massachusetts Bay, President of the Special Court of Admiralty, at the court-house of Boston, assisted by 18 gentlemen of the council; before whom they were found guilty of murder and piracy, condemned to be executed, and accordingly were executed the 12th of July. Fly was ordered to be hanged in chains at the entrance of the harbour of Boston. Thus ended the short reign of an obdurate wretch, who only wanted skill and power to be as infamous as any who scoured the seas. The names of the three pirates executed with him, were, Samuel Cole, George Condick, and Henry Greenvil.

The Capture of the *Manila Galleon*

by FLEMING MacLIESH and MARTIN L. KRIEGER

They stared, for the last time, at the vacant, meaningless line of sky and sea with which they had deluded themselves so long. No hope, said the emptiness, there is nothing. You can ride here and rot your lives out and the lives of your children and grandchildren and there will still be nothing. Only this rolling immensity indifferent to man.

There was no more to do here, or that could be done. It was finished. They gave up, and turned away. And then in the moment of turning away, the curve of sky and sea bulged and distended and the emptiness, extending off into unlimited space, produced a speck, a point—something almost protozoic or protoplasmic, and like that, it might be said, viable: because it grew and enlarged; until its masts became thin and short as a needle, carrying squares of canvas half the size of a thumbnail.

The lookout, high at the masthead of the *Duke,* yelled and yelled again. She was coming on with a good wind. She was coming on with her topsails filling, right for them. Here, here—the sky and sun and sea and the rolling horizon might have been saying—here, here, since you wanted it—in spite of everything, against all the impossible odds, here she is in your hands, in your laps, the ultimate, absolute prize, six months from Manila, in silks, pearls, spice, gauze, rubies.

But, of course, as might be expected after all that time, they couldn't entirely believe it. As the *Marquiss* three weeks before, had mistaken the *Duke* for the galleon, so now many said that what they took for the galleon was actually the *Marquiss*—particularly since no fore-topmast could be discerned. The *Marquiss* actually was undergoing final repairs for the long voyage west and was at anchor in the small natural harbor of Puerto Segura, near the Cape; but they thought that somehow, for some reason, she had slipped out and put to sea. This was merely a kind of uncontrollable trembling; a fit like buck fever. *Duke* hoisted her ensign and bore after the sail. It was morning of December 21st.

They closed the distance very slowly. There was little wind, and that began to drop. By afternoon the strange sail was only a little bit larger, maybe now the size of a stamp. Men laid money on whether it was the galleon or the *Marquiss,* the way some people will lay a bet against themselves on what they want most: partly, to insure that if they don't get it they'll at least pocket

467

something but, actually, to make a sort of sacrifice to fortune, so that the goddess will smile, collar the small bet and let them have the big one.

There was activity aboard *Dutchess*. She put out a boat and it returned. Rogers sent Frye in the yawl to reconnoiter, fired a gun and hoisted a French ensign; the stranger distantly answered. By nightfall Frye was back. The *Marquiss* was where she ought to be. What they had in front of them was nothing at all but the *Manila Galleon*. It was as good as done. Except, of course, for the business of taking her.

They kept a boat out that night with lights, in order not to lose her. At one point during the night *Dutchess* passed near this boat and twice fired on it wildly. The vessels rose and fell in the darkness, the occasional lights gave back nothing. It was almost as if the whale had sounded.

And then it was daybreak of December 22nd, and daybreak disclosed her, not a league away, off the weather bow, towering, huge: *Dutchess* ahead of her to leeward, and all riding silently in the still, first light.

Everyone knew now. On each ship the boatswain shouted, "Up all hammocks." Each man ran to his hammock, rolled it up, corded it and carried it to the quarterdeck, poop or forecastle, as assigned. The hammocks were stowed, under the direction of the quartermaster, between the two parts of the protective netting that ran along the decks, as a shield against small shot. Hammocks and bedding were also packed against bulkheads and cabin walls to stop the splinters. Other bulkheads, chests, casks, mess tables, everything movable that might splinter, had already been pitched into the hold.

The boatswain and his mates secured the lower yards, slinging them with chains and doubling the important sheets, ropes and braces. Nets were spread under the masts to catch any wreckage falling from aloft.

There was no wind, and the distance of even one league was still too great. They had to come to point-blank range. *Duke* got out eight of the big oars and began to row. Carpenters and their crews assembled the tools and spare parts to repair the iron machinery of the chain pumps, against a hit. They got out their shot-plugs and mauls, plugs of oakum and sheets of lead to jam against holes opened up by hits at or below the waterline.

On each ship the surgeons in the holds had their platforms spread with canvas and the chests ready, the lanterns lit, the water standing in tubs; basins, tourniquets, ligatures, linens, powders, forceps, saws, tape and tow. *And at the corner of the Platform you are to place two Vessels, one with Water to wash Hands in between each Operation, and to wet your dismembring Blades in, and for other Services; and the other to throw amputated Limbs into, till you have an opportunity to heave them overboard . . . also Basons to mix your Restrictives in. Pannikins to warm your Oyls in, and . . . have likewise your Cordial Bottle ready at hand to relieve men when they faint.*

A slight breeze sprang up. The oars were shipped. There was no liquor left; so Rogers had a kettle of chocolate made for the men.

Decks had been sanded, sails splashed with water to reduce the fire hazard. On the gun decks spongers and rammers were hooked to the beams above the guns. Spare matches, freshly soaked in saltpeter water, were coiled in small tubs. The heavy shot had been placed in shot racks beside each gunner, and from the magazines below the waterline stooping ship's boys had lugged up the cartridges in bucket brigades—charges of powder packed in canvas or parchment. The buckets were stowed amidships in barrels sealed with leather. Between the guns stood tubs of water: in some of them vinegar water for sponging the cannon; in others blankets soaking, to extinguish fires. The magazines were opened and hung with dripping blankets.

In each gun the cartridge had been rammed home: after the cartridge a wad of oakum; after that the ball, and then a second wad. The gunners opened the metal caps and filled the touchholes with priming powder. Rogers' ship was closing the range. *Dutchess,* still far back, couldn't come up. After the chocolate, the men of the *Duke* went to prayers; and while they were at prayers, the *Manila Galleon* opened fire on them.

The drums beat. At every hatchway the boatswain and his mates piped all hands to quarters. Gunports were opened, the lashings of the great guns cast loose, and the guns run out. All hatches were secured to prevent anyone deserting his post and hiding in the hold. In order that the force of the explosion might not blow the linstock from his hand, each gunner sprinkled a little train of powder from the touchhole to the base ring of his piece. The slow-matches lifted. The distance closed. From her stern-chase the galleon cannonaded them. Then the commands sang out, and the matches dropped, and the guns boomed.

Duke fired her fore-chase first, and then as she drew nearer, let go with a broadside. They were at point-blank musket range. One broadside and another and another. *Duke* fought alone. *Marquiss* was far off, and *Dutchess* almost becalmed.

The gunners stood on the opposite side of their pieces from the cartridges, to prevent sparks from their matches igniting the ammunition. They applied the matches to the base rings smartly, whipped back their hands and jumped aside to avoid the recoil. Through the smoke and the pounding of cannon as the shot smashed home, small arms banged and rattled from the tops, waist, forecastle and quarter-deck. The galleon replied in kind, but could not work her big guns as fast.

And then Rogers was down on the deck and in agony, hit in the face. He could not speak, but wrote out his orders, lying where he fell. A shot cracked the mizzenmast. As the guns roared and came back, they were scraped to remove the burning fragments of cartridge-casing, sponged, reloaded and run out, blasting again. *Duke* moved ahead of the galleon and lay athwart her hawse, raking her. And then in a blast of flame, iron, splinters and stinking, fire-streaked smoke the action was over; the galleon struck.

Dutchess, finally coming up, excitedly fired five of her guns and let go a musket volley; but the galleon, having by then submitted, did not reply. The action had lasted three glasses, an hour and a half, and the price for the English was one man killed and two wounded. Rogers had been shot through the left cheek, the bullet knocking out a lot of teeth and smashing his jaw. He was in horrible pain; but he still commanded.

He ordered the pinnace over to bring him the galleon's captain and other officers. Nobody spoke about cheering, as the crew sat or leaned to rest, staring at what they had got; it was too soon; it was a little grim.

And a lot more grim, certainly, for everyone on board the prize and for her captains and officers as they were rowed back in the pinnace. *I am gall; I am heartburn. God's most deep decree/Bitter would have me taste . . .*

After the longest, and most terrible, continuous voyage in the world—after the gales and storms and the gigantic seas; after the cold to the bone and perpetual thirst; the lice, rats, weevils, and maggots swimming in the broth; after the beriberi, and scurvy and the pickled bodies awash in the bilge, when the whole ship swelled and stank with one gigantic infection; after the Te Deums and the hilarious celebration when they finally sighted, two or three hundred miles off the California coast, the *señas*—sea lions—and seaweed, the welcome first signs of land, and thought they were home safe and alive and all right—they had had to be met at this last Cape and be taken. Everything they had endured and survived, all those last-chance escapes, wound up under the guns of people they did not know, of whom they had barely been informed, who had sailed to meet them from Bristol, England, nearly a year before they had ever left Manila. So it was for nothing and worse than nothing, because they had lost not only all the possible profits and compensations which made men willing to undergo so much, but would now have to pay, out of whatever credit they had left, ransom money for "That Voyage . . ." as Careri wrote, "which is enough to Destroy a Man, or make him unfit for anything as long as he lives."

Sea Storms

The Gale

by JOSEPH CONRAD

Meantime the *Narcissus,* with square yards, ran out of the fair monsoon. She drifted slowly, swinging round and round the compass, through a few days of baffling light airs. Under the patter of short warm showers, grumbling men whirled the heavy yards from side to side; they caught hold of the soaked ropes with groans and sighs, while their officers, sulky and dripping with rain water, unceasingly ordered them about in wearied voices. During the short respites they looked with disgust into the smarting palms of their stiff hands, and asked one another bitterly:—"Who would be a sailor, if he could be a farmer?" All the tempers were spoilt, and no man cared what he said. One black night, when the watch, panting in the heat and half-drowned with the rain, had been through four mortal hours hunted from brace to brace, Belfast declared that he would "chuck the sea for ever and go in a steamer." This was excessive, no doubt. Captain Allistoun, with great self-control, would mutter sadly to Mr. Baker:—"It is not so bad—not so bad," when he had managed to shove, and dodge, and manoeuvre his smart ship through sixty miles in twenty-four hours. From the doorstep of the little cabin, Jimmy, chin in hand, watched our distasteful labours with insolent and melancholy eyes. We spoke to him gently —and out of his sight exchanged sour smiles.

Then, again, with a fair wind and under a clear sky, the ship went on piling up the South Latitude. She passed outside Madagascar and Mauritius without a glimpse of the land. Extra lashings were put on the spare spars. Hatches were looked to. The steward in his leisure moments and with a worried air tried to fit washboards to the cabin doors. Stout canvas was bent with care. Anxious eyes looked to the westward, towards the cape of storms. The ship began to dip into a southwest swell, and the softly luminous sky of low latitudes took on a harder sheen from day to day above our heads: it arched high above the ship vibrating and pale, like an immense dome of steel, resonant with the deep voice of freshening gales. The sunshine gleamed cold on the white curls of black waves. Before the strong breath of westerly squalls the ship, with reduced sail, lay slowly over, obstinate and yielding. She drove to and fro in the unceasing endeavour to fight her way through the invisible violence of the winds: she pitched headlong into dark smooth hollows; she struggled upwards over the snowy ridges of great running seas; she rolled, restless, from side to side, like a thing in pain. Enduring and valiant, she answered to the call of men; and her slim spars waving for ever in abrupt semicircles, seemed to beckon in vain for help towards the stormy sky.

It was a bad winter off the Cape that year. The relieved helmsmen came off flapping their arms, or ran stamping hard and blowing into swollen, red fingers. The watch on deck dodged the sting of cold sprays or, crouching in sheltered corners, watched dismally the high and merciless seas boarding the ship time after time in unappeasable fury. Water tumbled in cataracts over the forecastle doors. You had to dash through a waterfall to get into your damp bed. The men turned in wet and turned out stiff to face the redeeming and ruthless exactions of their glorious and obscure fate. Far aft, and peering watchfully to windward, the officers could be seen through the mist of squalls. They stood by the weather-rail, holding on grimly, straight and glistening in their long coats; and in the disordered plunges of the hard-driven ship, they appeared high up, attentive, tossing violently above the grey line of a clouded horizon in motionless attitudes.

They watched the weather and the ship as men on shore watch the momentous chances of fortune. Captain Allistoun never left the deck, as though he had been part of the ship's fittings. Now and then the steward, shivering, but always in shirt sleeves, would struggle towards him with some hot coffee, half of which the gale blew out of the cup before it reached the master's lips. He drank what was left gravely in one long gulp, while heavy sprays pattered loudly on his oilskin coat, the seas swishing broke about his high boots; and he never took his eyes off the ship. He kept his gaze riveted upon her as a loving man watches the unselfish toil of a delicate woman upon the slender thread of whose existence is hung the whole meaning and joy of the world. We all watched her. She was beautiful and had a weakness. We loved her no less for that. We admired her qualities aloud, we boasted of them to one another, as though they had been our own, and the consciousness of her only fault we kept buried in the silence of our profound affection. She was born in the thundering peal of hammers beating upon iron, in black eddies of smoke, under a grey sky, on the banks of the Clyde. The clamorous and sombre stream gives birth to things of beauty that float away into the sunshine of the world to be loved by men. The *Narcissus* was one of that perfect brood. Less perfect than many perhaps, but she was ours, and, consequently, incomparable. We were proud of her. In Bombay, ignorant landlubbers alluded to her as that "pretty grey ship." Pretty! A scurvy meed of commendation! We knew she was the most magnificent sea-boat ever launched. We tried to forget that, like many good sea-boats, she was at times rather crank. She was exacting. She wanted care in loading and handling, and no one knew exactly how much care would be enough. Such are the imperfections of mere men! The ship knew, and sometimes would correct the presumptuous human ignorance by the wholesome discipline of fear. We had heard ominous stories about past voyages. The cook (technically a seaman, but in reality no sailor)—the cook, when unstrung by some misfortune, such as the rolling over of a saucepan, would mutter gloomily while he wiped the floor:—"There! Look at what she has done! Some voy'ge she will drown all hands! You'll see if she won't." To which the steward, snatching in the galley a moment to draw breath in the hurry of his worried life, would remark philosophically:—"Those that see won't tell, anyhow. I don't want to see it." We derided those fears. Our hearts went out to the old man when he pressed her hard so as to make her hold her own, hold to every inch gained to windward; when he made her, under reefed sails, leap obliquely at enormous waves. The men, knitted together aft into a ready group by the first sharp order of an officer coming to take charge of the deck in bad weather:—"Keep handy the watch," stood admiring her valiance. Their eyes blinked in the wind; their dark faces were wet with drops of water more salt and bitter than human tears; beards and moustaches, soaked, hung straight and dripping like fine seaweed. They were fantastically misshapen; in high boots, in hats like helmets, and swaying clumsily, stiff and bulky in glistening oilskins, they resembled men strangely equipped for some fabulous adventure. Whenever she rose easily to a towering green sea, elbows dug ribs, faces brightened, lips murmured:—"Didn't she do it cleverly," and all the heads turning like one watched with sardonic grins the foiled wave go roaring to leeward, white with the foam of a monstrous rage. But when she had not been quick enough and, struck heavily, lay over trembling under the blow, we clutched at ropes, and looking up at the narrow bands of drenched and strained sails waving desperately aloft, we thought in our hearts:—"No wonder. Poor thing!"

The thirty-second day out of Bombay began inauspiciously. In the morning a sea smashed one of the galley doors. We dashed in through lots of steam and found the cook very wet and indignant with the ship:—"She's getting worse every day. She's trying to drown me in front of my own stove!" He was very angry. We pacified him, and the carpenter, though washed away twice from there, managed to repair the door. Through that accident our dinner was not ready till late, but it didn't matter in the end because Knowles, who went to fetch it, got knocked down by a sea and the dinner went over the side. Captain Allistoun, looking more hard and thin-lipped than ever, hung on to full topsails and foresail, and would not notice that the ship, asked to do too much, appeared to lose heart altogether for the first time since we knew her. She refused to rise, and bored her way sullenly through the seas. Twice running, as though she had been blind or weary of life, she put her nose deliberately into a big wave and swept the decks from end to end. As the boatswain observed with marked annoyance, while we were splashing about in a body to try and save a worthless wash-tub:—"Every blooming thing in the ship is going overboard this afternoon." Venerable Singleton broke his habitual silence and said with a glance aloft:—"The old man's in a temper with the weather, but it's no good bein' angry with the winds of heaven." Jimmy had shut his door, of course. We knew he was dry and comfortable within his little cabin, and in our absurd way were pleased one moment, exasperated the next, by that certitude. Donkin skulked shamelessly, uneasy and miserable. He grumbled:—"I'm perishin' with cold outside in bloomin' wet rags, an' that 'ere black sojer sits dry on a blamed chest full of bloomin' clothes; blank his black soul!" We took no notice of him; we hardly gave a thought to Jimmy and his bosom friend. There was no leisure for idle probing of hearts. Sails blew adrift. Things broke loose. Cold and wet, we were washed about the deck while trying to repair damages. The ship tossed about, shaken furiously, like a toy in the hand of a lunatic. Just at sunset there was a rush to shorten sail before the menace of a sombre hail cloud. The hard gust of wind came brutal like the blow of a fist. The ship relieved of her canvas in time received it pluckily: she yielded reluctantly to the violent onset; then, coming up with a stately and irresistible motion, brought her spars to windward in the teeth of the screeching squall. Out of the abysmal darkness of the black cloud overhead white hail steamed on her, rattled on the rigging, leaped in handfuls off the yards, rebounded on the deck— round and gleaming in the murky turmoil like a shower of pearls. It passed away. For a moment a livid sun shot horizontally the last rays of sinister light between the hills of steep, rolling waves. Then a wild night rushed in— stamped out in a great howl that dismal remnant of a stormy day.

There was no sleep on board that night. Most seamen remember in their life one or two such nights of a culminating gale. Nothing seems left of the whole universe but darkness, clamour, fury—and the ship. And like the last vestige of a shattered creation she drifts, bearing an anguished remnant of sinful mankind, through the distress, tumult, and pain of an avenging terror. No one slept in the forecastle. The tin oil-lamp suspended on a long string, smoking, described wide circles; wet clothing made dark heaps on the glistening floor; a thin layer of water rushed to and fro. In the bed-places men lay booted, resting on elbows and with open eyes. Hung-up suits of oilskin swung out and in, lively and disquieting like reckless ghosts of decapitated seamen dancing in a tempest. No one spoke and all listened. Outside the night moaned and sobbed to the accompaniment of a continuous loud tremor as of innumerable drums beating far off. Shrieks passed through the air. Tremendous dull blows made the ship tremble while she rolled under the weight of the seas toppling on her deck. At times she soared up swiftly as if to leave this earth for ever, then during interminable moments fell through a void with all the hearts on board of her standing still, till a frightful shock, expected and sudden, started them off again with a big thump. After every dislocating jerk of the ship, Wamibo, stretched full length, his face on the pillow, groaned slightly with the pain of his tormented universe. Now and then, for the fraction of an intolerable second, the ship, in the fiercer burst of a terrible uproar, remained on her side, vibrating and still, with a stillness more appalling than the wildest motion. Then upon all those prone bodies a stir would pass, a shiver of suspense. A man would protrude his anxious head and a pair of eyes glistened in the sway of light glaring wildly. Some moved their legs a little as if making ready to jump out. But several, motionless on their backs and with one hand gripping hard the edge of the bunk, smoked nervously with quick puffs, staring upwards; immobilised in a great craving for peace.

At midnight, orders were given to furl the fore and mizen topsails. With immense efforts men crawled aloft through a merciless buffeting, saved the canvas and crawled down almost exhausted, to bear in panting silence the cruel battering of the seas. Perhaps for the first time in the history of the merchant service the watch, told to go below, did not leave the deck, as if compelled to remain there by the fascination of a venomous violence. At every heavy gust men, huddled together, whispered to one another:—"It can blow no harder"—and presently the gale would give them the lie with a piercing shriek, and drive their breath back into their throats. A fierce squall seemed to burst asunder the thick mass of sooty vapours; and above the wrack of torn clouds glimpses could be caught of the high moon rushing backwards with frightful speed over the sky, right into the wind's eye. Many hung their heads, muttering that it "turned their inwards out" to look at it. Soon the clouds closed up and the world again became a raging, blind darkness that howled, flinging at the lonely ship salt sprays and sleets.

About half-past seven the pitchy obscurity round us turned a ghastly grey, and we knew that the sun had risen. This unnatural and threatening daylight, in which we could see one another's wild eyes and drawn faces, was only an added tax on our endurance. The horizon seemed to have come on all sides within arm's length of the ship. Into that narrowed circle furious seas leaped in, struck, and leaped out. A rain of salt, heavy drops flew aslant like mist. The main-topsail had to be goose-winged, and with stolid resignation every one prepared to go aloft once more; but the officers yelled, pushed back, and at last we understood that no more men would be allowed to go on the yard than were absolutely necessary for the work. As at any moment the masts were likely to be jumped out or blown overboard, we concluded that the captain didn't want to see all his crowd go over the side at once. That was reasonable. The watch then on duty, led by Mr. Creighton, began to struggle up the rigging. The wind flattened them against the ratlines; then, easing a little, would let them ascend a couple of steps; and again, with a sudden gust, pin all up the shrouds the whole crawling line in attitudes of crucifixion. The other watch plunged down on the main deck to haul up the sail. Men's heads bobbed up as the water flung them irresistibly from side to side. Mr. Baker grunted encouragingly in our midst, spluttering and blowing amongst the tangled ropes like an energetic porpoise. Favoured by an ominous and untrustworthy lull, the work was done without any one being lost either off the deck or from the yard. For the moment the gale seemed to take off, and the ship, as if grateful for our efforts, plucked up heart and made better weather of it.

At eight the men off duty, watching their chance, ran forward over the flooded deck to get some rest. The other half of the crew remained aft for their turn of "seeing her through her trouble," as they expressed it. The two mates urged the master to go below. Mr. Baker grunted in his ear:—"Ough! surely now . . . Ough! . . . confidence in us . . . nothing more to do . . . she must lay it out or go. Ough! Ough!" Tall young Mr. Creighton smiled down at him cheerfully:—". . . She's as right as a trivet! Take a spell, sir." He looked at them stonily with bloodshot, sleepless eyes. The rims of his eyelids were scarlet, and he moved his jaws unceasingly with a slow effort, as though he had been masticating a lump of india-rubber. He shook his head. He repeated:— "Never mind me. I must see it out—I must see it out," but he consented to sit down for a moment on the skylight, with his hard face turned unflinchingly to windward. The sea spat at it—and stoical, it streamed with water as though he had been weeping. On the weather side of the poop the watch, hanging on to the mizen rigging and to one another, tried to exchange encouraging words. Singleton, at the wheel, yelled out:—"Look out for yourselves!" His voice reached them in a warning whisper. They were startled.

A big, foaming sea came out of the mist; it made for the ship, roaring wildly, and in its rush it looked as mischievous and discomposing as a mad-man with an axe. One or two, shouting, scrambled up the rigging; most, with a convulsive catch of the breath, held on where they stood. Singleton dug his knees under the wheel-box, and carefully eased the helm to the headlong pitch of the ship, but without taking his eyes off the coming wave. It towered close-to and high, like a wall of green glass topped with snow. The ship rose to it as though she had soared on wings, and for a moment rested poised upon the foaming crest as if she had been a great sea-bird. Before we could draw breath a heavy gust struck her, another roller took her unfairly under the weather bow, she gave a toppling lurch, and filled her decks. Captain Allistoun leaped up, and fell; Archie rolled over him, screaming:—"She will rise!" She gave another lurch to leeward; the lower deadeyes dipped heavily; the men's feet flew from under them, and they hung kicking above the slanting poop. They could see the ship putting her side in the water, and shouted all together:— "She's going!" Forward the forecastle doors flew open, and the watch below were seen leaping out one after another, throwing their arms up; and, falling on hands and knees, scrambled aft on all fours along the high side of the deck, sloping more than the roof of a house. From leeward the seas rose, pursuing them; they looked wretched in a hopeless struggle, like vermin fleeing before a flood; they fought up the weather ladder of the poop one after another, half naked and staring wildly; and as soon as they got up they shot to leeward in clusters, with closed eyes, till they brought up heavily with their ribs against the iron stanchions of the rail; then, groaning, they rolled in a confused mass. The immense volume of water thrown forward by the last scend of the ship had burst the lee door of the forecastle. They could see their chests, pillows, blan-kets, clothing, come out floating upon the sea. While they struggled back to windward they looked in dismay. The straw beds swam high, the blankets, spread out, undulated; while the chests, waterlogged and with a heavy list, pitched heavily like dismasted hulks, before they sank; Archie's big coat passed with outspread arms, resembling a drowned seaman floating with his head under water. Men were slipping down while trying to dig their fingers into the planks; others, jammed in corners, rolled enormous eyes. They all yelled unceasingly:—"The masts! Cut! Cut! . . ." A black squall howled low over the ship, that lay on her side with the weather yard-arms pointing to the clouds; while the tall masts, inclined nearly to the horizon, seemed to be of an immeasurable length. The carpenter let go his hold, rolled against the sky-light, and began to crawl to the cabin entrance, where a big axe was kept ready for just such an emergency. At that moment the topsail sheet parted, the end of the heavy chain racketed aloft, and sparks of red fire streamed down through the flying sprays. The sail flapped once with a jerk that seemed to tear our hearts out through our teeth, and instantly changed into a bunch of fluttering narrow ribbons that tied themselves into knots and became quiet along the yard. Captain Allistoun struggled, managed to stand up with his face near the deck, upon which men swung on the ends of ropes, like nest robbers upon a cliff. One of his feet was on somebody's chest; his face was purple; his lips moved. He yelled also; he yelled, bending down:—"No! No!" Mr. Baker, one leg over the binnacle-stand, roared out:—"Did you say no? Not cut?" He shook his head madly. "No! No!" Between his legs the crawling carpenter heard, collapsed at once, and lay full length in the angle of the skylight. Voices took up the shout—"No! No!" Then all became still. They waited for the ship to turn over altogether, and shake them out into the sea; and upon the terrific noise of wind and sea not a murmur of remonstrance came out from those men, who each would have given ever so many years of life to see "them damned sticks go overboard!" They all believed it their only chance; but a little hard-faced man shook his grey head and shouted "No!" without giving them as much as a glance. They were silent, and gasped. They gripped rails, they had wound ropes'-ends under their arms; they clutched ringbolts, they crawled in heaps where there was foothold; they held on with both arms, hooked themselves to anything to windward with elbows, with chins, almost with their teeth: and some, unable to crawl away from where they had been flung, felt the sea leap up, striking against their backs as they struggled up-wards. Singleton had stuck to the wheel. His hair flew out in the wind; the gale seemed to take its life-long adversary by the beard and shake his old head. He wouldn't let go, and, with his knees forced between the spokes, flew up and down like a man on a bough. As Death appeared unready, they began to look about. Donkin, caught by one foot in a loop of some rope, hung, head down, below us, and yelled, with his face to the deck:—"Cut! Cut!" Two men lowered themselves cautiously to him; others hauled on the rope. They caught him up, shoved him into a safer place, held him. He shouted curses at the master, shook his fist at him with horrible blasphemies, called upon us in filthy words to "Cut! Don't mind that murdering fool! Cut, some of you!" One of his rescuers struck him a back-handed blow over the mouth; his head banged on the deck, and he became suddenly very quiet, with a white face, breathing hard, and with a few drops of blood trickling from his cut lip. On the lee side another man could be seen stretched out as if stunned; only the washboard prevented him from going over the side. It was the steward. We had to sling him up like a bale, for he was paralysed with fright. He had rushed up out of the pantry when he felt the ship go over, and had rolled down helplessly, clutching a china mug. It was not broken. With difficulty we tore it away from him and when he saw it in our hands he was amazed. "Where did you get that thing?" he kept on asking us in a trembling voice. His shirt was blown to shreds; the ripped sleeves flapped like wings. Two men made him fast, and, doubled over the rope that held him, he resembled a bundle of wet rags. Mr. Baker crawled along the line of men, asking:—"Are you all there?" and looking them over. Some blinked vacantly, others shook convulsively; Wamibo's head hung over his breast; and in painful attitudes, cut by lashings, exhausted with clutching, screwed up in corners, they breathed heavily. Their lips twitched, and at every sickening heave of the overturned ship they opened them wide as if to shout. The cook, embracing a wooden stanchion, unconsciously repeated a prayer. In every short interval of the fiendish noises around he could be heard there, without cap or slippers, imploring in that storm the Master of our lives not to lead him into temptation. Soon he also became silent. In all that crowd of cold and hungry men, waiting wearily for a violent death, not a voice was heard; they were mute, and in sombre thoughtfulness listened to the horrible imprecations of the gale.

Hours passed. They were sheltered by the heavy inclination of the ship from the wind that rushed in one long unbroken moan above their heads, but cold rain showers fell at times into the uneasy calm of their refuge. Under the torment of that new infliction a pair of shoulders would writhe a little. Teeth chattered. The sky was clearing, and bright sunshine gleamed over the ship. After every burst of battering seas, vivid and fleeting rainbows arched over the drifting hull in the flick of sprays. The gale was ending in a clear blow, which gleamed and cut like a knife. Between two bearded shellbacks, Charley, fastened with somebody's long muffler to a deck ring-bolt, wept quietly, with rare tears wrung out by bewilderment, cold, hunger, and general misery. One of his neighbours punched him in the ribs asking roughly:—"What's the matter with your cheek? In fine weather there's no holding you, youngster." Turning about with prudence he worked himself out of his coat and threw it over the boy. The other man closed up, muttering:—" 'Twill make a bloomin' man of you, sonny." They flung their arms over and pressed against him. Charley drew his feet up and his eyelids dropped. Sighs were heard, as men, perceiving that they were not to be "drowned in a hurry," tried easier positions. Mr. Creighton, who had hurt his leg, lay amongst us with compressed lips. Some fellows belonging to his watch set about securing him better. Without a word or a glance he lifted his arms one after another to facilitate the operation, and not a muscle moved in his stern, young face. They asked him with solicitude:—"Easier now, sir?" He answered with a curt:—"That'll do." He was a hard young officer, but many of his watch used to say they liked him well enough because he had "such a gentlemanly way of damning us up and down the deck." Others unable to discern such fine shades of refinement, respected him for his smartness. For the first time since the ship had gone on her beam ends Captain Allistoun gave a short glance down at his men. He was almost upright—one foot against the side of the skylight, one knee on the deck; and with the end of the vang round his waist swung back and forth with his gaze fixed ahead, watchful, like a man looking out for a sign. Before his eyes the ship, with half her deck below water, rose and fell on heavy seas that rushed from under her flashing in the cold sunshine. We began to think she was wonderfully buoyant—considering. Confident voices were heard shouting:— "She'll do, boys!" Belfast exclaimed with fervour:—"I would giv' a month's pay for a draw at a pipe!" One or two, passing dry tongues on their salt lips, muttered something about a "drink of water." The cook, as if inspired, scrambled up with his breast against the poop water-cask and looked in. There was a little at the bottom. He yelled, waving his arms, and two men began to crawl backwards and forwards with the mug. We had a good mouthful all round. The master shook his head impatiently, refusing. When it came to Charley one of his neighbours shouted:—"That bloomin' boy's asleep." He slept as though he had been dosed with narcotics. They let him be. Singleton held to the wheel with one hand while he drank, bending down to shelter his lips from the wind. Wamibo had to be poked and yelled at before he saw the mug held before his eyes. Knowles said sagaciously:—"It's better'n a tot o'rum." Mr. Baker grunted:—"Thank ye." Mr. Creighton drank and nodded. Donkin gulped greedily, glaring over the rim. Belfast made us laugh when with grimacing mouth he shouted:—"Pass it this way. We're all taytottlers here." The master, presented with the mug again by a crouching man, who screamed up at him:—"We all had a drink, Captain," groped for it without ceasing to look ahead, and handed it back stiffly as though he could not spare half a glance away from the ship. Faces brightened. We shouted to the cook:— "Well done, Doctor!" He sat to leeward, propped by the water-cask and yelled back abundantly, but the seas were breaking in thunder just then, and we only caught snatches that sounded like: "Providence" and "born again." He was at his old game of preaching. We made friendly but derisive gestures at him, and from below he lifted one arm, holding on with the other, moved his lips; he beamed up to us, straining his voice—earnest, and ducking his head before the sprays.

Suddenly some one cried:—"Where's Jimmy?" and we were appalled once more. On the end of the row the boatswain shouted hoarsely:—"Has any one seed him come out?" Voices exclaimed dismally:—"Drowned—is he? . . . No! In his cabin! . . . Good Lord! . . . Caught like a bloomin' rat in a trap. . . . Couldn't open his door . . . Aye! She went over too quick and the water jammed it . . . Poor beggar! . . . No help for 'im . . . Let's go and see. . . ." "Damn him, who could go?" screamed Donkin.—"Nobody expects you to," growled the man next to him: "you're only a thing."—"Is there half a chance to get at 'im?" inquired two or three men together. Belfast untied himself with blind impetuosity, and all at once shot down to leeward quicker than a flash of lightning. We shouted all together with dismay; but with his legs overboard he held and yelled for a rope. In our extremity nothing could be terrible; so we judged him funny kicking there, and with his scared face. Some one began to laugh, and, as if hysterically infected with screaming merriment, all those haggard men went off laughing, wild-eyed, like a lot of maniacs tied up on a wall. Mr. Baker swung off the binnacle-stand and tendered him one leg. He scrambled up rather scared, and consigning us with abominable words to the "divvle." "You are . . . Ough! You're a foul-mouthed beggar, Craik," grunted Mr. Baker. He answered, stuttering with indignation:—"Look at 'em, sorr. The bloomin' dirty images! laughing at a chum going overboard. Call themselves men, too." But from the break of the poop the boatswain called out:—"Come along," and Belfast crawled away in a hurry to join him. The five men, poised and gazing over the edge of the poop, looked for the best way to get forward. They seemed to hesitate. The others, twisting in their lashings, turning painfully, stared with open lips. Captain Allistoun saw nothing; he seemed with his eyes to hold the ship up in a superhuman concentration of effort. The wind screamed loud in sunshine; columns of spray rose straight up; and in the glitter of rainbows bursting over the trembling hull the men went over cautiously, disappearing from sight with deliberate movements.

They went swinging from belaying pin to cleat above the seas that beat the half-submerged deck. Their toes scraped the planks. Lumps of green cold water toppled over the bulwark and on their heads. They hung for a moment on strained arms, with the breath knocked out of them, and with closed eyes— then, letting go with one hand, balanced with lolling heads, trying to grab some rope or stanchion further forward. The long-armed and athletic boatswain swung quickly, gripping things with a fist hard as iron, and remembering suddenly snatches of the last letter from his "old woman." Little Belfast scrambled in a rage spluttering "cursed nigger." Wamibo's tongue hung out with excitement; and Archie, intrepid and calm, watched his chance to move with intelligent coolness.

When above the side of the house, they let go one after another, and falling heavily, sprawled, pressing their palms to the smooth teak wood. Round them the backwash of waves seethed white and hissing. All the doors had become trap-doors, of course. The first was the galley door. The galley extended from side to side, and they could hear the sea splashing with hollow noises in there. The next door was that of the carpenter's shop. They lifted it, and looked down. The room seemed to have been devastated by an earthquake. Everything in it had tumbled on the bulkhead facing the door, and on the other side of that bulkhead there was Jimmy dead or alive. The bench, a half-finished meat-safe, saws, chisels, wire rods, axes, crowbars, lay in a heap besprinkled with loose nails. A sharp adze stuck up with a shining edge that gleamed dangerously down there like a wicked smile. The men clung to one another, peering. A sickening, sly lurch of the ship nearly sent them overboard in a body. Belfast howled "Here goes!" and leaped down. Archie followed cannily, catching at shelves that gave way with him, and eased himself in a great crash of ripped wood. There was hardly room for three men to move. And in the sunshiny blue square of the door, the boatswain's face, bearded and dark, Wamibo's face, wild and pale, hung over—watching.

Together they shouted: "Jimmy! Jim!" From above the boatswain contributed a deep growl: "You . . . Wait!" In a pause, Belfast entreated: "Jimmy, darlin' are ye aloive?" The boatswain said: "Again! All together, boys!" All yelled excitedly. Wamibo made noises resembling loud barks. Belfast drummed on the side of the bulkhead with a piece of iron. All ceased suddenly. The sound of screaming and hammering went on thin and distinct— like a solo after a chorus. He was alive. He was screaming and knocking below us with the hurry of a man prematurely shut up in a coffin. We went to work. We attacked with desperation the abominable heap of things heavy, of things sharp, of things clumsy to handle. The boatswain crawled away to find somewhere a flying end of a rope; and Wamibo, held back by shouts:—"Don't jump! . . . Don't come in here, muddlehead!"—remained glaring above us— all shining eyes, gleaming fangs, tumbled hair; resembling an amazed and half-witted fiend gloating over the extraordinary agitation of the damned. The boatswain adjured us to "bear a hand," and a rope descended. We made things fast to it and they went up spinning, never to be seen by man again. A rage to fling things overboard possessed us. We worked fiercely, cutting our hands and speaking brutally to one another. Jimmy kept up a distracting row; he screamed piercingly, without drawing breath, like a tortured woman; he banged with hands and feet. The agony of his fear wrung our hearts so terribly that we longed to abandon him, to get out of that place deep as a well and swaying like a tree, to get out of his hearing, back on the poop where we could wait passively for death in incomparable repose. We shouted to him to "shut up, for God's sake." He redoubled his cries. He must have fancied we could not hear him. Probably he heard his own clamour but faintly. We could picture him crouching on the edge of the upper berth, letting out with both fists at the wood, in the dark, and with his mouth wide open for that unceasing cry. Those were loathsome moments. A cloud driving across the sun would darken the doorway menacingly. Every movement of the ship was pain. We scrambled about with no room to breathe, and felt frightfully sick. The boatswain yelled down at us:—"Bear a hand! Bear a hand! We two will be washed away from here directly if you ain't quick!" Three times a sea leaped over the high side and flung bucketfuls of water on our heads. Then Jimmy, startled by the shock, would stop his noise for a moment—waiting for the ship to sink, perhaps—and began again, distressingly loud, as if invigorated by the gust of fear. At the bottom the nails lay in a layer several inches thick. It was ghastly. Every nail in the world, not driven in firmly somewhere, seemed to have found its way into that carpenter's shop. There they were, of all kinds, the remnants of stores from seven voyages. Tin-tacks, copper tacks (sharp as needles); pump nails with big heads, like tiny iron mushrooms; nails without any heads (horrible); French nails polished and slim. They lay in a solid mass more inabordable than a hedgehog. We hesitated, yearning for a shovel, while Jimmy below us yelled as though he had been flayed. Groaning, we dug our fingers in, and very much hurt, shook our hands, scattering nails and drops of blood. We passed up our hats full of assorted nails to the boatswain, who, as if performing a mysterious and appeasing rite, cast them wide upon a raging sea.

We got to the bulkhead at last. Those were stout planks. She was a ship, well finished in every detail—the *Narcissus* was. They were the stoutest planks ever put into a ship's bulkhead—we thought—and then we perceived that, in our hurry, we had sent all the tools overboard. Absurd little Belfast wanted to break it down with his own weight, and with both feet leaped straight up like a springbok, cursing the Clyde shipwrights for not scamping their work. Incidentally he reviled all North Britain, the rest of the earth, the sea—and all his companions. He swore, as he alighted heavily on his heels, that he would never, never any more associate with any fool that "hadn't savee enough to know his knee from his elbow." He managed by his thumping to scare the last remnant of wits out of Jimmy. We could hear the object of our exasperated solicitude darting to and fro under the planks. He had cracked his voice at last, and could only squeak miserably. His back or else his head rubbed the planks, now here, now there, in a puzzling manner. He squeaked as he dodged the invisible blows. It was more heartrending even than his yells. Suddenly Archie produced a crowbar. He had kept it back; also a small hatchet. We howled with satisfaction. He struck a mighty blow and small chips flew at our eyes. The boatswain above shouted:—"Look out! Look out there. Don't kill the man. Easy does it!" Wamibo, maddened with excitement, hung head down and insanely urged us:—"Hoo! Strook'im! Hoo! Hoo!" We were afraid he would fall in and kill one of us and, hurriedly, we entreated the boatswain to "shove the blamed Finn overboard." Then, all together, we yelled down at the planks:—"Stand from under! Get forward," and listened. We only heard the deep hum and moan of the wind above us, the mingled roar and hiss of the seas. The ship, as if overcome with despair, wallowed lifelessly, and our heads swam with that unnatural motion. Belfast clamoured:—"For the love of God, Jimmy, where are ye? . . . Knock! Jimmy darlint! . . . Knock! You bloody black beast! Knock!" He was as quite as a dead man inside a grave; and, like men standing above a grave, we were on the verge of tears— but with vexation, the strain, the fatigue; with the great longing to be done with it, to get away, and lie down to rest somewhere where we could see our danger and breathe. Archie shouted:—"Gi'e me room!" We crouched behind him, guarding our heads, and he struck time after time in the joint of planks. They cracked. Suddenly the crowbar went halfway in through a splintered oblong hole. It must have missed Jimmy's head by less than an inch. Archie withdrew it quickly, and that infamous nigger rushed at the hole, put his lips to it, and whispered "Help" in an almost extinct voice; he pressed his head to it, trying madly to get out through that opening one inch wide and three inches long. In our disturbed state we were absolutely paralysed by his incredible action. It seemed impossible to drive him away. Even Archie at last lost his composure. "If ye don't clear oot I'll drive the crowbar thro' your head," he shouted in a determined voice. He meant what he said, and his earnestness seemed to make an impression on Jimmy. He disappeared suddenly, and we set to prising and tearing at the planks with the eagerness of men trying to get at a mortal enemy, and spurred by the desire to tear him limb from limb. The wood split, cracked, gave way. Belfast plunged in head and shoulders and groped viciously. "I've got 'im! Got 'im," he shouted. "Oh! There! . . . He's

gone; I've got 'im! . . . Pull at my legs! . . . Pull!" Wamibo hooted unceasingly. The boatswain shouted directions:—"Catch hold of his hair,
Belfast; pull straight up, you two! . . . Pull fair!" We pulled fair. We pulled
Belfast out with a jerk, and dropped him with disgust. In a sitting posture,
purple-faced, he sobbed despairingly:—"How can I hold on to 'is blooming
short wool?" Suddenly Jimmy's head and shoulders appeared. He stuck half-
way, and with rolling eyes foamed at our feet. We flew at him with brutal
impatience, we tore the shirt off his back, we tugged at his ears, we panted
over him; and all at once he came away in our hands as though somebody had
let go his legs. With the same movement, without a pause, we swung him up.
His breath whistled, he kicked our upturned faces, he grasped two pairs of
arms above his head, and he squirmed up with such precipitation that he
seemed positively to escape from our hands like a bladder full of gas. Streaming with perspiration, we swarmed up the rope, and, coming into the blast of
cold wind, gasped like men plunged into icy water. With burning faces we
shivered to the very marrow of our bones. Never before had the gale seemed to
us more furious, the sea more mad, the sunshine more merciless and mock-
ing, and the position of the ship more hopeless and appalling. Every movement of her was ominous of the end of her agony and of the beginning of ours.
We staggered away from the door, and, alarmed by a sudden roll, fell down in
a bunch. It appeared to us that the side of the house was more smooth than
glass and more slippery than ice. There was nothing to hang on to but a long
brass hook used sometimes to keep back an open door. Wamibo held on to it
and we held on to Wamibo, clutching our Jimmy. He had completely collapsed now. He did not seem to have the strength to close his hand. We stuck
to him blindly in our fear. We were not afraid of Wamibo letting go (we
remembered that the brute was stronger than any three men in the ship), but
we were afraid of the hook giving way, and we also believed that the ship had
made up her mind to turn over at last. But she didn't. A sea swept over us. The
boatswain spluttered:—"Up and away. There's a lull. Away aft with you, or
we will all go to the devil here." We stood up surrounding Jimmy. We begged
him to hold up, to hold on, at least. He glared with his bulging eyes, mute as a
fish, and with all the stiffening knocked out of him. He wouldn't stand; he
wouldn't even as much as clutch at our necks; he was only a cold black skin
loosely stuffed with soft cotton wool; his arms and legs swung jointless and
pliable; his head rolled about; the lower lip hung down, enormous and heavy.
We pressed round him, bothered and dismayed; sheltering him we swung here
and there in a body; and on the very brink of eternity we tottered all together
with concealing and absurd gestures, like a lot of drunken men embarrassed
with a stolen corpse.

Something had to be done. We had to get him aft. A rope was tied slack
under his armpits, and, reaching up at the risk of our lives, we hung him on
the foresheet cleet. He emitted no sound; he looked as ridiculously lamentable
as a doll that had lost half it sawdust, and we started on our perilous journey
over the main deck, dragging along with care that pitiful, that limp, that

hateful burden. He was not very heavy, but had he weighed a ton he could not have been more awkward to handle. We literally passed him from hand to hand. Now and then we had to hang him up on a handy belaying-pin, to draw a breath and reform the line. Had the pin broken he would have irretrievably gone into the Southern Ocean, but he had to take his chance of that; and after a little while, becoming apparently aware of it, he groaned slightly, and with a great effort whispered a few words. We listened eagerly. He was reproaching us with our carelessness in letting him run such risks: "Now, after I got myself out from there," he breathed out weakly. "There" was his cabin. And he got himself out. We had nothing to do with it apparently! . . . No matter . . . We went on and let him take his chances, simply because we could not help it; for though at that time we hated him more than ever—more than anything under heaven—we did not want to lose him. We had so far saved him; and it had become a personal matter between us and the sea. We meant to stick to him. Had we (by an incredible hypothesis) undergone similar toil and trouble for an empty cask, that cask would have become as precious to us as Jimmy was. More precious, in fact, because we would have had no reason to hate the cask. And we hated James Wait. We could not get rid of the monstrous suspicion that this astounding black-man was shamming sick, had been malingering heartlessly in the face of our toil, of our scorn, of our patience—and now was malingering in the face of our devotion—in the face of death. Our vague and imperfect morality rose with disgust at his unmanly lie. But he stuck to it manfully—amazingly. No! It couldn't be. He was at all extremity. His cantankerous temper was only the result of the provoking invincibleness of that death he felt by his side. Any man may be angry with such a masterful chum. But, then, what kind of men were we—with our thoughts! Indignation and doubt grappled within us in a scuffle that trampled upon the finest of our feelings. And we hated him because of the suspicion; we detested him because of the doubt. We could not scorn him safely—neither could we pity him without risk to our dignity. So we hated him, and passed him carefully from hand to hand. We cried, "Got him?"—"Yes. All right. Let go." And he swung from one enemy to another, showing about as much life as an old bolster would do. His eyes made two narrow white slits in the black face. The air escaped through his lips with a noise like the sound of bellows. We reached the poop ladder at last, and it being a comparatively safe place, we lay for a moment in an exhausted heap to rest a little. He began to mutter. We were always incurably anxious to hear what he had to say. This time he mumbled peevishly, "It took you some time to come. I began to think the whole smart lot of you had been washed overboard. What kept you back? Hey? Funk?" We said nothing. With sighs we started again to drag him up. The secret and ardent desire of our hearts was the desire to beat him viciously with our fists about the head; and we handled him as tenderly as though he had been made of glass. . . .

The return on the poop was like the return of wanderers after many years amongst people marked by the desolation of time. Eyes were turned slowly in their sockets, glancing at us. Faint murmurs were heard, "Have you got 'im after all?" The well-known faces looked strange and familiar; they seemed faded and grimy; they had a mingled expression of fatigue and eagerness. They seemed to have become much thinner during our absence, as if all these men had been starving for a long time in their abandoned attitudes. The captain, with a round turn of a rope on his wrist, and kneeling on one knee, swung with a face cold and stiff; but with living eyes he was still holding the ship up, heeding no one, as if lost in the unearthly effort of that endeavour. We fastened up James Wait in a safe place. Mr. Baker scrambled along to lend a hand. Mr. Creighton, on his back, and very pale, muttered, "Well done," and gave us, Jimmy and the sky, a scornful glance, then closed his eyes slowly. Here and there a man stirred a little, but most of them remained apathetic, in cramped positions, muttering between shivers. The sun was setting. A sun enormous, unclouded and red, declining low as if bending down to look into their faces. The wind whistled across long sunbeams that, resplendent and cold, struck full on the dilated pupils of staring eyes without making them wink. The wisps of hair and the tangled beards were grey with the salt of the sea. The faces were earthy, and the dark patches under the eyes extended to the ears, smudged into the hollows of sunken cheeks. The lips were livid and thin, and when they moved it was with difficulty, as though they had been glued to the teeth. Some grinned sadly in the sunlight, shaking with cold. Others were sad and still. Charley, subdued by the sudden disclosure of the insignificance of his youth, darted fearful glances. The two smooth-faced Norwegians resembled decrepit children, staring stupidly. To leeward, on the edge of the horizon, black seas leaped up towards the glowing sun. It sank slowly, round and blazing, and the crests of waves splashed on the edge of the luminous circle. One of the Norwegians appeared to catch sight of it, and, after giving a violent start, began to speak. His voice, startling the others, made them stir. They moved their heads stiffly, or turning with difficulty, looked at him with surprise, with fear, or in grave silence. He chattered at the setting sun, nodding his head, while the big seas began to roll across the crimson disc; and over miles of turbulent waters the shadows of high waves swept with a running darkness the faces of men. A crested roller broke with a loud hissing roar, and the sun, as if put out, disappeared. The chattering voice faltered, went out together with the light. There were sighs. In the sudden lull that follows the crash of a broken sea a man said wearily, "Here's that blooming Dutchman gone off his chump." A seaman, lashed by the middle, tapped the deck with his open hand with unceasing quick flaps. In the gathering greyness of twilight a bulky form was seen rising aft, and began marching on all fours with the movements of some big cautious beast. It was Mr. Baker passing along the line of men. He grunted encouragingly over every one, felt their fastenings. Some, with half-open eyes, puffed like men oppressed by heat; others mechanically and in dreamy voices answered him, "Aye! aye! sir!" He went from one to another grunting, "Ough! . . . See her through it yet;" and unexpectedly, with loud angry outbursts, blew up Knowles for cutting off a long piece from the fall of the relieving tackle. "Ough!—Ashamed of yourself—Relieving tackle—Don't you know better!—Ough!—Able seaman! Ough!" The lame man was crushed. He muttered, "Get som'think for a lashing for myself, sir."—"Ough! Lashing—yourself. Are you a tinker or a sailor—What? Ough!—May want that tackle directly—Ough!—More use to the ship than your lame carcass. Ough!—Keep it!—Keep it, now you've done it." He crawled away slowly, muttering to himself about some men being "worse than children." It had been a comforting row. Low exclamations were heard: "Hallo . . . Hallo." . . . Those who had been painfully dozing asked with convulsive starts, "What's up? . . . What is it?" The answers came with unexpected cheerfulness: "The mate is going bald-headed for lame Jack about something or other." "No!" . . . "What 'as he done?" Some one even chuckled. It was like a whiff of hope, like a reminder of safe days. Donkin, who had been stupefied with fear, revived suddenly and began to shout:— " 'Ear 'im; that's the way they tawlk to us. Vy donch 'ee 'it 'im—one ov yer? 'It 'im. 'It 'im! Comin' the mate over us. We are as good men as 'ee! We're all goin' to 'ell now. We 'ave been starved in this rotten ship, an' now we're goin' to be drowned for them black 'earted bullies! 'It 'im!" He shrieked in the deepening gloom, he blubbered and sobbed, screaming:—" 'It 'im! 'It 'im!" The rage and fear of his disregarded right to live tried the steadfastness of hearts more than the menacing shadows of the night that advanced through the unceasing clamour of the gale. From aft Mr. Baker was heard:—"Is one of you men going to stop him—must I come along?" "Shut up!" . . . "Keep quiet!" cried various voices, exasperated, trembling with cold.—"You'll get one across the mug from me directly," said an invisible seaman, in a weary tone, "I won't let the mate have the trouble." He ceased and lay still with the silence of despair. On the black sky the stars, coming out, gleamed over an inky sea that, speckled with foam, flashed back at them the evanescent and pale light of a dazzling whiteness born from the black turmoil of the waves. Remote in the eternal calm they glittered hard and cold above the uproar of the earth; they surrounded the vanquished and tormented ship on all sides: more pitiless than the eyes of a triumphant mob, and as unapproachable as the hearts of men.

The icy south wind howled exultingly under the sombre splendour of the sky. The cold shook the men with a resistless violence as though it had tried to shake them to pieces. Short moans were swept unheard off the stiff lips. Some complained in mutters of "not feeling themselves below the waist;" while those who had closed their eyes, imagined they had a block of ice on their chests. Others, alarmed at not feeling any pain in their fingers, beat the deck feebly with their hands—obstinate and exhausted. Wamibo stared vacant and dreamy. The Scandinavians kept on a meaningless mutter through chattering teeth. The spare Scotchmen, with determined efforts, kept their lower jaws still. The West-country men lay big and stolid in an invulnerable surliness. A man yawned and swore in turns. Another breathed with a rattle in his throat. Two elderly hard-weather shellbacks, fast side by side, whispered dismally to one another about the landlady of a boarding-house in Sunderland, whom they both knew. They extolled her motherliness and her liberality; they tried to talk about the joint of beef and the big fire in the downstairs kitchen. The words dying faintly on their lips, ended in light sighs. A sudden voice cried into the cold night, "O Lord!" No one changed his position or took any notice of the cry. One or two passed, with a repeated and vague gesture, their hand over their faces, but most of them kept very still. In the benumbed immobility of their bodies they were excessively wearied by their thoughts, which rushed with the rapidity and vividness of dreams. Now and then, by an abrupt and startling exclamation, they answered the weird hail of some illusion; then, again, in silence contemplated the vision of known faces and familiar things. They recalled the aspect of forgotten shipmates and heard the voice of dead and gone skippers. They remembered the noise of gaslit streets, the steamy heat of tap-rooms or the scorching sunshine of calm days at sea.

Mr. Baker left his insecure place, and crawled, with stoppages, along the poop. In the dark and on all fours he resembled some carnivorous animal prowling amongst corpses. At the break, propped to windward of a stanchion, he looked down on the main deck. It seemed to him that the ship had a tendency to stand up a little more. The wind had eased a little, he thought, but the sea ran as high as ever. The waves foamed viciously, and the lee side of the deck disappeared under a hissing whiteness as of boiling milk, while the rigging sang steadily with a deep vibrating note, and, at every upward swing of the ship, the wind rushed with a long-drawn clamour amongst the spars. Mr. Baker watched very still. A man near him began to make a blabbing noise with his lips, all at once and very loud, as though the cold had broken brutally through him. He went on:—"Ba—ba—ba—brrr—brr—ba—ba."—"Stop that!" cried Mr. Baker, groping in the dark. "Stop it!" He went on shaking the leg he found under his hand.—"What is it, sir?" called out Belfast, in the tone of a man awakened suddenly; "we are looking after that 'ere Jimmy."—"Are you? Ough! Don't make that row then. Who's that near you?"—"It's me—the boatswain, sir," growled the West-country man; "we are trying to keep life in that poor devil."—"Aye, aye!" said Mr. Baker. "Do it quietly, can't you?"—"He wants us to hold him up above the rail," went on the boatswain, with irritation, "says he can't breathe here under our jackets."—"If we lift 'im we drop 'im overboard," said another voice, "we can't feel our hands with cold."—"I don't care. I am choking!" exclaimed James Wait in a clear tone.—"Oh, no, my son," said the boatswain, desperately, "you don't go till we all go on this fine night."—"You will see yet many a worse," said Mr. Baker, cheerfully.—"It's no child's play, sir!" answered the boatswain. "Some of us further aft, here, are in a pretty bad way."—"If the blamed sticks had been cut out of her she would be running along on her bottom now like any decent ship, an' giv' us all a chance," said some one, with a sigh.—"The old man wouldn't have it . . . much he cares for us," whispered another.—"Care for you!" exclaimed Mr. Baker, angrily. "Why should he care for you? Are you a lot of women passengers to be taken care of? We are here to take care of the ship—and some of you ain't up to that. Ough! . . . What have you done so very smart to be taken care of? Ough! . . . Some of you can't stand a bit of a breeze without crying over it."—"Come, sorr. We ain't so bad," protested Belfast, in a voice shaken by shivers; "we ain't . . . brr . . ."— "Again," shouted the mate, grabbing at the shadowy form; "again! . . . Why, you're in your shirt! What have you done?"—"I've put my oilskin and jacket over that half-dead nayggur—and he says he chokes," said Belfast, complainingly.—"You wouldn't call me nigger if I wasn't half dead, you Irish beggar!" boomed James Wait, vigorously.—"You . . . brr . . . You wouldn't be white if you were ever so well . . . I will fight you . . . brrr . . . in fine weather . . . brrr . . . with one hand tied behind my back . . . brrrrrr . . ."—"I don't want your rags—I want air," gasped out the other faintly, as if suddenly exhausted.

The sprays swept over whistling and pattering. Men disturbed in their peaceful torpor by the pain of quarrelsome shouts, moaned, muttering curses. Mr. Baker crawled off a little way to leeward where a watercask loomed up big, with something white against it. "Is it you, Podmore?" asked Mr. Baker. He had to repeat the question twice before the cook turned, coughing feebly.—"Yes, sir. I've been praying in my mind for a quick deliverance; for I am prepared for any call. . . . I—"—"Look here, Cook," interrupted Mr. Baker, "the men are perishing with cold."—"Cold!" said the cook, mournfully; "they will be warm enough before long."—"What?" asked Mr. Baker, looking along the deck into the faint sheen of frothing water.—"They are a wicked lot," continued the cook solemnly, but in an unsteady voice, "about as wicked as any ship's company in this sinful world! Now, I"—he trembled so that he could hardly speak; his was an exposed place, and in a cotton shirt, a thin pair of trousers, and with his knees under his nose, he received, quaking, the flicks of stinging, salt drops; his voice sounded exhausted—"now, I—any time . . . My eldest youngster, Mr. Baker . . . a clever boy . . . last Sunday on shore before this voyage he wouldn't go to church, sir. Says I, 'You go and clean yourself, or I'll know the reason why!' What does he do? . . . Pond, Mr. Baker—fell into the pond in his best rig, sir! . . . Accident? . . . 'Nothing will save you, fine scholar though you are!' says I . . . Accident! . . . I whopped him, sir, till I couldn't lift my arm. . . ." His voice faltered. "I whopped 'im!" he repeated, rattling his teeth; then, after a while, let out a mournful sound that was half a groan, half a snore. Mr. Baker shook him by the shoulders. "Hey! Cook! Hold up, Podmore! Tell me—is there any fresh water in the galley tank? The ship is lying along less, I think; I would try to get forward. A little water would do them good. Hallo! Look out! Look out!" The cook struggled.—"Not you, sir—not you!" He began to scramble to windward. "Galley! . . . my business!" he shouted.—"Cook's going crazy now," said several voices. He yelled:—"Crazy, am I? I am more ready to die than any of you, officers incloosive—there! As long as she swims I will cook! I will get you coffee."—"Cook, ye are a gentleman!" cried Belfast. But the cook was already going over the weather-ladder. He stopped for a moment to shout back on the poop:—"As long as she swims I will cook!" and disappeared as though he had gone overboard. The men who had heard sent after him a cheer that sounded like a wail of sick children. An hour or more afterwards some one said distinctly: "He's gone for good."—"Very likely," assented the boatswain; "even in fine weather he was as smart about the deck as a milch-cow on her first voyage. We ought to go and see." Nobody moved. As the hours dragged slowly through the darkness Mr. Baker crawled back and forth along the poop several times. Some men fancied they had heard him exchange murmurs with the master, but at that time the memories were incomparably more vivid than anything actual, and they were not certain whether the murmurs were heard now or many years ago. They did not try to find out. A mutter more or less did not matter. It was too cold for curiosity, and almost for hope. They could not spare a moment or a thought from the great mental occupation of wishing to live. And the desire of life kept them alive, apathetic and enduring, under the cruel persistence of wind and cold; while the bestarred black dome of the sky revolved slowly above the ship, that drifted, bearing their patience and their suffering, through the stormy solitude of the sea.

Huddled close to one another, they fancied themselves utterly alone. They heard sustained loud noises, and again bore the pain of existence through long hours of profound silence. In the night they saw sunshine, felt warmth, and suddenly, with a start, thought that the sun would never rise upon a freezing world. Some heard laughter, listened to songs; others, near the end of the poop, could hear loud human shrieks, and opening their eyes, were surprised to hear them still, though very faint, and far away. The boatswain said:— "Why, it's the cook, hailing from forward, I think." He hardly believed his own words or recognised his own voice. It was a long time before the man next to him gave a sign of life. He punched hard his other neighbour and said:— "The cook's shouting!" Many did not understand, others did not care; the majority further aft did not believe. But the boatswain and another man had the pluck to crawl away forward to see. They seemed to have been gone for hours, and were very soon forgotten. Then suddenly men who had been plunged in a hopeless resignation became as if possessed with a desire to hurt. They belaboured one another with fists. In the darkness they struck persistently anything soft they could feel near, and, with a greater effort than for a shout, whispered excitedly:—"They've got some hot coffee. . . . Boss'en got it. . . ." "No! . . . Where?" . . . "It's coming! Cook made it." James Wait moaned. Donkin scrambled viciously, caring not where he kicked, and anxious that the officers should have none of it. It came in a pot, and they drank in turns. It was hot, and while it blistered the greedy palates, it seemed incredible. The men sighed out parting with the mug:—"How 'as he done it?" Some cried weakly:—"Bully for you, Doctor!"

He had done it somehow. Afterwards Archie declared that the thing was "meeraculous." For many days we wondered, and it was the one ever-interesting subject of conversation to the end of the voyage. We asked the cook, in fine weather, how he felt when he saw his stove "reared up on end." We inquired, in the north-east trade and on serene evenings, whether he had to stand on his head to put things right somewhat. We suggested he had used his bread-board for a raft, and from there comfortably had stoked his grate; and we did our best to conceal our admiration under the wit of fine irony. He affirmed not to know anything about it, rebuked our levity, declared himself, with solemn animation, to have been thè object of a special mercy for the saving of our unholy lives. Fundamentally he was right, no doubt; but he need not have been so offensively positive about it—he need not have hinted so often that it would have gone hard with us had he not been there, meritorious and pure, to receive the inspiration and the strength for the work of grace. Had we been saved by his recklessness or his agility, we could have at length become recon-ciled to the fact; but to admit our obligation to anybody's virtue and holiness alone was as difficult for us as for any other handful of mankind. Like many benefactors of humanity, the cook took himself too seriously, and reaped the reward of irreverence. We were not ungrateful, however. He remained heroic. His saying—*the* saying of his life—became proverbial in the mouth of men as are the sayings of conquerors or sages. Later, whenever one of us was puzzled by a task and advised to relinquish it, he would express his determ-ination to persevere and to succeed by the words:—"As long as she swims I will cook!"

The hot drink helped us through the bleak hours that precede the dawn. The sky low by the horizon took on the delicate tints of pink and yellow like the inside of a rare shell. And higher, where it glowed with a pearly sheen, a small black cloud appeared, like a forgotten fragment of the night set in a border of dazzling gold. The beams of light skipped on the crests of waves. The eyes of men turned to the east-ward. The sunlight flooded their weary faces. They were giving themselves up to fatigue as though they had done for ever with their work. On Singleton's black oilskin coat the dried salt glistened like hoar frost. He hung on by the wheel, with open and lifeless eyes. Captain Allis-toun, unblinking, faced the rising sun. His lips stirred, opened for the first time in twenty-four hours, and with a fresh firm voice he cried, "Wear ship!"

The commanding sharp tones made all these torpid men start like a sudden flick of a whip. Then again, motionless where they lay, the force of habit made some of them repeat the order in hardly audible murmurs. Captain Allistoun glanced down at his crew, and several, with fumbling fingers and hopeless movements, tried to cast themselves adrift. He repeated impatiently, "Wear ship. Now then, Mr. Baker, get the men along. What's the matter with them?"—"Wear ship. Do you hear there?—Wear ship!" thundered out the boatswain suddenly. His voice seemed to break through a deadly spell. Men began to stir and crawl.—"I want the fore-top-mast stay-sail run up smartly," said the master, very loudly; "if you can't manage it standing up you must do it lying down—that's all. Bear a hand!"—"Come along! Let's give the old girl a chance," urged the boatswain.—"Aye! aye! Wear ship!" exclaimed quavering voices. The forecastle men, with reluctant faces, prepared to go forward. Mr. Baker pushed ahead, grunting, on all fours to show the way, and they followed him over the break. The others lay still with a vile hope in their hearts of not being required to move till they got saved or drowned in peace.

After some time they could be seen forward appearing on the forecastle head, one by one in unsafe attitudes; hanging on to the rails, clambering over the anchors; embracing the cross-head of the windlass or hugging the fore-capstan. They were restless with strange exertions, waved their arms, knelt, lay flat down, staggered up, seemed to strive their hardest to go overboard. Suddenly a small white piece of canvas fluttered amongst them, grew larger, beating. Its narrow head rose in jerks—and at last it stood distended and triangular in the sunshine.—"They have done it!" cried the voices aft. Captain Allistoun let go the rope he had round his wrist and rolled to leeward headlong. He could be seen casting the lee main braces off the pins while the backwash of waves splashed over him.—"Square the main yard!" he shouted up to us—who stared at him in wonder. We hesitated to stir. "The main brace, men. Haul! Haul anyhow! Lay on your backs and haul!" he screeched, half drowned down there. We did not believe we could move the main yard, but the strongest and the less discouraged tried to execute the order. Others assisted half-heartedly. Singleton's eyes blazed suddenly as he took a fresh grip of the spokes. Captain Allistoun fought his way up to windward.—"Haul, men! Try to move it! Haul, and help the ship." His hard face worked suffused and furious. "Is she going off, Singleton?" he cried.—"Not a move yet, sir," croaked the old seaman in a horribly hoarse voice.—"Watch the helm, Singleton," spluttered the master. "Haul, men! Have you no more strength than rats? Haul, and earn your salt." Mr. Creighton, on his back, with a swollen leg and a face as white as a piece of paper, blinked his eyes; his bluish lips twitched. In the wild scramble men grabbed at him, crawled over his hurt leg, knelt on his chest. He kept perfectly still, setting his teeth without a moan, without a sigh. The master's ardour, the cries of that silent man inspired us. We hauled and hung in bunches on the rope. We heard him say with violence to Donkin, who sprawled abjectly on his stomach,—"I will brain you with this belaying pin if you don't catch hold of the brace," and that victim of men's injustice, cowardly and cheeky, whimpered:—"Are you goin' to murder us now?" while with sudden desperation he gripped the rope. Men sighed, shouted, hissed meaningless words, groaned. The yards moved, came slowly square against the wind, that hummed loudly on the yard-arms.—"Going off, sir," shouted Singleton, "she's just started."—"Catch a turn with that brace. Catch a turn!" clamoured the master. Mr. Creighton, nearly suffocated and unable to move, made a mighty effort, and with his left hand managed to nip the rope.—"All fast!" cried some one. He closed his eyes as if going off into a swoon, while huddled together about the brace we watched with scared looks what the ship would do now.

She went off slowly as though she had been weary and disheartened like the men she carried. She paid off very gradually, making us hold our breath till we choked, and as soon as she had brought the wind abaft the beam she started to move, and fluttered our hearts. It was awful to see her, nearly overturned, begin to gather way and drag her submerged side through the water. The dead-eyes of the rigging churned the breaking seas. The lower half of the deck was full of mad whirlpools and eddies; and the long line of the lee rail could be seen showing black now and then in the swirls of a field of foam as dazzling and white as a field of snow. The wind sang shrilly amongst the spars; and at every slight lurch we expected her to slip to the bottom sideways from under our backs. When dead before it she made the first distinct attempt to stand up, and we encouraged her with a feeble and discordant howl. A great sea came running up aft and hung for a moment over us with a curling top; then crashed down under the counter and spread out on both sides into a great sheet of bursting froth. Above its fierce hiss we heard Singleton's croak:—"She is steering!" He had both his feet now planted firmly on the grating, and the wheel spun fast as he eased the helm.—"Bring the wind on the port quarter and steady her!" called out the master, staggering to his feet, the first man up from amongst our prostrate heap. One or two screamed with excitement:— "She rises!" Far away forward, Mr. Baker and three others were seen erect and black on the clear sky, lifting their arms, and with open mouths as though they had been shouting all together. The ship trembled, trying to lift her side, lurched back, seemed to give up with a nerveless dip, and suddenly with an unexpected jerk swung violently to windward, as though she had torn herself out from a deadly grasp. The whole immense volume of water, lifted by her deck, was thrown bodily across to starboard. Loud cracks were heard. Iron ports breaking open thundered with ringing blows. The water topped over the starboard rail with the rush of a river falling over a dam. The sea on deck, and the seas on every side of her, mingled together in a deafening roar. She rolled violently. We got up and were helplessly run or flung about from side to side. Men, rolling over and over, yelled,—"The house will go!"—"She clears herself!" Lifted by a towering sea she ran along with it for a moment, spouting thick streams of water through every opening of her wounded sides. The lee braces having been carried away or washed off the pins, all the ponderous yards on the fore swung from side to side and with appalling rapidity at every roll. The men forward were seen crouching here and there with fearful glances upwards at the enormous spars that whirled about over their heads. The torn canvas and the ends of broken gear streamed in the wind like wisps of hair. Through the clear sunshine, over the flashing turmoil and uproar of the seas, the ship ran blindly, dishevelled and headlong, as if fleeing for her life; and on the poop we spun, we tottered about, distracted and noisy. We all spoke at once in a thin babble; we had the aspect of invalids and the gestures of mani-acs. Eyes shone, large and haggard, in smiling, meagre faces that seemed to have been dusted over with powdered chalk. We stamped, clapped our hands, feeling ready to jump and do anything; but in reality hardly able to keep on our feet. Captain Allistoun, hard and slim, gesticulated madly from the poop at Mr. Baker: "Steady these fore-yards! Steady them the best you can!" On the main deck, men excited by his cries, splashed, dashing aimlessly here and there with the foam swirling up to their waists. Apart, far aft, and alone by the helm, old Singleton had deliberately tucked his white beard under the top button of his glistening coat. Swaying upon the din and tumult of the seas, with the whole battered length of the ship launched forward in a rolling rush before his steady old eyes, he stood rigidly still, forgotten by all, and with an attentive face. In front of his erect figure only the two arms moved crosswise with a swift and sudden readiness, to check or urge again the rapid stir of circling spokes. He steered with care.

Sea Survivors

Loss of the *Centaur* Man-of-War,

which foundered in the Atlantic Ocean,

in September 1782

compiled by CHARLES ELLMS

The greatest naval catastrophe that ever arose from the violence of the elements, occurred to the fleet under the command of Admiral Graves, in August 1782. All the trophies of Lord Rodney's victory, except the *Ardent*, perished in the storm; two British ships of the line foundered; an incredible number of merchantmen under convoy were lost; and the number of lives that perished, exceeded three thousand. Among the vessels which suffered most in the dreadful storm, was the *Centaur* man-of-war, commanded by Captain Inglefield.

The *Centaur* left Jamaica rather in a leaky condition, keeping two hand-pumps going, and, when it blew fresh, sometimes a spell at the chain-pump. But I had no apprehension that she was unable to encounter a common gale of wind.

A storm came on in the evening of the 16th of September, 1782, when the ship was prepared for the worst weather usually occurring in the same latitudes; the mainsail was reefed and set, the top-gallant-masts struck, and, though it did not at that time blow very strong, the mizen-yard was lowered down.

But towards night it blew a gale of wind, and the ship made so much water it was necessary to turn all hands up to the pumps. The leak continuing to increase, I entertained thoughts of trying the ship before the sea, and, happy should I probably have been in doing so, but the impropriety of leaving the convoy except in the last extremity, and the hopes of the weather growing moderate, weighed against the opinion of its being right.

About two in the morning the wind lulled, and we flattered ourselves that the gale was breaking. Soon after there was much thunder and lightning from the south-east, with rain, when strong gusts of wind began to blow, which obliged me to haul up the mainsail, the ship being then under bare poles. Scarce was this done, when a gust, exceeding in violence every thing of the kind I had ever seen, or could conceive, laid the ship on her beam-ends. The water forsook the hold and appeared between decks, so as to fill the men's hammocks to leeward, the ship lay motionless, and, to all appearance, irrecoverably overset. The water fast increasing, forced through the cells of the ports, and scuttled the ports themselves inwards, from the pressure of the ship. Immediate directions were given to cut away the main and mizen-masts, trusting, when the ship righted, to be able to wear her. On cutting one or two lanyards, the mizen-mast went first over, but without producing the smallest effect on the ship, and, on cutting the lanyard of one shroud, the main-mast followed. I had next the mortification to see the foremast and bowsprit also go over. On this the ship immediately righted, with great violence, and the motion was so quick that it was difficult for the men to work the pumps. Three guns broke loose on the main deck, which it took some time to secure. In attempting to do so several men were maimed, and every moveable was destroyed, either by shot thrown loose from the lockers, or the wreck of the deck. The officers, who had left their beds naked in the morning when the ship overset, had not an article of clothes to put on, nor could their friends supply them.

Before the masts had been ten minutes over the side, I was informed that the tiller had broke short in the rudder-head, and, before the chocks could be placed, the rudder itself was gone. Thus we lay, at the mercy of the wind and sea, under accumulated disasters. Yet I had one comfort, in finding that the pumps, if any thing, reduced the water in the hold, and, as the morning of the 17th advanced, the weather became more moderate.

At day-light I saw two line-of-battle ships to leeward, one of which had lost her mainmast, and the other her foremast and bowsprit. It was the general opinion on board, that the latter was the *Canada*, and the former the *Glorieux*. The *Ramillies* was not in sight, and only about fifteen sail of merchantmen.

About seven in the morning, another line-of-battle ship was seen ahead, which I soon distinguished to be the *Ville de Paris*, with all her masts standing. I immediately ordered a signal of distress to be made, by hoisting the ensign on the stump of the mizen-mast union downwards, and firing one of the forecastle guns. But the ensign, which was the only one we had remaining, blew away soon after being hoisted; however, I had the satisfaction of seeing the *Ville de Paris* wear and stand towards us. Several of the merchant ships also approached, and those that could, hailed us, and offered their assistance. Depending on the king's ship, I only thanked them, desiring, if they joined Admiral Graves, to acquaint him with our condition. I had not the smallest doubt of the *Ville de Paris* coming to us, as she appeared not to have suffered in the least by the storm, and, having seen her wear, we knew that she was under government of her helm. At this time also the weather was so moderate that the merchantmen set their topsails. But the *Ville de Paris* approaching within two miles to windward, passed us, which being observed by one of the merchantmen, she wore, and came under our stern, offering to carry any message to her. I desired the master to acquaint Captain Wilkinson that the *Centaur* had lost her rudder, as well as her masts, that she made a great deal of water, and I requested him to remain with her until the weather became moderate. I afterwards saw this merchantman approach near enough to speak with the *Ville de Paris*, but I fear that the condition of the latter was much worse than it appeared to be, as she continued on the same tack.

Meantime all the quarter-deck guns were thrown overboard, and the whole of those, except six which had overset, of the main-deck. The ship, lying in the trough of the sea, labored prodigiously. I got over one of the small anchors with a boom and several gun-carriages, veered out from the head-door, with a large hawser to keep the ship's bow to the sea. But this, with a top-gallant-sail set on the stump of the mizen-mast, had not the desired effect.

As the evening came on it grew hazy and blew in strong squalls. We lost sight of the *Ville de Paris*, but thought certainly to see her in the morning; and the night was passed in constant labor at the pumps. Sometimes when the wind lulled the water diminished, then blowing strong, and the sea rising, the water increased.

Towards the morning of the 18th I was informed that there was seven feet of water on the keelson; that one of the winches was broke; that the two spare ones would not fit, and that the hand-pumps were choked. These circumstances were sufficiently alarming, but, on opening the after-hold to get up some rum for the people, we found our condition much more so.

At this time the weather was more moderate, and a couple of spars were prepared for shears, to get up a jury-foremast; but as evening came on, the gale increased. We had seen nothing through the day but the ship which had lost her mainmast, and she appeared to be in as great want of assistance as ourselves, having fired guns of distress. Before night, I was told that her foremast was gone.

At day-light of the 19th, there was no vessel in sight, and flashes from guns having been seen in the night, we apprehended that the ship we had seen the preceding day had foundered.

All the officers, passengers, and boys, who were not seamen by profession, had been employed in thrumming a sail which was passed under the ship's bottom, and I thought had some effect. The shears were raised for the foremast, the weather looked promising, and the sea fell; and at night we were able to relieve at the pumps and baling every two hours. By the morning of the 20th, the fore-hold was cleared of water, and we had the comfortable promise of a fine day. It proved so, and I was determined to make use of it with every possible exertion.

As we had no other resource but bailing, I gave orders that scuttles should be cut through the decks, to introduce more buckets into the holds; and all the sail-makers were employed night and day in making canvas buckets. The orlop-deck having fallen in on the larboard side, I ordered the sheet cable to be roused overboard.

The morning of the 22d arrived, without any thing being seen, or any change in the weather; and the day was spent in equal struggles to keep the ship above water, by pumping and bailing at the hatchways and scuttles.

During the night the water increased; but about seven in the morning of the 23d, I was told that an unusual quantity had appeared all at once in the fore-hold, which, on my going forward to be convinced, I found but too true. The stowage of the hold ground tier was all in motion, so that in a short time not a whole cask was to be seen. We were satisfied that the ship had sprung a fresh leak. Another sail had been thrumming all night, and I was giving directions to place it over the bows, when I perceived the ship settling by the head, the lower-deck bow-ports being even with the water.

Every time of visiting the hatchway I observed that the water had increased, and at noon it washed even with the orlop-deck. The carpenter assured me that the ship could not swim long, and proposed making rafts to float the ship's company, whom it was not in my power to encourage any longer with a prospect of safety. Some appeared perfectly resigned, went to their hammocks and desired their messmates to lash them in; others were securing themselves to gratings and small rafts; but the most predominant idea, was that of putting on their best and cleanest clothes.

During the course of these preparations, the ship was gradually sinking, the orlop-deck having been blown up by the water in the hold, and the cables floated to the gun-deck. The men had for some time quitted their occupation of bailing, and the ship was left to her fate.

As evening approached the ship seemed little more than suspended in the water. There was no certainty that she would swim from one minute to another; and the love of life, which I believe was never exhibited later in the approach of death, now began to level all distinctions. It was impossible, indeed, for any man to deceive himself with the hopes of being saved on a raft in such a sea; besides, it was probable that the ship in sinking, would, to a certain surrounding distance, carry every thing down with her in a vortex.

It was near five o'clock, when coming from my cabin, I observed a number of people gazing very anxiously over the side; and looking myself, I saw that several men had forced the pinnace, and that more were attempting to get in. I had thoughts of securing this boat before she might be sunk by numbers; there appeared not a moment for consideration; to remain and perish with the ship's company, to whom I could no longer be of any use, or seize the opportunity, which seemed the only one of escaping, and leave the people with whom, on a variety of occasions I had been so well satisfied, that I thought I could give my life to preserve them. This was indeed a painful conflict, and of which, I believe, no man can form a just idea, who has not been placed in a similar situation.

The love of life prevailed; I called to Mr. Rainy the master, the only officer on deck, desired him to follow me, and immediately descended into the boat at the after part of the chains. But it was not without great difficulty that we got her clear of the ship, twice the number that she could carry pushing in, and many leaping into the water. Mr. Baylis, a young gentleman of fifteen years of age, leaped from the chains after the boat had got off, and was taken in.

It was now near five o'clock in the evening, and in half an hour we lost sight of the ship. Before it was dark, a blanket was discovered in the boat. This was immediately bent to one of the stretchers, and under it as a sail we scudded all night in expectation of being swallowed up by every wave: it being sometimes with great difficulty that we could clear the boat of the water before the return of the next great sea; all of us half drowned, and sitting, except those who baled, at the bottom of the boat, without actually perishing, I am sure no people ever endured more. In the morning the weather grew moderate, the wind having shifted to the southward, as we discovered by the sun. Having survived the night, we began to recollect ourselves, and think of future preservation.

When we quitted the ship the wind was at N. W. or W. N. W. and Fayal had bore E. S. E. 250 or 260 leagues. Had the wind continued for five or six days, there was a probability that, running before the sea, we might have fallen in with some one of the Western Islands. Its change was a death blow to our hopes, for should it begin to blow we knew there would be no preserving life, but by running before the sea, which would carry us again to the northward, where we must soon afterwards perish.

On examining what means we had of subsistence, I found a bag of bread, a small ham, a single piece of pork, two quart bottles of water, and a few French cordials.

The wind continued to the southward for eight or nine days, and providentially never blew so strong but we could keep the side of the boat to the sea; yet we were always most miserably wet and cold. We kept a sort of reckoning, but the sun and stars being sometimes hid from us for twenty-four hours, we had no very good opinion of our navigation. At this period we judged that we had made nearly an E. N. E. course, after the first night's run, which had carried us to the south-east, and expected to see the island of Corvo. We were disappointed, however, in our expectations, and dreaded that the southerly wind had driven us too far to the northward; thus we now prayed for a northerly wind.

Our condition began to be truly miserable, both from hunger and cold, for on the fifth day we had discovered that our bread was nearly all spoiled by salt water, and it was necessary to go to an allowance. One biscuit divided into twelve morsels for breakfast, and the same for dinner; the neck of a bottle broke off, with the cork in it, served for a glass; and this filled with water was the allowance for twenty-four hours to each man. The partition was made without any sort of partiality or distinction, but we must have perished, had we not previously caught six quarts of rain water, and this we should have not been blessed with, had we not found a pair of sheets in the boat, which by accident had been put there. These were spread when it rained, and when thoroughly wet, wrung into the kidd with which we baled the boat. We began to grow very feeble on this short allowance, which was rather tantalizing than sustaining in our comfortless condition, and our clothes being continually wet, our bodies were in many places chafed into sores.

Our sufferings were now as great as human strength could bear; but we were convinced that good spirits were a better support than great bodily strength; for on this day Thomas Mathews, quarter-master, perished from hunger and cold. On the day before he had complained of want of strength in his throat, as he expressed it, to swallow his morsel, and in the night grew delirious, and died without a groan. As it became next to certainty that we should all perish in the same manner in a day or two, it was somewhat comfortable to reflect, that dying of hunger was not so dreadful as our imaginations had represented.

Others had complained of the same symptoms in their throats; some had drank their own urine, and all but myself had drank salt water.

Hitherto despair and gloom had been successfully prohibited, and, as the evening closed in, the men had been encouraged, by turns, to sing a song, or relate a story, instead of a supper; but this evening I found it impossible to raise either. As the night came on it fell calm, and, about midnight, a breeze sprung up from the westward, as we guessed by the swell; but there not being a star to be seen, we were afraid of running out of our way, and waited impatiently for the rising of the sun to be our compass.

As soon as the dawn appeared we found the wind to be exactly as we had wished, at west-south-west, and immediately spread our sail, running before the sea at the rate of four miles an hour.

Our last breakfast had been served with the bread and water remaining, when John Gregory, quarter-master, declared, with much confidence, that he saw land in the south-east. We had seen fog-banks so often bearing the appearance of land, that I did not trust myself to believe it, and cautioned the people, who were extravagantly elated, that they might not feel the effects of disappointment.

At length one of them broke out into a most immoderate swearing fit of joy, which I could not restrain, and declared that had never seen land in his life if what he now saw was not so.

We immediately shaped our course for it, though on my part, with very little faith. The wind freshened; the boat went through the water at the rate of five or six miles an hour; and, in two hours time, the land was plainly seen by every man in the boat, but at a very great distance, so that we did not reach it before ten at night.

On nearing the shore we discovered a fishing canoe, which conducted us into the road of Fayal about midnight. The English consul treated us with the greatest humanity.

Of the company of the *Centaur* were saved, Captain Inglefield; the master Mr. Rainy; Robert Bayles, a midshipman; James Clark, surgeon's mate; the captain's coxswain; two quarter-masters; one of whom died in the boat; and five seamen. There were lost five lieutenants, the captain of marines, purser, surgeon, boatswain, gunner, carpenter, ten mates and midshipmen, and all the rest on board. This calamity happened in 48° 33' north latitude and 43° 20' longitude.

The Incredible Survival

by EDGAR ALLAN POE

It was now about one o'clock in the morning, and the wind was still blowing tremendously. The brig evidently laboured much more than usual, and it became absolutely necessary that something should be done with a view of easing her in some measure. At almost every roll to leeward she shipped a sea, several of which came partially down into the cabin during our scuffle, the hatchway having been left open by myself when I descended. The entire range of bulwarks to larboard had been swept away, as well as the caboose, together with the jollyboat from the counter. The creaking and working of the mainmast, too, gave indication that it was nearly sprung. To make room for more stowage in the after hold, the heel of this mast had been stepped between decks (a very reprehensible practice, occasionally resorted to by ignorant shipbuilders), so that it was in imminent danger of working from its step. But, to crown all our difficulties, we plummed the well, and found no less than seven feet water.

Leaving the bodies of the crew lying in the cabin, we got to work immediately at the pumps—Parker, of course, being set at liberty to assist us in the labour. Augustus's arm was bound up as well as we could effect it, and he did what he could, but that was not much. However, we found that we could just manage to keep the leak from gaining upon us by having one pump constantly going. As there were only four of us, this was severe labour; but we endeavoured to keep up our spirits, and looked anxiously for daybreak, when we hoped to lighten the brig by cutting away the mainmast.

In this manner we passed a night of terrible anxiety and fatigue, and, when the day at length broke, the gale had neither abated in the least, nor were there any signs of its abating. We now dragged the bodies on deck and threw them overboard. Our next care was to get rid of the mainmast. The necessary preparations having been made, Peters cut away at the mast (having found axes in the cabin), while the rest of us stood by the stays and lanyards. As the brig gave a tremendous lee-lurch, the word was given to cut away the weather-lanyards, which being done, the whole mass of wood and rigging plunged into the sea, clear of the brig, and without doing any material injury. We now found that the vessel did not labour quite as much as before, but our situation was still exceedingly precarious, and, in spite of the utmost exertions, we could not gain upon the leak without the aid of both pumps. The little assistance which Augustus could render us was not really of any importance. To add to our distress, a heavy sea, striking the brig to windward, threw her off several points from the wind, and, before she could regain her position, another broke completely over her, and hurled her full upon her beam-ends. The ballast now shifted in a mass to leeward (the stowage had been knocking about perfectly at random for some time), and for a few moments we thought nothing could save us from capsizing. Presently, however, we partially righted; but the ballast still retaining its place to larboard, we lay so much along that it was useless to think of working the pumps, which indeed we could not have done much longer in any case, as our hands were entirely raw with the excessive labour we had undergone, and were bleeding in the most horrible manner.

Contrary to Parker's advice, we now proceeded to cut away the foremast, and at length accomplished it after much difficulty, owing to the position in which we lay. In going overboard the wreck took with it the bowsprit, and left us a complete hulk.

So far we had had reason to rejoice in the escape of our longboat, which had received no damage from any of the huge seas which had come on board. But we had not long to congratulate ourselves; for the foremast having gone, and, of course, the foresail with it, by which the brig had been steadied, every sea now made a complete breach over us, and in five minutes our deck was swept from stem to stern, the longboat and starboard bulwarks torn off, and even the windlass shattered into fragments. It was, indeed, hardly possible for us to be in a more pitiable condition.

At noon there seemed to be some slight appearance of the gale's abating, but in this we were sadly disappointed, for it only lulled for a few minutes to blow with redoubled fury. About four in the afternoon it was utterly impossible to stand up against the violence of the blast; and, as the night closed in upon us, I had not a shadow of hope that the vessel would hold together until morning.

By midnight we had settled very deep in the water, which was now up to the orlop deck. The rudder went soon afterward, the sea which tore it away lifting the after portion of the brig entirely from the water, against which she thumped in her descent with such a concussion as would be occasioned by going ashore. We had all calculated that the rudder would hold its own to the last, as it was unusually strong, being rigged as I have never seen one rigged either before or since. Down its main timber there ran a succession of stout iron hooks, and others in the same manner down the stern-post. Through these hooks there extended a very thick wrought-iron rod, the rudder being thus held to the stern-post, and swinging freely on the rod. The tremendous force of the sea which tore it off may be estimated by the fact, that the hooks in the stern-post, which ran entirely through it, being clinched on the inside, were drawn every one of them completely out of the solid wood.

We had scarcely time to draw breath after the violence of this shock, when one of the most tremendous waves I had then ever known broke right on board of us, sweeping the companion-way clear off, bursting in the hatchways, and filling every inch of the vessel with water.

Luckily, just before night, all four of us had lashed ourselves firmly to the fragments of the windlass, lying in this manner as flat upon the deck as possible. This precaution alone saved us from destruction. As it was we were all more or less stunned by the immense weight of water which tumbled upon us, and which did not roll from above us until we were nearly exhausted. As soon as I could recover breath, I called aloud to my companions. Augustus alone replied, saying, "It is all over with us, and may God have mercy upon our souls." By-and-by both the others were enabled to speak, when they exhorted us to take courage, as there was still hope; it being impossible, from the nature of the cargo, that the brig could go down, and there being every chance that the gale would blow over by the morning. These words inspired me with new life; for, strange as it may seem, although it was obvious that a vessel with a cargo of empty oil-casks would not sink, I had been hitherto so confused in mind as to have overlooked this consideration altogether; and the danger which I had for some time regarded as the most imminent was that of foundering. As hope revived within me, I made use of every opportunity to strengthen the lashings which held me to the remains of the windlass, and in this occupation I soon discovered that my companions were also busy. The night was as dark as it could possibly be, and the horrible shrieking din and confusion which surrounded us it is useless to attempt describing. Our deck lay level with the sea, or rather we were encircled with a towering ridge of foam, a portion of which swept over us every instant. It is not too much to say that our heads were not fairly out of water more than one second in three. Although we lay close together, no one of us could see the other, or, indeed, any portion of the brig itself, upon which we were so tempestuously hurled about. At intervals we called one to the other, thus endeavouring to keep alive hope, and render consolation and encouragement to such of us as stood most in need of it. The feeble condition of Augustus made him an object of solicitude with us all; and as, from the lacerated condition of his right arm, it must have been impossible for him to secure his lashings with any degree of firmness, we were in momentary expectation of finding that he had gone overboard—yet to render him aid was a thing altogether out of the question. Fortunately, his station was more secure than that of any of the rest of us; for the upper part of his body lying just beneath a portion of the shattered windlass, the seas, as they tumbled in upon him, were greatly broken in their violence. In any other situation than this (into which he had been accidentally thrown after having lashed himself in a very exposed spot) he must inevitably have perished before morning. Owing to the brig's lying so much along, we were all less liable to be washed off than otherwise would have been the case. The heel, as I have before stated, was to larboard, about one half of the deck being constantly under water. The seas, therefore, which struck us to starboard were much broken by the vessel's side, only reaching us in fragments as we lay flat on our faces; while those which came from larboard, being what are called back-water seas, and obtaining little hold upon us on account of our posture, had not sufficient force to drag us from our fastenings.

In this frightful situation we lay until the day broke so as to show us more fully the horrors which surrounded us. The brig was a mere log, rolling about at the mercy of every wave; the gale was upon the increase, if anything, blowing indeed a complete hurricane, and there appeared to us no earthly prospect of deliverance. For several hours we held on in silence, expecting every moment that our lashings would either give way, that the remains of the windlass would go by the board, or that some of the huge seas, which roared in every direction around us and above us, would drive the hulk so far beneath the water that we should be drowned before it could regain the surface. By the mercy of God, however, we were preserved from these imminent dangers, and about midday were cheered by the light of the blessed sun. Shortly afterward we could perceive a sensible diminution in the force of the wind, when, now for the first time since the latter part of the evening before, Augustus spoke, asking Peters, who lay closest to him, if he thought there was any possibility of our being saved. As no reply was at first made to this question, we all concluded that the hybrid had been drowned where he lay; but presently, to our great joy, he spoke, although very feebly, saying that he was in great pain, being so cut by the tightness of his lashings across his stomach, that he must either find means of loosening them or perish, as it was impossible that he could endure his misery much longer. This occasioned us great distress, as it was altogether useless to think of aiding him in any manner while the sea continued washing over us as it did. We exhorted him to bear his sufferings with fortitude, and promised to seize the first opportunity which should offer itself to relieve him. He replied that it would soon be too late; that it would be all over with him before we could help him; and then, after moaning for some minutes, lay silent, when we concluded that he had perished.

As the evening drew on, the sea had fallen so much that scarcely more than one wave broke over the hulk from windward in the course of five minutes, and the wind had abated a great deal, although still blowing a severe gale. I had not heard any of my companions speak for hours, and now called to Augustus. He replied, although very feebly, so that I could not distinguish what he said. I then spoke to Peters and to Parker, neither of whom returned any answer.

Shortly after this period I fell into a state of partial insensibility, during which the most pleasing images floated in my imagination; such as green trees, waving meadows of ripe grain, processions of dancing girls, troops of cavalry, and other phantasies. I now remember that, in all which passed before my mind's eye, *motion* was a predominant idea. Thus, I never fancied any stationary object, such as a house, a mountain, or anything of that kind; but windmills, ships, large birds, balloons, people on horseback, carriages driving furiously, and similar moving objects, presented themselves in endless succession. When I recovered from this state, the sun was, as near as I could guess, an hour high. I had the greatest difficulty in bringing to recollection the various circumstances connected with my situation, and for some time remained firmly convinced that I was still in the hold of the brig, near the box, and that the body of Parker was that of Tiger.

When I at length completely came to my senses, I found that the wind blew no more than a moderate breeze, and that the sea was comparatively calm; so much so that it only washed over the brig amidships. My left arm had broken loose from its lashings, and was much cut about the elbow; my right was entirely benumbed, and the hand and wrist swollen prodigiously by the pressure of the rope, which had worked from the shoulder downward. I was also in great pain from another rope which went about my waist, and had been drawn to an insufferable degree of tightness. Looking round upon my companions, I saw that Peters still lived, although a thick line was pulled so forcibly around his loins as to give him the appearance of being cut nearly in two; as I stirred, he made a feeble motion to me with his hand, pointing to the rope. Augustus gave no indication of life whatever, and was bent nearly double across a splinter of the windlass. Parker spoke to me when he saw me moving, and asked me if I had not sufficient strength to release him from his situation; saying, that if I would summon up what spirits I could, and contrive to untie him, we might yet save our lives; but that otherwise we must all perish. I told him to take courage, and I would endeavour to free him. Feeling in my pantaloons' pocket, I got hold of my penknife, and, after several ineffectual attempts, at length succeeded in opening it. I then, with my left hand, managed to free my right from its fastenings, and afterward cut the other ropes which held me. Upon attempting, however, to move from my position, I found that my legs failed me altogether, and that I could not get up; neither could I move my right arm in any direction. Upon mentioning this to Parker, he advised me to lie quiet for a few minutes, holding on to the windlass with my left hand, so as to allow time for the blood to circulate. Doing this, the numbness presently began to die away, so that I could move first one of my legs, and then the other; and, shortly afterward, I regained the partial use of my right arm. I now crawled with great caution towards Parker, without getting on my legs, and soon cut loose all the lashings about him, when, after a short delay, he also recovered the partial use of his limbs. We now lost no time in getting loose the rope from Peters. It had cut a deep gash through the waistband of his woollen pantaloons, and through two shirts, and made its way into his groin, from which the blood flowed out copiously as we removed the cordage. No sooner had we removed it, however, than he spoke, and seemed to experience instant relief—being able to move with much greater ease than either Parker or myself—this was no doubt owing to the discharge of blood.

We had little hope that Augustus would recover, as he evinced no signs of life; but, upon getting to him, we discovered that he had merely swooned from loss of blood, the bandages we had placed around his wounded arm having been torn off by the water; none of the ropes which held him to the windlass were drawn sufficiently tight to occasion his death. Having relieved him from the fastenings, and got him clear of the broken wood about the windlass, we secured him in a dry place to windward, with his head somewhat lower than his body, and all three of us busied ourselves in chafing his limbs. In about half an hour he came to himself, although it was not until the next morning that he gave signs of recognising any of us, or had sufficient strength to speak. By the time we had got clear of our lashings it was quite dark, and it began to cloud up, so that we were again in the greatest agony lest it should come on to blow hard, in which event nothing could have saved us from perishing, exhausted as we were. By good fortune it continued very moderate during the night, the sea subsiding every minute, which gave us great hopes of ultimate preservation. A gentle breeze still blew from the N.W., but the weather was not at all cold. Augustus was lashed carefully to windward in such a manner as to prevent him from slipping overboard with the rolls of the vessel, as he was still too weak to hold on at all. For ourselves there was no such necessity. We sat close together, supporting each other with the aid of the broken ropes about the windlass, and devising methods of escape from our frightful situation. We derived much comfort from taking off our clothes and wringing the water from them. When we put them on after this, they felt remarkably warm and pleasant, and served to invigorate us in no little degree. We helped Augustus off with his, and wrung them for him, when he experienced the same comfort.

Our chief sufferings were now those of hunger and thirst, and, when we looked forward to the means of relief in this respect, our hearts sunk within us, and we were induced to regret that we had escaped the less dreadful perils of the sea. We endeavoured, however, to console ourselves with the hope of being speedily picked up by some vessel, and encouraged each other to bear with fortitude the evils that might happen.

The morning of the fourteenth at length dawned, and the weather still continued clear and pleasant, with a steady but very light breeze from the N.W. The sea was now quite smooth, and as, from some cause which we could not determine, the brig did not lie so much along as she had done before, the deck was comparatively dry, and we could move about with freedom. We had now been better than three entire days and nights without either food or drink, and it became absolutely necessary that we should make an attempt to get up something from below. As the brig was completely full of water, we went to this work despondingly, and with but little expectation of being able to obtain anything. We made a kind of drag by driving some nails which we broke out from the remains of the companion-hatch into two pieces of wood. Tying these across each other, and fastening them to the end of a rope, we threw them into the cabin, and dragged them to and fro, in the faint hope of being thus able to entangle some article which might be of use to us for food, or which might at least render us assistance in getting it. We spent the greater part of the morning in this labour without effect, fishing up nothing more than a few bedclothes, which were readily caught by the nails. Indeed, our contrivance was so very clumsy, that any greater success was hardly to be anticipated.

We now tried the forecastle, but equally in vain, and were upon the brink of despair, when Peters proposed that we should fasten a rope to his body, and let him make an attempt to get up something by diving into the cabin. This proposition we hailed with all the delight which reviving hope could inspire. He proceeded immediately to strip off his clothes with the exception of his pantaloons; and a strong rope was then carefully fastened around his middle, being brought up over his shoulders in such a manner that there was no possibility of its slipping. The undertaking was one of great difficulty and danger; for, as we could hardly expect to find much, if any provision in the cabin itself, it was necessary that the diver, after letting himself down, should make a turn to the right, and proceed under water a distance of ten or twelve feet, in a narrow passage, to the storeroom, and return, without drawing breath.

Everything being ready, Peters now descended into the cabin, going down the companion-ladder until the water reached his chin. He then plunged in, head first, turning to the right as he plunged, and endeavouring to make his way to the storeroom. In this first attempt, however, he was altogether unsuccessful. In less than half a minute after his going down we felt the rope jerked violently (the signal we had agreed upon when he desired to be drawn up). We accordingly drew him up instantly, but so incautiously as to bruise him badly against the ladder. He had brought nothing with him, and had been unable to penetrate more than a very little way into the passage, owing to the constant exertions he found it necessary to make in order to keep himself from floating up against the deck. Upon getting out he was very much exhausted and had to rest full fifteen minutes before he could again·venture to descend.

The second attempt met with even worse success; for he remained so long under water without giving the signal, that, becoming alarmed for his safety, we drew him out without it, and found that he was almost at the last gasp, having, as he said, repeatedly jerked at the rope without our feeling it. This was probably owing to a portion of it having become entangled in the balustrade at the foot of the ladder. This balustrade was, indeed, so much in the way, that we determined to remove it, if possible, before proceeding with our design. As we had no means of getting it away except by main force, we all descended into the water as far as we could on the ladder, and giving a pull against it with our united strength, succeeded in breaking it down.

The third attempt was equally unsuccessful with the two first, and it now became evident that nothing could be done in this manner without the aid of some weight with which the diver might steady himself, and keep to the floor of the cabin while making his search. For a long time we looked about in vain for something which might answer this purpose; but at length, to our great joy, we discovered one of the weather-forechains so loose that we had not the least difficulty in wrenching it off. Having fastened this securely to one of his ankles, Peters now made his fourth descent into the cabin, and this time succeeded in making his way to the door of the steward's room. To his inexpressible grief, however, he found it locked, and was obliged to return without effecting an entrance, as, with the greatest exertion, he could remain under water no more, at the utmost extent, than a single minute. Our affairs now looked gloomy indeed, and neither Augustus nor myself could refrain from bursting into tears, as we thought of the host of difficulties which encompassed us, and the slight probability which existed of our finally making an escape. But this weakness was not of long duration. Throwing ourselves on our knees to God, we implored his aid in the many dangers which beset us; and arose with renewed hope and vigour to think what could yet be done by mortal means towards accomplishing our deliverance.

Shortly afterward an incident occurred which I am induced to look upon as more intensely productive of emotion, as far more replete with the extremes first of delight and then of horror, then even any of the thousand chances which afterward befell me in nine long years, crowded with events of the most startling, and, in many cases, of the most unconceived and unconceivable character. We were lying on the deck near the companionway, and debating the possibility of yet making our way into the storeroom, when, looking towards Augustus, who lay fronting myself, I perceived that he had become all at once deadly pale, and that his lips were quivering in the most singular and unaccountable manner. Greatly alarmed, I spoke to him, but he made me no reply, and I was beginning to think that he was suddenly taken ill, when I took notice of his eyes, which were glaring apparently at some object behind me. I turned my head, and shall never forget the ecstatic joy which thrilled through every particle of my frame, when I perceived a large brig bearing down upon us, and not more than a couple of miles off. I sprung to my feet as if a musket bullet had suddenly struck me to the heart; and, stretching out my arms in the direction of the vessel, stood in this manner, motionless, and unable to articulate a syllable. Peters and Parker were equally affected, although in different ways. The former danced about the deck like a madman, uttering the most extravagant rhodomontades, intermingled with howls and imprecations, while the latter burst into tears, and continued for many minutes weeping like a child.

The vessel in sight was a large hermaphrodite brig, of a Dutch build, and painted black, with a tawdry gilt figurehead. She had evidently seen a good deal of rough weather, and, we supposed, had suffered much in the gale which had proved so disastrous to ourselves; for her foretopmast was gone, and some of her starboard bulwarks. When we first saw her, she was, as I have already said, about two miles off and to windward, bearing down upon us. The breeze was very gentle, and what astonished us chiefly was, that she had no other sails set than her foresail and mainsail, with a flying jib—of course she came down but slowly, and our impatience amounted nearly to phrensy. The awkward manner in which she steered, too, was remarked by all of us, even excited as we were. She yawed about so considerably, that once or twice we thought it impossible she could see us, or imagined that, having seen us, and discovered no person on board, she was about to tack and make off in another direction. Upon each of these occasions we screamed and shouted at the top of our voices, when the stranger would appear to change for a moment her intention, and again hold on towards us—this singular conduct being repeated two or three times, so that at last we could think of no other manner of accounting for it than by supposing the helmsman to be in liquor.

No person was seen upon her decks until she arrived within about a quarter of a mile of us. We then saw three seamen, whom by their dress we took to be Hollanders. Two of these were lying on some old sails near the forecastle, and the third, who appeared to looking at us with great curiosity, was leaning over the starboard bow near the bowsprit. This last was a stout and tall man, with a very dark skin. He seemed by his manner to be encouraging us to have patience, nodding to us in a cheerful although rather odd way, and smiling constantly, so as to display a set of the most brilliantly white teeth. As his vessel drew nearer, we saw a red flannel cap which he had on fall from his head into the water; but of this he took little or no notice, continuing his odd smiles and gesticulations. I relate these things and circumstances minutely, and I relate them, it must be understood, precisely as they *appeared* to us.

The brig came on slowly, and now more steadily than before, and—I cannot speak calmly of this event—our hearts leaped up wildly within us, and we poured out our whole souls in shouts and thanksgiving to God for the complete, unexpected, and glorious deliverance that was so palpably at hand. Of a sudden, and all at once, there came wafted over the ocean from the strange vessel (which was now close upon us) a smell, a stench, such as the whole world has no name for—no conception of—hellish—utterly suffocating—insufferable—inconceivable. I gasped for breath, and turning to my companions, perceived that they were paler than marble. But we had now no time left for question or surmise—the brig was within fifty feet of us, and it seemed to be her intention to run under our counter, that we might board her without her putting out a boat. We rushed aft, when, suddenly, a wide yaw threw her off full five or six points from the course she had been running, and, as she passed under our stern at the distance of about twenty feet, we had a full view of her decks. Shall I ever forget the triple horror of that spectacle? Twenty-five or thirty human bodies, among whom were several females, lay scattered about between the counter and the galley in the last and most loathsome state of putrefaction. We plainly saw that not a soul lived in that fated vessel! Yet we could not help shouting to the dead for help! Yes, long and loudly did we beg, in the agony of the moment, that those silent and disgusting images would stay for us, would not abandon us to become like them, would receive us among their goodly company! We were raving with horror and despair—thoroughly mad through the anguish of our grievous disappointment.

As our first loud yell of terror broke forth, it was replied to by something, from near the bowsprit of the stranger, so closely resembling the scream of a human voice that the nicest ear might have been startled and deceived. At this instant another sudden yaw brought the region of the forecastle for a moment into view, and we beheld at once the origin of the sound. We saw the tall stout figure still leaning on the bulwark, and still nodding his head to and fro, but his face was now turned from us so that we could not behold it. His arms were extended over the rail, and the palms of his hands fell outward. His knees were lodged upon a stout rope, tightly stretched, and reaching from the heel of the bowsprit to a cathead. On his back, from which a portion of the shirt had been torn, leaving it bare, there sat a huge seagull, busily gorging itself with the horrible flesh, its bill and talons deep buried, and its white plumage spattered all over with blood. As the brig moved further round so as to bring us close in view, the bird, with much apparent difficulty, drew out its crimsoned head, and, after eying us for a moment as if stupefied, arose lazily from the body upon which it had been feasting, and, flying directly above our deck, hovered there a while with a portion of clotted and liver-like substance in its beak. The horrid morsel dropped at length with a sullen splash immediately at the feet of Parker. May God forgive me, but now, for the first time, there flashed through my mind a thought, a thought which I will not mention, and I felt myself making a step towards the ensanguined spot. I looked upward, and the eyes of Augustus met my own with a degree of intense and eager meaning which immediately brought me to my senses. I sprang forward quickly, and, with a deep shudder, threw the frightful thing into the sea.

The body from which it had been taken, resting as it did upon the rope, had been easily swayed to and fro by the exertions of the carnivorous bird, and it was this motion which had at first impressed us with the belief of its being alive. As the gull relieved it of its weight, it swung round and fell partially over, so that the face was fully discovered. Never, surely, was any object so terribly full of awe! The eyes were gone, and the whole flesh around the mouth, leaving the teeth utterly naked. This, then, was the smile which had cheered us on to hope! this the—but I forbear. The brig, as I have already told, passed under our stern, and made its way slowly but steadily to leeward. With her and with her terrible crew went all our gay visions of deliverance and joy. Deliberately as she went by, we might possibly have found means of boarding her, had not our sudden disappointment, and the appalling nature of the discovery which accompanied it, laid entirely prostrate every active faculty of mind and body. We had seen and felt, but we could neither think nor act, until, alas, too late. How much our intellects had been weakened by this incident may be estimated by the fact, that, when the vessel had proceeded so far that we could perceive no more than the half of her hull, the proposition was seriously entertained of attempting to overtake her by swimming!

I have, since this period, vainly endeavoured to obtain some clew to the hideous uncertainty which enveloped the fate of the stranger. Her build and general appearance, as I have before stated, led us to the belief that she was a Dutch trader, and the dresses of the crew also sustained this opinion. We might have easily seen the name upon her stern, and, indeed, taken other observations which would have guided us in making out her character; but the intense excitement of the moment blinded us to everything of that nature. From the saffron-like hue of such of the corpses as were not entirely decayed, we concluded that the whole of her company had perished by the yellow fever, or some other virulent disease of the same fearful kind. If such were the case (and I know not what else to imagine), death, to judge from the positions of the bodies, must have come upon them in a manner awfully sudden and overwhelming, in a way totally distinct from that which generally characterizes even the most deadly pestilences with which mankind are acquainted. It is possible, indeed, that poison, accidentally introduced into some of their sea-stores, may have brought about the disaster; or that the eating some unknown venomous species of fish, or other marine animal, or oceanic bird, might have induced it—but it is utterly useless to form conjectures where all is involved, and will, no doubt, remain for ever involved, in the most appalling and unfathomable mystery.

We spent the remainder of the day in a condition of stupid lethargy, gazing after the retreating vessel until the darkness, hiding her from our sight, recalled us in some measure to our senses. The pangs of hunger and thirst then returned, absorbing all other cares and considerations. Nothing, however, could be done until the morning, and, securing ourselves as well as possible, we endeavoured to snatch a little repose. In this I succeeded beyond my expectations, sleeping until my companions, who had not been so fortunate, aroused me at daybreak to renew our attempts at getting up provision from the hull.

It was now a dead calm, with the sea as smooth as I have ever known it—the weather warm and pleasant. The brig was out of sight. We commenced our operations by wrenching off, with some trouble, another of the forechains; and having fastened both to Peters's feet, he again made an endeavour to reach the door of the store-room, thinking it possible that he might be able to force it open, provided he could get at it in sufficient time; and this he hoped to do, as the hulk lay much more steadily than before.

He succeeded very quickly in reaching the door, when, loosening one of the chains from his ankle, he made every exertion to force a passage with it, but in vain, the framework of the room being far stronger than was anticipated. He was quite exhausted with his long stay under water, and it became absolutely necessary that some other one of us should take his place. For this service Parker immediately volunteered; but, after making three ineffectual efforts, found that he could never even succeed in getting near the door. The condition of Augustus's wounded arm rendered it useless for him to attempt going down, as he would be unable to force the room open should he reach it, and it accordingly now devolved upon me to exert myself for our common deliverance.

Peters had left one of the chains in the passage, and I found, upon plunging in, that I had not sufficient balance to keep me firmly down. I determined, therefore, to attempt no more, in my first effort, than merely to recover the other chain. In groping along the floor of the passage for this I felt a hard substance, which I immediately grasped, not having time to ascertain what it was, but returning and ascending instantly to the surface. The prize proved to be a bottle, and our joy may be conceived when I say that it was found to be full of Port wine. Giving thanks to God for this timely and cheering assistance, we immediately drew the cork with my penknife, and, each taking a moderate sup, felt the most indescribable comfort from the warmth, strength, and spirits with which it inspired us. We then carefully recorked the bottle, and, by means of a handkerchief, swung it in such a manner that there was no possibility of its getting broken.

Having rested a while after this fortunate discovery, I again descended, and now recovered the chain, with which I instantly came up. I then fastened it on and went down for the third time, when I became fully satisfied that no exertions whatever, in that situation, would enable me to force open the door of the storeroom. I therefore returned in despair.

There seemed now to be no longer any room for hope, and I could perceive in the countenances of my companions that they had made up their minds to perish. The wine had evidently produced in them a species of delirium, which, perhaps, I had been prevented from feeling by the immersion I had undergone since drinking it. They talked incoherently, and about matters unconnected with our condition, Peters repeatedly asking me questions about Nantucket. Augustus, too, I remember, approached me with a serious air, and requested me to lend him a pocket-comb, as his hair was full of fish-scales, and he wished to get them out before going on shore. Parker appeared somewhat less affected, and urged me to dive at random into the cabin, and bring up any article which might come to hand. To this I consented, and, in the first attempt, after staying under a full minute, brought up a small leather trunk belonging to Captain Barnard. This was immediately opened in the faint hope that it might contain something to eat or drink. We found nothing, however, except a box of razors and two linen shirts. I now went down again, and returned without any success. As my head came above water I heard a crash on deck, and, upon getting up, saw that my companions had ungratefully taken advantage of my absence to drink the remainder of the wine, having let the bottle fall in the endeavour to replace it before I saw them. I remonstrated with them on the heartlessness of their conduct, when Augustus burst into tears. The other two endeavoured to laugh the matter off as a joke, but I hope never again to behold laughter of such a species; the distortion of countenance was absolutely frightful. Indeed, it was apparent that the stimulus, in the empty state of their stomachs, had taken instant and violent effect, and that they were all exceedingly intoxicated. With great difficulty I prevailed upon them to lie down, when they fell very soon into a heavy slumber, accompanied with loud stertorous breathing.

I now found myself, as it were, alone in the brig, and my reflections, to be sure, were of the most fearful and gloomy nature. No prospect offered itself to my view but a lingering death by famine, or, at the best, by being over-whelmed in the first gale which should spring up, for in our present exhausted condition we could have no hope of living through another.

The gnawing hunger which I now experienced was nearly insupportable, and I felt myself capable of going to any lengths in order to appease it. With my knife I cut off a small portion of the leather trunk, and endeavoured to eat it, but found it utterly impossible to swallow a single morsel, although I fan-cied that some little alleviation of my suffering was obtained by chewing small pieces of it and spitting them out. Towards night my companions awoke, one by one, each in an indescribable state of weakness and horror, brought on by the wine, whose fumes had now evaporated. They shook as if with a violent ague, and uttered the most lamentable cries for water. Their condition affected me in the most lively degree, at the same time causing me to rejoice in the fortunate train of circumstances which had prevented me from indulging in the wine, and consequently from sharing their melancholy and most distressing sensations. Their conduct, however, gave me great uneasiness and alarm; for it was evident that, unless some favourable change took place, they could afford me no assistance in providing for our common safety. I had not yet abandoned all idea of being able to get up something from below; but the attempt could not possibly be resumed until some one of them was sufficiently master of himself to aid me by holding the end of the rope while I went down. Parker appeared to be somewhat more in possession of his senses than the others, and I endeavoured, by every means in my power, to arouse him. thinking that a plunge in the sea-water might have a beneficial effect, I contrived to fasten the end of a rope around his body, and then, leading him to the companion-way (he remaining quite passive all the while), pushed him in, and immediately drew him out. I had good reason to congratulate myself upon having made this experiment; for he appeared much revived and invigorated, and, upon getting out, asked me, in a rational manner, why I had so served him. Having ex-plained my object, he expressed himself indebted to me, and said that he felt greatly better from the immersion, afterward conversing sensibly upon our situation. We then resolved to treat Augustus and Peters in the same way, which we immediately did, when they both experienced much benefit from the shock. This idea of sudden immersion had been suggested to me by reading in some medical work the good effect of the shower-bath in a case where the patient was suffering from *mania a potu*.

Finding that I could now trust my companions to hold the end of the rope, I again made three or four plunges into the cabin, although it was now quite dark, and a gentle but long swell from the northward rendered the hulk some-what unsteady. In the course of these attempts I succeeded in bringing up two case-knives, a three-gallon jug, empty, and a blanket, but nothing which could serve us for food. I continued my efforts, after getting these articles, until I was completely exhausted, but brought up nothing else. During the night Parker and Peters occupied themselves by turns in the same manner; but nothing coming to hand, we now gave up this attempt in despair, concluding that we were exhausting ourselves in vain.

We passed the remainder of this night in a state of the most intense mental and bodily anguish that can possibly be imagined. The morning of the sixteenth at length dawned, and we looked eagerly around the horizon for relief, but to no purpose. The sea was still smooth, with only a long swell from the northward, as on yesterday. This was the sixth day since we had tasted either food or drink, with the exception of the bottle of Port wine, and it was clear that we could hold out but a very little while longer unless something could be obtained. I never saw before, nor wish to see again, human beings so utterly emaciated as Peters and Augustus. Had I met them on shore in their present condition I should not have had the slightest suspicion that I had ever beheld them. Their countenances were totally changed in character, so that I could not bring myself to believe them really the same individuals with whom I had been in company but a few days before. Parker, although sadly reduced, and so feeble that he could not raise his head from his bosom, was not so far gone as the other two. He suffered with great patience, making no complaint, and endeavouring to inspire us with hope in every manner he could devise. For myself, although at the commencement of the voyage I had been in bad health, and was at all times of a delicate constitution, I suffered less than any of us, being much less reduced in frame, and retaining my powers of mind in a surprising degree, while the rest were completely prostrated in intellect, and seemed to be brought to a species of second childhood, generally simpering in their expressions, with idiotic smiles, and uttering the most absurd platitudes. At intervals, however, they would appear to revive suddenly, as if inspired all at once with a consciousness of their condition, when they would spring upon their feet in a momentary flash of vigour, and speak, for a short period, of their prospects, in a manner altogether rational, although full of the most intense despair. It is possible, however, that my companions may have entertained the same opinion of their own condition as I did of mine, and that I may have unwittingly been guilty of the same extravagances and imbecilities as themselves—this is a matter which cannot be determined.

About noon Parker declared that he saw land off the larboard quarter, and it was with the utmost difficulty I could restrain him from plunging into the sea with the view of swimming towards it. Peters and Augustus took little notice of what he said, being apparently wrapped up in moody contemplation. Upon looking in the direction pointed out, I could not perceive the faintest appearance of the shore—indeed, I was too well aware that we were far from any land to indulge in a hope of that nature. It was a long time, nevertheless, before I could convince Parker of his mistake. He then burst into a flood of tears, weeping like a child, with loud cries and sobs, for two or three hours, when, becoming exhausted, he fell asleep.

Peters and Augustus now made several ineffectual efforts to swallow portions of the leather. I advised them to chew it and spit it out; but they were too excessively debilitated to be able to follow my advice. I continued to chew pieces of it at intervals, and found some relief from so doing; my chief distress was for water, and I was only prevented from taking a draught from the sea by remembering the horrible consequences which thus have resulted to others who were similarly situated with ourselves.

The day wore on in this manner, when I suddenly discovered a sail to the eastward, and on our larboard bow. She appeared to be a large ship, and was coming nearly athwart us, being probably twelve or fifteen miles distant. None of my companions had as yet discovered her, and I forbore to tell them of her for the present, lest we might again be disappointed of relief. At length, upon her getting nearer, I saw distinctly that she was heading immediately for us, with her light sails filled. I could now contain myself no longer, and pointed her out to my fellow-sufferers. They immediately sprang to their feet, again indulging in the most extravagant demonstrations of joy, weeping, laughing in an idiotic manner, jumping, stamping upon the deck, tearing their hair, and praying and cursing by turns. I was so affected by their conduct, as well as by what I now considered a sure prospect of deliverance, that I could not refrain from joining in with their madness, and gave way to the impulses of my gratitude and ecstacy by lying and rolling on the deck, clapping my hands, shouting, and other similar acts, until I was suddenly called to my recollection, and once more to the extreme of human misery and despair, by perceiving the ship all at once with her stern fully presented towards us, and steering in a direction nearly opposite to that in which I had at first perceived it.

It was some time before I could induce my poor companions to believe that this sad reverse in our prospects had actually taken place. They replied to all my assertions with a stare and a gesture implying that they were not to be deceived by such misrepresentations. The conduct of Augustus most sensibly affected me. In spite of all I could say or do to the contrary, he persisted in saying that the ship was rapidly nearing us, and in making preparations to go on board of her. Some sea-weed floating by the brig, he maintained that it was the ship's boat, and endeavoured to throw himself upon it, howling and shrieking in the most heart-rending manner, when I forcibly restrained him from thus casting himself into the sea.

Having become in some degree pacified, we continued to watch the ship until we finally lost sight of her, the weather becoming hazy, with a light breeze springing up. As soon as she was entirely gone, Parker turned suddenly towards me with an expression of countenance which made me shudder. There was about him an air of self-possession which I had not noticed in him until now, and before he opened his lips my heart told me what he would say. He proposed, in a few words, that one of us should die to preserve the existence of the others.

I had, for some time past, dwelt upon the prospect of our being reduced to this last horrible extremity, and had secretly made up my mind to suffer death in any shape or under any circumstances rather than resort to such a course.

Nor was this resolution in any degree weakened by the present intensity of hunger under which I laboured. The proposition had not been heard by either Peters or Augustus. I therefore took Parker aside; and mentally praying to God for power to dissuade him from the horrible purpose he entertained, I expostulated with him for a long time, and in the most supplicating manner, begging him in the name of everything which he held sacred, and urging him by every species of argument which the extremity of the case suggested, to abandon the idea, and not to mention it to either of the other two.

He heard all I said without attempting to controvert any of my arguments, and I had begun to hope that he would be prevailed upon to do as I desired. But when I had ceased speaking, he said that he knew very well all I had said was true, and that to resort to such a course was the most horrible alternative which could enter into the mind of man; but that he had now held out as long as human nature could be sustained; that it was unnecessary for all to perish, when, by the death of one, it was possible, and even probable, that the rest might be finally preserved; adding that I might save myself the trouble of trying to turn him from his purpose, his mind having been thoroughly made up on the subject even before the appearance of the ship, and that only her heaving in sight had prevented him from mentioning his intention at an earlier period.

I now begged him, if he would not be prevailed upon to abandon his design, at least to defer it for another day, when some vessel might come to our relief; again reiterating every argument I could devise, and which I thought likely to have influence with one of his rough nature. He said, in reply, that he had not spoken until the very last possible moment; that he could exist no longer without sustenance of some kind; and that therefore in another day his suggestion would be too late, as regarded himself at least.

Finding that he was not to be moved by anything I could say in a mild tone, I now assumed a different demeanour, and told him that he must be aware I had suffered less than any of us from our calamities; that my health and strength, consequently, were at that moment far better than his own or than that either of Peters or Augustus; in short, that I was in a condition to have my own way by force if I found it necessary; and that, if he attempted in any manner to acquaint the others with his bloody and cannibal designs, I would not hesitate to throw him into the sea. Upon this he immediately seized me by the throat, and drawing a knife, made several ineffectual efforts to stab me in the stomach; an atrocity which his excessive debility alone prevented him from accomplishing. In the mean time, being roused to a high pitch of anger, I forced him to the vessel's side, with the full intention of throwing him overboard. He was saved from this fate, however, by the interference of Peters, who now approached and separated us, asking the cause of the disturbance. This Parker told before I could find means in any manner to prevent him.

The effect of his words was even more terrible than what I had anticipated. Both Augustus and Peters, who, it seems, had long secretly entertained the same fearful idea which Parker had been merely the first to broach, joined with him in his design, and insisted upon its immediately being carried into effect. I had calculated that one at least of the two former would be found still possessed of sufficient strength of mind to side with myself in resisting any attempt to execute so dreadful a purpose; and, with the aid of either one of them, I had no fear of being able to prevent its accomplishment. Being disappointed in this expectation, it became absolutely necessary that I should attend to my own safety, as a further resistance on my part might possibly be considered by men in their frightful condition a sufficient excuse for refusing me fair play in the tragedy that I knew would speedily be enacted.

I now told them I was willing to submit to the proposal, merely requesting a delay of about one hour, in order that the fog which had gathered around us might have an opportunity of lifting, when it was possible that the ship we had seen might be again in sight. After great difficulty I obtained from them a promise to wait thus long; and, as I had anticipated (a breeze rapidly coming in), the fog lifted before the hour had expired, when, no vessel appearing in sight, we prepared to draw lots.

It is with extreme reluctance that I dwell upon the appalling scene which ensued; a scene which, with its minutest details, no after events have been able to efface in the slightest degree from my memory, and whose stern recollection will embitter every future moment of my existence. Let me run over this portion of my narrative with as much haste as the nature of the events to be spoken of will permit. The only method we could devise for the terrific lottery, in which we were to take each a chance, was that of drawing straws. Small splinters of wood were made to answer our purpose, and it was agreed that I should be the holder. I retired to one end of the hulk, while my poor companions silently took up their station in the other with their backs turned towards me. The bitterest anxiety which I endured at any period of this fearful drama was while I occupied myself in the arrangement of the lots. There are few conditions into which man can possibly fall where he will not feel a deep interest in the preservation of his existence; an interest momentarily increasing with the frailness of the tenure by which that existence may be held. But now that the silent, definite, and stern nature of the business in which I was engaged (so different from the tumultuous dangers of the storm or the gradually approaching horrors of famine) allowed me to reflect on the few chances I had of escaping the most appalling of deaths—a death for the most appalling of purposes—every particle of that energy which had so long buoyed me up departed like feathers before the wind, leaving me a helpless prey to the most abject and pitiable terror. I could not, at first, even summon up sufficient strength to tear and fit together the small splinters of wood, my fingers absolutely refusing their office, and my knees knocking violently against each other. My mind ran over rapidly a thousand absurd projects by which to avoid becoming a partner in the awful speculation. I thought of falling on my knees to my companions, and entreating them to let me escape this necessity; of suddenly rushing upon them, and, by putting one of them to death, of rendering the decision by lot useless—in short, of everything but of going through with the matter I had in hand. At last, after wasting a long time in this imbecile conduct, I was recalled to my senses by the voice of Parker, who urged me to relieve them at once from the terrible anxiety they were enduring. Even then I could not bring myself to arrange the splinters upon the spot, but thought over every species of finesse by which I could trick some one of my fellow-sufferers to draw the short straw, as it had been agreed that whoever drew the shortest of four splinters from my hand was to die for the preservation of the rest. Before any one condemn me for this apparent heartlessness, let him be placed in a situation precisely similar to my own.

At length delay was no longer possible, and, with a heart almost bursting from my bosom, I advanced to the region of the forecastle, where my companions were awaiting me. I held out my hand with the splinters, and Peters immediately drew. He was free—*his*, at least, was not the shortest; and there was now another chance against my escape. I summoned up all my strength, and passed the lots to Augustus. He also drew immediately, and he also was free; and now, whether I should live or die, the chances were no more than precisely even. At this moment all the fierceness of the tiger possessed my bosom, and I felt towards my poor fellow-creature, Parker, the most intense, the most diabolical hatred. But the feeling did not last; and, at length, with a convulsive shudder and closed eyes, I held out the two remaining splinters towards him. It was full five minutes before he could summon resolution to draw, during which period of heart-rending suspense I never once opened my eyes. Presently one of the two lots was quickly drawn from my hand. The decision was then over, yet I knew not whether it was for me or against me. No one spoke, and still I dared not satisfy myself by looking at the splinter I held. Peters at length took me by the hand, and I forced myself to look up, when I immediately saw by the countenance of Parker that I was safe, and that he it was who had been doomed to suffer. Gasping for breath, I fell senseless to the deck.

I recovered from my swoon in time to behold the consummation of the tragedy in the death of him who had been chiefly instrumental in bringing it about. He made no resistance whatever, and was stabbed in the back by Peters, when he fell instantly dead. I must not dwell upon the fearful repast which immediately ensued. Such things may be imagined, but words have no power to impress the mind with the exquisite horror of their reality. Let it suffice to say that, having in some measure appeased the raging thirst which consumed us by the blood of the victim, and having by common consent taken off the hands, feet, and head, throwing them, together with the entrails, into the sea, we devoured the rest of the body, piecemeal, during the four memorable days of the seventeenth, eighteenth, nineteenth, and twentieth of the month.

On the nineteenth, there coming on a smart shower which lasted fifteen or twenty minutes, we contrived to catch some water by means of a sheet which had been fished up from the cabin by our drag just after the gale. The quantity we took in all did not amount to more than half a gallon; but even this scanty allowance supplied us with comparative strength and hope.

On the twenty-first we were again reduced to the last necessity. The weather still remained warm and pleasant, with occasional fogs and light breezes, most usually from N. to W.

On the twenty-second, as we were sitting close huddled together, gloomily revolving over our lamentable condition, there flashed through my mind all at once an idea which inspired me with a bright gleam of hope. I remembered that, when the foremast had been cut away, Peters, being in the windward chains, passed one of the axes into my hand, requesting me to put it, if possible, in a place of security, and that a few minutes before the last heavy sea struck the brig and filled her I had taken this axe into the forecastle, and laid it in one of the larboard berths. I now thought it possible that, by getting at this axe, we might cut through the deck over the store-room, and thus readily supply ourselves with provisions.

When I communicated this project to my companions, they uttered a feeble shout of joy, and we all proceeded forthwith to the forecastle. The difficulty of descending here was greater than that of going down in the cabin, the opening being much smaller, for it will be remembered that the whole framework about the cabin companion-hatch had been carried away, whereas the forecastle-way, being a simple hatch of only about three feet square, had remained uninjured. I did not hesitate, however, to attempt the descent; and a rope being fastened round my body as before, I plunged boldly in, feet foremost, made my way quickly to the berth, and, at the very first attempt, brought up the axe. It was hailed with the most ecstatic joy and triumph, and the ease with which it had been obtained was regarded as an omen of our ultimate preservation.

We now commenced cutting at the deck with all the energy of rekindled hope, Peters and myself taking the axe by turns, Augustus's wounded arm not permitting him to aid us in any degree. As we were still so feeble as to be scarcely able to stand unsupported, and could consequently work but a minute or two without resting, it soon became evident that many long hours would be requisite to accomplish our task—that is, to cut an opening sufficiently large to admit of a free access to the storeroom. This consideration, however, did not discourage us; and, working all night by the light of the moon, we succeeded in effecting our purpose by daybreak on the morning of the twenty-third.

Peters now volunteered to go down; and, having made all arrangements as before, he descended, and soon returned, bringing up with him a small jar, which, to our great joy, proved to be full of olives. Having shared these among us, and devoured them with the greatest avidity, we proceeded to let him down again. This time he succeeded beyond our utmost expectations, returning instantly with a large ham and a bottle of Madeira wine. Of the latter we each took a moderate sup, having learned by experience the pernicious consequences of indulging too freely. The ham, except about two pounds near the bone, was not in a condition to be eaten, having been entirely spoiled by the salt water. The sound part was divided among us. Peters and Augustus, not being able to restrain their appetite, swallowed theirs upon the instant; but I was more cautious, and ate but a small portion of mine, dreading the thirst which I knew would ensue. We now rested a while from our labours, which had been intolerably severe.

By noon, feeling somewhat strengthened and refreshed, we again renewed our attempt at getting up provision, Peters and myself going down alternately, and always with more or less success, until sundown. During this interval we had the good fortune to bring up, altogether, four more small jars of olives, another ham, a carboy containing nearly three gallons of excellent Cape Madeira wine, and, what gave us still more delight, a small tortoise of the Gallipago breed, several of which had been taken on board by Captain Barnard, as the *Grampus* was leaving port, from the schooner *Mary Pitts*, just returned from a sealing voyage in the Pacific.

In a subsequent portion of this narrative I shall have frequent occasion to mention this species of tortoise. It is found principally, as most of my readers may know, in the group of islands called the Gallipagos, which, indeed, derive their name from the animal—the Spanish word Gallipago meaning a fresh-water terrapin. From the peculiarity of their shape and action they have been sometimes called the elephant tortoise. They are frequently found of an enormous size. I have myself seen several which would weigh from twelve to fifteen hundred pounds, although I do not remember that any navigator speaks of having seen them weighing more than eight hundred. Their appearance is singular, and even disgusting. Their steps are very slow, measured, and heavy, their bodies being carried about a foot from the ground. Their neck is long, and exceedingly slender; from eighteen inches to two feet is a very common length, and I killed one, where the distance from the shoulder to the extremity of the head was no less than three feet ten inches. The head has a striking resemblance to that of a serpent. They can exist without food for an almost incredible length of time, instances having been known where they have been thrown into the hold of a vessel and lain two years without nourishment of any kind—being as fat, and, in every respect, in as good order at the expiration of the time as when they were first put in. In one particular these extraordinary animals bear resemblance to the dromedary, or camel of the desert. In a bag at the root of the neck they carry with them a constant supply of water. In some instances, upon killing them after a full year's deprivation of all nourishment, as much as three gallons of perfectly sweet and fresh water have been found in their bags. Their food is chiefly wild parsley and celery, with purslain, sea-kelp, and prickly-pears, upon which latter vegetable they thrive wonderfully, a great quantity of it being usually found on the hill-sides near the shore wherever the animal itself is discovered. They are excellent and highly nutritious food, and have, no doubt, been the means of preserving the lives of thousands of seamen employed in the whale-fishery and other pursuits in the Pacific.

The one which we had the good fortune to bring up from the storeroom was not of a large size, weighing probably sixty-five or seventy pounds. It was a female, and in excellent condition, being exceedingly fat, and having more than a quart of limpid and sweet water in its bag. This was indeed a treasure;

and, falling on our knees with one accord, we returned fervent thanks to God for so seasonable a relief.

We had great difficulty in getting the animal up through the opening, as its struggles were fierce and its strength prodigious. It was upon the point of making its escape from Peters's grasp, and slipping back into the water, when Augustus, throwing a rope with a slip-knot around its throat, held it up in this manner until I jumped into the hole by the side of Peters, and assisted him in lifting it out.

The water we drew carefully from the bag into the jug, which, it will be remembered, had been brought up before from the cabin. Having done this, we broke off the neck of a bottle so as to form, with a cork, a kind of glass, holding not quite half a gill. We then each drank one of these measures full, and resolved to limit ourselves to this quantity per day as long as it should hold out.

During the last two or three days, the weather having been dry and pleasant, the bedding we had obtained from the cabin, as well as our clothing, had become thoroughly dry, so that we passed this night (that of the twenty-third) in comparative comfort, enjoying a tranquil repose, after having supped plentifully on olives and ham, with a small allowance of the wine. Being afraid of losing some of our stores overboard during the night, in the event of a breeze springing up, we secured them as well as possible with cordage to the fragments of the windlass. Our tortoise, which we were anxious to preserve alive as long as we could, we threw on its back, and otherwise carefully fastened.

July 24. This morning saw us wonderfully recruited in spirits and strength. Notwithstanding the perilous situation in which we were still placed, ignorant of our position, although certainly at a great distance from land, without more food than would last us for a fortnight even with great care, almost entirely without water, and floating about at the mercy of every wind and wave, on the merest wreck in the world, still the infinitely more terrible distresses and dangers from which we had so lately and so providentially been delivered caused us to regard what we now endured as but little more than an ordinary evil—so strictly comparative is either good or ill.

At sunrise we were preparing to renew our attempts at getting up something from the storeroom, when, a smart shower coming on, with some lightning, we turned our attention to the catching of water by means of the sheet we had used before for this purpose. We had no other means of collecting the rain than by holding the sheet spread out with one of the forechain-plates in the middle of it. The water, thus conducted to the centre, was drained through into our jug. We had nearly filled it in this manner, when, a heavy squall coming on from the northward, obliged us to desist, as the hulk began once more to roll so violently that we could no longer keep our feet. We now went forward, and, lashing ourselves securely to the remnant of the windlass as before, awaited the event with far more calmness than could have been anticipated, or would have been imagined possible under the circumstances. At noon the wind had freshened into a two-reef breeze, and by night into a stiff gale, accompanied with a tremendously heavy swell. Experience having taught us, however, the best method of arranging our lashings, we weathered this dreary night in tolerable security, although thoroughly drenched at almost every instant by the sea, and in momentary dread of being washed off. Fortunately, the weather was so warm as to render the water rather grateful than otherwise.

July 25. This morning the gale had diminished to a mere ten-knot breeze, and the sea had gone down with it so considerably that we were able to keep ourselves dry upon the deck. To our great grief, however, we found that two jars of our olives, as well as the whole of our ham, had been washed overboard, in spite of the careful manner in which they had been fastened. We determined not to kill the tortoise as yet, and contented ourselves for the present with a breakfast on a few of the olives, and a measure of water each, which latter we mixed, half and half, with wine, finding great relief and strength from the mixture, without the distressing intoxication which had ensued upon drinking the Port. The sea was still far too rough for the renewal of our efforts at getting up provision from the storeroom. Several articles, of no importance to us in our present situation, floated up through the opening during the day, and were immediately washed overboard. We also now observed that the hulk lay more along than ever, so that we could not stand an instant without lashing ourselves. On this account we passed a gloomy and uncomfortable day. At noon the sun appeared to be nearly vertical, and we had no doubt that we had been driven down by the long succession of northward and northwesterly winds into the near vicinity of the equator. Towards evening we saw several sharks, and were somewhat alarmed by the audacious manner in which an enormously large one approached us. At one time, a lurch throwing the deck very far beneath the water, the monster actually swam in upon us, floundering for some moments just over the companion-hatch, and striking Peters violently with his tail. A heavy sea at length hurled him overboard, much to our relief. In moderate weather we might have easily captured him.

July 26. This morning, the wind having greatly abated, and the sea not being very rough, we determined to renew our exertions in the storeroom. After a great deal of hard labour during the whole day, we found that nothing further was to be expected from this quarter, the partitions of the room having been stove during the night, and its contents swept into the hold. This discovery, as may be supposed, filled us with despair.

July 27. The sea nearly smooth, with a light wind, and still from the northward and westward. The sun coming out hotly in the afternoon, we occupied ourselves in drying our clothes. Found great relief from thirst, and much comfort otherwise, by bathing in the sea; in this, however, we were forced to use great caution, being afraid of sharks, several of which were seen swimming around the brig during the day.

July 28. Good weather still. The brig now began to lie along so alarmingly that we feared she would eventually roll bottom up. Prepared ourselves as well as we could for this emergency, lashing our tortoise, waterjug, and two remaining jars of olives as far as possible over to the windward, placing them outside the hull, below the main-chains. The sea very smooth all day, with little or no wind.

July 29. A continuance of the same weather, Augustus's wounded arm began to evince symptoms of mortification. He complained of drowsiness and excessive thirst, but no acute pain. Nothing could be done for his relief beyond rubbing his wounds with a little of the vinegar from the olives, and from this no benefit seemed to be experienced. We did everything in our power for his comfort, and trebled his allowance of water.

July 30. An excessively hot day, with no wind. An enormous shark kept close by the hulk during the whole of the forenoon. We made several unsuccessful attempts to capture him by means of a noose. Augustus much worse, and evidently sinking as much from want of proper nourishment as from the effect of his wounds. He constantly prayed to be released from his sufferings, wishing for nothing but death. This evening we ate the last of our olives, and found the water in our jug so putrid that we could not swallow it at all without the addition of wine. Determined to kill our tortoise in the morning.

July 31. After a night of excessive anxiety and fatigue, owing to the position of the hulk, we set about killing and cutting up our tortoise. He proved to be much smaller than we had supposed, although in good condition—the whole meat about him not amounting to more than ten pounds. With a view of preserving a portion of this as long as possible, we cut it into fine pieces, and filled with them our three remaining olive-jars and the wine-bottle (all of which had been kept), pouring in afterward the vinegar from the olives. In this manner we put away about three pounds of the tortoise, intending not to touch it until we had consumed the rest. We concluded to restrict ourselves to about four ounces of the meat per day; the whole would thus last us thirteen days. A brisk shower, with severe thunder and lightning, came on about dusk, but lasted so short a time that we only succeeded in catching about half a pint of water. The whole of this, by common consent, was given to Augustus, who now appeared to be in the last extremity. He drank the water from the sheet as we caught it (we holding it above him as he lay so as to let it run into his mouth), for we had now nothing left capable of holding water, unless we had chosen to empty out our wine from the carboy, or the stale water from the jug. Either of these expedients would have been resorted to had the shower lasted.

The sufferer seemed to derive but little benefit from the draught. His arm was completely black from the wrist to the shoulder, and his feet were like ice. We expected every moment to see him breathe his last. He was frightfully emaciated; so much so that, although he weighed a hundred and twenty-seven pounds upon his leaving Nantucket, he now did not weigh more than *forty or fifty at the farthest*. His eyes were sunk far in his head, being scarcely perceptible, and the skin of his cheeks hung so loosely as to prevent his masticating any food, or even swallowing any liquid, without great difficulty.

August 1.   A continuance of the same calm weather, with an oppressively hot sun. Suffered exceedingly from thirst, the water in the jug being absolutely putrid and swarming with vermin. We contrived, nevertheless, to swallow a portion of it by mixing it with wine—our thirst, however, was but little abated. We found more relief by bathing in the sea, but could not avail ourselves of this expedient except at long intervals, on account of the continual presence of sharks. We now saw clearly that Augustus could not be saved; that he was evidently dying. We could do nothing to relieve his sufferings, which appeared to be great. About twelve o'clock he expired in strong convulsions, and without having spoken for several hours. His death filled us with the most gloomy forebodings, and had so great an effect upon our spirits that we sat motionless by the corpse during the whole day, and never addressed each other except in a whisper. It was not until some time after dark that we took courage to get up and throw the body overboard. It was then loathsome beyond expression, and so far decayed that, as Peters attempted to lift it, an entire leg came off in his grasp. As the mass of putrefaction slipped over the vessel's side into the water, the glare of phosphoric light with which it was surrounded plainly discovered to us seven or eight large sharks, the clashing of whose horrible teeth, as their prey was torn to pieces among them, might have been heard at the distance of a mile. We shrunk within ourselves in the extremity of horror at the sound.

August 2.   The same fearfully calm and hot weather. The dawn found us in a state of pitiable dejection as well as bodily exhaustion. The water in the jug was now absolutely useless, being a thick gelatinous mass; nothing but frightful-looking worms mingled with slime. We threw it out, and washed the jug well in the sea, afterward pouring a little vinegar in it from our bottles of pickled tortoise. Our thirst could now scarcely be endured, and we tried in vain to relieve it by wine, which seemed only to add fuel to the flame, and excited us to a high degree of intoxication. We afterward endeavoured to relieve our sufferings by mixing the wine with sea-water; but this instantly brought about the most violent retchings, so that we never again attempted it. During the whole day we anxiously sought an opportunity of bathing, but to no purpose; for the hulk was now entirely besieged on all sides with sharks—no doubt the identical monsters who had devoured our poor companion on the evening before, and who were in momentary expectation of another similar feast. This circumstance occasioned us the most bitter regret, and filled us with the most depressing and melancholy forebodings. We had experienced indescribable relief in bathing, and to have this resource cut off in so frightful a manner was more than we could bear. Nor, indeed, were we altogether free from the apprehension of immediate danger, for the least slip or false movement would have thrown us at once within reach of these voracious fish, who frequently thrust themselves directly upon us, swimming up to leeward. No shouts or exertions on our part seemed to alarm them. Even when one of the largest was struck with an axe by Peters, and much wounded, he persisted in his attempts to push in where we were. A cloud came up at dusk, but, to our extreme anguish, passed over without discharging itself. It is quite impossible to conceive our sufferings from thirst at this period. We passed a sleepless night, both on this account and through dread of the sharks.

August 3. No prospect of relief, and the brig lying still more and more along, so that we could not maintain a footing upon deck at all. Busied ourselves in securing our wine and tortoise-meat, so that we might not lose them in the event of our rolling over. Got out two stout spikes from the forechains, and, by means of the axe, drove them into the hull to windward within a couple of feet of the water; this not being very far from the keel, as we were nearly upon our beam-ends. To these spikes we now lashed our provisions, as being more secure than their former position beneath the chains. Suffered great agony from thirst during the whole day—no chance of bathing on account of the sharks, which never left us for a moment. Found it impossible to sleep.

August 4. A little before daybreak we perceived that the hulk was heeling over, and aroused ourselves to prevent being thrown off by the movement. At first the roll was slow and gradual, and we contrived to clamber over to windward very well, having taken the precaution to leave ropes hanging from the spikes we had driven in for the provisions. But we had not calculated sufficiently upon the acceleration of the impetus; for, presently the heel became too violent to allow of our keeping pace with it; and, before either of us knew what was to happen, we found ourselves hurled furiously into the sea, and struggling several fathoms beneath the surface, with the huge hull immediately above us.

In going under the water I had been obliged to let go my hold upon the rope; and finding that I was completely beneath the vessel, and my strength utterly exhausted, I scarcely made a struggle for life, and resigned myself, in a few seconds, to die. But here again I was deceived, not having taken into consideration the natural rebound of the hull to windward. The whirl of the water upward, which the vessel occasioned in rolling partially back, brought me to the surface still more violently than I had been plunged beneath. Upon coming up, I found myself about twenty yards from the hulk, as near as I could judge. She was lying keel up, rocking furiously from side to side, and the sea in all directions around was much agitated, and full of strong whirlpools. I could see nothing of Peters. An oil-cask was floating within a few feet of me, and various other articles from the brig were scattered about.

My principal terror was now on account of the sharks, which I knew to be in my vicinity. In order to deter these, if possible, from approaching me, I splashed the water vigorously with both hands and feet as I swam towards the hulk, creating a body of foam. I have no doubt that to this expedient, simple as it was, I was indebted for my preservation; for the sea all around the brig, just before her rolling over, was so crowded with these monsters, that I must have been, and really was, in actual contact with some of them during my progress. By great good fortune, however, I reached the side of the vessel in safety, although so utterly weakened by the violent exertion I had used that I should never have been able to get upon it but for the timely assistance of Peters, who now, to my great joy, made his appearance (having scrambled up to the keel from the opposite side of the hull), and threw me the end of a rope—one of those which had been attached to the spikes.

Having barely escaped this danger, our attention was now directed to the dreadful imminency of another; that of absolute starvation. Our whole stock of provision had been swept overboard in spite of all our care in securing it; and seeing no longer the remotest possibility of obtaining more, we gave way both of us to despair, weeping aloud like children, and neither of us attempting to offer consolation to the other. Such weakness can scarcely be conceived, and to those who have never been similarly situated will, no doubt, appear unnatural; but it must be remembered that our intellects were so entirely disordered by the long course of privation and terror to which we had been subjected, that we could not justly be considered, at that period, in the light of rational beings. In subsequent perils, nearly as great, if not greater, I bore up with fortitude against all the evils of my situation, and Peters, it will be seen, evinced a stoical philosophy nearly as incredible as his present childlike supineness and imbecility—the mental condition made the difference.

The overturning of the brig, even with the consequent loss of the wine and turtle, would not, in fact, have rendered our situation more deplorable than before, except for the disappearance of the bedclothes by which we had been hitherto enabled to catch rainwater, and of the jug in which we had kept it when caught; for we found the whole bottom, from within two or three feet of the bends as far as the keel, together with the keel itself, *thickly covered with large barnacles, which proved to be excellent and highly nutritious food.* Thus, in two important respects, the accident we had so greatly dreaded proved a benefit rather than an injury; it had opened to us a supply of provisions, which we could not have exhausted, using it moderately, in a month; and it had greatly contributed to our comfort as regards position, we being much more at our ease, and in infinitely less danger, than before.

The difficulty, however, of now obtaining water blinded us to all the benefits of the change in our condition. That we might be ready to avail ourselves, as far as possible, of any shower which might fall, we took off our shirts, to make use of them as we had of the sheets—not hoping, of course, to get more in this way, even under the most favourable circumstances, than half a gill at a time. No signs of a cloud appeared during the day, and the agonies of our thirst were nearly intolerable. At night, Peters obtained about an hour's disturbed sleep, but my intense sufferings would not permit me to close my eyes for a single moment.

August 5. To-day, a gentle breeze springing up, carried us through a vast quantity of seaweed, among which we were so fortunate as to find eleven small crabs, which afforded us several delicious meals. Their shells being quite soft, we ate them entire, and found that they irritated our thirst far less than the barnacles. Seeing no trace of sharks among the seaweed, we also ventured to bathe, and remained in the water for four or five hours, during which we experienced a very sensible diminution of our thirst. Were greatly refreshed, and spent the night somewhat more comfortably than before, both of us snatching a little sleep.

August 6. This day we were blessed by a brisk and continual rain, lasting from about noon until after dark. Bitterly did we now regret the loss of our jug and carboy; for, in spite of the little means we had of catching the water, we might have filled one, if not both of them. As it was, we contrived to satisfy the cravings of thirst by suffering the shirts to become saturated, and then wringing them so as to let the grateful fluid trickle into our mouths. In this occupation we passed the entire day.

August 7. Just at daybreak we both at the same instant descried a sail to the eastward, and *evidently coming towards us!* We hailed the glorious sight with a long, although feeble shout of rapture; and began instantly to make every signal in our power, by flaring the shirt in the air, leaping as high as our weak condition would permit, and even by hallooing with all the strength of our lungs, although the vessel could not have been less than fifteen miles distant. However, she still continued to near our hulk, and we felt that, if she but held her present course, she must eventually come so close as to perceive us. In about an hour after we first discovered her, we could clearly see the people on her decks. She was a long, low, and rakish-looking topsail schooner, with a black ball in her foretopsail, and had, apparently, a full crew. We now became alarmed, for we could hardly imagine it possible that she did not observe us, and were apprehensive that she meant to leave us to perish as we were—an act of fiendish barbarity, which, however incredible it may appear, has been repeatedly perpetrated at sea, under circumstances very nearly similar, and by beings who were regarded as belonging to the human species. In this instance however, by the mercy of God, we were destined to be most happily deceived; for presently we were aware of a sudden commotion on the deck of the stranger, who immediately afterward ran up a British flag, and hauling her wind, bore up directly upon us. In half an hour more we found ourselves in her cabin. She proved to be the *Jane Guy*, of Liverpool, Captain Guy, bound on a sealing and trading voyage to the South Seas and Pacific.

The Open Boat

by STEPHEN CRANE

I

None of them knew the colour of the sky. Their eyes glanced level, and were fastened upon the waves that swept toward them. These waves were of the hue of slate, save for the tops, which were of foaming white, and all of the men knew the colours of the sea. The horizon narrowed and widened, and dipped and rose, and at all times its edge was jagged with waves that seemed thrust up in points like rocks.

Many a man ought to have a bath-tub larger than the boat which here rode upon the sea. These waves were most wrongfully and barbarously abrupt and tall, and each froth-top was a problem in small-boat navigation.

The cook squatted in the bottom and looked with both eyes at the six inches of gunwale which separated him from the ocean. His sleeves were rolled over his fat forearms, and the two flaps of his unbuttoned vest dangled as he bent to bail out the boat. Often he said: "Gawd! That was a narrow clip." As he remarked it he invariably gazed eastward over the broken sea.

The oiler, steering with one of the two oars in the boat, sometimes raised himself suddenly to keep clear of water that swirled in over the stern. It was a thin little oar and it seemed often ready to snap.

The correspondent, pulling at the other oar, watched the waves and wondered why he was there.

The injured captain, lying in the bow, was at this time buried in that profound dejection and indifference which comes, temporarily at least, to even the bravest and most enduring when, willy nilly, the firm fails, the army loses, the ship goes down. The mind of the master of a vessel is rooted deep in the timbers of her, though he commanded for a day or a decade, and this captain had on him the stern impression of a scene in the greys of dawn of seven turned faces, and later a stump of a top-mast with a white ball on it that slashed to and fro at the waves, went low and lower, and down. Thereafter there was something strange in his voice. Although steady, it was deep with mourning, and of a quality beyond oration or tears.

"Keep 'er a little more south, Billie," said he.

" 'A little more south,' sir," said the oiler in the stern.

A seat in this boat was not unlike a seat upon a bucking broncho, and, by the same token, a broncho is not much smaller. The craft pranced and reared, and plunged like an animal. As each wave came, and she rose for it, she seemed like a horse making at a fence outrageously high. The manner of her scramble over these walls of water is a mystic thing, and, moreover, at the top of them were ordinarily these problems in white water, the foam racing down from the summit of each wave, requiring a new leap, and a leap from the air. Then, after scornfully bumping a crest, she would slide, and race, and splash down a long incline, and arrive bobbing and nodding in front of the next menace.

A singular disadvantage of the sea lies in the fact that after successfully surmounting one wave you discover that there is another behind it just as important and just as nervously anxious to do something effective in the way of swamping boats. In a ten-foot dingey one can get an idea of the resources of the sea in the line of waves that is not probable to the average experience which is never at sea in a dingey. As each slaty wall of water approached, it shut all else from the view of the men in the boat, and it was not difficult to imagine that this particular wave was the final outburst of the ocean, the last effort of the grim water. There was a terrible grace in the move of the waves, and they came in silence, save for the snarling of the crests.

In the wan light, the faces of the men must have been grey. Their eyes must have glinted in strange ways as they gazed steadily astern. Viewed from a balcony, the whole thing would doubtlessly have been weirdly picturesque. But the men in the boat had no time to see it, and if they had had leisure there were other things to occupy their minds. The sun swung steadily up the sky, and they knew it was broad day because the colour of the sea changed from slate to emerald-green, streaked with amber lights, and the foam was like tumbling snow. The process of the breaking day was unknown to them. They were aware only of this effect upon the colour of the waves that rolled toward them.

In disjointed sentences the cook and the correspondent argued as to the difference between a life-saving station and a house of refuge. The cook had said: "There's a house of refuge just north of the Mosquito Inlet Light, and as soon as they see us, they'll come off in their boat and pick us up."

"As soon as who see us?" said the correspondent.

"The crew," said the cook.

"Houses of refuge don't have crews," said the correspondent. "As I understand them, they are only places where clothes and grub are stored for the benefit of shipwrecked people. They don't carry crews."

"Oh, yes, they do," said the cook.

"No, they don't," said the correspondent.

"Well, we're not there yet, anyhow," said the oiler, in the stern.

"Well," said the cook, "perhaps it's not a house of refuge that I'm thinking of as being near Mosquito Inlet Light. Perhaps it's a life-saving station."

"We're not there yet," said the oiler, in the stern.

II

As the boat bounced from the top of each wave, the wind tore through the hair of the hatless men, and as the craft plopped her stern down again the spray slashed past them. The crest of each of these waves was a hill, from the top of which the men surveyed, for a moment, a broad tumultuous expanse, shining and wind-riven. It was probably splendid. It was probably glorious, this play of the free sea, wild with lights of emerald and white and amber.

"Bully good thing it's an on-shore wind," said the cook. "If not, where would we be? Wouldn't have a show."

"That's right," said the correspondent.

The busy oiler nodded his assent.

Then the captain, in the bow, chuckled in a way that expressed humour, contempt, tragedy, all in one. "Do you think we've got much of a show now, boys?" said he.

Whereupon the three were silent, save for a trifle of hemming and hawing. To express any particular optimism at this time they felt to be childish and stupid, but they all doubtless possessed this sense of the situation in their mind. A young man thinks doggedly at such times. On the other hand, the ethics of their condition was decidedly against any open suggestion of hopelessness. So they were silent.

"Oh, well," said the captain, soothing his children, "we'll get ashore all right."

But there was that in his tone which made them think, so the oiler quoth: "Yes! If this wind holds!"

The cook was bailing: "Yes! If we don't catch hell in the surf."

Canton flannel gulls flew near and far. Sometimes they sat down on the sea, near patches of brown seaweed that rolled over the waves with a movement like carpets on a line in a gale. The birds sat comfortably in groups, and they were envied by some in the dingey, for the wrath of the sea was no more to them than it was to a covey of prairie chickens a thousand miles inland. Often they came very close and stared at the men with black bead-like eyes. At these times they were uncanny and sinister in their unblinking scrutiny, and the men hooted angrily at them, telling them to be gone. One came, and evidently decided to alight on the top of the captain's head. The bird flew parallel to the boat and did not circle, but made short sidelong jumps in the air in chicken-fashion. His black eyes were wistfully fixed upon the captain's head. "Ugly brute," said the oiler to the bird. "You look as if you were made with a jack-knife." The cook and the correspondent swore darkly at the creature. The captain naturally wished to knock it away with the end of the heavy painter; but he did not dare do it, because anything resembling an emphatic gesture would have capsized this freighted boat, and so with his open hand, the captain gently and carefully waved the gull away. After it had been discouraged from the pursuit the captain breathed easier on account of his hair, and others breathed easier because the bird struck their minds at this time as being somehow grewsome and ominous.

In the meantime the oiler and the correspondent rowed. And also they rowed.

They sat together in the same seat, and each rowed an oar. Then the oiler took both oars; then the correspondent took both oars; then the oiler; then the correspondent. They rowed and they rowed. The very ticklish part of the business was when the time came for the reclining one in the stern to take his turn at the oars. By the very last star of truth, it is easier to steal eggs from under a hen than it was to change seats in the dingey. First the man in the stern slid his hand along the thwart and moved with care, as if he were of Sèvres. Then the man in the rowing seat slid his hand along the other thwart. It was all done with the most extraordinary care. As the two sidled past each other, the whole party kept watchful eyes on the coming wave, and the captain cried: "Look out now! Steady there!"

The brown mats of sea-weed that appeared from time to time were like islands, bits of earth. They were travelling, apparently, neither one way nor the other. They were, to all intents, stationary. They informed the men in the boat that it was making progress slowly toward the land.

The captain, rearing cautiously in the bow, after the dingey soared on a great swell, said that he had seen the lighthouse at Mosquito Inlet. Presently the cook remarked that he had seen it. The correspondent was at the oars then, and for some reason he too wished to look at the lighthouse, but his back was toward the far shore and the waves were important, and for some time he could not seize an opportunity to turn his head. But at last there came a wave more gentle than the others, and when at the crest of it he swiftly scoured the western horizon.

"See it?" said the captain.

"No," said the correspondent slowly, "I didn't see anything."

"Look again," said the captain. He pointed. "It's exactly in that direction."

At the top of another wave, the correspondent did as he was bid, and this time his eyes chanced on a small still thing on the edge of the swaying horizon. It was precisely like the point of a pin. It took an anxious eye to find a lighthouse so tiny.

"Think we'll make it, Captain?"

"If this wind holds and the boat don't swamp, we can't do much else," said the captain.

The little boat, lifted by each towering sea, and splashed viciously by the crests, made progress that in the absence of seaweed was not apparent to those in her. She seemed just a wee thing wallowing, miraculously top-up, at the mercy of five oceans. Occasionally, a great spread of water, like white flames swarmed into her.

"Bail her, cook," said the captain serenely.

"All right, Captain," said the cheerful cook.

III

It would be difficult to describe the subtle brotherhood of men that was here established on the seas. No one said that it was so. No one mentioned it. But it dwelt in the boat, and each man felt it warm him. They were a captain, an oiler, a cook, and a correspondent, and they were friends, friends in a more curiously iron-bound degree than may be common. The hurt captain, lying against the water-jar in the bow, spoke always in a low voice and calmly, but he could never command a more ready and swiftly obedient crew than the motley three of the dingey. It was more than a mere recognition of what was best for the common safety. There was surely in it a quality that was personal and heartfelt. And after this devotion to the commander of the boat there was this comradeship that the correspondent, for instance, who had been taught to be cynical of men, knew even at the time was the best experience of his life. But no one said that it was so. No one mentioned it.

"I wish we had a sail," remarked the captain. "We might try my overcoat on the end of an oar and give you two boys a chance to rest." So the cook and the correspondent held the mast and spread wide the overcoat. The oiler steered, and the little boat made good way with her new rig. Sometimes the oiler had to scull sharply to keep a sea from breaking into the boat, but otherwise sailing was a success.

Meanwhile the lighthouse had been growing slowly larger. It had now almost assumed colour, and appeared like a little grey shadow on the sky. The man at the oars could not be prevented from turning his head rather often to try for a glimpse of this little grey shadow.

At last, from the top of each wave the men in the tossing boat could see land. Even as the lighthouse was an upright shadow on the sky, this land seemed but a long black shadow on the sea. It certainly was thinner than paper. "We must be about opposite New Smyrna," said the cook, who had coasted this shore often in schooners. "Captain, by the way, I believe they abandoned that life-saving station there about a year ago."

"Did they?" said the captain.

The wind slowly died away. The cook and the correspondent were not now obliged to slave in order to hold high the oar. But the waves continued their old impetuous swooping at the dingey, and the little craft, no longer under way, struggled woundily over them. The oiler or the correspondent took the oars again.

Shipwrecks are à propos of nothing. If men could only train for them and have them occur when the men had reached pink condition, there would be less drowning at sea. Of the four in the dingey none had slept any time worth mentioning for two days and two nights previous to embarking in the dingey, and in the excitement of clambering about the deck of a foundering ship they had also forgotten to eat heartily.

For these reasons, and for others, neither the oiler nor the correspondent was fond of rowing at this time. The correspondent wondered ingenuously how in the name of all that was sane could there be people who thought it amusing to row a boat. It was not an amusement; it was a diabolical punishment, and even a genius of mental aberrations could never conclude that it was anything but a horror to the muscles and a crime against the back. He mentioned to the boat in general how the amusement of rowing struck him, and the weary-faced oiler smiled in full sympathy. Previously to the foundering, by the way, the oiler had worked double-watch in the engine-room of the ship.

"Take her easy, now, boys," said the captain. "Don't spend yourselves. If we have to run a surf you'll need all your strength, because we'll sure have to swim for it. Take your time."

Slowly the land arose from the sea. From a black line it became a line of black and a line of white, trees and sand. Finally, the captain said that he could make out a house on the shore. "That's the house of refuge, sure," said the cook. "They'll see us before long, and come out after us."

The distant lighthouse reared high. "The keeper ought to be able to make us out now, if he's looking through a glass," said the captain. "He'll notify the life-saving people."

"None of those other boats could have got ashore to give word of the wreck," said the oiler, in a low voice. "Else the lifeboat would be out hunting us."

Slowly and beautifully the land loomed out of the sea. The wind came again. It had veered from the north-east to the south-east. Finally, a new sound struck the ears of the men in the boat. It was the low thunder of the surf on the shore. "We'll never be able to make the lighthouse now," said the captain. "Swing her head a little more north, Billie," said he.

" 'A little more north,' sir," said the oiler.

Whereupon the little boat turned her nose once more down the wind, and all but the oarsman watched the shore grow. Under the influence of this expansion doubt and direful apprehension was leaving the minds of the men. The management of the boat was still most absorbing, but it could not prevent a quiet cheerfulness. In an hour, perhaps, they would be ashore.

Their backbones had become thoroughly used to balancing in the boat, and they now rode this wild colt of a dingey like circus men. The correspondent thought that he had been drenched to the skin, but happening to feel in the top pocket of his coat, he found therein eight cigars. Four of them were soaked with sea-water; four were perfectly scatheless. After a search, somebody produced three dry matches, and thereupon the four waifs rode impudently in their little boat, and with an assurance of an impending rescue shining in their eyes, puffed at the big cigars and judged well and ill of all men. Everybody took a drink of water.

IV

"Cook," remarked the captain, "there don't seem to be any signs of life about your house of refuge."

"No," replied the cook. "Funny they don't see us!"

A broad stretch of lowly coast lay before the eyes of the men. It was of

dunes topped with dark vegetation. The roar of the surf was plain, and sometimes they could see the white lip of a wave as it spun up the beach. A tiny
house was blocked out black upon the sky. Southward, the slim lighthouse
lifted its little grey length.

Tide, wind, and waves were swinging the dingey northward. "Funny they
don't see us," said the men.

The surf's roar was here dulled, but its tone was, nevertheless, thunderous
and mighty. As the boat swam over the great rollers, the men sat listening to
this roar. "We'll swamp sure," said everybody.

It is fair to say here that there was not a life-saving station within twenty
miles in either direction, but the men did not know this fact, and in consequence they made dark and opprobrious remarks concerning the eyesight of
the nation's life-savers. Four scowling men sat in the dingey and surpassed
records in the invention of epithets.

"Funny they don't see us."

The light-heartedness of a former time had completely faded. To their
sharpened minds it was easy to conjure pictures of all kinds of incompetency
and blindness and, indeed, cowardice. There was the shore of the populous
land, and it was bitter and bitter to them that from it came no sign.

"Well," said the captain, ultimately, "I suppose we'll have to make a try for
ourselves. If we stay out here too long, we'll none of us have strength left to
swim after the boat swamps."

And so the oiler, who was at the oars, turned the boat straight for the shore.
There was a sudden tightening of muscles. There was some thinking.

"If we don't all get ashore—" said the captain. "If we don't all get ashore,
I suppose you fellows know where to send news of my finish?"

They then briefly exchanged some addresses and admonitions. As for the
reflections of the men, there was a great deal of rage in them. Perchance they
might be formulated thus: "If I am going to be drowned—if I am going to be
drowned—if I am going to be drowned, why, in the name of the seven mad
gods who rule the sea, was I allowed to come thus far and contemplate sand
and trees? Was I brought here merely to have my nose dragged away as I was
about to nibble the sacred cheese of life? It is preposterous. If this old ninny-
woman, Fate, cannot do better than this, she should be deprived of the management of men's fortunes. She is an old hen who knows not her intention. If
she has decided to drown me, why did she not do it in the beginning and save
me all this trouble? The whole affair is absurd. . . . But no, she cannot mean
to drown me. She dare not drown me. She cannot drown me. Not after all this
work." Afterward the man might have had an impulse to shake his fist at the
clouds: "Just you drown me, now, and then hear what I call you!"

The billows that came at this time were more formidable. They seemed
always just about to break and roll over the little boat in a turmoil of foam.
There was a preparatory and long growl in the speech of them. No mind
unused to the sea would have concluded that the dingey could ascend these

sheer heights in time. The shore was still afar. The oiler was a wily surfman. "Boys," he said swiftly, "she won't live three minutes more, and we're too far out to swim. Shall I take her to sea again, Captain?"

"Yes! Go ahead!" said the captain.

The oiler, by a series of quick miracles, and fast and steady oarsmanship, turned the boat in the middle of the surf and took her safely to sea again.

There was a considerable silence as the boat bumped over the furrowed sea to deeper water. Then somebody in gloom spoke. "Well, anyhow, they must have seen us from the shore by now."

The gulls went in slanting flight up the wind toward the grey desolate east. A squall, marked by dingy clouds, and clouds brick-red, like smoke from a burning building, appeared from the south-east.

"What do you think of those life-saving people? Ain't they peaches?"

"Funny they haven't seen us."

"Maybe they think we're out here for sport! Maybe they think we're fishin'. Maybe they think we're damned fools."

It was a long afternoon. A changed tide tried to force them southward, but wind and wave said northward. Far ahead, where coast-line, sea, and sky formed their mighty angle, there were little dots which seemed to indicate a city on the shore.

"St. Augustine?"

The captain shook his head. "Too near Mosquito Inlet."

And the oiler rowed, and then the correspondent rowed. Then the oiler rowed. It was a weary business. The human back can become the seat of more aches and pains than are registered in books for the composite anatomy of a regiment. It is a limited area, but it can become the theatre of innumerable muscular conflicts, tangles, wrenches, knots, and other comforts.

"Did you ever like to row, Billie?" asked the correspondent.

"No," said the oiler. "Hang it."

When one exchanged the rowing-seat for a place in the bottom of the boat, he suffered a bodily depression that caused him to be careless of everything save an obligation to wiggle one finger. There was cold sea-water swashing to and fro in the boat, and he lay in it. His head, pillowed on a thwart, was within an inch of the swirl of a wave crest, and sometimes a particularly obstreperous sea came in-board and drenched him once more. But these matters did not annoy him. It is almost certain that if the boat had capsized he would have tumbled comfortably out upon the ocean as if he felt sure that it was a great soft mattress.

"Look! There's a man on the shore!"

"Where?"

"There! See 'im? See 'im?"

"Yes, sure! He's walking along."

"Now he's stopped. Look! He's facing us!"

"He's waving at us!"

"So he is! By thunder!"

"Ah, now we're all right! Now we're all right! There'll be a boat out here for us in half-an hour."

"He's going on. He's running. He's going up to that house there."

The remote beach seemed lower than the sea, and it required a searching glance to discern the little black figure. The captain saw a floating stick and they rowed to it. A bath-towel was by some weird chance in the boat, and, tying this on the stick, the captain waved it. The oarsman did not dare turn his head, so he was obliged to ask questions.

"What's he doing now?"

"He's standing still again. He's looking, I think. . . . There he goes again. Towards the house . . . . Now he's stopped again."

"Is he waving at us?"

"No, not now! He was, though."

"Look! There comes another man!"

"He's running."

"Look at him go, would you."

"Why, he's on a bicycle. Now he's met the other man. They're both waving at us. Look!"

"There comes something up the beach."

"What the devil is that thing?"

"Why, it looks like a boat."

"Why, certainly it's a boat."

"No, it's on wheels."

"Yes, so it is. Well, that must be the life-boat. They drag them along shore on a wagon."

"That's the life-boat, sure."

"No, by—, it's—it's an omnibus."

"I tell you it's a life-boat."

"It is not! It's an omnibus. I can see it plain. See? One of these big hotel omnibuses."

"By thunder, you're right. It's an omnibus, sure as fate. What do you suppose they are doing with an omnibus? Maybe they are going around collecting the life-crew, hey?"

"That's it, likely. Look! There's a fellow waving a little black flag. He's standing on the steps of the omnibus. There come those other two fellows. Now they're all talking together. Look at the fellow with the flag. Maybe he ain't waving it."

"That ain't a flag, is it? That's his coat. Why certainly, that's his coat."

"So it is. It's his coat. He's taken it off and is waving it around his head. But would you look at him swing it."

"Oh, say, there isn't any life-saving station there. That's just a winter resort hotel omnibus that has brought over some of the boarders to see us drown."

"What's that idiot with the coat mean? What's he signaling, anyhow?"

"It looks as if he were trying to tell us to go north. There must be a life-saving station up there."

"No! He thinks we're fishing. Just giving us a merry hand. See? Ah, there, Willie."

"Well, I wish I could make something out of those signals. What do you suppose he means?"

"He don't mean anything. He's just playing."

"Well, if he'd just signal us to try the surf again, or to go to sea and wait, or go north, or go south, or go to hell—there would be some reason in it. But look at him. He just stands there and keeps his coat revolving like a wheel. The ass!"

"There come more people."

"Now there's quite a mob. Look! Isn't that a boat?"

"Where? Oh, I see where you mean. No, that's no boat."

"That fellow is still waving his coat."

"He must think we like to see him do that. Why don't he quit it? It don't mean anything."

"I don't know. I think he is trying to make us go north. It must be that there's a life-saving station there somewhere."

"Say, he ain't tired yet. Look at 'im wave."

"Wonder how long he can keep that up. He's been revolving his coat ever since he caught sight of us. He's an idiot. Why aren't they getting men to bring a boat out? A fishing boat—one of those big yawls—could come out here all right. Why don't he do something?"

"Oh, it's all right, now."

"They'll have a boat out here for us in less than no time, now that they've seen us."

A faint yellow tone came into the sky over the low land. The shadows on the sea slowly deepened. The wind bore coldness with it, and the men began to shiver.

"Holy smoke!" said one, allowing his voice to express his impious mood, "if we keep on monkeying out here! If we've got to flounder out here all night!"

"Oh, we'll never have to stay here all night! Don't you worry. They've seen us now, and it won't be long before they'll come chasing out after us."

The shore grew dusky. The man waving a coat blended gradually into this gloom, and it swallowed in the same manner the omnibus and the group of people. The spray, when it dashed uproariously over the side, made the voyagers shrink and swear like men who were being branded.

"I'd like to catch the chump who waved the coat. I feel like soaking him one, just for luck."

"Why? What did he do?"

"Oh, nothing, but then he seemed so damned cheerful."

In the meantime the oiler rowed, and then the correspondent rowed, and then the oiler rowed. Grey-faced and bowed forward, they mechanically, turn by turn, plied the leaden oars. The form of the lighthouse had vanished from the southern horizon, but finally a pale star appeared, just lifting from the sea. The streaked saffron in the west passed before the all-merging darkness, and the sea to the east was black. The land had vanished, and was expressed only by the low and drear thunder of the surf.

"If I am going to be drowned—if I am going to be drowned—if I am going to be drowned, why, in the name of the seven mad gods who rule the sea, was I allowed to come thus far and contemplate sand and trees? Was I brought here merely to have my nose dragged away as I was about to nibble the sacred cheese of life?"

The patient captain, drooped over the water-jar, was sometimes obliged to speak to the oarsman.

" 'Keep her head up! Keep her head up!' "

"Keep her head up,' sir." The voices were weary and low.

This was surely a quiet evening. All save the oarsman lay heavily and list-lessly in the boat's bottom. As for him, his eyes were just capable of noting the tall black waves that swept forward in a most sinister silence, save for an occasional subdued growl of a crest.

The cook's head was on a thwart, and he looked without interest at the water under his nose. He was deep in other scenes. Finally he spoke. "Billie," he murmured, dreamfully, "what kind of pie do you like best?"

V

"Pie," said the oiler and the correspondent, agitatedly. "Don't talk about those things, blast you!"

"Well," said the cook, "I was just thinking about ham sandwiches, and—"

A night on the sea in an open boat is a long night. As darkness settled finally, the shine of the light, lifting from the sea in the south, changed to full gold. On the northern horizon a new light appeared, a small bluish gleam on the edge of the waters. These two lights were the furniture of the world. Otherwise there was nothing but waves.

Two men huddled in the stern, and distances were so magnificent in the dingey that the rower was enabled to keep his feet partly warmed by thrusting them under his companions. Their legs indeed extended far under the rowing-seat until they touched the feet of the captain forward. Sometimes, despite the efforts of the tired oarsman, a wave came piling into the boat, an icy wave of the night, and the chilling water soaked them anew. They would twist their bodies for a moment and groan, and sleep the dead sleep once more, while the water in the boat gurgled about them as the craft rocked.

The plan of the oiler and the correspondent was for one to row until he lost the ability, and then arouse the other from his sea-water couch in the bottom of the boat.

The oiler plied the oars until his head drooped forward, and the overpowering sleep blinded him. And he rowed yet afterward. Then he touched a man in the bottom of the boat, and called his name. "Will you spell me for a little while?" he said, meekly.

"Sure, Billie," said the correspondent, awakening and dragging himself to a sitting position. They exchanged places carefully, and the oiler, cuddling down in the sea-water at the cook's side, seemed to go to sleep instantly.

The particular violence of the sea had ceased. The waves came without snarling. The obligation of the man at the oars was to keep the boat headed so that the tilt of the rollers would not capsize her, and to preserve her from filling when the crests rushed past. The black waves were silent and hard to be seen in the darkness. Often one was almost upon the boat before the oarsman was aware.

In a low voice the correspondent addressed the captain. He was not sure that the captain was awake, although this iron man seemed to be always awake. "Captain, shall I keep her making for that light north, sir?"

The same steady voice answered him. "Yes. Keep it about two points off the port bow."

The cook had tied a life-belt around himself in order to get even the warmth which this clumsy cork contrivance could donate, and he seemed almost stove-like when a rower, whose teeth invariably chattered wildly as soon as he ceased his labour, dropped down to sleep.

The correspondent, as he rowed, looked down at the two men sleeping under-foot. The cook's arm was around the oiler's shoulders, and, with their fragmentary clothing and haggard faces, they were the babes of the sea, a grotesque rendering of the old babes in the wood.

Later he must have grown stupid at his work, for suddenly there was a growling of water, and a crest came with a roar and a swash into the boat, and it was a wonder that it did not set the cook afloat in his life-belt. The cook continued to sleep, but the oiler sat up, blinking his eyes and shaking with the new cold.

"Oh, I'm awful sorry, Billie," said the correspondent contritely.

"That's all right, old boy," said the oiler, and lay down again and was asleep.

Presently it seemed that even the captain dozed, and the correspondent thought that he was the one man afloat on all the oceans. The wind had a voice as it came over the waves, and it was sadder than the end.

There was a long, loud swishing astern of the boat, and a gleaming trail of phosphorescence, like blue flame, was furrowed on the black waters. It might have been made by a monstrous knife.

Then there came a stillness, while the correspondent breathed with the open mouth and looked at the sea.

Suddenly there was another swish and another long flash of bluish light, and this time it was alongside the boat, and might almost have been reached with an oar. The correspondent saw an enormous fin speed like a shadow through the water, hurling the crystalline spray and leaving the long glowing trail.

The correspondent looked over his shoulder at the captain. His face was hidden, and he seemed to be asleep. He looked at the babes of the sea. They certainly were asleep. So, being bereft of sympathy, he leaned a little way to one side and swore softly into the sea.

But the thing did not then leave the vicinity of the boat. Ahead or astern, on one side or the other, at intervals long or short, fled the long sparkling streak, and there was to be heard the whiroo of the dark fin. The speed and power of the thing was greatly to be admired. It cut the water like a gigantic and keen projectile.

The presence of this biding thing did not affect the man with the same horror that it would if he had been a picnicker. He simply looked at the sea dully and swore in an undertone.

Nevertheless, it is true that he did not wish to be alone. He wished one of his companions to awaken by chance and keep him company with it. But the captain hung motionless over the water-jar, and the oiler and the cook in the bottom of the boat were plunged in slumber.

VI

"If I am going to be drowned—if I am going to be drowned—if I am going to be drowned, why, in the name of the seven mad gods who rule the sea, was I allowed to come thus far and contemplate sand and trees?"

During this dismal night, it may be remarked that a man would conclude that it was really the intention of the seven mad gods to drown him, despite the abominable injustice of it. For it was certainly an abominable injustice to drown a man who had worked so hard, so hard. The man felt it would be a crime most unnatural. Other people had drowned at sea since galleys swarmed with painted sails, but still—

When it occurs to a man that nature does not regard him as important, and that she feels she would not maim the universe by disposing of him, he at first wishes to throw bricks at the temple, and he hates deeply the fact that there are no bricks and no temples. Any visible expression of nature would surely be pelleted with his jeers.

Then, if there be no tangible thing to hoot he feels, perhaps, the desire to confront a personification and indulge in pleas, bowed to one knee, and with hands supplicant, saying: "Yes, but I love myself."

A high cold star on a winter's night is the word he feels that she says to him. Thereafter he knows the pathos of his situation.

The men in the dingey had not discussed these matters, but each had, no doubt, reflected upon them in silence and according to his mind. There was seldom any expression upon their faces save the general one of complete weariness. Speech was devoted to the business of the boat.

To chime the notes of his emotion, a verse mysteriously entered the correspondent's head. He had even forgotten that he had forgotten this verse, but it suddenly was in his mind.

> A soldier of the Legion lay dying in Algiers,
> There was lack of woman's nursing, there was dearth of woman's tears;
> But a comrade stood beside him, and he took that comrade's hand,
> And he said: "I shall never see my own, my native land."

In his childhood, the correspondent had been made acquainted with the fact that a soldier of the Legion lay dying in Algiers, but he had never regarded the fact as important. Myriads of his school-fellows had informed him of the soldier's plight, but the dinning had naturally ended by making him perfectly indifferent. He had never considered it his affair that a soldier of the Legion lay dying in Algiers, nor had it appeared to him as a matter for sorrow. It was less to him than the breaking of a pencil's point.

Now, however, it quaintly came to him as a human, living thing. It was no longer merely a picture of a few throes in the breast of a poet, meanwhile drinking tea and warming his feet at the grate; it was an actuality—stern, mournful, and fine.

The correspondent plainly saw the soldier. He lay on the sand with his feet out straight and still. While his pale left hand was upon his chest in an attempt to thwart the going of his life, the blood came between his fingers. In the far Algerian distance, a city of low square forms was set against a sky that was faint with the last sunset hues. The correspondent, plying the oars and dreaming of the slow and slower movements of the lips of the soldier, was moved by a profound and perfectly impersonal comprehension. He was sorry for the soldier of the Legion who lay dying in Algiers.

The thing which had followed the boat and waited, had evidently grown bored at the delay. There was no longer to be heard the slash of the cut-water, and there was no longer the flame of the long trail. The light in the north still glimmered, but it was apparently no nearer to the boat. Sometimes the boom of the surf rang in the correspondent's ears, and he turned the craft seaward then and rowed harder. Southward, some one had evidently built a watch-fire on the beach. It was too low and too far to be seen, but it made a shimmering, roseate reflection upon the bluff back of it, and this could be discerned from the boat. The wind came stronger, and sometimes a wave suddenly raged out like a mountain-cat, and there was to be seen the sheen and sparkle of a broken crest.

The captain, in the bow, moved on his water-jar and sat erect. "Pretty long night," he observed to the correspondent. He looked at the shore. "Those life-saving people take their time."

"Did you see that shark playing around?"

"Yes, I saw him. He was a big fellow, all right."

"Wish I had known you were awake."

Later the correspondent spoke into the bottom of the boat.

"Billie!" There was a slow and gradual disentanglement. "Billie, will you spell me?"

"Sure," said the oiler.

As soon as the correspondent touched the cold comfortable sea-water in the bottom of the boat, and had huddled close to the cook's life-belt he was deep in sleep, despite the fact that his teeth played all the popular airs. This sleep was so good to him that it was but a moment before he heard a voice call his name in a tone that demonstrated the last stages of exhaustion. "Will you spell me?"

"Sure, Billie."

The light in the north had mysteriously vanished, but the correspondent took his course from the wide-awake captain.

Later in the night they took the boat farther out to sea, and the captain directed the cook to take one oar at the stern and keep the boat facing the seas. He was to call out if he should hear the thunder of the surf. This plan enabled the oiler and the correspondent to get respite together. "We'll give those boys a chance to get into shape again," said the captain. They curled down and, after a few preliminary chatterings and trembles, slept once more the dead sleep. Neither knew they had bequeathed to the cook the company of another shark, or perhaps the same shark.

As the boat caroused on the waves, spray occasionally bumped over the side and gave them a fresh soaking, but this had no power to break their repose. The ominous slash of the wind and the water affected them as it would have affected mummies.

"Boys," said the cook, with the notes of every reluctance in his voice, "she's drifted in pretty close. I guess one of you had better take her to sea again." The correspondent, aroused, heard the crash of the toppled crests.

As he was rowing, the captain gave him some whisky-and-water, and this steadied the chills out of him. "If I ever get ashore and anybody shows me even a photograph of an oar—"

At last there was a short conversation.

"Billie . . . Billie, will you spell me?"

"Sure," said the oiler.

VII

When the correspondent again opened his eyes, the sea and the sky were each of the grey hue of the dawning. Later, carmine and gold was painted upon the waters. The morning appeared finally, in its splendour, with a sky of pure blue, and the sunlight flamed on the tips of the waves.

On the distant dunes were set many little black cottages, and a tall white windmill reared above them. No man, nor dog, nor bicycle appeared on the beach. The cottages might have formed a deserted village.

The voyagers scanned the shore. A conference was held in the boat. "Well," said the captain, "if no help is coming we might better try a run through the surf right away. If we stay out here much longer we will be too weak to do anything for ourselves at all." The others silently acquiesced in this reasoning. The boat was headed for the beach. The correspondent wondered if none ever ascended the tall wind-tower, and if then they never looked seaward. This tower was a giant, standing with its back to the plight of the ants. It represented in a degree, to the correspondent, the serenity of nature amid the struggles of the individual—nature in the wind, and nature in the vision of men. She did not seem cruel to him then, nor beneficent, nor treacherous, nor wise. But she was indifferent, flatly indifferent. It is, perhaps, plausible that a man in this situation, impressed with the unconcern of the universe, should see the innumerable flaws of his life, and have them taste wickedly in his mind and wish for another chance. A distinction between right and wrong seems absurdly clear to him, then, in this new ignorance of the grave-edge, and he understands that if he were given another opportunity he would mend his conduct and his words, and be better and brighter during an introduction or at a tea.

"Now, boys," said the captain, "she is going to swamp, sure. All we can do is to work her in as far as possible, and then when she swamps, pile out and scramble for the beach. Keep cool now, and don't jump until she swamps sure."

The oiler took the oars. Over his shoulders he scanned the surf. "Captain," he said, "I think I'd better bring her about, and keep her head-on to the seas and back her in."

"All right, Billie," said the captain. "Back her in." The oiler swung the boat then and, seated in the stern, the cook and the correspondent were obliged to look over their shoulders to contemplate the lonely and indifferent shore.

The monstrous in-shore rollers heaved the boat high until the men were again enabled to see the white sheets of water scudding up the slanted beach. "We won't get in very close," said the captain. Each time a man could wrest his attention from the rollers, he turned his glance toward the shore, and in the expression of the eyes during this contemplation there was a singular quality. The correspondent, observing the others, knew that they were not afraid, but the full meaning of their glances was shrouded.

As for himself, he was too tired to grapple fundamentally with the fact. He tried to coerce his mind into thinking of it, but the mind was dominated at this time by the muscles, and the muscles said they did not care. It merely occurred to him that if he should drown it would be a shame.

There were no hurried words, no pallor, no plain agitation. The men simply looked at the shore. "Now, remember to get well clear of the boat when you jump," said the captain.

Seaward the crest of a roller suddenly fell with a thunderous crash, and the long white comber came roaring down upon the boat.

"Steady now," said the captain. The men were silent. They turned their eyes from the shore to the comber and waited. The boat slid up the incline, leaped at the furious top, bounced over it, and swung down the long back of the wave. Some water had been shipped and the cook bailed it out.

But the next crest crashed also. The tumbling boiling flood of white water caught the boat and whirled it almost perpendicular. Water swarmed in from all sides. The correspondent had his hands on the gunwale at this time, and when the water entered at that place he swiftly withdrew his fingers, as if he objected to wetting them.

The little boat, drunken with this weight of water, reeled and snuggled deeper into the sea.

"Bail her out, cook! Bail her out," said the captain.

"All right, Captain," said the cook.

"Now, boys, the next one will do for us, sure," said the oiler. "Mind to jump clear of the boat."

The third wave moved forward, huge, furious, implacable. It fairly swallowed the dingey, and almost simultaneously the men tumbled into the sea. A piece of lifebelt had lain in the bottom of the boat and as the correspondent went overboard he held this to his chest with his left hand.

The January water was icy, and he reflected immediately that it was colder than he had expected to find it off the coast of Florida. This appeared to his dazed mind as a fact important enough to be noted at the time. The coldness of the water was sad; it was tragic. This fact was somehow so mixed and confused with his opinion of his own situation that it seemed almost a proper reason for tears. The water was cold.

When he came to the surface he was conscious of little but the noisy water. Afterward he saw his companions in the sea. The oiler was ahead in the race. He was swimming strongly and rapidly. Off to the correspondent's left, the cook's great white and corked back bulged out of the water, and in the rear the captain was hanging with his one good hand to the keel of the overturned dingey.

There is a certain immovable quality to a shore, and the correspondent wondered at it amid the confusion of the sea.

It seemed also very attractive, but the correspondent knew that it was a long journey, and he paddled leisurely. The piece of life-preserver lay under him, and sometimes he whirled down the incline of a wave as if he were on a hand-sled.

But finally he arrived at a place in the sea where travel was beset with difficulty. He did not pause swimming to inquire what manner of current had caught him, but there his progress ceased. The shore was set before him like a bit of scenery on a stage, and he looked at it and understood with his eyes each detail of it.

As the cook passed, much farther to the left, the captain was calling to him, "Turn over on your back, cook! Turn over on your back and use the oar."

"All right, sir." The cook turned on his back, and, paddling with an oar, went ahead as if he were a canoe.

Presently the boat also passed to the left of the correspondent with the captain clinging with one hand to the keel. He would have appeared like a man raising himself to look over a board fence, if it were not for the extraordinary gymnastics of the boat. The correspondent marvelled that the captain could still hold to it.

They passed on, nearer to shore—the oiler, the cook, the captain—and following them went the water-jar, bouncing gaily over the seas.

The correspondent remained in the grip of this strange new enemy—a current. The shore, with its white slope of sand and its green bluff, topped with little silent cottages, was spread like a picture before him. It was very near to him then, but he was impressed as one who in a gallery looks at a scene from Brittany or Holland.

He thought: "I am going to drown? Can it be possible? Can it be possible? Can it be possible?" Perhaps an individual must consider his own death to be the final phenomenon of nature.

But later a wave perhaps whirled him out of this small deadly current, for he found suddenly that he could again make progress toward the shore. Later still, he was aware that the captain, clinging with one hand to the keel of the dingey, had his face turned away from the shore and toward him, and was calling his name. "Come to the boat! Come to the boat!"

In his struggle to reach the captain and the boat, he reflected that when one gets properly wearied, drowning must really be a comfortable arrangement, a cessation of hostilities accompanied by a large degree of relief, and he was glad of it, for the main thing in his mind for some moments had been horror of the temporary agony. He did not wish to be hurt.

Presently he saw a man running along the shore. He was undressing with most remarkable speed. Coat, trousers, shirt, everything flew magically off him.

"Come to the boat," called the captain.

"All right, Captain." As the correspondent paddled, he saw the captain let himself down to bottom and leave the boat. Then the correspondent performed his one little marvel of the voyage. A large wave caught him and flung him with ease and supreme speed completely over the boat and far beyond it. It struck him even then as an event in gymnastics, and a true miracle of the sea. An overturned boat in the surf is not a plaything to a swimming man.

The correspondent arrived in water that reached only to his waist, but his condition did not enable him to stand for more than a moment. Each wave knocked him into a heap, and the under-tow pulled at him.

Then he saw the man who had been running and undressing, and undressing and running, come bounding into the water. He dragged ashore the cook, and then waded towards the captain, but the captain waved him away, and sent him to the correspondent. He was naked, naked as a tree in winter, but a halo was about his head, and he shone like a saint. He gave a strong pull, and a long drag, and a bully heave at the correspondent's hand. The correspondent, schooled in the minor formulae, said: "Thanks, old man." But suddenly the man cried: "What's that?" He pointed a swift finger. The correspondent said: "Go."

In the shallows, face downward, lay the oiler. His forehead touched sand that was periodically, between each wave, clear of the sea.

The correspondent did not know all that transpired afterward. When he achieved safe ground he fell, striking the sand with each particular part of his body. It was as if he had dropped from a roof, but the thud was grateful to him.

It seems that instantly the beach was populated with men with blankets, clothes, and flasks, and women with coffee-pots and all the remedies sacred to their minds. The welcome of the land to the men from the sea was warm and generous, but a still and dripping shape was carried slowly up the beach, and the land's welcome for it could only be the different and sinister hospitality of the grave.

When it came night, the white waves paced to and fro in the moonlight, and the wind brought the sound of the great sea's voice to the men on shore, and they felt that they could then be interpreters.

The Landsman's Tale

by FRANK STOCKTON

Into a little town on the New England coast there came, one day in mild October weather, a quiet man without an object; at least, this was the opinion of the villagers.

This opinion was not formed until the stranger had lived for five or six days in their midst, having lodgings at the inn, but spending his days and even parts of his evenings in the open air—sometimes in the village streets, sometimes in the surrounding country, and very often on the sands and among the rocks of the ocean beach.

It was his manner of spending his time which proved that he was a man without an object. At first it was supposed that he was an artist—so many wandering strangers are artists; but he never sketched, and it did not appear that he had brought with him even an umbrella or a camp-stool. He had probably not come for his health, for he seemed in good physical condition. And he had not come for the usual seaside society, for it was not the time of the year for that; all the summer boarders had gone, and there was no one left in the little village but the regular inhabitants thereof. The water was now too cold for sea-bathing, and, besides, he had casually mentioned that he did not care for that sort of thing. And, what was stranger than all, he had not come there to sail upon the ocean.

Several times it had been proposed to him that he should go out in one of the numerous cat-boats or sloops which were idly lying at anchor in the little bay, for in the middle of the day the weather was just as good for a sail as it had been in August or September. But only once did the stranger heed such suggestions, and then he hired the best boat in the bay, which was sailed by one of the oldest skippers, assisted by a weather-beaten mariner, and it may be therefore supposed that it was very well sailed. Whether the stranger liked the little excursion or not, it was impossible for the skipper to say. He had expressed no opinion on the subject, either while he was in the boat or after he landed; but as he did not go out again during his stay in the village, it was generally believed that he had not liked it.

It might have been supposed that he came to this quiet little place for the sake of living cheaply, had it not been for the fact that he occupied the largest and most expensive room at the hotel, and that, being the only lodger at the inn, he ordered the best living that the landlord could procure for him, and at dinner-time indulged in the unusual extravagance of a glass or two of wine.

So it was not long before the villagers made up their minds that the quiet man at the inn was without an object. As he cared for nothing which they or their village could offer him, it was plain enough that he had no reason for coming there. But the investigations and consultations of the villagers had a positive as well as a negative result. They proved, without the shadow of a doubt, that this person was a thorough landsman. He did not seem to care for the ocean or anything connected with it; and on the one occasion when he had gone out in a boat it was manifest to the skipper and to the mariner who was with him that this stranger knew nothing whatever about navigation, about boats, about sails, about sheets, or even about a tiller.

He did not seem to mind the motion of the waves, but it was remarked, when the subject was discussed that evening, that it was very probable that he did not know enough about the ocean to be aware that people unaccustomed to it were made to feel badly when the sea was rough, and on that day it had been a little rough.

The stranger now occupied a peculiar position in the village: he was the only landsman therein. All the men in the place were nautical, in some degree or other, and there was not one of them over thirty years of age who was not called captain. They had not all commanded a vessel, but it would have been considered discourteous in that region to cast upon a man old enough to be a captain the imputation that he had not attained that distinction. Not to be able to sail a boat would have been considered in a citizen of the village a condition of denser ignorance than inability to read.

But, of course, conditions were different in the case of a thorough landsman: he would not know anything about the sea, but he might know something about the land, and in the inferior sphere in which he moved he might hold a very fair position. Consequently, when it was agreed that the man at the inn was an out-and-out landsman, he rose in the esteem of the villagers. To be sure, he did not know anything about the sea, but then he did not pretend to know anything; such a man they had never seen before.

Many men had come down there in the summertime who, although they did not know the difference between a sliding keel and a shuffleboard, hitched up their trousers, walked with a rolling gait, wore little caps with visors, and were perfectly willing to take the helm if they should find any one fool enough to let them do it. These men had always been looked upon with the contempt proper to their pretensions. But here was a man who pretended nothing: a good, honest, square, outright, unvarnished landsman. As such they recognized him, and as such they gave him a position—not a very high one, but one they believed he deserved.

When the season for seaside visitors was over, and when the evenings were cold, it was the custom of some of the captains of the village to gather, after supper, in the large room of the inn, and to sit around the great fireplace to smoke and to talk; and now the landsman often found it pleasant to sit there and listen to them as he smoked his cigar. He was not much of a talker, but he was a very good listener, and for this the captains liked him. It often happened that when an old skipper told a tale of adventures in far-away seas, and told it ostensibly to the assembled company, he really told it to the landsman; and all the rest knew it, and the more evidently such tales were directed at the landsman, and the better they were adapted to his want of comprehension of nautical subjects, the better they were liked by the rest of the assembled company.

One evening there was a public meeting in the large room of the inn, composed not only of the captains of the place, but of their wives, their daughters, and their sisters. This had been called together for the purpose of considering the establishment of a library in the village. The captains, old and young, as well as their wives and daughters, were always glad to have something to read during the long evenings of winter, and as their stock of reading matter was very limited, and as they had heard a great deal about village libraries from their summer visitors, they had now determined to establish a little library for themselves. So this meeting was called, and it was hoped that it might result in encouraging subscriptions.

The landlord of the inn, who had taken part in public meetings elsewhere, was called upon to preside, and the exercises consisted in speeches from the more prominent captains present. These speeches were all of the same character; they had the same object, and they were constructed on the same general plan. They recounted the speaker's love of reading, which always began in his boyhood; they told how difficult it had been for him to get access to books; and how he had always longed for first-class, A No. 1, copper-fastened literature; and they all ended with remarks on the great advantages of an institution which should supply reading matter to nautical people, and of the peculiar need of their own village for such an institution.

These speeches, most of them autobiographical to an extent not required by the subject, were listened to with great attention, and when every captain who desired to speak had spoken, it was evident that the audience would be pleased with a continuation of the interesting proceedings.

With this idea in his mind the landlord stood up and glanced toward the landsman. "There is a gentleman present," he said, "who is not a seafaring person and for that reason is not likely to feel as we do about the needs of mariners and their families for books; but he may be able to say something on the subject which will be useful, and perhaps he may get from what has happened to him in his inland life a point or two which may come in well upon an occasion like this. It may be that some of us mariners have got into the way of thinking that this world is all water—that is, all the parts that are good for much; but that isn't the right way of thinking: there are plenty of things which have happened on land that are well worth hearing about. So, if the gentleman would not mind, I am sure we would all be very glad to have him say something to us, something which may come in with the general drift of the public feeling in this village in the direction of a library."

All eyes were now directed toward the landsman, who, without hesitation, rose in his place.

"Mr. Chairman," said he, "I am very willing to make some remarks upon this occasion, but I should prefer not to divert the very interesting and instructive current in which the proceedings of this evening have been flowing. I therefore ask that you will allow me to tell you, instead of a story of the land, which would not harmonize with the tenor of the narrations to which we have listened with such pleasure this evening, a story of the sea."

At this everybody stared in surprise. What could this landsman know about the sea? Of course he might have heard of something which happened at sea, but how could he repeat it? That would be as if one of their townsmen should overhear a couple of Welshmen talking in their native tongue and should endeavor to give the points of their conversation. It was odd, truly, that this landsman should want to tell a sea story, but for that very reason everybody wanted to hear it.

"It was some time ago," the landsman said, "exactly how long I cannot state, that a good-sized schooner was sailing on the Pacific Ocean. It was an American schooner, and was manned by a crew of ten thoroughbred seamen, a captain, and a boy. I don't know to what port this schooner was bound, but I think it very likely she was going to the Sandwich Islands; nor do I know what her cargo was, but that would be of no interest to us.

"Her crew were all respectable mariners; on such a vessel a foreigner would have been decidedly out of place. These men cared not only for their bodies, but for their minds. They would not have been satisfied with enough to eat and to drink, good clothes to wear, and not too much work to do; they must have more than this: they must have food for the mind—they must have reading matter. Every one of them, including the captain and the boy, was fond of books.

"It may well be supposed that a crew with tastes of that sort would not start out of port without taking along, among their other stores, a store of books; and so this schooner had on board a library. This was a very small one, and was contained in a portable bookcase not much larger than a soap-box; but the books were all in small type,—for a sailor who has not good eyes can't be much of a sailor,—and as it takes a long time to read a book at sea, where there are so many interruptions in the way of watches and storms and meals and going to the masthead to look out for whales and sails, the contents of the little portable bookcase had never failed to give the crew all the reading matter they wanted, no matter how long a voyage might be. Even if a rapid reader had got through with the whole of them before the schooner reached the port to which she was bound, he would have been very willing to begin again and read them all the second time, for they were good books. Consequently great care was taken of this portable library, and whenever there was rough weather the doors of the little bookcase were battened down, so that the precious volumes should not be tumbled out."

At this some of the captains looked at each other. It was all right to batten down hatches when there was a storm, but nobody ever battened down the doors of a bookcase; however, this person was a landsman.

"They had been sailing," the speaker continued, "for some weeks, and, as there had been many calms, the men had had unusual opportunities for reading, and all of them had become very much interested in the books they had in hand. This state of things was pleasant, although not profitable; but it soon came to an end, for one morning just after breakfast a violent wind arose, and soon became so strong that the captain was quite sure that a tornado or a hurricane would soon be upon them. He gave orders to take in all the sails; but before this could be done one of the small ones in front was blown entirely away from the ropes which held it, and went whirling out to sea, far in advance of the vessel.

"The wind came from the south, and therefore the schooner was soon scudding along under bare poles as if she intended to dash through the water to the region of the polar bears, and, as the captain had expected, this wind-storm grew into a hurricane, and the masts of the schooner, although they were good ones, could not stand it. First the topmast of the foremast went; then the other topmast followed; then the thicker part of the masts snapped off one after the other, just about the middle, and, jerking themselves loose from the rope ladders and all the cords which held them, they went off through the air as if they had been birds, and none of them touched water until they had gone at least a mile ahead.

"Now the booms, which held the two large sails wrapped up upon them, blew away from the half-masts on which they swung, and went up into the air; and the violence of the wind was such that the little cords which held the sails to the booms were broken, and the sails spread out like great kites, and higher and higher they went up into the air, until they seemed like little white specks against the black, tempestuous sky.

"Now the ends of the masts which had been left standing broke off with a great crack and disappeared as suddenly as if each one of them had been the flame of a candle when it is blown out, and after them the bowsprit was wrenched from its fastenings and hurled forward like a javelin cast into the wild waste ahead."

At this point the captains, who had been listening with eager interest, looked at each other, and the landsman noticed it.

"That may seem somewhat strange," he said, "but this wind was now acquiring the character of an irregular cyclone, and as it passed the schooner its corkscrew-like movements drew out the bowsprit as if it had been the stopper from a bottle. And now the small boats, which had been so firmly fastened to the irons which held them like pots suspended from an old-fashioned crane in a fireplace, upheaved themselves and blew away; and when this happened the heart of each one of the crew, including the captain and the boy, sank as if it had been the lead on a line. But there was no need for such mental depression, for those sailors soon saw that they would have been no better off in such a storm as that with the boats than without them.

"There were two of these boats, a long-boat and a shorter one, and the crew gazed with amazement at their behavior. The boats were in front of them, not very far away, and for a time did not seem to be blown along any faster than the schooner; but their motions were wonderful. First the long-boat rose high in the air, then it turned bow down and stern up and plunged into the ocean, dipping up a boatful of water, and, rising again into the air, turned completely over, upsetting its whole load of water upon the other boat, which was just beneath it. This made the shorter boat sink; but it soon came up some distance ahead, and flew into the air, followed hard by the long-boat, which seemed to be trying to bump it.

"The two rose and fell together, sometimes high, sometimes low, the long-boat always in pursuit of the shorter boat, like a hawk after a pigeon, until at last they came together, with their hollow parts toward each other like the two shells of a clam. The shock was so great that they burst into fragments with a great noise, as if they had exploded, and little pieces of them scattered themselves over the sea like hail. To think of their fate had they been in those boats was enough to make that crew shiver.

"Now the wind grew stronger and stronger. It was a real, full-grown tornado, and every man of the crew, including the captain and the boy, was obliged to lie flat upon the deck and hold on to some ring or bar to keep himself from being blown away. They did this none too soon, for in a few minutes the wind began to blow the bulwarks off that schooner, and if the stern-rail had not lifted itself a little as it flew over the schooner and out ahead, it would have wiped every man off that deck as neatly as you would peel the skin from a banana."

The captains did not look at each other now, but they stared steadfastly at the landsman. Even their wives, their daughters, and their sisters were impressed with the intensity of the storm that was being described. Their nerves were in a state of tension; if one of their hair-pins had dropped, it would have startled them.

"On went that schooner," continued the landsman, "faster and faster, before that awful, howling, shrieking wind. It seemed as if the waves behind were yelling to the waves in front to turn and stop the flying vessel so that they might leap on board. The captain, flat on his face on the deck, kept his hand upon the helm, and so steered the schooner that she sped straight forward over the waves and before the wind. Now the whole ocean was boiling under the hot fury of the tempest, and great waves seemed to rise perpendicularly out of the depths, and one of these, coming up under the schooner, lifted her stern high into the air. This was only for a moment, but it was an eventful one, for the wild blast struck the rudder, now exposed to its fury, and tore it from the stern as if it had been the stem of a strawberry. Over the sea now skipped that rudder, as a stone from the hand of a boy skims and jumps over the smooth surface of a mill-pond.

"Now, of course, the schooner could be no longer directed or controlled. On she still went before the maddened gale, but not as before,—bows in front and stern behind,—but sometimes stern foremost, sometimes whirling around like a top, sometimes brushing broadside over the waves as if she were trying to smooth them down. On, on, still on she plunged and dashed and spun, until the men clinging to her deck were sometimes almost dizzy with the motion; but still the heart of the captain did not falter. 'Hold on, my men,' he cried, whenever the roaring tempest would allow him to be heard; 'we have yet a good hull beneath us, and the wind may fall.'

"But now a terrible thing happened. The schooner was down in the trough of the sea, and as she rose, a fierce blast, blowing close to the surface of the water, struck her broadside and turned her over upon her beam-ends—so far over, indeed, that the men clung to the deck as if they had been hanging against the side of a perpendicular wall. She went over still farther, and every one felt that she was going to capsize entirely. Just at this moment there came over the sea the wildest and most furious blast that had yet blown, and in one mad whiff it blew off the keel of that schooner."

As the landsman now gazed in the faces of his audience, it seemed as if each one of the captains had been transformed into a wooden image. With open eyes, with close-closed lips, and without a sign of emotion upon their rigid faces, they sat and listened. In the eyes of some of the women were tears; others had their mouths open. The landsman paused for a few seconds, and then continued:

"That schooner did not capsize. As soon as her keel was gone she righted, and went plunging, bounding, whirling, northward. But the wind had done its worst. There was nothing about that vessel which could be blown away except the crew, and they stuck so close to the deck that the wind passed over them as if they had been mere knobs or pimples on the surface of the vessel.

"Having done its worst, the wind did really begin to fall, and the storm passed away almost as suddenly as it had risen, and before long the hull of the schooner was rising and falling and rolling on the great swells which had followed the tempest. Now the crew could sit up and look about them; but there wasn't much to look at, for everything of wood or iron which had projected from the hull of that schooner had been blown away.

"The captain folded his arms and considered the case. It was a hard thing for him to make up his mind to desert his vessel. Under ordinary circumstances he would have rigged up some sort of a rudder; he would have made some sort of a mast; he would have hoisted sails, even if they had been table-cloths and sheets—he would have endeavored to make his way to the nearest port. But now it was of no use for him to try to do any of these things. You all know as well as he did that when a vessel has lost her keel in the ocean, the time has come to give her up.

"So the captain addressed his crew. 'My men' he said, we must leave this vessel; her keel is gone, and she is of no further use. Down below, with our freight, there is a boat which was shipped in sections; it is a hunting-boat, which can be taken apart and carried over the land when necessary. Of course this boat does not belong to us, but under the circumstances we are warranted in using it. We will get this boat on deck and put it together; there are oars belonging to it, and in it we will row away to the nearest land. Of course I don't know how near such land may be, and I can't take any observations now;

but by dead reckoning, and I have been doing a good deal of this since I have been lying here on the deck, I think I have a fair idea where we are. We sailed on pretty near the same line of latitude from the time I took my observation yesterday until the storm struck us this morning, and then I dead-reckoned that that wind must have been blowing at the rate of sixty miles an hour, and, although it could not carry us along as fast as that, it must have taken us thirty-five miles an hour, and so in the five hours in which it blew we must have sailed northward one hundred and seventy-five miles.

"'Now, according to the chart as I remember it, there are some desert islands about forty-five miles to the northeast of us, and it will not be difficult for us to row to them in that boat. So, my men, let us get to work and launch her.'

"The men sprang up with a will, and in a short time the boat was hauled up on deck, put together, and lowered to the water.

"The crew of the schooner now got down into the boat, and as they did so it seemed doubtful to the captain whether or not the little hunting-craft would hold them all; but they crowded in until they were all aboard except the captain, who, of course, would be the last to leave his ship. They were packed tightly together, barely leaving room for the oarsmen to move their arms; but there was still a vacant space at the stern which had been left for the captain.

"But this good man, instead of descending, stood on the edge of the deck and looked down into the boat.

"'Hurry, captain,' said the first mate, 'and come down; we have got a good way to row, and we ought to be starting; there is room for you here.'

"'I see that,' said the captain, 'and I have been considering that vacant space. Hold on a few moments; I will be with you directly.'

"Now the captain hurried down into the hold, but soon reappeared, carrying under each arm a box. These he placed on the edge of the deck and stood between them.

"'My men,' 'he said, addressing the crew, 'I have calculated that if I sit with my knees drawn up there is room in that boat for one of these boxes; and as that is all the additional load which the boat can carry, it will not be possible to put both boxes into her. Now one of these is a box I have always kept packed, to be used in a case of emergency like this; it contains condensed food of various kinds, sufficient to last us all for some days. As to water, I don't think we shall suffer for that, for I see it is going to rain. The other box is our portable library; it contains our precious books. Now, my men, we can take but one of these boxes, and I leave it to you to decide which it shall be. Please come to an agreement among yourselves as quickly as possible, and I will lower down to you one of the boxes and then get in myself.'

"The men in the boat now held a consultation; it was an earnest one, but did not last long. The first mate rose in his place and spoke for the others.

"'Captain,' said he, 'we have made up our minds. If it is only forty-five miles to the nearest land, we can easily row that far without eating. When we reach the island, even if it should be a desert one, it is not unlikely that we shall find some sort of food,—berries, birds, or breadfruit,—and almost certainly some fish in the adjacent water; but there is no reason to suppose that upon such islands we shall find books. Therefore, we have unanimously agreed that we will take with us our library. There's not a man among us who is not interested in a story or in a historical volume, and to leave our books behind would be a wrench, Captain, which, in all deference to your opinion, if it be otherwise, we truly think we ought not to be obliged to give ourselves.'

"In a faltering voice the captain spoke. 'My men,' said he, 'you have chosen wisely; I will lower the library to the boat.'

"When this had been done, he got down himself, and the boat pushed off from the hull of the schooner and rowed away to the northeast."

The speaker ceased. For a moment there was absolute silence in the room, but on the face of every captain there seemed to be a shadow which grew darker and darker as grows the sky before a storm.

The landsman, who appeared to be possessed of a certain amount of weather wisdom, advanced toward the chairman of the meeting. "I have told my little tale," said he, "and now allow me to make this contribution to your library fund, and to bid you good evening."

Laying a bank-note on the table before the presiding officer, he bowed and withdrew; after which, without any motion being made to that effect, the meeting adjourned.

There was a great deal of talking as the people went home. Some of the captains who were in the habit of refraining from swearing in the presence of their wives, their daughters, and their sisters, now swerved from their usual custom.

"Do you suppose," said Captain Ephraim Smolley to Captain Daniel Yates, "that that confounded fool came here for nothing else than to get the chance to spin us that all-fired yarn?"

"Dunno," said Captain Daniel; "but as there wasn't nothin' else that he could have come for, it must have been that."

Miss Amelia Brindley, a young woman with a high color and a quick step, who was to be the librarian of the library when it should be founded, said to her mother when she got home: "What nettles me most is not thinking of the story he told to us to-night, but thinking of the story he is going to tell about us when he goes somewhere else; they say he has ordered himself driven to the cars early in the morning."

My Rescue from the *Titanic*

by WILLIAM INGLIS

Saved from the wreck of the Titanic *in a way so casual as to seem miraculous, Henry Sleeper Harper told me, soon after he came ashore, the following astonishing story of his experiences—a story probably unique in the history of maritime narratives. A keen and competent observer, this narrator, who never loses his mental balance, has been familiar with the sea since boyhood, and often crossed the Atlantic. His story was told in response to a few questions. Things he had not actually seen and heard he would neither affirm nor deny. Here is his narrative:*

I was fast asleep when the *Titanic* struck, for I had been kept in my stateroom by tonsillitis ever since coming aboard the ship. Our stateroom was pretty well forward on the starboard side and was perhaps thirty feet or more above the water. I remember that the sea was quite smooth when we went to sleep. As to how fast the ship was going I have no knowledge.

I am inclined to believe the statements of many passengers that the *Titanic* was going at the pace of twenty-three knots an hour when she ran over the submerged edge of the berg that ripped a long gash in her bottom and sank her. My first knowledge about it was that of being awakened by a grinding sound that seemed to come from far below our deck. It was not a loud crash; it was felt almost as much as heard. But years before I had been in a ship that ran over a reef and was sunk, and I remembered that the impact and thrill then were so slight that I thought we were simply running over a fishing-smack that bumped and scraped under our keel. So the moment I was awakened by the noise and heard the same sort of sound I sat up in bed and looked out of the nearest port.

I saw an iceberg only a few feet away, apparently racing aft at high speed and crumbling as it went. I knew right away what that meant.

"Get dressed quickly," I told my wife. "We must go on deck."

"Wait," she replied. "I'll ask Mrs.—— across the way if she has heard any word."

"You haven't a moment for talk," I insisted. "Get dressed—at once."

She dressed much faster than I did, for I was pretty weak from my sickness, and she hurried to the stateroom of the ship's doctor.

"I wish you'd speak to my husband," she said. "He insists upon going on deck and he won't mind me."

The doctor came in and ordered me to undress and go back to bed. He said he was sure there was nothing serious.

"Damn it, man," I told him, "this ship has hit an iceberg! How can you say there's nothing serious?"

I'm sorry now that I cussed him out, but it made me hot to hear him make little of such a grave danger.

"Well, stay here awhile," he said, "and I'll see what's up." He was gone only a few moments, and then popped his head in at my door.

"They tell me the trunks are floating around in the hold," he said. "You may as well go on deck."

So I put on my overcoat and my wife put on her fur coat and we started up. I suppose this was a quarter of an hour after the ship struck, for we were completely dressed as if we were going ashore—shoes all laced up and tied, and all that sort of thing.

We walked very slowly up the steps of the big stairways, for I was pretty weak, and when we got to the next deck above I sat down on a lounge and rested five or six minutes. Then we climbed up to the next deck, and so on. At last we got up to the gymnasium, which was on the top deck, and I sat down beside my wife. Men and women were standing about in groups talking. I have heard some talk since about excitement, but I saw none then. Everybody seemed confident that the ship was all right. She certainly *seemed* all right. The engines had been stopped soon after we struck and by this time she had slowly lost headway and was standing still. The sea was quiet, a flat calm, but all the ship's lights were lit and there was not a suggestion of excitement anywhere. A few people were talking about the life-boats, but they were laughed at.

"Life-boats!" said a woman near me. "What do they need of life-boats? This ship could smash a hundred icebergs and not feel it. Ridiculous!"

After a little time, word was passed among the passengers that we'd better go back to bed.

"The ship will be delayed two hours," the stewards said, "and then go on to New York."

At this a great many people went away from our neighborhood. Whether they went back to bed or not I don't know; but I can't remember seeing their faces again. They dropped away a few at a time—casually drifted off. Funny thing to remember how they scattered here and there—two or three crossing over from one group to another and two or three going from that group to still another. They all seemed curious, not a bit anxious. The reassurance that the ship would be delayed only two hours seemed to satisfy the curiosity of most of them, though, and the crowds soon dwindled. However, there were still a few dozens of us left, in our neighborhood, on the upper deck.

Perhaps a quarter of an hour later word was passed that we'd better put on life-preservers. Some people put on the life-belts and others laughed at them. Then came a long wait. I was surprised that there was no officer in sight to direct people where to go or to warn them or reassure them. We were left to ourselves. It was rather like a stupid picnic where you don't know anybody and wonder how soon you can get away from such a boresome place. I couldn't help wondering what had become of all the fine sea discipline I had heard and read about so much. I said to myself: These steamship men are hotel-keepers rather than sailor-men. They hear there are icebergs ahead, and instead of swinging out of their way they simply turn on more steam as a hotel man would do with a cold-wave coming, and then go plunging right into the iceberg. They hit an iceberg and then tell their guests they'd better go back to bed. I was pretty sore by that time, and I think any one would be who knows anything about seafaring.

Not long after the passengers began telling one another that we were ordered to put on life-preservers, stewards came around our neighborhood and began calling out: "All women to go to the lower deck!" Some women went. Others were escorted down the companionway by their husbands. I take it that they all understood, as we certainly did, that the women were to be kept together there ready to be sent off in the first boats if it should become necessary to abandon the ship. My wife and I said nothing to each other, but simply sat still and waited.

Presently a number of stewards and other men of the ship's company began to fuss with the tackle of a couple of life-boats near where we were on the upper deck. I say "fuss" with them, but I might as well say "make a mess of them." They seemed quite unused to handling boat gear. They took away a section of the deck rail near each boat and then climbed into the boat and hoisted away on the falls so as to swing the boat clear on the davits and let her down so that the gunwale was flush with the deck. We passengers still remaining on the deck gathered around and watched the men at work. Very slowly, and stumbling here and there, the people began to get in. It was like stepping down, say, from this table to the chair alongside. We took a look at both boats. My wife thought the one farther off was better because there would be hardly a dozen people left to go in it after the big boat beside us was filled. I looked them both over, saw that the farther boat had no watertight compartments in it while the one near had; so I said: "No; let's take this. It will float longest."

With that I handed my wife down into the nearer, bigger boat, and she comfortably seated herself on a thwart. Other women and other men climbed aboard. An old dragoman of mine who had come with me from Alexandria— because he wanted "to see the country all the crazy Americans came from," as he explained it—made his way into the unfamiliar boat and settled himself. He made himself quite at home. Four or five stokers or some such men came along and jumped into the boat at the forward end. The sailor who seemed to be in charge of the boat laughed a little.

"Huh!" he said; "I suppose I ought to go and get my gun and stop this." But he did not go and get any gun, and neither did he order the stokers out. Everybody seemed to take what was happening as a matter of course and there wasn't a word of comment.

I stepped in and sat down among the stokers. There was no one in sight on the decks. I had on my arm a little brown Pekingese spaniel we had picked up in Paris and named Sun Yat Sen in honor of his country's first President. The little dog kept very quiet. I found out, after boarding the *Carpathia*, that several dogs had been rescued in the same way in the early boats. There seemed to be lots of room, and nobody made any objection. The sailor who seemed to be in charge ordered, "Lower away!" The gang at each end of the boat began to pay out the boat-falls, so that our life-boat went down, first by the head, then by the stern, in a series of jerks. Lower by machinery? Not an inch—so far as I saw. It was all done by hand, and very clumsily done. If there had been any sea running, I feel sure our boat would have been smashed against the ship's side. A boat that had descended fifteen or twenty feet was hailed by a man on the upper deck—a second-class passenger, an Australian going out to America to see his mother, it transpired later. He leaned out over the edge and called: "Hey! Will you take me in that boat?"

"No," said the man who seemed to be in charge.

"But you've lots of room in your boat," the man on deck insisted.

"Yes," replied the sailor, "but we're too far down now for you to jump in. You'd hurt yourself."

"Yes; but I can slide down the ropes," the passenger answered.

"Very well. Come on," the sailor agreed. Whereupon the crew ceased lowering, and the passenger twined arms and legs around the falls, slid down to the boat, said, "Thanks," and sat down. More lowering by fits and starts, and at last our boat was afloat. Then we had more trouble—they didn't know how to cast loose the tackle. They fussed and fiddled, and the life-boat grated up against the ship's black hull for minutes. Just imagine how we'd have pounded to pieces if there had been any sort of sea running!

Somehow or other they got her clear at last, and the four men at the oars began to row. And such rowing! You've seen the young man who hires a boat on Central Park lake on Sunday and tries to show off? Well, about like that—skying the oar on every recover, burying the blade on the pull or missing it altogether. There was only one man in the four who knew how to row. The steering was worse. The four oarsmen paddled as briskly as they could, and our boat, with, say, some forty people in it, began to move away from the ship, slowly but not surely. For the man at the tiller would pull it toward himself for a while and send her around to port, or push the tiller away and swerve her around to starboard.

"Ow!" he exclaimed; "let's get on. There'll be a big wave when she goes under—ow! a terrible big wave!—so let's get out of her way!"

But the poor fellow was so anxious to escape from the neighborhood of the *Titanic* that he kept steering in half-circles or worse. At last he headed the boat clear around so that her bow was pointed straight toward the ship. I couldn't stand that.

"Here!" I cried, "do you want to run the ship down? I guess you may have steered with a wheel, but surely you've never handled a tiller. Shove the tiller the opposite to the way you want to go, and you'll be all right."

He got her straightened out then, and our poor crew paddled very slowly away from the *Titanic*. I suppose by this time it must have been about one o'clock in the morning. There was a very little bit of the moon in the sky—the last quarter, I suppose. The water was smooth as a lake, not a piece of ice anywhere except the big iceberg that had wrecked us, far astern; and at every stroke of the oars great glares of greenish-yellow phosphorescent light would swirl aft from the blades and drip in globules like fire from the oars as they swung forward. The phosphorescence was so brilliant that it almost dazzled us at first. I have never seen it so fine.

As we drew away from the *Titanic* she was brightly lighted as ever and not a sound came from her. I have heard since coming ashore about rioting and shooting, but throughout the whole incident I did not hear a shot fired or a loud voice. Of course, there may have been something like this as the later boats were loaded, but there was nothing like it in our vicinity. We seemed deserted on our part of the deck before launching our life-boat, and I guess whatever violence there was happened on the lower deck to which the women were ordered some time before we left.

Nor did I see much of a list in the ship's body as I looked at her from the boat. She seemed a little down by the head, but as we moved away from her she looked like a great mountain of strength that would last forever. Her lights were all burning as it seemed to us, and she made a wonderful picture. The air was so clear that we could see plainly such details as her rails and bits of the rigging, standing out like lines in an engraving. We were lying off perhaps a quarter of a mile from her when I heard several bursts of cheering. I suppose that was when the people on board received the news by wireless that other ships were hurrying to the rescue.

After an hour or more—I had no way of seeing the exact time, but it seemed very long—the lights of the *Titanic* suddenly went out and we began to think her end could not be very far away. I have heard a lot of talk about explosions in the *Titanic;* that her boilers blew up and tore her body apart. I certainly heard nothing that sounded like an explosion. I did hear a great roar mingled with hissing coming from the direction of the ship. I supposed that this was caused by the sea-water rising in the hull high enough to put out the fires under the boilers. Water thus heated would hardly make boilers explode, I should think. No one in our boat said a word, but I feel sure the seriousness of the situation began to depress everybody. Very slowly the giant black hull began to diminish against the skyline. It was a frightful thing to feel that the ship was going, faster and faster, and that we could do nothing for the people on her. Not a sound came from the ship until the very last, and then there rose in the air a sort of wild maniacal chorus, a mingling of cries and yells in which I could distinguish voices of different tones. Many of the people, I fear, had gone mad as they felt the ship settle for her final plunge to the depths. No one gave any command, but our crew began to row as hard as they could away from the awful sounds, and then in the twinkling of an eye we were all alone on the dark sea. There was no talking in our boat, nothing but the rattling of the oars in the rowlocks. But the air still resounded with the long-drawn wail of agony that rose from the ship. These were the most awful moments in the whole experience. Bravery was shown by the people in every phase of the emergency; but flesh and blood could not withstand that gasping cry of horror as the sea rose to them. After a time our boat passed out of reach of the cry and we were alone indeed.

One sailor called to another: "Did you put the plugs in the bottom of this boat before she was launched?"

"Well," the other replied, meditating, "I'm sure I put in one plug an' I *hope* I put in both, for I don't feel any water about our feet."

Either the men didn't know where to look or they couldn't grope their way among the passengers to find out; but we found out later that both plugs were in place. After a long silence some one cried out that there was a green light dead ahead.

"Must be the starboard light of a fishing-smack," another voice answered. I felt pretty sure it couldn't be, since very few fishermen will waste their money on kerosene for side-lights; but our crew made for the green light just the same. When we got a mile nearer to the light we found that it was the reflection of the stars shining on the side of an iceberg. A wind was blowing off the ice that seemed to bite as it struck us, it was so cold. No picture I have ever seen gives a fair idea of the size and the menace of a berg. This one looked fearful, and seemed to breathe out the threat of death. Nevertheless no one in our boat was frozen. We were all well wrapped up and we sat so close together that we kept one another comfortably warm. As the wind freshened up to what would be a good sailing breeze, the sea rose with it, and we began to pitch and roll.

They say it was a little before four o'clock in the morning when the *Carpathia* came in sight. Her lights looked very low and dim at first, but within a short time after we sighted her she came up near us and stopped. I remember thinking how tiny she looked, all picked out against the sky by her rows of lights, compared with the great bulk of the *Titanic* which we had seen all lighted up only a few hours before. Within a few minutes the sun began to show its edge above the horizon and soon rose clear of the sea. I never saw a finer sight than that ship which had raced through fifty miles of field ice and bergs to come to our rescue. I saw some of the bergs later, and they looked as big as the pyramids.

The little life-boats began racing toward the *Carpathia* as fast as their crews could row. They couldn't do much more than paddle, but soon they came alongside. Presently our boat came up to where they had a chair rigged to a whip and let down for our people, one by one. The third person to leave our boat—a woman of substantial size—was stepping forward to take her place in the chair when, to the utter amazement of everybody, another woman, clad only in nightgown and kimono, sprang from nowhere and sat up on the floor of the boat.

"Look at that horrible woman!" she cried, pointing at the astonished lady in the chair. "Horrible! She stepped on my stomach. Horrible creature!"

The unhappy woman in the kimono had been lying for all of the four hours on the floor of the life-boat, either unconscious or too frightened to speak. She was next up in the chair after her oppressor.

When it finally came my turn to go up I found myself hoisted aloft quickly. A pair of hands was thrust out to keep me from bumping my head against the ship as I ascended. At the deck one man seized me to hold me up, while another wrapped a blanket, warmed in advance, completely around me. A third man assisted me into a room where a cup of hot coffee and a big drink of brandy were served to me—the whole process from the moment of lifting me out of the chair taking about half a minute.

It seems to me now as if I should remember these details as long as I live. And, of course, all I saw and heard was a very small part of all the happenings of that awful night.

Sea Whalers and Sealers

The Chase

by HERMAN MELVILLE

That night, in the mid-watch, when the old man—as his wont at intervals—stepped forth from the scuttle in which he leaned, and went to his pivot-hole, he suddenly thrust out his face fiercely, snuffing up the sea air as a sagacious ship's dog will, in drawing nigh to some barbarous isle. He declared that a whale must be near. Soon that peculiar odour, sometimes to a great distance given forth by the living sperm whale, was palpable to all the watch; nor was any mariner surprised when, after inspecting the compass, and then the dog-vane, and then ascertaining the precise bearing of the odour as nearly as possible, Ahab rapidly ordered the ship's course to be slightly altered, and the sail to be shortened.

The acute policy dictating these movements was sufficiently vindicated at daybreak, by the sight of a long sleek on the sea directly and lengthwise ahead, smooth as oil, and resembling in the pleated watery wrinkles bordering it, the polished metallic-like marks of some swift tide-rip, at the mouth of a deep, rapid stream.

"Man the mast-heads! Call all hands!"

Thundering with the butts of three clubbed handspikes on the forecastle deck, Daggoo roused the sleepers with such judgment claps that they seemed to exhale from the scuttle, so instantaneously did they appear with their clothes in their hands.

"What d'ye see?" cried Ahab, flattening his face to the sky.

"Nothing, nothing, sir!" was the sound hailing down in reply.

"T'gallant sails! Stunsails alow and aloft, and on both sides!"

All sail being set, he now cast loose the life-line, reserved for swaying him to the main royal-mast head; and in a few moments they were hoisting him thither, when, while but two-thirds of the way aloft, and while peering ahead through the horizontal vacancy between the main-top-sail and top-gallant-sail, he raised a gull-like cry in the air, "There she blows!—There she blows! A hump like a snow-hill! It is Moby Dick!"

Fired by the cry which seemed simultaneously taken up by the three look-outs, the men on deck rushed to the rigging to behold the famous whale they had so long been pursuing. Ahab had now gained his final perch, some feet above the other look-outs, Tashtego standing just beneath him on the cap of the top-gallant-mast, so that the Indian's head was almost on a level with Ahab's heel. From this height the whale was now seen some mile or so ahead, at every roll of the sea revealing his high sparkling hump, and regularly jetting his silent spout into the air. To the credulous mariners it seemed the same silent spout they had so long ago beheld in the moonlit Atlantic and Indian Oceans.

"And did none of ye see it before?" cried Ahab, hailing the perched men all around him.

"I saw him almost that same instant, sir, that Captain Ahab did, and I cried out," said Tashtego.

"Not the same instant; not the same—no, the doubloon is mine, Fate reserved the doubloon for me. *I* only; none of ye could have raised the White Whale first. There she blows! there she blows!—there she blows! There again!—there again!" he cried, in long-drawn, lingering, methodic tones, attuned to the gradual prolongings of the whale's visible jets. "He's going to sound! In stunsails! Down top-gallant-sails! Stand by three boats. Mr. Starbuck, remember, stay on board, and keep the ship. Helm there! Luff, luff a point! So; steady, man, steady! There go flukes! No, no; only black water! All ready the boats there? Stand by, stand by! Lower me, Mr. Starbuck; lower, lower,—quick, quicker!" and he slid through the air to the deck.

"He is heading straight to leeward, sir," cried Stubb, "right away from us; cannot have seen the ship yet."

"Be dumb, man! Stand by the braces! Hard down the helm!—brace up! Shiver her!—shiver her! So; well that! Boats, boats!"

Soon all the boats but Starbuck's were dropped; all the boat-sails set—all the paddles plying; with rippling swiftness, shooting to leeward; and .hab heading the onset. A pale, death-glimmer lit up Fedallah's sunken eyes; a hideous motion gnawed his mouth.

Like noiseless nautilus shells, their light prows sped through the sea; but only slowly they neared the foe. As they neared him, the ocean grew still more smooth; seemed drawing a carpet over its waves; seemed a noon-meadow, so serenely it spread. At length the breathless hunter came so nigh his seemingly unsuspecting prey, that his entire dazzling hump was distinctly visible, sliding along the sea as if an isolated thing, and continually set in a revolving ring of finest, fleecy, greenish foam. He saw the vast involved wrinkles of the slightly projecting head beyond. Before it, far out on the soft Turkish-rugged waters, went the glistening white shadow from his broad, milky forehead, a musical rippling playfully accompanying the shade; and behind, the blue waters interchangeably flowed over into the moving valley of his steady wake; and on either hand bright bubbles arose and danced by his side. But these were broken again by the light toes of hundreds of gay fowl softly feathering the sea, alternate with their fitful flight; and like to some flag-staff rising from the painted hull of an argosy, the tall but shattered pole of a recent lance projected from the white whale's back; and at intervals one of the cloud of soft-toed fowls hovering, and to and fro skimming like a canopy over the fish, silently perched and rocked on this pole, the long tail feathers streaming like pennons.

A gentle joyousness—a mighty mildness of repose in swiftness, invested

the gliding whale. Not the white bull Jupiter swimming away with ravished
Europa clinging to his graceful horns; his lovely, leering eyes sideways intent
upon the maid; with smooth bewitching fleetness, rippling straight for the
nuptial bower in Crete; not Jove, not that great majesty Supreme! did surpass
the glorified White Whale as he so divinely swam.

On each soft side—coincident with the parted swell, that but once leaving
him, then flowed so wide away—on each bright side, the whale shed off
enticings. No wonder there had been some among the hunters who namelessly
transported and allured by all this serenity, had ventured to assail it; but had
fatally found that quietude but the vesture of tornadoes. Yet calm, enticing
calm, oh, whale! thou glidest on, to all who for the first time eye thee, no
matter how many in that same way thou may'st have bejuggled and destroyed
before.

And thus, through the serene tranquillities of the tropical sea, among waves
whose hand-clappings were suspended by exceeding rapture, Moby Dick
moved on, still withholding from sight the full terrors of his submerged trunk,
entirely hiding the wrenched hideousness of his jaw. But soon the fore part of
him slowly rose from the water; for an instant his whole marbleized body
formed a high arch, like Virginia's Natural Bridge, and warningly waving his
bannered flukes in the air, the grand god revealed himself, sounded, and went
out of sight. Hoveringly halting, and dipping on the wing, the white sea-fowls
longingly lingered over the agitated pool that he left.

With oars apeak, the paddles down, the sheets of their sails adrift, the three
boats now stilly floated, awaiting Moby Dick's reappearance.

"An hour," said Ahab, standing rooted in his boat's stern; and he gazed
beyond the whale's place, towards the dim blue spaces and wide wooing vacancies to leeward. It was only an instant; for again his eyes seemed whirling
round in his head as he swept the watery circle.The breeze now freshened; the
sea began to swell.

"The birds!—the birds!" cried Tashtego.

In long Indian file, as when herons take wing, the white birds were now all
flying towards Ahab's boat; and when within a few yards began fluttering over
the water there, wheeling round and round, with joyous, expectant cries. Their
vision was keener than man's; Ahab could discover no sign in the sea. But
suddenly as he peered down and down into its depths, he profoundly saw a
white living spot no bigger than a white weasel, with wonderful celerity uprising, and magnifying as it rose, till it turned, and then there were plainly revealed two long crooked rows of white, glistening teeth, floating up from the
undiscoverable bottom. It was Moby Dick's open mouth and scrolled jaw; his
vast, shadowed bulk still half blending with the blue of the sea. The glittering
mouth yawned beneath the boat like an open-doored marble tomb; and giving
one sidelong sweep with his steering oar, Ahab whirled the craft aside from
this tremendous apparition. Then, calling upon Fedallah to change places with
him, went forward to the bows, and seizing Perth's harpoon, commanded his
crew to grasp their oars and stand by to stern.

Now, by reason of this timely spinning round the boat upon its axis, its bow, by anticipation, was made to face the whale's head while yet under water. But as if perceiving this stratagem, Moby Dick, with that malicious intelligence ascribed to him, sidelingly transplanted himself, as it were, in an instant, shooting his plated head lengthwise beneath the boat.

Through and through; through every plank and each rib, it thrilled for an instant, the whale obliquely lying on his back, in the manner of a biting shark, slowly and feelingly taking its bows full within his mouth, so that the long, narrow, scrolled lower jaw curled high up into the open air, and one of the teeth caught in a row-lock. The bluish pearl-white of the inside of the jaw was within six inches of Ahab's head, and reached higher than that. In this attitude the White Whale now shook the slight cedar as a mildly cruel cat her mouse. With unastonished eyes Fedallah gazed, and crossed his arms; but the tiger-yellow crew were tumbling over each other's heads to gain the uttermost stern.

And now, while both elastic gunwales were springing in and out, as the whale dallied with the doomed craft in this devilish way; and from his body being submerged beneath the boat, he could not be darted at from the bows, for the bows were almost inside of him, as it were; and while the other boats involuntarily paused, as before a quick crisis impossible to withstand, then it was that monomaniac Ahab, furious with this tantalizing vicinity of his foe, which placed him all alive and helpless in the very jaws he hated; frenzied with all this, he seized the long bone with his naked hands, and wildly strove to wrench it from its gripe. As now he thus vainly strove, the jaw slipped from him; the frail gunwales bent in, collapsed, and snapped, as both jaws, like an enormous shears, sliding further aft, bit the craft completely in twain, and locked themselves fast again in the sea, midway between the two floating wrecks. These floated aside, the broken ends drooping, the crew at the stern-wreck clinging to the gunwales, and striving to hold fast to the oars to lash them across.

At that preluding moment, ere the boat was yet snapped, Ahab, the first to perceive the whale's intent, by the crafty upraising of his head, a movement that loosed his hold for the time; at that moment his hand had made one final effort to push the boat out of the bite. But only slipping further into the whale's mouth, and tilting over sideways as it slipped, the boat had shaken off his hold on the jaw; spilled him out of it, as he leaned to the push; and so he fell flat-faced upon the sea.

Ripplingly withdrawing from his prey, Moby Dick now lay at a little distance, vertically thrusting his oblong white head up and down in the billows; and at the same time slowly revolving his whole spindled body; so that when his vast wrinkled forehead rose—some twenty or more feet out of the water—the now rising swells, with all their confluent waves, dazzling broke against it; vindictively tossing their shivered spray still higher into the air. So, in the gale, the but half baffled Channel billows only recoil from the base of the Eddystone, triumphantly to overleap its summit with their scud.

But soon resuming his horizontal attitude, Moby Dick swam swiftly round and round the wrecked crew; sideways churning the water in his vengeful wake, as if lashing himself up to still another and more deadly assault. The sight of the splintered boat seemed to madden him, as the blood of grapes and mulberries cast before Antiochus's elephants in the book of Maccabees. Meanwhile Ahab half smothered in the foam of the whale's insolent tail, and too much of a cripple to swim,—though he could still keep afloat, even in the heart of such a whirlpool as that; helpless Ahab's head was seen, like a tossed bubble which the least chance shock might burst. From the boat's fragmentary stern, Fedallah incuriously and mildly eyed him; the clinging crew, at the other drifting end, could not succour him; more than enough was it for them to look to themselves. For so revolvingly appalling was the White Whale's aspect, and so planetarily swift the ever-contracting circles he made, that he seemed horizontally swooping upon them. And though the other boats, unharmed, still hovered hard by; still they dared not pull into the eddy to strike, lest that should be the signal for the instant destruction of the jeopardised castaways, Ahab and all; nor in that case could they themselves hope to escape. With straining eyes, then, they remained on the outer edge of the direful zone, whose centre had now become the old man's head.

Meantime, from the beginning all this had been descried from the ship's mast heads; and squaring her yards, she had borne down upon the scene; and was now so nigh, that Ahab in the water hailed her;—"Sail on the"—but that moment a breaking sea dashed on him from Moby Dick, and whelmed him for the time. But struggling out of it again, and chancing to rise on a towering crest, he shouted,—"Sail on the whale!—Drive him off!"

The Pequod's prows were pointed; and breaking up the charmed circle, she effectually parted the white whale from his victim. As he sullenly swam off, the boats flew to the rescue.

Dragged into Stubb's boat with blood-shot, blinded eyes, the white brine caking in his wrinkles; the long tension of Ahab's bodily strength did crack, and helplessly he yielded to his body's doom: for a time, lying all crushed in the bottom of Stubb's boat, like one trodden under foot of herds of elephants. Far inland, nameless wails came from him, as desolate sounds from out ravines.

But this intensity of his physical prostration did but so much the more abbreviate it. In an instant's compass, great hearts sometimes condense to one deep pang, the sum total of those shallow pains kindly diffused through feebler men's whole lives. And so, such hearts, though summary in each one suffering; still, if the gods decree it, in their life-time aggregate a whole age of woe, wholly made up of instantaneous intensities; for even in their pointless centres, those noble natures contain the entire circumferences of inferior souls.

"The harpoon," said Ahab, half-way rising, and draggingly leaning on one bended arm—"is it safe?"

"Aye, sir, for it was not darted; this is it," said Stubb, showing it.

"Lay it before me;—any missing men?"

"One, two, three, four, five;—there were five oars, sir, and here are five men."

"That's good.—Help me, man; I wish to stand. So, so, I see him! there! there! going to leeward still; what a leaping spout!—Hands off from me! The eternal sap runs up in Ahab's bones again! Set the sail; out oars; the helm!"

It is often the case when a boat is stove, its crew, being picked up by another boat, help to work that second boat; and the chase is thus continued with what is called double-banked oars. It was thus now. But the added power of the boat did not equal the added power of the whale, for he seemed to have treble-banked his every fin; swimming with a velocity which plainly showed, that if now, under these circumstances, pushed on, the chase would prove an indefinitely prolonged, if not a hopeless one; nor could any crew endure for so long a period, such an unintermitted, intense straining at the oar; a thing barely tolerable only in some one brief vicissitude. The ship itself, then, as it sometimes happens, offered the most promising intermediate means of overtaking the chase. Accordingly, the boats now made for her, and were soon swayed up to their cranes—the two parts of the wrecked boat having been previously secured by her—and then hoisting everything to her side, and stacking her canvas high up, and sideways outstretching it with stun-sails, like the double-jointed wings of an albatross; the Pequod bore down in the leeward wake of Moby Dick. At the well known, methodic intervals, the whale's glittering spout was regularly announced from the manned mast-heads; and when he would be reported as just gone down, Ahab would take the time, and then pacing the deck, binnacle-watch in hand, so soon as the last second of the allotted hour expired, his voice was heard.—"Whose is the doubloon now? D'ye see him?" and if the reply was, No, sir! straightway he commanded them to lift him to his perch. In this way the day wore on; Ahab, now aloft and motionless; anon, unrestingly pacing the planks.

As he was thus walking, uttering no sound, except to hail the men aloft, or to bid them hoist a sail still higher, or to spread one to a still greater breadth—thus to and fro pacing, beneath his slouched hat, at every turn he passed his own wrecked boat, which had been dropped upon the quarter-deck, and lay there reversed; broken bow to shattered stern. At last he paused before it; and as in the already over-clouded sky fresh troops of clouds will sometimes sail across, so over the old man's face there now stole some such added gloom as this.

Stubb saw him pause; and perhaps intending, not vainly, though, to evince his own unabated fortitude, and thus keep up a valiant place in his Captain's mind, he advanced, and eyeing the wreck exclaimed—"The thistle the ass refused; it pricked his mouth too keenly, sir; ha! ha!"

"What soulless thing is this that laughs before a wreck? Man, man! did I not know thee brave as fearless fire (and as mechanical) I could swear thou wert a poltroon. Groan nor laugh should be heard before a wreck."

"Aye, sir," said Starbuck drawing near, " 'tis a solemn sight; an omen, and an ill one."

"Omen? omen?—the dictionary! If the gods think to speak outright to man, they will honourably speak outright; not shake their heads, and give an old wives' darkling hint.—Begone! Ye two are the opposite poles of one thing; Starbuck is Stubb reversed, and Stubb is Starbuck; and ye two are all mankind; and Ahab stands alone among the millions of the peopled earth, nor gods nor men his neighbours! Cold, cold—I shiver!—How now? Aloft there! D'ye see him? Sing out for every spout, though he spout ten times a second!"

The day was nearly done; only the hem of his golden robe was rustling. Soon, it was almost dark, but the lookout men still remained unset.

"Can't see the spout now, sir;—too dark"—cried a voice from the air.

"How heading when last seen?"

"As before, sir,—straight to leeward."

"Good! he will travel slower now 'tis night. Down royals and top-gallant stun-sails, Mr. Starbuck. We must not run over him before morning; he's making a passage now, and may heave-to a while. Helm there! keep her full before the wind!—Aloft! come down!—Mr. Stubb, send a fresh hand to the fore-mast head, and see it manned till morning."—Then advancing towards the doubloon in the mainmast—"Men, this gold is mine, for I earned it; but I shall let it abide here till the White Whale is dead; and then, whosoever of ye first raises him, upon the day he shall be killed, this gold is that man's; and if on that day I shall again raise him, then, ten times its sum shall be divided among all of ye! Away now!—the deck is thine, sir."

And so saying, he placed himself half-way within the scuttle, and slouching his hat, stood there till dawn, except when at intervals rousing himself to see how the night wore on.

Second Day

At daybreak, the three mast-heads were punctually manned afresh.

"D'ye see him?" cried Ahab, after allowing a little space for the light to spread.

"See nothing, sir."

"Turn up all hands and make sail! He travels faster than I thought for;—the top-gallant sails!—aye, they should have been kept on her all night. But no matter—'tis but resting for the rush."

Here be it said, that this pertinacious pursuit of one particular whale, continued through day into night, and through night into day, is a thing by no means unprecedented in the South Sea fishery. For such is the wonderful skill, prescience of experience, and invincible confidence acquired by some great natural geniuses among the Nantucket commanders; that from the simple observation of a whale when last descried, they will, under certain given circumstances, pretty accurately foretell both the direction in which he will continue to swim for a time, while out of sight, as well as his probable rate of progression during that period. And, in these cases, somewhat as a pilot, when about losing sight of a coast, whose general rending he well knows, and which he desires shortly to return to again, but at some further point; like as this pilot stands by his compass, and takes the precise bearing of the cape at present visible, in order the more certainly to hit aright the remote, unseen headland, eventually to be visited: so does the fisherman, at his compass, with the whale; for after being chased, and diligently marked, through several hours of daylight, then, when night obscures the fish, the creature's future wake through the darkness is almost as established to the sagacious mind of the hunter, as the pilot's coast is to him. So that to this hunter's wondrous skill, the proverbial evanescence of a thing writ in water, a wake, is to all desired purposes well-nigh as reliable as the steadfast land. And as the mighty iron Leviathan of the modern railway is so familiarly known in its every pace, that, with watches in their hands, men time his rate as doctors that of a baby's pulse; and lightly say of it, the up train or the down train will reach such or such a spot, at such or such an hour; even so, almost, there are occasions when these Nantucketers time that other Leviathan of the deep, according to the observed humour of his speed; and say to themselves, so many hours hence this whale will have gone two hundred miles, will have about reached this or that degree of latitude or longitude. But to render this acuteness at all successful in the end, the wind and the sea must be the whaleman's allies; for of what present avail to the becalmed or windbound mariner is the skill that assures him he is exactly ninety-three leagues and a quarter from his port? Inferable from these statements, are many collateral subtile matters touching the chase of whales.

The ship tore on; leaving such a furrow in the sea as when a cannon-ball, missent, becomes a ploughshare and turns up the level field.

"By salt and hemp!" cried Stubb, "but this swift motion of the deck creeps up one's legs and tingles at the heart. This ship and I are two brave fellows!— Ha! ha! Some one take me up, and launch me, spine-wise, on the sea,—for by live-oaks! my spine's a keel. Ha, ha! we go the gait that leaves no dust behind!"

"There she blows—she blows!—she blows!—right ahead!" was now the mast-head cry.

"Aye, aye!" cried Stubb, "I knew it—ye can't escape—blow on and split your spout, O whale! the mad fiend himself is after ye! blow your trump— blister your lungs!—Ahab will dam off your blood, as a miller shuts his water-gate upon the stream!"

And Stubb did but speak out for well-nigh all that crew. The frenzies of the chase had by this time worked them bubblingly up, like old wine worked anew. Whatever pale fears and forebodings some of them might have felt before; these were not only now kept out of sight through the growing awe of Ahab, but they were broken up, and on all sides routed, as timid prairie hares that scatter before the bounding bison. The hand of Fate had snatched all their souls; and by the stirring perils of the previous day; the rack of the past night's suspense; the fixed, unfearing, blind, reckless way in which their wild craft went plunging towards its flying mark; by all these things, their hearts were bowled along. The wind that made great bellies of their sails, and rushed the vessel on by arms invisible as irresistible; this seemed the symbol of that unseen agency which so enslaved them to the race.

They were one man, not thirty. For as the one ship that held them all; though it was put together of all contrasting things—oak, and maple, and pine wood; iron, and pitch, and hemp—yet all these ran into each other in the one concrete hull, which shot on its way, both balanced and directed by the long central keel; even so, all the individualities of the crew, this man's valour, that man's fear; guilt and guiltiness, all varieties were wedded into oneness, and were all directed to that fatal goal which Ahab their one lord and keel did point to.

The rigging lived. The mast-heads, like the tops of tall palms, were outspreadingly tufted with arms and legs. Clinging to a spar with one hand, some reached forth the other with impatient wavings; others, shading their eyes from the vivid sunlight, sat far out on the rocking yards; all the spars in full bearing of mortals, ready and ripe for their fate. Ah! how they still strove through that infinite blueness to seek out the thing that might destroy them!

"Why sing ye not out for him, if ye see him?" cried Ahab, when, after the lapse of some minutes since the first cry, no more had been heard. "Sway me up, men: ye have been deceived; not Moby Dick casts one odd jet that way, and then disappears."

It was even so; in their headlong eagerness, the men had mistaken some other thing for the whale-spout, as the event itself soon proved; for hardly had Ahab reached his perch; hardly was the rope belayed to its pin on deck, when he struck the key-note to an orchestra, that made the air vibrate as with the combined discharges of rifles.The triumphant halloo of thirty buckskin lungs was heard, as—much nearer to the ship than the place of the imaginary jet, less than a mile ahead—Moby Dick bodily burst into view! For not by any calm and indolent spoutings; not by the peaceable gush of that mystic fountain in his head, did the White Whale now reveal his vicinity; but by the far more wondrous phenomenon of breaching. Rising with his utmost velocity from the furthest depths, the Sperm Whale thus booms his entire bulk into the pure element of air, and piling up a mountain of dazzling foam, shows his place to the distance of seven miles and more. In those moments, the torn, enraged waves he shakes off, seem his mane; in some cases, this breaching is his act of defiance.

"There she breaches! there she breaches!" was the cry, as in his immeasurable bravadoes the White Whale tossed himself salmon-like to Heaven. So suddenly seen in the blue plain of the sea, and relieved against the still bluer margin of the sky, the spray that he raised, for the moment, intolerably glittered and glared like a glacier; and stood there gradually fading and fading away from its first sparkling intensity, to the dim mistiness of an advancing shower in a vale.

"Aye, breach your last to the sun, Moby Dick!" cried Ahab, "thy hour and thy harpoon are at hand!—Down! down all of ye, but one man at the fore. The boats!—stand by!"

Unmindful of the tedious rope-ladders of the shrouds, the men, like shooting stars, slid to the deck, by the isolated backstays and halyards; while Ahab, less dartingly, but still rapidly, was dropped from his perch.

"Lower away," he cried, so soon as he had reached his boat—a spare one, rigged the afternoon previous. "Mr. Starbuck, the ship is thine—keep away from the boats, but keep near them. Lower, all!"

As if to strike a quick terror into them, by this time being the first assailant himself, Moby Dick had turned, and was now coming for the three crews. Ahab's boat was central; and cheering his men, he told them he would take the whale head-and-head,—that is, pull straight up to his forehead,—a not uncommon thing; for when within a certain limit, such a course excludes the coming onset from the whale's sidelong vision. But ere that close limit was gained, and while yet all three boats were plain as the ship's three masts to his eye; the White Whale churning himself into furious speed, almost in an instant as it were, rushing among the boats with open jaws, and a lashing tail, offered appalling battle on every side; and heedless of the irons darted at him from every boat, seemed only intent on annihilating each separate plank of which those boats were made. But skillfully manoeuvred, incessantly wheeling like trained chargers in the field; the boats for a while eluded him; though, at times, but by a plank's breadth; while all the time, Ahadb's unearthly slogan tore every other cry but his to shreds.

But at last in his untraceable evolutions, the White Whale so crossed and recrossed, and in a thousand ways entangled the slack of the three lines now fast to him, that they fore-shortened, and, of themselves, warped the devoted boats towards the planted irons in him; though now for a moment the whale drew aside a little, as if to rally for a more tremendous charge. Seizing that opportunity, Ahab first paid out more line: and then was rapidly hauling and jerking in upon it again—hoping that way to disencumber it of some snarls— when lo!—a sight more savage than the embattled teeth of sharks!

Caught and twisted—corkscrewed in the mazes of the line, loose harpoons and lances, with all their bristling barbs and points, came flashing and dripping up to the chocks in the bows of Ahab's boat. Only one thing could be done. Seizing the boat-knife, he critically reached within—through—and then, without—the rays of steel; dragged in the line beyond, passed it, inboard, to the bowsman, and then, twice sundering the rope near the chocks— dropped the intercepted fagot of steel into the sea; and was all fast again. That instant, the White Whale made a sudden rush among the remaining tangles of the other lines; by so doing, irresistibly dragged the more involved boats of Stubb and Flask towards his flukes; dashed them together like two rolling husks on a surf-beaten beach, and then, diving down into the sea, disappeared in a boiling maelstrom, in which, for a space, the odorous cedar chips of the wrecks danced round and round, like the grated nutmeg in a swiftly stirred bowl of punch.

While the two crews were yet circling in the waters, reaching out after the revolving line-tubs, oars, and other floating furniture, while aslope little Flask bobbed up and down like an empty vial, twitching his legs upwards to escape the dreaded jaws of sharks; and Stubb was lustily singing out for some one to ladle him up; and while the old man's line—now parting—admitted of his pulling into the creamy pool to rescue whom he could;—in that wild simultaneousness of a thousand concreted perils,—Ahab's yet unstricken boat seemed drawn up towards Heaven by invisible wires,—as, arrow-like, shooting perpendicularly from the sea, the White Whale dashed his broad forehead against its bottom, and sent it, turning over and over, into the air; till it fell again—gunwale downwards—and Ahab and his men struggled out from under it, like seals from a sea-side cave.

The first uprising momentum of the whale—modifying its direction as he struck the surface—involuntarily launched him along it, to a little distance from the centre of the destruction he had made; and with his back to it, he now lay for a moment slowly feeling with his flukes from side to side; and whenever a stray oar, bit of plank, the least chip or crumb of the boats touched his skin, his tail swiftly drew back, and came sideways, smiting the sea. But soon, as if satisfied that his work for that time was done, he pushed his pleated forehead through the ocean, and trailing after him the intertangled lines, continued his leeward way at a traveller's methodic pace.

As before, the attentive ship having descried the whole fight, again came bearing down to the rescue, and dropping a boat, picked up the floating mariners, tubs, oars, and whatever else could be caught at, and safely landed them on her decks. Some sprained shoulders, wrists, and ankles, livid contusions; wrenched harpoons and lances: inextricable intricacies of rope; shattered oars and planks; all these were there; but no fatal or even serious ill seemed to have befallen any one. As with Fedallah the day before, so Ahab was now found grimly clinging to his boat's broken half, which afforded a comparatively easy float; nor did it so exhaust him as the previous day's mishap.

But when he was helped to the deck, all eyes were fastened upon him; as instead of standing by himself he still half-hung upon the shoulder of Starbuck, who had thus far been the foremost to assist him. His ivory leg had been snapped off, leaving but one short sharp splinter.

"Aye aye, Starbuck, 'tis sweet to lean sometimes, be the leaner who he will; and would old Ahab had leaned oftener than he has."

"The ferrule has not stood, sir," said the carpenter, now coming up; "I put good work into that leg."

"But no bones broken, sir, I hope," said Stubb with true concern.

"Aye! and all splintered to pieces, Stubb!—d'ye see it.—But even with a broken bone, old Ahab is untouched; and I account no living bone of mine one jot more me, than this dead one that's lost. Nor white whale, nor man, nor fiend, can so much as graze old Ahab in his own proper and inaccessible being. Can any lead touch yonder floor, any mast scrape yonder roof?— Aloft there! which way?"

"Dead to leeward, sir."

"Up helm, then; pile on the sail again, ship keepers! down the rest of the spare boats and rig them—Mr. Starbuck away, and muster the boat's crews."

"Let me first help thee towards the bulwarks, sir."

"Oh, oh, oh! how this splinter gores me now! Accursed fate! that the un-conquerable captain in the soul should have such a craven mate!"

"Sir?"

"My body, man, not thee. Give me something for a cane—there, that shivered lance will do. Muster the men. Surely I have not seen him yet. By heaven it cannot be!—missing?—quick! call them all."

The old man's hinted thought was true. Upon mustering the company, the Parsee was not there.

"The Parsee!" cried Stubb—"he must have been caught in—"

"The black vomit wrench thee!—run all of ye above, alow, cabin, forecastle—find him—not gone—not gone!"

But quickly they returned to him with the tidings that the Parsee was nowhere to be found.

"Aye, sir," said Stubb—"caught among the tangles of your line—I thought I saw him dragging under."

"*My* line! *my* line? Gone?—Gone? What means that little word?—What death-knell rings in it, that old Ahab shakes as if he were the belfry. The harpoon, too!—toss over the litter there,—d'ye see it?—the forged iron, men, the white whale's—no, no, no,—blistered fool! this hand did dart it!— 'tis in the fish!—Aloft there! Keep him nailed—Quick!—all hands to the rigging of the boats—collect the oars—harpooners! the irons, the irons!— hoist the royals higher—a pull on all the sheets!—helm there! steady, steady for your life! I'll ten times girdle the unmeasured globe; yea and dive straight through it, but I'll slay him yet!"

"Great God! but for one single instant show thyself," cried Starbuck; "never never wilt thou capture him, old man.—In Jesus' name no more of this, that's worse than devil's madness. Two days chased; twice stove to splinters; thy very leg once more snatched from under thee; they evil shadow gone—all good angels mobbing thee with warnings:—what more wouldst thou have?—Shall we keep chasing this murderous fish till he swamps the last man? Shall we be dragged by him to the bottom of the sea? Shall we be towed by him to the infernal world? Oh, oh,—Impiety and blasphemy to hunt him more!"

"Starbuck, of late I've felt strangely moved to thee; ever since that hour we both saw—thou know'st what, in one another's eyes. But in this matter of the whale, be the front of thy face to me as the palm of this hand—a lipless, unfeatured blank. Ahab is for ever Ahab, man. This whole act's immutably decreed. 'Twas rehearsed by thee and me a billion years before this ocean rolled. Fool! I am the Fates' lieutenant; I act under orders. Look thou, underling! that thou obeyest mine.—Stand round me, men. Ye see an old man cut down to the stump; leaning on a shivered lance; propped up on a lonely foot. 'Tis Ahab—his body's part; but Ahab's soul's a centipede, that moves upon a hundred legs. I feel strained, half stranded, as ropes that tow dismasted frigates in a gale; and I may look so. But ere I break, ye'll hear me crack; and till ye hear *that*, know that Ahab's hawser tows his purpose yet. Believe ye, men, in the things called omens? Then laugh aloud, and cry encore! For ere they drown, drowning things will twice rise to the surface; then rise again, to sink for evermore. So with Moby Dick—two days he's floated—tomorrow will be the third. Aye, men, he'll rise once more,—but only to spout his last! D'ye feel brave men, brave?"

"As fearless fire," cried Stubb.

"And as mechanical," muttered Ahab. Then as the men went forward, he muttered on:—"The things called omens! And yesterday I talked the same to Starbuck there, concerning my broken boat. Oh! how valiantly I seek to drive out of others' hearts what's clinched so fast in mine!—The Parsee—the Parsee!—gone, gone? and he was to go before:—but still was to be seen again ere I could perish—How's that?—There's a riddle now might baffle all the lawyers backed by the ghosts of the whole line of judges:—like a hawk's beak it pecks my brain. *I'll, I'll* solve it, though!"

When dusk descended, the whale was till in sight to leeward.

So once more the sail was shortened, and everything passed nearly as on the previous night; only, the sound of hammers, and the hum of the grindstone was heard till nearly daylight, as the men toiled by lanterns in the complete and careful rigging of the spare boats and sharpening their fresh weapons for the morrow. Meantime, of the broken keel of Ahab's wrecked craft the carpenter made him another leg; while still as on the night before, slouched Ahab stood fixed within his scuttle; his hid heliotrope glance anticipatingly gone backward on its dial; sat due eastward for the earliest sun.

Third Day

The morning of the third day dawned fair and fresh, and once more the solitary night-man at the fore-mast-head was relieved by crowds of the daylight look-outs, who dotted every mast and almost every spar.

"D'ye see him?" cried Ahab; but the whale was not yet in sight.

"In his infallible wake, though; but follow that wake, that's all. Helm there; steady, as thou goest, and hast been going. What a lovely day again! were it a new-made world, and made for a summer-house to the angels, and this morning the first of its throwing open to them, a fairer day could not dawn upon that world. Here's food for thought, had Ahab time to think; but Ahab never thinks; he only feels, feels, feels, *that's* tingling enough for mortal man! to think's audacity. God only has that right and privilege. Thinking is, or ought to be, a coolness and a calmness; and our poor hearts throb, and our poor brains beat too much for that. And yet, I've sometimes thought my brain was very calm—frozen calm, this old skull cracks so, like a glass in which the contents turn to ice, and shiver it. And still this hair is growing now; this moment growing, and heat must breed it; but no, it's like that sort of common grass that will grow anywhere, between the earthly clefts of Greenland ice or in Vesuvius lava. How the wild winds blow it; they whip it about me as the torn shreds of split sails lash the tossed ship they cling to. A vile wind that has no doubt blown ere this through prison corridors and cells, and wards of hospitals, and ventilated them, and now comes blowing hither as innocent as fleeces. Out upon it!—it's tainted. Were I the wind, I'd blow no more on such a wicked, miserable world. I'd crawl somewhere to a cave, and slink there. And yet, 'tis a noble and heroic thing, the wind! who ever conquered it? In every fight it has the last and bitterest blow. Run tilting at it, and you but run through it. Ha! a coward wind that strikes stark naked men, but will not stand to receive a single blow. Even Ahab is a braver thing—a nobler thing than *that*. Would now the wind but had a body; but all the things that most exasperate and outrage mortal man all these things are bodiless, but only bodiless as objects, not as agents. There's a most special, a most cunning, oh, a most malicious difference! And yet, I say again, and swear it now, that there's something all glorious and gracious in the wind. These warm Trade Winds, at least, that in the clear heavens blow straight on, in strong and steadfast, vigorous mildness; and veer not from their mark, however the baser currents of the sea may turn and tack, and mightiest Mississippi of the land swift and swerve about, uncertain where to go at last. And by the eternal Poles! these same Trades that so directly blow my good ship on; these Trades, or something like them—something so unchangeable, and full as strong, blow my keeled soul along! To it! Aloft there! What d'ye see?"

"Nothing, sir."

"Nothing! and noon at hand! The doubloon goes a-begging! See the sun! Aye, aye, it must be so. I've oversailed him. How, got the start? Aye, he's chasing *me* now; not I, *him*—that's bad; I might have known it, too. Fool! the lines—the harpoons he's towing. Aye, aye, I have run him by last night. About! about! Come down, all of ye, but the regular look-outs! Man the braces!"

Steering as she had done, the wind had been somewhat on the Pequod's quarter, so that now being pointed in the reverse direction, the braced ship sailed hard upon the breeze as she rechurned the cream in her own white wake.

"Against the wind he now steers for the open jaw," murmured Starbuck to himself, as he coiled the new-hauled main-brace upon the rail. "God keep us, but already my bones feel damp within me, and from the inside wet my flesh. I misdoubt me that I disobey my God in obeying him!"

"Stand by to sway me up!" cried Ahab, advancing to the hempen basket. "We should meet him soon."

"Aye, aye, sir," and straightway Starbuck did Ahab's bidding, and once more Ahab swung on high.

A whole hour passed; gold-beaten out to ages. Time itself now held long breaths with keen suspense. But at last, some three points off the weather-bow, Ahab descried the spout again, and instantly from the three mast-heads three shrieks went up as if the tongues of fire had voiced it.

"Forehead to forehead I meet thee, this third time, Moby Dick! On deck there!—brace sharper up; crowd her into the wind's eye. He's too far off to lower yet, Mr. Starbuck. The sails shake! Stand over that helmsman with a top-maul! So, so; he travels fast, and I must down. But let me have one more round look aloft here at the sea; there's time for that. An old, old sight, and yet somehow so young; aye, and not changed a wink since I first saw it, a boy, from the sand-hills of Nantucket! The same!—the same!—the same to Noah as to me. There's a soft shower to leeward. Such lovely leewardings! They must lead somewhere—to something else than common land, more palmy than the palms. Leeward! the white whale goes that way; look to windward, then; the better if the bitterer quarter. But good-bye, good-bye, old mast-head! What's this?—green? aye, tiny mosses in these warped cracks. No such green weather stains on Ahab's head! There's the difference now between man's old age and matter's. But aye, old mast, we both grow old together; sound in our hulls, though, are we not, my ship? Aye, minus a leg, that's all. By heaven this dead wood has the better of my live flesh every way. I can't compare with it; and I've known some ships made of dead trees outlast the lives of men made of the most vital stuff of vital fathers. What's that he said? he should still go before me, my pilot; and yet to be seen again? But where? Will I have eyes at the bottom of the sea, supposing I descend those endless stairs? and all night I've been sailing from him, wherever he did sink to. Aye, aye, like many more thou told'st direful truth as touching thyself, O Parsee; but, Ahab, there thy shot fell short. Good-bye, mast-head—keep a good eye upon the whale, the while I'm gone. We'll talk to-morrow, nay, to-night, when the white whale lies down there, tied by head and tail."

He gave the word; and still gazing round him, was steadily lowered through the cloven blue air to the deck.

In due time the boats were lowered; but as standing in his shallop's stern, Ahab just hovered upon the point of the descent, he waved to the mate,—who held one of the tackle-ropes on deck—and bade him pause.

"Starbuck!"

"Sir?"

"For the third time my soul's ship starts upon this voyage, Starbuck."

"Aye, sir, thou wilt have it so."

"Some ships sail from their ports, and ever afterwards are missing, Starbuck!"

"Truth, sir: saddest truth."

"Some men die at ebb tide; some at low water; some at the full of the flood;—and I feel now like a billow that's all one crested comb, Starbuck. I am old;—shake hands with me, man."

Their hands met; their eyes fastened; Starbuck's tears the glue.

"Oh, my captain, my captain!—noble heart—go not—go not!—see, it's a brave man that weeps; how great the agony of the persuasion then!"

"Lower away!"—cried Ahab, tossing the mate's arm from him. "Stand by the crew!"

In an instant the boat was pulling round close under the stern.

"The sharks! the sharks!" cried a voice from the low cabin-window there; "O master, my master, come back!"

But Ahab heard nothing; for his own voice was high-lifted then; and the boat leaped on.

Yet the voice spake true; for scarce had he pushed from the ship, when numbers of sharks, seemingly rising from out the dark waters beneath the hull, maliciously snapped at the blades of the oars, every time they dipped in the water; and in this way accompanied the boat with their bites. It is a thing not uncommonly happening to the whale-boats in those swarming seas; the sharks at times apparently following them in the same prescient way that vultures hover over the banners of marching regiments in the east. But these were the first sharks that had been observed by the *Pequod* since the White Whale had been first descried; and whether it was that Ahab's crew were all such tiger-yellow barbarians, and therefore their flesh more musky to the senses of the sharks—a matter sometimes well known to affect them,—however it was, they seemed to follow that one boat without molesting the others.

"Heart of wrought steel!" murmured Starbuck gazing over the side, and following with his eyes the receding boat—"canst thou yet ring boldy to that sight?—lowering thy keel among ravening sharks, and followed by them, open-mouthed to the chase; and this the critical third day?—For when three days flow together in one continuous intense pursuit; be sure the first is the morning, the second the noon, and the third the evening and the end of that thing—be that end what it may. Oh! my God! what is this that shoots through me, and leaves me so deadly calm, yet expectant,—fixed at the top of a shudder! Future things swim before me, as in empty outlines and skeletons; all the past is somehow grown dim. Mary, girl! thou fadest in pale glories behind me; boy! I seem to see but thy eyes grown wondrous blue. Strangest problems of life seem clearing; but clouds sweep between—Is my journey's end coming? My legs feel faint; like his who has footed it all day. Feel thy heart,—beats it yet?—Stir thyself, Starbuck!—stave it off—move, move! speak aloud!—Mast-head there! See ye my boy's hand on the hill? —Crazed;—aloft there!—keep thy keenest eye upon the boats:—mark well the whale!—Ho! again!—drive off that hawk! see! he pecks—he tears the vane"—pointing to the red flag flying at the main-truck—"Ha! he soars away with it!—Where's the old man now? sees't thou that sight, oh Ahab!—shudder, shudder!"

The boats had not gone very far, when by a signal from the mast-heads—a downward pointed arm, Ahab knew that the whale had sounded; but intending to be near him at the next rising, he held on his way a little sideways from the vessel; the becharmed crew maintaining the profoundest silence, as the head-beat waves hammered and hammered against the opposing bow.

"Drive, drive in your nails, oh ye waves! to their utter-most heads drive them in! ye but strike a thing without a lid; and no coffin and no hearse can be mine:—and hemp only can kill me! Ha! ha!"

Suddenly the waters around them slowly swelled in broad circles; then quickly upheaved, as if sideways sliding from a submerged berg of ice, swiftly rising to the surface. A low rumbling sound was heard; a subterraneous hum; and then all held their breaths; as bedraggled with trailing ropes, and harpoons, and lances, a vast form shot lengthwise, but obliquely from the sea. Shrouded in a thin drooping veil of mist, it hovered for a moment in the rainbowed air; and then fell swamping back into the deep. Crushed thirty feet upwards, the waters flashed for an instant like heaps of fountains, then brokenly sank in a shower of flakes, leaving the circling surface creamed like new milk round the marble trunk of the whale.

"Give way!" cried Ahab to the oarsmen, and the boats darted forward to the attack; but maddened by yesterday's fresh irons that corroded in him, Moby Dick seemed combinedly possessed by all the angels that fell from heaven. The wide tiers of welded tendons overspreading his broad white forehead, beneath the transparent skin, looked knitted together; as head on, he came churning his tail among the boats; and once more flailed them apart; spilling out the irons and lances from the two mates' boats, and dashing in one side of the upper part of their bows, but leaving Ahab's almost without a scar.

While Daggoo and Queequeg were stopping the strained planks; and as the whale swimming out from them, turned, and showed one entire flank as he shot by them again; at that moment a quick cry went up. Lashed round and round to the fish's back; pinioned in the turns upon turns in which, during the past night, the whale had reeled the involutions of the lines around him, the half torn body of the Parsee was seen; his sable raiment frayed to shreds; his distended eyes turned full upon old Ahab.

The harpoon dropped from his hand.

"Befooled, befooled!"—drawing in a long lean breath—"Aye, Parsee! I see thee again.—Aye, and thou goest before; and this, *this* then is the hearse that thou didst promise. But I hold thee to the last letter of thy word. Where is the second hearse? Away, mates, to the ship! those boats are useless now; repair them if ye can in time, and return to me; if not, Ahab is enough to die— Down, men! the first thing that but offers to jump from this boat I stand in, that thing I harpoon. Ye are not other men, but my arms and my legs; and so obey me.—Where's the whale? gone down again?"

But he looked too nigh the boat; for as if bent upon escaping with the corpse he bore, and as if the particular place of the last encounter had been but a stage in his leeward voyage, Moby Dick was now again steadily swimming forward; and had almost passed the ship,—which thus far had been sailing in the contrary direction to him, though for the present her headway had been stopped. He seemed swimming with his utmost velocity, and now only intent upon pursuing his own straight path in the sea.

"Oh! Ahab," cried Starbuck, "not too late is it, even now, the third day, to desist. See! Moby Dick seeks thee not. It is thou, thou, that madly seekest him!"

Setting sail to the rising wind, the lonely boat was swiftly impelled to leeward, by both oars and canvas. And at last when Ahab was sliding by the vessel, so near as plainly to distinguish Starbuck's face as he leaned over the rail, he hailed him to turn the vessel about, and follow him, not too swiftly, at a judicious interval. Glancing upwards, he saw Tashtego, Queequeg, and Daggoo, eagerly mounting to the three mast-heads; while the oarsmen were rocking in the two staved boats which had but just been hoisted to the side, and were busily at work in repairing them. One after the other, through the portholes, as he sped, he also caught flying glimpses of Stubb and Flask, busying themselves on deck among bundles of new irons and lances. As he saw all this; as he heard the hammers in the broken boats; far other hammers seemed driving a nail into his heart. But he rallied. And now marking that the vane or flag was gone from the main-mast-head, he shouted to Tashtego, who had just gained that perch, to descend again for another flag, and a hammer and nails, and so nail it to the mast.

Whether fagged by the three days' running chase, and the resistance to his swimming in the knotted hamper he bore; or whether it was some latent deceitfulness and malice in him: whichever was true, the White Whale's way now began to abate, as it seemed, from the boat so rapidly nearing him once more; though indeed the whale's last start had not been so long a one as before. And still as Ahab glided over the waves the unpitying sharks accompanied him; and so pertinaciously stuck to the boat; and so continually bit at the plying oars, that the blades became jagged and crunched, and left small splinters in the sea, at almost every dip.

"Heed them not! those teeth but give new rowlocks to your oars. Pull on! 'tis the better rest, the shark's jaw than the yielding water."

"But at every bite, sir, the thin blades grow smaller and smaller!"

"They will last long enough! pull on!—But who can tell"—he muttered—"whether these sharks swim to feast on the whale or on Ahab?—But pull on! Aye, all alive, now—we near him. The helm! take the helm; let me pass,"—and so saying, two of the oarsmen helped him forward to the bows of the still flying boat.

At length as the craft was cast to one side, and ran ranging along with the White Whale's flank, he seemed strangely oblivious of its advance—as the whale sometimes will—and Ahab was fairly within the smoky mountain mist, which, thrown off from the whale's spout, curled round his great, Monadnock hump; he was even thus close to him; when, with body arched back, and both arms lengthwise high-lifted to the poise, he darted his fierce iron, and his far fiercer curse into the hated whale. As both steel and curse sank to the socket, as if sucked into a morass, Moby Dick sideways writhed; spasmodically rolled his nigh flank against the bow, and, without staving a hole in it, so suddenly canted the boat over, that had it not been for the elevated part of the gunwale to which he then clung, Ahab would once more have been tossed into the sea. As it was, three of the oarsmen—who foreknew not the precise instant of the dart, and were therefore unprepared for its effects—these were flung out; but so fell, that, in an instant two of them clutched the gunwale again, and rising to its level on a combing wave, hurled themselves bodily inboard again; the third man helplessly dropping astern, but still afloat and swimming.

Almost simultaneously, with a mighty volition of ungraduated, instantaneous swiftness, the White Whale darted through the weltering sea. But when Ahab cried out to the steersman to take new turns with the line, and hold it so; and commanded the crew to turn round on their seats, and tow the boat up to the mark; the moment the treacherous line felt that double strain and tug, it snapped in the empty air!

"What breaks in me? Some sinew cracks!—'tis whole again; oars! oars! Burst in upon him!"

Hearing the tremendous rush of the sea-crashing boat, the whale wheeled round to present his blank forehead at bay; but in that evolution, catching sight of the nearing black hull of the ship; seemingly seeing in it the source of all his persecutions; bethinking it—it may be—a larger and nobler foe; of a sudden, he bore down upon its advancing prow, smiting his jaws amid fiery showers of foam.

Ahab staggered; his hand smote his forehead. "I grow blind; hands! stretch out before me that I may yet grope my way. Is't night?"

"The whale! The ship!" cried the cringing oarsmen.

"Oars! oars! Slope downwards to thy depths, O sea, that ere it be for ever too late, Ahab may slide this last, last time upon his mark! I see: the ship! the ship! Dash on, my men! Will ye not save my ship?"

But as the oarsmen violently forced their boat through the sledge-hammering seas, the before whale-smitten bow-ends of two planks burst through, and in an instant almost, the temporarily disabled boat lay nearly level with the waves; its half-wading, splashing crew, trying hard to stop the gap and bale out the pouring water.

Meantime, for that one beholding instant, Tashtego's mast-head hammer remained suspended in his hand; and the red flag, half-wrapping him as with a plaid, then streamed itself straight out from him, as his own forward-flowing heart; while Starbuck and Stubb, standing upon the bowsprit beneath, caught sight of the down-coming monster just as soon as he.

"The whale, the whale! Up helm, up helm! Oh, all ye sweet powers of air, now hug me close! Let not Starbuck die, if die he must, in a woman's fainting fit. Up helm, I say—ye fools, the jaw! the jaw! Is this the end of all my bursting prayers? all my life-long fidelities? Oh, Ahab, Ahab, lo, thy work. Steady! helmsman, steady. Nay, nay! Up helm again! He turns to meet us! Oh, his unappeasable brow drives on towards one, whose duty tells him he cannot depart. My God, stand by me now!"

"Stand not by me, but stand under me, whoever you are that will now help Stubb; for Stubb, too, sticks here. I grin at thee, thou grinning whale! Who ever helped Stubb, or kept Stubb awake, but Stubb's own unwinking eye? And now poor Stubb goes to bed upon a mattress that is all too soft; would it were stuffed with brushwood! I grin at thee, thou grinning whale! Look ye, sun, moon and stars! I call ye assassins of as good a fellow as ever spouted up his ghost. For all that, I would yet ring glasses with ye, would ye but hand the cup! Oh, oh, oh, oh! thou grinning whale, but there'll be plenty of gulping soon! Why fly ye not, O Ahab? For me, off shoes and jacket to it; let Stubb die in his drawers! A most mouldy and over salted death, though;—cherries! cherries! cherries! Oh, Flask, for one red cherry ere we die!"

"Cherries? I only wish that we were where they grow. Oh, Stubb, I hope my poor mother's drawn my part-pay ere this; if not, few coppers will now come to her, for the voyage is up."

From the ship's bows, nearly all the seamen now hung inactive; hammers, bits of plank, lances, and harpoons, mechanically retained in their hands, just as they had darted from their various employments; all their enchanted eyes intent upon the whale, which from side to side strangely vibrating his pre-destinating head, sent a broad band of overspreading semicircular foam before him as he rushed. Retribution, swift vengeance, eternal malice were in his whole aspect, and spite of all that mortal man could do, the solid white buttress of his forehead smote the ship's starboard bow, till men and timbers reeled. Some fell flat upon their faces. Like dislodged trucks, the heads of the harpooners aloft shook on their bull-like necks. Through the breach, they heard the waters pour, as mountain torrents down a flume.

"The ship! The hearse!—the second hearse!" cried Ahab from the boat; "its wood could only be American!"

Diving beneath the settling ship, the whale ran quivering along its keel; but turning under water, swiftly shot to the surface again, far off the other bow, but within a few yards of Ahab's boat, where, for a time, he lay quiescent.

"I turn my body from the sun. What ho, Tashtego! let me hear thy hammer. Oh! ye three unsurrendered spires of mine; thou uncracked keel; and only god-bullied hull; thou firm deck, and haughty helm, and Pole-pointed prow,—death-glorious ship! must ye then perish, and without me? Am I cut off from the last fond pride of meanest shipwrecked captains? Oh, lonely death on lonely life! Oh, now I feel my topmost greatness lies in my topmost grief. Ho, ho! from all your furthest bounds, pour ye now in, ye bold billows of my whole foregone life, and top this one piled comber of my death! Towards thee I roll, thou all-destroying but unconquering whale; to the last I grapple with thee; from hell's heart I stab at thee; for hate's sake I spit my last breath at thee. Sink all coffins and all hearses to one common pool! and since neither can be mine let me then tow to pieces, while still chasing thee, though tied to thee, thou damned whale! Thus, I give up the spear!"

The harpoon was darted; the stricken whale flew forward; with igniting velocity the line ran through the groove;—ran foul. Ahab stooped to clear it; he did clear it; but the flying turn caught him round the neck, and voicelessly as Turkish mutes bowstring their victim, he was shot out of the boat, ere the crew knew he was gone. Next instant, the heavy eyesplice in the rope's final end flew out of the stark-empty tub, knocked down an oarsman, and smiting the sea, disappeared in its depths.

For an instant, the tranced boat's crew stood still; then turned. "The ship? Great God, where is the ship?" Soon they through dim, bewildering mediums saw her sidelong fading phantom, as in the gaseous Fata Morgana; only the uppermost masts out of water; while fixed by infatuation, or fidelity, or fate, to their once lofty perches, the pagan harpooners still maintained their sinking lookouts on the sea. And now, concentric circles seized the lone boat itself, and all its crew, and each floating oar, and every lance-pole, and spinning, animate and inanimate, all round and round in one vortex, carried the smallest chip of the Pequod out of sight.

But as the last whelmings intermixingly poured themselves over the sunken head of the Indian at the mainmast, leaving a few inches of the erect spar yet visible, together with long streaming yards of the flag, which calmly undulated, with ironical coincidings, over the destroying billows they almost touched;—at that instant, a red arm and a hammer hovered backwardly uplifted in the open air, in the act of nailing the flag faster and yet faster to the subsiding spar. A sky-hawk that tauntingly had followed the main-truck downwards from its natural home among the stars, pecking at the flag, and incommoding Tashtego there; this bird now chanced to intercept its broad fluttering wing between the hammer and the wood; and simultaneously feeling that etherial thrill, the submerged savage beneath, in his death-gasp, kept his hammer frozen there; and so the bird of heaven, with archangelic shrieks, and his imperial beak thrust upwards, and his whole captive form folded in the flag of Ahab, went down with his ship, which, like Satan, would not sink to hell till she had dragged a living part of heaven along with her, and helmeted herself with it.

Now small fowls flew screaming over the yet yawning gulf; a sullen white surf beat against its steep sides; then all collapsed, and the great shroud of the sea rolled on as it rolled five thousand years ago.

Whaling Near the Falklands

by CAPTAIN W. H. MACY

No more whales were seen till the *Arethusa* had passed the latitude of 48 degrees south, and was nearly up with the Falklands. The wind was fresh from south-west, and the ship close-hauled on the south-south-east tack, diving into a head sea under whole topsails, making wet weather of it; while the aspect of the heavens was threatening, and indicated more wind before night. Mr. Dunham, who went to the masthead in the forenoon, reported a large "breach" on the weather quarter five miles distant. The ship stood on for a short time, and then going about, headed up nearly in the direction where the breach was seen. In an hour after tacking, spouts were seen, and were soon made out beyond question to be those of three large sperm whales going slowly to leeward. When they went down again they were not more than two miles from us; but it was by this time high noon, and the wind and sea had increased, so that the ship was brought down to double-reefed topsails. The chances were not at all favorable for chasing whales with much prospect of success. But Captain Upton and his officers were not to be daunted by trifles, with sperm whales in sight; and their doctrine was, that as long as a boat could live she could tackle a whale and kill him. So everything was cleared for action, and after standing on till he judged the ship near enough, the captain ordered the maintopsail hauled aback, and the boats hoisted and swung. This was hardly accomplished when the whales broke water within half a dozen ship's lengths of the lee-beam.

"Lower away!" was the word, and down went all three boats, the starboard boat having the advantage in this case from being on the lee quarter, and getting clear of the ship in advance of the rest.

The whales were as yet apparently undisturbed, and the chance of striking what would be considered a sure one, as they would not readily take the alarm in such weather. There was no need of spreading a sail to a breeze like this; it was only necessary to head the boat off before the wind and sea, and giving her a slight impetus with the paddle-strokes, to drive quietly down upon the prey.

The two mates, as they shoved astern of the ship, saw the exact state of things, and merely suffered their boats to run to leeward, without effort, so as to be at hand to support the captain if he should strike, without interfering with his chance by competition. Seated at the bow thwart next the boatsteerer, I had a fair view of the advance to the attack, and regarded the progress of the starboard boat with eager interest, not unmixed with anxiety, as I thought of the difficulty and danger of grappling with these monsters in such weather. Mr. Johnson stood up in the head of his boat grasping the bight of the warp in his left hand, the right resting on his "iron poles," while the other four continued dipping their paddles to add to the speed of the lively boat, which was sliding down to leeward, as it were, at a rate that promised soon to place her within striking distance. Already she was within a ship's length of the right hand one, for which the captain was steering, when the off whale of the three took the alarm, as was evinced by his elevating his head rather more than usual, and then cutting out a corner of his flukes with that peculiar movement known to whalemen as indicative of an intention to leave soon. The panic spread to the others instantly, by that sort of magnetic communication which whales seem to employ even when miles apart. A sudden and convulsive movement was observed in all three of them at the same instant. It was evident that like Macbeth's guests, they would "stand not upon the order of their going." The left-hand whale, who had first perceived the danger, was gone like a flash, his tail skimming out just above the surface; his next neighbor shot ahead half his length with a sudden effort, and threw his flukes high in air; the third, who had just blown off his spout, attempted the same manoeuvre, but it was too late; the boat was shooting too quick for him. As he threw up his body, the head of the boat was just abreast of his "small," rushing down the declivity of a wave.

"Dart!" cried Captain Upton, in a voice that rose high above the roaring of the wind and sea; "dart, and try him!"

Quick as thought the flashing iron sped on its mission from the long, sinewy arms of the mulatto, and its sudden stoppage, and the quiver of the pole in the "suds" as his keen eye noted it, told him it had found its mark. Already the second one was drawn back for a dart; Father Grafton had roared, "Spring ahead! He's fast!" when the air was darkened by the ponderous tail of the infuriated monster, which seemed to hang poised for an instant—a cry of "Stern! stern hard! !"—a crash—and the starboard boat was buried in a cloud of foam. "Spring, men! he stove!" shouted the mate, and with the heave of the next sea the wreck seemed to struggle up through the boiling vortex, the crew striking out for their lives to meet the approaching boats. No whale was to be seen; but what struck a chill to every heart, only five heads could be counted!

"Spring, men, do! they're all swimming for it! Peak your oar, Bunker, and stand by to lend them a hand! Don't look for the whale now! Two—three—four—five—O God! where's Mr. Johnson?"

The oath must have been overlooked by the recording angel. The third mate had sunk to rise no more till the great day of reckoning. The whole head of the boat, as far as the bow-thwart, was crushed to splinters by the fearful blow; and the bowman seemed to have escaped by a miracle. The half-drowned men were pulled into the other two boats; and the line was found to be cut, but no one seemed clearly to know how, when, or by whom. Anxious eyes peered round, hoping against hope, to see the head of the lost man; but a moment's reflection served to convince Captain Upton of the impossibility of his having escaped. He was silent for a short space after he stood by the side of his mate; then pointing significantly at the crushed fragments of the boat's bow, "He must have been killed instantly, Mr. Grafton," he said, and a tear started from the eye of the strong man, and was lost among the briny drops that were streaming from every thread of his clothing.

Father Grafton answered only by a nod of assent, showing his full conviction of the worst. A moment and the captain was himself again! He had paid the tribute of a full heart, and was once more the whaling captain, alive to the emergency of the moment.

"Pull ahead, and pick up the wreck! We'll save all the craft we can, Mr. Dunham, but never mind the boat. We must let her go, and bear a hand aboard—it's breezing on all the time, and I expect we shall have it harder tonight. Don't stop for small matters; save the oars and line—boat's sail if you can. Set your waif, Mr. Grafton, for the ship—never mind, he's coming; I see her falling off now. Lay off a little from the wreck, boys; don't, for Heaven's sake, stave another boat now. There, that'll do; stand by to pull ahead. What's 'Cooper' running so far for? I wonder if he'll think to come to on the starboard tack, so as to hoist these boats to leeward. Yes! all right! there he braces up his mizzen topsail! Pull ahead, and let's get snug before night!"

The *Arethusa* came flying up to the wind with her topsails run down on the caps, and the jib at the boom-end slatting at a furious rate, as the overloaded boats pulled alongside under her lee.

"Keep your tackles up clear till we give the word! Look out on deck for some of this lumber! Bear a hand—what are you all staring at?" for the shipkeepers seemed to be paralyzed with dread, at not seeing the third mate in either of the boats.

"Light out now, all but two to hook on! Here, come to the falls, everybody, and stand by to run the boat up. Now's your time, Mr. Grafton—hook on—all ready, Bunker? *Fore and aft!* Quick, boys, and take her out of water!"

The boats were fortunately secured in the cranes, without accident. The wind was piping on to a gale and a thick, driving mist, bringing an icy sensation with it from the southward, gave evidence that we were approaching the Cape Horn latitudes.

"Clew the fore and mizzentopsails right up, Mr. Grafton! Send some hands out to stow the jib—never mind hauling down the foretack—we shall have to reef the foresail soon. Make all snug as fast as you can, and have some small tackles ready for securing the lee-boats to-night." And the "old man" went below to find some dry clothing, and to indulge his feeling now that he had leisure to reflect upon the loss of Mr. Johnson.

The *Arethusa* was soon careening to the blast under her close-reefed maintopsail and staysails, the whole heavens shrouded in gloom, and, as the shades of night drew down upon the wild scene, each one seemed to realize that we had cause of congratulation in the fact of our timely arrival on board, and shuddered to think what might have been our fate, if exposed an hour or two longer in open boats, had the whale run us some distance from the ship before the thick weather shut down hiding her from view. It is at such times that the seaman feels his own nothingness, and realizes his dependence on the mercy of Heaven. The whaleman, in particular, has frequent cause to feel how narrowly he has escaped such dangers. Even other mariners have little idea of the risks encountered by this class of men; for whalemen form the only branch of the profession who may be truly said to make their home on the ocean; to "go *down* to the sea in ships," while others skim across it; and in a literal sense, to "*do business* on the great waters."

Little was said among the officers about the dreadful casualty which had so suddenly removed one of their number, but many a thrilling story went round the forecastle that night from the old hands, the more impressive from the circumstance of the speakers lying in their berths, with the darkness relieved by only one dimly-burning lamp, swaying and flickering with the motion of the ship in the gale—of men who had met violent deaths in various ways, and of hairbreadth escapes of others, in most of which latter cases, the narrator was, of course, himself the hero of the adventure.

Morning broke upon the stout ship still lying to under short canvas, the wind howling through the rigging, the decks drenched with spray, and everything cold and cheerless. The gale, however, now came in fitful gusts, with lulls between; in evidence that it had spent its force, and was breaking up. The morning watch were collected aft on the lee side of the deck, while Father Grafton, wrapped in pilotcloth, stood holding on by the weather quarter rail, and gazing at the sky to windward, observing the signs of better weather. As he turned and threw his glance casually off to leeward, a sudden lighting up of his countenance told that something had arrested his attention. He changed his position for a better view, and, in a moment more, spoke:

"There it is again. Blo-o-ows! Sperm whale—there's white water! wounded whale, too—I know by the way he spouts. That must be the whale we struck yesterday—Blo-o-ows! Steward! tell Captain Upton there's a sperm whale off the lee-beam!"

It was unnecessary to tell him, for he was just stepping out of the cabin at the moment.

"Where away, Mr. Grafton?" Then, as his quick eye caught the smoke of the spout blowing off, "Ah! yes! I see him—there's white water. Yes, that's the whale that killed Mr. Johnson. O, if we only had good weather to pay him off for it!"

Then looking to windward, "How *is* the weather, anyhow? Can't we go down and have a dig at him? No, no, it's no use to put boats down into this sea. By thunder! how he lies there, aggravating us! badly hurt, too; he can't go much. Got both irons in him, I expect—I couldn't tell about the second iron. Can't we keep the run of him till the weather moderates?"

"I think we can," said the mate, "if he don't work to windward—and I don't think he will. He must have gone just about the drift of the ship through the night. We might kill him from the ship, but then we couldn't secure him afterwards, and we should drift to leeward of him."

"I'd like to have the killing of him!" said the captain, eagerly. "I want a little revenge on that whale, and I would rather kill him than any other one in the ocean." Another impatient look to windward, "No, no, we can't use the boats. The-e-ere's white water again! We'll try him with the ship anyhow. Get some lances ready, and we'll run down there and have a fling at him—if we lose a lance or two it's no great matter—we'll have revenge at any rate. It's moderating every minute, eh, Mr. Grafton?"

"Yes, sir; and there's the sun trying to break through the clouds yonder. I think we shall have good weather in an hour or two."

"Yes, but it will take some time for the sea to go down. Get your lances ready! Here, Blacksmith, bend the end of that line to the lance warp. We mustn't check too short, Mr. Grafton, or we'll lose all our lances."

The whale was not more than a quarter of a mile off, bearing a little abaft the beam, or nearly dead to leeward, and appeared to be too badly hurt to go down. All hands were on deck to assist in the sport, and lances were hastily prepared at various points along the starboard side of the ship.

"Hard up your helm, there!" shouted the captain. "Run down the mizzen-staysail, and shiver in the mainyard! Here, Jeff, I want you at the wheel, and mind the word, quick. See the whale now, Mr. Dunham? Yes, there he is—let her go off more yet. *Well*, the mainyard! Belay that—haul taut the lee-braces. *Stead-y!* meet her, quick, Jeff—stand by your lances now." And Captain Upton ran to his place by the starboard fore-swifter, and Mr. Grafton into the fore-chains abaft him, while the second mate stood ready in the waist, and the boatsteerers, armed with similar weapons, found eligible stations still further in reserve.

The ship was now booming off under good headway, rolling heavily in the trough of the sea. "Starboard a little, Jeff—so, steady! meet her, quick, meet her. Port a little—so, steady as you go now!" said the eager and excited captain, coursing the ship so as to shave just clear of the whale, who lay "sogging" up and down in his element, and occasionally blowing, the spout having a faint and broken appearance as if forced from him by a painful effort.

As we drew near, the iron could be distinctly seen in his back, the pole hanging down by his side, and soon as he raised his flukes to thrash the sea in his agony, the other one was discovered in his "small." The last effort of a dying man had driven it home!

"Now, then, stand by, all of you," said the captain, in a suppressed voice. "We shall have a good chance but it's awkward darting, if we don't catch the roll of the ship right. If I *miss* him, Mr. Grafton, *don't you!*"

At the moment the whale was abreast the martingale, he moved his hand to port the helm, and stand by the braces.

"Now's our time!" as the next roll of the ship brought her fore-channels nearly into the water just at the right moment, and both lances entered the whale's body at the same instant, driven to the socket.

"Hard a port! Brace up the mainyard! Bear a hand, and let her come to the wind!"

The whale had buried himself beneath the surface, on receiving the deadly steel. The captain's lance drew out, but Mr. Grafton's warp was snapped like a thread, and the lance was left in his body. The reserves had no chance to grease their weapons.

"Run up that mizzen-staysail!" shouted the "old man," as the ship was brought rapidly to the wind, shipping a considerable body of water forward, which luckily did no damage.

"Where's the whale? I see the bloody water here on the quarter. Up aloft, two or three of ye, and keep a sharp eye out for him!"

The order was superfluous, for half a dozen were already in the rigging at different points.

"Loose the foresail, Mr. Grafton, fore and mizzentop-sails, too. We mustn't drift off any more—it's going to moderate; and we may be able to keep the run of him. There he blo-o-ows! right astern! *blood thick as tar!*" roared Captain Upton, wild with excitement, as the immense spermaceti rose in the ship's wake, and the blood-red cloud blown off to leeward from his spiracle, told that the death of Mr. Johnson was avenged.

The weather had materially improved by the time the topsails were sheeted home and set. Vigilant eyes at the masthead observed the whale's movement, and in time the ship wore round and stood along near him in time to see him go in his dying "flurry" within a short distance of his relentless enemies. The sea would not admit of a boat being lowered to take possession; but he was kept in sight by watching the "slick," and manoeuvring on short tacks all the forenoon.

After dinner, the gale having abated to a whole topsail breeze, and the sea gone down so that a boat with a picked crew and careful management might venture to cut a hole, the larboard boat was lowered, and after considerable difficulty he was hauled alongside and fluked. The cutting gear was got up, and the work driven with all possible expedition, for moderate weather was not to be depended upon for any length of time in these latitudes. Still, it was three o'clock by the time we got fairly hooked on, and what with surging and parting, and tearing out hooks, little progress was made, and at dark we "lashed down," and knocked off our arduous duty with one blanket piece in the blubber-room, the whale's body riding by the large flukechain, and the head cut off and secured alongside by the small chain and two parts of a large new hawser. The wind was hauling to the westward, and blowing on another gale. All sail was taken in, and the watches set; darkness shut down its dread pall around, and the howling of the night storm was rendered more dismal by the screams of thousands of ravenous albatrosses sitting in the "slick" to windward of the ship, and the clanking and surging of the fluke-chain as it quivered under the terrific strain. At midnight the small chain attached to the head parted, but by veering away a longer scope on the ropes the ponderous mass seemed to ride easier than before. The ropes held bravely till four o'clock, when weakened by long-continued stretch, strain and chafe, they gave way; and the valuable head, containing at least forty barrels of sperm, went dancing off upon a mountain wave, and could be seen from time to time flashing up through the darkness, till it was lost to view in the gloom to windward.

The fluke-chain still hung, but the gale and sea increasing every moment, the strain at last became too powerful even for its great strength, and it snapped about daylight with the report of a gun. The wind had hauled round gradually by north-west, and was now nearly at north, and fair for the course on which we were bound. Captain Upton was on deck when the chain parted, and looked with longing eyes off the weather quarter at the lost prize till it could be seen no longer; then, satisfied no more could be done to save it, he ordered the helm up, and, setting the foresail and close-reefed fore and maintopsails, the proud ship once more bounded before the favorable gale, laying her course inside of the Falklands for Cape Horn.

Christmas Dinner Aboard a Whale

by FRANK BULLEN

Christmas Day drew near, beloved of Englishmen all the world over, thought little of by Americans. The two previous ones spent on board the *Cachalot* have been passed over without mention, absolutely no notice being taken of the season by any one on board, to all appearance. In English ships some attempt is always made to give the day somewhat of a festive character, and to maintain the national tradition of good-cheer and goodwill in whatever part of the world you may happen to be. For some reason or other, perhaps because of the great increase in comfort we had all experienced lately, I felt the approach of the great Christian anniversary very strongly; although, had I been in London, I should probably have spent it in lonely gloom, having no relatives or friends whom I might visit. But what of that? Christmas is Christmas; and, if we have no home, we think of the place where our home should be; and whether, as cynics sneer, Dickens invented the English Christmas or not, its observance has taken deep root among us. May its shadow never be less!

On Christmas morning I mounted to the crow's-nest at daybreak, and stood looking with never-failing awe at the daily marvel of the sunrise. Often and often have I felt choking for words to express the tumult of thoughts aroused by this sublime spectacle. Hanging there in cloudland, the tiny microcosm at one's feet forgotten, the grandeur of the celestial outlook is overwhelming. Many and many a time I have bowed my head and wept in pure reverence at the majesty manifested around me while the glory of the dawn increased and brightened, till with one exultant bound the sun appeared.

For some time I stood gazing straight ahead of me with eyes that saw not, filled with wonder and admiration. I must have been looking directly at the same spot for quite a quarter of an hour, when suddenly, as if I had but just opened my eyes, I saw the well-known bushy spout of a sperm whale. I raised the usual yell, which rang through the stillness discordantly, startling all hands out of their lethargy like bees out of a hive. After the usual preliminaries, we were all afloat with sails set, gliding slowly over the sleeping sea towards the unconscious objects of our attention. The captain did not lower this time, as there only appeared to be three fish, none of them seeming large. Though at any distance it is extremely difficult to assess the size of whales, the spout being very misleading. Sometimes a full-sized whale will show a small spout, while a twenty-barrel cow will exhale a volume of vapour extensive enough for two or three at once.

Now although, according to etiquette, I kept my position in the rear of my superior officers, I had fully determined in my own mind, being puffed up with previous success, to play second fiddle to no one, if I could help it, this time. Samuela was decidedly of the same opinion; indeed, I believe he would have been delighted to tackle a whole school single-handed, while my crew were all willing and eager for the fight. We had a long, tedious journey before we came up with them, the wind being so light that even with the occasional assistance of the paddles our progress was wretchedly slow. When at last we did get into their water, and the mate's harpooner stood up to dart, his foot slipped, and down he came with a clatter enough to scare a cachalot twenty miles away. It gallied our friends effectually, sending them flying in different directions at the top of their speed. But being some distance astern of the other boats, one of the fish, in his headlong retreat, rose for a final blow some six or seven fathoms away, passing us in the opposite direction. His appearance was only momentary, yet in that moment Samuela hurled his harpoon into the air, where it described a beautiful parabola, coming down upon the disappearing monster's back just as the sea was closing over it. Oh, it was a splendid dart, worthy of the finest harpooner that ever lived! There was no time for congratulations, however, for we spun round as on a pivot, and away we went in the wake of that fellow at a great rate. I cast one look astern to see whether the others had struck, but could see nothing of them; we seemed to have sprung out of their ken in an instant.

The speed of our friend was marvellous, but I comforted myself with the knowledge that these animals usually run in circles—sometimes, it is true, of enormous diameter, but seldom getting far away from the starting-point. But as the time went on, and we seemed to fly over the waves at undiminished speed, I began to think this whale might be the exception necessary to prove the rule, so I got out the compass and watched his course. Due east, not a degree to north or south of it, straight as a bee to its hive. The ship was now far out of sight astern, but I knew that keen eyes had been watching our movements from the masthead, and that every effort possible would be made to keep the run of us. The speed of our whale was not only great, but unflagging. He was more like a machine than an animal capable of tiring; and though we did our level best, at the faintest symptom of slackening, to get up closer and lance him, it was for some time impossible. After, at a rough estimate, running in a direct easterly course for over two hours, he suddenly sounded, without having given us the ghost of a chance to "land him one where he lived." Judging from his previous exertions, though, it was hardly possible he would be able to stay down long, or get very deep, as the strain upon these vast creatures at any depth is astonishingly exhausting. After a longer stay below than usual, when they have gone extra deep, they often arrive at the surface manifestly "done up" for a time. Then, if the whaleman be active and daring, a few well-directed strokes may be got in which will promptly settle the business out of hand.

Now, when my whale sounded he was to all appearance as frightened a beast as one could wish—one who had run himself out endeavouring to get away from his enemies, and as a last resource had dived into the quietness below in the vain hope to get away. So I regarded him, making up my mind to wait on him with diligence upon his arrival, and not allow him to get breath before I had settled him. But when he did return, there was a mighty difference in him. He seemed as if he had been getting some tips on the subject from some school below where whales are trained to hunt men; for his first move was to come straight for me with a furious rush, carrying the war into the enemy's country with a vengeance. It must be remembered that I was but young, and a comparatively new hand at this sort of thing; so when I confess that I felt more than a little scared at this sudden change in the tactics of my opponent, I hope I shall be excused. Remembering, however, that all our lives depended on keeping cool, I told myself that even if I was frightened I must not go all to pieces, but compel myself to think and act calmly, since I was responsible for others. If the animal had not been in so blind a fury, I am afraid my task would have been much harder; but he was mad, and his savage rushes were, though disquieting, unsystematic and clumsy. It was essential, however, that he should not be allowed to persist too long in his evil courses; for a whale learns with amazing rapidity, developing such cunning in an hour or two that all a man's smartness may be unable to cope with his newly-acquired experience. Happily, Samuela was perfectly unmoved. Like a machine, he obeyed every gesture, every look even, swinging that boat "off" or "on" the whale with such sweeping strokes of his mighty oar that she revolved as if on a pivot, and encouraging the other chaps with his cheerful cries and odd grimaces, so that the danger was hardly felt. During a momentary lull in the storm, I took the opportunity to load my bomb-gun, much as I disliked handling the thing, keeping my eye all the time on the water around where I expected to see mine enemy popping up murderously at any minute. Just as I had expected, when he rose, it was very close, and on his back, with his jaw in the first biting position, looking ugly as a vision of death. Finding us little out of reach, he rolled right over towards us, presenting as he did so the great rotundity of his belly. We were not twenty feet away, and I snatched up the gun, levelled it, and fired the bomb point-blank into his bowels. Then all was blank. I do not even remember the next moment. A rush of roaring waters, a fighting with fearful, desperate energy for air and life, all in a hurried, flurried phantasmagoria about which there was nothing clear except the primitive desire for life, life, life! Nor do I know how long this struggle lasted, except that, in the nature of things, it could not have been very long.

When I returned to a consciousness of external things, I was for some time perfectly still, looking at the sky, totally unable to realize what had happened or where I was. Presently the smiling, pleasant face of Samuela bent over me. Meeting my gratified look of recognition, he set up a perfect yell of delight. "So glad, so glad you blonga life! No go Davy Jonesy dis time, hay?" I put my hand out to help myself to a sitting posture, and touched blubber. That startled me so that I sprang up as if shot. Then I took in the situation at a glance. There were all my poor fellows with me, stranded upon the top of our late antagonist, but no sign of the boat to be seen. Bewildered at the state of affairs, I looked appealingly from one to the other for an explanation. I got it from Abner, who said, laconically, "When yew fired thet ole gun, I guess it mus' have bin loaded fer bear, fer ye jest tumbled clear head over heels backwards outen the boat. Et that very same moment I suspicion the bomb busted in his belly, fer he went clean rampageous loony. He rolled right over an' over to'rds us, n' befo' we c'd rightly see wat wuz comin', we cu'dnt see anythin' 'tall; we wuz all grabbin' at nothin', some'rs underneath the whale. When I come to the top, I lit eout fer the fust thing I c'd see to lay holt of, which wuz old squarehead himself, deader'n pork. I guess that ar bomb o' yourn kinder upset his commissary department. Anyway, I climbed up onto him, 'n bimeby the rest ov us histed themselves alongside ov me. Sam Weller here; he cum last, towin' you 'long with him. I don'no whar he foun' ye, but ye was very near a goner, 'n's full o' pickle as ye c'd hold." I turned a grateful eye upon my dusky harpooner, who had saved my life, but was now apparently blissfully unconscious of having done anything meritorious.

Behold us, then, a half-drowned row of scarecrows perched, like some new species of dilapidated birds, upon the side of our late foe. The sun was not so furiously hot as usual, for masses of rain-laden *nimbi* were filling the sky, so that we were comparatively free from the awful roasting we might have expected; nor was our position as precarious for a while as would be thought. True, we had only one harpoon, with its still fast line, to hold on by; but the side of the whale was somehow hollowed, so that, in spite of the incessant movement imparted to the carcass by the swell, we sat fairly safe, with our feet in the said hollow. We discussed the situation in all its bearings, unable to extract more than the faintest gleam of hope from any aspect of the case. The only reasonable chance we had was, that the skipper had almost certainly taken our bearings, and would, we were sure, be anxiously seeking us on the course thus indicated. Meanwhile, we were ravenously hungry and thirsty. Samuela and Polly set to work with their sheath-knives, and soon excavated a space in the blubber to enable them to reach the meat. Then they cut off some good-sized junks, and divided it up. It was not half bad; and as we chewed on the tough black fibre, I could hardly help smiling as I thought how queer a Christmas dinner we were having. But eating soon heightened our thirst, and our real sufferings then began. We could eat very little, once the want of drink made itself felt. Hardly two hours had elapsed, though, before one of the big-bellied clouds which had been keeping the sun off us most considerately emptied out upon us a perfect torrent of rain. It filled the cavity in the whale's side in a twinkling; and though the water was greasy, stained with blood, and vilely flavoured, it was as welcome a drink as I have ever tasted. Thus fed, and with our thirst slaked, we were able to take a more hopeful view of things, while the prospect of our being found seemed much more probable than it had done before the rain fell.

Still, we had to endure our pillory for a long while yet. The sharks and birds began to worry us, especially the former, who in their eagerness to get a portion of the blubber fought, writhed, and tore at the carcass with tireless energy. Once, one of the smaller ones actually came sliding up right into our hollow; but Samuela and Polly promptly dispatched him with a cut throat, sending him back to encourage the others. The present relieved us of most of their attentions for a short time at least, as they eagerly divided the remains of their late comrade among them.

To while away the time we spun yarns—without much point, I am afraid; and sung songs, albeit we did not feel much like singing—till after a while our poor attempts at gaiety fizzled out like a damp match, leaving us silent and depressed. The sun, which had been hidden for some time, now came out again, his slanting beams revealing to us ominously the flight of time and the near approach of night. Should darkness overtake us in our present position, we all felt that saving us would need the performance of a miracle; for in addition to the chances of the accumulated gases within the carcass bursting it asunder, the unceasing assault of the sharks made it highly doubtful whether they would not in a few hours more have devoured it piecemeal. Already they had scooped out some deep furrows in the solid blubber, making it easier to get hold and tear off more, and their numbers were increasing so fast that the surrounding sea was fairly alive with them. Lower and lower sank the sun, deeper and darker grew the gloom upon our faces, till suddenly Samuela leaped to his feet in our midst, and emitted a yell so ear-piercing as to nearly deafen us. He saw the ship! Before two minutes had passed we all saw her— God bless her—coming down upon us like some angelic messenger. There were no fears among us that we should be overlooked. We knew full well how anxiously and keenly many pairs of eyes had been peering over the sea in search of us, and we felt perfectly sure they had sighted us long ago. On she came, gilded by thet evening glow, till she seemed glorified, moving in a halo of celestial light, all her homeliness and clumsy build forgotten in what she then represented to us.

Never before or since has a ship looked like that to me, nor can I ever forget the thankfulness, the delight, the reverence, with which I once more saw her approaching. Straight down upon us she bore, rounding to within a cable's length, and dropping a boat simultaneously with her windward sweep. They had no whale—well for us they had not. In five minutes we were on board, while our late resting-place was being hauled alongside with great glee.

The captain shook hands with me cordially, pooh-poohing the loss of the boat as an unavoidable incident of the trade, but expressing his heart-felt delight at getting us all back safe. The whale we had killed was ample compensation for the loss of several boats, though such was the vigour with which the sharks were going for him, that it was deemed advisable to cut in at once, working all night. We who had been rescued, however, were summarily ordered below by the skipper, and forbidden, on pain of his severe displeasure, to reappear until the following morning. This great privilege we gladly availed ourselves of, awaking at daylight quite well and fit, not a bit the worse for our queer experience of the previous day.

The whale proved a great acquisition, for although not nearly so large as many we had caught, he was so amazingly rich in blubber that he actually yielded twelve and a half tuns of oil, in spite of the heavy toll taken of him by the hungry multitudes of sharks. In addition to the oil, we were fortunate enough to secure a lump of ambergris, dislodged perhaps by the explosion of my bomb in the animal's bowels. It was nearly black, wax-like to the touch, and weighed seven pounds and a half. At the current price, it would be worth about £200, so that, taken altogether, the whale very nearly approached in value the largest one we had yet caught. I had almost omitted to state that incorporated with the substance of the ambergris were several of the horny cuttle-fish beaks, which, incapable of being digested, had become in some manner part of this peculiar product.

The *Ghost* Loses Her
Seal-Hunting Boats

by JACK LONDON

Strange to say, in spite of the general foreboding, nothing of especial moment happened on the *Ghost*. We ran on to the north and west till we raised the coast of Japan and picked up with the great seal herd. Coming from no man knew where in the illimitable Pacific, it was travelling north on its annual migration to the rookeries of Bering Sea. And north we travelled with it, ravaging and destroying, flinging the naked carcasses to the shark and salting down the skins so that they might later adorn the fair shoulders of the women of the cities.

It was wanton slaughter, and all for woman's sake. No man ate of the seal meat or the oil. After a good day's killing I have seen our decks covered with hides and bodies, slippery with fat and blood, the scuppers running red; masts, ropes, and rails spattered with the sanguinary color; and the men, like butchers plying their trade, naked and red of arm and hand, hard at work with ripping and flensing-knives, removing the skins from the pretty sea-creatures they had killed.

It was my task to tally the pelts as they came aboard from the boats, to oversee the skinning and afterward the cleansing of the decks and bringing things shipshape again. It was not pleasant work. My soul and my stomach revolted at it; and yet, in a way, this handling and directing of many men was good for me. It developed what little executive ability I possessed, and I was aware of a toughening or hardening which I was undergoing and which could not be anything but wholesome for "Sissy" Van Weyden.

One thing I was beginning to feel, and that was that I could never again be quite the same man I had been. While my hope and faith in human life still survived Wolf Larsen's destructive criticism, he had nevertheless been a cause of change in minor matters. He had opened up for me the world of the real, of which I had known practically nothing and from which I had always shrunk. I had learned to look more closely at life as it was lived, to recognize that there were such things as facts in the world, to emerge from the realm of mind and idea and to place certain values on the concrete and objective phases of existence.

I saw more of Wolf Larsen than ever when we had gained the grounds. For when the weather was fair and we were in the midst of the herd, all hands were away in the boats, and left on board were only he and I, and Thomas Mugridge, who did not count. But there was no play about it. The six boats, spreading out fan-wise from the schooner until the first weather boat and the last lee boat were anywhere from ten to twenty miles apart, cruised along a straight course over the sea till nightfall or bad weather drove them in. It was our duty to sail the *Ghost* well to leeward of the last lee boat, so that all the boats should have fair wind to run for us in case of squalls or threatening weather.

It is no slight matter for two men, particularly when a stiff wind has sprung up, to handle a vessel like the *Ghost*, steering, keeping lookout for the boats, and setting or taking in sail; so it devolved upon me to learn and learn quickly. Steering I picked up easily, but running aloft to the crosstrees and swinging my whole weight by my arms when I left the ratlines and climbed still higher, was more difficult. This, too, I learned, and quickly, for I felt somehow a wild desire to vindicate myself in Wolf Larsen's eyes, to prove my right to live in ways other than of the mind. Nay, the time came when I took joy in the run of the masthead and in the clinging on by my legs at that precarious height while I swept the sea with glasses in search of the boats.

I remember one beautiful day, when the boats left early and the reports of the hunters' guns grew dim and distant and died away as they scattered far and wide over the sea. There was just the faintest wind from the westward; but it breathed its last by the time we managed to get to leeward of the last lee boat. One by one,—I was at the masthead and saw,—the six boats disappeared over the bulge of the earth as they followed the seal into the west. We lay, scarcely rolling on the placid sea, unable to follow. Wolf Larsen was apprehensive. The barometer was down, and the sky to the east did not please him. He studied it with unceasing vigilance.

"If she comes out of there," he said, "hard and snappy, putting us to windward of the boats, it's likely there'll be empty bunks in steerage and fo'c'sle."

By eleven o'clock the sea had become glass. By midday, though we were well up in the northerly latitudes, the heat was sickening. There was no freshness in the air. It was sultry and oppressive, reminding me of what the old Californians term "earthquake weather." There was something ominous about it, and in intangible ways one was made to feel that the worst was about to come. Slowly the whole eastern sky filled with clouds that overtowered us like some black sierra of the infernal regions. So clearly could one see cañon, gorge, and precipice, and the shadows that lie therein, that one looked unconsciously for the white surf-line and bellowing caverns where the sea charges on the land. And still we rocked gently, and there was no wind.

"It's no squall," Wolf Larsen said. "Old Mother Nature's going to get up on her hind legs and howl for all that's in her, and it'll keep us jumping, Hump, to pull through with half our boats. You'd better run up and loosen the topsails."

"But if it is going to howl, and there are only two of us?" I asked, a note of protest in my voice.

"Why, we've got to make the best of the first of it and run down to our boats before our canvas is ripped out of us. After that I don't give a rap what happens. The sticks'll stand it, and you and I will have to, though we've plenty cut out for us."

Still the calm continued. We ate dinner, a hurried and anxious meal for me with eighteen men abroad on the sea and beyond the bulge of the earth and with that heaven-rolling mountain range of clouds moving slowly down upon us. Wolf Larsen did not seem affected, however; though I noticed, when we returned to the deck, a slight twitching of the nostrils, a perceptible quickness of movement. His face was stern, the lines of it had grown hard, and yet in his eyes,—blue, clear blue this day,—there was a strange brilliancy, a bright scintillating light. It struck me that he was joyous, in a ferocious sort of way; that he was glad there was an impending struggle; that he was thrilled and upborne with knowledge that one of the great moments of living, when the tide of life surges up in flood, was upon him.

Once, and unwitting that he did so or that I saw, he laughed aloud, mockingly and defiantly, at the advancing storm. I see him yet, standing there like a pygmy out of the "Arabian Nights" before the huge front of some malignant genie. He was daring destiny, and he was unafraid.

He walked to the galley. "Cooky, by the time you've finished pots and pans you'll be wanted on deck. Stand ready for a call."

"Hump," he said, becoming cognizant of the fascinated gaze I bent upon him, "this beats whiskey, and is where your Omar misses. I think he only half lived after all."

The western half of the sky had by now grown murky. The sun had dimmed and faded out of sight. It was two in the afternoon, and a ghostly twilight, shot through by wandering purplish lights, had descended upon us. In this purplish light Wolf Larsen's face glowed and glowed, and to my excited fancy he appeared encircled by a halo. We lay in the midst of an unearthly quiet, while all about us were signs and omens of oncoming sound and movement. The sultry heat had become unendurable. The sweat was standing on my forehead, and I could feel it trickling down my nose. I felt as though I should faint, and reached out to the rail for support.

And then, just then, the faintest possible whisper of air passed by. It was from the east, and like a whisper it came and went. The drooping canvas was not stirred, and yet my face had felt the air and been cooled.

"Cooky," Wolf Larsen called in a low voice. Thomas Mugridge turned a pitiable, scared face. "Let go that fore-boom tackle and pass it across, and when she's willing let go the sheet and come in snug with the tackle. And if you make a mess of it, it will be the last you ever make. Understand?

"Mr. Van Weyden, stand by to pass the head-sails over. Then jump for the topsails and spread them quick as God'll let you—the quicker you do it the easier you'll find it. As for Cooky, if he isn't lively bat him between the eyes."

I was aware of the compliment and pleased, in that no threat had accompanied my instructions. We were lying head to northwest, and it was his intention to jibe over all with the first puff.

"We'll have the breeze on our quarter," he explained to me. "By the last guns the boats were bearing away slightly to the south'ard."

He turned and walked aft to the wheel. I went forward and took my station at the jibs. Another whisper of wind, and another, passed by. The canvas flapped lazily.

"Thank Gawd she's not comin' all of a bunch, Mr. Van Weyden," was the Cockney's fervent ejaculation.

And I was indeed thankful, for I had by this time learned enough to know, with all our canvas spread, what disaster in such event awaited us. The whispers of wind became puffs, the sails filled, the *Ghost* moved. Wolf Larsen put the wheel hard up, to port, and we began to pay off. The wind was now dead astern, muttering and puffing stronger and stronger, and my head-sails were pounding lustily. I did not see what went on elsewhere, though I felt the sudden surge and heel of the schooner as the wind-pressures changed to the jibing of the fore- and main-sails. My hands were full with the flying-jib, jib, and staysail; and by the time this part of my task was accomplished the *Ghost* was leaping into the southwest, the wind on her quarter and all her sheets to starboard. Without pausing for breath, though my heart was beating like a trip-hammer from my exertions, I sprang to the topsails, and before the wind had become too strong we had them fairly set and were coiling down. Then I went aft for orders.

Wolf Larsen nodded approval and relinquished the wheel to me. The wind was strengthening steadily and the sea rising. For an hour I steered, each moment becoming more difficult. I had not the experience to steer at the gait we were going on a quartering course.

"Now take a run up with the glasses and raise some of the boats. We've made at least ten knots, and we're going twelve or thirteen now. The old girl knows how to walk."

I contented myself with the fore crosstrees, some seventy feet above the deck. As I searched the vacant stretch of water before me, I comprehended thoroughly the need for haste if we were to recover any of our men. Indeed, as I gazed at the heavy sea through which we were running, I doubted that there was a boat afloat. It did not seem possible that such frail craft could survive such stress of wind and water.

I could not feel the full force of the wind, for we were running with it; but from my lofty perch I looked down as though outside the *Ghost* and apart from her, and saw the shape of her outlined sharply against the foaming sea as she tore along instinct with life. Sometimes she would lift and send across some great wave, burying her starboard rail from view, and covering her deck to the hatches with the boiling ocean. At such moments, starting from a windward roll, I would go flying through the air with dizzying swiftness, as though I clung to the end of a huge, inverted pendulum, the arc of which, between the greater rolls, must have been seventy feet or more. Once, the terror of this giddy sweep overpowered me, and for a while I clung on, hand and foot, weak and trembling, unable to search the sea for the missing boats or to behold aught of the sea but that which roared beneath and strove to overwhelm the *Ghost*.

But the thought of the men in the midst of it steadied me, and in my quest for them I forgot myself. For an hour I saw nothing but the naked, desolate sea. And then, where a vagrant shaft of sunlight struck the ocean and turned its surface to wrathful silver, I caught a small black speck thrust skyward for an instant and swallowed up. I waited patiently. Again the tiny point of black projected itself through the wrathful blaze a couple of points off our port-bow. I did not attempt to shout, but communicated the news to Wolf Larsen by waving my arm. He changed the course, and I signalled affirmation when the speck showed dead ahead.

It grew larger, and so swiftly that for the first time I fully appreciated the speed of our flight. Wolf Larsen motioned for me to come down, and when I stood beside him at the wheel gave me instructions for heaving to.

"Expect all hell to break loose," he cautioned me, "but don't mind it. Yours is to do your own work and to have Cooky stand by the fore-sheet."

I managed to make my way forward, but there was little choice of sides, for the weather-rail seemed buried as often as the lee. Having instructed Thomas Mugridge as to what he was to do, I clambered into the fore rigging a few feet. The boat was now very close, and I could make out plainly that it was lying head to wind and sea and dragging on its mast and sail, which had been thrown overboard and made to serve as a sea-anchor. The three men were bailing. Each rolling mountain whelmed them from view, and I would wait with sickening anxiety, fearing that they would never appear again. Then, and with black suddenness, the boat would shoot clear through the foaming crest, bow pointed to the sky, and the whole length of her bottom showing, wet and dark, till she seemed on end. There would be a fleeting glimpse of the three men flinging water in frantic haste, when she would topple over and fall into the yawning valley, bow down and showing her full inside length to the stern upreared almost directly above the bow. Each time that she reappeared was a miracle.

The *Ghost* suddenly changed her course, keeping away, and it came to me with a shock that Wolf Larsen was giving up the rescue as impossible. Then I realized that he was preparing to heave to, and dropped to the deck to be in readiness. We were now dead before the wind, the boat far away and abreast of us. I felt an abrupt easing of the schooner, a loss for the moment of all strain and pressure, coupled with a swift acceleration of speed. She was rushing around on her heel into the wind.

As she arrived at right angles to the sea, the full force of the wind, (from which we had hitherto run away), caught us. I was unfortunately and ignorantly facing it. It stood up against me like a wall, filling my lungs with air which I could not expel. And as I choked and strangled, and as the *Ghost* wallowed for an instant, broadside on and rolling straight over and far into the wind, I beheld a huge sea rise far above my head. I turned aside, caught my breath, and looked again. The wave overtopped the *Ghost*, and I gazed sheer up and into it. A shaft of sunlight smote the over-curl, and I caught a glimpse of translucent, rushing green, backed by a milky smother of foam.

Then it descended, pandemonium broke loose, everything happened at once. I was struck a crushing, stunning blow, nowhere in particular and yet everywhere. My hold had been broken loose, I was under water, and the thought passed through my mind that this was the terrible thing of which I had heard, the being swept in the trough of the sea. My body struck and pounded as it was dashed helplessly along and turned over and over, and when I could hold my breath no longer, I breathed the stinging salt water into my lungs. But through it all I clung to the one idea—*I must get the jib backed over to windward*. I had no fear of death. I had no doubt but that I should come through somehow. And as this idea of fulfilling Wolf Larsen's order persisted in my dazed consciousness, I seemed to see him standing at the wheel in the midst of the wild welter, pitting his will against the will of the storm and defying it.

I brought up violently against what I took to be the rail, breathed, and breathed the sweet air again. I tried to rise, but struck my head and was knocked back on hands and knees. By some freak of the waters I had been swept clear under the forecastle-head and into the eyes. As I scrambled out on all fours, I passed over the body of Thomas Mugridge, who lay in a groaning heap. There was no time to investigate. I must get the jib backed over.

When I emerged on deck it seemed that the end of everything had come. On all sides there was a rending and crashing of wood and steel and canvas. The *Ghost* was being wrenched and torn to fragments. The foresail and fore topsail, emptied of the wind by the manoeuvre, and with no one to bring in the sheet in time, were thundering into ribbons, the heavy boom threshing and splintering from rail to rail. The air was thick with flying wreckage, detached ropes and stays were hissing and coiling like snakes, and down through it all crashed the gaff of the foresail.

The spar could not have missed me by many inches, while it spurred me to action. Perhaps the situation was not hopeless. I remembered Wolf Larsen's caution. He had expected all hell to break loose, and here it was. And where was he? I caught sight of him toiling at the main sheet, heaving it in and flat with his tremendous muscles, the stern of the schooner lifted high in the air and his body outlined against a white surge of sea sweeping past. All this, and more,—a whole world of chaos and wreck,—in possibly fifteen seconds I had seen and heard and grasped.

I did not stop to see what had become of the small boat, but sprang to the jib-sheet. The jib itself was beginning to slap, partially filling and emptying with sharp reports; but with a turn of the sheet and the application of my whole strength each time it slapped, I slowly backed it. This I know: I did my best. I pulled till I burst open the ends of all my fingers; and while I pulled, the flying-jib and staysail split their cloths apart and thundered into nothingness.

Still I pulled, holding what I gained each time with a double turn until the next slap gave me more. Then the sheet gave with greater ease, and Wolf Larsen was beside me, heaving in alone while I was busied taking up the slack.

"Make fast!" he shouted. "And come on!"

As I followed him, I noted that in spite of rack and ruin a rough order obtained. The *Ghost* was hove to. She was still in working order, and she was still working. Though the rest of her sails were gone, the jib, backed to windward, and the mainsail hauled down flat, were themselves holding, and holding her bow to the furious sea as well.

I looked for the boat, and, while Wolf Larsen cleared the boat-tackles, saw it lift to leeward on a big sea and not a score of feet away. And, so nicely had he made his calculation, we drifted fairly down upon it, so that nothing remained to do but hook the tackles to either end and hoist it aboard. But this was not done so easily as it is written.

In the bow was Kerfoot, Oofty-Oofty in the stern, and Kelly amidships. As we drifted closer, the boat would rise on a wave while we sank in the trough, till almost straight above me I could see the heads of the three men craned overside and looking down. Then, the next moment, we would lift and soar upward while they sank far down beneath us. It seemed incredible that the next surge should not crush the *Ghost* down upon the tiny eggshell.

But, at the right moment, I passed the tackle to the Kanaka, while Wolf Larsen did the same thing forward to Kerfoot. Both tackles were hooked in a trice, and the three men, deftly timing the roll, made a simultaneous leap aboard the schooner. As the *Ghost* rolled her side out of water, the boat was lifted snugly against her, and before the return roll came, we had heaved it in over the side and turned it bottom up on the deck. I noticed blood spouting from Kerfoot's left hand. In some way the third finger had been crushed to a pulp. But he gave no sign of pain, and with his single right hand helped us lash the boat in its place.

"Stand by to let that jib over, you Oofty!" Wolf Larsen commanded, the very second we had finished with the boat. "Kelly, come aft and slack off the main-sheet! You, Kerfoot, go for'ard and see what's become of Cooky! Mr. Van Weyden, run aloft again, and cut away any stray stuff on your way!"

And having commanded, he went aft with his peculiar tigerish leaps, to the wheel. While I toiled up the foreshrouds the *Ghost* slowly paid off. This time, as we went into the trough of the sea and were swept, there were no sails to carry away. And, halfway to the crosstrees and flattened against the rigging by the full force of the wind so that it would have been impossible for me to have fallen, the *Ghost* almost on her beam ends and the masts parallel with the water, I looked, not down, but at almost right angles from the perpendicular, to the deck of the *Ghost*. But I saw, not the deck, but where the deck should have been, for it was buried beneath a wild tumbling of water. Out of this water I could see the two masts rising, and that was all. The *Ghost,* for the moment, was buried beneath the sea. As she squared off more and more, escaping from the side pressure, she righted herself and broke her deck, like a whale's back, through the ocean surface.

Then we raced, and wildly, across the wild sea, the while I hung like a fly in the crosstrees and searched for the other boats. In half an hour I sighted the second one, swamped and bottom up, to which were desperately clinging Jock Horner, fat Louis, and Johnson. This time I remained aloft, and Wolf Larsen succeeded in heaving to without being swept. As before, we drifted down upon it. Tackles were made fast and lines flung to the men, who scrambled aboard like monkeys. The boat itself was crushed and splintered against the schooner's side as it came inboard; but the wreck was securely lashed, for it could be patched and made whole again.

Once more the *Ghost* bore away before the storm, this time so submerging herself that for some seconds I thought she would never reappear. Even the wheel, quite a deal higher than the waist, was covered and swept again and again. At such moments I felt strangely alone with God, alone with him and watching the chaos of his wrath. And then the wheel would reappear, and Wolf Larsen's broad shoulders, his hands gripping the spokes and holding the schooner to the course of his will, himself an earth-god, dominating the storm, flinging its descending waters from him and riding it to his own ends. And oh, the marvel of it! the marvel of it! That tiny men should live and breathe and work, and drive so frail a contrivance of wood and cloth through so tremendous an elemental strife!

As before, the *Ghost* swung out of the trough, lifting her deck again out of the sea, and dashed before the howling blast. It was now half-past five, and half an hour later, when the last of the day lost itself in a dim and furious twilight, I sighted a third boat. It was bottom up, and there was no sign of its crew. Wolf Larsen repeated his manoeuvre, holding off and then rounding up to windward and drifting down upon it. But this time he missed by forty feet, the boat passing astern.

"Number four boat!" Oofty-Oofty cried, his keen eyes reading its number in one second when it lifted clear of the foam and upside down.

It was Henderson's boat, and with him had been lost Holyoak and Williams, another of the deep-water crowd. Lost they indubitably were; but the boat remained, and Wolf Larsen made one more reckless effort to recover it. I had come down to the deck, and I saw Horner and Kerfoot vainly protest against the attempt.

"By God, I'll not be robbed of my boat by any storm that ever blew out of hell!" he shouted, and though we four stood with our heads together that we might hear, his voice seemed faint and far, as though removed from us an immense distance.

"Mr. Van Weyden!" he cried, and I heard through the tumult as one might hear a whisper. "Stand by that jib with Johnson and Oofty! The rest of you tail aft to the main sheet! Lively now! Or I'll sail you all into Kingdom come! Understand?"

And when he put the wheel hard over and the *Ghost's* bow swung off, there was nothing for the hunters to do but obey and make the best of a risky chance. How great the risk I realized when I was once more buried beneath the pounding seas and clinging for life to the pinrail at the foot of the foremast. My fingers were torn loose, and I swept across to the side and over the side into the sea. I could not swim, but before I could sink I was swept back again. A strong hand gripped me, and when the *Ghost* finally emerged, I found that I owed my life to Johnson. I saw him looking anxiously about him and noted that Kelly, who had come forward at the last moment, was missing.

This time, having missed the boat and not being in the same position as in the previous instances, Wolf Larsen was compelled to resort to a different manoeuvre. Running off before the wind with everything to starboard, he came about and returned close-hauled on the port tack.

"Grand!" Johnson shouted in my ear, as we successfully came through the attendent deluge, and I knew he referred, not to Wolf Larsen's seamanship, but to the performance of the *Ghost* herself.

It was now so dark that there was no sign of the boat; but Wolf Larsen held back through the frightful turmoil as if guided by unerring instinct. This time, though we were continually half-buried, there was no trough in which to be swept, and we drifted squarely down upon the upturned boat, badly smashing it as it was heaved inboard.

Two hours of terrible work followed, in which all hands of us,—two hunters, three sailors, Wolf Larsen, and I,—reefed, first one and then the other, the jib and mainsail. Hove to under this short canvas, our decks were comparatively free of water, while the *Ghost* bobbed and ducked amongst the combers like a cork.

I had burst open the ends of my fingers at the very first, and during the reefing I had worked with tears of pain running down my cheeks. And when all was done, I gave up like a woman and rolled upon the deck in the agony of exhaustion.

In the meantime Thomas Mugridge, like a drowned rat, was being dragged out from under the forecastle head where he had cravenly ensconced himself. I saw him pulled aft to the cabin and noted with a shock of surprise that the galley had disappeared. A clean space of deck showed where it had stood.

In the cabin I found all hands assembled, sailors as well, and while coffee was being cooked over the small stove we drank whiskey and crunched hardtack. Never in my life had food been so welcome. And never had hot coffee tasted so good. So violently did the *Ghost* pitch and toss and tumble that it was impossible for even the sailors to move about without holding on, and several times, after a cry of "Now she takes it!" we were heaped upon the wall of the port cabins as though it had been the deck.

"To hell with a lookout," I heard Wolf Larsen say when we had eaten and drunk our fill. "There's nothing can be done on deck. If anything's going to run us down we couldn't get out of its way. Turn in, all hands, and get some sleep."

The sailors slipped forward, setting the side-lights as they went, while the two hunters remained to sleep in the cabin, it not being deemed advisable to open the slide to the steerage companionway. Wolf Larsen and I, between us, cut off Kerfoot's crushed finger and sewed up the stump. Mugridge, who, during all the time he had been compelled to cook and serve coffee and keep the fire going, had complained of internal pains, now swore that he had a broken rib or two. On examination we found that he had three. But his case was deferred to next day, principally for the reason that I did not know anything about broken ribs and would first have to read it up.

"I don't think it was worth it," I said to Wolf Larsen, "a broken boat for Kelly's life."

"But Kelly didn't amount to much," was the reply. "Good night."

After all that had passed, suffering intolerable anguish in my finger ends, and with three boats missing, to say nothing of the wild capers the *Ghost* was cutting, I should have thought it impossible to sleep. But my eyes must have closed the instant my head touched the pillow, and in utter exhaustion I slept throughout the night, the while the *Ghost*, lonely and undirected, fought her way through the storm.

Sea Wrecks

St. Paul Averts a Shipwreck

And when it was determined that we should sail into Italy, they delivered Paul and certain other prisoners unto *one* named Julius, a centurion of Augustus' band.

2 And entering into a ship of Ăd-ră-mўt-ti-ŭm, we launched, meaning to sail by the coasts of Asia; one Ăr-is-tär-chŭs, a Macedonian of Thĕss-ă-lō-ní-că, being with us.

3 And the next *day* we touched at Sidon. And Julius courteously entreated Paul, and gave *him* liberty to go unto his friends to refresh himself.

4 And when we had launched from thence, we sailed under Cyprus, because the winds were contrary.

5 And when we had sailed over the sea of Ci-líc-iă and Păm-phўl-i-a, we came to Myra, *a city* of Lyć-i-a.

6 And there the centurion found a ship of Alexandria sailing into Italy; and he put us therein.

7 And when we had sailed slowly many days, and scarce were come over against Cní-dĭs, the wind not suffering us, we sailed under Crete, over against Săl-mŏ-nē;

8 And, hardly passing it, came unto a place which is called The fair havens; nigh whereunto was the city *of* Lă-sē-ă.

9 Now when much time was spent, and when sailing was now dangerous, because the fast was now already past, Paul admonished *them*,

10 And said unto them, Sirs, I perceive that this voyage will be with hurt and much damage, not only of the lading and ship, but also of our lives.

11 Nevertheless the centurion believed the master and the owner of the ship, more than those things which were spoken by Paul.

12 And because the haven was not commodious to winter in, the more part advised to depart thence also, if by any means they might attain to Phē-nĭ-cĕ, *and there* to winter; *which is* an haven of Crete, and lieth toward the south-west and north-west.

13 And when the south wind blew softly, supposing that they had obtained *their* purpose, loosing *thence,* they sailed close by Crete.

14 But not long after there arose against it a tempestuous wind, called *Eu-rŏć-lў-don.*

15 And when the ship was caught, and could not bear up into the wind, we let *her* drive.

16 And running under a certain island which is called Clauda, we had much work to come by the boat:

17 Which when they had taken up, they used helps, undergirding the ship; and, fearing lest they should fall into the quicksands, strake sail, and so were driven.

18 And we being exceedingly tossed with a tempest, the next *day* they lightened the ship;

19 And the third *day* we cast out with our own hands the tackling of the ship.

20 And when neither sun nor stars in many days appeared, and no small tempest lay on *us,* all hope that we should be saved was then taken away.

21 But after long abstinence Paul stood forth in the midst of them, and said, Sirs, ye should have hearkened unto me, and not have loosed from Crete, and to have gained this harm and loss.

22 And now I exhort you to be of good cheer: for there shall be no loss of *any man's* life among you, but of the ship.

23 For there stood by me this night the angel of God, whose I am, and whom I serve,

24   Saying, Fear not, Paul; thou must be brought before Caesar: and, lo, God hath given thee all them that sail with thee.

25   Wherefore, sirs, be of good cheer: for I believe God, that it shall be even as it was told me.

26   Howbeit we must be cast upon a certain island.

27   But when the fourteenth night was come, as we were driven up and down in Adria, about midnight the shipmen deemed that they drew near to some country;

28   And sounded, and found *it* twenty fathoms: and when they had gone a little further, they sounded again, and found *it* fifteen fathoms.

29   Then fearing lest we should have fallen upon rocks, they cast four anchors out of the stern, and wished for the day.

30   And as the shipmen were about to flee out of the ship, when they had let down the boat into the sea, under colour as though they would have cast anchors out of the foreship.

31   Paul said to the centurion and to the soldiers, Except these abide in the ship, ye cannot be saved.

32   Then the soldiers cut off the ropes of the boat, and let her fall off.

33   And while the day was coming on, Paul besought *them* all to take meat, saying, This day is the fourteenth day that ye have tarried and continued fasting, having taken nothing.

34   Wherefore I pray you to take *some* meat: for this is for your health: for there shall not an hair fall from the head of any of you.

35   And when he had thus spoken, he took bread, and gave thanks to God in presence of them all: and when he had broken *it*, he began to eat.

36   Then were they all of good cheer, and they also took *some* meat.

37   And we were in all in the ship two hundred threescore and sixteen souls.

38   And when they had eaten enough, they lightened the ship, and cast out the wheat into the sea.

39   And when it was day, they knew not the land: but they discovered a certain creek with a shore, into the which they were minded, if it were possible, to thrust in the ship.

40   And when they had taken up the anchors, they committed *themselves* unto the sea, and loosed the rudder bands, and hoisted up the mainsail to the wind, and made toward shore.

41   And falling into a place where two seas met, they ran the ship aground; and the forepart stuck fast, and remained unmoveable, but the hinder part was broken with the violence of the waves.

42   And the soldiers' counsel was to kill the prisoners, lest any of them should swim out, and escape.

43   But the centurion, willing to save Paul, kept them from *their* purpose; and commanded that they which could swim should cast *themselves* first *into the sea*, and get to land:

44   And the rest, some on boards, and some on *broken pieces* of the ship. And so it came to pass, that they escaped all safe to land.

The Loss of
the *Halsewell* East Indiaman

by ARCHIBALD DUNCAN

The *Halsewell* East Indiaman, of 758 tons burthen, Richard Pierce, Esq. commander, having been taken up by the Directors to make her third voyage to Coast and Bay, fell down to Gravesend the 16th of November, 1785, and there completed her lading. Having taken the ladies and other passengers on board at the Hope, she sailed through the Downs on Sunday, January the 1st, 1786, and the next morning, being abreast of Dunnose, it fell calm.

The ship was one of the finest in the service, and supposed to be in the most perfect condition for her voyage; and the commander a man of distinguished ability and exemplary character. His officers possessed unquestioned knowledge in their profession; the crew, composed of the best seamen that could be collected, was as numerous as the establishment admits. The vessel likewise contained a considerable body of soldiers, destined to recruit the forces of the Company in Asia.

The passengers were: Miss Eliza Pierce, and Miss Mary Anne Pierce, daughters of the commander; Miss Amy Paul, and Miss Mary Paul, daughter of Mr. Paul, of Somersetshire, and relations of Captain Pierce; Miss Elizabeth Blackburne, daughter of Captain B. likewise in the service of the East India Company; Miss Mary Haggard, sister to an officer on the Madras establishment; Miss Ann Mansell, a native of Madras, but of European parents, who had received her education in England; and John George Schutz, Esq., returning to Asia, where he had long resided, to collect a part of his fortune which he had left behind.

On Monday, the 2d of January, at three P.M. a breeze springing up from the south, they ran in shore to land the pilot. The weather coming on very thick in the evening, and the wind baffling, at nine they were obliged to anchor in eighteen fathom water. They furled their top-sails, but were unable to furl their courses, the snow falling thick and freezing as it fell.

Tuesday, the 3d, at four A.M. a violent gale came on from E. N. E. and the ship driving, they were obliged to cut their cables and run out to sea. At noon they spoke with a brig bound to Dublin, and having put their pilot on board of her, bore down channel immediately. At eight in the evening the wind freshening, and coming to the southward, they reefed such sails as were judged necessary. At ten it blew a violent gale at south, and they were obliged to carry a press of sail to keep the ship off the shore. In this situation, the hawse-plugs which, according to a recent improvement, were put inside, were washed in, and the hawse-bags washed away, in consequence of which they shipped a great quantity of water on the gun-deck.

Upon sounding the well they found that the vessel had sprung a leak, and had five feet water in her hold; they clued up the main top-sail, hauled up the main-sail and immediately endeavoured to furl both, but failed in the attempt. All the pumps were set to work on the discovery of the leak.

Wednesday the 4th, at two A.M. they endeavoured to wear the ship, but without success. The mizen-mast was instantly cut away, and a second attempt made to wear, which succeeded no better than the former. The ship having now seven feet water in her hold, and the leak gaining fast on the pumps, it was thought expedient, for the preservation of the ship, which appeared to be in immediate danger of foundering, to cut away the main-mast. In its fall Jonathan Moreton, coxswain, and four men, were carried overboard by the wreck and drowned. By eight o'clock the wreck was cleared, and the ship got before the wind. In this position she was kept about two hours, during which the pumps reduced the water in the hold two feet.

At ten in the morning the wind abated considerably, and the ship labouring extremely, rolled the foretop-mast over on the larboard side, which, in the fall, tore the foresail to pieces. At eleven the wind came to the westward, and the weather clearing up, the Berry Head was distinguishable, at the distance of four or five leagues. Having erected a jury main-mast, and set a top gallant-sail, for a main-sail, they bore up for Portsmouth, and employed the remainder of the day in getting up a jury mizen mast.

On Thursday, the 5th, at two in the morning the wind came to the southward, blew fresh, and the weather was very thick. At noon Portland was seen bearing north and by east, distant two or three leagues. At eight at night it blew a strong gale at south; the Portland lights were seen bearing north-west, distant four or five leagues, when they wore ship and got her head to the westward. Finding they lost ground on that tack, they wore her again, and kept stretching to the eastward, in the hope of weathering Peverel-point, in which case they intended to have anchored in Studland Bay. At eleven they saw St. Alban's Head, a mile and a half to the leeward, upon which they took in sail immediately, and let go the small bower anchor, which brought up the ship at a whole cable, and she rode for about an hour, but then drove. They now let go the sheet anchor, and wore away a whole cable; the ship rode about two hours longer, when she drove again.

In this situation the captain sent for Mr. Henry Meriton, the chief officer, and asked his opinion concerning the probability of saving their lives. He replied, with equal candor and calmness, that he apprehended there was very little hope, as they were then driving fast on the shore, and might expect every moment to strike. It was agreed that the boats could not then be of any use, but it was proposed that the officers should be confidentially requested, in case an opportunity presented itself, of making them serviceable, to reserve the long boat for the ladies and themselves, and this precaution was accordingly taken.

About two in the morning of Friday, the 6th, the ship still driving, and approaching the shore very fast, the same officer again went into the cuddy where the captain then was. Captain Pierce expressed extreme anxiety for the preservation of his beloved daughters, and earnestly asked Mr. Meriton, if he could devise any means of saving them. The latter expressed his fears that it would be impossible, adding, that their only chance would be to wait for the morning, upon which the captain lifted up his hands in silent distress.

At this moment the ship struck with such violence as to dash the heads of those who were standing in the cuddy against the deck above them, and the fatal blow was accompanied by a shriek of horror, which burst at the same instant from every quarter of the ship.

The seamen, many of whom had been remarkable inattentive and remiss in their duty during great part of the storm, and had actually skulked in their hammocks, leaving the exertions of the pump, and the other labors required by their situation, to the officers, roused to a sense of their danger, now poured upon the deck, to which the utmost endeavors of their officers could not keep them while their assistance might have been useful. But it was now too late; the ship continued to beat upon the rock, and soon bulged, falling with her broadside towards the shore. When the ship struck, several of the men caught hold of the ensign-staff, under the apprehension of her going to pieces immediately.

At this critical juncture Mr. Meriton offered his unhappy companions the best advice that could possibly be given. He recommended that they should all repair to that side of the ship which lay lowest on the rocks, and take the opportunities that might then present themselves of escaping singly to the shore. He then returned to the round-house, where all the passengers and most of the officers were assembled. The latter were employed in affording consolation to the unfortunate ladies, and, with unparalleled magnanimity, suffering their compassion for the amiable companions of their misfortunes to overcome the sense of their own danger, and the dread of almost inevitable destruction. At this moment what must have been the feelings of a father—of such a father as Captain Pierce?

The ship had struck on the rocks near Seacombe, on the island of Purbeck, between Peverel-point and St. Alban's Head. On this part of the shore the cliff is of immense height, and rises almost perpendicularly. In this particular spot the cliff is excavated at the base, presenting a cavern ten or twelve yards in depth, and equal in breadth to the length of a large ship. The sides of the cavern are so nearly upright as to be extremely difficult of access, and the bottom of it is strewed with sharp and uneven rocks which appear to have been rent from above by some convulsion of nature. It was at the mouth of this cavern that the unfortunate vessel lay stretched almost from side to side, and presented her broadside to the horrid chasm. But, at the time the ship struck it was too dark to discover the extent of the danger, and the extreme horror of their situation.

The number in the round-house was now increased to nearly fifty, by the admission of three black women and two soldiers' wives, with the husband of one of the latter, though the sailors, who had demanded entrance to get a light, had been opposed and kept out by the officers. Captain Pierce was seated on a chair, or some other moveable, between his two daughters, whom he pressed alternately to his affectionate bosom. The rest of the melancholy assembly were seated on the deck, which was strewed with musical instruments, and the wreck of furniture, boxes, and packages.

Here Mr. Meriton, after having lighted several wax candles, and all the glass lanterns he could find, likewise took his seat, intending to wait till day light, in the hope that it would afford him an opportunity of effecting his own escape, and also of rendering assistance to the partners of his danger. But, observing that the ladies appeared parched and exhausted, he fetched a basket of oranges from some part of the round-house, with which he prevailed on some of them to refresh themselves.

On his return he perceived a considerable alteration in the appearance of the ship. The sides were visibly giving way, the deck seemed to heave, and he discovered other evident symptoms that she could not hold together much longer. Attempting to go forward to look out, he instantly perceived that the ship had separated in the middle and that the fore-part had changed its position, and lay rather farther out towards the sea. In this emergency he determined to seize the present moment, as the next might have been charged with his fate, and to follow the example of the crew and the soldiers, who were leaving the ship in numbers, and making their way to a shore, with the horrors of which they were yet unacquainted.

To favor their escape an attempt had been made to lay the ensign-staff from the ship's side to the rocks, but without success, for it snapped to pieces before it reached them. By the light of a lantern, however, Mr. Meriton discovered a spar, which appeared to be laid from the ship's side to the rocks, and upon which he determined to attempt his escape. He accordingly lay down upon it, and thrust himself forward, but soon found that the spar had no communication with the rock. He reached the end and then slipped off, receiving a violent contusion in his fall. Before he could recover his legs he was washed off by the surge, in which he supported himself by swimming till the returning wave dashed him against the back of the cavern. Here he laid hold of a small projection of the rock, but was so benumbed that he was on the point of quitting it, when a seaman, who had already gained a footing, extending his hand and assisted him till he could secure himself on a little shelf of the rock, from which he clambered still higher till he was out of the reach of the surf.

Mr. Rogers, the third mate, remained with the captain and the ladies nearly twenty minutes after Mr. Meriton had left the ship. The latter had not long quitted the round-house before the captain enquired what was become of him, when Mr. Rogers replied that he had gone upon deck to see what could be done. A heavy sea soon afterwards broke over the ship, upon which the ladies expressed great concern at the apprehension of his loss. Mr. Rogers proposed to go and call him, but this they opposed, fearful lest he might share the same fate.

The sea now broke in at the fore-part of the ship, and reached as far as the main-mast. Captain Pierce and Mr. Rogers, then went together, with a lamp, to the stern gallery, where, after viewing the rocks, the captain asked Mr. Rogers if he thought there was any possibility of saving the girls. He replied he feared not; for they could discover nothing but the black surface of the perpendicular rock, and not the cavern which afforded shelter to those who had escaped. They then returned to the round-house, where Captain Pierce again seated himself between his two daughters, struggling to suppress the parental tear which then started into his eye.

The sea continuing to break in very fast, Mr. Rogers, Mr. Shutz, and Mr. M'Manus, a midshipman, with a view to attempt their escape, made their way to the poop. They had scarcely reached it, when a heavy sea breaking over the wreck, the round-house gave way, and they heard the ladies shriek at the intervals, as if water had reached them; the noise of the sea at other times drowning their voices.

Mr. Brimer had followed Mr. Rogers to the poop, where, on the coming of the fatal sea, they jointly seized a hen coop, and the same wave which whelmed those who remained below in destruction, carried him and his companion to the rock, on which they were dashed with great violence and miserably bruised.

On this rock were twenty-seven men; but it was low water, and being convinced that, upon the flowing of the tide, they must all be washed off, many endeavored to get to the back or sides of the cavern beyond the reach of the returning sea. Excepting Mr. Rogers and Mr. Brimer, scarcely more than six succeeded in this attempt. Of the remainder some experienced the fate they sought to avoid, and others perished in endeavoring to get into the cavern.

Mr. Rogers and Mr. Brimer, however, having reached the cavern, climbed up the rock, on the narrow shelves of which they fixed themselves. The former got so near to his friend, Mr. Meriton, as to exchange congratulations with him; but between these gentlemen there were about twenty men, none of whom could stir but at the most imminent hazard of his life. When Mr. Rogers reached this station his strength was so nearly exhausted that had the struggle continued a few minutes longer he must inevitably have perished.

They soon found that though many, who had reached the rocks below, had perished in attempting to ascend, yet that a considerable number of the crew, seamen, soldiers, and some of the inferior officers, were in the same situation with themselves. What that situation was they had still to learn. They had escaped immediate death; but they were yet to encounter a thousand hardships for the precarious chance of escape. Some part of the ship was still discernible, and they cheered themselves, in this dreary situation, with the hope that it would hold together till day break. Amidst their own misfortunes the sufferings of the females filled their minds with the acutest anguish; every returning sea increased their apprehensions for the safety of their amiable and helpless companions.

But, alas! too soon were these apprehensions realized! A few minutes after

Mr. Rogers had gained the rock, a general shriek, in which the voice of female distress was lamentably distinguishable, announced the dreadful catastrophe! In a few moments all was hushed, excepting the warring winds and the dashing waves. The wreck was whelmed in the bosom of the deep, and not an atom of it was ever discovered. Thus perished the *Halsewell*—and with her, worth, honor, skill, beauty and accomplishments!

This stroke was a dreadful aggravation of woe to the trembling and scarcely half-saved wretches, who were clinging about the sides of the horrid cavern. They felt for themselves, but they wept for wives, parents, fathers, brothers, sisters—perhaps lovers!—all cut off from their dearest, fondest hopes!

Their feelings were not less agonized by the subsequent events of that ill-fated night. Many who had gained the precarious stations on the rocks, exhausted with fatigue, weakened by bruises, and benumbed with cold, quitted their holds, and falling headlong, either upon the rocks below, or into the surf, perished beneath the feet of their wretched associates, and by their dying groans and loud exclamations, awakened terrific apprehension of a similar fate in the survivors.

At length, after three hours of the keenest misery, the day broke on them, but, far from bringing with it the expected relief, it served only to discover to them all the horrors of their situation. They were convinced that, had the country been alarmed by the guns of distress, which they continued to fire several hours before the ship struck, but which, from the violence of the storm, were unheard, they could neither be observed by the people above, as they were completely ingulphed in the cavern, and overhung by the cliff; nor was any part of the wreck remaining to indicate their probable place of refuge. Below, no boat could live to search them out, and had it been possible to acquaint those who were willing to assist them with their exact situation, they were at a loss to conceive how any ropes could be conveyed into the cavern to facilitate their escape.

The only method that afforded any prospect of success was to creep along the side to its outer extremity, to turn the corner on a ledge scarcely as broad as a man's hand, and to climb up the almost perpendicular precipices, nearly two hundred feet in height. In this desperate attempt some succeeded, while others, trembling with terror, and exhausted with bodily and mental fatigue, lost their precarious footing, and perished.

The first men who gained the summit of the cliff were the cook, and James Thompson, a quarter-master. By their individual exertions they reached the top, and instantly hastened to the nearest house, to make known the situation of their fellow-sufferers. Eastington, the habitation of Mr. Garland, steward, or agent, to the proprietors of the Purbeck quarries, was the house at which they first arrived. That gentleman immediately assembled the workmen under his directions, and with the most zealous humanity exerted every effort for the preservation of the surviving part of the crew of the unfortunate ship.

Mr. Meriton had, by this time, almost reached the edge of the precipice. A soldier, who preceded him, stood upon a small projecting rock, or stone, and upon the same stone Mr. Meriton had fastened his hands to assist his progress.

Just at this moment the quarrymen arrived, and seeing a man so nearly within their reach, they dropped a rope, of which he immediately laid hold. By a vigorous effort, to avail himself of the advantage, he loosened the stone, which giving way, Mr. Meriton must have been precipitated to the bottom, had not a rope been lowered to him at the instant, which he seized, while in the act of falling, and was safely drawn to the summit.

The fate of Mr. Brimer was peculiarly severe. He had been married, only nine days before the ship sailed, to the daughter of Captain Norman, of the Royal Navy, came on shore, as it has been observed, with Mr. Rogers, and, like him, got up the side of the cavern. Here he remained till the morning, when he crawled out; a rope was thrown him, but he was either so benumbed with the cold as to fasten it about him improperly, or so agitated as to neglect to fasten it at all. Whatever was the cause, the effect proved fatal; at the moment of his supposed preservation he fell from his stand, and was unfortunately dashed to pieces, in the sight of those who could only lament the deplorable fate of an amiable man and a skilful officer.

The method of affording help was remarkable, and does honor to the humanity and intrepidity of the quarrymen. The distance from the top of the rock to the cavern, over which it projected, was at least one hundred feet: ten of these formed a declivity to the edge, and the remainder was perpendicular. On the very brink of this precipice stood two daring fellows, with a rope tied round them, and fastened above to a strong iron bar fixed into the ground. Behind these, in like manner, stood others, two and two. A strong rope. likewise properly secured, passed between them, by which they might hold, and support themselves from falling. Another rope, with a noose ready fixed, was then let down below the cavern, and the wind blowing hard, it was sometimes forced under the projecting rock, so that the sufferers could reach it without crawling to the edge. Whoever laid hold of it put the noose round his waist, and was drawn up with the utmost care and caution by their intrepid deliverers.

In this attempt, however, many shared the fate of the unfortunate Mr. Brimer. Unable, through cold, perturbation of mind, weakness, or the inconvenience of the stations they occupied, to avail themselves of the succor that was offered them, they were precipitated from the stupendous cliff, and either dashed to pieces on the rocks, or, falling into the surge, perished in the waves.

Among these unhappy sufferers the death of a drummer was attended with circumstances of peculiar distress. Being either washed off the rocks by the sea, or falling into the surf, he was carried by the returning waves beyond the breakers. His utmost efforts to regain them were ineffectual; he was drawn farther out to sea, and being a remarkable good swimmer, continued to struggle with the waves, in the view of his commiserating companions, till his strength was exhausted, and he sunk,—to rise no more!

It was late in the day before all the survivors were carried to a place of safety, excepting William Trenton, a soldier, who remained on his perilous stand till the morning of Saturday, the 7th, exposed to the united horrors of extreme personal danger, and the most acute disquietude of mind.

The surviving officers, seamen, and soldiers, being assembled at the house of their benevolent deliverer, Mr. Garland, they were mustered, and found to amount to 74, out of rather more than 240, which was nearly the number of the crew, and passengers, when she sailed through the Downs. Of the rest it is supposed that fifty or more sunk with the Captain and the ladies in the round-house, and that upwards of seventy reached the rocks, but were washed off, or perished, in falling from the cliffs. All those who reached the summit survived, excepting two or three, who expired while being drawn up, and a black, who died a few hours after he was brought to the house. Many, however, were so miserably bruised, that their lives were doubtful, and it was a considerable time before they perfectly recovered their strength.

The benevolence and generosity of the master of the Crown Inn, at Blandford, deserves the highest praise. When the distressed seamen arrived at that town, he sent for them all to his house, and having given them the refreshment of a comfortable dinner, he presented each man with half a crown to help him on his journey.

Loss of the *Kent* East Indiaman

by SIR DUNCAN MacGREGOR

Y ou are aware that the *Kent,* Captain Henry Cobb, a fine new ship of 1350 tons, bound to Bengal and China, left the Downs on the 19th February; with 20 officers, 344 soldiers, 43 women, and 66 children, belonging to the 31st regiment; with 20 private passengers, and a crew (including officers) of 148 men, on board.

With a fine fresh breeze from the north-east, the stately *Kent,* in bearing down the Channel, speedily passed many a well-known spot on the coast, dear to our remembrance; and on the evening of the 23d, we took our last view of happy England, and entered the wide Atlantic, without the expectation of again seeing land until we reached the shores of India.

With slight interruptions of bad weather, we continued to make way until the night of Monday the 28th, when we were suddenly arrested in lat. 47° 30′, long. 10°, by a violent gale from the south-west, which gradually increased during the whole of the following morning.

The activity of the officers and seamen of the *Kent* appeared to keep ample pace with that of the gale. Our larger sails were speedily taken in, or closely reefed; and about ten o'clock on the morning of the 1st of March, after having struck our top-gallant yards, we were lying to, under a triple reefed main top-sail only, with our dead lights in, and with the whole watch of soldiers attached to the life-lines, that were run along the deck for this purpose.

The rolling of the ship, which was vastly increased by a dead weight of some hundred tons of shot and shells that formed a part of its lading, became so great about half-past eleven or twelve o'clock, that our main chains were thrown by every lurch considerably under water; and the best cleated articles of furniture in the cabins and the *cuddy* were dashed about with so much noise and violence, as to excite the liveliest apprehensions of individual danger.

It was a little before this period that one of the officers of the ship, with the well-meant intention of ascertaining that all was fast below, descended with two of the sailors into the hold, where they carried with them, for safety, a light in the patent lantern; and seeing that the lamp burned dimly, the officer took the precaution to hand it up to the orlop deck to be trimmed. Having afterwards discovered one of the spirit casks to be adrift, he sent the sailors for some billets of wood to secure it; but the ship in their absence having made a heavy lurch, the officer unfortunately dropped the light; and letting go his hold of the cask in his eagerness to recover the lantern, it suddenly stove, and the spirits communicating with the lamp, the whole place was instantly in a blaze.

I know not what steps were then taken, but I received from Captain Spence, the Captain of the day, the alarming information that the ship was on fire in the after-hold; on hastening to the hatchway, whence smoke was slowly ascending, I found Captain Cobb and other officers already giving orders, which seemed to be promptly obeyed by the seamen and troops, who were using every exertion, by means of the pumps, buckets of water, wet sails, hammocks, etc. to extinguish the flames.

As long as the devouring element appeared to be confined to the spot where the fire originated, and which we were assured was surrounded on all sides by the water casks, we ventured to cherish hopes that it might be subdued; but no sooner was the light blue vapour that at first arose succeeded by volumes of thick dingy smoke, which speedily ascending through all the four hatchways, rolled over every part of the ship, than all farther concealment became impossible, and almost all hope of preserving the vessel was abandoned. "The flames have reached the cable tier" was exclaimed by some individuals, and the strong pitchy smell that pervaded the deck confirmed the truth of the exclamation.

In these awful circumstances, Captain Cobb, with an ability and decision of character that seemed to increase with the imminence of the danger, resorted to the only alternative now left him, of ordering the lower decks to be scuttled, the combings of the hatches to be cut, and the lower ports to be opened, for the free admission of the waves.

These instructions were speedily executed by the united efforts of the troops and seamen; but not before some of the sick soldiers, one woman, and several children, unable to gain the upper deck, had perished. On descending to the gun deck with Colonel Fearon, Captain Bray, and one or two other officers of the 31st regiment, to assist in opening the ports, I met, staggering towards the hatchway, in an exhausted and nearly senseless state, one of the mates, who informed us that he had just stumbled over the dead bodies of some individuals who must have died from suffocation, to which it was evident that he himself had almost fallen a victim. So dense and oppressive was the smoke, that it was with the utmost difficulty we could remain long enough below to fulfil Captain Cobb's wishes; which were no sooner accomplished, than the sea rushed in with extraordinary force, carrying away, in its resistless progress to the hold, the largest chests, bulk-heads, etc.

Such a sight, under any other conceivable circumstances, was well calculated to have filled us with horror; but in our natural solicitude to avoid the more immediate peril of explosion, we endeavoured to cheer each other, as we stood up to our knees in water. The immense quantity of water that was thus introduced into the hold, had indeed the effect, for a time, of checking the fury of the flames; but the danger of sinking having increased as the risk of explosion was diminished, the ship became water-logged, and presented other indications of settling, previous to her going down.

Death in two of its most awful forms now encompassed us, and we seemed left to choose the terrible alternative. But always preferring the more remote, though equally certain crisis, we tried to shut the ports again, to close the hatches, and to exclude the external air, in order if possible to prolong our existence, the near and certain termination of which appeared inevitable.

The scene of horror that now presented itself, baffles all description—

> Then rose from sea to sky the wild farewell;
> Then shriek'd the timid, and stood still the brave.

The upper deck was covered with between six and seven hundred human beings, many of whom, from previous sea-sickness, were forced on the first alarm to flee from below in a state of absolute nakedness. While some were standing in silent resignation, or in stupid insensibility to their impending fate, others were yielding themselves up to the most frantic despair. Some on their knees were earnestly imploring, with significant gesticulations and in noisy supplications, the mercy of Him, whose arm, they exclaimed, was at length outstretched to smite them; others were to be seen hastily crossing themselves, and performing the various external acts required by their peculiar persuasion, while a number of the older and more stout-hearted soldiers and sailors sullenly took their seats directly over the magazine, hoping, as they stated, that by means of the explosion which they every instant expected, a speedier termination might thereby be put to their sufferings.

It was at this time when "all hope that we should be saved was now taken away," that it occurred to Mr. Thomson, the fourth mate, to send a man to the foretop, rather with the ardent wish, than the expectation, that some friendly sail might be discovered on the face of the waters. The sailor, on mounting, threw his eyes round the horizon for a moment,—a moment of unutterable suspense,—and waving his hat, exclaimed, "a sail on the lee bow!" The joyful announcement was received with deep-felt thanksgivings, and with three cheers upon deck. Our flags of distress were instantly hoisted, and our minute guns fired; and we endeavoured to bear down under our three top-sails and fore-sail upon the stranger, which afterwards proved to be the *Cambria*, a small brig of 200 tons burden—Cook—bound to Vera Cruz, having on board twenty or thirty Cornish miners, and other agents of the Anglo-Mexican Company.

For ten or fifteen minutes we were left in doubt whether the brig perceived our signals, or perceiving them, was either disposed or able to lend us any assistance. From the violence of the gale, it seems that the report of our guns was not heard; but the ascending volumes of smoke from the ship, sufficiently announced the dreadful nature of our distress; and we had the satisfaction, after a short period of dark suspense, to see the brig hoist British colours, and crowd all sail to hasten to our relief.

Although it was impossible, and would have been improper to repress the rising hopes that were pretty generally diffused amongst us by the unexpected sight of the *Cambria*, yet I confess, that when I reflected on the long period our ship had been already burning—on the tremendous sea that was running—on the extreme smallness of the brig, and the immense number of human beings to be saved,—I could only venture to hope that a few might be spared; but I durst not for a moment contemplate the possibility of my own preservation.

While Captain Cobb, Colonel Fearon, and Major MacGregor of the 31st regiment, were consulting together, as the brig was approaching us, on the necessary preparations for getting out the boats, etc., one of the officers asked Major M. in what order it was intended the officers should move off; to which the other replied, "Of course in funeral order," which injunction was instantly confirmed by Colonel Fearon, who said, "Most undoubtedly the juniors first—but see that any man is cut down who presumes to enter the boats before the means of escape are presented to the women and children."

To prevent the rush to the boats, as they were being lowered, which, from certain symptoms of impatience manifested both by soldiers and sailors, there was reason to fear; some of the military officers were stationed over them with drawn swords. But from the firm determination which these exhibited, and the great subordination observed, with few exceptions, by the troops, this proper precaution was afterwards rendered unnecessary.

Arrangements having been considerately made by Captain Cobb for placing in the first boat, previous to letting it down, all the ladies, and as many of the soldiers' wives as it could safely contain, they hurriedly wrapt themselves up in whatever articles of clothing could be most conveniently found; and I think about two, or half-past two o'clock a most mournful procession advanced from the after-cabins to the starboard cuddy port, outside of which the cutter was suspended. Scarcely a word was uttered—not a scream was heard—even the infants ceased to cry, as if conscious of the unspoken and unspeakable anguish that was at that instant rending the hearts of their parting parents—nor was the silence of voices in any way broken, except in one or two cases, where the ladies plaintively entreated permission to be left behind with their husbands. But on being assured that every moment's delay might occasion the sacrifice of a human life, they successively suffered themselves to be torn from the tender embrace, and with the fortitude which never fails to characterise and adorn their sex on occasions of overwhelming trial, were placed, without a murmur, in the boat, which was immediately lowered into a sea so tempestuous, as to leave us only "to hope against hope" that it should live in it for a single moment.

After one or two unsuccessful attempts to place the little frail bark fairly upon the surface of the water, the command was at length given to unhook; the tackle at the stern was, in consequence, immediately cleared; but the ropes at the bow having got foul, the sailor there found it impossible to obey the order. In vain was the axe applied to the entangled tackle. The moment was inconceivably critical; as the boat, which necessarily followed the motion of the ship, was gradually rising out of the water, and must, in another instant, have been hanging perpendicularly by the bow, and its helpless passengers launched into the deep, had not a most providential wave suddenly struck and lifted up the stern, so as to enable the seamen to disengage the tackle; and the boat, being dexterously cleared from the ship, was seen, after a little while, from the poop, battling with the billows; now raised, in its progress to the brig, like a speck on their summit, and then disappearing for several seconds, as if engulfed "in the horrid vale" between them.

The *Cambria* having prudently lain to at some distance from the *Kent,* lest she should be involved in her explosion, or exposed to the fire from our guns, which, being all shotted, afterwards went off as the flames successively reached them, the men had a considerable way to row; and the success of this first experiment seeming to be the measure of our future hopes, the movements of this precious boat—incalculably precious, without doubt, to the agonized husbands and fathers immediately connected with it—were watched with intense anxiety by all on board. The better to balance the boat in the raging sea through which it had to pass, and to enable the seamen to ply their oars, the women and children were stowed promiscuously under the seats; and consequently exposed to the risk of being drowned by the continual dashing of the spray over their heads, which so filled the boat during the passage, that before their arrival at the brig, the poor females were sitting up to the breast in water, and their children kept with the greatest difficulty above it.

However, in the course of twenty minutes, or half an hour, the little cutter was seen alongside the "ark of refuge"; and the first human being that happened to be admitted, out of the vast assemblage that ultimately found shelter there, was the infant son of Major MacGregor, a child of only a few weeks, who was caught from his mother's arms, and lifted into the brig, by Mr. Thomson, the fourth mate of the *Kent,* the officer who had been ordered to take charge of the ladies' boat.

It being impossible for the boats, after the first trip, to come alongside the *Kent,* a plan was adopted for lowering the women and children by ropes from the stern, by tying them two and two together. But from the heaving of the ship, and the extreme difficulty in dropping them at the instant the boat was underneath, many of the poor creatures were unavoidably plunged repeatedly under water; and much as humanity may rejoice that no woman was eventually lost by this process.

Seeing that the tardy means employed for the escape of the women and children necessarily consumed a great deal of time that might be partly devoted to the general preservation, orders were given, that, along with the females, each of the boats should also admit a certain portion of the soldiers; several of whom, in their impatience to take advantage of this permission, flung themselves overboard, and sunk in their ill-judged and premature efforts for deliverance.

I ought to state, that three out of the six boats we originally possessed, were either completely stove or swamped in the course of the day, one of them with men in it, some of whom were seen floating in the water for a moment before they disappeared; and it is suspected that one or two of those who went down, must have sunk under the weight of their spoils, the same individuals having been seen eagerly plundering the cuddy cabins.

As the day was rapidly drawing to a close and the flames were slowly, but perceptibly extending, Colonel Fearon and Captain Cobb evinced an increasing anxiety to relieve the remainder of the gallant men under their charge.

To facilitate this object, a rope was suspended from the extremity of the spanker boom, along which the men were recommended to proceed, and thence slide down by the rope into the boats. But as, from the great swell of the sea, and the constant heaving of the ship, it was impossible for the boats to preserve their station for a moment; those who adopted this course incurred so great a risk of swinging for some time in the air, and of being repeatedly plunged under water, or dashed against the sides of the boats underneath, that many of the landsmen continued to throw themselves out of the stern windows on the upper deck, preferring what appeared to me the more precarious chance of reaching the boats by swimming. Rafts made of spars, hencoops, etc., were also ordered to be constructed, for the twofold purpose of forming an intermediate communication with the boats,—a purpose, by the bye, which they very imperfectly answered,—and of serving as a last point of retreat, should the farther extension of the flames compel us to desert the vessel altogether: directions were at the same time given that every man should tie a rope round his waist, by which he might afterwards attach himself to the rafts, should he be suddenly forced to take to the water.

Some time after the shades of night had enveloped us, I descended to the cuddy, in quest of a blanket to shelter me from the increasing cold; and the scene of desolation that there presented itself was melancholy in the extreme. The place which, only a few short hours before, had been the seat of kindly intercourse and of social gaiety, was now entirely deserted, save by a few miserable wretches, who were either stretched in irrecoverable intoxication on the floor, or prowling about like beasts of prey, in search of plunder. The sofas, drawers, and other articles of furniture, the due arrangement of which had cost so much thought and pains, were now broken into a thousand pieces, and scattered in confusion around me. Some of the geese and other poultry, escaped from their confinement, were cackling in the cuddy; while a solitary pig, wandering from its sty in the forecastle, was ranging at large in undisturbed possession of the Brussels carpet that covered one of the cabins. Glad to retire from a scene so cheerless and affecting, and rendered more dismal by the smoke which was oozing up from below, I returned to the poop, where I again found amongst the few officers that remained, Captain Cobb, Colonel Fearon, Lieutenants Ruxton, Booth, and Evans, superintending with unabated zeal, the removal of the rapidly diminishing sufferers, as the boats successively arrived for their conveyance.

It was now imperative on Captain Cobb to reiterate his threats, as well as his entreaties, that not an instant should be lost, but seemed to render it expedient for one of the officers of the troops, who had expressed his intention of remaining to the last, to limit, in the hearing of those around him, the period of his own stay. Seeing however, between nine and ten o'clock, that some individuals were consuming the precious moments, by obstinately hesitating to proceed, while others were making the inadmissible request to be lowered down as the women had been; learning from the boatmen, that the wreck, which was already nine or ten feet below the ordinary water mark, had sunk two feet lower since their last trip; and calculating, besides, that the two boats then under the stern, with that which was in sight on its return from the brig, would suffice for the conveyance of all who seemed in a condition to remove; the three remaining officers of the 31st regiment seriously prepared to take their departure.

As I cannot perhaps convey to you so correct an idea of the condition of others as by describing my own feelings and situation under the same circumstances, I shall make no apology for detailing the manner of my individual escape, which will sufficiently mark that of many hundreds that preceded it.

The spanker boom of so large a ship as the *Kent,* which projects, I should think, 16 or 18 feet over the stern, rests on ordinary occasions about 19 or 20 feet above the water; but in the position in which we were placed, from the great height of the sea, and consequent pitching of the ship, it was frequently lifted to a height of not less than 30 or 40 feet from the surface.

To reach the rope, therefore, that hung from its extremity, was an operation that seemed to require the aid of as much dexterity of hand as steadiness of head. For it was not only the nervousness of creeping along the boom itself, or the extreme difficulty of afterwards seizing on, and sliding down by the rope, that we had to dread, and that had occasioned the loss of some valuable lives, by deterring the men from adopting this mode of escape; but as the boat, which the one moment was probably close under the boom, might be carried the next, by the force of the waves, 15 or 20 yards away from it, the unhappy individual, whose best calculations were thus defeated, was generally left swinging for some time in mid-air, if he was not repeatedly plunged several feet under water, or dashed with dangerous violence against the sides of the returning boat,—or, what not unfrequently happened, was forced to let go his hold of the rope altogether. As there seemed, however, no alternative, I did not hesitate, notwithstanding my comparative inexperience and awkwardness in such a situation, to throw my leg across the perilous stick; and with a heart extremely grateful that such means of deliverance, dangerous as they appeared, were still extended to me; and more grateful still that I had been enabled, in common with others, to discharge my honest duty to my sovereign and to my fellow soldiers;—I proceeded, after confidently committing my spirit, the great object of my solicitude, into the keeping of Him who had formed and redeemed it, to creep slowly forward, feeling at every step the increasing difficulty of my situation. On getting nearly to the end of the boom, the young officer whom I followed and myself were met with a squall of wind and rain, so violent as to make us fain to embrace closely the slippery stick, without attempting for some minutes to make any progress, and to excite our apprehension that we must relinquish all hope of reaching the rope. But our fears were disappointed: and after resting for a while at the boom end, while my companion was descending to the boat, which he did not find until he had been plunged once or twice over head in the water, I prepared to follow; and instead of lowering myself, as many had imprudently done, at the moment when the boat was inclining toward us,—and consequently being unable to descend the whole distance before it again receded,—I calculated that while the boat was retiring I ought to commence my descent, which would probably be completed by the time the returning wave brought it underneath; by which means I was, I believe, almost the only officer or soldier who reached the boat with being either severely bruised or immersed in the water. But my friend Colonel Fearon had not been so fortunate: for after swinging for some time, and being repeatedly struck against the side of the boat, and at one time drawn completely under it, he was at last so utterly exhausted, that he must instantly have let go his hold of the rope and perished, had not some one in the boat seized him by the hair of the head and dragged him into it, almost senseless and alarmingly bruised.

Captain Cobb, in his immoveable resolution to be the last if possible to quit his ship, and in his generous anxiety for the preservation of every life intrusted to his charge, refused to seek the boat, until he again endeavoured to urge onward the few still around him, who seemed struck dumb and powerless with dismay. But finding all his entreaties fruitless, and hearing the guns, whose tackle was burst asunder by the advancing flames, successively exploding in the hold into which they had fallen,—this gallant officer, after having nobly pursued, for the preservation of others, a course of exertion that has been rarely equalled either in its duration or difficulty, at last felt it right to provide for his own safety, by laying hold on the topping-lift, or rope that connects the driver boom with the mizen-top, and thereby getting over the heads of the infatuated men who occupied the boom, unable to go either backward or forward, and ultimately dropping himself into the water.

After the arrival of the last boat, the flames, which had spread along the upper deck and poop, ascended with the rapidity of lightning to the masts and rigging, forming one general conflagration, that illumined the heavens to an immense distance, and was strongly reflected upon several objects on board the brig. The flags of distress, hoisted in the morning, were seen for a considerable time waving amid the flames until the masts to which they were suspended successively fell, like stately steeples, over the ship's side. At last, about half-past one o'clock in the morning, the devouring element having communicated to the magazine, the long threatened explosion was seen, and the blazing fragments of the once magnificent *Kent* were instantly hurried, like so many rockets, high into the air; leaving, in the comparative darkness that succeeded, the deathful scene of that disastrous day floating before the mind like some feverish dream.

Shortly afterwards the brig, which had been gradually making sail, was running at the rate of nine or ten miles an hour towards the nearest port.

After the first burst of mutual gratulation, and of becoming acknowledgment of the Divine mercy, on account of our unlooked for deliverance, had subsided, none of us felt disposed to much interchange of thought, each being rather inclined to wrap himself up in his own reflections; yet we did not, during this first night, view with the alarm it warranted, the extreme misery and danger to which we were still exposed, by being crowded together, in a gale of wind, with upwards of 600 human beings in a small brig of 200 tons, at a distance, too, of several hundred miles from any accessible port. Our little cabin, which was only calculated, under ordinary circumstances, for the accommodation of eight or ten persons, was now made to contain nearly eighty individuals, many of whom had no sitting room, and even some of the ladies no room to lie down. Owing to the continued violence of the gale, and to the bulwarks on one side of the brig having been driven in, the sea beat so incessantly over our deck, as to render it necessary that the hatches should only be lifted up between the returning waves, to prevent absolute suffocation below, where the men were so closely packed together, that the steam arising from their respiration excited at one time an apprehension that the vessel was on fire; while the impurity of the air they were inhaling became so marked, that the lights occasionally carried down amongst them were almost instantly extinguished. Nor was the condition of the hundreds who covered the deck less wretched than that of their comrades below; since they were obliged night and day to stand shivering, in their wet and nearly naked state, ankle-deep in water; some of the older children and females were thrown into fits, while the infants were pitifully crying for that nourishment which their nursing mothers were no longer able to give them.

Our only hope, amid these great and accumulating miseries was, that the same compassionate Providence which had already so marvellously interposed on our behalf, would not permit the wind to abate or change, until we reached some friendly port; for we were all convinced that a delay of a very few days longer at sea, must inevitably involve us in famine, pestilence, and a complication of the most dreadful evils. Our hopes were not disappointed. The gale continued with even increasing violence; and our able Captain, crowding all sail at the risk of carrying away his masts, so nobly urged his vessel onward, that in the afternoon of Thursday the 3d, the delightful exclamation from aloft was heard, "Land a-head!" In the evening we descried the Scilly lights; and running rapidly along the Cornish coast, we joyfully cast anchor in Falmouth harbour, about half-past 12 o'clock on the following morning.

Crusoe Visits the Wreck

by DANIEL DEFOE

When I waked it was broad day, the weather clear, and the storm abated, so that the sea did not rage and swell as before; but that which surprised me most was, that the ship was lifted off in the night from the sand where she lay, by the swelling of the tide, and was driven up almost as far as the rock which I first mentioned, where I had been so bruised by the dashing me against it. This being within about a mile from the shore where I was, and the ship seeming to stand upright still, I wished myself on board, that at least I might save some necessary things for my use.

When I came down from my apartment in the tree, I looked about me again, and the first thing I found was the boat, which lay, as the wind and the sea had tossed her up upon the land, about two miles on my right hand. I walked as far as I could upon the shore to have got to her, but found a neck, or inlet, of water between me and the boat, which was about half a mile broad; so I came back for the present, being more intent upon getting at the ship, where I hoped to find something for my present subsistence.

A little after noon I found the sea very calm, and the tide ebbed so far out that I could come within a quarter of a mile of the ship; and here I found a fresh renewing of my grief, for I saw evidently that, if we had kept on board, we had all been safe—that is to say, we had all got safe on shore, and I had not been so miserable as to be left entirely destitute of all comfort and company as I now was. This forced tears from my eyes again, but as there was little relief in that, I resolved, if possible, to get to the ship; so I pulled off my clothes, for the weather was hot to extremity, and took the water. But when I came to the ship, my difficulty was still greater to know how to get on board, for as she lay aground, and high out of the water, there was nothing within my reach to lay hold of. I swam round her twice, and the second time I spied a small piece of rope, which I wondered I did not see at first, hang down by the fore-chains, so low as that with great difficulty I got hold of it, and by the help of that rope got into the forecastle of the ship. Here I found that the ship was bilged, and had a great deal of water in her hold; but that she lay so on the side of a bank of hard sand, or rather earth, and her stern lay lifted up upon the bank, and her head low, almost to the water. By this means all her quarter was free, and all that was in that part was dry; for you may be sure my first work was to search and to see what was spoiled and what was free: and first I found that all the ship's provisions were dry and untouched by the water; and being very well disposed to eat, I went to the bread-room, and filled my pockets with biscuit, and ate it as I went about other things, for I had no time to lose. I also found some rum in the great cabin, of which I took a large dram, and which I had indeed need enough of, to spirit me for what was before me. Now I wanted nothing but a boat, to furnish myself with many things which I foresaw would be very necessary to me.

He Constructs a Raft

It was in vain to sit still and wish for what was not to be had, and this extremity roused my application; we had several spare yards, and two or three spars of wood, and a spare topmast or two in the ship. I resolved to fall to work with these, and flung as many of them overboard as I could manage of their weight, tying every one with a rope, that they might not drive away. When this was done, I went down the ship's side, and pulling them to me, I tied four of them fast together at both ends, as well as I could, in the form of a raft, and laying two or three short pieces of plank upon them crossways, I found I could walk upon it very well, but that it was not able to bear any great weight, the pieces being too light; so I went to work, and with the carpenter's saw I cut a spare topmast into three lengths, and added them to my raft, with a great deal of labour and pains. But the hope of furnishing myself with necessaries encouraged me to go beyond what I should have been able to have done upon another occasion.

His Choice of Provisions

My raft was now strong enough to bear any reasonable weight. My next care was what to load it with, and how to preserve what I laid upon it from the surf of the sea. But I was not long considering this. I first laid all the planks, or boards, upon it that I could get, and having considered well what I most wanted, I first got three of the seamen's chests, which I had broken open and emptied, and lowered them down upon my raft. The first of these I filled with provisions, viz, bread, rice, three Dutch cheeses, five pieces of dried goats' flesh (which we lived much upon), and a little remainder of European corn which had been laid by for some fowls which we had brought to sea with us, but the fowls were killed. There had been some barley and wheat together, but, to my great disappointment, I found afterwards that the rats had eaten or spoiled it all. As for liquors, I found several cases of bottles belonging to our skipper, in which were some cordial waters, and, in all, about five or six gallons of rack. These I stowed by themselves, there being no need to put them into the chests, nor no room for them. While I was doing this I found the tide began to flow, though very calm, and I had the mortification to see my coat, shirt, and waistcoat, which I had left on shore upon the sand, swim away; as for my breeches which were only linen and open-kneed, I swam on board in them and my stockings. However this put me upon rummaging for clothes, of which I found enough, but took no more than I wanted for present use, for I had other things which my eye was more upon, as first, tools to work with on shore; and it was after long searching that I found out the carpenter's chest, which was indeed a very useful prize to me, and much more valuable than a ship loading of gold would have been at that time. I got it down to my raft, even whole as it was, without losing time to look into it, for I knew in general what it contained.

My next care was for some ammunition and arms. There were two very good fowling-pieces in the great cabin, and two pistols; these I secured first, with some powder-horns and a small bag of shot, and two old rusty swords. I knew there were three barrels of powder in the ship, but knew not where our gunner had stowed them, but with much search I found them, two of them dry and good, the third had taken water. Those two I got to my raft, with the arms. And now I thought myself pretty well freighted, and began to think how I should get to shore with them having neither sail, oar, nor rudder; and the least capful of wind would have overset all my navigation.

I had three encouragements: 1. A smooth, calm sea. 2. The tide rising, and setting in to the shore. 3. What little wind there was blew me towards the land. And thus, having found two or three broken oars belonging to the boat, and besides the tools which were in the chest, I found two saws, an axe, and a hammer; and with this cargo I put to sea. For a mile, or thereabouts, my raft went very well, only that I found it drive a little distant from the place where I had landed before, by which I perceived that there was some indraft of the water, and consequently I hoped to find some creek or river there, which I might make use of as a port to get to land with my cargo.

As I imagined, so it was: there appeared before me a little opening of land, and I found a strong current of the tide set into it; so I guided my raft as well as I could, to keep in the middle of the stream. But here I had like to have suffered a second shipwreck, which, if I had, I think verily would have broke my heart; for, knowing nothing of the coast, my raft ran aground at one end of it upon a shoal, and not being aground at the other end, it wanted but a little that all my cargo had slipped off towards that end that was afloat, and so fallen into the water. I did my utmost, by setting my back against the chests, to keep them in their places, but could not thrust off the raft with all my strength; neither durst I stir from the posture I was in, but holding up the chests with all my might, stood in that manner near half an hour, in which time the rising of the water brought me a little more upon a level; and a little after, the water still rising, my raft floated again, and I thrust her off with the oar I had into the channel, and then, driving up higher, I at length found myself in the mouth of a little river, with land on both sides, and a strong current or tide running up. I looked on both sides for a proper place to get to shore, for I was not willing to be driven too high up the river, hoping, in time, to see some ship at sea, and therefore resolved to place myself as near the coast as I could.

At length I spied a little cove on the right shore of the creek, to which, with great pain and difficulty, I guided my raft, and at last got so near as that, reaching ground with my oar, I could thrust her directly in; but here I had like to have dipped all my cargo into the sea again, for that shore lying pretty steep, that is to say, sloping, there was no place to land, but where one end of my float, if it ran on shore, would lie so high, and the other sink lower, as before, that it would endanger my cargo again. All that I could do was to wait till the tide was at the highest, keeping the raft with my oar, like an anchor, to hold the side of it fast to the shore, near a flat piece of ground which I expected the water would flow over; and so it did. As soon as I found water enough, for my raft drew about a foot of water, I thrust her upon that flat piece of ground, and there fastened or moored her, by sticking my two broken oars into the ground, one on one side near one end, and one on the other side near the other end; and thus I lay till the water ebbed away, and left my raft and all my cargo safe on shore.

What He Brought Off Next Day

I got on board the ship as before, and prepared a second raft; and having had experience of the first, I neither made this so unwieldy, nor loaded it so hard, but yet I brought away several things very useful to me: as, first, in the carpenter's stores, I found two or three bags full of nails and spikes, a great screw-jack, a dozen or two of hatchets, and, above all, that most useful thing called a grindstone. All these I secured together, with several things belonging to the gunner, particularly two or three iron crows, and two barrels of musket bullets, seven muskets, and another fowling-piece, with some small quantity of powder more, a large bag full of small shot, and a great roll of sheet lead; but this last was so heavy I could not hoist it up to get it over the ship's side.

Besides these things, I took all the men's clothes that I could find, and a spare fore-topsail, hammock, and some bedding; and with this I loaded my second raft, and brought them all safe on shore to my very great comfort.

I was under some apprehensions, during my absence from the land, that at least my provisions might be devoured on shore; but, when I came back, I found no sign of any visitor, only there sat a creature like a wild cat upon one of the chests, which, when I came towards it, ran away a little distance and then stood still. She sat very composed and unconcerned, and looked full in my face, as if she had a mind to be acquainted with me. I presented my gun at her, but as she did not understand it she was perfectly unconcerned at it, nor did she offer to stir away, upon which I tossed her a bit of biscuit, though, by the way, I was not very free of it, for my store was not great; however, I spared her a bit, I say, and she went to it, smelled of it, and ate it, and looked, as pleased, for more; but I thanked her, and could spare no more, so she marched off.

Having got my second cargo on shore—though I was fain to open the barrels of powder and bring them by parcels, for they were too heavy, being large casks—I went to work to make me a little tent with the sail and some poles which I cut for that purpose, and into this tent I brought everything that I knew would spoil, either with rain or sun; and I piled all the empty chests and casks up in a circle round the tent, to fortify it from any sudden attempt either from man or beast.

When I had done this, I blocked up the door of the tent with some boards within, and an empty chest set up on end without; and spreading one of the beds upon the ground, laying my two pistols just at my head, and my gun at length by me, I went to bed for the first time, and slept very quietly all night; for I was very weary and heavy, for the night before I had slept little, and had laboured very hard all day, as well to fetch all those things from the ship as to get them on shore.

I had the biggest magazine of all kinds now that ever was laid up, I believe, for one man; but I was not satisfied still, for while the ship sat upright in that posture, I thought I ought to get everything out of her I could: so every day, at low water, I went on board and brought away something or other; but particularly the third time I went, I brought away as much of the rigging as I could, as also all the small ropes and rope-twine I could get, with a piece of spare canvas, which was to mend the sails upon occasion, and the barrel of wet gunpowder. In a word, I brought away all the sails, first and last, only that I was fain to cut them in pieces, and bring as much at a time as I could; for they were no more useful to be sails, but as mere canvas only.

But that which comforted me more still was, that, at last of all, after I had made five or six such voyages as these, and thought I had nothing more to expect from the ship that was worth my meddling with,—I say, after all this, I found a great hogshead of bread, and three large runlets of rum or spirits, and a box of sugar and a barrel of fine flour; this was surprising to me, because I had given over expecting any more provisions, except what was spoiled by the water. I soon emptied the hogshead of that bread and wrapped it up, parcel by parcel, in pieces of the sails, which I cut out; and, in a word, I got all this safe on shore also.

The next day I made another voyage, and now, having plundered the ship of what was portable and fit to hand out, I began with the cables, and cutting the great cable into pieces such as I could move, I got two cables and a hawser on shore, with all the iron work I could get; and, having cut down the spritsail-yard and the mizzen-yard, and everything I could, to make a large raft, I loaded it with all those heavy goods, and came away: but my good luck began now to leave me; for this raft was so unwieldy and so over laden, that after I was entered the little cove where I had landed the rest of my goods, not being able to guide it so handily as I did the other, it overset, and threw me and all my cargo into the water. As for myself, it was no great harm, for I was near the shore; but as to my cargo, it was a great part of it lost, especially the iron, which I expected would have been of great use to me. However, when the tide was out, I got most of the pieces of cable ashore, and some of the iron, though with infinite labour; for I was fain to dip for it into the water, a work which fatigued me very much. After this I went every day on board, and brought away what I could get.

Last Trip to the Wreck

I had been now thirteen days on shore, and had been eleven times on board the ship, in which time I had brought away all that one pair of hands could well be supposed capable to bring; though, I believe verily, had the calm weather held, I should have brought away the whole ship, piece by piece; but preparing the twelfth time to go on board, I found the wind began to rise. However, at low water, I went on board, and though I thought I had rummaged the cabin so effectually, as that nothing more could be found, yet I discovered a locker with drawers in it, in one of which I found two or three razors, and one pair of large scissors, with some ten or a dozen of good knives and forks; in another I found about thirty-six pounds value in money, some European coin, some Brazil, some pieces of eight, some gold, some silver.

I smiled to myself at the sight of this money. "O drug!" said I aloud, "what art thou good for? Thou art not worth to me, no, not the taking off the ground; one of those knives is worth all this heap: I have no manner of use for thee; e'en remain where thou art, and go to the bottom, as a creature whose life is not worth saving." However, upon second thoughts, I took it away; and wrapping all this in a piece of canvas, I began to think of making another raft; but while I was preparing this, I found the sky overcast, and the wind began to rise, and in a quarter of an hour it blew a fresh gale from the shore. It presently occurred to me, that it was in vain to pretend to make a raft with the wind off shore, and that it was my business to be gone before the tide of flood began, otherwise I might not be able to reach the shore at all. Accordingly I let myself down into the water, and swam across the channel which lay between the ship and the sands, and even that with difficulty enough, partly with the weight of the things I had about me, and partly the roughness of the water; for the wind rose very hastily, and before it was quite high water it blew a storm.

But I was gotten home to my little tent, where I lay with all my wealth about me, very secure. It blew very hard all that night and in the morning, when I looked out, behold, no more ship was to be seen! I was a little surprised, but recovered myself with this satisfactory reflection, viz, that I had lost no time, nor abated no diligence, to get everything out of her that could be useful to me, and that indeed there was little left in her that I was able to bring away, if I had had more time.

His Reflections on Fate

I had a dismal prospect of my condition; for as I was not cast away upon that island without being driven, as is said, by a violent storm quite out of the course of our intended voyage, and a great way, viz, some hundreds of leagues, out of the ordinary course of the trade of mankind, I had great reason to consider it as a determination of Heaven that, in this desolate place, and in this desolate manner, I should end my life. The tears would run plentifully down my face when I made these reflections, and sometimes I would expostulate with myself why Providence should thus completely ruin its creatures, and render them so absolutely miserable,—so without help abandoned, so entirely depressed, that it could hardly be rational to be thankful for such a life.

But something always returned swift upon me to check these thoughts, and
to reprove me; and particularly one day walking with my gun in my hand by
the seaside, I was very pensive upon the subject of my present condition,
when reason, as it were, expostulated with me the other way thus: "Well, you
are in a desolate condition, it is true; but, pray remember, where are the rest of
you? Did not you come eleven of you into the boat? Where are the ten? Why
were not they saved, and you lost? Why were you singled out? Is it better to be
here or there?"

Then it occurred to me again, how well I was furnished for my subsistence,
and what would have been my case if it had not happened, which was a hundred thousand to one, that the ship floated from the place where she first
struck, and was driven so near to the shore that I had time to get all these
things out of her: what would have been my case, if I had been to have lived in
the condition in which I at first came on shore, without necessaries of life, or
necessaries to supply and procure them? "Particularly," said I aloud (though
to myself), "what should I have done without a gun, without ammunition,
without any tools to make anything or to work with, without clothes, bedding,
a tent, or any manner of coverings?" And that now I had all these to a sufficient quantity, and was in a fair way to provide myself in such a manner as to
live without my gun, when my ammunition was spent, so that I had a tolerable
view of subsisting, without any want, as long as I lived; for I considered, from
the beginning, how I would provide for the accidents that might happen, and
for the time that was to come, not only after my ammunition should be spent,
but even after my health or strength should decay.